APPLICATIONS OF SOCIAL RESEARCH METHODS TO QUESTIONS IN INFORMATION AND LIBRARY SCIENCE

APPLICATIONS OF SOCIAL RESEARCH METHODS TO QUESTIONS IN INFORMATION AND LIBRARY SCIENCE

Barbara M. Wildemuth

LIBRARIES
U N L I M I T E D
A Member of the Greenwood Publishing Group
Westport, Connecticut • London

Library of Congress Cataloging-in-Publication Data

Wildemuth, Barbara M.
  Applications of social research methods to questions in information and library science /
Barbara M. Wildemuth.
    p.   cm.
  Includes bibliographical references and indexes.
  ISBN 978–1–59158–503–9 (alk. paper)
  1. Library science—Research—Methodology.   2. Information science—Research—Methodology.
I. Title.
  Z669.7.W55   2009
  020.72—dc22   2008053745

British Library Cataloguing in Publication Data is available.

Library of Congress Catalog Card Number: 2008053745
ISBN: 978–1–59158–503–9

First published in 2009

Libraries Unlimited, 88 Post Road West, Westport, CT 06881
A Member of the Greenwood Publishing Group, Inc.
www.lu.com

Printed in the United States of America

The paper used in this book complies with the
Permanent Paper Standard issued by the National
Information Standards Organization (Z39.48–1984).

10 9 8 7 6 5 4 3 2 1

Contents

Acknowledgments

As with any other intellectual endeavor, the development of this book relied on the support of many people. I would particularly like to acknowledge the contributions of the following:

- The authors of the examples discussed in these chapters. Without a large body of excellent research from which to select examples, this book would not have been possible. Thank you for your scholarly efforts, both in their creativity and their rigor.
- My coauthors. All of the chapter coauthors were doctoral students at the University of North Carolina at Chapel Hill when these chapters were originally written. Thank you for your intellectual curiosity and your high standards for the quality of your work.
- My colleagues at the University of North Carolina. Thank you for the many ideas you gave me as I worked on particular chapters in this book and for your collegiality during the process of completing it.
- The School of Information and Library Science at the University of North Carolina at Chapel Hill, the Fulbright Scholar Program, and the Institute of Information Studies and Librarianship at Charles University (Prague). Thank you for your financial and material support during my work on this manuscript.
- My editor, Sue Easun. Thank you for your willingness to take on this project and for your guidance throughout the process.
- My family and friends, with particular thanks to my husband, Gaylen Brubaker. Thank you for your gentle nudges to complete this manuscript and for your never-failing encouragement.

PART I

INTRODUCTION

I

Using Research Results to Improve Practice in the Information Professions

Barbara M. Wildemuth

Research is formalized curiosity. It is poking and prying with a purpose. It is a seeking that he who wishes may know the cosmic secrets of the world and that they dwell therein.

—Zora Neale Hurston (1942)

Information and library science (ILS) is a field that includes the profession of librarianship as well as a variety of other information professions (systems designer, database administrator, and information architect, to name a few). While these professions are diverse in some aspects, in each case, their practice assumes a close interaction between the following:

- Information content, that is, the substance of the information being created, communicated, stored, and/or transformed
- The people who interact with the content, including the creators of information, recipients of information, or intermediaries in the communication process
- The technology used to support the creation, communication, storage, or transformation of the content

As with other professional fields, the research conducted in the field of information and library science tends to be oriented toward the improvement of practice in these professions. Basic research may not have an impact on practice for a decade or more after it has been conducted, while more applied research and evaluation studies may have an impact on practice almost immediately. All along this research continuum, the researcher defines questions and conducts research studies that are motivated by the desire to improve practice in the information professions.

From the practitioner's perspective, best practices can often be developed through significant amounts of direct experience. However, they can also be developed through an examination and application of research findings, as noted by Kaske (1993). For example, a study of student and faculty expectations of instant messaging for providing library reference services may guide the development of those services so that they are acceptable to and accepted by the intended users. This type of application of research results—to improve professional practice—is called *evidence-based practice*, a variation of the term *evidence-based medicine*, which came into vogue over a decade ago (Cochrane Collaboration, 2004).

Two things need to happen for the information professions to profit from evidence-based practice. The first is that effective research studies need to be completed; the second is that their results need to be applied to particular situations and questions that occur in practice. The aim of this book is to support this first effort by improving our ability to conduct effective research studies. Most information professionals receive formal education in research methods during their master's degree education. The research method courses in graduate ILS programs are primarily supported by textbooks in related disciplines such as sociology and psychology. While a number of these textbooks are well written and cover methods appropriate to our field, none of them contains examples illustrating how methods can be applied to ILS research questions. This book is intended to fill this gap, augmenting current research method textbooks. Specifically, it provides critical analyses of the application of a variety of social research methods to exemplary research questions in ILS.

INTENDED AUDIENCES

The field of information and library science is not large, so we must all contribute to the improvement of practice by conducting research and evaluation studies and publishing their results. This book is intended to be useful to all who are engaging in this enterprise. It can support research methods courses in ILS schools and is expected to be useful to both doctoral and master's students as they learn how to conduct research. It is also intended to be useful to practitioners who are interested in conducting their own studies and who would benefit from examples illustrating how particular methods can be applied to their research and evaluation questions. Finally, it is also intended to be useful to experienced researchers, particularly when they are considering a method with which they are unfamiliar. The critical analyses of exemplar studies included in this book should prove useful in guiding each of these groups as they design and carry out their own research studies in ILS.

SELECTION OF RESEARCH METHODS

One of the challenges in developing this book was to select the research methods to be included. To support this effort, the textbooks used for master's-level research methods courses in ILS schools were examined. In addition, some recent examinations of the ILS research literature (Julien & Duggan, 2000; Powell, 1999; Yuan & Meadow, 1999) and discussions of the research methods employed (Dervin, 2003; Tague-Sutcliffe, 1996; Wilson, 2002) provided guidance concerning which methods are in use by ILS researchers. Finally, frequently cited ILS journals (*Journal of the American Society for Information Science and Technology*; *Journal of Documentation*; *Information Processing and Management*; *College and Research Libraries*) were examined in a review of the articles published over the last several years to identify the methods used in those studies. While the chapters in this book do not include *every* research method used in ILS research, they do include those methods used most frequently.[1]

The discussion of each method is intended to complement, rather than repeat, the content of typical social research methods textbooks. Specifically, each method is discussed in terms of its applicability to ILS research questions, its strengths and weaknesses, and the precautions that researchers should take when applying the method to ILS research questions. Each chapter includes a brief list of additional sources that describe and discuss the method in more detail.

SELECTION OF EXEMPLARY STUDIES

The primary purpose of this book is to provide and critically analyze examples of each of the methods presented. Each chapter contains two (or more) exemplary studies that have applied the method appropriately. After a brief description of each example study, the example study is analyzed in terms of pitfalls the authors avoided (or were unable to avoid), ways in which the application of the method might have been improved, and lessons that can be learned from the example. To my knowledge, no other ILS research methods book has taken this approach: relying primarily on exemplary studies as models for future research.

The example studies are all strong in terms of the way they apply the research method being examined. In fact, an effort was made to identify and include award-winning studies (such as winners of the American Society for Information Science and Technology Best *JASIST* Paper Award or the Association for Library and Information Science Education Methodology Award). Thus readers can look to these examples as studies to emulate in terms of how a particular research method can be applied to an ILS research question.

While the example studies were selected to provide positive models, it is not possible for a research study to be conducted flawlessly. The real world requires that compromises be made if we are to complete any studies at all. Thus the discussion of each example will attempt to point out some of the trade-offs made by the study authors. In some cases, other choices might have made the study stronger; in other cases, alternative methods that, at first, could appear to be a better choice might have weakened the study overall. Our hope is that open discussion of these methodological issues will help all of us develop stronger studies in the future.

USING THIS BOOK

As I was writing this book, I was envisioning a student or colleague sitting in my office, asking me questions about how to conduct a particular study using a particular method. Thus it is very conversational in tone. I am hopeful that it will answer some of the questions you have about how to conduct your own research.

Parts of this book are organized in terms of the process of conducting a research study. Thus Part 2 considers the research questions that are asked in the field of information and library science, and how these questions can arise from practice and direct observation or from existing theories. After a brief introductory chapter, discussing the general process of identifying and defining a research question, several chapters discuss how questions arise in practice settings, how they might be oriented to describing a particular phenomenon or setting, how they might test hypotheses about relationships, and how they may be related to the validation or development of theory. These question sources are not mutually exclusive, but instead illustrate the diversity of question sources in ILS.

Part 3 considers a variety of research designs and the sampling issues associated with those designs. The research designs discussed include case studies, naturalistic research, longitudinal studies, Delphi studies, and quasi-experimental and experimental designs. The chapters include some designs that are more appropriate for quantitative research and others that are more appropriate for qualitative research. They include some methods that are more interpretive in their research orientation and some that are more positivist in their perspective. Part 3 concludes with three chapters focused on sampling issues: one discusses sampling for extensive studies, one discusses sampling for intensive studies, and one addresses the issues associated with studying special populations (i.e., groups rarely studied by ILS researchers).

Part 4 moves on to methods for collecting data. Methods of data collection in social research are diverse, to say the least. While surveys and different types of interviews (the most commonly used methods in ILS) are discussed, other methods that are not as frequently used are also given space. These include such varied approaches as historical and documentary studies, transaction log analysis, diaries, and participant observation.

Part 5 focuses on methods for analyzing the data gathered. Basic statistical methods are, of course, included, as are both quantitative and thematic content analysis. Some additional methods, not often used in ILS, are included such as analytic induction and discourse analysis. While this part is not comprehensive in its coverage of analysis methods, it does provide a good starting point for those wishing to engage in ILS research.

In Part 6, the book concludes with a chapter discussing the ways in which these research methods might be combined for a particular study. In most cases, you will want to read one or more chapters in each part in developing your plans for a particular study. As you are contemplating a study, check the chapters in Part 2, on defining your question, and read any that might be useful to you. As you develop your study design, explore the relevant chapters in Part 3. As you select particular methods for data collection and data analysis, look over the relevant chapters in Parts 4 and 5.

In each chapter, read over the introductory section to get a basic grasp of the method being discussed. If it seems to fit your needs, examine the example studies presented in that chapter. One or more of them may serve as excellent models for your research plans. The experiences of the researchers discussed in those examples may also help you avoid some problems in executing your research plan.

This book is not intended to be read cover to cover. Instead, it is intended as a guide to the many research methods available to those conducting evaluation and research studies in ILS. Select those chapters that address your need for a particular study, and leave the remaining chapters to examine as you plan your *next* study.

NOTE

1. One group of methods commonly used in ILS was excluded: bibliometric methods and similar approaches. These methods were excluded because they are described in a number of books, including in discussions of examples from our field. Thus further discussion of their use in ILS was considered unnecessary.

WORKS CITED

Cochrane Collaboration. (2004). *What is the Cochrane Collaboration?* Retrieved July 8, 2004, from http://www.cochrane.org/docs/descrip.htm.

Dervin, B. (2003). Human studies and user studies: A call for methodological inter-disciplinarity. *Information Research, 9*(1). Retrieved July 9, 2004, from http://informationr.net/ir/9-1/paper166.html.

Hurston, Z. N. (1942). *Dust Tracks on a Road: An Autobiography.* Philadelphia: J. P. Lippincott.

Julien, H., & Duggan, L. J. (2000). A longitudinal analysis of the information needs and uses literature. *Library and Information Science Research, 22*(3), 291–309.

Kaske, N. K. (1993). Research methodologies and transaction log analysis: Issues, questions and a proposed model. *Library Hi Tech, 11*(2), 79–86.

Powell, R. R. (1999). Recent trends in research: A methodological essay. *Library and Information Science Research, 21*(1), 91–119.

Tague-Sutcliffe, J. M. (1996). Some perspectives on the evaluation of information retrieval systems. *Journal of the American Society for Information Science, 47*(1), 1–3.

Wilson, T. (2002). "Information science" and research methods. *Knižnicná a informacná veda (Library and Information Science)* [in Slovak]. Retrieved June 10, 2004, from http://informationr.net/tdw/publ/papers/slovak02.html [in English].

Yuan, W., & Meadow, C. T. (1999). A study of the use of variables in information retrieval user studies. *Journal of the American Society for Information Science, 50*(2), 140–150.

PART II
THE QUESTIONS ASKED

2

Developing a Research Question

Barbara M. Wildemuth

The scientific mind does not so much provide the right answers as ask the right questions.
—Claude Lévi-Strauss (1969)

INTRODUCTION

The first, and most important, step in conducting a research study is to define your research question. Having a clear statement of your research question in hand allows you to design your study (including your overall strategy and your specific data collection procedures). It guides your selection of a sample for the study, your selection of a research design, your approach to data collection, and how you will analyze your data. A clear statement of your research question will also help you justify the costs of conducting the research, to external funding sources or to yourself (Maxwell, 2005). In addition, a clear statement of your research question will help you to stay focused through the study's completion.

But let's start back at the beginning. Where would an idea for a research question come from? There are two general ways in which research questions originate. First, your research question may come from your own experience or direct observation of some situation or event, through discussion with your colleagues, or through exposure to current topics in the field (Gray, 2004; Locke et al., 2007; Robson, 2002). In other words, a situation you encounter in information and library science (ILS) practice presents a problem that you're interested in solving. For example, you may wonder whether college students would learn searching skills if they were taught by their discipline's faculty, rather than the library faculty (example adapted from Eldredge, 2001). A second source of research questions is the logical gaps that exist in our current state of knowledge of the field (Locke et al., 2007). There may be a recent study that provides some new information about how students interact with online resources, but it didn't investigate such interactions by faculty. There may be a theory that has been proposed, but you're not sure of whether it can explain what's happening in a new situation. Usually, these ideas come from reading or browsing the literature, conversations with colleagues, and your own reflections on your knowledge of the field (Locke et al., 2007). Whichever of these two avenues leads you to your research question(s), the most important consideration is that you're personally interested in and motivated to answer the question(s).

The process of developing a research question begins with clarifying what *problem* you are trying to solve. Your primary task at this point is to clarify the meanings of the concepts involved in the problem (Punch, 1998). A good understanding of the problem, as experienced in practice or encountered in prior research/theory, will lead to the *research question*, defined as "a statement of what you wish to know about some unsatisfactory situation" (Locke et al., 2007, p. 45). In addition, you will want to clarify the *purposes* or *goals* of the study—your motivations or intentions for undertaking the study (Locke et al., 2007; Maxwell, 2005). This chapter will guide you in the development of your research question(s).

UNDERSTANDING WHAT IT IS THAT YOU WANT TO ASK

Once you are able to state your research question, you need to unpack it a bit (O'Leary, 2005). Begin by exploring your personal perspectives on the question. Do you have any direct experiences that are related to the question? If so, how will they affect your plans for the study? Next, you should consider the perspectives of other stakeholders. Stakeholders include anyone who has a vested interest in the outcomes of your research. These might include the users of an information system or library, managers or employees within a particular organization, trustees or advisors to an organization, and corporations (including vendors) that have a commercial interest in the study, among others. Which of these stakeholders will be supportive of your research, and which may try to block the study? Viewed from the perspective of a particular stakeholder, you may want to revise your question to take into account a relevant idea that you had not previously considered. Finally, you will want to consider the cultural context of your research question, including the prevailing worldview that may have shaped it. Are you making assumptions that are consistent with that worldview but may not be accurate? Does your question reflect the interests of the dominant groups in society and ignore the interests of marginalized groups? Through this unpacking process, you can strengthen and solidify your understanding of your question.

All research ideas occur within an intellectual context. Whether your idea originated in your own experience, in conversations with colleagues, or through your reading of the literature, you will need to begin the process of defining your research question by reading some more (O'Leary, 2005). You need to be sure that the question's answer hasn't already been discovered by someone else. You need to know what other people have found about the same phenomenon in other settings. You need to know what other people have found about related phenomena in settings that are similar to yours. You need to understand how your research will be relevant and important to the field. You need to identify any theories or models that could help you conceptualize your research question. You need to know which methods other researchers have used to investigate the phenomenon in which you're interested. To identify the readings you need, you will want to gather recommendations from colleagues, conduct literature searches (including citation searches), and check the footnotes or references on the important articles you read. With the knowledge you gain, you will be in a better position to clearly state the question you want to answer.

As you consider alternative research questions, there are four important matters to consider. The first is that a question isn't really a question unless there is some uncertainty about the answer (Booth, 2006; Robson, 2002). For example, you might be interested in whether a three-session information literacy course will improve the academic work of first-year college students. As you read the literature, you find a number of studies of this question or closely related questions. If you find that these studies, across multiple settings and providing multiple types of instruction, consistently conclude that there is little or no effect on students' academic achievement, you will not want to conduct a study of the same question that has been investigated in the past. However, if you find that these studies have mixed results, you will need to delve deeper, to find out which types of programs were successful in which settings. Within those contexts that are similar to yours, there may or may not be consensus among the studies' findings. On the basis of what you find in past studies, you will want to define a research question that has not yet been answered.

The second important matter to consider is the importance of the question. Locke et al. (2007) suggest asking yourself, "What don't we know that matters?" (p. 44). In the first part of their question, they're raising the issue we just discussed; in the second part, they're raising the issue of the importance of your question, that is, the impact that finding the answer will have. Will the results have an impact on practice? Will they have an impact on our general knowledge of the field, leading to development of improved or new theories? The amount of effort to be invested in the study should be in balance with the level of the contribution that will be made by its findings (Losee & Worley, 1993).

A third matter to consider is what Gill and Johnson (1997) call the *symmetry of potential outcomes* (p. 17). What they mean is that no matter whether you confirm or refute your initial hypotheses, the findings of the study will be useful. For example, if you're studying the relative effectiveness of two styles of library reference interviews, you would like to know which of the two is more effective. Even if there is no difference between the two styles of interview, the results will be useful because then you can use other criteria to select a style, or you can adopt both styles as acceptable for use within your library. So, as you consider alternative research questions, take into account what will happen if you don't get the results for which you hope.

The fourth matter to consider at this point is the feasibility of answering the question in which you're interested (Miles & Huberman, 1984; Robson, 2002). As Barrett (2006) notes, a question must not only be "interesting, important, or useful"; it must also lead to a study that is "realistic and feasible" (p. 27) to conduct. It's very possible to develop a research question that cannot be answered, given the resources available to you. In most cases, you will address this issue by constraining the scope of your question(s). Keeping all these considerations in mind, you're now ready to write your problem statement.

WRITING A PROBLEM STATEMENT

While Hernon (2001) delineates several components of a problem statement (including a lead-in, a claim for originality based on a literature review, and a justification of the study's value), we will focus on making the research question(s) explicit. This is an iterative process; as you draft a research question, you will identify ambiguities in it or find that it's too broad or too narrow. Each iteration will make it clearer and more useful in completing your "research journey" (O'Leary, 2005, p. 32).

A research question is situated within a conceptual framework: the system of concepts to be studied as well as the relationships between them (Miles & Huberman, 1984; Maxwell, 2005). It can be represented either graphically (e.g., as a concept map) or in narrative form. It also makes explicit the researcher's "assumptions, expectations, beliefs and theories" about the phenomenon under study (Maxwell, 2005, p. 33). While you may be relying heavily on a preexisting theory or model, keep in mind that your conceptual framework will be constructed or synthesized based on your integration of ideas from other researchers and your own reflections on current knowledge in the field. Because it provides the context for your specific research questions, a well-formulated conceptual framework can both focus the research question and bound its scope. A good example of applying such a conceptual framework in formulating a research question is discussed in the chapter on testing hypotheses: Sundar et al.'s (2007) study of the effects of peripheral cues on people's evaluations of newsbot displays. It would have been easy for the authors to pose their research question, ignoring the underlying concepts that framed their work. For example, they could have posed the question as a straightforward study of the usability of newsbot displays of various kinds. Instead, they firmly embedded their work within the context of earlier work on the types of cues that affect people's interactions with information, integrating concepts from two different theories about those interactions. While not all studies need to have such a strong theoretical foundation, those that do will provide results that have more far-reaching impact than those that are not situated within a clear conceptual framework.

On the basis of the conceptual framework, you will identify one or more research questions that are of particular interest. They will focus the attention of your study on the most important aspects of the conceptual framework (Creswell, 2003; Miles & Huberman, 1984; Robson, 2002). A particular research question may be important because its answer has the potential to change particular practices in ILS or because it helps us to more fully understand a crucial aspect of people's information behaviors or the information systems with which they interact. Making your research question(s) explicit allows you "to get clear about what, in the general domain, is of most interest" (Miles & Huberman, 1984, p. 35). Stone (2002) reinforces this point when he argues that "formulating the research question . . . acts as a guard against sloppy thinking" (p. 265).

Several authors have provided sound advice about how to state your research question(s), and all of them begin by saying that you need to write them down. You should be able to state each research question as a single sentence (Losee & Worley, 1993). If it is too broad, it will not provide sufficient guidance for developing your study design; if it is too narrow, you may be blinded to relevant data or alternative ways to achieve your research purposes (Maxwell, 2005). Booth (2006) recommends that you incorporate several components (setting, perspective, intervention, comparison, evaluation) in your research question. To illustrate this point, he provides an example question: "From the perspective of an undergraduate student (perspective) in a university library (setting), is provision of a short term loan collection (intervention) more effective than a general collection (comparison) in terms of the percentage availability of recommended texts (evaluation)?" (p. 363). You need to be able to define each concept or component of the question (Barrett, 2006). For instance, in Booth's (2006) example, you need to define what is meant by a short-term loan collection and a general collection. Your definitions should be clear enough that they can be used to design your study methods.

In summary, a good research question has several attributes: (1) it is clear, unambiguous, and easily understood; (2) it is specific enough to suggest the data that need to be collected during your study; (3) it is answerable, in the sense that it is feasible to collect the needed data; (4) it is interconnected with important concepts or phenomena; and (5) it is substantively relevant to the field (Punch, 1998).

THE IMPLICATIONS OF THE RESEARCH QUESTION FOR THE RESEARCH DESIGN

As Punch (1998) notes, "a well stated research question indicates what data will be necessary to answer it" (p. 46). While research into scientists' behavior has indicated that at least some researchers are ambivalent about the dominance of the research question over the research methods (Bryman, 2007), there is almost universal promotion of the idea that your research question will guide the development of your study methods. Booth (2001) provides several examples of the way in which the connection between the research question and the data needed to answer it will influence the design of the study. As you consider different methods for your study, you will want to select the approach that "has the most strengths and fewest weaknesses in the context of the problem statement and objectives" (Hernon, 2001, p. 84).

While the preceding section encouraged the development of very precise research questions, there is actually a spectrum of approaches. At one end of this spectrum are the most precise research questions, often specified as hypotheses to be tested. This type of question would call for a tightly structured research design, resulting in data that are also well structured (Punch, 1998). Robson (2002) describes these research designs as fixed because all their components are determined in advance of the study being carried out. At the other end of the spectrum are research questions that are intended to provide general guidance to the research effort but that are more exploratory and open in their conception. Such questions call for research approaches that are more loosely structured and that will evolve as they proceed. The data collected are often open ended and less structured. Robson (2002) describes these research designs as flexible because they may be altered as the research progresses. Maxwell (2005) proposes an interactive approach to developing such designs, with the goals and research questions interacting with the selection of study methods during the course of the study; both the goals and questions and the methods are expected to change during the course of the study.

The research question(s) you are asking have implications for several aspects of the study design. First, they have implications for the sample that will participate in the study. You will need to decide which people, organizations, settings, and so on, are of interest. This component of the study design is reflected in the perspective and setting components of the research question suggested by Booth (2006). Second, the questions have implications for the data to be collected. As you define each of the concepts incorporated in your question, you will need to decide what data can be used as an indicator for each. Mason (2002) suggests that you ask yourself, "Which of my research questions does each method or data source help me to address?" (p. 27). In this way, you can tightly link your data collection efforts (including both which data will be collected and how they will be collected) to answering your research questions. Finally, the research questions have implications for your data analysis methods. You will want to use those analysis methods that will help you focus your attention on answering your research questions.

MAKING YOUR PROJECT HAPPEN

In this chapter, we've discussed how to develop your research questions and how they will be used to design your study. One of the criteria for a good research question is that it leads to a study that is feasible to complete. In this section, we will briefly discuss a few of the issues you will want to consider to ensure that your study design is feasible to carry out (Barrett, 2006). As Moore (1987) points out, it is "necessary to keep the scale of the research in tune with the size of the problem" (p. 3).

The first issue to consider is your access to the people that you'd like to include as participants in your study. You will need to know how to identify and locate them. You will need to be able to convince a sample of them to participate in your study. You may need to retain their participation over a period of time, depending on your study design. You will need to make sure that they have the ability to complete the procedures required for data collection (e.g., you can't conduct a Web survey of people who don't have easy access to the Web).

Second, you will need to consider the equipment and other material resources that may be needed to conduct your study. Your study procedures may involve specialized computer equipment or software (e.g., a way to capture people's interactions with a new information system). They may involve printing and mailing of surveys. They may involve audio or video recording of interviews. They may involve providing financial incentives to your study participants. In summary, you need to make sure you have the resources to obtain the equipment and materials you will need to carry out the study. In addition, you need to make sure that you or a member of your research team has the expertise to use specialized equipment or software effectively.

Finally, you need to consider the political support you will need to carry out the study. Particularly if the study is to be carried out within the context of an organization, you will need the approval and support of the organization's management. You may also encounter resistance to your study among your potential participants if the research question is sensitive in some way. For example, if you are studying the ways in which a particular computer system can improve the efficiency of the workers using it, they may believe that the purpose of the study is to calculate how many workers can be laid off. In such a setting, you will face political obstacles in conducting the research.

If you find that you do have access to your potential study participants, you have a means to obtain the equipment and materials needed, and you have the political support of the study's stakeholders, you are ready to proceed. Otherwise, you may need to rethink your research questions (Robson, 2002; Stone, 2002).

The Role of Funding Agencies in Shaping Your Problem Statement

In some cases, you do not have the resources to carry out a research study, but there is a funding source that might be convinced to support it. Both private sources (foundations and corporations) and public sources of funding (local, state, and federal government agencies) should be considered. Possible funding sources might be identified by searching specialized databases, by searching the Web, and by checking the acknowledgments in related articles discovered during your reading on the topic. Once you've identified a few possible funding sources, check what types of projects they've funded in the past. Also check any initiatives they've recently announced. If you have a research question that you think is important for the field, it's very possible that you can convince others of its importance.

In some cases, you may also want to modify your research question somewhat to correspond more closely to a funding source's interests. For instance, a foundation may fund exactly the type of study you're interested in conducting, but they limit their support to studies in the state in which their offices are located. If such a compromise is still of interest to you, you may be persuaded by the funding source's views. In other cases, you will want to seek other sources of funding. Careful reflection on the significance of your research question will guide you in making this decision.

EXAMPLES

In each chapter within this book, examples illustrate the way in which the chapter's topic has been applied in specific research studies. To illustrate the ways in which research questions are developed, I will instead briefly summarize the examples used in the rest of this section, with special emphasis on how each research question was developed. The examples are discussed more fully in the other chapters in which they are presented.

Chapter 3 focuses on research questions that are grounded in information and library practice. Such research questions are motivated by specific problems that arise in the everyday lives of information professionals. Some of these studies are carried out by those professionals, while others are carried out by academic researchers (usually working closely with practicing professionals). The three examples discussed in this chapter include a study designed to help a branch library in a large university develop its marketing plan for a particular subset of its user population (Song, 2006), a study that uses the logs of user searches of a Web site to develop a menu structure for a portion of that Web site (Huntington & Nicholas, 2006), and a statewide study of school libraries and the ways in which they can help students learn (Todd, 2003).

Chapter 4 focuses on descriptive studies: those that are intended to fully describe some phenomenon of interest. Descriptive studies address such questions as, What is this phenomenon? What occurred at this event, and who participated in it? When and where is the phenomenon occurring? How frequently is this phenomenon occurring? or What is the meaning of this occurrence? The four examples discussed in this chapter include a study of library users' understanding of relationships among sets of works (e.g., multiple versions of Dickens's *A Christmas Carol*; Carlyle, 2001), a study of chemists' perceptions of e-prints (Brown, 2003), the role of reading in the lives of lesbian and queer young women (Rothbauer, 2004a, 2004b), and a study of imposed queries brought to public libraries (Gross & Saxton, 2001). Because the phenomena of interest in ILS are changing rapidly, there is a strong need for high-quality descriptive studies.

Testing specific hypotheses is the focus of Chapter 5. In some situations, we already have a basic understanding of a phenomenon and can begin to formulate hypotheses about the relationships between that phenomenon and other phenomena. Such is the case for the studies examined in this chapter: a study of people's desire for control of information retrieval interactions (White & Ruthven, 2006), a study of the effect of a workshop on clinicians' information seeking behaviors and attitudes (Cheng, 2003), and a study of the effects of peripheral cues on people's evaluations of newsbot displays (Sundar et al., 2007). As you can see, these types of studies generally focus on relationships between phenomena or the effect of one phenomenon on another.

Finally, Chapter 6 examines questions related to theory, either by attempting to develop new theory or to validate existing theory. The field of information and library science is still young in comparison with other disciplines. Thus we are still in the process of developing theories of information behaviors and other phenomena of interest to the field. Two examples illustrating theory development are discussed in this chapter: a study defining a typology of relationships between personal growth and Internet use (Kari & Savolainen, 2007) and a study developing a model of factors that affect sense making within an organizational context (Solomon, 1997a, 1997b, 1997c). In addition, a third example is used to illustrate how an existing theory can be validated; in this case, Fisher et al.'s (2004) concept of *information grounds* is validated by testing its extension into a new setting.

In Part 2, we've devoted four chapters to four different kinds of research questions. These are not the only types of research questions that need to be investigated in ILS, nor are the boundaries of these four types clearly defined. They are meant only to demonstrate that the research questions that we might ask are quite diverse and may be inspired by many different sources. In each case, the examples provided can show you how an ILS research question can be successfully formulated.

WORKS CITED

Barrett, M. (2006). Practical and ethical issues in planning research. In G. M. Breakwell, S. Hammond, C. Fife-Schaw, & J. A. Smith (Eds.), *Research Methods in Psychology* (3rd ed., pp. 24–49). London: Sage.

Booth, A. (2001). Asking questions, knowing answers. *Health Information and Libraries Journal, 18*(4), 238–240.

Booth, A. (2006). Clear and present questions: Formulating questions for evidence based practice. *Library Hi Tech, 24*(3), 355–368.

Brown, C. (2003). The role of electronic preprints in chemical communication: Analysis of citation, usage, and acceptance in the journal literature. *Journal of the American Society for Information Science and Technology, 54*(5), 362–371.

Bryman, A. (2007). The research question in social research: What is its role? *International Journal of Social Research Methodology, 10*(1), 5–20.

Carlyle, A. (2001). Developing organized information displays for voluminous works: A study of user clustering behavior. *Information Processing and Management, 37*(5), 677–699.

Cheng, G.Y.T. (2003). Educational workshop improved information seeking skills, knowledge, attitudes and the search outcome of hospital clinicians: A randomised controlled trial. *Health Information and Libraries Journal, 20*(Suppl. 1), 22–33.

Creswell, J. W. (2003). *Research Design: Qualitative, Quantitative, and Mixed Method Approaches*. Thousand Oaks, CA: Sage.

Eldredge, J. (2001). The most relevant and answerable research questions facing the practice of health sciences librarianship. *Hypothesis, 15*(1), 9–14, 17.

Fisher, K. E., Durrance, J. C., & Hinton, M. B. (2004). Information grounds and the use of need-based services by immigrants in Queens, New York: A context based, outcome evaluation approach. *Journal of the American Society for Information Science and Technology, 55*(8), 754–766.

Gill, J., & Johnson, P. (1997). *Research Methods for Managers* (2nd ed.). London: P. Chapman.

Gray, D. E. (2004). *Doing Research in the Real World*. London: Sage.

Gross, M., & Saxton, M. L. (2001). Who wants to know? Imposed queries in the public library. *Public Libraries*, *40*(3), 170–176.

Hernon, P. (2001). Components of the research process: Where do we need to focus attention? *Journal of Academic Librarianship*, *27*(2), 81–89.

Huntington, P., & Nicholas, D. (2006). Improving the relevance of Web menus using search logs: A BBCi case study. *Aslib Proceedings*, *58*(1), 118–128.

Kari, J., & Savolainen, R. (2007). Relationships between information seeking and context: A qualitative study of Internet searching and the goals of personal development. *Library and Information Science Research*, *29*(1), 47–69.

Lévi-Strauss, C. (1969). *The Raw and the Cooked*. J. Weightman & D. Weightman (Trans.). New York: Harper and Row.

Locke, L. F., Spirduso, W. W., & Silverman, S. J. (2007). *Proposals That Work: A Guide for Planning Dissertations and Grant Proposals*. Thousand Oaks, CA: Sage.

Losee, R. M., Jr., & Worley, K. A. (1993). *Research and Evaluation for Information Professionals*. San Diego: Academic Press.

Mason, J. (2002). *Qualitative Researching* (2nd ed.). London: Sage.

Maxwell, J. A. (2005). *Qualitative Research Design: An Interactive Approach*. Thousand Oaks, CA: Sage.

Miles, M. B., & Huberman, A. M. (1984). *Qualitative Data Analysis: A Sourcebook of New Methods*. Newbury Park, CA: Sage.

Moore, N. (1987). *How to Do Research*. London: Library Association.

O'Leary, Z. (2005). *Researching Real-World Problems: A Guide to Methods of Inquiry*. London: Sage.

Punch, K. F. (1998). *Introduction to Social Research: Quantitative and Qualitative Approaches*. Thousand Oaks, CA: Sage.

Robson, C. (2002). *Real World Research: A Resource for Social Scientists and Practitioner-Researchers* (2nd ed.). Oxford: Blackwell.

Rothbauer, P. (2004a). The Internet in the reading accounts of lesbian and queer young women: Failed searches and unsanctioned reading. *Canadian Journal of Information and Library Science*, *28*(4), 89–110.

Rothbauer, P. (2004b). "People aren't afraid any more, but it's hard to find books": Reading practices that inform the personal and social identities of self-identified lesbian and queer young women. *Canadian Journal of Information and Library Science*, *28*(3), 53–74.

Solomon, P. (1997a). Discovering information behavior in sense making. I. Time and timing. *Journal of the American Society for Information Science*, *48*, 1097–1108.

Solomon, P. (1997b). Discovering information behavior in sense making. II. The social. *Journal of the American Society for Information Science*, *48*, 1109–1126.

Solomon, P. (1997c). Discovering information behavior in sense making. III. The person. *Journal of the American Society for Information Science*, *48*, 1127–1138.

Song, Y.-S. (2006). Evidence-based marketing for academic librarians. *Evidence Based Library and Information Practice*, *1*(1), 69–80.

Stone, P. (2002). Deciding upon and refining a research question. *Palliative Medicine*, *16*, 265–267.

Sundar, S. S., Knobloch-Westerwick, S., & Hastall, M. R. (2007). News cues: Information scent and cognitive heuristics. *Journal of the American Society for Information Science and Technology*, *58*(3), 366–378.

Todd, R. (2003). *Student learning through Ohio school libraries: A summary of the Ohio Research Study*. Retrieved December 17, 2007, from http://www.oelma.org/StudentLearning/documents/OELMAResearchStudy8page.pdf.

White, R. W., & Ruthven, I. (2006). A study of interface support mechanisms for interactive information retrieval. *Journal of the American Society for Information Science and Technology, 57*(7), 933–948.

3

Questions Originating in Library and Information Practice

Barbara M. Wildemuth

We may base our practice on our own experience, or we may supplement that experience with the experience of others.

—J. T. Gerould (1906)

Question formulation, and indeed question answering, is a key competency for our profession.

—Andrew Booth (2006)

WHY ASK PRACTICE-BASED QUESTIONS?

As early as 1906, Gerould was encouraging information professionals to use more than their own personal experience to make decisions about how best to provide information services. This call has been taken up in the last decade in the form of the evidence-based information practice movement (e.g., Booth & Brice, 2004) and the related call for evidence-based information systems (Atkins & Louw, 2000). The basic idea of evidence-based information practice is that information professionals should base their decisions on the strongest evidence available. As they make decisions about initiating new services, designing new systems, changing current policies, or a myriad of other issues that arise, they should use the current literature base and conduct their own research to identify evidence that can inform those decisions. As Davies (2002) points out, "what is most important is the intelligent use and interpretation of suitable evidence by those who determine policy, allocate resources and manage" (p. 129). In addition, information professionals should not only react to problems that arise in their professional practice. They should proactively question their current practices, constantly seeking ways to improve the resources and services they provide (Booth, 2006).

Most of the attention in the evidence-based information practice movement is on identifying and using the conclusions of existing studies to inform decisions about information practice. However, the body of research in information and library science is small (Haddow, 1997) and will continue to remain small if the creation of new knowledge is seen as the province of only the academic researchers in our field. To increase the research base of the field, practitioners will also need to conduct their own studies and report their results to the wider community (Crumley & Koufogiannakis, 2002). Information professionals "need to start filling the gaps and mending the seams of our professional body of knowledge in order for our profession to advance" (Koufogiannakis & Crumley, 2006, p. 338). While practitioners face a number of barriers to conducting research (e.g., lack of employer support for research, lack of external funding, lack of training/expertise in research methods, and lack of examples in the current literature), it is critical for them to overcome these barriers if we are to develop a robust knowledge base that can support evidence-based practice (Koufogiannakis & Crumley, 2006).

One way for practitioners to overcome many of these barriers is to team up with researchers in nearby universities. Such an arrangement is advantageous for both parties because the practitioner will get some evidence on which to base a decision and the academic researcher will get access to practical questions that can motivate studies that will have an immediate impact on the field. Even if there is no information and library science school nearby, an information professional may collaborate virtually or may team up with a researcher in a related department. For instance, a school librarian might team up with a researcher in education, or the developer of some social software might team up with a sociologist. In these ways, practitioners and academic researchers can, together, strengthen the field's knowledge base.

FORMULATING A PRACTICE-BASED QUESTION

The challenge with formulating a practice-based question is that there are so many interesting questions from which to choose. If you sat down with any group of a half-dozen information professionals, it would be easy to generate dozens of questions in an hour of discussion. These questions would likely be very closely associated with particular issues that have arisen for those information professionals in their day-to-day work. But the effort necessary to conduct a study means that you will need to select a question that is important, as discussed in Chapter 2. Most often, you will want to select a question related to one of your core activities, rather than just the newest technologies or procedures (Booth, 2006). Davies (2002) recommends gathering evidence about "inputs, outputs, outcomes, and impacts" (p. 131). The practitioners in studies by Eldredge (2001) and Lewis and Cotter (2007) believe that management, education, and reference services were the three core areas that could yield important research and evaluation questions. The answers to questions in these areas will have an enduring impact on information practice.

Before the research study can be designed, the question will need to be expressed in a somewhat more abstract form so that it is of interest beyond the local setting. Yet it should not become so abstract or generalized that it is no longer of interest in the local setting (i.e., so abstract that it will no longer provide evidence that can support the decision that motivated the original question).[1] Stating your research question at the appropriate level of abstractness will make the effort you invest in it more meaningful.

CARRYING OUT YOUR STUDY

Once you have clearly defined your research question, you are ready to conduct your study. The process of conducting a study of a practice-based question is similar to any other type of study, with one possible exception: often you are conducting the research in an organization of which you are a member. For example, if you were comparing two different approaches to bibliographic instruction for college students, it's likely you'd be working with a sample of the students at your own institution. Or if you were investigating the usability of your organization's Web site, you're likely to need to convey the results to designers within your organization. Your own closeness to the participants (or other stakeholders) in your research can carry with it some political issues that need to be resolved (O'Leary, 2005). Be sure to think these through as you're designing your study. Plan for how you will handle any potential problems that may arise.

The final step in the process is applying the results of your research to improve the services you offer. As O'Leary (2005) points out, the research you conduct "can be instrumental to your ability to either: (a) modify, refine and improve what it is that you do, or (b) make recommendations that can influence the practices of others within a particular setting" (p. 8). In the first case, you should be able to apply your research results as strong evidence related to the decision you'll make about your current practices. In the second case, you'll need to link your results to earlier work on the same question, pointing out how your results reinforce or differ from the results of those previous studies (Plutchak, 2005). In either case, you should disseminate your results by publishing them so that they can be of use to others facing similar questions in their local settings (Crumley & Koufogiannakis, 2002). In this way, your work can benefit you directly as well as build the body of information and library science knowledge.

EXAMPLES

Each of the three examples discussed here is based on a practice-based research question, and the results of each have important implications for that practice. The first was conducted by a single branch of an academic library but still has implications for the development of marketing strategies for academic libraries more generally. The second examines one way in which existing data (transaction logs of searches conducted on a particular Web site) can be used to help Web site designers make decisions during the design process. The third example is a statewide study of school libraries, with implications for ways in which they can more effectively support student learning.

Example 1: An Evidence-based Marketing Plan

As the Business and Economics Library (BEL) at the University of Illinois at Urbana-Champaign (UIUC) was considering new services to offer, one of the librarians there (Song, 2006) undertook a marketing study "to understand how business students perceived BEL and its current services" (p. 70). It was expected that understanding library users' attitudes about current services would help the librarians identify new services that would be most valuable to this audience.

The goal of the study was to survey all the graduate business students at UIUC. Two of the three research questions were intended to help the BEL design a general marketing strategy. These were: (1) "What services do graduate business students want to receive from BEL?" and (2) "With whom should BEL partner to increase visibility at the College of Business?" (Song, 2006, p. 72). Because over half of the students in the College of Business (the library's primary target audience) were international students, and approximately 70 percent of those international students were from East

Asia, the third research question focused on this subpopulation: "Should BEL develop marketing strategies differently for East Asian business students?" (Song, 2006, p. 72). Both open-ended and close-ended survey questions were used to generate results that addressed these questions.

This study illustrates the way in which a local library's planning needs can be addressed, while still conducting a study that will be of interest beyond the local setting. Very concrete results were obtained to provide support to the BEL's efforts in planning a marketing strategy. At the same time, it is likely that those results would also be applicable to other institutions (i.e., other large universities with a departmental business library that includes a high proportion of international students). By making these results available through publication, Song has added to our knowledge base for marketing academic libraries.

Example 2: Developing a Web Site's Menu Structure

Huntington and Nicholas (2006) argue that because "the search terms entered by users reveal their information need" (p. 119), the logs of user searches can be used effectively to design a Web site's menu structure. The design of a site's menu structure is a core problem faced by Web site designers in their daily practice; while the authors of this study are not practitioners, they have selected a research problem that has important implications for practice.

From a population of over 4 million searches, the authors analyzed the 1,838 searches that were related to diabetes. These searches included 384 different search expressions, with the top 20 search expressions accounting for 58 percent of all the searches. The search expressions (excluding the single term *diabetes*) were then classified into 19 broad subject categories. These categories were compared to the menu structures already implemented on three Internet-based diabetes information services (including the British Broadcasting Corporation [BBC] site, from which the transaction logs were collected). None of these menu structures was completely effective in covering the 19 broad subject categories identified from the user searches. The authors conclude by proposing a six-item menu structure that will provide good coverage of the subject categories derived from user searches.

The purpose of this paper was to demonstrate that transaction log data could be used as the basis for the design of Web site menu structures. Using one health-related topic (diabetes) as an example, Huntington and Nicholas (2006) were able to derive a menu structure that provided good coverage of the types of information needs that searchers of the BBC site expressed in their searches. To be applied to a wider range of topics (e.g., all health-related topics, or even more broadly, all topics covered on the BBC Web site) would require a significant additional investment. Nevertheless, the approach they espouse could be taken by designers of well-focused sites and could improve the menu structures on those sites.

Example 3: Evaluating School Libraries

Like many other states, Ohio was interested in investigating the potential links between investments in school libraries and student learning outcomes. To pursue this interest, the state awarded a grant to the Ohio Educational Library Media Association in 2002 to conduct a statewide study of the ways in which libraries help students learn. The connection between the research question and its implications for improving practice are made clear in Todd's (2003) summary of the study[2]: "On the basis of how students benefit from effective school libraries, this study sought to provide recommendations for professional practice, educational policy development, further research, and tools for school librarians to chart their libraries' impacts on learning. The project team also sought to focus on evidence-based practice by providing statewide data on best practices and promising practices in school librarianship that could serve as a basis for dialogue, continuous improvement and professional development across Ohio" (p. 1).

The study focused on 39 effective school libraries in Ohio. Students in grades 3 to 12 were invited to complete a Web-based survey of the ways in which the school library helped them learn; almost 900 of their teachers completed a similar survey. The survey consisted primarily of 48 sentences, each describing a way in which the library might help a student learn (e.g., "The school library has helped me be more careful about information I find on the Internet"); the students and faculty were to rate each "help" on its level of helpfulness.

In a later critique of the study findings, Logan (Everhart & Logan, 2005) outlines several ways in which the findings can be applied to practice in school libraries. They can use the findings to develop a shared vision or to develop new services for students (e.g., checking their bibliographies before they hand in a paper). This study also serves as a model for the way in which individual school librarians might evaluate their current or planned programs and services or might use student input in other ways. While this example study was conducted on a large scale, it can still serve as a model investigation of the practice-based question, How do school libraries help students learn?

CONCLUSION

As can be seen from these examples and many others not discussed here, it is important for the development of our knowledge base in information and library science to study research questions derived from the context of practice. As you consider undertaking a study based on such a question, you might find O'Leary's (2005) checklist useful:

Is the question right for you?
Does the question have significance for an organization, an institution, a group, a field, etc.?
Can it lead to tangible situation improvement?
Is the question well articulated?
Is the question researchable?
Does the question have a level of political support? (pp. 35–36)

If you responded yes to each of O'Leary's questions, then you're ready to embark on the design of your study. Once it's completed, the dissemination of your results will add to the body of knowledge that we can use to support evidence-based practice.

NOTES

1. It is likely that differing views about the appropriate level of abstractness for research questions is what leads practitioners to believe that the questions formulated by academic researchers are not useful (Booth, 2001; Lewis & Cotter, 2007).

2. Additional details on the study are available at http://www.oelma.org/StudentLearning/default.asp.

WORKS CITED

Atkins, C., & Louw, G. (2000). *Reclaiming knowledge: A case for evidence-based information systems.* Paper presented at the 8th European Conference on Information Systems. Retrieved November 28, 2007, from http://is2.lse.ac.uk/asp/aspecis/20000022.pdf.

Booth, A. (2001). Research: Turning research priorities into answerable questions. *Health Information and Libraries Journal, 18*(2), 130–132.

Booth, A. (2006). Clear and present questions: Formulating questions for evidence based practice. *Library Hi Tech, 24*(3), 355–368.

Booth, A., & Brice, A. (2004). Why evidence-based information practice? In A. Booth & A Brice (Eds.), *Evidence-Based Practice for Information Professionals: A Handbook* (pp. 1–12). London: Facet.

Crumley, E., & Koufogiannakis, D. (2002). Developing evidence-based librarianship: Practical steps for implementation. *Health Information and Libraries Journal, 19*(2), 61–70.

Davies, J. E. (2002). What gets measured, gets managed: Statistics and performance indicators for evidence based management. *Journal of Librarianship and Information Science, 34*(3), 129–133.

Eldredge, J. (2001). The most relevant and answerable research questions facing the practice of health sciences librarianship. *Hypothesis, 15*(1), 9–14, 17.

Everhart, N., & Logan, D. K. (2005). Building the effective school library media center using the Student Learning through Ohio School Libraries Research Study. *Knowledge Quest, 34*(2), 51–54.

Gerould, J. T. (1906). A plan for the compilation of comparative university and college library statistics. *Library Journal, 31,* 761–763.

Haddow, G. (1997). The nature of journals of librarianship: A review. *LIBRES, 7*(1). Retrieved November 28, 2007, from http://libres.curtin.edu.au/libre7n1/haddow.htm.

Huntington, P., & Nicholas, D. (2006). Improving the relevance of Web menus using search logs: A BBCi case study. *Aslib Proceedings, 58*(1), 118–128.

Koufogiannakis, D., & Crumley, E. (2006). Research in librarianship: Issues to consider. *Library Hi Tech, 24*(3), 324–340.

Lewis, S., & Cotter, L. (2007). Have the most relevant and answerable research questions facing librarians changed between 2001 and 2006? *Evidence Based Library and Information Practice, 2*(1), 107–120.

O'Leary, Z. (2005). *Researching Real-World Problems: A Guide to Methods of Inquiry.* London: Sage.

Plutchak, T. S. (2005). Building a body of evidence. *Journal of the Medical Library Association, 93*(2), 193–195.

Song, Y.-S. (2006). Evidence-based marketing for academic librarians. *Evidence Based Library and Information Practice, 1*(1), 69–80.

Todd, R. (2003). *Student learning through Ohio school libraries: A summary of the Ohio Research Study.* Paper presented to the Ohio Educational Library Media Association. Retrieved December 17, 2007, from http://www.oelma.org/StudentLearning/documents/OELMAResearchStudy8page.pdf.

4

Descriptions of Phenomena or Settings

Barbara M. Wildemuth

To describe is to draw a picture of what happened, or of how things are proceeding, or of what a situation or a person or an event is like. Description is concerned with making complicated things understandable.

—Keith Punch (1998)

INTRODUCTION

As Punch (1998) suggests in the epigraph, descriptive studies are conducted for the purpose of understanding a phenomenon or setting that is complicated—it is too complex to take in with just a superficial observation of it. When it is important to understand a phenomenon or setting, and we do not yet understand that phenomenon or setting, then a descriptive study should be undertaken. The research questions represented by descriptive studies ask such things as, What is this phenomenon? What occurred at this event, and who participated in it? When and where is this phenomenon occurring? How frequently is this phenomenon occurring? or What is the meaning of this occurrence?

There are a number of specific reasons for conducting a descriptive study, and often you will be using several of them in your rationale for a single study. The first, and most obvious, is that you need to explore a new phenomenon or construct. For example, not so long ago, there was no such thing as the World Wide Web. When the Web became a reality, it was not at all clear how people might go about searching for Web materials and navigating among Web sites. Many exploratory, descriptive studies have been undertaken to understand these phenomena, and more are needed as the capabilities provided by the Web evolve. A second reason for conducting a descriptive study is that you may wish to understand a phenomenon in more depth. It may be that a particular behavior has been found among a particular group, and you want to find out if another group of interest also displays the same behavior and, if not, how that group behaves differently. For example, previous studies may have found that middle school children read fantasy books as an escape mechanism, and you want to find out if this same motivation holds true for younger children. A third reason for conducting a descriptive study is to understand a particular phenomenon for the particular purpose of using that understanding to improve a system's or program's design. For example, you may want to understand your library's users' reactions to your summer reading program so that you can make improvements in that program. Or you may want to understand how people formulate their Web search strategies so that you can better support their searching of your new Web-based online library catalog. A fourth reason for conducting a descriptive study is that the study will be the first step in the development of a new theory. Because this purpose takes on some additional dimensions not present in other types of descriptive studies, a separate chapter is devoted to developing research questions related to theory development and validation (Chapter 6).

EXAMPLES

Four studies will be examined here, with our attention focused on the questions being asked and the rationale for those questions. In addition, we'll take a brief look at the ways in which the outcomes of the example studies addressed the research questions posed. The examples represent a variety of participant groups, from teenage girls to astronomers, and a variety of research designs and data collection methods, including surveys, in-depth interviewing, and direct observation. The variety of study methods is intended to illustrate that descriptive studies can draw on the full range of social research methods available.

Example 1: Library Users' Understanding of Relationships among Sets of Works

Carlyle (2001)[1] investigated "the ways in which people group or categorize documents associated with a voluminous work" (p. 677). She defined a voluminous work as "a large group of documents sharing a variety of relationships that evolve out of and are linked to a common originator document" (p. 678). For example, a keyword search on *shakespeare* and *romeo and juliet* in my university's online catalog today yielded 434 items. That list included the original play in various editions; books about Shakespeare and his plays; audio versions of the play or books about it; recordings of musical compositions inspired by the play; recordings of productions of the play; and modern adaptations of the play. They were not in any order that I could easily discern (e.g., the first occurrence of the actual play was fifth on the list).

The rationale for Carlyle's (2001) study was based on her desire to improve known-item searching in online catalogs. In particular, she was interested in improving the display of the results of a known-item search (Carlyle, 1997). Most current catalogs list a group of related documents with little or no indication of the relationships between the individual items in the group. Carlyle (2001) argues that "easily scanned, single-screen summary displays that group records or documents by type of relationship" (p. 679) would be more useful. Therefore she asked the research question, How would library users group the items in a voluminous work? By understanding how library users would group such works, system designers can match online catalog displays to users' expectations, thus providing better support for known-item searching in library catalogs.

Carlyle (2001) used Dickens's *A Christmas Carol* as the voluminous work in her study; it included a set of 47 documents. She asked her study participants to group the actual documents based on how similar they were to each other. Fifty adult participants were recruited in a local mall, and the study was conducted there. The data from the participants were analyzed through cluster analysis, identifying six different clusters: sound recordings, non–English language versions, paperback versions, video recordings, hardcover versions, and children's and activity versions. These clusters represent the mental models that people have concerning the items in a voluminous work and the relationships among those items. Carlyle went on to discuss the implications of these results in terms of the design of catalog displays (suggesting a possible way to display voluminous works), in terms of the metadata needed to implement such a display, and in terms of the design of digital libraries. In this way, her results are likely to have an impact on the design of online catalogs and similar systems.

Example 2: Chemists' Perceptions of E-Prints

Brown (2003)[2] investigated the acceptance of e-prints by chemists. This question originated from two different perspectives. The first was the launch of the Chemistry Preprint Server (CPS) by Elsevier in August 2000. At that time, it included 20 papers; by the end of 2001, when the study was conducted, it included 362 papers. In addition to allowing authors to post electronic preprints of papers, CPS also supported the evaluation (through reader rankings of them) and discussion (through an online discussion board) of those papers. The system provides listings of the most viewed, most discussed, and highest-ranking articles as well as the most recently posted articles. The availability of this novel service was one motivation for trying to describe the ways in which chemists accept and use it. The second motivation was the prior literature on other disciplines in the natural sciences and the ways in which they communicate within their "invisible colleges." In particular, a number of studies of physicists' use of electronic preprints have been undertaken, so a comparison of chemists' and physicists' scholarly communication behaviors would be of interest.

Given these motivations for the study, Brown (2003) wanted to describe the acceptance of the CPS by chemists as well as the ways in which they were using it. She analyzed citations to the e-prints included in CPS as well as their own referencing of electronic preprints. She examined the relationships between the citation data and the usage, ranking, and discussion data from CPS. She surveyed the authors of CPS papers concerning their perceptions of and interactions with CPS. Finally, she surveyed the editors of leading chemistry journals. She found that chemists had come to value the interactions associated with publication of electronic preprints and were "becoming increasingly aware of the utility, versatility, and validity of the e-print mode of communication" (p. 369).

Brown's (2003) research question was purely descriptive. She was interested in understanding a new phenomenon—the use of e-prints by chemists—in terms of both the chemists' behaviors and the chemists' perceptions of the utility of e-prints. This question, while partially motivated by the appearance of a new technology, was well situated within the context of studies of scholarly communication and builds on prior research in that area. Such snapshots of phenomena as they occur can be very useful, in the long term, for increasing our understanding of those phenomena and how they evolve.

Example 3: The Role of Reading in the Lives of Lesbian and Queer Young Women

For her dissertation, Rothbauer (2004a, 2004b)[3] "explored the role of reading in the lives of self-identified lesbian or queer young women" (2004a, p. 89). Part of her motivation was very personal—wondering whether others shared her "experience of the shock of self-recognition when [she] encountered a lesbian character in a novel for the first time" (2004a, p. 90). Rothbauer is not unique in the way her personal experiences shaped her research interests. It is often true that research questions are derived from the personal experiences of a researcher, for example, an encounter with a troublesome help desk client may lead to a study of help desk services, or an observation of a coworker's rejection of a new technology may lead to a study of technology resistance among information professionals. Your personal experiences can often launch a particular line of study.

In addition, Rothbauer (2004a) was motivated by a particular thread in the literature of library practice. As she notes, "an argument is often made in the literature for librarians that libraries ought to provide access to a broad selection of lesbian and gay literature, especially for young readers who may turn to library resources as a way to explore what it means to be lesbian, gay, bisexual, trans-, or queer" (p. 90). In an earlier, related study, she argued that public libraries, in particular, should provide access to literature for young adults that "reflects the reality of their lives" (Rothbauer & McKechnie, 1999, p. 32). Such calls for action in the literature often motivate a research study. As in this case, when somebody argues that libraries should do something, it can lead to a question about whether they actually heed that prescription.

Rothbauer worked her way around this question through a series of studies, first investigating whether Canadian public libraries included gay and lesbian fiction in their collections (Rothbauer & McKechnie, 1999) and subsequently studying how such fiction is reviewed in several of the reviewing tools used by librarians (Rothbauer & McKechnie, 2000). These studies eventually led to the research that is our focus here—an investigation of the role of reading such literature in the lives of young women. Using an interpretive approach to her research, Rothbauer (2004b) "conducted flexibly structured, in-depth, conversational interviews" (p. 62) with 17 young women who self-identified as lesbian or queer. In addition, four of the participants completed writing exercises, and Rothbauer kept field notes and diaries of her work. Her findings help us to understand the ways in which this particular population uses reading as an "opportunity to engage with the larger world" (Rothbauer, 2004b, p. 63) and the potential (though currently unfulfilled) role for public libraries in supporting these women's reading.

Example 4: Imposed Queries

Gross and Saxton (2001) position their research question within the context of the field's quest for an understanding of the ways in which public libraries are used. Specifically, they are interested in understanding imposed queries in a public library context. But the interest in public library services is only one of the roots of this question. The other starting point is in Gross's (1995) earlier work, developing the concept of an imposed query. An *imposed query* is defined as "a question that is developed by one person and then given to someone else who will receive, hold and transact the query for that person" (Gross & Saxton, 2001, pp. 170–171). For example, a student might be pursuing a question assigned by his or her teacher, or a husband might be pursuing a question originally raised by his wife. In each case, the information need is imposed on an agent, who will search for a response and communicate it to the original imposer of the question. Gross (1995) argues that the concept of the imposed query complements the concept of a self-generated query, augmenting our understanding of the information needs of library users and others.

In this study, Gross and Saxton (2001) want to find out the extent to which such queries are brought to public library reference desks, the characteristics of the agents bringing the questions, and the characteristics of the persons initially posing the question (i.e., the imposers). This type of question can be traced back to Gross's (1995) observation that "it is unclear with what frequency people seek information on the behalf of others, and the types of situations that elicit this behavior have not been fully enumerated" (p. 241). Here, Gross and Saxton (2001) begin to build our understanding of imposed queries addressed to public libraries. Additional descriptive studies in other library and information settings will be needed to more fully understand this phenomenon. In addition, researchers can begin to study the differences between user behaviors associated with self-generated queries and those associated with imposed queries. The findings of such studies will have important implications for providing reference services as well as designing computer-mediated library services.

CONCLUSION

The four studies examined in this chapter show us some of the variety of types of descriptive questions that might be asked. Some of them (e.g., Carlyle, 2001) will originate from professional practices that are in need of improvement. Some of them (e.g., Brown, 2003) will originate in the invention of a new technology. Some of them will arise from the practice literature (e.g., Gross & Saxton, 2001; Rothbauer, 2004a, 2004b) or the research literature (e.g., Brown, 2003; Gross & Saxton, 2001). Some of them (e.g., Rothbauer, 2004a, 2004b) will originate in the personal experiences of the researcher. In all the examples examined here, the first priority was to describe the phenomenon of interest, whether it was the publishing behaviors and attitudes of chemists or the reading behaviors and attitudes of young lesbian women.

Most often, descriptive questions arise at the beginning of a program of study, when the phenomenon of interest has not yet been fully defined. The goal is for the research to provide a detailed description of the phenomenon of interest and, possibly, its relationships to other phenomena. Eventually, a theory about it may be formed and hypotheses about that theory generated and tested. Examples of such questions are examined in other chapters in Part 2.

NOTES

1. This paper received the 2000 Bohdan S. Wynar Research Paper Award from the Association for Library and Information Science Education.

2. This paper received the 2004 Wiley Best *JASIST* Paper Award from the American Society for Information Science and Technology.

3. These two articles are based on Rothbauer's dissertation, which received the 2005 Garfield Dissertation Award from the Association for Library and Information Science Education.

WORKS CITED

Brown, C. (2003). The role of electronic preprints in chemical communication: Analysis of citation, usage, and acceptance in the journal literature. *Journal of the American Society for Information Science and Technology, 54*(5), 362–371.

Carlyle, A. (1997). Fulfilling the second objective in the online catalog: Schemes for organizing author and work records into usable displays. *Library Resources and Technical Services, 41*(2), 79–100.

Carlyle, A. (2001). Developing organized information displays for voluminous works: A study of user clustering behavior. *Information Processing and Management, 37*(5), 677–699.

Gross, M. (1995). The imposed query. *RQ, 35*(2), 236–243.

Gross, M., & Saxton, M. L. (2001). Who wants to know? Imposed queries in the public library. *Public Libraries, 40*(3), 170–176.

Punch, K. F. (1998). *Introduction to Social Research: Quantitative and Qualitative Approaches.* London: Sage.

Rothbauer, P. (2004a). The Internet in the reading accounts of lesbian and queer young women: Failed searches and unsanctioned reading. *Canadian Journal of Information and Library Science, 28*(4), 89–110.

Rothbauer, P. (2004b). "People aren't afraid any more, but it's hard to find books": Reading practices that inform the personal and social identities of self-identified lesbian and queer young women. *Canadian Journal of Information and Library Science, 28*(3), 53–74.

Rothbauer, P. M., & McKechnie, L.E.F. (1999). Gay and lesbian fiction for young adults: A survey of holdings in Canadian public libraries. *Collection Building, 18*(1), 32–39.

Rothbauer, P. M., & McKechnie, L.E.F. (2000). The treatment of lesbian and gay fiction for young adults in selected prominent reviewing media. *Collection Building, 19*(1), 5–16.

5

Testing Hypotheses

Barbara M. Wildemuth

The great tragedy of science—the slaying of a beautiful hypothesis by an ugly fact.
—Thomas Henry Huxley (1907)

DEFINITION OF A HYPOTHESIS

Kerlinger (1986) defines a hypothesis as "a conjectural statement of the relation between two or more variables" (p. 17). Thus, when we say that we will test a hypothesis, we mean that we have made a statement that we assume, for the sake of argument, to be true. But the research study itself will be designed to test the truth of the statement. In Kumar's (2005) words, it must be "capable of verification" (p. 76). So, as Huxley (1907) points out, it is the task—and the great tragedy—of research to be obligated to test our hypotheses against reality.

In most cases, research hypotheses in social science research make a statement about the relationship between two variables. For example, I might hypothesize that the amount a person uses an information system is related to his or her satisfaction with that system. This example is typical in that the hypothesis states that the two variables are related but does not state that one causes the other. In this example, more use may cause an increase in satisfaction, or higher satisfaction may cause increased use, or there may be some other (as yet unknown) variable that leads to both more use and higher satisfaction. We often want to find out whether one phenomenon causes another. As Punch (1998) points out, "the concept of causation is deeply ingrained in our culture, and saturates our attempts to understand and explain the world" (p. 51). To move from testing for the existence of a hypothesized relationship to concluding that one of the phenomena causes the other, we usually must rely on additional data or forms of reasoning.

SOURCES OF HYPOTHESES

There are many sources from which you might develop a hypothesis. One possibility is that you have direct experience with a phenomenon and, in your personal experience, find it to be related to another phenomenon. You might decide to carry out a research study to determine whether this relationship holds in settings other than the one you have observed. While it is possible that you may design your study to test your hypothesis, you may face challenges in the study design if the phenomena of interest are not well defined. If you are the first to investigate these phenomena, there may be no methods established for measuring them. In that case, you will need to conduct a more descriptive study first, to more clearly define each phenomenon of interest. A second source of hypotheses is the evidence provided by prior studies. It is possible (even likely) that some studies have already investigated the phenomena in which you're interested. Even if they have not investigated the specific relationship you're hypothesizing, their results may have suggested that the relationship exists. On the basis of the foundation formed by the prior studies, you can formulate and test your hypothesis. A third source of hypotheses is theory. On the basis of extensive bodies of research, some theories about information phenomena have been established. For example, Rogers's (2003) diffusion theory might be relevant to studies of the diffusion of chat reference, or social network theory (e.g., Haythornthwaite, 1996, 2007) might be relevant to studies of the relationships formed through social software. If your hypothesis is based on an established theory, you are most likely trying to determine if it holds true in your specific situation. No matter what the source of your hypothesis, you have an obligation to test its accuracy to the best of your ability.

TESTING HYPOTHESES

The first step in testing a hypothesis is to state it clearly (Kumar, 2005). Most likely, it began as a question, possibly ill formed. First try to write it out as a question. Then examine each noun in the question and define each clearly. Next, examine each adjective and verb in the question. Do they have clear implications for how your study will be designed, or is there some ambiguity about their roles? Let's look at an example. Say that my question is, "Is the new library catalog better than the old one?" The nouns of interest are *the new library catalog* and *the old library catalog*. It is likely that they are clearly defined, though that may not be the case if the implementation of the new catalog was gradual and occurred in multiple phases. The adjective in the question—*better*—is too vague. You need to decide what it means for your situation. Does it mean that the user can identify a known item faster? Does it mean that the user can find all the works on a particular subject and not miss any relevant works? There are many possible meanings for *better*, and you'll have to more clearly define it before you can test the hypothesis that the new catalog is better than the old one.

Once you begin to design your study, you will find it useful to state your hypothesis as a null hypothesis, that is, the hypothesis that there is no relationship between the variables or no difference between one thing and another. In our example, we might hypothesize that the level of user satisfaction with the new catalog is no different than the level of user satisfaction with the old catalog. The statistical analyses you will want to conduct for your study can only test null hypotheses, so you need to conceptualize your hypothesis in this way.

EXAMPLES

Three examples of hypothesis testing will be discussed here. In each case, I will emphasize the process through which the hypothesis was formulated, based on the introduction and background presented by the author(s) of the study. The first example (White & Ruthven, 2006) is typical of information retrieval experiments involving human subjects and investigates people's desire for control over particular aspects of the retrieval interaction. The second example (Cheng, 2003) examines the effects of a workshop on physicians' information seeking behaviors and attitudes. It was an experiment conducted within a practice (rather than an academic) setting and was clearly influenced by medical research methodologies. The third example (Sundar et al., 2007) is more cognitive in focus, and the formulation of the research question clearly relies on a theoretical base: information foraging theory. While the authors of each of these examples have formulated their hypotheses in a different way, all clearly describe the sources of the hypotheses and state the hypotheses explicitly.

Example 1: People's Desire for Control of Information Retrieval Interactions

White and Ruthven (2006) developed their research question based on past empirical studies in information retrieval and, particularly, studies of the ways in which people reformulate their queries through relevance feedback. They were especially interested in three aspects of people's interactions with search systems: formulating and reformulating queries, indicating that particular items are relevant to the information need motivating the query, and deciding whether to stop or continue with a search. Their purpose in conducting the study was "to establish how much control users *actually want*" (p. 934) over these three aspects of their search interactions.

The research question is embedded within the assumption that it is worth pursuing the use of relevance feedback for improving search effectiveness. This assumption is based on past studies of information retrieval on "batch" systems, in which relevance feedback has proved effective. To inform the design of this study, the authors reviewed past studies of the ways in which people formulate and re-formulate queries, provide relevance feedback by identifying relevant documents, and indicate that a search should continue rather than stop. This literature provided some background information on people's behaviors, but it did not answer the question of how much control people would like to exert when conducting a search.

To address this question, the authors developed three different systems, each allocating control for search processes to the user or to the system in different ways. The "manual" system allowed the user to fully control relevance indication, query construction, and query execution. The "assisted" system delegated relevance indication to the system; the system assumed that, if the user interacted with the representations of a particular document, that document should be considered relevant, even though the user did not explicitly mark it as relevant. In the "assisted" system, responsibility for query construction and query execution were shared by the user and the system. A third system, the "automatic" system, placed control for all three activities with the system.

Given these three systems, the next challenge for the authors was to decide on the criteria that should be used to compare the systems. Because they were interested in people's desire for control, rather than user or system performance, they chose to evaluate people's affective responses to the systems. Each study participant interacted with each system, then rated their reactions to those interactions through a series of questionnaires.

The primary question investigated by this study can, thus, be stated as the null hypothesis that there is no difference in users' attitudes toward and preferences for these three systems. If a difference was discovered (leading the researchers to reject the null hypothesis), we would infer that future systems should delegate control of the search interaction to the user or the system in a way that mimics the preferred system in this study. Overall, White and Ruthven (2006) found that the participants wanted the system to infer relevance from their interactions, but that they wanted to retain control over the query formulation and query execution processes.

This study is a good example of how a research question can be derived from prior empirical studies and can lead to further research questions. The research question was based on the many studies of relevance feedback in so-called batch retrieval systems that preceded this study as well as the many studies of how people interact with search systems. These prior studies helped the authors to narrow their focus on the question of how much control of the search process should be allocated to the searcher and how much to the system. Furthermore, the authors argued persuasively that it was necessary to understand people's desire for control before investigating the particular interface mechanisms that would provide them with that control. Their study leaves us with a clear path to these future interface-oriented research questions.

The authors developed an experiment, based on their research question, to test the (null) hypothesis that there was no difference between the systems in terms of their ability to support people's desires for control of the search process. While this research question could have been framed in a way that led to another type of research design, it was very appropriate for the authors to develop the three systems with clearly articulated differences in level of user control and to formally test the differences in users' attitudes toward them. Both the types of control that might be delegated to the system and the measurement of users' attitudes toward system effectiveness were relatively well understood. The first dimension (i.e., level of control) could be manipulated to set up the needed comparisons. The second dimension (i.e., user perceptions) could be reliably measured. This is the ideal situation in which a formal hypothesis can be tested.

Example 2: The Effect of a Workshop on Clinicians' Information Seeking Behaviors and Attitudes

Cheng's (2003) research question was motivated by her own prior research and her experiences in her information center. Her dissertation research (Cheng, 2002) suggested that clinicans' success in problem solving was related to both their satisfaction with electronic databases and other resources and their use of those resources. In addition, usage statistics from her own institution, the Hong Kong Hospital Authority, indicated that use of electronic resources increased after the Knowledge Management Unit offered workshops on searching these resources. She then put these two links together to form a chain of reasoning from the offering of workshops, to greater use/satisfaction with electronic resources, to improved clinical problem solving. Her study was intended to find out whether these relationships actually exist, as she hypothesized.

In this study, Cheng (2003) is relatively explicit in her desire to establish a causal relationship between the workshops on searching and improved problem solving. It is much easier to establish that there is some kind of relationship than it is to establish that one phenomenon causes another. Nevertheless, Cheng's study design largely succeeds in doing so. She had a pool of clinicians (doctors, nurses, and allied health professionals) who were interested in a workshop on searching. She randomly assigned half of them to attend a workshop in the first month the workshops were offered (the experimental group, $n = 257$ out of the 400 participants originally recruited for this group) and delayed the other half until the next month (the control group, $n = 287$ out of the 400 participants originally recruited for this group). After the workshop, the experimental group answered a questionnaire about their preferences for and attitudes toward electronic resources and their knowledge and skill in selecting appropriate electronic resources, formulating appropriate queries, and conducting searches. The link between the workshop and physician problem solving was weaker; the physicians did provide a self-assessment of whether "the problem in hand" (p. 25) had been solved, but it is not clear what exactly was asked in this questionnaire. The control group responded to the same questionnaires before they attended the workshops. As the knowledge test was scored and the attitude questionnaire was analyzed, those evaluating the clinicians' responses did not know which were in the experimental group and which were in the control group (i.e., they were blinded to the participants' group assignments).

The random assignment of the participants to the two groups and the blind review of their responses support Cheng's (2003) claim that the workshops caused the effects observed. Often, claims of causal relationships rest on the researcher's ability to rule out all other possible causes of those effects. In Cheng's study, one possible cause for differences in the groups would be if the groups had been different before attending the workshops; for example, one group might have had more experience with electronic databases than the other. Through random assignment, this possibility can be ruled out. The only weakness in this argument being applied to Cheng's study is the attrition between the time people signed up for the workshops and when the data were collected. For the experimental group, one had to have attended the workshops and completed the questionnaires to be considered a study participant; for the control group, one only needed to have completed the questionnaires. So it would be worthwhile to confirm that those who participated in each group were similar to those in the other group in terms of such characteristics as professional experience, occupational category, years of search experience, or frequency of searching, and so on. If Cheng carried out these analyses, she did not report them, possibly due to lack of space.

If we accept the argument that there were no important differences between the experimental group and the control group, then the case for the workshops causing any differences discovered between the groups' attitudes and knowledge/skills is quite strong. This was, in fact, what happened in this study. Cheng (2003) found quite large differences between the groups. Her null hypothesis, that there would be no effect from attending the workshops, was rejected.

Example 3: Effects of Peripheral Cues on People's Evaluations of Newsbot Displays

Sundar et al. (2007) based their hypotheses on two theories. The first of these is *information foraging theory* (Pirolli & Card, 1999), which postulates that people use proximal cues about the relevance of distal information to make decisions about whether to pursue that information. For example, you might use the text of a hyperlink (a proximal cue) to make a decision about whether to click and go to the page at the far end of the hyperlink (the distal information). Using a biological metaphor, the theory postulates that if the information scent of the proximal cue is strong enough, a person will follow that scent to the distal information. Part of the motivation for the Sundar and colleagues study is to find out whether the proximal cues provided in result lists from Web-based news aggregators (e.g., http://news.google.com) have enough information scent to influence people's interpretations of the credibility of the news story listed.

The second theory relevant to the current study is a *dual-route theory of persuasion* (Petty, 1994). This theory postulates that there are two different processes by which someone might be persuaded to take an action: through the careful scrutiny of issue-relevant arguments or through the processing of peripheral cues. The proximal cues defined in information foraging theory fit the definition of peripheral cues in this dual-route theory of persuasion. The idea is that the cue (i.e., the hyperlink anchor) persuades the person to follow it. This second theory provides much more detail about how people cognitively process peripheral cues, either individual cues or combinations of cues. Because Sundar et al. (2007) wanted to examine the influence of three types of cues, and those influences may be cumulative, they relied on this theory to formulate their hypotheses.

The two theories that provide the foundation for this study are both fairly abstract. They have been applied to many different specific contexts, each of which encompasses specific instances of the abstract concepts in the theory. For instance, information foraging theory has been applied to people's navigation behaviors on the Web; in that context, the proximal cues are always link anchors and the distal information is always the Web page to which the link is connected. When study hypotheses are derived from theories, as in this case, it is almost always the case that the researcher wants to know whether the abstract concepts in the theory (and the postulated relationships between them) will hold true in a particular context of interest to the researcher. The context under study by Sundar et al. (2007) is news aggregators. While Web-based news aggregators, like other contexts examined from the perspectives of one or both of these theories, are also different because they offer different forms of proximal cue beyond the link anchor (i.e., the title of the news story), specifically, Sundar and colleagues wanted to study the potential influences of the source of the story (i.e., which news organization posted it on the Web), the recency of its posting, and the number of related articles that had been posted. They formulated five specific hypotheses about these influences: (1) the effect of source on the story's credibility, (2) the effect of the number of re-lated articles on the story's credibility, (3) the effect of the number of related articles on the perceived newsworthiness of the story, (4) the effect of the number of related articles on the likelihood that someone will click through to the story, and (5) the ef-fect of the story's recency on its perceived newsworthiness. In addition, they used the dual-route theory of persuasion to conduct a more exploratory investigation of the ways in which these three types of proximal/peripheral cues affect people's perceptions and behaviors.

Sundar et al. (2007) carried out their study by having people review result listings of news stories, which systematically varied on each of the three types of cues. For example, some of the stories were described as having been posted just minutes ago, while others were described as having been posted almost two days ago. Each study participant was exposed to the descriptions of 12 stories and then responded to a questionnaire about each story's credibility, its newsworthiness, and the likelihood they would click on the description to read the full story. In summary, this study is an example of the way in which a theory (with well-defined constructs and relationships) can be used to generate specific hypotheses that can be tested for their applicability in a new context.

CONCLUSION

Many studies are conducted to test specific hypotheses. These hypotheses may be derived from personal experience (as with the Cheng, 2003, study), from prior research (as with the White & Ruthven, 2006, study), or from a theoretical foundation (as with the Sundar et al., 2007, study). No matter what the source for the hypotheses is, the hypothesis must be stated clearly for it to be tested. Hypotheses may be listed explicitly, as in the Sundar and colleagues study, or they may be stated as research questions and transformed into null hypotheses only for statistical analyses. However, it is critical that each construct or phenomenon under investigation be defined clearly and that each criterion evaluated or aspect examined be characterized in a way that can lead to its valid measurement.

WORKS CITED

Cheng, G.Y.T. (2002). *Measuring Electronic Information Services: The Use of the Information Behaviour Model*. Canberra, ACT: University of Canberra.

Cheng, G.Y.T. (2003). Educational workshop improved information seeking skills, knowledge, attitudes and the search outcome of hospital clinicians: A randomised controlled trial. *Health Information and Libraries Journal*, *20*(Suppl. 1), 22–33.

Haythornthwaite, C. (1996). Social network analysis: An approach and technique for the study of information exchange. *Library and Information Science Research*, *18*, 323–342.

Haythornthwaite, C. (2007). Social networks and online community. In A. N. Joinson, K.Y.A. McKenna, T. Postmes, & U.-D. Reips (Eds.), *The Oxford Handbook of Internet Psychology* (pp. 121–138). New York: Oxford University Press.

Huxley, T. H. (1907). Reflection #219. In H. A. Huxley (Ed.), *Aphorisms and Reflections*. London: Macmillan.

Kerlinger, F. N. (1986). *Foundations of Behavioral Research* (3rd ed.). New York: Holt, Rinehart and Winston.

Kumar, R. (2005). *Research Methodology: A Step-by-Step Guide for Beginners* (2nd ed.). London: Sage.

Petty, R. E. (1994). Two routes to persuasion: State of the art. In G. d'Ydewalle, P. Eelen, & P. Bertelson (Eds.), *International Perspectives on Psychological Science: Vol. 2. The State of the Art* (pp. 229–247). Hillsdale, NJ: Erlbaum.

Pirolli, P., & Card, S. (1999). Information foraging. *Psychological Review*, *106*(4), 643–675.

Punch, K. (1998). *Introduction to Social Research: Quantitative and Qualitative Approaches*. Thousand Oaks, CA: Sage.

Rogers, E. M. (2003). *Diffusion of Innovations* (5th ed.). New York: Free Press.

Sundar, S. S., Knobloch-Westerwick, S., & Hastall, M. R. (2007). News cues: Information scent and cognitive heuristics. *Journal of the American Society for Information Science and Technology*, *58*(3), 366–378.

White, R. W., & Ruthven, I. (2006). A study of interface support mechanisms for interactive information retrieval. *Journal of the American Society for Information Science and Technology*, *57*(7), 933–948.

6

Questions Related to Theory

Chad Morgan and Barbara M. Wildemuth

There never comes a point where a theory can be said to be true. The most that one can claim for any theory is that it has shared the successes of all its rivals and that it has passed at least one test which they have failed.

—Sir A. J. Ayer (1982)

INTRODUCTION

When considering a research question related to theoretical concepts or propositions, you'll first need to figure out what you mean by *theory*. That term means (a lot of) different things to different people. In everyday speech, *theory* may describe a casual hunch or assumption about a given phenomenon. Merriam-Webster's Online Dictionary (http://www.merriam-webster.com/) defines it as "the analysis of a set of facts in their relation to one another." To physicist Stephen Hawking (1988), a theory must meet two criteria: "It must accurately describe a large class of observations on the basis of a model which contains only a few arbitrary elements, and it must make definite predictions about the results of future observations" (p. 10). Merton (1968) summarizes the problem when he notes that the term *theory* refers to many different things, "including everything from minor working hypotheses, through comprehensive but vague and unordered speculations, to axiomatic systems of thought" (p. 39). Yet even such widely cast nets do not ensnare everything that scholars seem to mean when they invoke the *T* word.

Understandably, at least one researcher has found it easier to say what theory is not. Mintzberg (2005) began his contemplation of the topic by enumerating those things not falling under the rubric of theory. He concluded that theory was, first of all, not true. Instead, theories are simplifications of always-more-complicated realities; they are useful ways of looking at and understanding a world that persistently resists even the most formidable logic. Because theories are not true, it follows that theory development is neither objective nor deductive, according to Mintzberg. Developing theory is by definition inductive—it moves from the particular to the general. *Testing* theory, on the other hand, is deductive. Mintzberg goes on to bemoan the fact that often only theory testing is thought of as proper science. Instead, he encourages young scholars to work at developing new theory by pointing out the satisfaction it brings. "What makes me salivate is induction: inventing explanations about things. Not finding them—that's truth; inventing them," he writes. "We don't discover theory; we create it. And that's great fun" (Mintzberg, 2005, p. 357). A world where the testing of theory counts as the only real science is also one where progress is not possible. A theoretical model is not defeated by the discovery of exceptions to the theory, but only by the evolution of a better model, or at least one that better answers the questions that scientists are asking at a given time.

Kuhn (1996) reinforces this argument by pointing out that there are certain circumstances under which the development of new theories becomes especially appropriate. These circumstances are moreover tied to the process of theory testing and the discovery of anomalies that do not fit in with the currently dominant model. In Kuhn's formulation, what he calls "normal" science "is predicated on the assumption that the scientific community knows what the world is like" (p. 5). In other words, it is based on the idea that theories are essentially, if not actually, true; they describe whatever phenomenon they purport to describe at least as well as any other existing theory. But because theories are by definition not true, a theory works only until a critical mass of anomalies and exceptions to it are found, at which point, it becomes untenable and must be replaced by a new theoretical model.

One of the hallmarks of such a new theory is that it is unexpected. "No matter how accepted eventually, theory is of no use unless it initially surprises—that is, changes perceptions" (Mintzberg, 2005, p. 361). Useful theory gives us new ways of looking at phenomena. The process of arriving at a new perspective is, according to Mintzberg, ineffable. Normal science can tell us how to test existing theory; that requires that one look at data and assess how it comports with the theory. But theory formation is the process of generalizing beyond one's data, moving from the particular to the general, and there are no sure methods for doing that. Another way of putting it would be to say that one can teach rigor, that is, the systematic testing of data; but insight—seeing the broader implications of one's data—is, at its core, an act of creation. And creativity cannot be taught (though it can be developed).

So when *is* it most appropriate to develop theory? Should doctoral students and junior scholars, as Mintzberg suggests, busy themselves more with inventing theories and less with testing them? Or are theories really frameworks within which scholars in mature scientific communities work as long as they remain plausible, as Kuhn argues, and therefore something which it is only necessary to revise every generation or so? There is less tension between these two positions than there might at first appear, and a lot of the apparent tension stems from the different definitions employed by Mintzberg and Kuhn. While Mintzberg's theories comprise everything from simple typologies to full-blown paradigms, Kuhn means only the latter when he writes of theory. He's talking about the cosmos-defining "grand" theories advanced by Newton, Darwin, Marx, Freud, Einstein, and the like.

Obviously, this chapter will not tell you how to develop such grand theories. Instead, it will focus on the development and validation of what Merton (1968) calls *middle-range theories*. These theories are at a middle point on the continuum between what he calls *special theories*, which are applicable only to a very small range of phenomena, and *general theories*, which are highly abstract and applicable to a broad range of phenomena.

Middle-range theories are concrete enough to clearly apply to phenomena of interest to a professional field like information and library science, while simultaneously being abstract enough to apply to settings beyond the context in which they were originally developed (Poole, 1985).

Glaser and Strauss's (1967) approach to *grounded theory* development provides some structure for the development of middle-range theories. They argued for "grounding theory in social research itself—for generating it from the data" (p. viii). Specific methods for developing grounded theory were developed more fully by Strauss and Corbin (1990). The basic idea behind grounded theory is that theory emerges simultaneously with data collection—it isn't a separate process. Rather than testing an existing theory, this approach begins to formulate a theory that fits the data as the data emerge. At the heart of the process is an overwhelming familiarity of the researcher with his or her materials. The barest of outlines of grounded theory development would go something like the following. As the researcher reads and rereads the interview transcripts and other raw data, common themes and theoretical concepts will begin to emerge. The researcher codes (i.e., identifies and defines) these themes or concepts whenever they crop up in the data. During coding, theoretical propositions (i.e., relationships between variables) will occur to the researcher, and these propositions are written up in theoretical memos. These memos provide a record of the evolution of the theoretical framework, including documentation of conflicting evidence found in the data and the researcher's questions about the findings. The content of these memos continually sends the researcher back to the raw data, comparing the conclusions being drawn and the current version of the theory to the data from which it has been induced. A final prewriting process, sorting, is then undertaken. During the sorting process, the researcher brings the memos together to assess their relative importance and how they fit together into a (it is hoped) cogent and unified theory.

Unquestionably, the grounded theory approach has given the analysis of qualitative data a level of rigor it previously lacked. Still, it doesn't quite tell you how to develop theory. It gives you a set of steps to follow that should *allow* you to develop theory. And the constant comparison and rereading of data that are at the heart of grounded theory are well designed to eliminate, insofar as possible, discrepancies between what different researchers will conclude from a given data set. But even then, the process by which a researcher arrives at those conclusions is conditioned by personal predilection. Thus the process is both subjective and inductive, and every theory must be validated in a variety of contexts.

EXAMPLES

It is hoped that the present chapter, by examining a few examples of the development of theory at different levels—a typology (Kari & Savolainen, 2007), then a more fully developed middle-range theory (Solomon, 1997a, 1997b, 1997c)—will shed some light on that process. In keeping with our call for the validation of existing theories, we will also examine one example (Fisher et al., 2004) in which an existing theory is validated in a setting that is different from the context in which it was originally developed.

Example 1: A Typology of Relationships between Personal Growth and Internet Use

This first example illustrates the development of a typology, a comprehensive list of theoretical concepts or categories, and their definitions. Kari and Savolainen (2007) set out to explain "how exactly information processes relate to their context" (p. 47). Their purpose was to develop a typology of such relationships. More specifically, they addressed the following research question: "What kinds of relationships are there between individual developmental objectives and information searching via the Internet?" (p. 50).

After sending an e-mail asking for study volunteers to five local organizations (e.g., a public library, a computer club for seniors), Kari and Savolainen (2007) obtained 18 suitable participants for their study. These were individuals who simply expressed an interest in using the Internet to facilitate their personal growth; no other criteria were considered. The subjects were mostly female (12 of the 18) but came from a diversity of occupations, educational backgrounds, and ages. The study data came from five sources. The first was a primary interview, during which the researchers ascertained subjects' "general orientation of a partaker's self-development, Internet use, and Web searching" (p. 54). There followed a presearch interview focused on the circumstances that precipitated the participant's search for personal growth. The third step comprised observing and listening to the participant think aloud as he or she conducted a search. After that, the researchers debriefed the participant about the search results in a post-search interview. Finally, Kari and Savolainen conducted a last interview via telephone, in which they inquired what information the subjects had ascertained in subsequent, unsupervised searching sessions and how that information had affected their pursuit of personal development.

From these interviews and observations, the researchers identified 11 different kinds of relationships between Internet searching and personal growth. For example, there were "affecting" relationships, where the Internet affected a subject's personal growth or vice versa (i.e., growth influenced search); "causing" relationships, where the desire for personal growth moved a subject to search the Internet or vice versa; and "illustrating" relationships, where the Internet provided users with examples of how they hoped to grow. While some of the 11 types of relationships appear to overlap substantially, and others appear not to be relationships at all, it must be concluded that Kari and Savolainen (2007) have taken a major step forward in enumerating every conceivable type of linkage between Web searching and the goals of personal development.

If theirs is not the final word on the relationships they sought to study, this is only to say that Kari and Savoleinen's (2007) article is a true work of theory: not true and highly subjective. As the authors themselves put it, "these findings are not an end in themselves, but an instrument to be utilized in further research.... The work started here could be continued by testing the relationships with different sorts of information seeking or in different contexts; by measuring the distribution, strength and significance of the connections; or by analyzing each of them in more detail" (p. 57). In other words, they have created a typology that can serve as a spur to further research. This typology must now stand up to testing until it no longer can and a new typology becomes necessary to replace it.

Example 2: A Model of Factors Affecting Sense Making within an Organizational Context

Rather than merely categorizing phenomena, Solomon (1997a) posited relationships among several factors affecting "sense making of participants in the annual work planning of a unit of a public agency" (p. 1097). The unnamed government agency Solomon observed in his study was responsible for "provid[ing] technical assistance on natural resource conservation matters primarily to nonprofit community groups" (p. 1099) but had recently been incorporated into a larger parent organization. His research design was ethnographic, and his data collection methods included "observation, participant logs, interviews, and documentary traces" (p. 1101).

The theory-developing nature of his study is obvious from the beginning, as he wrote, "Research is a creative process that builds on a foundation of interests, ideas, anomalies, questions and intuitions; takes advantage of opportunities; and works around barriers and constraints" (Solomon, 1997a, p. 1097). In this three-part article,[1] the author attempts to isolate specific factors—timing, social context, and personal predilections—and how they affect sense making within an organizational context. Although clearly ambitious, Solomon is not trying to present a general theory of information behavior; his focus is narrower than that, and he is presenting what might be called a limited model—one that explains certain aspects of information behavior but doesn't try to explain everything in a given phenomenological universe.

In the first article of the series, to take just one example, Solomon (1997a) sought to describe the time and timing aspects of sense making over a three-year work-planning process. Specifically, he sought to capture exactly what comprised the work-planning process, how the process changed over time, and whether changes indicated progress or breakdowns. From observing this agency over several years, Solomon drew some conclusions that could be characterized as theoretical propositions. Among them were the following: "it takes time for people to build common ground and develop meaning from uncertain and ambiguous evidence" (p. 1107) and "information has a time value and timing of information gathering has important productivity implications" (p. 1107). He also draws some more specific conclusions with practical implications such as an "early start may actually limit productivity" because "information systems that support process may help in managing and planning for time" (p. 1107). Yet even the latter types of statements are pitched at a high level of abstraction, a hallmark of theoretical propositions.

Solomon paints with similarly broad strokes in other sections of the articles. In his contemplation of the social, he finds that "participants do not think of information or actions to collect, process, or use information as something separate from the task or problem at hand" (Solomon, 1997b, p. 1125). And in the series's third article, addressing the person, Solomon (1997c) concludes that different people, often reflecting their role in the organization, also have different sense-making styles. These styles included cognition, "where people develop an appreciation of an object in a way that builds on their previous knowledge and experience" (p. 1128); affect, which connoted the emotional side of sense making, including "outbursts of anger and expressions of frustration," in addition to "excitement, laughter, and other evidence of satisfaction" (p. 1129); and conation, meaning "action instincts" or people's natural preferences in information behavior, whether they be information gathering, information processing, innovation, or following through on an existing plan. Taken together, all these individual insights led Solomon (1997c) to the "fundamental insight . . . that information is embedded in people's lives" (p. 1137). It follows, therefore, that those of us who create information systems must "ground our designs in an understanding of the variety, uncertainty, and complexity of the role of information in people's lives" (p. 1137).

In effect, Solomon (1997a, 1997b, 1997c) is calling for more attention to be paid to the context of people's information behavior, based on the empirically grounded theory developed in this set of articles. As Brown and Duguid (2000) would later point out, the world of information is much richer than some designers of information systems would have us believe. But whereas Brown and Duguid concentrated on the social dimension of information and information behavior, Solomon sees a richer context still, one that also embraces time and personal proclivity. Solomon comes to these conclusions based not on some exhaustive survey of all varieties of information behavior—such a survey would be impossible, in the first place—but on the actions of a small number of individuals within one particular organizational context.

As mentioned at the outset, Solomon's (1997a, 1997b, 1997c) articles represent a higher level of theory than Kari and Savolainen's (2007) article because Solomon has attempted to explain the interrelationships among phenomena, rather than just to categorize them. Of course, he has proven nothing, but that is the nature of theory development. The test of his theory will be whether it explains sense making in any of the millions of other organizational milieux in the world.

Example 3: Validating a Theoretical Concept

Our third exemplar is not an instance of theory formation, but of theory validation. It is included here to illustrate the connection between the two processes. Fisher et al. (2004)[2] set out to test the validity of Fisher's *information grounds* concept, which she first discussed in relation to her study of the ways in which nurses and their elderly patients shared information at a monthly foot clinic (Pettigrew, 1999). As recapitulated in this article, an information ground is defined as an "environment temporarily created by the behavior of people who have come together to perform a given task, but from which emerges a social atmosphere that fosters the spontaneous and serendipitous sharing of information" (Fisher et al., 2004, p. 756). This definition and its applicability in a new context were validated in the 2004 study.

The new context was a set of "programs in literacy and coping skills run by the Queens Borough Public Library (QBPL)" (Fisher et al., 2004, p. 758). Fisher and her coauthors were seeking to understand, in part, "whether these programs might function as information grounds" (p. 758). By looking at whether the information grounds concept works in this specific context, they were evaluating the validity and usefulness of Fisher's theory. Their data came from three sources: interviews with library administrators about the effectiveness of the programs in gaining desired outcomes; interviews with immigrants about the same; and another round of follow-up interviews with library staff to "assess the efficacy of the survey instrument" (p. 758).

The results of the study "suggest[ed] that the QBPL literacy and coping skills model does indeed function as information ground" (Fisher et al., 2004, p. 762). The participants mostly got the information they needed through "communicating with other program attendees and their families and with program staff" (p. 762), which constitutes a key feature of information grounds. The QBPL programs also conformed to the proposed definition of an information ground inasmuch as they catered to similar social types; participants came "for the same instrumental purpose"; information sharing was multidirectional and both formal and informal; and attendees obtained "diverse outcomes and benefits" (p. 762). Given that the validity of this theoretical concept was being evaluated by its originator, it's not particularly surprising that the results were positive. Nevertheless, this study is a good example of the ways in which even the early formulations of a theory can be validated empirically. How useful the concept of information grounds remains will depend on its further validation in other contexts.

CONCLUSION

One would do well to keep certain guidelines in mind when developing and/or validating theory. First, you should plan to work with theories in the middle range—broad and abstract enough to be useful to the information and library science community generally, but concrete and well defined enough to be applicable to specific questions in the field. As you work on developing your own theory, base it on (i.e., ground it in) the most thorough examination of your data possible. Finally, as a general rule, make modest claims that accurately explain what is in your data set. Perhaps your theory will be applicable in other contexts, and perhaps it will not. That is something for repeated validity studies—not you alone—to decide.

NOTES

1. These papers received the 1999 John Wiley Best *JASIST* Paper Award, the Special Award for a Series, from the American Society for Information Science and Technology.
2. This paper received the 2005 Jesse H. Shera Award for Excellence in Published Research from the American Library Association Library Research Round Table.

WORKS CITED

Ayer, A. J. (1982). *Philosophy in the Twentieth Century*. New York: Random House.

Brown, J. S., & Duguid, P. (2000). *The Social Life of Information*. Boston: Harvard Business School Press.

Fisher, K. E., Durrance, J. C., & Hinton, M. B. (2004). Information grounds and the use of need-based services by immigrants in Queens, New York: A context based, outcome evaluation approach. *Journal of the American Society for Information Science and Technology*, 55(8), 754–766.

Glaser, B. G., & Strauss, A. L. (1967). *The Discovery of Grounded Theory: Strategies for Qualitative Research*. Chicago: Aldine.

Hawking, S. (1988). *A Brief History of Time: From the Big Bang to Black Holes*. New York: Bantam.

Kari, J., & Savolainen, R. (2007). Relationships between information seeking and context: A qualitative study of Internet searching and the goals of personal development. *Library and Information Science Research*, 29(1), 47–69.

Kuhn, T. S. (1996). *The Structure of Scientific Revolutions* (3rd ed.). Chicago: University of Chicago Press.

Merton, R. K. (1968). On sociological theories of the middle range. In *Social Theory and Social Structure* (Exp. ed., pp. 39–72). New York: Free Press.

Mintzberg, H. (2005). Developing theory about the development of theory. In M. Hitt & K. Smith (Eds.), *Great Minds in Management: The Process of Theory Development* (pp. 355–372). New York: Oxford University Press.

Pettigrew, K. E. (1999). Waiting for chiropody: Contextual results from an ethnographic study of the information behaviour among attendees at communication clinics. *Information Processing and Management*, 35(6), 801–818.

Poole, H. L. (1985). *Theories of the Middle Range*. Norwood, NJ: Ablex.

Solomon, P. (1997a). Discovering information behavior in sense making. I. Time and timing. *Journal of the American Society for Information Science*, 48, 1097–1108.

Solomon, P. (1997b). Discovering information behavior in sense making. II. The social. *Journal of the American Society for Information Science, 48*, 1109–1126.

Solomon, P. (1997c). Discovering information behavior in sense making. III. The person. *Journal of the American Society for Information Science, 48*, 1127–1138.

Strauss, A., & Corbin, J. (1990). *Basics of Qualitative Research: Grounded Theory, Procedures, and Techniques*. Newbury Park, CA: Sage.

PART III

RESEARCH DESIGNS
AND SAMPLING

7

Case Studies

Songphan Choemprayong and Barbara M. Wildemuth

> The case is one among others. In any given study, we will concentrate on the one. The time we spend concentrating on the one may be a day or a year, but while we so concentrate we are engaged in case study.
>
> —Robert E. Stake (1995)

Like other social science research, information and library science (ILS) scholars have adopted case study methods for decades. According to Fitzgibbons and Callison (1991), case study research became an acceptable method in the ILS field in the 1980s, although it was infrequently used. However, the number of studies employing case studies dramatically increased during the late 1980s and 1990s (Callison, 1997). This chapter will introduce the concept as well as explore the possible implications of applying case studies to ILS research questions.

WHAT IS A CASE STUDY?

The definition of a case study has been discussed in a couple of different ways. For teaching purposes, a case study is defined as a description of a particular situation or event. The description of the case serves as a learning tool, providing a framework for discussion. In a research context, a case study is defined as a research study focused on a single case or set of cases. Here we are interested in this second sense of the term *case study*. We will think of it as a research approach, rather than a specific research design, because a variety of designs and methods of data collection and analysis can be used to accomplish the goals of a particular case study.

Although the standardization of its definition and scope is still debatable, Benbasat et al. (1987) listed 11 key characteristics of case studies:

1. The phenomenon is examined in a natural setting.
2. Data are collected by multiple means

3. One or a few entities (person, group, or organization) are examined.
4. The complexity of the unit is studied intensively.
5. Case studies are more suitable for the exploration, classification, and hypothesis development stages of the knowledge-building process; the investigator should have a receptive attitude toward exploration.
6. No experimental controls or manipulation are involved.
7. The investigator may not specify the set of independent and dependent variables in advance.
8. The results derived depend heavily on the integrative powers of the investigator.
9. Changes in site selection and data collection methods could take place as the investigator develops new hypotheses.
10. Case research is useful in the study of *why* and *how* questions because these deal with operational links to be traced over time, rather than with frequency or incidence.
11. The focus is on contemporary events.

Most often, case studies are qualitative and conducted in the field (e.g., Darke et al., 1998; Edgars, 2004; Fidel, 1984; McTavish & Loether, 1999). However, you should not ignore the multimethod aspects of case study research. Yin (2003) pointed out that the evidence collected in case studies may be either qualitative or quantitative, or both. In particular, the combination of both types of evidence could contribute to the validity of the method.

Additionally, the flexibility of this method could be considered a strength or a weakness. If data analysis is conducted at the same time as data collection, the investigator has an opportunity to review and revise the procedures and instruments during the study (e.g., Eisenhardt, 1989; Fidel, 1984). However, Yin (2003) warns us that the research procedures should only be changed after careful consideration because such a change may decrease the rigor of the study.

WHEN SHOULD CASE STUDIES BE USED?

Your specific research question is the most critical criterion in selecting your research method. Specifically, the following questions should be taken into consideration to judge the appropriateness of using a case study as your research strategy:

Does the phenomenon of interest have to be studied in a natural setting?
Does the phenomenon of interest focus on contemporary events?
Does the research question aim to answer how and why questions?
Does the phenomenon of interest include a variety of factors and relationships that can be directly observed?

Case studies are often used in exploratory studies to define phenomena worth studying further. For example, to explore the relationship between information search strategies and personal development theory, Kari (2006) conducted a case study of a single person by interviewing and observing information seeking on the Internet. When the research is highly exploratory, a case study can be used as a pilot study for trying out particular data collection methods in a specific context or to help the investigator become more familiar with the phenomenon in a specific context.

A case study may also be used to follow up on an exploratory study conducted with another method. For example, Boyd-Byrnes and Rosenthal (2005) conducted a study to examine roles of librarians in remote access and their impact on the quality and effectiveness of the research process. Open-ended interviews were conducted at the preliminary stage to ascertain the important factors to investigate further. Then the case study protocol was used to follow up on those factors. While a case study can be used to follow up on a preliminary study, its weakness is its lack of generalizability. Thus the research findings, rather than contributing to theory development or testing directly, usually provide evidence for hypothesis generation (Darke et al., 1998).

A case study approach can also be used in descriptive research to depict comprehensively the phenomenon of interest. For instance, to examine the organizational restructuring of an academic library from decentralization to centralization, Moran (2005) selected Oxford University's libraries as perhaps the largest and most complex case with which to examine this phenomenon. Because the Oxford libraries were in the process of restructuring, she was able to follow this process over a seven-year period. In this particular study, the case study method allowed an investigator to describe different aspects of the restructuring, including chronological, operational, and role-based foci.

Case studies also can facilitate evaluation research. In ILS, evaluation research is often applied in specific organizational contexts—natural "cases" available for study. As Darke et al. (1998) point out, case study research "is well suited to understanding the interactions between information technology-related innovations and organizational contexts" (p. 274) as well as other aspects of organizational behavior. Used in this way, case study results can be directly applied to the improvement of information and library practice.

In summary, case studies are useful in many different types of research studies: both exploratory and confirmatory, descriptive and evaluative. As Gray (2004) notes, "the case study method is ideal when a 'how' or 'why' question is being asked about a contemporary set of events over which the researcher has no control" (p. 124).

DESIGNING A CASE STUDY

As with other research approaches, the first step in designing a case study is to clearly define your research question. Because many case studies are exploratory, the theoretical and empirical literature may provide only a sketchy foundation for your study (Eisenhardt, 1989). Nevertheless, a thorough literature review will be your first step. Other critical steps include identifying your unit of analysis, selecting the case or cases that will be the focus of your study, and planning your data collection procedures. Each of these steps is discussed here.

Identifying the Unit of Analysis

The unit of analysis "is the major entity that you are analyzing in your study" (Trochim, 2006). Most studies focus on individuals as the unit of analysis, but other possibilities include aggregate entities like groups or organizations; projects; or events such as decisions made or information seeking episodes. A primary defining characteristic of a case study is that it focuses on a single instance of the unit of analysis. For example, a case study may focus on a single person, a single organization, or a single event. Within the focus on the single case, the study is likely to take multiple perspectives by gathering data based on multiple units of analysis, then aggregating it to understand the case that is the focus of the study. For instance, Tan et al. (2005) used a case study approach to examine how knowledge had been managed in one organization: the National I.T. Literacy Program (NITLP) in Singapore. The unit of analysis is one team within one organization: the implementation team within the NITLP. To fully understand knowledge management within the team, the researchers examined interactions among team members, interactions between the team and other parts of the organization, and the perspectives of individual members of the team. This approach exemplifies the multifaceted character of case studies.

Selecting a Case

Instead of randomly selecting a case from a population of cases, you will strategically select a case (or several cases) based on your theoretical purposes and the relevance of a case to those purposes (Eisenhardt, 1989; Glaser & Strauss, 1967). Stake (2000) advises us to choose the case from which we can learn the most. If the case is chosen because of its theoretical dimensions, case selection is called *theoretical sampling*, and the goal is to choose a case or cases that are likely to replicate or extend an emergent theory. Both purposive sampling and theoretical sampling are quite different from *statistical sampling*, which focuses on selecting study participants that are representative of a population of interest.

Some studies will focus on a single case, while others may compare two or more cases. A single case study provides in-depth investigation of and rich detail about phenomena. Yin (2003) identified five possible reasons for selecting a particular case: (1) it is a *representative* or *typical* case that captures the circumstances and conditions of an everyday or commonplace situation; (2) it is a *critical* case that is essential for testing a well-formulated theory; (3) it is an *extreme* or *unique* case that represents a rare phenomenon that needs to be documented and analyzed; (4) it is a *revelatory* case that illuminates previously inaccessible knowledge; or (5) it is a *longitudinal* case that can be repeatedly studied at several different points in time. For example, Kari's (2006) study of the relationship between information searching and personal development employs a single case study method. Only one person was selected to represent a revelatory case, so that the investigator was able to empirically observe the whole searching experience of the study participant. In addition, it was a typical case, based on sex, age, location, education, employment, and Internet experience.

Multiple-case studies (also called *comparative case studies*) are basically a combination of two or more single case studies. This approach contributes to cross-case analysis and the extension of theory to additional individuals or settings. There are two logics supporting a multiple-case study design: literal replication and theoretical replication. *Literal replication* selects cases that are very similar to each other, and the researcher expects the same outcomes from each. *Theoretical replication* selects cases that differ from each other in theoretically important ways, and the researcher expects either to expand the scope of the underlying theory or to rule out the theory's applicability in certain settings. The second example presented in this chapter exemplifies this approach: Hughes (1998, 1999) conducted a series of four case studies, then compared the results across the cases.

Collecting Data

Because a case study is intended to generate rich data concerning a particular case, it is almost inevitable that multiple methods of data collection will be used. These methods might include analysis of existing documentation and archival records, interviews, direct observation, participant observation, and examination of physical artifacts (Yin, 2003). In addition, quantitative methods, such as questionnaires, may be incorporated into the research design. Among these methods, direct observation is most frequently used and, because direct observation is a major research tool for field studies, some investigators (e.g., Fidel, 1984; McTavish & Loether, 1999) equate case studies with field studies. Yin (2003) noted that even though most case studies use direct observation, data collection methods for case studies are not limited to direct observation.

The results from the different data collection methods are combined through *triangulation*. This approach to data integration was developed by Denzin (1978) for use in sociological studies. Stake (2000) defines it as "a process of using multiple perceptions to clarify meaning, verifying the repeatability of an observation or interpretation" (p. 443). Four types of triangulation were identified by Denzin (1978): (1) *data triangulation* (combining data from different sources); (2) *investigator triangulation* (combining data collected by multiple researchers); (3) *methodological triangulation* (combining data collected via different methods); and (4) *theory triangulation* (combining data collected from multiple theoretical perspectives). This fourth type, though possible, is quite rare in ILS and other social science research. The others have all been used in ILS studies and, in fact, could all be included within a single case study. For example, imagine that you and a couple of colleagues are studying the metadata generation practices in a particular organization. You will need to integrate the data collected by each researcher, requiring investigator triangulation. In terms of data triangulation, you may have data from several sources: cataloging staff, executive staff, policy and procedures manuals, and Web server transaction logs. In terms of methodological triangulation, you may have used direct observation of the workplace, interviews (with staff), content analysis (with policy manuals), and transaction log analysis (with the Web server logs). In each case, the triangulation process will require the comparison of findings from each investigator/source/method, cross-checking carefully to ensure that the study findings are valid conclusions drawn from the data.

STRENGTHS AND WEAKNESSES OF CASE STUDIES

The lack of generalizability of the study findings is the weakness of case studies most cited by its critics. There is no basis for generalizing the findings of case study beyond the setting(s) in which it was conducted. But turning this weakness on its head, Stake (1995) insists that "the real business of a case study is particularization, not generalization" (p. 8). Thus Stake is pointing to the greatest strength of a case study: the richness with which a particular setting or phenomenon can be described using this approach. Yin (2003) addresses the initial criticism in another way, by arguing that the results from case studies are generalizable to theoretical propositions. Hammersley (1992) concurs, arguing that theory can be tested through case study research if cases are selected "in such a way as to open the theory up to maximal threat" (p. 182). In this way, a single case can be used to test a theory against a particular set of empirical circumstances, even though it cannot be treated as a representative sample from a population.

The overall quality of case study research has sometimes been criticized. When evaluating the strength of a particular study, the study report will be the focus of attention. A reader should be able to evaluate how good the study is by reading the research report. Therefore Lincoln and Guba (1990) identify four classes of criteria relevant to the quality of a case study research report:

1. *Resonance criteria* focus on the degree to which the report fits, overlaps with, or reinforces the selected theoretical framework.
2. *Rhetorical criteria* deal with the form, structure, and presentational characteristics of the report. Such criteria include unity, overall organization, simplicity or clarity, and craftsmanship.
3. *Empowerment criteria* refer to the ability to evoke and facilitate action on the part of readers. Empowerment-related characteristics may include fairness, educativeness, and actionability.
4. *Applicability criteria* focus on the feasibility of making inferences from the case study results and applying them in the reader's context or situation. It is important to note that to transfer findings from one context to another, the relevant characteristics of both contexts should be the same.

As you plan your own case study, you can apply these criteria in advance to ensure that your research design and procedures will yield findings that are valid and useful.

A final consideration for case studies is more practical: it is the large amount of qualitative data that will need to be organized and analyzed. As noted earlier, a variety of data sources and data collection methods are likely to be used. These might include field notes, documents, transcripts of interviews, correspondence with people in the setting, and so on. The sheer volume of data might overwhelm the investigator. Therefore you need to develop consistent and thoughtful procedures for organizing and analyzing your data. Computer-based tools may be useful in this regard. Yin (2003) suggests developing a database to manage your data; qualitative data analysis software is also useful for case study research.

EXAMPLES

Two case studies will be presented here, as examples of the potential of this research method. The first (Tang & Solomon, 1998) is based on close examination of the Internet searching behaviors of a single person. The second (Hughes, 1998, 1999) is a comparative case study, examining the impact of a particular approach to reading instruction (the whole language approach) on school libraries and librarians.

Example 1: The Relevance Judgments Made by a Single Person

Tang and Solomon (1998) used a case study approach to investigate empirically the dynamic nature of a person's mental model of his or her information need, as represented by the process and product of the relevance judgments made in relation to particular documents. They observed the relevance judgments made by a single person as she worked on a term paper assignment. Their research question was as follows: "From a cognitive and situational perspective, how do relevance judgments evolve during the process of information retrieval?" (p. 240).

The study was framed in terms of Kuhlthau's (1993) proposition that end users' judgments shift from *relevance* to *pertinence* during the information seeking process. This view was supported by additional theoretical work concerning the dynamic nature of people's relevance judgment processes (Schamber et al., 1990), situational influences on those judgments (Wilson, 1973), and the fluid nature of mental model development (Holland et al., 1986). Data were gathered with these theories in mind, with an eye toward testing their validity. As the authors argue, "the case study is appropriate for studying the research question here because the approach allows the collection of the kind of detailed data that intensively reflects the patterns and properties of the relevance judgment process" (Tang & Solomon, 1998, p. 242).

The selected single case, as a revelatory representation, was a first-year female graduate student in information studies. She was enrolled in an archives-related course for which a term paper was required. This assignment provided the context for the study. This individual was the unit of analysis; data were collected about her process of searching for articles that would be useful for writing her paper.

Adopting data and method triangulations, data collection occurred during two observation sessions. The first session began with a presession interview to collect background information on the search topic and the subject's perceptions of "an ideal relevant document" (Tang & Solomon, 1998, p. 243). She was directly observed while conducting searches of two major ILS databases and while evaluating the retrieved records. During these processes, the subject was asked to "read- and speak-aloud" (p. 243); these verbalizations were recorded and field notes were taken. All the documents used during the processes (e.g., marked-up lists of search results) also were collected. The first part of the session ended with a discussion about the subject's perceptions of her progress. She and the researcher then retrieved the relevant articles from the library collection, and the observation continued as the subject evaluated the documents' full texts. The session then concluded with a brief interview concerning the subject's overall feelings about the session.

The second observation session occurred one month later; by then, the subject had outlined her term paper. The session began with the subject describing what she had done in the intervening month. She then evaluated each of the articles initially judged relevant, commenting on the annotations she had added since the first session. She also had identified six additional relevant articles, and they were discussed. A final postsession interview focused on the subject's increased knowledge and skill in making judgments about the relevance of the retrieved documents.

The richness of this data set is clear. The data collected include transcriptions of interviews and verbal protocols, field notes on what was observed, and retrieval data (i.e., the annotated lists of search results and a quantitative analysis of the terms/topics represented by those judged relevant). The different data sources (i.e., the subject and the documents) involve data triangulation; the different data collection methods (i.e., interviews, verbal protocols, observation notes, quantitative content analysis of relevance judgments made) involve method triangulation. Both of these types of triangulation strengthen the validity of the study findings. In addition, it is clear that the researchers achieved their goal of observing the natural behaviors of the subject. For example, when the subject asked to "go back and re-evaluate" records already seen in the first observation session (Tang & Solomon, 1998, p. 244), she was allowed to do this, and this request was added to the analysis as a data point.

One possible criticism of this study is the general weakness of case studies, in terms of their generalizability. However, the goals of this study did not include generalizing the findings to a larger population. Instead, the authors were interested in understanding one person's experience of making relevance judgments. From the data they gathered, they could then provide support for several of the theoretical models underlying the study. While the findings are not generalizable in the statistical sense, they are useful for the purpose of theory validation.

The only real weakness of this study relates to the timing and frequency of the observation sessions. There were only two observation sessions, and they were conducted one month apart. The discontinuity of direct observation during that one-month period means that the investigators could not confirm at what stage/period the subject's judgment shifted from relevance to pertinence. The subject identified additional articles during that month and further studied the original set of retrieved articles. These unobserved behaviors could not be fully taken into account as the data were analyzed. Although the interview at the beginning of the second observation session provided the subject's description of the intervening activity, her memory of those events could not have been as complete as a researcher's direct observation of them.

Example 2: The Impact of Whole Language Instruction on Four School Libraries

The *whole language* approach is "a method of teaching reading and writing that emphasizes learning whole words and phrases by encountering them in meaningful contexts rather than by phonics exercises" (Merriam-Webster Online Dictionary, http://www.merriam-webster.com/). It is characterized by its reliance on whole pieces of literature (as opposed to basal readers), its emphasis on student choice in selecting reading assignments, and the integration of language-based experiences (reading and writing), rather than instruction on specific skill sequences (Jeynes & Littell, 2000). It seems likely that the introduction of this approach in an elementary school would affect the functioning of the library in that school. Thus Hughes (1998, 1999) conducted a comparative case study to help us understand how "the implementation and continuation of the [whole language] philosophy affect[ed] the library programs and the librarians" (Hughes, 1998, p. 5) in four elementary schools in Virginia.

While the study drew on theories of educational change and the role of change agents (librarians might serve as change agents in this context), it did not use these theories to frame the research design. Instead, Hughes (1998, 1999) allowed the specific research methods to emerge as they were needed during the processes of data collection and analysis. The emergent character of the research methods used in this study is typical of many qualitative or interpretive studies.

Because the study would eventually compare the results from multiple cases, the selection of those cases was intended to simultaneously minimize the differences between cases (so that they could be considered comparable) and to maximize the differences between cases (so that the effects of each case's context would be visible). Thus Hughes selected schools that were similar in two important ways: they were all successful in implementing the whole language approach, and the school librarians had experience with more traditional approaches using textbooks or basal readers. To maximize the differences between the cases, Hughes selected schools that were different from each other in terms of the income and educational levels of the parents, the ethnic or racial backgrounds of the students, and the size of the school. All four cases were selected from the Jefferson County (Virginia) School System, which had received national recognition for its implementation of the whole language approach. In addition, the diversity among the county's residents allowed the selection of four schools that differed from each other.

The data were collected through multiple methods, from multiple sources. Hughes spent one month in each school as a participant observer. She conducted formal interviews with librarians, teachers, and the principals in each school as well as engaging in less formal conversations with the school librarians. In addition, she examined a variety of documentary evidence: "correspondences between the librarian and the teachers, newsletters, student and teacher handbooks, library schedules, lesson plans, and annual school plans" (Hughes, 1998, p. 77). Thus data triangulation involved integration of data from multiple sources: teachers, librarians, principals, and documents. Method triangulation involved integration of data collected through multiple methods: observation, interviews, and document analysis. In addition, Hughes improved the trustworthiness of the study's findings through prolonged and persistent engagement at each site, peer debriefing, and member checks.

The results from each site were described in terms of the ways in which each library program had changed since implementation of the whole language approach (scheduling, the collection, and the librarian's role) and how each librarian had reacted to the implementation of the whole language approach. After examining what happened in each of the four schools, a cross-site analysis was conducted. In relation to some themes, the four schools had similar outcomes, but differences between schools were also identified. For instance, two of the librarians were much more comfortable with the process of change than the other two librarians. This difference in librarian knowledge affected the ways in which the library programs changed (Hughes, 1999).

Overall, this comparative case study was successful in achieving its purposes. The sample was carefully selected. Access to each site was gained, and a rich body of data was collected at each site. After an initial analysis of the themes that emerged at each site, the findings were analyzed across sites. Some similarities were found, but some differences were also identified. It is likely that the success of this study is at least partially due to the careful pilot study conducted by Hughes (1993). Given the intensive nature of case studies, a small pilot study is always advisable.

CONCLUSION

By aiming to answer *how* and *why* questions, the case study method focuses on examining contemporary events in a natural setting. A single case can be used to define a general conceptual category or property, while multiple cases can confirm the definition (Glaser & Strauss, 1967). The strength of the case study approach primarily focuses on the flexibility of this research strategy and its incorporation of a rich array of data collection techniques. Triangulation of multiple data sources and data collection methods will increase the rigor of this approach. In addition, it can be used to support theory testing and development as well as simply to describe a phenomenon of interest.

WORKS CITED

Benbasat, I., Goldstein, D. K., & Mead, M. (1987). The case research strategy in studies of information systems. *MIS Quarterly, 11*(3), 369–386.

Boyd-Byrnes, M. K., & Rosenthal, M. (2005). Remote access revisited: Disintermediation and its discontents. *Journal of Academic Librarianship, 31*(3), 216–224.

Callison, D. (1997). Evolution of methods to measure student information use. *Library and Information Science Research, 19*(4), 347–357.

Darke, P., Shanks, G., & Broadbent, M. (1998). Successfully completing case study research: Combining rigour, relevance and pragmatism. *Information Systems Journal, 8*(4), 273–289.

Denzin, K. (1978). *The Research Act*. New York: McGraw-Hill.

Edgars, W. (2004). Corporate library impact, Part II: Methodological trade-off. *Library Quarterly, 74*(2), e1–e18.

Eisenhardt, K. M. (1989). Building theories from case study research. *Academy of Management Review, 14*(4), 532–550.

Fidel, R. (1984). The case study method: A case study. *Library and Information Science Research, 6*(3), 273–288.

Fitzgibbons, S. A., & Callison, D. (1991). Research needs and issues in school librarianship. In C. R. McClure & P. Hernon (Eds.), *Library and Information Science Research: Perspectives and Strategies for Improvement* (pp. 296–315). Norwood, NJ: Ablex.

Glaser, B. G., & Strauss, A. L. (1967). *The Discovery of Grounded Theory: Strategies for Qualitative Research*. Chicago: Aldine.

Gray, D. E. (2004). *Doing Research in the Real World*. London: Sage.

Hammersley, M. (1992). *What's Wrong with Ethnography? Methodological Explorations*. London: Routledge.

Holland, J. H., Holyoak, K. J., Nisbett, R. E., & Thagard, P. R. (1986). *Induction: Processes of Inference, Learning, and Discovery*. Cambridge, MA: MIT Press.

Hughes, S. M. (1993). The impact of whole language on four elementary school libraries. *Language Arts, 70*(5), 393–399.

Hughes, S. M. (1998). *The impact of whole language on four elementary school libraries*. Unpublished doctoral dissertation, University of North Carolina.

Hughes, S. (1999). The impact of whole language on four elementary school libraries: Results from a comparative case study. In *Unleash the Power! Knowledge—Technology—Diversity: Papers Presented at the Third International Forum on Research in School Librarianship, Annual Conference of the International Association of School Librarianship* (pp. 83–94). (ERIC Document Reproduction Service No. ED437059)

Jeynes, W. H., & Littell, S. W. (2000). A meta-analysis of studies examining the effect of whole language instruction on the literacy of low-SES students. *Elementary School Journal, 101*(1), 21–33.

Kari, J. (2006). Evolutionary information seeking: A case study of personal development and Internet searching. *First Monday, 11*(1). Retrieved February 13, 2006, from http://firstmonday.org/issues/issue11_1/kari/index.html.

Kuhlthau, C. C. (1993). *Seeking Meaning: A Process Approach to Library and Information Services*. Norwood, NJ: Ablex.

Lincoln, Y. S., & Guba, E. G. (1990). Judging the quality of case study reports. *Qualitative Studies in Education, 3*(1), 53–59.

McTavish, D., & Loether, H. (1999). *Social Research*. New York: Addison-Wesley.

Moran, B. B. (2005). Continuity and change: The integration of Oxford University's libraries. *Library Quarterly, 75*(3), 262–294.

Schamber, L., Eisenberg, M. B., & Nilan, M. S. (1990). A reexamination of relevance: Toward a dynamic situational definition. *Information Processing and Management, 26,* 755–776.

Stake, R. E. (1995). *The Art of Case Study Research*. Thousand Oaks, CA: Sage.

Stake, R. E. (2000). Case studies. In N. K. Denzin & Y. S. Lincoln (Eds.), *Handbook of Qualitative Research* (2nd ed., pp. 435–454). Thousand Oaks, CA: Sage.

Tan, C. W., Pan, S. L., Lim, E.T.K., & Chan, C.M.L. (2005). Managing knowledge conflicts in an interorganizational project: A case study of the Infocomm Development Authority of Singapore. *Journal of the American Society for Information Science and Technology, 56*(11), 1187–1199.

Tang, R., & Solomon, P. (1998). Toward an understanding of the dynamics of relevance judgment: An analysis of one person's search behavior. *Information Processing and Management, 34*(2/3), 237–256.

Trochim, W. M. K. (2006). *Unit of analysis.* Retrieved February 4, 2008, from http://www .socialresearchmethods.net/kb/unitanal.php.

Wilson, P. (1973). Situational relevance. *Information Storage and Retrieval, 9,* 457–469.

Yin, R. K. (2003). *Case Study Research: Design and Method* (3rd ed.). London: Sage.

ADDITIONAL RECOMMENDED READING

Myers, M. D. (Ed.). (2005). *Qualitative research in information systems: References on case study research.* Retrieved January 31, 2009, from http://www.qual.auckland.ac.nz/case.aspx.

8

Naturalistic Research

Abe J. Crystal and Barbara M. Wildemuth

I keep six honest serving-men
(They taught me all I knew);
Their names are What and Where and When
And How and Where and Who.

—Rudyard Kipling (1893)

INTRODUCTION

Suppose you have some burning question about how people behave. Perhaps you are fascinated by the problem of how people formulate and revise queries for use in search engines, or your job demands a better understanding about why people seek (or avoid) the help of a librarian.

You have some time and resources you can devote to answering your question—but how to go about answering it? You could bring people into a controlled environment and have them perform some sort of experiment (see Chapter 12). For example, you could ask your participants to search for information on a set series of topics, and then answer questions about how they formulated their queries. This approach would enable you to control specific manipulations such as the topics and search engines used. In addition, it would enable you to determine exactly which variables you would measure such as how satisfied participants were with their experience.

Suppose, though, that you were concerned about how people use search engines on their own, including how they come up with their own topics and use the results of searches in their everyday lives. You want data that more closely reflect the real, lived experiences of the population of interest. To gather this kind of data, you could conduct *naturalistic research*. Naturalistic research attempts to conduct studies that approximate natural, uncontrived conditions. This approach can be exciting and inspiring and lead to research results that illuminate new areas of behavior. At the same time, it raises difficult philosophical issues, along with a host of practical problems. This chapter will introduce you to the basics of naturalistic research, including the major methodological issues.

THE CHALLENGE OF VALIDITY

For decades, social scientists have conducted laboratory studies to gain insight into human behaviors and characteristics. Though these studies have been highly successful, a long line of dissenters have argued that they lead to an incomplete view of how people think and behave. In particular, laboratory studies fail to

- Gather a detailed, unprejudiced record of people's behaviors, beliefs and preferences
- Explore people's behavior in the context of their own work and life
- Intensively observe particular elements of context such as settings and artifacts
- Uncover the tacit meanings and understandings that are common in communication and social interaction

To address this gap, a variety of naturalistic research methods have been developed and used. In general, these methods seek to study people in their natural environment, either by going into the field to observe people in their own homes or offices or by replicating elements of the natural environment elsewhere. This approach may seem reasonable and intuitive, but it has raised challenging philosophical issues about the nature of social scientific research.

In particular, there is a basic tension between naturalism and positivism (or rationalism) as modes of inquiry (Park, 1994; Potts & Newstetter, 1997). In essence, advocates of naturalistic inquiry argue that it is not merely about adding some new tools to your methodological arsenal; rather, it is a fundamentally different philosophical approach that is in direct opposition to traditional scientific norms such as causality, reality, generalizability, and objectivity (see Table 8.1). In a sense, naturalistic inquiry calls for radical humility on the part of the researcher—acknowledging that research findings are idiographic, reflecting only one view of one environment.

The description of naturalistic inquiry presented in Table 8.1 is what Potts and Newstetter (1997) would call a "strong" view of this approach to research. However, it is the "weak" view that guides most naturalistic research and that is the focus of this chapter. In this view, naturalistic inquiry axioms are taken as practical warnings (rather than fundamental philosophical issues); naturalistic methods are used to illuminate complex work processes; researchers are to be alert to political and social issues within organizations; and multiple viewpoints are recognized. Thus it is possible to engage in naturalistic research without pursuing the implications of its philosophical baggage to their logical conclusions.

DOING NATURALISTIC RESEARCH

As with any research problem, your first step is to move from a specific research question to a design that helps you to answer that question. Let's consider an example: understanding how people look for information in a university library. One approach would be to use a carefully designed and validated survey to collect detailed quantitative

Table 8.1. Positivistic versus naturalistic views of research

Positivistic (rationalistic) view	Naturalistic view
Most actions can be explained by real (temporally precedent or simultaneous, manipulable, probabilistic) causes.	Cause and effect are intertwined; all entities interact and shape each other (feedforward and feedback).
Context-free generalizations can be developed and form a consistent body of knowledge.	Working hypotheses, closely bound to specific, individual cases, help illuminate particular contexts.
The scientist and the participant or object of inquiry are independent.	The scientist and the participant or object of inquiry are mutually dependent—inseparable.
A single, observable reality exists and can be divided into specific variables, which in turn can be studied, controlled, and predicted.	Reality is made of multiple individually constructed viewpoints that can be only partially understood.
Scientific inquiry is value-free.	Scientific inquiry is value-bound.

information about how people use and perceive the library. Another approach, as implemented by Crabtree et al. (2000), would be to listen in on a number of reference transactions, taking extensive notes on what the patrons and librarians said and did. This second approach is more naturalistic in the sense that it enables direct observation of people in their natural environment (in this case, a library). The environment is natural in the sense that they have chosen to come to the library and make use of its services as part of their ordinary life.

What did Crabtree and colleagues (2000) learn from this research? There were no neat and tidy conclusions or clear recommendations for practice; rather, they identified patterns and themes as well as illustrative extracts of their field notes intended to deepen our understanding of library use. For example, they trailed "Craig," a law student, as he used a variety of strategies for finding information: consulting a seminar reading list, browsing the stacks, looking up citations he sees, and finally, moving on to legal databases. They found that he relied on "signs and other conventions" to assess the information available to him. In particular, the actual physical layout of the stacks and of the books and articles he consulted served to orient him and help him make sense of a complex situation. In another example, they observed two students using a CD-ROM database to search for articles on stress. They watched the students struggle with online help, and then try to guess how the system operated ("What's it doing now?," one wondered). Crabtree and colleagues concluded that the students were having difficulty "filling in the gap" between the ostensibly clear instructions in the online help and the practical reality of changing databases, executing searches, and so forth.

Not surprisingly, this naturalistic approach was no silver bullet. But, as Crabtree et al. (2000) argued, it is worthwhile to document the "recurrent ways in which discrete activities are produced, performed, and accomplished by members time and time again" (p. 680). Careful analysis of these patterns can be used to develop better theories and models of behavior, and better programs and systems to support peoples' search for and use of information.

APPROACHES AND TRADE-OFFS

Naturalistic techniques can be applied in many different ways to many different types of problems. Different approaches work better in different situations. These approaches can be organized along three main dimensions: degree of naturalism, type of insight, and resources required.

Degree of Naturalism

Not all naturalistic studies are created equal. The Crabtree et al. (2000) study discussed previously, for example, has a high degree of naturalism in that the situations and interactions they observed were uncontrived and occurred in the context of participants' own work and experience (as well as the real physical context of the library). Compared to participant observation techniques (see Chapter 21), though, Crabtree and colleagues' study could be considered less naturalistic because the researchers did not engage directly in the community. They did not, for example, go to the reference desk with problems of their own or try to assist patrons with a search.

Type of Insight

You can't answer any research question completely and definitively (you'd need infinite time to collect the data, and infinite time to analyze them). So you need to specify the types of insight that are particularly relevant to your interests. If you were responsible for the architecture of a new library, you might be concerned with how people navigate and orient themselves within the library. You would design your study to focus on how and when people get confused in the library. On the other hand, if you were responsible for fundraising and marketing of the new library, you might be more concerned with how people talk about the library and how they relate to it as part of their professional, personal, and social lives. You would design your study to focus on people's feelings about the library, both when they're in it and when they're not. You will most likely choose to conduct a naturalistic study in situations when you want to gain insight into people's naturally occurring behaviors in natural settings.

Resources Required

Naturalistic research can demand vast amounts of time because of the practical issues involved in gaining access to natural settings and because of the rich data that must be collected and interpreted. As a result, a wide array of naturalistic techniques have been developed, which offer researchers different trade-offs and are appropriate for different research problems. Lightweight approaches (sometimes called *rapid assessment techniques*) try to quickly gain insight via brief and focused forays into natural settings or incorporating elements of naturalism into otherwise controlled designs. Full-blown approaches (often taking a stronger naturalistic perspective) seek to engage fully with the chosen domain, often through direct participation in the activities being studied. These approaches emphasize open-ended exploration and understanding, rather than answering particular, focused questions.

SPECIFIC TECHNIQUES

Once you've decided that naturalistic inquiry is the best approach with which to address your research question, you still have numerous decisions to make about the particulars of your research design, data collection methods, and data analysis methods. Some of the most frequently selected options are briefly described here. Field observation and ethnography are approaches adopted from anthropology and qualitative sociology; contextual inquiry and cognitive work analysis are approaches adopted from information systems design; and quasi-experimental research is an approach adopted from psychology and education. With the exception of contextual inquiry and cognitive work analysis (methods adopted from information systems design), each of these methods is discussed in more detail in its own chapter in this book.

Field Observation

Observing people in their natural environments (i.e., in the field) is one of the most basic ways to gain insight into their natural behavior. Field observation differs from participant observation (see Chapter 21) in that the researcher is not attempting to become *engaged* in the activities and rituals of a community; rather, the researcher is present only as an observer.

There are two basic observational strategies: continuous monitoring and sampling. With continuous monitoring, you watch a person or small group nonstop for set periods of time. With sampling, you choose (typically randomly) specific locations, times, and individuals, then observe what the individuals are doing at each given location and time. With either technique, a variety of detailed data can be collected. For example, you could record all the books a person looked at during a single trip to a library. Or you could see which magazines in an open reading room were being read over the course of a few months. A variety of direct and indirect observation methods are discussed in Part 4 (see Chapters 18–22).

Ethnography

Ethnography (literally, writing the culture) entails "detailed, in-depth observation of people's behavior, beliefs, and preferences" (Ireland, 2003, p. 26). It is the core research method of anthropology (Bernard, 1995) and is commonly used in sociology as well. In most cases, ethnography is a form of participant observation because it involves "being in the presence of others on an ongoing basis and having some nominal status for them as someone who is part of their daily lives" (Schwartz & Jacob, 1979, p. 46). See Chapter 21 for further discussion of participant observation in the information and library science (ILS) context.

Unfortunately, true ethnography takes months or years of fieldwork—and as much or more time to structure, interpret, and write about the vast trove of data (Myers, 1999). Few practitioners (and even few academics) have the time to devote to such a project. But the detailed insights of ethnographic inquiry are still desirable in many situations, so researchers have developed lightweight or rapid forms of ethnography to gain useful insight in less time. The key change is to refocus and sharply limit the ethnographic inquiry. Rather than ranging over the whole of human behavior, the idea is to target a few specific hypotheses that are relevant to the problem. For example, if a new information retrieval system is being designed, and there is concern over how the system should support saving and printing of retrieved documents, the ethnographer would focus closely on how people use documents in their current work.

Contextual Inquiry

Contextual inquiry (Beyer & Holtzblatt, 1999) is a technique for rapidly gathering information about people's work practices in their own environments. It was developed for use within information system design projects to help the analyst/designer gather useful data to support the design process. The researcher (i.e., the analyst/designer) spends several hours (over the course of one to a few days) with the participant (i.e., the "customer" of the system being designed). The researcher takes on the role of apprentice to the participant's master, as the participant teaches the researcher about the work practices of interest. This process enables the researcher to learn quickly about the participant's ordinary work, including the tacit understandings and unacknowledged assumptions that people would gloss over in an interview. As Beyer and Holtzblatt (1995) say, "Customers do not generally have the skills to talk about their work effectively; this is not their job. But customers can talk about their work as it unfolds. They do not have to develop a way to present it or figure out what their motives are. All they have to do is explain what they are doing" (p. 46).

Cognitive Work Analysis

Vicente (1999) developed an approach to understanding people's work processes that is similar to contextual inquiry, yet has some unique aspects. Like contextual inquiry, it is a descriptive approach in that it is a method that can be used to help us understand how people actually perform their work. This goal is different than trying to understand how people are supposed to complete their work or even from what they will tell you about their work. In addition to emphasizing the importance of gaining a realistic understanding of the task a person performs, cognitive work analysis takes into account "the environment in which it is carried out, and the perceptual, cognitive, and ergonomic attributes of the people who typically do the task" (Fidel et al., 2004, p. 942). Fidel and her colleagues have applied this technique to a study of collaborative information retrieval conducted to support the decision making of a design team at Microsoft. In addition to reporting the results of their case study, they provided details of the ways in which they applied cognitive work analysis in this research, which was a naturalistic study carried out within a corporate setting. Specifically, they identified and explored seven attributes or dimensions that served as a framework for their data collection and analysis. The seven dimensions were (1) the environment, (2) the work domain, (3) the organization, (4) the task in work domain terms, (5) the task in decision-making terms, (6) the task in terms of the strategies that can be used, and (7) the actors' resources and values. The multifaceted nature of cognitive work analysis makes it a useful tool for naturalistic research.

Quasi-experiments

In addition to the exploratory and descriptive approaches just presented, naturalistic research can be conducted as a quasi-experiment (see Chapter 11). A quasi-experiment is a fixed research design, similar to an experiment, in which participants are assigned to conditions in some systematic way (by the researcher or by some process outside the researcher's control). Since assigning people randomly to particular conditions is basically antinaturalistic, quasi-experiments are a way to introduce naturalistic elements into a study, while maintaining some control. For example, suppose you are interested in the effects of information literacy instruction on people's use of online library catalogs. You could observe two groups of people, one group that had a taken a class and one that had not. Since you couldn't randomly assign people to one group or another, this would be a quasi-experiment. See the examples in Chapter 11 as well as the Barry (1994) example (later in this chapter) for further discussion of quasi-experimental methods.

EXAMPLES

Two naturalistic studies will be discussed here to provide examples of how such research can be conducted effectively. The first example (Heidorn, 2001; Heidorn et al., 2002) is a study that was not only naturalistic in its research approach, but was conducted out in nature, working with teams that were conducting biodiversity surveys as part of the Illinois Eco Watch program. The second example (Barry, 1994) aimed to identify the criteria people use to make relevance judgments when evaluating documents. Each of these examples illustrates a different method of data collection and analysis, but they are alike in striving to investigate information behaviors in a naturalistic context.

Example 1: Naturalistic Research in a Natural Setting

If you were responsible for designing a system to help students and teachers document the plants and trees that grow in their area, what kinds of research would you do? What kinds of evidence would you need? The Biological Information Browsing Environment (BIBE) project team (Heidorn, 2001; Heidorn et al., 2002) took on this challenge and came up with a multifaceted answer. They argue that a variety of user-centered research methods should be used as these provide different and complementary data.

Like many naturalistic researchers, Heidorn et al.'s (2002) research questions were concerned with context, which they defined as "the task, the goals, and the skills of the participants" (p. 1252). Of course, context can be defined much more broadly, but in this case, providing a specific definition for context likely helped the researchers to narrow their focus and identify the precise types of research they needed to carry out. They were also focused on a particular domain: people conducting biodiversity surveys.

The BIBE team took an explicitly intensive approach (Sayer, 1984) to their research: "We are closely studying a small sample of people" (Heidorn et al., 2002, p. 1252). They chose data collection methods appropriate to this approach: interviews, focus groups, field observation, and immersion. These may be contrasted with the techniques that might be used for a large-scale extensive study such as a survey.

They conducted interviews (see Chapter 24) with professional botanists and biology teachers and focus groups (see Chapter 25) with high school students. While these methods had naturalistic elements, and certainly complemented the other techniques, they were not as explicitly naturalistic as the field observation and immersion work, further discussed here.

One technique the researchers used to attain a better understanding of context was field observation. This was not an open-ended, exploratory observation process, as in participant observation and ethnography (see Chapter 21); rather, the researchers had a specific agenda: "to determine where the participants made mistakes, why the mistakes are made, and to find solutions" (Heidorn et al., 2002, p. 1253). The researchers evidently operated from a positivist perspective, assuming that clear causality could be established and used as a basis for design. At the same time, they strove to gather rich data about context and to develop a more nuanced understanding of the participants' work. This approach proved practical and effective for their research problem.

Even close observation in the field is still just observation. One way to gain different insights into a particular task is to actually *do* the task, in the domain and situation of interest. Heidorn et al. (2002) immersed themselves in the world of volunteer biodiversity surveyors by becoming certified ForestWatch volunteers. They discussed this experience as an example of contextual inquiry (Beyer & Holtzblatt, 1995, 1998), although their particular approach was somewhat different than contextual inquiry as it is ordinarily practiced. Generally, a systems analyst or designer uses the contextual inquiry methodology to become an apprentice to a business user (e.g., a marketing specialist) for a few hours or days. Heidorn and colleagues instead participated in a formal training program and conducted a practice survey in the forest. Their description of their experience as immersion seems accurate and is somewhat unique in ILS research—the opportunity as an outsider to participate in training, and then in the actual activity, is rare.

Given the data collection methods, it is not surprising to find that the data collected for this study included *artifacts*, descriptions of *processes*, and notes on *problems and breakdowns*. The primary artifact examined was the data input form used by Forest-Watch volunteers. This enabled them to determine the types of information volunteers needed such as tree species and size. They also saw the various guides that volunteers used to help identify trees, including laminated color pages with plant images and descriptions, printouts of Web descriptions, and published field guides (e.g., *Forest Trees of Illinois*). The team gathered descriptions of processes using video and field notes, recording how the volunteers went through the forest and identified trees. The researchers also compared this process with the process used by two experts surveying the same area. Idealized models of process flows often assume that everything proceeds swimmingly toward the expected or right outcome. In reality, of course, people make mistakes of all sorts. In this case, students misidentified about 20 percent of the trees, so the researchers also attempted to understand and classify these problems and breakdowns.

Heidorn et al. (2002) argued that the synergy generated by using a variety of different naturalistic (and not-so-naturalistic) methods can address several issues associated with naturalistic research. The first issue is how to elicit information about "unspoken goals and motives" (p. 1257). Careful interviewing can bring people's motives to the surface, but interviews are still subject to misinterpretation and oversimplification. Field observations can make the complexities of actual practice apparent. The second issue emerges from a desire to study the complexity of people's work. Field observations can capture so much data as to become overwhelming. Additional structure and context are needed to help researchers make sense of the messiness of raw field data. The BIBE team found that interviews and focus groups helped provide this structure. The third issue is that experts and novices not only have different knowledge, but can express what they know in different ways. Because novices are still learning, they are better able to articulate what they are doing, and why. In contrast, experts have a much deeper knowledge base, but much of their knowledge is tacit, and they perform complex activities (such as distinguishing two similar trees) without reflection. This makes it difficult for researchers to understand what the experts are doing, and why. Collecting data from both experts and novices in different ways helped to overcome this problem by bringing different issues to light. It is apparent that the four data collection methods used by the BIBE team complemented each other in achieving the study goals.

The next step was to use the data collected in this naturalistic research study to develop tools to support biodiversity surveys. However, mapping naturalistic research findings to design (whether of a system, a particular user interface, an outreach program, or a marketing strategy) is never easy. "The difficulty comes," the BIBE team wrote, "in interpreting the data and deciding how this interpretation should affect design" (Heidorn et al., 2002, p. 1257). As you consider engaging in naturalistic research, think about how you will draw on your findings to achieve your larger objectives. In many cases, this requires adaptation and combination of multiple naturalistic approaches. The pragmatic approach illustrated here—focused on gathering a relevant, broad base of evidence—can serve as a model.

Example 2: Criteria Used in Making Relevance Judgments

Information retrieval systems, such as search engines, often return vast amounts of information in response to users' requests. When faced with such a deluge of information, how do people evaluate documents and decide which ones to pursue? Of course, their principal concern is whether a given document is on topic. But in many cases, that's not their only concern. A wide range of other considerations might come into play. Developing a good understanding of these extratopical factors might enable the creation of better retrieval systems. Barry's (1994)[1] study intended to identify these factors, using a study design with important naturalistic elements.

Barry's (1994) research was driven by naturalistic concerns—specifically, the desire to study users with real and current information need situations. She sought to capture the range of issues that affect these situations (such as prior knowledge, expected use of information, emotional state, and so forth) by working directly with people motivated by some information need. Thus she sought participants who were "motivated users involved in current information need situations" and observed them "evaluating information within an actual information seeking and use situation" (p. 153). This emphasis on a naturalistic design with authentically motivated users may be contrasted with laboratory experiments using participants recruited because of convenience (e.g., students seeking extra credit for a class) and assigned to complete tasks in which they had little or no interest.

Although it emphasized naturalistic design, this study was not based on open-ended observation; rather, a specific research question guided the inquiry: What criteria allow users to determine whether connections or lack of connections exist between the information within documents and the users' information need situations? To answer this question, a specific procedure was designed.

Participants (18 students and faculty from a university) were asked to submit written search requests. These search requests represented real information needs, originating from class assignments, theses and dissertations, and professional presentations and publications. A preliminary online search and a presearch interview were then used to refine the search request. Then a final online search was conducted to retrieve citations related to the participant's information need. Fifteen documents were randomly selected from the search results, and document representations (containing, e.g., citations, abstracts, indexing terms, etc.) were constructed for each document. In addition, three documents were randomly selected from the search results, and the full text was retrieved.

These document representations were presented, in random order, to the participant, who was asked to circle (or cross out) each portion of the representation that prompted a reaction to pursue (or not pursue) the citation. After all the representations and documents had been annotated in this way, the researcher interviewed the participant, asking neutral questions to elicit his or her reasons for circling (or crossing out) each aspect. The responses to these interviews were then inductively analyzed to identify and describe the criteria used in making judgments about whether to pursue the citation/document or not. The 989 responses (to 242 distinct documents) yielded 444 instances of 23 categories of criteria. These categories were then grouped into seven major groups. For example, the group "criteria pertaining to the document as physical entity" included the criteria obtainability and cost.

To what extent did Barry's (1994) research examine users' information behavior in a naturalistic way? On one hand, she was able to recruit motivated users with real needs and observe them in an "actual information seeking and use situation." This should be applauded, given the relatively contrived situations that are often seen in studies of information behaviors. On the other hand, the presentation, ordering, and analysis of documents were still quite contrived in this study, and participants were required to circle or cross out particular regions, a potentially artificial imposition. In addition, the study did not address many subtler aspects of how people evaluate information in their natural environment. The social (e.g., showing a citation to a colleague) and physical (e.g., referring to an out-of-print reference work stored in an office) aspects of context were not incorporated into the study design. Moreover, the research was based on an assumed model of information retrieval—that people retrieve document representations, then systematically evaluate them. In reality, information retrieval behavior is much more fluid, dynamic, and messy (Bates, 1989).

On the other hand, this study provides something that more naturalistic research (e.g., an ethnographic study that involved observations in participants' offices, homes, etc.) might not: a well-organized list of particular criteria that people use when evaluating documents. This list filled an important void in researchers' understanding and inspired many subsequent studies (as evidenced by its being cited over 100 times). Research that makes an impact must often make trade-offs between naturalism and control. It is the effectiveness of the trade-off that makes the difference, and this should be foremost in your mind as you pursue naturalistic research.

CONCLUSION

Naturalistic techniques are an essential element of a researcher's repertoire. They represent social science at both its most exciting and its most frustrating. Naturalistic research is exciting because it reveals the fascinating complexity of human behavior and enables the collection of rich visual, verbal, and physical data. It is frustrating because of the elusiveness of what you want to measure and the seeming infinity of techniques for doing so. That is why, within a particular research program, you'll want to combine the richness of naturalistic techniques with the rigor of controlled studies and validated instruments.

NOTE

1. This paper received the Best *JASIS* Paper Award from the American Society for Information Science in 1995.

WORKS CITED

Barry, C. L. (1994). User-defined relevance criteria: An exploratory study. *Journal of the American Society for Information Science, 45*, 149–159.

Bates, M. (1989). The design of browsing and berrypicking techniques for the online search interface. *Online Review, 13*, 407–424.

Bernard, H. R. (1995). *Research Methods in Anthropology* (2nd ed.). Walnut Creek, CA: AltaMira.

Beyer, H. R., & Holtzblatt, K. (1995). Apprenticing with the customer. *Communications of the ACM, 38*(5), 45–52.

Beyer, H., & Holtzblatt, K. (1999). Contextual design. *Interactions, 6*(1), 32–42.

Crabtree, A., Nichols, D. M., O'Brien, J., Rouncefield, M., & Twidale, M. B. (2000). Ethnomethodologically-informed ethnography and information systems design. *Journal of the Ameican Society for Information Science, 51*(7), 666–682.

Fidel, R., Pejtersen, A. M., Cleal, B., & Bruce, H. (2004). A multidimensional approach to the study of human-information interaction: A case study of collaborative information retrieval. *Journal of the American Society for Information Science and Technology, 55*(11), 939–953.

Heidorn, P. B. (2001). A tool for multipurpose use of online flora and fauna: The Biological Information Browsing Environment (BIBE). *First Monday, 6*(2). Retrieved January 31, 2009, from http://firstmonday.org/htbin/cgiwrap/bin/ojs/index.php/fm/article/view/835/744.

Heidorn, P. B., Mehra, B., & Lokhaiser, M. (2002). Complementary user-centered methodologies for information seeking and use. *Journal of the American Society for Information Science, 53*(14), 1251–1258.

Ireland, C. (2003). Qualitative methods: From boring to brilliant. In B. Laurel (Ed.), *Design Research* (pp. 23–29). Cambridge, MA: MIT Press.

Kipling, R. (1893). *The Kipling Reader for Elementary Grades*. New York: D. Appleton.

Myers, M. D. (1999). Investigating information systems with ethnographic research. *Communication of the AIS, 2*(2), 1–20.

Park, T. K. (1994). Toward a theory of user-based relevance: A call for a new paradigm of inquiry. *Journal of the American Society for Information Science, 45*, 135–141.

Potts, C., & Newstetter, W. (1997). Naturalistic inquiry and requirements engineering: Reconciling their theoretical foundations. In *Proceedings of the 3rd International Symposium on Requirements Engineering (RE'97)* (pp. 118–127). New York: IEEE Computer Society Press.

Sayer, A. (1984). *Method in Social Science: A Realist Approach*. London: Hutchinson.

Schwartz, H., & Jacob, J. (1979). *Qualitative Sociology: A Method to the Madness*. New York: Free Press.

Vicente, K. J. (1999). *Cognitive Work Analysis: Toward Safe, Productive and Healthy Computer-based Work*. Mahwah, NJ: Erlbaum.

9

Longitudinal Studies

Barbara M. Wildemuth

Doing a longitudinal study means wrapping an albatross around one's neck, placing a monkey on one's back, mounting a tiger, and grabbing a bear by its tail.

—Jack Block and Jeanne H. Block (2006)

SCOPE

As indicated by the epigraph, longitudinal studies should not be undertaken unless you have a good reason. The primary reason for using a longitudinal study design is because you're interested in a process that occurs over time, and you need to observe it over time to understand it more fully. For example, you might be interested in how people's information seeking behaviors change as the searchers learn more and progress through the project motivating their information behaviors (see, e.g., Kuhlthau, 1991). As Plewis (1985) notes, "many of the interesting questions in the social sciences are about change and process and cause, questions about dynamics, and they cannot be answered with static descriptions and associations" (p. 1).

The term *longitudinal research* can be used to refer to a whole family of different research designs (Menard, 2002), including repeated cross-sectional studies (i.e., a series of observations, not necessarily including the same study participants in each, e.g., Tenopir et al., 2006) and retrospective panel designs (i.e., in which people are asked, once, about multiple past occasions). However, in this chapter, we will focus on the narrower definition of longitudinal research (sometimes called *prospective panel designs*), including only those studies "in which (a) data are collected for each item or variable for two or more distinct time periods; (b) the subjects or cases analyzed are the same or at least comparable from one period to the next; and (c) the analysis involves some comparison of data between or among periods" (Menard, 2002, p. 2). The participants may be individual people or individual organizations such as libraries or other organizations (Van de Ven & Huber, 1990). Two or more participant panels may be included to improve the robustness of the design (Bauer, 2004; Menard, 2002; Singer & Willett, 1996).

Most often, data are collected on at least three occasions so that the trajectory of change can be observed (Singer & Willett, 1996). Using these criteria, we are left with a research design that is well suited to investigations of processes—including change processes—that occur over time.

ADVANTAGES OF LONGITUDINAL RESEARCH

When considering whether to conduct a longitudinal study, you are most likely comparing its strengths and weaknesses to those of cross-sectional research designs. There are two primary advantages that longitudinal research, as defined previously, has over cross-sectional studies. The first is that longitudinal research can examine changes or other processes that occur over time, within individuals (Bauer, 2004). Because the same panel of subjects or cases is involved in the study on each data collection occasion, the researcher can examine the ways in which each participant has changed from one time to the next. In addition, the researcher can examine the duration of particular episodes or phenomena (Ruspini, 1999). This type of individual analysis is not possible with cross-sectional research, in which different participants are involved on each occasion.

The second advantage of longitudinal research designs is that they provide a stronger basis for drawing conclusions about cause and effect. There are three important criteria that must be met to establish that cause and effect: the two variables must covary, this relationship between them must not be attributable to any other cause, and the variable believed to be the cause must precede or be simultaneous with the effect (Menard, 2002). The first two criteria can be met through cross-sectional designs, but the third cannot (unless the cause is something inherent in the individual, e.g., sex or educational status). Therefore researchers interested in making the strongest case that one variable causes another should consider a longitudinal study design.

DATA COLLECTION AND ANALYSIS IN LONGITUDINAL STUDIES

Almost any type of data might be included in a longitudinal study (Bergman & Magnusson, 1990). You can directly observe the phenomena of interest. You might use interviews, questionnaires, or other types of measures to ask study participants about the phenomena of interest. You might collect data from existing records, for example, library circulation records. The only rule of thumb is that equitable data must be gathered over multiple occasions (Singer & Willett, 1996) so that you can make comparisons based on those data. You should keep in mind that this rule of thumb may not be easy to implement. Because of the different rates at which information behaviors occur, you may need to gather data about some of your variables very frequently and about others only periodically. Also, if you are undertaking a very long study, measures that were appropriate at the beginning of the study may not be appropriate by the end. As you plan your data collection methods, be sure to think through the full length of the study to ensure that your data will support the comparisons between time periods that are the focus of the study.

You will also need to plan for how many times you will collect data and how they will be timed. These plans will depend on many things, both theoretical and practical. One of the most important considerations is the life cycle of the process you are trying to observe and how quickly it occurs (Block & Block, 2006). For instance, a longitudinal study of library use while writing a dissertation may occur over several years, and data collection might be scheduled for every few months; a different study might be examining the ways that people use Web sites to plan their vacations, so data collection might be scheduled weekly for a couple of months.

Once the data have been collected, you will need to analyze them to answer your research question(s). A variety of methods, both qualitative and quantitative, might be appropriate. Qualitative approaches will most likely take a life history approach, treating each subject as a case study and trying to understand the dynamic nature of the phenomenon of interest. Quantitative analysis may involve a number of statistical techniques (e.g., repeated measures analysis of variance, structural equation modeling, longitudinal multilevel methods, regression analysis, or event history analysis), and it would be appropriate to get advice from a statistical consultant on how to proceed.

CHALLENGES IN COLLECTING AND ANALYZING LONGITUDINAL DATA

As indicated by the epigraph, many challenges are associated with conducting longitudinal research. They include challenges associated with your sample and attrition from your sample, the difficulty of measuring the same variables on each occasion, and the effects of extraneous events (including your study procedures) on the phenomenon being observed. In each case, you will need to plan for the study that you want to conduct and, in addition, plan for the study you will need to conduct when your original plans don't work. Try to anticipate the challenges you might face, and plan for how to address them if they do occur (Bauer, 2004).

Because longitudinal studies occur over extended periods of time, selecting or recruiting a sample that is willing to participate can be more challenging than for a study that will occur at only one point in time. Because those who will volunteer to participate in a longitudinal study are likely to be different than those who won't, even your original sample may be biased (Bauer, 2004). In addition, attrition (i.e., people dropping out of the study after it's begun) could introduce even more bias because those who drop out are likely to be different from those who continue in the study (Bergman & Magnusson, 1990). There are a number of things you can do to minimize attrition (Bauer, 2004; Murphy, 1990). First, you will want to carefully track all your participants so that, when you need to follow up with them for the next data collection, you will be able to find them. At the first data collection session, be sure you record accurate contact information for each participant (Goldstein, 1979). Second, you should consider ways in which you can develop rapport with the study participants (e.g., having the same interviewer contact each participant on each occasion) to encourage participants to continue. A personal relationship with the researcher will lessen attrition. Third, be sure that the frequency of data collection or the amount of time required for each data collection session is not too much of a burden on the participants. Finally, consider offering an incentive (e.g., cash or a gift of some kind) to participants. If necessary, the value of the incentive can be increased for later data collection sessions. For instance, if you were conducting a study of college students' use of the library over their undergraduate careers, you might provide them with gift certificates to the campus bookstore, with the amount of the gift certificate increasing each year. With appropriate planning and study procedures, a valid sample can be recruited and maintained over the course of the study. You might also consider using multiple panels simultaneously to be better able to evaluate the effects of attrition within each of them.

There are also challenges associated with the measurements to be taken during a longitudinal study, particularly with measures of psychological constructs (i.e., individual characteristics that cannot be directly observed such as attitudes or satisfaction). Since your goal is to observe changes over time, you need to be able to compare the measures over time. Thus, as Singer and Willett (1996) point out, they need to be equitable, if not exactly the same. Once you have valid measures to use for data collection, you will want to consider how to analyze those changes: as simple change scores (i.e., the difference between scores at one time and scores at another time) or some type of residual change score, taking into account the expected trajectory of change and looking for divergence from that trajectory (Bauer, 2004; Bergman & Magnusson, 1990). You may need to seek statistical consulting advice to resolve these issues.

Finally, several challenges are associated with the context of any given study. The most obvious is the possibility of *history effects* (Bauer, 2004; Stanley & Campbell, 1963). The danger here is that some extraneous event occurs during the course of the study that has an effect on the phenomenon of interest, influencing it in unusual ways. The longer the study, the more likely that something unexpected will occur. Even for relatively short studies, researchers should be continually monitoring the environment to be able to take into account such unexpected and unwanted influences. A second problem is called *panel conditioning* (Ruspini, 1999) and is equivalent to the testing effects described by Stanley and Campbell (1963). Because the same measurements will be taken on multiple occasions, the process of data collection may influence the behavior of the participants. For example, if you were studying the development of information literacy skills among middle school students, the skills test you administer to them every two months may have an effect on their skill development, in addition to the training they are receiving. Thus the data collection procedures themselves influence the process being studied. A third issue is that while some change is linear, for many phenomena of interest in information and library science (ILS), linear change cannot be assumed (Plewis, 1985). Instead, there are "fluctuations over time" (p. 2). None of these problems can be easily resolved, but careful consideration of them while planning your study procedures will allow you to minimize their negative effects on the validity of your results.

EXAMPLES

Given the narrow definition of longitudinal research that we are using here, there are not many examples of this research design in the ILS literature. Both the examples to be discussed here have relatively small sample sizes, making them more feasible for an individual researcher or a small research team to conduct. They vary in their length; the longer the study, the more planning and resources it requires. In spite of the challenges of conducting longitudinal research, these two examples illustrate that longitudinal research is possible and that it can yield rich rewards. The first is a study of Web users' information behaviors and the contexts in which they occur, and the second is a study of scholars' information use.

Example 1: The Effects of Context on Information Behaviors

Kelly's (2004,[1] 2006a, 2006b) dissertation research investigated the role of context as doctoral students sought information on the Web over the course of one semester.

Seven doctoral students were provided with laptops instrumented with logging software. They were interviewed and completed a questionnaire at the beginning of a semester and indicated a set of tasks and topics of interest at the time. Each week during the semester, they returned to the researcher's office to review some of the documents they had retrieved during the past week. They classified each document in relation to the task and topic for which it was retrieved and rated its usefulness. During these weekly sessions, they could also add tasks and topics to their active lists. Each week, they also rated the endurance of each task, the frequency with which they had worked on each task, the stage of their progress in completing the task, and the persistence of each topic and their familiarity with that topic. At the end of the 14-week semester, they were interviewed about the tasks and topics, the process of classifying the documents by task and topic, the history of their work on each task and topic, and their reactions to the study procedures.

Our discussion here will focus on the aspects of this study design that define it as a longitudinal study. It clearly meets the first criterion of collecting data on each variable over multiple time periods—14, in this case. It also meets the second criterion, that the study participants were the same people on each occasion. Finally, it also meets the third criterion because the analysis of the results includes a focus on changes in endurance, frequency, and stage ratings of the tasks, and changes in the persistence and familiarity ratings of each topic.

While Kelly (2004, 2006a, 2006b) began the study with a small convenience sample, she was able to retain all the members of that sample throughout the 14 weeks of the study. Several of her procedures promoted continuing participation. By meeting personally with the participants each week, she established a relationship with them, increasing their motivation to continue in the study. The weekly meetings were scheduled often enough to develop rapport and to become a routine part of each participant's schedule, but were not so frequent that they would be burdensome. She restricted the number of documents to be reviewed each week to control the level of the burden on the participants. She provided the laptop and printer to the participants at the end of the study—a significant incentive for them to participate in all 14 data collection sessions. This combination of procedures was successful in avoiding attrition in the study sample.

The study procedures also demonstrate the benefits of careful advance planning for the study. In advance of the beginning of the study, the data collection instruments were developed and pilot tested. While the topic familiarity ratings were still not as reliable as desired, the pilot testing did allow Kelly (2004, 2006a, 2006b) to minimize any problems with the data collection procedures. In particular, they allowed her to use the same data collection procedures at all 14 occasions, making the longitudinal data comparable across occasions. The use of Web logs was also supported by careful planning. The PCs were instrumented to collect data, plus a copy of each Web site visited was captured by a proxy server, through which all the participants' Web sessions were routed. Finally, at the end of the study, Kelly implemented clear procedures for "cleaning" the laptops and legally transferring them to the participants. This combination of procedures contributed to the quality of the data collected during the study.

The data analysis for this study focused on two types of questions typical of longitudinal studies: the history of change in the outcome variables over the course of the study, and the relationships among variables over the course of the study. The first type of analysis is illustrated in the longitudinal analysis of participants' perceptions of their stage of task completion. While there were a small number of participants, there

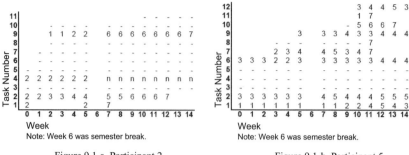

Figure 9.1-a. Participant 2

Figure 9.1-b. Participant 5

Figure 9.1. Ratings of task stage by participants 2 and 5 (from 1, started, to 7, finished; dash indicates not applicable). Adapted from Kelly (2006b, Fig. 1). Reprinted with permission of John Wiley & Sons, Inc.

were a large number of cases (i.e., 127 tasks) included in this analysis. The results for participants 2 and 5 are shown in Figure 9.1. The goal of this analysis was to try to detect patterns that occurred over time. From the results for all seven participants, Kelly was able to conclude that very few tasks were completed during the semester: participant 2 (Figure 9.1a) completed only 2 of 11, and participant 5 (Figure 9.1b) completed only 4 of 12. In addition, while it would be expected that each task would progress toward completion as the semester proceeded (as illustrated by participant 2), this was not always the case. Participant 5 rated half of the tasks as progressing forward but then moving further away from completion later in the semester. During the exit interviews, this phenomenon was explored and explained by the participants as times when "you get thrown back . . . because you hit a little snafu" (Kelly, 2006b, p. 1866). While Kelly needed to develop these analysis procedures specifically for this study, they were quite effective in helping her to understand changes in her participants' stages of task completion over time.

The second type of question addressed with these data focuses on relationships among the variables. Specifically, Kelly investigated the relationships between the context variables (i.e., attributes of the tasks and topics) and the participants' ratings of Web site usefulness. She used two different statistical analysis techniques to examine these relationships. First, she checked the correlations among the context variables and usefulness ratings (see Kelly, 2006b, table 6). While there were a number of relationships between context variables that seemed to warrant further study (e.g., for six of the participants, the endurance of a task was related to its stage of completion), this analysis provided relatively little evidence that the context variables were related to ratings of Web site usefulness. A second analysis examined the question of whether usefulness ratings varied based on the particular task or topic. For this analysis, chi-square was used (even with some concerns that the sample size was insufficient to draw valid conclusions). Nevertheless, the analyses did indicate that usefulness ratings did vary by task and topic for all seven participants. As in many longitudinal studies, this type of question is somewhat less concerned with the longitudinal nature of the data and might also be investigated with a cross-sectional study design.

In summary, Kelly's use of a longitudinal study design demonstrated many of the ways in which a researcher can address the challenges associated with this approach. Her careful planning of the study procedures was exemplary, in particular in relation to keeping the data collection procedures comparable across occasions and minimizing sample attrition. It serves as a good example of how to apply this research design to questions related to change over time.

Example 2: A Longitudinal Study of Scholars' Use of Information

Over the course of several years, Wang and her colleagues[2] studied scholars' selection, reading, and citing of documents originally identified in an online search. Twenty-five agricultural economists (11 faculty and 14 graduate students) were recruited to participate in the study, which began in 1992. At that time, an online search was conducted to support a project of each participant; the participants then reviewed the retrieved items and identified those that would be relevant to their projects. Three years later, 15 of the same participants were interviewed concerning which of the documents they had read and which they had cited. There are a number of aspects of this study design that are of interest to others planning a longitudinal study, including the timing of the data collection waves, the ways in which retrospective data collection was combined with concurrent data collection (including the use of external stimuli to improve recall), and finally, the timing of the publication of results from the study.

The information behavior of interest for this study was the selection, reading, and citing behavior of the participants as they worked on intellectual projects (e.g., articles, book chapters, and dissertations). Each of these three types of behaviors happens intermittently: intensely during some periods, and rarely during other periods. In addition, each of these types of information behavior can continue over an extended period of time. Therefore the study began in 1992 (Wang & Soergel, 1993, 1998), when each participant was beginning a particular project. At that time, the participants provided think-aloud protocols while they identified relevant papers on which they expected to follow up during the project. Wang and White (1995, 1996, 1999; White & Wang, 1997a, 1997b) contacted each participant a second time, in 1995, three years later. At that point, 10 of the original 25 participants had dropped their projects or modified them so significantly that they could not provide data appropriate to the study. Of the remaining 15, 3 were not able to provide data about citing decisions: "two participants still had research in progress and the third was a joint author whose colleague had made the citing decisions" (White & Wang, 1997b, p. 124). Thus the three-year interval between the two waves of data collection was appropriate for most of the participants, but still too short for some.

Another point of interest is that this study was concerned with three information behaviors (selection, reading, and citing of documents) that occur at different times, but data were collected on only two occasions. Data about selection of relevant documents were collected through concurrent think-aloud protocols while the participants reviewed their search results. Data about reading and citing of documents were collected retrospectively, that is, after the behaviors had occurred. In some cases, this would have been years after the behavior had occurred. For example, it is easy to imagine a participant who identified a few relevant items from the search in 1992 and, within months, had read several of those items. It was not until 1995 that the participant was asked about that reading behavior and, at the same time, was asked about whether the item had been cited in project publications. It's very possible that the results of this study were not as complete or unbiased as would be desirable because participants had forgotten how they reacted to the document when they read it or decided to cite it. Wang and her colleagues tried to overcome this problem, primarily, by encouraging the participants to use external stimuli to aid their memories. For example, one participant referred to referee comments on an article to see if the referee had recommended a particular citation. Others referred to their notes, drafts of publications, and other documentary evidence. An ideal study design would have the researcher present with each participant as each reading or citing decision was made. However, in the real (rather than ideal) world, the use of retrospective recall of reading and citing decisions, aided by external stimuli, was an appropriate approach to increasing the validity of the study data.

Finally, it is worthwhile to take note of the publications that resulted from this study because the timing of longitudinal study results can be an issue. The results of the 1992 interviews were published in Wang's (1994) dissertation. In addition, preliminary results were reported in an American Society for Information Science and Technology paper (Wang & Soergel, 1993), and the full results were reported in a *Journal of the American Society for Information Science and Technology* (*JASIST*) article (Wang & Soergel, 1998). There is no evidence that when the original study was undertaken, it was planned as the first phase of a longitudinal study; thus the second wave of data collection, in 1995, appears to have been opportunistic. It resulted in several more publications: a report of preliminary results in two ASIST papers (Wang & White, 1995, 1996), a *JASIST* article reporting the results (Wang & White, 1999), a technical report (White & Wang, 1997a), and a *Library Quarterly* article examining scholars' citing behaviors in more detail (White & Wang, 1997b). This is a typical pattern for publishing the results of longitudinal studies that occur over a period of years. Usually, the first wave of data collection is of interest, even without the additional comparisons that will be possible after the follow-up data are collected. Most often, the second and later waves of results are published in combination with the earlier waves of data, comparing the results over time.

Wang's work, in collaboration with Soergel and White, resulted in a fairly unique view of scholars' selection, reading, and citing behaviors as they occurred over time. The interviews regarding selection decisions allowed the later data on reading and citing decisions to be explicitly anchored in a set of documents that could be used to stimulate the study participants' memories. While all the original study participants were available and willing to participate in the second wave of data collection, the phenomenon of interest resulted in some natural attrition from the sample. Though a longitudinal study design presented several challenges, it allowed these researchers to advance our understanding of scholarly use of research materials.

CONCLUSION

If you want to use a longitudinal study design in your research, you can use the examples provided by Kelly and Wang to think through some of the challenges you will face. Always keep in mind that your goal is to understand, on the individual level, a phenomenon that occurs over time. As you select your sample, consider how you will hold on to all your study participants over the course of the study. Be careful in selecting your methods for measuring the variables of interest so that the measurements taken on the multiple occasions of the study can be compared with each other. Try to anticipate any extraneous events (including your study procedures) that could have a biasing effect on your results. With care, you can plan and implement a successful longitudinal study.

NOTES

1. Kelly's dissertation received the 2006 Eugene Garfield Doctoral Dissertation Award from the Association for Library and Information Science Education.

2. Wang and Soergel (1998) were the recipients of the 1999 Best *JASIST* Paper Award from the American Society for Information Science and Technology (ASIST). Dagobert Soergel was the recipient of the 1997 ASIST Award of Merit.

WORKS CITED

Bauer, K. W. (2004). Conducting longitudinal studies. *New Directions for Institutional Research*, *121*, 75–90.

Bergman, L. R., & Magnusson, D. (1990). General issues about data quality in longitudinal research. In D. Magnusson & L. R. Bergman (Eds.), *Data Quality in Longitudinal Research* (pp. 1–31). Cambridge: Cambridge University Press.

Block, J., & Block, J. H. (2006). Venturing a 30-year longitudinal study. *American Psychologist*, *61*(4), 315–327.

Goldstein, H. (1979). *The Design and Analysis of Longitudinal Studies*. London: Academic Press.

Kelly, J. D. (2004). *Understanding implicit feedback and document preference: A naturalistic user study*. Unpublished doctoral dissertation, Rutgers University. Retrieved July 19, 2007, from http://ils.unc.edu/~dianek/diane-kelly-dissertation.htm.

Kelly, D. (2006a). Measuring online information seeking context, part 1: Background and method. *Journal of the American Society for Information Science and Technology*, *57*(13), 1729–1739.

Kelly, D. (2006b). Measuring online information seeking context, part 2: Findings and discussion. *Journal of the American Society for Information Science and Technology*, *57*(14), 1862–1874.

Kuhlthau, C. C. (1991). Inside the search process: Information seeking from the user's perspective. *Journal of the American Society for Information Science*, *42*(5), 361–371.

Menard, S. W. (2002). *Longitudinal Research* (2nd ed.). Thousand Oaks, CA: Sage.

Murphy, M. (1990). Minimizing attrition in longitudinal studies: Means or end? In D. Magnusson & L. R. Bergman (Eds.), *Data Quality in Longitudinal Research* (pp. 148–156). Cambridge: Cambridge University Press.

Plewis, I. (1985). *Analysing Change: Measurement and Explanation Using Longitudinal Data*. Chichester, England: John Wiley.

Ruspini, E. (1999). Longitudinal research and the analysis of social change. *Quality and Quantity*, *33*, 219–227.

Singer, J. D., & Willett, J. B. (1996). Methodological issues in the design of longitudinal research: Principles and recommendations for a quantitative study of teachers' careers. *Educational Evaluation and Policy Analysis*, *18*(4), 265–283.

Stanley, D. T., & Campbell, J. C. (1963). *Experimental and Quasi-experimental Designs for Research*. Dallas, TX: Houghton Mifflin.

Tenopir, C., King, D. W., Boyce, P., Grayson, M., & Paulson, K.-L. (2006). Relying on electronic journals: Reading patterns of astronomers. *Journal of the American Society for Information Science and Technology*, *56*(8), 786–802.

Van de Ven, A. H., & Huber, G. P. (1990). Longitudinal field research methods for studying processes of organizational change. *Organization Science*, *1*(3), 213–219.

Wang, P. (1994). *A cognitive model of document selection of real users of information retrieval systems.* Unpublished doctoral dissertation, University of Maryland.

Wang, P., & Soergel, D. (1993). Beyond topical relevance: Document selection behavior of real users of IR systems. *ASIS '93 Proceedings, 30,* 87–92.

Wang, P., & Soergel, D. (1998). A cognitive model of document use during a research project. Study I. Document selection. *Journal of the American Society for Information Science, 49*(2), 115–133.

Wang, P., & White, M. D. (1995). Document use during a research project: A longitudinal study. *ASIS '95 Proceedings, 32,* 181–188.

Wang, P., & White, M. D. (1996). A qualitative study of scholars' citation behavior. *ASIS '96 Proceedings, 33,* 255–261.

Wang, P., & White, M. D. (1999). A cognitive model of document use during a research project. Study II: Decisions at the reading and citing stages. *Journal of the American Society for Information Science and Technology, 50*(2), 98–114.

White, M. D., & Wang, P. (1997a). Document selection and relevance assessments during a research project. CLIS Technical Report No. 97–02. College Park, MD: University of Maryland, College of Library and Information Services.

White, M. D., & Wang, P. (1997b). A qualitative study of citing behavior: Contributions, criteria, and metalevel documentation concerns. *Library Quarterly, 67*(2), 122–154.

White, R. T., & Ariz, H. J. (2005). Longitudinal studies: Designs, validity, practicality, and value. *Research in Science Education, 35,* 137–149.

10

Delphi Studies

Lili Luo and Barbara M. Wildemuth

Oracle: Something that is foretold by or as if by supernatural means: divination, prophecy, soothsaying, vaticination, vision.

Roget's II: The New Thesaurus, 3rd edition (1995)

INTRODUCTION AND DEFINITION

Pythia, the Delphic oracle, was the medium through whom the Greek god Apollo spoke. She was purportedly able to foresee the future. The Delphi technique was named for this oracle because it has primarily been employed in forecasting future events based on the opinions of experts. It is a technique for gleaning and refining the subjective input from a group of people, usually experts, in an attempt to achieve consensus about some aspect of the present or the future (Fischer, 1978). A formal definition was provided by Linstone and Turoff (1975):

Delphi may be characterized as a method for structuring a group communication process so that the process is effective in allowing a group of individuals, as a whole, to deal with a complex problem. To accomplish this "structured communication" there is provided: some feedback of individual contributions of information and knowledge; some assessment of the group judgment or view; some opportunity for individuals to revise views; and some degree of anonymity for the individual responses. (p. 3)

The Delphi technique was developed in an Air Force–sponsored RAND Corporation study (Linstone & Turoff, 1975) aiming to "obtain the most reliable consensus of opinion of a group of experts . . . by a series of intensive questionnaires interspersed with controlled opinion feedback" (Dalkey & Helmer, 1963, p. 458). It was not used outside the defense community until 1964, when Gordon and Helmer published a RAND paper titled "Report on a Long-Range Forecasting Study," which attempted to forecast future developments in science and technology and their probable impacts on society and the world. Now the Delphi technique has been applied in a diverse range of disciplines, primarily supporting both short- and long-range planning, allocation of resources, and decision making.

Although forecasting future events has been the major application of the Delphi technique, it is a versatile research tool that can be used in a wide variety of situations. Researchers have developed variations of this method so that it can be used for different problem types and outcome objectives, including soliciting experts' opinions, assessing the relative importance of issues, and developing a concept or theoretical framework (Okoli & Pawlowski, 2004).

CHARACTERISTICS OF THE DELPHI METHOD

As stated previously, the Delphi method is conducted through group communication on the premise of some degree of anonymity. In other words, the participants involved in the Delphi method, as opposed to those in face-to-face communication, are anonymous to each other. Each works on an individual basis. The way they communicate with the rest of the group is not through direct discussion, but through the report of organized group results from the researchers. Both face-to-face meetings and Delphi studies are alternatives to solicit opinions from a group of people. However, with the aim of reaching consensus, the Delphi method is considered more efficient and accurate. It has the following advantages in overcoming biases inherent in face-to-face communications (Fischer, 1978; Linstone & Turoff, 1975):

- It allows more people to participate in the study than can effectively interact face-to-face. The method controls the communication flow and helps the group to stay focused.
- It allows participants from diverse backgrounds and with diverse (even opposing) views to interact without being concerned that severe disagreement (e.g., over political views) would lead to vehement reaction.
- The influences of dominant individuals are avoided. The strength of personality, eloquence, and other personal influential factors are much less visible because of the anonymity provided in Delphi studies.
- Group pressure for conformity is avoided. Individual participants are exempted from the direct pressure to conform to majority opinions.
- The effects of feelings and information communicated through body language, such as tone of voice, gestures, or the look of an eye, are minimized. Without seeing each other face-to-face, participants in Delphi studies are not affected by these nonverbal communications.
- Time and cost are reduced. Frequent face-to-face group meetings are costly and time consuming. Less time and cost are needed in Delphi studies to conduct the same number of rounds of data gathering.

While anonymity is a primary characteristic of the Delphi method, providing controlled feedback in the form of statistical summaries of group opinions (Fischer, 1978) is also important. The researchers summarize the results from a questionnaire by means of statistical analysis, such as calculating the means, interquartile range, standard deviation, and so on, and return the summary of the group responses to each individual participant. Through this controlled feedback, participants have access to the overall picture of the group's views and the distribution of different kinds of responses. In this way, an individual participant can compare his or her own opinions with those of the rest of the group and then decide whether to change them or not. Usually, opinions tend to have a large range at the beginning of the study, but through the successive rounds of data collection, the range is significantly narrowed and consensus starts to form (Dalkey & Helmer, 1963).

The iteration of several rounds of data collection is a third major characteristic of this technique. Helmer and Rescher (1959) proposed that the Delphi method "replaces direct debate by a carefully designed program of sequential individual interrogations (best conducted by questionnaires) interspersed with information and opinion feedback derived by computed consensus from the earlier parts of the program" (p. 47). Usually, a Delphi study has to go through three or four rounds to obtain a reasonable level of consensus within the group. In each round, the questionnaire is somewhat different from that of earlier rounds because each questionnaire will include feedback about the group's responses on the previous round.

Another characteristic of the Delphi method is asking participants to provide justification or an explanation when their opinions fall out of the range of group consensus. You can gain a better understanding of the quantitative results by having participants state their underlying reasons for their own opinions, though this is not an essential part of the method.

Whether or not the Delphi method is appropriate for a study depends on the nature of the research. Generally, if the problem "does not lend itself to precise analytical techniques but can benefit from subjective judgments on a collective basis" (Linstone & Turoff, 1975, p. 4), the Delphi method can be considered a feasible approach to tackle the problem. As for the length and scale of the study, such as how many rounds need to be conducted and how many participants need to be recruited, you should take into consideration the specific requirements of your research question/purpose to make those decisions. These concerns will be discussed in relation to the two example studies discussed later.

CONDUCTING A DELPHI STUDY

A hypothetical example is provided here to walk you through the basic steps in conducting a Delphi study. Let us suppose that some researchers in the field of digital reference are interested in finding out the frequently encountered difficulties/problems in implementing and managing digital reference services in academic libraries and which of those are the most urgent. Therefore the researchers design a Delphi study to ask experts in this field to identify these difficulties/problems and prioritize them according to their urgency. The steps involved in conducting such a Delphi study are listed and briefly described here.

First, the researchers would need to select experts in the field of digital reference to serve on the study panel. The criteria for selecting experts might include knowledge in this field; practical experience in implementing, managing, and evaluating digital reference services; research experience in studying digital reference as a new form of reference service; publications on this topic, and so on. A review of relevant literature, organization directories, Listservs, and blogs would result in a list of experts as potential participants for this study. The target sample size for the study will vary, depending on the goals of the study, but it is likely to be between 10 and 100 people. An invitation letter is sent out to explain the purpose/nature of the study and to invite the experts to participate. A consent form is attached for those who are willing to take part in the study to sign and send back.

The first-round questionnaire is distributed, asking participants to generate 20 problems they consider most difficult when implementing and managing digital reference services in a library. The content of this questionnaire will vary, of course, but it is often a short series of open-ended questions.

For the second-round questionnaires, the researchers consolidate the responses from the first round and produce a list of identified problems. With each problem listed, the researchers report the number of experts who identified this problem in the first round. This list is sent back to the participants, and they are asked to rate the urgency of these problems on a 5-point Likert-like scale.

In the third round, the researchers calculate the means and standard deviations of the ratings of each problem, based on the second-round responses, and order the problems according to their mean ratings. Problems with mean ratings below a certain cutoff point are dropped for this round. These results are presented back to the participants, and they are asked to rate these problems again in light of the statistical summary of group responses. For those who rate a problem over one standard deviation lower or higher than the group mean, the researchers ask them to provide explanations for their ratings.

The final results are summarized based on the responses from the third round. Means and standard deviations are computed again for each item. In the end, a list of problems, ordered according to their mean ratings, is generated, and explanations for ratings outside the consensus are summarized. With this final result, the researchers would be able to provide suggestions for the long-range planning of digital reference services development in libraries.

CRITICISM OF THE DELPHI METHOD

The Delphi method has been widely (though not universally) accepted as a reliable and valid method for forecasting the future. Nevertheless, we need to take a critical look at it. Criticism of the Delphi method has centered on five areas: lack of statistical tests, lack of demographic description of participants, selection of experts, lack of explanatory quality, and degree of anonymity. Each of these will be briefly described.

Lack of Statistical Tests

Although the Delphi method incorporates statistical summarization when reporting results, Sackman (1975) found that Delphi studies usually ignore tests for statistical significance and other analytical methods such as standard error of estimates, systematic correlations of items, factor analysis, and so on. He suggested that the Delphi method should be evaluated by the same standards, in terms of statistical methods, as other social science methods.

Lack of Demographic Description of Participants

Traditional Delphi studies do not report key characteristics of the participants such as age, gender, occupation, education and expertise, and so on (Sackman, 1975). It can be argued that such a description is not necessary because the only participant characteristic of interest is their expertise. As Ludwig and Starr (2005) note, "the validity of a Delphi study depends not on the number of participants polled, but rather on the expertise of the panel who participate" (p. 316). However, a description of the study sample may bolster the argument that the panel has the appropriate expertise. If appropriate, you could ask demographic questions in the first-round questionnaire, tailoring this kind of question to your specific purpose: collecting general demographic data or data providing a more detailed description of the participants' expertise.

Selection of Experts

Deciding on the criteria to be used in expert selection has always been a challenge in Delphi studies. Expertise, experience, and knowledge in a particular field are currently the primary criteria for judging an expert's ability to forecast future events. However, different experts may have different pursuits and interests in different subfields, and their opinions can be biased by their background and interest so as to make the group consensus less reliable than expected. One possible way of solving this problem, self-rating of expertise, was proposed by one of the Delphi reports published by RAND (Fischer, 1978). Participants were asked to rate the knowledge they thought they had about each item on a Delphi questionnaire when they responded to it.

Lack of Explanatory Quality

In Delphi studies, participants are asked to elaborate on their answers only when they are outside the range of group consensus. The lack of provision of explanations justifying the *convergence* of opinions is a weakness of the Delphi method (Gordon & Helmer, 1964; Passig, 1997; Weaver, 1971). To make the method more useful, the questionnaires should incorporate explanations for all responses, rather than just the outliers.

Degree of Anonymity

Different levels of anonymity (rather than complete anonymity) could be incorporated in a Delphi study. In some cases, revealing the identity of the participants to each other could be of help in soliciting input because the prestige of some participants would be an incentive for others to put a lot of thought into responding to the questionnaire. Even in such cases, individual responses are not linked to specific names so that partial anonymity still remains (Passig, 1997). While attractive in some ways, this approach is also very likely to have negative effects if some participants do not like some of the others because of different views or ideologies. You will need to be very careful in deciding what degree of anonymity is appropriate when designing your Delphi study.

THINGS TO AVOID IN CONDUCTING A DELPHI STUDY

At first glance, the Delphi method does not seem to be a very complicated research tool. However, it is not simple, and a lack of careful consideration of the problems involved in implementing such a study could lead to failure in achieving the research objective. Linstone and Turoff (1975) summarized a few things of which researchers need to be aware and which they need to avoid when conducting a Delphi study:

- Imposing your own preconceptions of a problem on the respondent group by overspecifying the Delphi questionnaires and not allowing for the contribution of other perspectives related to the problem

- Inadequately summarizing and presenting the group response
- Not ensuring common interpretations of the evaluation scales used in the questionnaires
- Ignoring, rather than exploring, disagreements so that discouraged dissenters drop out and an artificial consensus is generated
- Underestimating the demanding nature of a multiround Delphi study and not properly compensating the participants for their time and effort
- Ignoring misunderstandings that may "arise from differences in language and logic if participants come from diverse cultural backgrounds" (Linstone & Turoff, 1975, p. 7)

Although the Delphi method can be tailored to specific research designs in different studies, the preceding problems are the most common pitfalls of which you should be aware when planning a Delphi study.

EXAMPLES

Two Delphi studies will be examined here. The first (Neuman, 1995), focused on problems and issues associated with using electronic resources in high school libraries, was conducted in four rounds with a panel of 25 library media specialists. The second (Ludwig & Starr, 2005), focused on the future role of health sciences libraries, was conducted in three rounds with a panel of 30 librarians, building designers, and other stakeholders. Each study exemplifies a slightly different approach to the Delphi technique.

Example 1: High School Students' Use of Databases

Neuman (1995) conducted a nationwide Delphi study to identify high school students' most difficult problems in using electronic databases, potential solutions to these problems, and the most important policy issues related to the use of electronic resources in schools. The rationale for employing the Delphi method was that schools' use of electronic information resources was just beginning, and "insights of early adopters" (p. 285) would provide crucial guidance for further development and application of these tools.

The first step was to identify a panel representative of early adopters of electronic information resources in high schools. Seven national experts in the use of databases with students suggested several lists of potential participants for this study. Neuman (1995) did not describe how these experts were identified or what criteria they were given for nominating potential panelists; however, this general approach seems appropriate. All the high school library media specialists (LMSs) on these lists were invited to participate through telephone calls. Eventually, 25 LMSs from 22 schools in 13 states formed the panel, including seven winners of Dialog's Excellence in Online Education Award. The school was the unit of analysis for this study, so the schools' demographic characteristics, such as size, location, ethnicity, and years of experience using online and CD-ROM systems, were described in this article, addressing Sackman's (1975) concern that the demographic characteristics of Delphi panels are rarely provided. Although the purposive sampling of Delphi studies restricts the generalizability of the results, Neuman used these demographic data to make the case that the panel in her study was representative of the population of LMSs who use electronic information resources with high school students nationwide.

An important question in the design of a Delphi study is the source of the items on the first-round questionnaire. For this study, Neuman (1995) developed 226 statements in nine categories by combining the findings of two foundational case studies about students,' teachers,' and LMSs' behaviors and perceptions regarding database use, and Malcolm Fleming's (as cited in Neuman, 1995) five categories of effective instructional presentations. The marriage of empirical data and a well-established conceptual framework resulted in a comprehensive list of items covering the issues related to use and development of electronic information resources in schools. To further validate the initial questionnaire, Neuman asked several colleagues and LMSs to review it for the clarity of its direction and content.

The Delphi study was conducted in four rounds over 18 months. In the first round, the panelists were asked to rate 226 statements under 18 categories and subcategories on a 4-point Likert-type scale ranging from 0 (*not important*) to 4 (*critically important*) and to select those that were the most important in each category or subcategory. The second round was a replication of the first round, intended for the panel "to proceed toward consensus" (Neuman, 1995, p. 287). For each rated item, the range within one standard deviation above and below the means was reported, and each panelist needed to decide whether to move his or her rating within this range. A rationale was to be provided for any rating left outside the range of consensus. A similar procedure was followed to reach consensus about the "most important" statements. Each panelist's first-round responses were highlighted so that he or she could easily compare his or her own choices with the consensus of the group's responses. This was a thoughtful action, allowing the panelists to keep track of their own responses and to make any revisions in light of the group's responses. Since the primary goal of the Delphi method is to reach a consensus of opinions, defining the consensus range becomes an inherent part of any Delphi study. Neuman explicitly stated her definition of the consensus range, allowing her readers to understand how much consensus was achieved.

The design of the third and fourth rounds was considerably different from the first two rounds. In the third round, the identified "most important" statements were grouped into five categories, and under each category these statements were ordered according to the frequency with which they had garnered votes in the second round. Panelists were asked to rank the statements within each category. In the fourth round, the statements were reordered based on the results of the third round, and panelists were asked to provide the final rankings for these statements.

As with most Delphi studies, the sample size dwindled with the progression through the four rounds of questionnaires. The original panel consisted of 28 panelists from 26 schools in 16 states, but according to Neuman (1995), "panelists from two schools and one state dropped out in the first round, and panelists from two more schools in two states dropped out in the second; one panelist joined a colleague in completing the instruments for the study" (p. 285). Because the questionnaires used in Delphi studies are often fairly complex and/or long, it is rare that a study can be completed with all the panelists that begin the first round. Because the data from each round are used primarily to inform the design of the next round, input from all the panelists in each round is included in the analysis (i.e., data are not removed from previous rounds when a panelist drops out in a later round).

Because the third and fourth rounds took a different approach than the first two rounds, two sets of results are presented. The results from the first two rounds are the mean ratings for the problems and solutions listed in the questionnaire. From these mean ratings, a rank ordering of importance can be established indirectly. The results from the last two rounds were based on the panelists' votes for which statements were most important. Thus they are presented as a list of statements, ordered by importance. These two approaches to data collection and analysis provide slightly differing findings—two perspectives on the same issues. The differences illustrate the effects of your methods of data collection and analysis.

For the most part, Neuman's (1995) study was rigorously designed and could be considered a good model for readers who are interested in using the Delphi method in identifying and prioritizing research issues. She used an unusual but reasonable method for selecting a panel of experts. The initial questionnaire had a firm foundation in the past research literature. The four rounds of the study led to significant consensus among the panelists. In particular, her clear explanation of her study procedures can help guide others in designing a Delphi study.

Example 2: The Future of Health Sciences Libraries

Ludwig and Starr (2005) conducted a Delphi study to investigate experts' opinions about the future of health sciences libraries, with particular emphasis on the "library as place." On the basis of experts' statements about change in libraries, a three-round Delphi study was conducted with a panel of 30 experts.

The study began by assembling a small team of experts: 14 people (librarians, architects, and space planners) who had recently been involved in designing health sciences libraries. In response to open-ended questions, this group generated 80 pages of commentary, from which Ludwig and Starr (2005) extracted 200 "change statements." From this set of statements, they removed any "that the experts generally agreed on, that described fairly common-place activities, or that were vague and/or difficult to interpret" (p. 317), leaving the 78 statements that formed the first-round questionnaire. As noted previously, one of the challenges of a Delphi study is to develop the items to be evaluated/ranked during the study. These are often generated during the first round, by the panel itself, in response to open-ended questions; a variation of this approach was used in this study. This open-ended expression of opinion was incorporated as a preliminary step in the iterative cycle of the Delphi study.

The panel recruited for the Delphi study included the 14 people who had participated in generating the first-round questionnaire. This group was augmented by recruiting additional members through postings to several e-mail lists "for key opinion leaders in health care, librarianship, information technologies, and building and design" (Ludwig & Starr, 2005, p. 317). The process used in this study for ensuring that the panel was composed of experts is clearly not foolproof. While the final panel does represent a diverse set of stakeholders in library planning (librarians, library building designers, information technology managers, library building consultants, and health care administrators), their expertise in these areas was not vetted prior to including them on the panel. The panel consisted of 30 participants; no mention is made of any attrition in this sample through the three rounds.

The first round of the Delphi study asked the panel to rate each of the 78 change statements on five different scales: "'Likelihood of Change,' 'Desirability of Change,' 'Certainty of Answer,' 'Date Change Will Occur,' and 'Impact on Design'" (Ludwig & Starr, 2005, p. 317). The panel was also asked to explain the reasons for their responses. The second-round questionnaire was somewhat shorter; statements on which consensus

Table 10.1. Excerpt from Ludwig and Starr's study, showing the ways in which results were aggregated and presented

Consensus ranking	Agree (%)	Disagree (%)	Statement	Desirability and impact
4	92	8	By 2015, many academic health sciences libraries will be integrated into multifunctional buildings.	Somewhat to highly desirable; substantial design impact
5	8	92	By 2015, few institutions will have a health sciences library due to the easy, yet secured, ability of desktop access to information.	Undesirable; substantially different design
13	82	14	By 2007, the majority of faculty will regard health sciences librarians as partners in curriculum development teams.	Some design changes if classrooms and labs are part of the equation

Source: From Ludwig and Starr (2005, Table 1). Reprinted with permission of the authors.

was reached in the first round were eliminated, as were statements "for which there was substantial confusion" (p. 317). The panelists were provided with the mean ratings on each scale for each of the remaining items. The open-ended comments from the first-round questionnaire were also summarized on the second-round questionnaire, as *why* or *why not* commentary on the relevant change statement. In the second round, then, panelists were asked to rate each statement and provide their reasons, just as they had done in the first round. The same procedures were followed in the second round for analyzing the questionnaire responses. For the third round, the questionnaire was again shortened by eliminating those statements on which consensus had been reached or for which Ludwig and Starr concluded that there would be no consensus. The third round was then conducted.

Ludwig and Starr (2005) do not explicitly state a particular consensus level that needed to be reached for each statement to be included in the results. However, from the results included in the paper, we can conclude that they required that at least 65 percent of the panelists to concur about a particular statement. It appears that these results are based primarily on the ratings on the 'Likelihood of Change' scale. Responses to the 'Desirability of Change' and the 'Impact on Design' scales are incorporated into the summary of results as commentary on the statement. Results from the 'Date Change Will Occur' ratings were added to the original statements in the report of results. To illustrate the way in which these results were aggregated and presented, an excerpt from table 1 of the paper (presenting the results for all 78 statements) is shown here as Table 10.1. Given the quantity and qualitative nature of much of the data, this is an excellent overview of the findings from this study.

This study illustrates the way in which the Delphi method can be used to predict the future for libraries. While the future is always uncertain, we still need to plan for it. Using the consensus of a trusted panel of experts, as in this case, can provide a basis for such planning. Here Ludwig and Starr (2005) were particularly concerned with the physical aspects of library space and how that might be affected by other developments in library services. They recruited an appropriate panel of stakeholders in library buildings—those groups that are most likely to have thought about the questions of interest. If such a group reaches consensus about a trend, it is reasonable to conclude that you should take account of that trend in your own planning.

CONCLUSION

As can be seen from the two example studies discussed here, the Delphi technique is most appropriate in situations where the truth of the matter cannot be known through direct observation. Instead, we want to leverage the expertise of people who have thought about a particular issue or problem, seeking to find the consensus of their views on the matter. Through the careful selection of panelists and the iterative surveying of their opinions (with feedback), a Delphi study can provide results that will be useful in planning for the future.

WORKS CITED

Dalkey, N., & Helmer, O. (1963). An experimental application of the Delphi method to the use of experts. *Management Science, 9*(3), 458–467.

Fischer, R. G. (1978). The Delphi method: A description, review, and criticism. *Journal of Academic Librarianship, 4*(2), 64–70.

Gordon, T. J., & Helmer, O. (1964). *Report on a Long-Range Forecasting Study.* Retrieved January 6, 2009, from https://www.rand.org/pubs/papers/2005/P2982.pdf.

Helmer, O., & Rescher, N. (1959). On the epistemology of the inexact sciences. *Management Science, 6*, 25–52.

Linstone, H. A., & Turoff, M. (1975). *The Delphi Method: Techniques and Applications.* Reading, MA: Addison-Wesley.

Ludwig, L., & Starr, S. (2005). Library as place: Results of a Delphi study. *Journal of the Medical Library Association, 93*(3), 315–326.

Neuman, D. (1995). High school students' use of databases: Results of a national Delphi study. *Journal of the American Society for Information Science, 46*(4), 284–298.

Okoli, C., & Pawlowski, S. D. (2004). The Delphi method as a research tool: An example, design considerations and applications. *Information and Management, 42*, 15–29.

Passig, D. (1997). Imen-Delphi: A Delphi variant procedure for emergence. *Human Organization, 56*, 53–63.

Sackman, H. (1975). *Delphi Critique: Expert Opinion, Forecasting, and Group Process.* Lexington, MA: Lexington Books.

Weaver, W. T. (1971). Delphi forecasting method. *Phi Beta Kappan, 52*(5), 267–271.

11

Quasi-experimental Studies

Carolyn Hank and Barbara M. Wildemuth

From the standpoint of the final interpretation of an experiment and the attempt to fit it into the developing science, every experiment is imperfect.
—Donald T. Campbell and Julian C. Stanley (1963)

DEFINITION

Experimental methods are used for assessing causal relationships by determining "the impact of an intervention (e.g., a teaching technique, electronic database, or collection development policy) on an outcome or effect of interest" (Lorenzetti, 2007, p. 4). Campbell and Stanley (1963) present and discuss a family of these quantitative, experimental research designs, including *preexperimental designs, true experimental designs*, and *quasi-experimental designs*. This last set of designs is the focus of this chapter. They are used in natural settings, when some control over the experimental conditions can be exerted, yet full control is either not possible or not desirable. To better understand quasi-experimental designs, it is helpful to distinguish first how these differ from those other types of designs—the preexperiment and the true experiment.

The amount of control exerted on extraneous variables is the primary distinction between quasi-experimental studies and true experimental studies. In particular, it is the lack of control associated with the absence of random assignment that is the focus of any description of quasi-experimental designs (Campbell & Stanley, 1963; Fife-Schaw, 2000; Lorenzetti, 2007; Powell & Connaway, 2004). Typically, quasi-experimental designs involve naturally occurring groups (Lorenzetti, 2007; Powell & Connaway, 2004). Use of more than one group of subjects is a feature shared with true experimental designs (Koufogiannakis & Wiebe, 2006), but only in true experiments are individual subjects randomly assigned to particular experimental conditions. To borrow the words of Campbell and Stanley (1963), quasi-experimental methods are designed for settings "where better designs are not feasible" (p. 34). The "better" designs—true experiments—allow the researcher to control the effects of extraneous variables on the study's outcomes. However, when it is not possible to exert such control (through random assignment or in some other way), quasi-experimental designs offer an alternative for the researcher.

By employing quasi-experimental designs, the researcher recognizes from the outset of the study that the design lacks complete experimental control (Campbell & Stanley, 1963). While quasi-experiments are, in some ways, weaker than true experiments (Powell & Connaway, 2004), they are the most appropriate approach for many studies of interest in information and library science (ILS). Often, a quasi-experimental design can be implemented in a more naturalistic setting (rather than in a more controlled laboratory setting), thereby increasing the ecological validity of the study results. Thus the researcher can be more confident that the effect or treatment under investigation may be attainable in real-world settings, whereas controlled experimentation in a laboratory setting may not translate to success if implemented in less controlled, natural contexts.

USE OF QUASI-EXPERIMENTAL DESIGNS IN INFORMATION AND LIBRARY SCIENCE

Powell and Connaway (2004) reported that experimental designs (presumably including quasi-experimental designs) are applied to 8 percent to 10 percent of research studies in the field of ILS. Julien (1996) reported a lower percentage in her earlier investigation of the information needs and uses literature, a specific subtopic within ILS. Of the 163 research studies she identified, 6 percent used an experimental design. Additional evidence suggests that true experimental designs are used considerably less frequently than quasi-experimental designs. For example, Ondrusek (2004) reviewed 163 research studies for an investigation of end user online searching behavior, finding that only 1 of these 163 studies (0.06%) qualified as a true experimental design. Nineteen, or 12 percent, were identified as quasi-experimental designs. Koufogiannakis and Wiebe (2006) identified 122 relevant studies for consideration in their examination of effective library instruction methods; 48.4 percent of these employed quasi-experimental designs.

Applications of quasi-experimental designs are typically pragmatic, rather than theoretical, in nature and take the form of applied research. Additionally, quasi-experiments in ILS often fall within the framework of action research designs due to the intent of the research enterprise—to positively and directly impact procedures and services within a practice setting. Quasi-experimental designs have been applied in several ILS-specific research areas, including instruction, evaluation, information seeking, and professional development.

SPECIFIC DESIGNS

Within the broad classification of quasi-experimental designs provided by Campbell and Stanley (1963), they identified a number of specific single- and multigroup designs. Three are summarized here: time series designs, nonequivalent control group designs, and counterbalanced designs. These three distinct designs were selected because they demonstrate useful designs that may be particularly appropriate for application in ILS practice settings. You will want to consult Campbell and Stanley (1963) or other research design texts concerning additional quasi-experimental designs that may suit your purposes.

In borrowing from the graphical treatments of Campbell and Stanley (1963), the following descriptions include a formulaic representation of these distinct quasi-experimental designs—O represents a measurement or observation of the dependent variable(s) and X represents subjects' exposure to a treatment, the independent variable (e.g., a particular instructional method or a particular information system). Each row of a diagram represents one group of subjects and the treatment (Xs) and observations (Os) applied to that group (in the order shown). For multigroup designs, each row of the diagram depicts application of the treatment and observations for a particular group.

Time Series Design

The time series design is based on intermittent measurements taken before and after exposure to a treatment (Campbell & Stanley, 1963; Powell & Connaway, 2004). Simply put, this design tests for changes over time due to a treatment that occurs at a particular point in time. Time series designs are referred to as *within-subjects designs* because the comparison of interest is within each subject's performance before and after the treatment.

Fife-Schaw (2000) characterizes this design as having a minimum of two data collection points in total, pre- and posttreatment, but encourages use of more than this minimum to allow for sufficient opportunities to assess the effects of the treatment. A time series design with six observation points is represented as follows:

$$O_1 \quad O_2 \quad O_3 \quad X \quad O_4 \quad O_5 \quad O_6$$

Data would be collected at three points prior to the treatment (X) and at three points after the treatment. One hypothetical case in which such a design might be used is to investigate the effectiveness of a new tool developed for catalogers. Productivity resulting from this new tool, or treatment, could be ascertained by observing productivity each month for several months before the tool is introduced. Following introduction of the tool, or treatment, productivity would continue to be measured monthly, for several months, to assess the impact of the tool. It is important to take measurements on several occasions before and after the tool is introduced to make sure that the evaluation takes into account normal variability in productivity.

Nonequivalent Control Group Design

The *nonequivalent control group design* is likely the most frequently applied type of quasi-experimental design (Fife-Schaw, 2000; Trochim, 2006). This design is also referred to as the *nonequivalent groups design* (Campbell & Stanley, 1963; Trochim, 2006); the *pretest-posttest nonequivalent control group design* (Powell & Connaway, 2004); and the *controlled comparison study* (Lorenzetti, 2007). The nonequivalent control group design can be diagramed as follows:

Experimental group: O   X   O
Control group: O   O

There are two groups of study participants/subjects; often, they are naturally occurring groups such as two classes. One group receives the treatment and the other (the control group) does not. This design can be expanded to more groups if there are multiple forms of the treatment.

Although individual subjects are not randomly assigned to one group or the other, the groups should be formed so that they are as equivalent to each other as possible under existing conditions. For example, if evaluating a new method of library instruction, you would want to select two groups of students with similar characteristics such as the same class, age, college, and so on (Lorenzetti, 2007).

Each group is administered a pretest, and following application of the treatment to the experimental group, a posttest is administered. The pretest helps you to understand the ways in which the experimental group differs from the control group, even before the treatment is implemented. If there is no difference between the two groups on the pretest, then the comparison of their posttest scores is relatively straightforward. In addition, the pretest serves as a comparison with the posttest in determining the effects of the treatment.

This research design is referred to as a *between-subjects design*. Each subject participates in only one group, so comparisons between groups are comparisons between two independent sets of subjects.

Counterbalanced Design

In the multigroup *counterbalanced design*, multiple treatments, or interventions, are applied to each of the subjects. Since the comparison of interest is within each subject's performance in the multiple treatment conditions, this design is referred to as a within-subjects design. The counterbalanced design is particularly useful for situations when pretesting is unavailable or inappropriate. This design can be implemented in a variety of ways, depending on the number of treatments to be compared. The following example is depicted as a Latin square, to compare four treatments:

Group 1: X_1 O X_2 O X_3 O X_4 O
Group 2: X_2 O X_4 O X_1 O X_3 O
Group 3: X_3 O X_1 O X_4 O X_2 O
Group 4: X_4 O X_3 O X_2 O X_1 O

A typical study using this design might be trying to compare four different Web search engines and users' effectiveness in conducting searches with them. Group 1 would conduct searches on search engine 1, then search engine 2, then search engine 3, then search engine 4. The observation of user performance with each might be the amount of time taken to search or the number of relevant items retrieved with each. The second group of subjects would interact with search engine 2 first, then 4, then 1, then 3. By counterbalancing the order in which the subjects are exposed to the search engines, you will eliminate concerns about the learning that might occur as users get more and more practice with searching during the course of the study.

Like the nonequivalent control group design, counterbalanced designs are not considered true experiments because the researcher is not able to randomly assign individual subjects to the four groups. Instead, it is most common that intact groups are used. For example, four sections of an introductory English course might be used as the four experimental groups. While not a true experimental design, this is the most rigorous of the three designs discussed in this chapter and is more similar to true experimental designs than nonequivalent control group designs and time series designs.

RISKS TO DESIGN AND INTERPRETATION

The intent of a quasi-experimental design is to demonstrate that any difference in the results can be attributed to the treatment or intervention imposed by the researcher. To effectively demonstrate this connection, researchers must exclude other variables that may affect the results. First, the researcher must identify what other variables might affect the results. Whenever possible, the researcher should design the study to eliminate the possible effects of the extraneous variables. When that is not possible, the researcher should investigate the likelihood that these uncontrolled factors had an effect. Campbell and Stanley (1963) noted that "the more implausible this [effect of the uncontrolled factors] becomes, the more 'valid' the experiment" (p. 36).

These extraneous effects pose threats to the internal and external validity of the study results. *Internal validity* represents the degree to which the treatment actually affected the dependent variable, as evidenced by the resulting measurements and observations— posed as a question, "Did, in fact, the experimental treatments make a difference [in a] specific experimental instance" (Campbell & Stanley, 1963, p. 5)? *External validity* is concerned with the degree to which the research findings from a particular study can be generalized—posed as a question, "To what populations, settings, treatment variables, and measurement variables can this effect be generalized" (Campbell & Stanley, 1963, p. 5)? Threats to these two types of validity may manifest themselves in many ways. Some threats to validity that are likely to occur in ILS research (and discussed later) include selection bias and mortality effects, history effects, and testing effects (Campbell & Stanley, 1963; Fife-Schaw, 2000; Powell & Connaway, 2004).

Selection Bias and Mortality Effects

Selection bias and mortality effects are associated with multigroup designs. Selection bias occurs when the groups being compared are different from each other in some systematic way; mortality effects occur when study participants drop out of the study, resulting in nonequivalent groups. In either case, the effects observed in the study may not be a result of the treatment or intervention because they may be the result of differences between the participating groups (Campbell & Stanley, 1963; Powell & Connaway, 2004). For example, in a study on the impact of Web-based bibliographic instruction, if subjects in the treatment group have more experience in Web-based instruction than subjects in the control group, the study results can be attributed to this initial difference, rather than to the instruction provided.

The inability to randomly assign subjects to particular treatment conditions is a primary cause of selection bias. While random assignment may not be possible, researchers employing quasi-experimental designs may exert *some* control in combating selection bias and mortality effects. Foremost, for multigroup designs, researchers should select groups that are as comparable as possible. Mortality effects may be minimized by providing appropriate incentives to subjects to encourage their continued participation.

History Effects

Another threat to multigroup designs is the effect of unrelated events associated with the study participants, that is, their history during the course of the study (Campbell

& Stanley, 1963; Fife-Schaw, 2000; Powell & Connaway, 2004; Trochim, 2006). These types of effects may occur in any design that takes multiple measures and/or is making comparisons over time. For example, you might have selected two classes of first-year English students for a study examining search strategies used in the library catalog. The treatment group receives instruction from a librarian on how to conduct effective searches, while the control group does not. However, following the pretest, the English course teaching assistant provides similar instruction to the control group, in preparation for their literature review assignment. The results may indicate no difference in search strategy effectiveness between the two groups, but it is hard to know whether this lack of effect is because the librarian instruction was ineffective or because the history of the control group improved their performance.

There is no way to guarantee that there will be no history effects threatening the validity of your study. The chances of history effects can be reduced if the period between the observations is shorter, but even in the shortest study, something could occur that will have an effect on the validity of your results. Be aware of this threat, and try to discern whether anything has occurred during the course of your study that could affect your results.

Testing Effects

Asking subjects to complete a pretest of some kind may influence the validity of your study results in two ways. First, if the pretest and posttest are administered close together in time, subjects may recall their responses on the pretest and either match those responses or change them for the posttest. For example, you may try to study whether students' knowledge of a topic changes during the course of a search session on that topic. To assess their baseline knowledge, you administer a pretest; then you have them search for 15 to 30 minutes and administer a posttest. So that the pretest and posttest are directly comparable, you use the same test items, just in a different order. It is likely that many of your subjects will recall how they responded to the questions the first time, and this memory may affect how they respond to the same questions on the posttest. Second, the pretest questions may actually condition your subjects' responses to the intervention, causing them to interact with it differently than if they had not completed the pretest (this type of effect is called the *reactive effect* of testing). Using the same hypothetical study of topic knowledge, it is likely that the questions asked on the pretest will condition your subjects to pay particular attention to the items that they could not answer correctly, and during the searching period, they may attempt to fill those gaps in their knowledge. While it is true that they learned something about the topic from the searching activity, it is likely that the posttest inflates your conclusions about how much they had learned if you want to generalize your results to a more natural setting in which no pretest is administered.

Additional Threats to Validity

Several major threats to the validity of quasi-experimental studies have been outlined here, and suggestions were made for minimizing the likelihood that they will occur. There are several other threats to internal and external validity against which researchers should guard. Those associated with particular quasi-experimental designs are identified and discussed by Campbell and Stanley (1963).

EXAMPLES

The designs described earlier are idealized in the sense that they do not necessarily represent the additional compromises that must be made when research is conducted "in the field." Nevertheless, they can be implemented in this ideal form, as shown by the example studies discussed here. The first study (Hicks, 1980) examined the effects of charging public library user fees on library circulation using a time series design. The second study (Van Scoyoc, 2003) compared the effects of different forms of library instruction on students' library anxiety using a nonequivalent control group design. The third study (Jansen & McNeese, 2004, 2005) investigated the effects of automatic search assistance on search performance using a counterbalanced design. Each of these designs is well matched to the purposes of the respective studies.

Example 1: Effects of User Fees on Library Circulation (Time Series Design)

Hicks (1980) was concerned about the potential impact of charging user fees for public library services. Specifically, he investigated the impact of a small user fee, charged to suburban users of the Dallas Public Library system, on library circulation. The assumption was that such a user fee would have a negative impact on circulation because at least some of those users who had received services for free in the past would no longer be library users.

The study was conducted within the context of the Dallas Public Library system, which includes the central library and 17 branches (there were circulation data for only 14 of the branches, so only those libraries were included in the study). Monthly circulation data were used to represent level of library use. These data were available for a 12-year period, from 1965 through 1976. Thus the time series included 144 data points—clearly more than the minimum of three or four recommended by most authors writing about this method. This extended data set allowed Hicks (1980) to use more sophisticated statistical analysis methods than would have been appropriate with a smaller data set. In Campbell and Stanley's (1963) notation, it would look like the following:

$$O_1 \quad O_2 \quad O_3 \quad \ldots \quad O_{131} \quad O_{132} \quad X \quad O_{133} \quad O_{134} \quad \ldots \quad O_{144}$$

In January 1976 (designated by the X in the preceding diagram), a small user fee was established for suburban users of the city's public libraries. The rationale was that the suburban users were not supporting the libraries with their tax dollars and so should be asked to provide support through a user fee. The fee was very modest ($8.50) and was based on "the annual per capita costs of providing public library services in Dallas" (Hicks, 1980, p. 460). The implementation of this user fee would be considered the treatment, or intervention, in this time series design. It occurred at a particular point in time and would be expected to affect circulation levels after it was implemented.

Hicks used several different statistical methods to analyze the data. Each of them was trying to determine whether there was a difference in the slope of the trend line between the period prior to the user fees and after the user fees had been implemented. Because there is seasonal fluctuation in circulation levels, the long time period included in the analysis helped to gauge the trend more accurately, and the analysis methods could take the short-term fluctuations into account. The statistical analysis also took chance fluctuations into account. There was a "high degree of convergence" across the four statistical methods, and Hicks (1980) concluded that "for a majority of libraries there is evidence of a significant decline in circulation levels as a consequence of a nonresident fee card program" (pp. 470–471). While further discussion of the implications of this finding for library policy was necessary (and was undertaken by Hicks), it is clear that this research design allowed him to determine that the user fees had an impact on library circulation/use.

Example 2: Effectiveness of Bibliographic Instruction in Reducing Library Anxiety (Nonequivalent Control Group Design)

Van Scoyoc (2003) used a nonequivalent control group design to examine whether library instruction could reduce first-year college students' library anxiety, i.e., the "discomforts many students feel about library research" (p. 330). Library anxiety in three groups was compared: a group receiving in-class bibliographic instruction, a group receiving computer-assisted bibliographic instruction, and a control group receiving no instruction. Because Van Scoyoc could not randomly assign individual students to these three groups, she used a nonequivalent control group design.

The study sample was drawn from the first-year class of a Research I university. All the instructors of the English composition and rhetoric classes "were asked whether they were interested in having their classes participate in the study" (Van Scoyoc, 2003, p. 332). Participation in a library instruction session, using both a face-to-face bibliographic instruction session offered by a librarian and the instructor-assigned, computer-assisted instruction method, was an existing component of the class curriculum, making this a convenient setting in which to conduct this study.

Fifteen of the instructors were willing to have their classes participate (approximately 15% to 20% of the classes[1]). Ultimately, 297 students participated, with 238 providing a complete set of usable data. Because intact classes would be involved in the study, it was not possible to assign individual subjects to particular treatments. Thus a quasi-experimental research design was used: the nonequivalent control groups design. Each class was randomly assigned to one of the three groups: in-class instruction (84 students), computer-assisted instruction (58 students), or no instruction (the control group, 96 students). While this approach to defining the groups was the most rigorous possible, it does not exclude the possibility that a particular group might contain the students with the most previous library experience or the lowest/highest levels of library anxiety. Administering a pretest did allow Van Scoyoc to take prior differences into account during the data analysis phase of the study.

All groups were given a pretest and an identical posttest, incorporating Bostick's (1992) Library Anxiety Scale as well as measures of library knowledge and prior library experience. The pretest was administered to all groups during the regular English composition and rhetoric class, prior to any library-related instruction. The control group was administrated the posttest approximately one week after the pretest. The in-class instruction group completed the posttest within one week after participating in their instruction session. The computer-assisted instruction group was to complete the online tutorial within one week following the pretest; the posttest was administered in class at the conclusion of that week.

Both instruction methods entailed lessons in the use of library electronic resources. The in-class instruction was delivered by library staff for a scheduled, 30- to 40-minute period. The computer-assisted instruction was delivered via the Internet in the form of an interactive, online tutorial, expected to take 30 to 45 minutes to complete. The control group received instruction also, but not until after all study data were collected.

The design of the study is depicted in the following diagram. Those receiving in-class instruction are represented as X_1, and X_2 represents the computer-assisted instruction treatment. Because the control group did not receive treatment, there is no corresponding X to represent this group in the diagram. Thus this implementation of a nonequivalent control group design can be depicted as follows:

Experimental group 1:	O	X_1	O
Experimental group 2:	O	X_2	O
Control group:	O		O

As noted by Campbell and Stanley (1963), there are several threats to the validity of the findings from this research design. Because the individual subjects cannot be randomly assigned to groups, the groups may not be equivalent. Van Scoyoc (2003) evaluated group equivalency through comparisons of the pretest results. These revealed that the groups were not equivalent, with pretests for both treatment groups (X_1 and X_2) showing lower levels of library anxiety than the control group. Thus the statistical analysis approach (analysis of covariance) was designed to take this difference into account. Maturation also threatens this design because subjects may change during the period between the pretest and the posttest. In this study, this period was only one week, so we would expect only a minimal maturation effect, if any at all. Van Scoyoc (2003) also did everything possible to ensure that participants did not receive any library instruction, other than that planned in the study design, thus avoiding the most problematic type of history effect.

In summary, this is a very good example of a nonequivalent control group design, using a pretest and a posttest to collect data. Results can be compared across groups and across time, allowing the researcher to fully understand the effects of two methods of library instruction on students' library anxiety. While this quasi-experimental study design cannot protect the findings from all the possible threats to their validity, Van Scoyoc (2003) was aware of these threats and was careful to guard against them or take them into account during data analysis.

Example 3: The Benefits of Automated Search Assistance (Counterbalanced Design)

Jansen and McNeese (2004, 2005) applied a counterbalanced design in their investigation of the potential benefits of automated search assistance. One objective of the study was to determine whether automated search assistance improved search performance. Specifically, searchers' performance with a system incorporating automated search assistance was compared to their performance with a system offering no assistance.

A total of 40 subjects were recruited from two classes in an information science and technology program at a major U.S. university. Each subject completed a different search (drawn from a pool of six topics) with each of two systems, trying to find as many relevant documents as possible within a 15-minute time limit. The two systems were identical in all aspects—computer systems, browser, retrieval systems, search processing time, and document collection—except that one provided automatic search assistance and the other did not. The automated assistance application used "implicit feedback to build a model of user-system interactions using action-object pairs" (Jansen & McNeese, 2005, p. 1485), providing support for query reformulation and refinement (including reformulation based on similar queries), spelling correction, and relevance feedback. For the automated assistance system, subjects were informed of the automatic feature and shown a screen shot of the assistance button. Subjects were informed of the choice to select or ignore the assistance feature, represented as a clickable button. No other instructions were provided.

In this study, two variables need to be counterbalanced. First, the primary independent variable—which system was used to search—needed to be counterbalanced to avoid so-called order effects (i.e., the possibility that one system would be found to be more effective, just because it was always the second system used and the subject had more time to practice). To achieve this counterbalancing, the first subject was assigned to the basic system,[2] and the system assignment was then alternated for each subject. Second, the topics assigned for each search needed to be counterbalanced to avoid the possibility that the easy topics were assigned to one system more than the other. There were six topics, selected at random from those used in the Text REtrieval Conference (TREC), volumes 4 and 5. The first subject searched the first topic on the basic system and the second topic on the system with assistance. The second subject searched the third topic on the basic system and the fourth topic on the system with assistance. The third subject searched the fifth topic on the basic system and the sixth topic on the system with assistance. This rotation among the topics was then repeated for the remaining subjects. In this way, each of the topics was searched the same number of times on each of the systems. These two counterbalancing schemes are depicted in the following diagram, with each row representing a different subject (6 of the 40 subjects are shown here), with X_n representing the systems and t_n representing the topics:

$$
\begin{array}{lllll}
\text{Subject 1:} & X_1\,t_1 & O & X_2\,t_2 & O \\
\text{Subject 2:} & X_2\,t_3 & O & X_1\,t_4 & O \\
\text{Subject 3:} & X_1\,t_5 & O & X_2\,t_6 & O \\
\text{Subject 4:} & X_2\,t_1 & O & X_1\,t_2 & O \\
\text{Subject 5:} & X_1\,t_3 & O & X_2\,t_4 & O \\
\text{Subject 6:} & X_2\,t_5 & O & X_1\,t_6 & O \\
\end{array}
$$

While this type of careful counterbalancing scheme approaches the goal achieved in a true experiment, one aspect of the study did suffer from the almost-natural search interactions observed during the study. When subjects were assigned to use the system with automatic assistance, it was still up to the subject to choose when or if to invoke the assistance. To achieve the study's purpose of understanding when people would seek assistance, it was necessary to allow subjects to choose whether to use the automatic assistance. However, this naturalistic aspect of the study design resulted in 10 of the 40 subjects not interacting with the automated assistance search system at all, threatening the study's internal validity due to the effects of experimental mortality; that is, the dropout of subjects may contribute to differences in posttest comparisons (or lack of differences).

In summary, this is a very good example of the way in which a quasi-experimental design can straddle the gap between experimental control and a more naturalistic approach. Through a careful counterbalancing plan, significant control was exerted over possible order effects (of treatment exposure) and the effects of differences in topic difficulty. However, subjects were allowed to act naturally in deciding whether to invoke the automatic assistance available in one of the systems.

CONCLUSION

Quasi-experimental designs, such as those discussed in this chapter and others described by Campbell and Stanley (1963), can be very useful in situations in which it is impossible to implement a true experiment. In particular, when you want to make comparisons (e.g., between one group's performance and another's) but cannot randomly assign research subjects to the two groups, a quasi-experimental design may allow you to address your research question with a balanced combination of rigor and naturalism.

NOTES

1. Based on personal correspondence with the author.
2. Based on personal correspondence with B. J. Jansen.

WORKS CITED

Bostick, S. L. (1992). *The development and validation of the Library Anxiety Scale*. Unpublished doctoral dissertation, Wayne State University.

Campbell, D. T., & Stanley, J. C. (1963). *Experimental and Quasi-experimental Designs for Research*. Chicago: Rand-McNally.

Fife-Schaw, C. (2000). Quasi-experimental designs. In *Research Methods in Psychology* (2nd ed., pp. 75–87). London: Sage.

Hicks, D. A. (1980). Diversifying fiscal support by pricing public library services: A policy impact analysis. *Library Quarterly*, *50*(4), 453–474.

Jansen, B. J., & McNeese, M. D. (2004). Investigating automated assistance and implicit feedback for searching systems. *ASIS&T Proceedings 2004*, *41*, 280–286.

Jansen, B. J., & McNeese, M. D. (2005). Evaluating the effectiveness of and patterns of interactions with automated searching assistance. *Journal of the American Society for Information Science and Technology*, *56*(14), 1480–1503.

Julien, H. (1996). A content analysis of the recent information needs and uses literature. *Library and Information Science Research*, *18*, 53–65.

Koufogiannakis, D., & Wiebe, N. (2006). Effective methods for teaching information literacy skills to undergraduate students: A systematic review and meta-analysis. *Evidence Based Library and Information Practice*, *1*(3), 3–43.

Lorenzetti, D. (2007). Identifying appropriate quantitative study designs for library research. *Evidence Based Library and Information Practice*, *2*(1), 3–14.

Ondrusek, A. L. (2004). The attributes of research on end-user online searching behavior: A retrospective review and analysis. *Library and Information Science Research*, *26*, 221–265.

Powell, R. R., & Connaway, L. S. (2004). *Basic Research Methods for Librarians* (4th ed.). Westport, CT: Libraries Unlimited.

Trochim, W. (2006) *Research Methods Knowledge Base.* Available from http://www .socialresearchmethods.net/kb/quasiexp.php.

Van Scoyoc, A. M. (2003). Reducing library anxiety in first-year students: The impact of computer-assisted instruction and bibliographic instruction. *Reference and User Services Quarterly, 42*(4), 329–341.

12

Experimental Studies

Barbara M. Wildemuth and Leo L. Cao

What is a scientist? . . . We give the name scientist to the type of man who has felt experiment to be a means guiding him to search out the deep truth of life, to lift a veil from its fascinating secrets, and who, in this pursuit, has felt arising within him a love for the mysteries of nature, so passionate as to annihilate the thought of himself.

—Maria Montessori (1909/1964)

A DEFINITION, AND A BIT OF VOCABULARY

"By experiment we refer to that portion of research in which variables are manipulated and their effects upon other variables observed" (Campbell & Stanley, 1963, p. 1). This basic definition provides a strong framework for understanding the primary characteristics of a true experiment. First, some variables (i.e., phenomena that can vary in level or intensity, called *independent variables*) are manipulated. That means that we must exert control over their variation to be sure that we can understand the effects of their variation. The variable of primary interest is often called the *treatment* or *intervention* under study. The independent variables can be understood as the input to the experiment. Second, we will observe those effects on other variables (called dependent variables). The dependent variables can be understood as the output from the experiment. For instance, we may want to know the effects of a new system design on the efficiency with which it allows its users to complete particular kinds of tasks. We will manipulate the system with which the study participants work to complete the task; for example, we might give one group a particular version of the system and another group a different version of the system. Then we will measure (i.e., observe) the efficiency with which the task is performed with each system. As you can see from our definition of experiments, they are appropriate for those research questions with clearly stated hypotheses that can be tested in a well-controlled setting.

Experiments are characterized by control: the idea is that all the possibilities for variation are either controlled (i.e., held the same for all study participants) or they are varied systematically (e.g., the study participants experience either a high level or a low level of a variable of interest). A secondary characteristic of experiments is randomization as a means to exert control. Study participants may be randomly selected from a particular population. Study participants may be randomly assigned to one treatment or another. In each case, the randomization is performed to avoid any bias in the experiment's outcomes. It should be noted that randomization is a particular statistical process, not just a haphazard process, and procedures for randomization will be described later. Experimental control and randomization allow you to rule out all the possible causes of the observed effects other than the effects of the phenomenon of interest. Thus it can be argued that experiments are the only form of empirical research that provides leverage for discerning the causes of the phenomenon under study (Haas & Kraft, 1984).

THREE EXPERIMENTAL DESIGNS

Campbell and Stanley (1963) identify only three true experimental designs; two of those are most likely to be implemented in studies in information and library science and are briefly outlined here. In addition, factorial designs are discussed here. You will find that one characteristic they all have in common is the random assignment of participants to groups. How to carry out this aspect of the design will be discussed after this introduction to the designs themselves.

Pretest-posttest Control Group Design

This design, using Campbell and Stanley's (1963) notation, is depicted here:

$$\text{Group 1:} \quad R \quad O \quad X_1 \quad O$$
$$\text{Group 2:} \quad R \quad O \quad X_2 \quad O$$

From left to right, the columns represent the progression of time or stages of the experiment. Each row represents a group of study participants. For example, if we were comparing two information retrieval (IR) systems, one group would work with one of the systems and the other group would work with the other system. The R at the beginning of each row indicates that study participants were randomly assigned to one or the other group. Each O represents an observation in the study. Each of the groups in this design is observed both before and after it has interacted with the system. For instance, you might want to know if interacting with your experimental IR system will improve people's attitudes toward searching. You will ask them to fill out an attitude questionnaire before they use the system and also after they use the system. Each X represents the intervention or treatment, that is, the experience that your study participants will have. For instance, they may interact with a particular system, or they may attend a particular workshop. In some studies, one of the groups will be designated as a control group and not receive any treatment at all. For example, if you were implementing a new bibliographic instruction program in an academic library, you might have half of the first-year students attend it and not the other half (until after the study is over). Another common design variation is that the control group does experience an intervention, but it is normal practice, such as the current system in use or the current bibliographic instruction program. For our purposes here, we've designated two interventions; in other similar diagrams, there may be an intervention for only one of the groups. It should also be noted that this design can be extended to three or more groups.

To recap, this design assigns subjects randomly to group 1 or group 2. A pretest is conducted with each group, and then each group experiences the experimental intervention appropriate for it (if any). Then a posttest is conducted with each group. On the basis of your results, you can determine the effects of each intervention by comparing the posttest scores with the pretest scores (creating a change score for each group, i.e., a comparison across time). You can also compare the relative effect of the interventions by comparing the change scores between the two groups. In addition, you can verify that the random assignment to the two groups eliminated any bias by comparing the two groups' pretest scores. This design is powerful because it eliminates the possibility of bias in group assignment and allows you to investigate the changes caused by experiencing the intervention.

Posttest-only Control Group Design

As the name suggests, the posttest-only control group design (shown here) doesn't have a pretest, and that's the main difference between it and the previous design. The disadvantage is that you can't track any changes in a particular individual as he or she experiences the intervention. You are also completely reliant on randomization to make sure that the two groups are equivalent prior to the intervention:

$$\text{Group 1:} \quad R \quad X_1 \quad O$$
$$\text{Group 2:} \quad R \quad X_2 \quad O$$

However, there are also two important advantages (in addition to the obvious one, that you don't have to administer a pretest). First, if the pretest and posttest were to be administered within a short period of time, the pretest could affect participants' responses to the posttest. The participants might remember their responses on the pretest and either try to match them or try to change them. Second, depending on the focus of the study, the pretest can sometimes cause the study participants to experience the intervention differently than they would if they had not taken the pretest. For example, imagine that you plan to offer a course designed to lower people's computer anxiety. If you administer a pretest focusing on how anxious they feel when using a computer, it seems likely that they would react to the course differently than if the pretest had not been administered. With the posttest-only control group design, you can avoid the problems of the pretest affecting responses on the posttest or interacting with the intervention.

Factorial Design

In the first two designs, described previously, your research question is generally of the form, "Does this intervention make a difference in this outcome variable?" The independent variable in such a question can be thought of as a factor to be manipulated. If you want to manipulate multiple factors in the same experiment, a factorial design can be used. A factorial design simultaneously investigates the effects of all the independent variables (individually and in combination) on the dependent variables. The most basic factorial design is a 2×2 design, in which there are two factors (represented by the fact that there are two numbers in the name of the design), and each of them has two levels

SPECIALIZED
REFERENCE ASSISTANCE

		YES	NO
ATTEND WORKSHOP	YES	GROUP 1	GROUP 2
	NO	GROUP 3	GROUP 4

(represented by the fact that both numbers are 2). A research question for which a 2×2 factorial design would be appropriate is illustrated here:

Imagine that your library has two new ways to improve students' success in locating appropriate source materials for their honors theses. The first is a small-group workshop in which the students review the most important sources in their disciplines; the second is specialized reference assistance, with each honors student having an individual appointment with a reference librarian early in their research process. You would like to know which of these two methods was most effective and if they have an additive effect.

The full sample of study participants would be randomly divided into four groups, based on the preceding diagram. Group 1 would both attend the workshop and receive specialized reference assistance. Group 2 would attend the workshop but would not receive specialized reference assistance. Group 3 would receive specialized reference assistance but would not attend the workshop. Group 4, a true control group, would receive neither intervention. (Please note that this example is used to illustrate the workings of a factorial design; the ethical issues associated with providing services to some groups and not others are being set aside for this discussion.)

Using this research design, then, you can see the effects of specialized reference assistance by comparing groups 1 and 3 (combined) against groups 2 and 4 (combined). You can see the effects of the workshops by comparing groups 1 and 2 against groups 3 and 4. You can also detect interactions between the two interventions by comparing the four group means. For example, those participants in group 1 may experience benefits that are more than the additive effects of the two interventions.

Just as the previous designs can be generalized to compare three or more interventions, this design can also be generalized. More factors can be added. In our hypothetical example, you might also investigate the effects of the students' disciplines on their outcomes. If you grouped the disciplines into three groups (e.g., natural sciences, social sciences, and humanities), you would end up with a $3 \times 2 \times 2$ design. You can also have more than two levels of a factor, as was just illustrated by having three levels of the factor discipline. Thus this experimental design is very flexible and very robust.

RANDOMIZATION

"The most adequate all-purpose assurance of lack of initial biases between groups is randomization" (Campbell & Stanley, 1963, p. 25). Random assignment of study participants to the different groups is a simple procedure that goes a long way in mitigating potential biases, thus increasing the internal validity of your study.

As mentioned previously, random assignment is not a haphazard process. It must be carried out very systematically, based on a random number table or a random number generator in an electronic spreadsheet. Many statistics textbooks include random number tables in their appendices; all spreadsheet software includes the capability to generate random numbers through some type of random number generator function (e.g., RAND( ) in Excel). This simple function generates a random number between 0 and 1; if you want to use it to randomly assign your study participants into two groups, you can just generate a random number for each person; if it's greater than 0.5, they're in one group, and if it's less than 0.5, they're in the other group.

THE VALIDITY OF YOUR EXPERIMENT

There are two types of validity that you're trying to achieve with your experiment. The first is *internal validity*, defined as "the validity of assertions regarding the effects of the independent variable(s) on the dependent variable(s)" (Pedhazur & Schmelkin, 1991, p. 224). If you can achieve internal validity, then you can claim that the results you observed are due to the variables you manipulated, rather than other (i.e., extraneous) variables. As Campbell and Stanley (1963) declared, "internal validity is the basic minimum without which any experiment is uninterpretable: Did in fact the experimental treatments make a difference in this specific experimental instance?" (p. 5).

Once you've established the internal validity of your findings, you can move on to the bigger challenge of establishing their external validity (Bernard, 2000). *External validity* can be defined as the "generalizability of the findings *to* or *across* target populations, settings, times, and the like" (Pedhazur & Schmelkin, 1991, p. 229). You will be trying to achieve external validity so that you can apply your results (and the conclusions drawn from them) to people beyond your study participants and settings beyond the laboratory. "External validity asks the question of generalizability: To what populations, settings, treatment variables and measurement variables can this effect be generalized?" (Campbell & Stanley, 1963, p. 5).

There are known threats to both internal validity and external validity (Campbell & Stanley, 1963; Haas & Kraft, 1984; Pedhazur & Schmelkin, 1991) that you should try to avoid. Two threats to internal validity (attrition and contamination across groups) and two threats to external validity (interactions between pretesting and the intervention and interactions between selection/attrition and the intervention) are discussed here.

Threats to Internal Validity

In Piper's (1998) paper on conducting social science lab experiments on the Web, she outlined how the same threats to internal validity described in Campbell and Stanley's (1963) work are manifested in the context of information and library science research. Their description of these threats is a good one, so we will send you there for a full treatment of this topic. Here we'll mention only two threats that are not eliminated through random assignment: attrition during the study and contamination across groups.

Attrition is the loss of some of your participants during the course of the study. They may leave the study for a variety of reasons. If you lose only a few of your participants after the study has begun (i.e., after they've been assigned to their groups), it's not a serious problem. However, the more attrition you have, the bigger problem it is. At some point, the random assignment with which you began is no longer protecting you from bias because those who drop out of one group may be different from those who drop out of the other group. You should try to plan your recruitment processes, the study procedures, and the incentives for participation to minimize attrition among your participants.

The second threat to internal validity that you may need to watch for, even with an experimental design, is contamination across groups. Such contamination means that members of the two groups have communicated with each other about the intervention and so may be influencing each other's reactions to it. For example, imagine that one group is interacting with a very novel visualization interface for your IR system interface and the other group is interacting with a typical list of results from their searches. If the control group hears about the novel visualization interface, they may be less satisfied with the traditional interface than they would have been otherwise. Plan your study procedures to avoid contamination across groups; it is appropriate to ask your participants not to describe the intervention to anyone else during the period when data are being collected for the study.

Threats to External Validity

It is almost impossible to have experimental results for which you can confidently claim external validity (i.e., results that can confidently be generalized to the population of interest and a range of relevant settings). First, you would have to have a sample of study participants that was drawn randomly from the population to which you'd like to generalize; this is rarely feasible. Second, the control exerted through an experimental design cannot ever truly reflect the messiness of the everyday situations to which we'd like to generalize our results. This problem is an inherent drawback of experimental methods and is sometimes referred to as the issue of *ecological validity*, or, alternatively, as the *reactive effects* of an experiment. Nevertheless, there are a few other threats to external validity that you should try to avoid through your sampling methods or experimental design (Campbell & Stanley, 1963; Pedhazur & Schmelkin, 1991).

One possible problem is an interaction between pretesting and the intervention under study. Pretesting can change the perspective of the study participants, potentially introducing unwanted and unknown factors into the experiment. Campbell and Stanley (1963) recommend study designs without pretesting as a means of avoiding this interaction effect, thus increasing external validity.

A second possible problem is an interaction between the selection of study participants and the intervention. Comparable problems occur if the study sample suffers from attrition because the sample is no longer representative of the population of interest. Pedhazur and Schmelkin (1991) describe this phenomenon as "treatments-attributes interaction," appropriately placing the emphasis on the attributes of the study participants. For example, if you are studying how people interact with a college's online library catalog and want to generalize your results to all library users, then your sample needs to represent the full range of user attributes. The sample needs to include faculty, staff, and graduate students as well as undergraduate students to represent the full range of ages and levels of experience in using the catalog. If the attributes of the population are not well represented in the study sample, generalizability of the results to the population is limited.

ADDITIONAL ISSUES TO CONSIDER WHEN DESIGNING AN EXPERIMENT

In addition to selecting a particular experimental design for your study, and making every effort to avoid threats to internal and external validity, there are three more issues that you need to consider when designing an experiment: whether to conduct the experiment in the lab or in the field, whether to use a within-subjects or between-subjects design, and the ethical issues that may arise in your interactions with your study participants.

Experimental Setting: Lab or Field?

Conducting your experiment in the lab gives you the most control over extraneous variables. For example, you know that every participant used the same computer with the same network connections under the same conditions. While this level of control is a core strength of experimental designs, it may limit the external validity of the study's findings, as noted previously. Conducting your experiment in the field may increase its external validity. For example, participants are using the computer and network connections that they actually have available to them, and the conditions are more realistic. However, it is often the case that a field experiment provides so little control that you can no longer consider it an experiment. You will need to carefully consider the goals of your study to decide whether the lab or the field is a more appropriate setting for your study. You will want to pay special attention to how the two examples discussed later in this chapter handled this decision because one (Yu & Roh, 2002) was conducted in the lab and the other (Churkovich & Oughtred, 2002) was conducted in the field.

Within- versus Between-subjects Designs

One of the basic questions you face in setting up your experimental design is whether you are using independent groups (i.e., a participant is in only one group and experiences only one intervention) or overlapping groups (i.e., each participant experiences multiple interventions). The first of these cases is called a *between-subjects design* because the comparisons made during data analysis are comparisons between subjects. The second of these cases is called a *within-subjects design* because the comparisons made during data analysis are comparisons within subjects (i.e., between each individual's outcomes with one intervention and the same individual's outcomes with another intervention).

There are some situations that definitely call for a between-subjects design. For instance, if the interaction with the first intervention would have a very strong impact on the interaction with the second intervention, you can only avoid this threat to the internal validity of your study by using a between-subjects design. This type of situation often arises when you are investigating the effects of different instructional approaches, as in the Churkovich and Oughtred (2002) study discussed later. If your study procedures are quite demanding or take a long time to complete, you should also plan to use a between-subjects design to minimize the burden on each participant. For example, if you want your participants to complete six to eight searches with a novel search engine, filling out a brief questionnaire after each search, it may be asking too much of them to then repeat the entire process with a second search engine. The biggest disadvantage of using a between-subjects design is that it requires you to recruit more subjects. Thus it is more costly, and a within-subjects design might therefore be preferred.

A within-subjects design is more efficient in terms of the use of your subjects because each person will contribute two or more data points to your analysis. It also allows you to ask your participants for a direct comparison of the interventions (e.g., system) under investigation. In addition, it minimizes the variation in individual characteristics, making your statistical analysis more powerful. If you use this design, you need to be aware of potential learning effects from the specific order of the tasks that subjects complete or the interventions they experience. You can control for these effects by counterbalancing the order in which they're completed. For example, if you have group 1 and group 2 with interventions A and B, you will run intervention A, then B, for group 1, and intervention B, then A, for group 2 (this example is depicted here):

$$\text{Group 1:} \quad R \quad X_A \quad O \quad X_B \quad O$$
$$\text{Group 2:} \quad R \quad X_B \quad O \quad X_A \quad O$$

The Latin square experimental design is a formalized method for arranging the order of the tasks and/or interventions for even more complex situations (Cotton, 1993).

Ethical Issues in Experiments

Experiments, like other forms of research, require the ethical treatment of your study participants. In addition, there are two aspects of experiments that are unique and warrant some mention here. The first is that the experimental setting sometimes imposes demands on the subjects that they don't experience in other activities. Your research procedures may bring on excessive fatigue (if very demanding) or excessive boredom, especially if the session is long. As you plan your research procedures, consider their effects on your participants. Second, the use of a control group implies that some of your subjects will not experience the planned intervention. In cases where your research hypothesis is that the intervention will have significant advantages, withholding it from a portion of your subjects may be unethical. Thus you need to plan for ways to provide access to the intervention for the control group (usually after the experiment is completed; thus their access is just delayed, not denied). As with all kinds of research, it is your responsibility to ensure that the burdens of research participation are not unreasonable and are fairly distributed, and that the benefits accrue to all your participants in an equitable way.

EXAMPLES

The two examples discussed here vary in multiple ways. The first (Yu & Roh, 2002) uses a posttest-only control group design and the second (Churkovich & Oughtred, 2002) uses a pretest-posttest control group design. The first is a within-subjects design and the second is a between-subjects design. The first is a laboratory study and the second is a field experiment. Thus a lot can be learned from looking at them side by side.

Example 1: Users' Preferences and Attitudes toward Menu Designs

To investigate the effects of menu design on the performance and attitudes of users of a shopping Web site, Yu and Roh (2002) used a posttest-only control group design. The posttest in this study consisted of observations of the speed with which the study participants could complete assigned searching and browsing tasks and the participants' perceptions of the appeal of the Web site and whether they were disoriented when using it. Even though the measurements of time were actually collected during the interactions, they're still considered part of the posttest.

There was no true control group, but each of three types of menu designs was compared with the others: a simple hierarchical menu design, a menu design supporting both global and local navigation, and a pull-down menu design. The selection of the posttest-only control group design was a sound one. There was no interest in examining how the participants changed during their interactions with the Web sites, so there was no need for a pretest. This experimental design is often used to compare users' reactions to different system designs.

The authors used a within-subjects design, with each of the 17 participants interacting with each of the three menu designs. These three iterations of the research procedures occurred over three separate sessions, each a week apart. The authors chose to space out the research sessions to avoid memory effects (the same browsing and searching tasks were used each time). Unfortunately, this decision did result in some attrition from the sample. Of the original 21 subjects recruited for the study, 4 (almost 20%) were not included in the final analysis because they missed at least one of the sessions. An alternative would have been to develop three parallel sets of browsing and searching tasks and administer all of them in a single session, counterbalancing the design so that all tasks were performed on all three systems. The research procedures that were used took about a half hour to complete; if they had been combined into one session, participant fatigue may have been an issue. If a study is planned to be implemented over repeated sessions, it would also be appropriate to recruit a larger sample than needed to ensure that the final sample size is large enough.

With a within-subjects design, the order in which the interventions are presented can become an issue. The authors handled this issue through random assignment. At the first session, each participant was randomly assigned to a particular menu design (represented by a prototype Web site). At the second session, each participant was randomly assigned to one of the two Web sites he or she had not yet seen. At the third session, the participant interacted with the remaining Web site. Through this careful randomization (an alternative to the counterbalancing discussed earlier), the authors could be sure that any effects on the dependent variables were not due to the order in which people interacted with the three menu designs.

In this study, each participant completed 10 searching tasks and 5 browsing tasks with each of the three menu designs. The order in which these tasks were completed could also have an effect on the outcomes (though it's less likely than the potential for effects from the order in which the systems were presented). To guard against this possible threat, "the task cards were shuffled beforehand to ensure that the sequence of tasks was random" (Yuh & Row, 2002, p. 930). I would not agree that shuffling cards ensures random ordering; the authors could have used a random number generator to select the task order for each participant for each session. Nevertheless, the precautions they took were reasonable, given the low potential risk to the validity of the study results.

In summary, this example of a posttest-only control group design is typical of many studies comparing two or more alternative information systems. It was conducted in a lab, and adequate control was exerted over the procedures so that most threats to the study's validity were addressed. While it is somewhat unusual to spread the data collection over three sessions, the authors provided their reasons for this decision. The within-subjects design was very efficient, allowing them to discover differences between the menu designs while using only 17 subjects.

Example 2: Comparison of Bibliographic Instruction Methods

Churkovich and Oughtred (2002) were interested in the question of whether online tutorials would be as effective as face-to-face bibliographic instruction for first-year college students. They explicitly posed the question, Could first-year students be trained successfully by an online tutorial without the presence of a librarian? Their actual research design reveals that their research question was a bit more complex than this. They compared three conditions: traditional face-to-face bibliographic instruction, independent instruction through two modules of an online tutorial, and mediated (i.e., librarian-assisted) instruction through two modules of the online tutorial.

To investigate this question, they used a pretest-posttest control group design. This design allowed the researchers to gauge the increase in students' knowledge and changes in their attitudes due to the instruction received. The pretest consisted of 14 multiple-choice questions covering three types of basic information skills: identifying and searching for citations, keyword searching, and knowledge of library resources. In addition, the students responded to two attitudinal questions concerning their comfort with asking for library assistance and the importance of library skills for college students. The same questions were administered on the posttest, in addition to a question concerning their confidence as a result of the tutorial. Given that the pretest and the posttest were administered within about one hour of each other, it's very possible that the pretest may have interacted with the posttest and with the students' experiences of the instructional intervention. However, since the point of the study was to compare the three instructional approaches and all the students received the same pretest, this type of interaction should not have affected the outcomes of the study.

The students signed up for an instruction session, then the groups were randomly assigned to one of the three instructional approaches. Sixty students in three groups received the face-to-face instruction (this group would be considered the control group), 45 students in two groups received the mediated online tutorial, and 68 students in four groups received the online tutorial worked independently. If the groups had not been randomly assigned to the three types of instruction, this would have been a quasi-experiment. Even the approach used, though random, does not eliminate the potential for bias due to initial differences between the groups. Ideally, the students would have been individually assigned (randomly) to a particular intervention. But that is not the way students' lives work; they want control over when they will receive this type of instruction. Thus they were given the freedom to sign up for a group, and random assignment was at the group level. By using a pretest, the researchers were able to verify that there were no significant differences between the groups prior to the instruction being offered.

This study used a between-subjects design. Each participant received only one of the instructional interventions. Because the interventions were covering the same material, it is clear that it would be inappropriate to have each student repeat the instruction three times. Thus a between-subjects design was the only feasible option.

In summary, this is a typical example of a practice-based field experiment intended to compare three different forms of bibliographic instruction. Churkovich and Oughtred's (2002) primary research question was whether the online tutorial was effective enough to replace face-to-face instruction. Their interest in the changes brought about by the instruction indicated that a pretest-posttest design of some type would be appropriate. Likewise, a between-subjects design was the obvious choice for comparing instructional interventions. While they could not randomly assign individual subjects to particular interventions, they did randomly assign intact groups to the three forms of instruction, thus finding an appropriate compromise between control and feasibility.

CONCLUSION

The principles of experimentation are relatively simple: randomly assign the subjects to two or more groups and measure the outcomes resulting from the intervention experienced by each group. But once you move beyond this basic characterization of experiments, you will find that there are a number of decisions to make about your experimental design. It is crucial that you understand your research question thoroughly and state it clearly. Then you will be able to identify which independent variables should be manipulated and which dependent variables (i.e., outcomes) should be measured. A dose of common sense, some reading of prior research related to your question, and a bit of sketching and analyzing of the Xs and Os will go a long way toward a good experimental design for your study.

WORKS CITED

Bernard, H. R. (2000). *Social Research Methods: Qualitative and Quantitative Approaches.* Thousand Oaks, CA: Sage.

Campbell, D., & Stanley, J. (1963). *Experimental and Quasi-experimental Designs for Research.* Chicago: Rand-McNally.

Churkovich, M., & Oughtred, C. (2002). Can an online tutorial pass the test for library instruction? An evaluation and comparison of library skills instruction methods for first year students at Deakin University. *Australian Academic and Research Libraries, 33*(1), 25–38.

Cotton, J. W. (1993). Latin square designs. In L. K. Edwards (Ed.), *Applied Analysis of Variance in Behavioral Science* (pp. 147–196). New York: Marcel Dekker.

Haas, D. F., & Kraft, D. H. (1984). Experimental and quasi-experimental designs for research in information science. *Information Processing and Management, 20*(1–2), 229–237.

Montessori, M. (1964). *The Montessori Method.* A. E. George (Trans.). New York: Schocken. (Original work published 1909)

Pedhazur, E. J., & Schmelkin, L. P. (1991). *Measurement, Design, and Analysis: An Integrated Approach.* Hillsdale, NJ: Erlbaum.

Piper, A. I. (1998). Conducting social science laboratory experiments on the World Wide Web. *Library and Information Science Research, 20*(1), 5–21.

Yu, B.-M., & Roh, S.-Z. (2002). The effects of menu design on information seeking performance and user's attitude on the World Wide Web. *Journal of the American Society for Information Science, 53*(11), 923–933.

13

Sampling for Extensive Studies

Barbara M. Wildemuth

The tendency of the casual mind is to pick out or stumble upon a sample which supports or
defies its prejudices, and then to make it the representative of a whole class.
— Walter Lippmann (1922/2007)

INTRODUCTION

The conclusions you draw from your research will apply to a particular set of people or
organizations. While you may have studied all the people or organizations that are of
interest, it's more likely that you did not have the resources to conduct such a census
study. Instead, you selected a sample of people or organizations to study and plan to
generalize your findings to all of the people or organizations represented by that sample.
Thus the practice of sampling is intended to achieve greater efficiency (because you
collect data from a smaller number of people or organizations). Simultaneously, if done
properly, it results in more accurate findings because you can control your data collection
procedures and other aspects of the research more fully.

The challenge, then, is to select a sample that is representative of the population
in which you're interested. As Loether and McTavish (1993) note, "if the sample is
representative, we can feel justified in generalizing the findings from the sample data
to the population" (p. 381). To select a representative sample, you need to design your
sampling procedures carefully. The selection of particular people or organizations to
participate in your study will be based on a set of rules that will be applied to a carefully
defined population (Czaja & Blair, 2005).

Most statistical analyses are based on the assumption that you selected a probability
sample from the population of interest, so the procedures for selecting such a sample
will be reviewed subsequently. For many studies, however, it is not possible to select
a probability sample, so some additional approaches to sampling are also reviewed.
After a discussion of sample size and some of the challenges associated with selecting

and recruiting a representative sample, three studies will be examined in terms of their sampling procedures.

PROBABILITY SAMPLING: CONCEPTS AND DEFINITIONS

In general, a sample is a set of elements selected from a particular population of interest, based on specified rules and operations (Pedhazur & Schmelkin, 1991; Scheaffer et al., 1996). The population is the "collection of elements about which we wish to make an inference" (Scheaffer et al., 1996, p. 42). An element is "an object on which a measurement is taken" (Scheaffer et al., 1996, p. 42). For example, if you were trying to survey the help desk users at your university, each person who had used the help desk would be an element in the population of interest. The *sampling frame* is a list of all eligible elements in the population (Scheaffer et al., 1996), so in this example, it would be a list of all the help desk users.

A probability sample is a kind of sample that has two specific characteristics. First, "every element of the population of interest has a known nonzero probability of being selected into the sample" (Pedhazur & Schmelkin, 1991, p. 321). This characteristic is important because the data analyses to be conducted as part of a study rely on knowing the probability with which each element could be included in the sample. The second important characteristic is that the elements be selected randomly at some point in the process (Czaja & Blair, 2005; Pedhazur & Schmelkin, 1991). As Loether and McTavish (1993) note, "random selection *does not mean haphazard selection*" (p. 381); rather, it is a very systematic process of selection, based on the theory of probability, that will help you to avoid bias in your sample.

Procedures for Selecting a Probability Sample

The first step in developing a probability sample is to carefully define your population of interest. Taking up the example presented previously, your rough definition of your population is the users of your university's help desk. As you more carefully define the population of interest for your study, you may decide to survey only those people who have used the help desk within the past year, only those who have used the help desk more than three times within the past year, or only the faculty who have used the help desk within the past two years. Each is a different definition of the population of interest, and the definition you select will depend on the goals of your study.

Sometimes it is not really feasible to sample from the population in which you're truly interested. In such a case, you may choose to compromise the definition of the study population to make your sampling plan possible to carry out (Fan & Wang, 1999). If this is the case, you should define both your target (i.e., desired) population and the actual study population, making the difference between the two clear to the audience for your research results.

An important aspect of the population's definition is the unit of analysis. You might be studying individual people, as in the preceding example. Alternatively, you may want to study particular groups, such as the student organizations on a campus, or organizations, such as branch libraries. In such a case, each group or organization is an element in the population. By specifying the unit of analysis, you are making clear which elements are eligible for inclusion in your sample.

The next step is to identify or construct the sampling frame, or list of elements in the study population. For some studies, this will be relatively straightforward, but for others, it will be very challenging. In many cases, there may be no existing list that fully matches the definition of your study population. Existing lists may contain elements that are really not eligible for the study (e.g., a list of public library users that also includes "honorary" residents of the community). A list may be missing some portion of the target population (e.g., a list of college student e-mail addresses may not include those who have opted out of having their addresses displayed in the directory). Some lists may be complete, but the contact information in them is missing or inaccurate for some elements (e.g., missing addresses, phone numbers, etc.). Some lists may have duplications (e.g., a university directory that has more than one listing for an individual, as a student and again as a staff member). As you consider the use of a particular sampling frame, be cautious; if the list itself is flawed, you may be implicitly redefining your population (Bookstein, 1974).

The final step is to select particular elements from the sampling frame. In this step, you will be identifying the specific people or organizations to recruit for participation in your study. The procedures you use will depend on the type of probability sample you use, several of which are described in the next few sections.

Simple Random Sampling

When you use this sampling method, you are working with a single sampling frame, and all the elements in it will have an equal chance of being selected for participation in the study. First, you will number the elements in the sampling frame. Next, you will generate a set of random numbers with a spreadsheet or use a random number table to obtain a set of numbers. Work through the random numbers, one by one, selecting the element that matches each number, until you have the sample size you need. Bookstein (1974) provides a good discussion of how (and how not) to use a random number table. To see an example of how simple random sampling can be used, refer to the study of the ways in which people find information about genetics conducted by Case and colleagues (2004). It incorporated random digit dialing, an algorithmic approach to random selection based on people's phone numbers.

Systematic Sampling

With a large sampling frame, simple random sampling can become extremely tedious and error-prone. Thus many researchers will use systematic sampling instead. Using this approach, a random number is chosen to select the first element to be included in the sample. From there, every nth element is selected; n varies based on the size of the sample you need and the size of the sampling frame. For example, if your sampling frame was the 3,500 first-year students at your university, and you needed a sample of 350, you would select the first student to include by identifying a random number between 1 and 10. If the first random number your spreadsheet generated was 6, you would choose the sixth student on the list. Because you want to generate a sample that is one-tenth the size of the sampling frame, you would go on to choose every tenth student after the first, that is, you would choose the sixteenth student, the twenty-sixth student, and so on. Systematic sampling was used by Baker et al. (2004) to select members from one chapter of the Medical Library Association to respond to a survey of attitudes toward the Academy of Health Information Professionals.

There is one type of situation in which systematic sampling should *not* be used. If the sampling frame's order has some type of pattern, it could introduce bias into the sample. For example, if the sampling frame were grouped in blocks of 20 elements and each block was in order by a variable of interest, and the sampling plan called for sampling every tenth or twentieth element, then a biased sample would be created. While this hypothetical example artificially inflates the chances for bias, sampling frames do exist that have this type of periodic or cyclic ordering. Therefore, when you are considering the use of systematic sampling, be sure to check the order of your sampling frame to identify any potential for bias.

Stratified Sampling

With stratified sampling, the population is divided into strata first. For example, a population of public library users might be stratified by gender, with men and women making up separate strata. Then, elements are randomly sampled from each stratum. The goal of this approach is to reduce the variability within each stratum, thus improving the power of your statistical analyses. Using this approach, it may be possible to use a smaller sample size, thus making your research more efficient. In one example (McKenna et al., 2005) discussed later in this chapter, stratified sampling was used to survey occupational therapists in Australia about their use of an online database.

There are several decisions you will need to make if you use this approach. First, you will need to define the strata, that is, you will need to select a variable (like gender) that will be used to divide your population into strata. Usually, this decision is based on the variable's relationship to the goals of the study; you will want to select a variable that relates to the other important variables in the study. Second, you will need to decide on the number of strata. This decision, for a variable like gender, is relatively straightforward. However, if the variable is continuous (e.g., income level), you will need to make some decisions to be able to decide which elements in the sampling frame are high income and which are low income. Finally, you will need to decide on the sample size for each stratum. In most cases, you would select a sample that is proportionate to that stratum's size in the population. For example, if men make up 48 percent of the population you're studying, then you would expect that 48 percent of your final sample will be men. While this proportionate approach is most common, there may be reasons for increasing or decreasing the sample size for particular strata. You may want to consult with a statistician before making your final decision to ensure that the sample size from each stratum will support the analyses you are planning.

Cluster Sampling

In cluster sampling, the sampling units are clusters of elements, rather than individuals. For example, you may use classrooms as sampling units or groups using the library as sampling units. The idea is that you will begin the sampling procedure by randomly selecting a sample of clusters from the population of clusters that is of interest for your study. In single-stage cluster sampling, you would then include in your sample all the elements within the selected clusters. Multistage cluster sampling is also possible. For example, you might want to interview a sample of public library users within your state.

In the first stage, you would randomly select a sample of the public library systems within the state. In the second stage, you would randomly select a sample of branch libraries from each of the selected systems. Finally, you would select a random sample of users to interview from each of the selected branch libraries. McKenna et al. (2005) used single-stage cluster sampling to draw a second sample, surveying the therapists working in a random sample of the occupational therapy facilities in two states.

The goal of this approach is to minimize the cost of collecting data from a (geographically) widespread sample; in the preceding example, you wanted to avoid having to drive to every county in the state to interview just a few people in each county. With multistage clustering, you could more efficiently travel to just a few of the counties and easily arrange interviews in just a few branch libraries in each county.

NONPROBABILITY SAMPLING: CONCEPTS AND DEFINITIONS

While probability samples have the necessary properties to support statistical analyses of the data collected, sometimes it is not possible to select a random sample from the population in which you're interested. Most often, this situation arises because it is not possible to identify or create a valid sampling frame. For example, if you want to generalize your results to all users of the Web, it would not be possible to specify a sampling frame that could represent this population. In such situations, some type of nonprobability sample will need to be defined. There are several possible approaches you might consider, including quota sampling, purposive sampling, snowball sampling, and convenience sampling.

Quota Sampling

The first step in quota sampling is to determine which characteristics of the population are of interest. Then you set a quota for each level of each characteristic. Usually this quota is based on the proportion of that characteristic in the population as a whole, if it's known. Finally, you begin recruiting people until you have met your "quota" for each characteristic. For example, say that you are trying to recruit a sample to test the usability of a new type of social networking software designed specifically for engineers. You suspect that male engineers might react differently to it than females, and you also suspect that older engineers might react differently to it than younger engineers. You might decide to conceptualize your sample as being made up of two levels of gender (male and female) and three levels of age (21–35, 36–50, and 51 and above). If you're lucky, you can use statistics from professional engineering associations or workforce studies to estimate the proportion of your population that would fit each of the six profiles of interest. You would then set a quota for each profile (e.g., young woman, middle-aged man, etc.) and begin your recruiting.

This procedure superficially resembles stratified sampling, but it differs from stratified sampling in a very important way: there is no random selection of elements from a sampling frame. This difference in the procedures may result in several weaknesses in the sample. Because you cannot control which elements are selected, they could lead to a biased sample. Unless you keep careful records of which people were invited to participate and declined, you cannot estimate your response rate. The probability of selection of each element in the population is unknown, so it is not really valid to generalize to the population of all engineers. Thus, while quota sampling has some advantages over other types of nonprobability sampling procedures, it still has significant weaknesses.

Purposive Sampling

A purposive sample might also be called a judgment sample (Loether & McTavish, 1993) because it relies on the expert judgments of the person selecting the sample. Using this approach, particular people are selected from the population of interest based on their individual characteristics. The intent is to recruit a sample that is representative of the population in terms of both central tendency and range on characteristics of interest. For example, if you wanted to study the teamwork among library systems staff, you would want a sample that would represent those staff. You might try to include both a typical staff member (in terms of age, longevity in the job, level of responsibility, current number of teams, etc.) and people that represent more extreme cases (e.g., the newest member of the staff, the most senior member, the staff member on the most teams, etc.). It is obvious that there is the potential for bias in a sample selected purposively, but for some studies, this approach is the best that you can do.

Snowball Sampling

For studies in which the topic is particularly sensitive or when eligible members of the sample will be particularly difficult to identify, snowball sampling might be the approach to use. With snowball sampling, you first identify a few eligible members of your sample. Then you ask each participant for suggestions for additional people who meet your inclusion and exclusion criteria. A study in which this approach was appropriately used was focused on the prevalence and impact of cyberstalking (Bocij, 2003). Bocij began with an initial pool of five potential participants. Each was asked to forward the survey to five more people. In the time period allotted for data collection, he received a total of 169 completed questionnaires. As with the other nonprobability sampling methods, it is unlikely that this method will yield a representative sample of the population of interest. Nevertheless, it is the most appropriate choice for some studies.

Convenience Sampling

When you have no other options, you may need to recruit a convenience sample. Its name accurately reflects this procedure: you will try to recruit people because they are available. You can still impose inclusion and/or exclusion criteria, specifying the characteristics of the people who are eligible for study participation. In this way, you can try to balance the convenience of recruitment with an attempt to match the population definition. But the inclusion and exclusion criteria are your only means for improving the representativeness of your sample.

SAMPLE SIZE

To conduct your study as efficiently as possible, you will want to recruit and collect data from as small a sample as possible. Unfortunately, as Cohen (1965) noted when discussing psychology research, there are a number of problems with the ways that many researchers decide on their sample sizes:

As far as I can tell, decisions about n in much psychological research are generally arrived at by such considerations as local tradition ("At Old Siwash U., 30 cases are enough for a dissertation"); subject-matter precedent ("I'll use samples of 20 cases, since that's how many Hook and Crook used when they studied conditioning under anxiety"); data availability ("I can't study more idiots savants than we have in the clinic, can I?"); intuition or one of its more presumptuous variants, "experience"; and negotiation ("If I give them the semantic differential, too, then it's only fair that I cut my sample to 40"). (p. 98)

Despite the temptation of using one of these "standard" methods, we hope you'll try to be more rational in deciding how big your sample should be.

If you're conducting a descriptive study, you'll be using data from your sample to estimate characteristics (i.e., parameters) of your population. There are three aspects to the decision about sample size in this situation. The first, and most important, is the confidence interval around the estimate (Czaja & Blair, 2005). This is the amount of error that you can tolerate in the parameter estimates. For example, if you want to know the percentage of your computer help desk users who use the Windows operating system, you might be comfortable with a confidence interval that is five percentage points above or below the estimate that is derived from the sample, but in another study, you might need to estimate the population values within two percentage points above or below the estimate. There is no fixed criterion for setting the acceptable confidence interval; you need to balance the importance of the accuracy of the estimates for the goals of your study with the extra cost of collecting data from a larger sample. The second aspect of your decision is concerned with the probability that the true value for the population falls within the confidence interval you desire. Usually, you will want a small probability (5% or 1%) that the true population parameter falls outside the confidence interval (Rea & Parker, 1997). Finally, you need to take into account the variability expected within the population. If the characteristic you are estimating varies widely within the population (e.g., the number of times each person in a community visits the library each year), you'll need a larger sample to estimate its value accurately. Once you've made decisions about or know each of these attributes of your situation, there are simple formulas for estimating what sample size you will need.

If you're conducting a study in which you will be testing hypotheses, you will be concerned with the power of your statistical analyses. In these cases, there are four aspects of the study that you need to consider in deciding what sample size is appropriate. The first, and most important, is the effect size that you want to be able to detect (Asraf & Brewer, 2004). Let's imagine that you are trying to determine if the number of terms used in a Web search is related to the searcher's expertise on the topic of the search. You will be collecting measures of topic expertise and you will capture searches to determine how many search terms are used in each. In such a study, the effect is the difference in the number of search terms. Is it important for you to know that on average, experts use one more term than nonexperts? Or is it sufficient to be able to detect that experts use three more terms than nonexperts? The substance of your research question will help you to determine how small an effect you want to be able to detect. The smaller the effect you need to detect, the larger the sample you will need. The next aspect to consider is the probability of rejecting a null hypothesis when you shouldn't. This is the most obvious consideration in hypothesis testing and is sometimes called a *type I error*. Using our Web search example, you would be committing a type I error if you said that there is a difference between experts and nonexperts when there really isn't.

For most studies, this value (alpha) is set at 0.05. This would mean that you're willing to accept only a 5 percent chance of being wrong if you reject the hypothesis that there is no difference between experts and nonexperts. The next aspect to consider is the probability of making a type II error: *not* rejecting the null hypothesis when you really should. Using our Web search example, you would be committing a type II error if you said that there is no difference between experts and nonexperts when there really is. This aspect is sometimes referred to as the power of a statistical test, formally defined as 1—the probability of a type II error—or as the probability of correctly rejecting a null hypothesis (Howell, 2004). Cohen (1988) recommends that you set the probability of a type II error to 0.20 so that you will be achieving a power of 0.80. Finally, as with estimating population parameters, you need to take into account the variability expected within the population. Once you've made decisions or know about these four aspects of your study, you can use the formulas given by Cohen (1988) or Howell (2004) or use an online power calculator (e.g., Lenth, 2006) to determine the sample size needed.

A Special Case: Usability Testing

Usability testing is a special case, when it comes to deciding on sample size, because some experts (e.g., Nielsen, 1993) have argued that just five or six users can identify 80 percent of the usability problems there are, while others (e.g., Faulkner, 2003; Spool & Schroder, 2001) have found that a larger sample size is needed to identify a significant proportion of the usability problems in a new system or Web site. Lewis (2006) demonstrates how the sample size needed depends on the goals of the usability study.

THE EFFECTS OF NONRESPONSE ON A SAMPLE

You will be selecting your sample at the very beginning of your study. But as you collect your data, some of those participants that you selected for your sample will not accept your invitation to participate in the study. A recent study of surveys published in three core information and library science journals from 1996 to 2001 found that on average, they achieved response rates of only 63 percent (Burkell, 2003). This level of nonresponse (i.e., 37%) can negatively affect the representativeness of the sample you actually include in your study results. While you can oversample to increase the number of participants you include, this practice will not necessarily help you avoid a biased sample. Therefore you should try to do everything you can to improve your response rate.

The primary method for improving your response rate is to use appropriate data collection procedures. In your recruitment materials, use wording that will motivate potential participants. Lower the burden of participation by using well-designed questionnaires or study procedures, making it easy and pleasurable to be a study participant. Offer concrete incentives to the participants, for example, gift certificates, cash, or other items. Dillman's (2007) tailored design method for surveys has many additional suggestions for improving survey response rates, and many of these will apply to other types of studies as well. Once you've completed your study, you should assess the sampling bias that might have been caused by nonresponse. You can compare the respondents with the population as a whole to see if they are representative. You can compare the respondents with the nonrespondents to see if they differ. As you try to interpret your results, you should keep in mind that the nonrespondents are likely to have responded more like the late responders than those who responded early in the recruitment period. Finally, if you have a low participation/response rate, be cautious about the conclusions you draw from the results.

EXAMPLES

Three different studies will be discussed here, each using a different approach to defining and recruiting a sample. The first (McKenna et al., 2005) incorporated two samples, one a stratified sample and the other a cluster sample. The second (Uhegbu & Opeke, 2004) combined cluster sampling with quota sampling. The third (Thorpe, 1986) used quota sampling to recruit participants from a particularly challenging population.

Example 1: A Study of Occupational Therapists' Database Use

McKenna and her colleagues (2005) were interested in studying the extent to which occupational therapists (OTs) were using OTseeker, a database of evidence regarding the effectiveness of various OT practices. They conducted a survey in two phases. In the first phase, they selected a stratified sample of members of OT Australia, a professional organization. The population of interest was all occupational therapists in Australia, but the study population was limited to members of OT Australia. Given that therapists that joined a professional association were also more likely to be incorporating evidence-based practice into their routines, this compromise was a reasonable one. The OT Australia membership list was the sampling frame and included approximately 4,500 members. It was stratified by state/territory. A proportionate random sample was then selected from each state/territory, that is, each stratum. The sample was 400 members; the authors do not provide an explanation of why this sample size was selected. These sampling procedures are very appropriate; unfortunately, a low response rate (31%) made the validity of the study results questionable. Therefore the authors undertook a second phase, drawing a second sample.

In the second sample, the research team focused their efforts in two states. The two states, Queensland and New South Wales, were selected because they were the home states of members of the team. They believed that the occupational therapists in those states were most likely to have used the OTseeker database because they would have heard of it through local sources; thus they were more likely to respond to a questionnaire about their database use. A cluster sampling approach was used for this phase. The sampling frame for Queensland was "a directory of facilities employing occupational therapists who are members of OT AUSTRALIA Queensland" (McKenna et al., 2005, p. 207), and in New South Wales, the sampling frame was "a university's directory of facilities that provide fieldwork placements for occupational therapy students" (p. 207). The number of clusters (i.e., facilities) selected from each part of the sample was in proportion to the number of clusters in each sampling frame. Altogether, 95 facilities were selected for inclusion in the sample. Each facility received enough questionnaire packets for all the occupational therapists working at that facility. Of the 326 questionnaires distributed, 27 percent were returned.

Clearly these authors made every attempt to select and recruit a representative sample of occupational therapists in Australia, even going so far as to conduct a follow-up phase of the study to increase their sample size. Their study procedures also included follow-ups with potential respondents in an effort to improve their response rate. Even with these efforts, it would be hard to argue that the study results are based on a representative sample, as noted in the authors' discussion of the study's limitations. In that discussion, they also noted that members of OT Australia are a biased sample of all OTs in Australia and that respondents might have differed from nonrespondents in their familiarity with and use of the OTseeker database. We can conclude that the sampling procedures for this study were quite appropriate but that the conclusions are weakened by the effects of nonresponse.

Example 2: Interactive Interpersonal Networking among Rural Women in Nigeria

As rural Nigeria experiences an increasing flow of information, there is evidence that women are not fully participating in this flow due to barriers to information flow among themselves. They are believed to be "secretive" (Uhegbu & Opeke, 2004, p. 521), to their detriment. Therefore this study was undertaken to understand the factors that affect information flows among rural women in one state in Nigeria and to describe the character of the information dissemination that does occur among them. The methodological challenges presented by this study make it an interesting example to examine in depth.

Uhegbu and Opeke (2004) clearly define their population as "women who are indigenes of Imo State and resident therein" (p. 523). They go on to further define their target population in terms of the women's marital status, including only those who are or have been married. Unfortunately, the census data that provides a basis for their sampling plan do not designate the marital status of each person; this issue will be resolved in the final stages of the sampling procedures. The first stage of the sampling procedure was to stratify the 27 local government areas (LGAs) in Imo State into three zones. Two LGAs were then selected from each of the three zones for participation in the study. The next stage of the sampling procedures involved proportionate quota sampling. The number of women to be included in the sample from each LGA was proportional to the female population within that LGA, in relation to the state's female population. In addition, the quota sampling strategy was intended to eliminate unmarried females, include equal numbers of literate and illiterate women, and include proportionate numbers of rural- and suburban-dwelling women. A total sample of 500 women was selected; of those, 485 participated in the study. It is not clear whether additional women were invited to participate and declined.

Because a quota sampling approach was used in combination with the stratified sampling approach, it is possible that the sample was biased. In addition, nonresponse may have been an issue that was not reported. While these authors addressed many of the challenges associated with studying this population, our understanding of their results would have been strengthened with a more complete consideration of the possibilities for bias in the study sample.

Example 3: Non-users of a Public Library

To identify factors affecting non-use of the Enfield North section of the Enfield (England) Public Libraries, a quota sample of people was selected and interviewed (Thorpe, 1986). They were asked about their reasons for not using the library, whether they knew where it was, and other questions intended to guide the library's marketing activities.

The population for the study was those people who lived in the Enfield North section of town but did not use the library. Three characteristics of the members of the population were used to select the sample. First, the section of town was divided into 10 wards. Each ward was proportionately represented in the final sample. The other two characteristics considered were age and gender. There were four age categories: 16–24, 25–44, 45–64, and 65+. The goal was to recruit three or four individuals from each ward/age/sex category to be broadly representative of the community. Thorpe (1986) considered adding social class as a fourth attribute that could be used for the quota sampling because social class has been found to be related to library use. This possibility was eventually rejected because of the complexity it would have added to the sampling and data collection procedures, possibly lowering the response rate because of the increased burden on participants.

Altogether, 1,049 people were approached and invited to participate in the study. Of those, many did not meet the inclusion criteria for the study: they were users of the library (i.e., they had used at least one library service at some time within the previous year; $n = 253$) or they lived outside Enfield North ($n = 278$). Of those invited to participate, 234 declined. So, of those meeting the inclusion criteria, 54 percent were included in the final sample.

This study is a good example of how quota sampling can be used in a community-based study. In particular, the use of a three-dimensional quota sampling plan improved the likelihood that the participants were representative of their community. While both the sampling method and the level of nonresponse weaken the generalizability of the results, Thorpe (1986) is appropriately cautious in his interpretations of the findings.

CONCLUSION

These three studies illustrate both the challenges that researchers may face in developing an adequate sampling plan and some creative approaches to addressing those challenges. In each case, the authors were very careful to apply the sampling methods correctly. By using several different sampling techniques in combination, they were able to overcome some of the problems. They were aware of, and made the reader aware of, the limitations of their sampling methods.

One weakness that all these examples displayed is the lack of a rationale for their sample size. None of them worked with particularly small samples, so they may not have felt the need to justify their sample size. Nevertheless, it is worthwhile to consider the effects of your sample size on the achievement of your research goals while you are planning a study. This process can only strengthen the validity of your study findings.

WORKS CITED

Asraf, R. M., & Brewer, J. K. (2004). Conducting tests of hypotheses: The need for an adequate sample size. *Australian Educational Researcher, 31*(1), 79–94.

Baker, L. M., Kars, M., & Petty, J. (2004). Health sciences librarians' attitudes toward the Academy of Health Information Professionals. *Journal of the Medical Library Association, 92*(3), 323–333.

Bocij, P. (2003). Victims of cyberstalking: An exploratory study of harassment perpetrated via the Internet. *First Monday, 8*(10). Retrieved August 1, 2007, from http://firstmonday.org/issues/issue8_10/bocij/index.html.

Bookstein, A. (1974). How to sample badly. *Library Quarterly, 44*(2), 124–132.

Burkell, J. (2003). The dilemma of survey nonresponse. *Library and Information Science Research, 25*(3), 239–263.

Case, D. O., Johnson, J. D., Andrews, J. E., Allard, S. L., & Kelly, K. M. (2004). From two-step flow to the Internet: The changing array of sources for genetics information seeking. *Journal of the American Society for Information Science and Technology, 55*(8), 660–669.

Cohen, J. (1965). Some statistical issues in psychological research. In B. B. Wolman (Ed.), *Handbook of Clinical Psychology* (pp. 95–121). New York: McGraw-Hill.

Cohen, J. (1988). *Statistical Power Analysis for the Behavioral Sciences* (2nd ed.). Hillsdale, NJ: Erlbaum.

Czaja, R., & Blair, J. (2005). *Designing Surveys: A Guide to Decisions and Procedures.* Thousand Oaks, CA: Pine Forge Press.

Dillman, D. A. (2007). *Mail and Internet Surveys: The Tailored Design Method* (2nd ed.). New York: John Wiley.

Fan, X., & Wang, L. (1999, November 3–6). *Practical guidelines for evaluating sampling designs in survey studies.* Paper presented at the annual meeting of the American Evaluation Association, Orlando, FL. (ERIC Document Reproduction Service No. ED435701)

Faulkner, L. (2003). Beyond the five-user assumption: Benefits of increased sample sizes in usability testing. *Behavior Research Methods Instruments and Computers, 35*(3), 379–383.

Howell, D. C. (2004). Power. In *Fundamental Statistics for the Behavioral Sciences* (5th ed., pp. 332–354). Belmont, CA: Brooks / Cole.

Lenth, R. V. (2006). Java Applets for Power and Sample Size [Computer software]. Retrieved July 25, 2007, from http://www.stat.uiowa.edu/~rlenth/Power/.

Lewis, J. R. (2006). Sample sizes for usability tests: Mostly math, not magic. *Interactions, 13*(6), 29–33.

Lippmann, W. (2007). *Public Opinion.* Bibliobazaar. (Original work published 1922.)

Loether, H. J., & McTavish, D. G. (1993). *Descriptive and Inferential Statistics: An Introduction.* Boston: Allyn and Bacon.

McKenna, K., Bennett, S., Dierselhuis, Z., Hoffmann, T., Tooth, L., & McCluskey, A. (2005). Australian occupational therapists' use of an online evidence-based practice database (OTseeker). *Health Information and Libraries Journal, 22*, 205–214.

Nielsen, J. (1993). *Usability Engineering.* Boston: AP Professional.

Pedhazur, E. J., & Schmelkin, L. P. (1991). *Measurement, Design, and Analysis: An Integrated Approach.* Hillsdale, NJ: Erlbaum.

Rea, L. M., & Parker, R. A. (1997). *Designing and Conducting Survey Research: A Comprehensive Guide.* San Francisco: Jossey-Bass.

Scheaffer, R. L., Mendenhall, W., III, & Ott, L. (1996). *Elementary Survey Sampling* (5th ed.). Belmont, CA: Duxbury Press.

Spool, J., & Schroeder, W. (2001). Testing Web sites: Five users is nowhere near enough. *CHI 2001 Abstracts,* 285–286.

Thorpe, S. (1986). Market research in Enfield Libraries. *Public Library Journal, 1*(4), 49–54.

Uhegbu, A. N., & Opeke, R. O. (2004). Deterrents to effective interactive interpersonal information networking of rural women in Imo State, Nigeria. *Journal of Information Science, 30*(6), 520–527.

ADDITIONAL RECOMMENDED READING

Hernon, P. (1994). Determination of sample size and selection of the sample: Concepts, general sources, and software. *College and Research Libraries, 55*(2), 171–179.

Rosenthal, R., & Rosnow, R. L. (1984). Indices of effect size. In *Essentials of Behavioral Research: Methods and Data Analysis* (pp. 361–365). New York: McGraw-Hill.

Sudman, S. (1976). *Applied Sampling*. New York: Academic Press.

14

Sampling for Intensive Studies

Barbara M. Wildemuth and Leo L. Cao

Patience and tenacity of purpose are worth more than twice their weight of cleverness.
—Thomas Henry Huxley (1870/1893)

INTRODUCTION

An intensive study is one in which "the primary questions concern how some causal process works out in a particular case or limited number of cases" (Sayer, 1984, p. 221). This type of study is contrasted with an extensive study, intended to discover common properties of or patterns that hold within a population. A variety of research designs might be used to conduct an intensive study, including case studies, naturalistic field studies, and ethnographic research, among others.

When you are planning an intensive study, you will want to select study participants who will be able to provide valuable insights into the phenomena of interest. You will be looking for those participants who will be most likely to provide rich "cultural data" on the phenomena you intend to study (Bernard, 2000, p. 144). As Sayer (1984) notes, "specific, identifiable individuals are of interest in terms of their properties and their mode of connection to others" (p. 221). Selecting an appropriate sample for an intensive study requires that you, the researcher, understand enough about the research setting and the phenomena of interest to be able to identify and select the most appropriate participants. Thus the sampling plan tends to evolve as the study is conducted; results from early data analyses may suggest that additional participants be added to the sample to cover new ground.

INTENSIVE SAMPLING TECHNIQUES

Most, if not all, intensive sampling involves nonprobability sampling. Since intensive studies are aimed at attempting to learn more about a particular setting or phenomenon, a nonprobabilistic approach to sampling can be a much more efficient method of focusing on the research questions being posed. The two approaches most appropriate for intensive studies will be discussed here: *purposive sampling* and *theoretical sampling*. (Other approaches to nonprobability sampling are briefly described in the previous chapter.)

Several common themes run through these two approaches to sampling. The first is that the quality of the sample relies on the judgment of the researcher. As you develop your sample, you will rely on your knowledge of the research question and its context as well as your knowledge of the particular setting in which you are collecting data. You will have particular reasons for including each participant, and the final sample should "present a balanced perspective" on the research questions (Rubin & Rubin, 2005, p. 64).

Purposive Sampling

Purposive sampling, as suggested by its name, is about purposively selecting specific participants for the study. Most qualitative research, especially research involving special populations, relies on the use of purposive sampling. It is intended to "maximize discovery of the heterogeneous patterns and problems that occur in the particular context under study" and to maximize "the researcher's ability to identify emerging themes that take adequate account of contextual conditions and cultural norms" (Erlandson et al., 1993, p. 82). You will try to identify those participants who can provide you with the richest data on the phenomena in which you're interested.

While you are not using probability sampling to draw a statistically representative sample from a population, you do need to understand the relationship between your sample and the wider universe or population to which it relates (Mason, 2002). You may be selecting a purposive sample that is, in some sense, *representative* of a population of interest. If so, you will want your sample to have the same characteristics (both in central tendency and variability) as the population. An alternative approach is to *sample strategically*, maximizing your ability to make theoretical comparisons of interest. This approach is usually called theoretical sampling and is discussed in the next section. A third possibility is that you want your sample to be *illustrative* or evocative of the phenomena of interest. Using this approach, you are likely to include a sample that vividly illustrates particular aspects of the phenomena under study.

You will also need to make a decision about the units that you will be sampling (Mason, 2002). These units may be individual people, but they may also be settings or environments, events or incidents, objects or artifacts, or texts. In many studies, you will be sampling a variety of types of units, each making a potential contribution to the study. The use of multiple types of units in combination can strengthen the validity of your findings.

Next, you will need to develop a strategy for selecting the sample. There are a number of strategies you can use. (Patton, 2002, lists 15 different strategies, only a few of which are described here.) For some studies, you may want to select "typical" cases. With this strategy, you are generally trying to argue that the elements included in your sample are similar to those not included in your sample, along a variety of dimensions that are pertinent to the study. For some studies, you may want to select extreme cases. For example, in a study of the chat reference services provided in your library, you may want to examine those online interactions that were most interactive, that is, those in which each of the participants "spoke" the most often. For some studies, you may want to select cases to maximize the variability in your sample. For instance, in a study of the handling of help desk requests, you might include some cases that were handled on first contact, some that required two to five follow-up interactions, and some that required more than five follow-up interactions. In many situations, it is important to include participants who have opposing views so that you can reach a balanced interpretation of the phenomena of interest (Rubin & Rubin, 2005). For some studies, you may want to focus on a particular type of case, minimizing the variability of your sample. For instance, you might want to examine only those help desk requests coming from humanities departments.

The purpose of your study and the research questions you are asking should guide your sampling plan. In general, you will want to select participants who are experienced with the phenomena of interest, who are knowledgeable about the research questions, and who hold various perspectives on the issues under study (Rubin & Rubin, 2005).

Theoretical Sampling

Glaser and Strauss (1967) introduced the concept of theoretical sampling as one component of their grounded theory development approach. Taking this approach, the goal of the sample is to provide data that will support the development of theory. Each element in the sample should help you "to define the properties of [your] categories; to identify the contexts in which they are relevant; to specify the conductions under which they arise, are maintained, and vary; and to discover their consequences" (Charmaz, 2000, p. 519). The focus is on the contribution to theory development that can be made by each new data source, and the simultaneous collection and analysis of data is an essential aspect of the research process. Coyne (1997) suggests that it might more accurately be called "analysis driven purposeful sampling" (p. 629) because new elements are added to the sample based on prior analysis.

"The aim of theoretical sampling is to maximize opportunities to compare events, incidents, or happenings to determine how a category varies in terms of its properties and dimensions" (Strauss & Corbin, 1998, p. 202). So how does this really work? You would initially select a setting in which to conduct your study (based on your research questions) and some initial data sources (e.g., participants, documents, artifacts, etc.). Here, at the beginning, you are using a relatively open sampling technique to broaden your data set. It is a purposive sample, as discussed previously (Coyne, 1997). Once you've collected some initial data, you analyze and make some initial interpretations of it. On the basis of these initial interpretations, you select additional data sources that are likely to provide comparable data. At this stage, you are trying to compare new findings, based on the new data collected, with the initial interpretations derived from your initial data collection. As Charmaz (2000) describes it, you are trying to "tease out less visible properties of [your] concepts and the conditions and limits of their applicability" (p. 519). Particular data sources might be selected because of the likelihood that they will yield data that support the examination of relationships among concepts or variations in the definitions of those concepts.

A hypothetical example may help to clarify this process. Let's assume that you are trying to understand (i.e., generate a theory that will explain) the process through which library patrons adopt new chat reference services being offered by the library. Your initial data may be collected through interviews with a few reference librarians who provide chat reference services and a few "friends" of the library who have used the chat reference services as well as the logs of their chat sessions. Later waves of data collection may include an interview with a reference librarian hired directly from library school to get his perceptions of the training provided by the library concerning chat reference and how this was similar to or different than the education received while in school. You might interview a chat reference user who is from another community to understand why that person approached your library's reference service. You might examine records from the local cable company because some of your participants have mentioned that chat would only be possible if they had access to high-speed Internet services through their cable company. Each of these data sources is different from the others, and each can provide a unique perspective on the developing theory.

Similarities and Differences Between Purposive and Theoretical Sampling

Purposive and theoretical sampling approaches are so similar that some authors use the two terms interchangeably. Others argue that theoretical sampling is a type of purposive sampling (Coyne, 1997). Both are done purposively. However, it is a requirement of theoretical sampling that it be incremental, with the sample being developed as the researcher completes the data analysis and develops the theory that will be the outcome of the study. Purposive sampling may also be conducted incrementally, but there is also the possibility that the sample can be identified at the beginning of the study and remain relatively unchanged throughout the course of the research.

SAMPLE SIZE

Intensive studies in information and library science are focused on the richness and quality of the data collected, rather than the number of study participants. While this eliminates discussion of statistical power and other factors, it does raise two related issues: how many different participants should be included in the sample, and how much data should be collected from each participant?

In situations where purposive sampling is being used, you will need to return to your research questions and the purpose of your study to guide your decisions about sample size. If a particular body of data is intended to address a particular research question, is it adequate? Have you collected enough data so that you fully understand the concept of interest and its relationship to other concepts? Have you checked for negative examples, for example, have you included data sources that are likely to contradict your preliminary theory? Think back to the original logic of your sampling plan: were you intending a representative sample, or an illustrative sample? You should be able to justify the adequacy of your sample in terms of its ability to fully address your research questions.

In situations where theoretical sampling is being used, you will stop collecting additional data when you have reached theoretical saturation, that is, when you're hearing the same concepts discussed in the same way by your participants, with no additional information being added to your understanding of the theory you're developing. Over time, the data cumulates, and later data are collected in a more focused way (based on the emerging theory) than when you started your data collection. Being able to tell when you've reached theoretical saturation depends on an iterative cycle of collecting and analyzing data so that as you collect additional data, you will know whether it is expanding your understanding of the phenomena of interest. If it is not, then there is no need to collect additional data from participants who are likely to repeat what you already know. The aim of this iterative process is "to refine *ideas*, not to increase the size of the original sample" (Charmaz, 2000, p. 519).

During this process, you will want to alternate between strategies of maximizing differences among the study participants and minimizing those differences. You will begin with the minimizing strategy so that you can identify some important concepts and gain an initial understanding of them. Then you will switch to the strategy of maximizing differences so that you can spot differences in the concepts, resulting in their refinement. With this strategy, you can also find the boundaries of the phenomena or settings to which your emerging theory applies.

Whatever your sample size and whatever sampling approach you use, you need to describe your procedures and rationale in detail. Any decisions you made about who to include in the sample should be explained. You should also discuss how the selection of the sample affected the findings of the study.

ADDITIONAL ISSUES RELATED TO SAMPLING IN INTENSIVE STUDIES

Issues of access, including both initial recruitment of participants and maintenance of access over the course of the study, often present a challenge for both purposive and theoretical sampling. Many researchers simply opt for a convenience sample because the cost in time and resources of recruiting a more appropriate sample is too high to bear. Other researchers have worked very hard to obtain and retain a sample that suits their study purposes very well. Some applicable strategies include taking on both insider and outsider roles to gain access to potential participants, establishing rapport and building trust, and recruiting gatekeepers that can provide access to a particular setting or group (Carey et al., 2001). These strategies can help you to overcome some of the challenges of recruiting a sample for an intensive study.

Finally, no discussion of sampling for intensive studies would be complete without raising the issue of generalizability. The idea of generalizability is applicable to extensive studies, in which probability sampling and statistical methods are used to generalize to a particular population of interest. However, as Hara et al. (2003) note, "it is not the intent of an intensive study to generalize. Rather, the intent is to describe, define, identify, etc., patterns of behavior that might lead to theory, concept, or framework development" (p. 954). Most often, researchers conducting intensive studies are interested in the transferability of their findings. The question is, To what extent can the findings of a particular study be transferred to another context or setting? It is the joint responsibility of the researcher and the reader of the research results to make reasonable inferences about the transferability of the findings, based on the methods used to collect the data (including the sampling methods) and the "thick description" of the context in which those data were collected (Denzin, 2001; Erlandson et al., 1993). As the researcher writes up the findings, he or she should consider the contexts in which the findings might also hold true; as subsequent readers consider the findings, they must also make judgments about whether the findings might apply in the contexts of interest to them.

EXAMPLES

Two intensive studies will be discussed to illustrate issues in sampling. The first, the dissertation work of S. E. Zach (2002) and L. Zach (2005,[1] 2006), uses purposive sampling to select museum and symphony orchestra administrators as informants for understanding their information needs and information seeking behaviors. The second, by Prekop (2002), uses theoretical sampling to study the collaborative information seeking behaviors of a military team conducting a command and control support study.

Example 1: Information Seeking Behavior of Senior Arts Administrators

The purpose of S. E. Zach's (2002) and L. Zach's (2005, 2006) dissertation research was to study the information seeking behavior of a particular group: arts administrators. To represent this group in her study, she selected subsamples from two settings: symphony orchestras and art museums. Her goal was to understand how nonprofit arts managers go about identifying and acquiring the information they need to complete their work, including where they look for information, how they obtain such information, and how they determine when enough is enough. She used a multiple case study design, incorporating an extensive interview protocol with a replication strategy. Other than in her dissertation, her 2005 *Journal of the American Society for Information Science and Technology* article provides the most detail about her approach to sampling.

The sample included in the study was composed of two subsamples, enabling S. E. Zach (2002) and L. Zach (2005, 2006) to make some interesting comparisons. The orchestra sample was selected first. Because of her familiarity with symphony orchestras and their administrators, Zach attempted to avoid bias in her sample selection by relying on an outside listing of potential participants. At the time, the Andrew W. Mellon Foundation was conducting a study of symphony orchestras, so the administrators of the 14 orchestras participating in that study were the initial pool of participants. One of the 14 was eliminated because he had already participated in an earlier phase of Zach's research. Two more orchestras were eliminated because they were experiencing a transition in their leadership. Three more orchestras (the smallest) were eliminated to make the final sample more homogeneous. Zach assumed that size and budget of the orchestra would have an impact on the administrators' information seeking behaviors and wanted to reduce the variability in the data during this study. Her final sample of orchestra administrators included seven people.

A second sample of art museum administrators was selected so that findings across the two settings could be compared. To make these comparisons valid, S. E. Zach (2002) and L. Zach (2005, 2006) sought art museums that were similar to the orchestras already studied in terms of administrative staff size and level of sophistication. In this phase, access to the study participants also became an issue because Zach had no previous connections with this group. Therefore staff size and sophistication were used as inclusion criteria for developing a convenience sample based on referrals. The referrals came from two sources: participants in the orchestra subsample and art museum board members with whom Zach was already acquainted. This strategy allowed Zach to recruit a sample of five art museum administrators.

S. E. Zach (2002) and L. Zach's (2005, 2006) sampling strategy, overall, was a reasonable compromise between the ideal and the feasible. By using external guidance (from the Mellon study), she attempted to avoid bias in her sample of orchestra administrators. She eliminated some of that pool to make her sample more homogeneous, then leveraged that homogeneity to specify inclusion criteria for her sample of art museum administrators. There was no feasible way to achieve the ideal sample of art museum administrators (i.e., a sample that was comparable in all important ways to her orchestra administrator sample). The use of inclusion criteria to select museum administrators from the pool to which she had access was very appropriate. Zach's sampling strategy was purposive, but it was not theoretical sampling; to be considered a theoretical sample, participant selection would have had to have been influenced by particular concepts uncovered in the initial data collection and the need to pursue those concepts further.

Example 2: Collaborative Information Seeking

The Prekop (2002) study illustrates the use of theoretical sampling. The purpose of the study was to understand the collaborative information seeking behaviors of a particular group. The group was conducting a "large and complex review of the Australian Defence Force's (ADF) command and control capability" (p. 533); the review was conducted over a three-year period.

As is typical of a theoretical sampling strategy, the data were of various types and were collected at different points in time. The initial data set consisted of the minutes of the group's meetings: 40 meetings, each lasting a couple of hours. The minutes were analyzed, and concepts of interest to the research goals were identified. This initial set of concepts was then used to plan the second stage of data collection and analysis, intended to further define the concepts and understand the relationships between them.

During the second stage, data were collected through interviews with five of the review participants. Over the three years of the review, 28 people were involved in it. Due to staffing changes over time, nine people, on average, were actively involved in the review process at any given point. The five study participants were selected from the eight people involved in the review's final stages. Two of them were representatives of the Defence Science and Technology Organisation (DSTO) in the Department of Defense, and the other three were representatives of the ADF. The DSTO representatives had been involved throughout the review process; the ADF representatives had been involved for at least the final year of the review process. The five study participants were asked about their information seeking behaviors during the review, and these behaviors were compared with those identified from the meeting minutes. In addition, these interviews illuminated the importance of context, which influenced both the roles that people played and the information behaviors they performed.

During a third stage, additional interviews were conducted to define more clearly the concepts identified in earlier stages. It is assumed that these interviews were conducted with the same five study participants, but that is not explicitly stated in the report of the research (Prekop, 2002). In addition to achieving its goal, this third round of data collection and analysis identified one additional role that had not been discovered in the previous rounds.

The primary defining characteristic of theoretical sampling is that its iterations are anchored in the theoretical findings from previous data collection and analysis efforts. This study clearly demonstrates how theoretical sampling could work. While it requires a commitment to multiple rounds of data collection and analysis, it can result in findings that are well grounded in the context under study.

CONCLUSION

Sampling for an intensive study relies almost solely on the researcher's judgment and his or her understanding of the context (both theoretical and logistical) of the study. Whether purposive sampling or theoretical sampling is used, it is likely that you will need to make some compromises in your sampling plan to make your study feasible to complete. In particular, your (lack of) access to potential study participants may be a barrier that you will have to overcome. In any case, it is critical that you provide a clear account of your sampling methods and a thick description of the context of your study so that your audience can make valid judgments about how your findings may apply to the settings in which they're interested.

NOTE

1. L. Zach (2005) received the 2006 Best *JASIST* Paper Award from the American Society for Information Science and Technology.

WORKS CITED

Bernard, H. R. (2000). *Social Research Methods: Qualitative and Quantitative Research Approaches*. Thousand Oaks, CA: Sage.

Carey, R. F., McKechnie, L. E. F., & McKenzie, P. J. (2001). Gaining access to everyday life information seeking. *Library and Information Science Research*, *23*(4), e319–e334.

Charmaz, K. (2000). Grounded theory: Objectivist and constructivist methods. In N. K. Denzin & Y. S. Lincoln (Eds.), *Handbook of Qualitative Research* (2nd ed., pp. 509–535). Thousand Oaks, CA: Sage.

Coyne, I. T. (1997). Sampling in qualitative research. Purposeful and theoretical sampling; merging or clear boundaries? *Journal of Advanced Nursing*, *26*(3), 623–630.

Denzin, N. K. (2001). *Interpretive Interactionism* (2nd ed.). Thousand Oaks, CA: Sage.

Erlandson, D. A., Harris, E. L., Skipper, B. L., & Allen, S. D. (1993). *Doing Naturalistic Inquiry: A Guide to Methods*. Newbury Park, CA: Sage.

Glaser, B. G., & Strauss, A. L. (1967). Theoretical sampling. In *The Discovery of Grounded Theory: Strategies for Qualitative Research* (pp. 45–78). New York: Aldine De Gruyter.

Hara, N., Solomon, P., Kim, S.-L., & Sonnenwald, D. H. (2003). An emerging view of scientific collaboration: Scientists' perspectives on collaboration and factors that impact collaboration. *Journal of the American Society for Information Science and Technology*, *54*(10), 952–965.

Huxley, T. H. (1893). On medical education. An address to the students of the Faculty of Medicine in University College, London. In *Collected Essays* (Vol. 3). New York: D. Appleton. (Original work published 1870.)

Mason, J. (2002). Sampling and selection in qualitative research. In *Qualitative Researching* (2nd ed., pp. 120–144). Thousand Oaks, CA: Sage.

Patton, M. Q. (2002). *Qualitative Research and Evaluation Methods*. Thousand Oaks, CA: Sage.

Prekop, P. (2002). A qualitative study of collaborative information seeking. *Journal of Documentation*, *58*(5), 533–547.

Rubin, H. J., & Rubin, I. S. (2005). *Qualitative Interviewing: The Art of Hearing Data* (2nd ed.). Thousand Oaks, CA: Sage.

Sayer, A. (1984). *Method in Social Science: A Realist Approach*. London: Hutchinson.

Strauss, A., & Corbin, J. (1998). Theoretical sampling. In *Basics of Qualitative Research: Techniques and Procedures for Developing Grounded Theory* (2nd ed., pp. 201–215). Thousand Oaks, CA: Sage.

Zach, L. (2005). When is "enough" enough? Modeling the information seeking and stopping behavior of senior arts administrators. *Journal of the American Society for Information Science and Technology*, *56*(1), 23–35.

Zach, L. (2006). Using a multiple-case studies design to investigate the information seeking behavior of arts administrators. *Library Trends, 55*(1), 4–21.

Zach, S. E. (2002). *When is "enough" enough? An investigation of the information seeking and stopping behavior of senior arts administrators.* Unpublished doctoral dissertation, University of Maryland, College Park.

15

Studying Special Populations

Carol L. Perryman and Barbara M. Wildemuth

DEFINITION

What are special populations? While the American Library Association[1] defines special populations as people with special needs, we will try to define special populations from a research perspective. Much is known about the information behaviors and information environments of certain groups of people (e.g., college students and faculty), but the information environments of other groups remain unexamined, resulting in a perceptible gap. Special populations, then, are groups whose information behaviors and environments have not been extensively studied. Special populations include, for example, individuals living or working in unique environments, such as online communities, or gathered in inner-city community centers. Perhaps they are unique due to demography, purpose, or condition, as with four-year-old girls in a public library, patients newly diagnosed with cancer, or battered women seeking support. It might be too facile, however, to dismiss well-examined groups as not meeting our criteria because some members of the academic population may qualify as special when unique characteristics are considered (e.g., the information needs of gay, lesbian, transgendered, or transsexual students new to a university setting).

The challenge will be to understand the contexts and information-related needs and practices that make the group you are studying unique. Taylor (1991) calls this set of contexts and needs an *information use environment* (IUE), which he defines as "the set of those elements that (a) affect the flow and use of information messages into, within, and out of any definable entity; and (b) determine the criteria by which the value of information messages will be received" (p. 218).

For the purposes of a research study, any group defined as special should be of a size that is large enough to be considered meaningful in the context of professional practice. Populations shift and grow, so the best resource to begin with is your own observation and local data, followed by a thorough investigation of the literature. Even beyond that, the question might be whether existing studies accurately reflect the realities of your own environment. Because such groups may not have been conceptualized or identified as a discrete population, your approach to your research requires creativity and sensitivity to considerations not normally required in more frequently examined settings. Little can be presumed prior to beginning your study, and the processes of negotiating an approach to a group, collecting data from study participants, and ensuring confidentiality may be completely different from a population whose normal working lives include awareness of research studies.

Once you have identified such a group, it is easy to become paralyzed by indecision: Where to begin? What should I look for, and *how*? Although many of the particulars are dealt with in detail by other chapters in this book, this chapter will highlight issues specific to population definition, sampling, and recruiting study participants.

IDENTIFYING A SAMPLE

The first challenge in working with a special population is to define exactly who is included in that group. For example, I might be interested in working with young children to find out about their perceptions and use of a library. Who will be included in my population? A clearer definition might be children aged four to seven. But is that a clear enough definition? I might really only be interested in children, aged four to seven, who have been brought to the library at least once by a parent or guardian. You can see that each succeeding definition is more specific. In defining the population for your study, you should make it as clear and unambiguous as possible. Consider who should be included and who should be excluded.

Next, you should consider what is already known about this population. Check the research literature for other studies of this population. Check statistical sources for basic demographic data on this population. If you're studying young children, as in the preceding example, data from the U.S. Department of Education and the Census Bureau may be helpful. Prior research studies might be located through the education literature as well as the literature in information and library science (ILS). Taking another example, if you're interested in Haitian immigrants who have recently entered the United States, take a look at what's known more generally about the country—its culture, politics, and demographic characteristics. It's important to study special populations in the context of *their* lives, not your own.

DEFINING THE SAMPLE AND DEVELOPING A SAMPLING FRAME

Developing a sampling frame for a special population entails at least as many challenges as developing a sampling frame for any population (Sudman & Kalton, 1986). The first step is to figure out a way to list all the members of the population. For some populations, this process will be relatively straightforward. For instance, you may want to study all the people who use the senior center in your town; it's likely that the senior center has a list of active participants that they would be willing to share with you. In other situations, enumerating the population of interest will be very difficult. Sometimes this process is difficult or impossible because the population is very large such as in the preceding example study of young children. In such situations, you will need to compromise your expectations and develop a sampling frame that is not ideal, but workable. For instance, you might include in your sampling frame all those children, aged four to seven, who are enrolled in the local public school system (including kindergarten).

For some studies, you will be selecting a purposive sample, rather than attempting to select a random sample. In these studies, you will be selecting particular people because they play a particular role in the setting or have particular characteristics that are relevant to your research question. Because such studies are generally conducted within a particular setting, it is likely that you will be able to define the characteristics needed and identify study participants who have those characteristics.

RECRUITING STUDY PARTICIPANTS

Most often, the people in a special population have not been the focus of a research study before. Thus they will be unfamiliar with the recruiting process and the implications of study participation. Therefore it's important that you be particularly concerned with the ethical treatment of your potential study participants. Make sure that they understand that their participation is completely voluntary. Make sure that they understand the study procedures before they are asked to consent to their participation. Make sure that you have procedures in place to adequately protect their privacy (through anonymizing your data set or through strict security procedures). If you've taken these precautions in designing your study procedures, then you can proceed with the recruitment process.

For some studies, you will be recruiting study participants via letter or e-mail. In other studies, recruitment will be through direct contact with the potential study participant. In either case, you should be aware of how you might be perceived by the potential study participants. In many cases, you will be an "outsider" (i.e., not a member of the population of interest). You may differ from your study participants in some obvious and not-so-obvious ways. Because of these differences, you will need to pilot test your recruitment materials (and other study materials) with members of the population of interest to ensure that they will be understood. For example, if you are asking a young child to draw a map of the library, including the places he or she most likes to visit, you will need to make sure the instructions are expressed in a style that can be understood by the young child.

In summary, when working with a special population, you need to pay special attention to every aspect of the design of your study. Sampling issues have been discussed here, but you will also need to take into account the characteristics of your study population as you design your study procedures and the materials you'll use to carry out those procedures. With special populations, it's particularly important to pilot test these procedures and materials with members of the population before carrying out your study.

EXAMPLES

We'll use two very different studies to exemplify approaches to research with special populations. In the first study, Agada (1999) used semistructured interviews to explore the information needs of 20 inner-city information gatekeepers. In the second example, Bilal (2000, 2001, 2002) used a carefully structured mixed-methods approach to understanding the searching processes of seventh-grade children in Tennessee. Our critical examination of these two studies will focus on the methods employed and their suitability for the population being studied.

Example 1: African American Gatekeepers in Milwaukee

Twenty African American gatekeepers in a Milwaukee, Wisconsin, neighborhood became the focus of Agada's (1999) study. After exploring the literature, Agada concluded that though a descriptive model had been devised for other ethnic communities, it had not been applied to African American populations. Beginning with a fairly detailed exploration of the physical environment—the Harambee neighborhood itself—Agada justified his selection of gatekeepers based on his understanding of the important and unique role he felt they played within the community. He explained that within this community, people tended not to use "official" resources, such as libraries, but relied instead on trusted community members.

This study is of value because it demonstrates a number of issues of which you need to be aware as you consider your own research with a new community. Agada (1999) drew on existing literature to find what, if anything, had been done with similar populations. From this literature search, he constructed a beginning typology, which became the basis for exploration and helped to build the interview guide (which is included in the paper). His description of the Harambee neighborhood is extensive, and although this chapter is not focused on research settings, it seems worth pointing out that, especially when your population is outside of your own organization, setting plays a crucial role in your attempts to understand the community.

From a beginning list of 27 people, Agada (1999) ended with a purposive sample of 20 individuals who had been identified as gatekeepers within the community through contacts with local organizers and leaders in two community organizations. Three of this number were interviewed for a pilot study, leaving a total sample of 17. The two local organizations were approached because of their roles in neighborhood development and support, identifying areas of concern such as employment, drug abuse, and home ownership.

Not only is it important to nurture relationships with local agencies already involved in the location and with the population you wish to study, but also, contacts gathered in this way can provide valuable background information and assist you in finding study participants. Agada (1999) was directed to his respondents by others in the organization, a method that helped both with gathering participants and with easing his entry into the setting by having worked through the community's own structure.

With special populations, issues of participant protection may arise. Agada (1999) described the process of sharing interview responses with others within the community but failed to explain how he both protected the confidentiality of the individual respondents and gained their permission to share their comments. These issues should be addressed in any study, but particularly in studies in which the participants are likely to know each other.

The importance of negotiating access to an environment or population cannot be overemphasized as it can have an enormous impact on trust and, therefore, on the quality of data you can gather. Lofland and Lofland (1995) identified four aspects of gaining and maintaining access to a particular setting:

- Connections (use who you know, or focus on leaders within the community you wish to study)
- Accounts (provide your intended participants with a clear, audience-appropriate, and unambiguous explanation of your purpose)

- Knowledge (cast yourself as a learner within the community, rather than an expert)
- Courtesy (treat participants with the same respect you would expect)

The interviews comprised 60 open- and closed-ended questions in 19 categories designed to gather information on demography, characterization of information needs and uses, preferred sources, and perceptions of source quality. Although the questions were derived from other studies, participants were encouraged to add their own categories if they felt that those provided were incomplete. Even if you have every reason to believe, at the outset, that your population closely resembles another, be careful to allow for flexibility in your data collection methods and in coding and analysis.

Interview data were shared with the participants as a fact-check procedure and to encourage additional commentary. The data were also shared with individuals who worked within the community but who were not included in the study. There is no statement that participants' permission was obtained before their statements were shared with these nonparticipating individuals, which is an important component of ensuring confidentiality. In conducting your own research and in writing up your results, be sure to incorporate information about this crucial aspect of the study.

Viewing this study of a particular neighborhood through the lens of the *insider-outsider* experience is very appropriate. Derived from the field of sociology, insider-outsider research considers the sociological mechanisms in play when an individual or group differs from those in the larger society. This viewpoint has been applied in prior ILS studies (e.g., Chatman, 1996). It has great bearing on this study because it assumes that only those who live as insiders can truly understand what that's like. This assumption implies that while studying special populations, issues of trust and access, verification and comprehensiveness of data need to be carefully taken into account. Agada (1999) did this well, with his cross-checking and secondary verification of findings, but more discussion would have helped future researchers understand this process more thoroughly.

Agada's (1999) study demonstrates an exemplary exploration of one neighborhood and sensitivity to the political currents and issues of trust among a population defined by both geography and ethnicity. He began with his own perceptions of the community but was careful to examine the literature, then incorporated into the study the question of whether existing studies described his Harambee population's reality.

Example 2: The Information Behaviors of Middle School Children

The second study to be discussed is one of a series of publications generated by the author's detailed inquiry into the information behaviors of a group of seventh-grade students drawn from three science classes in a middle school in Knoxville, Tennessee. Bilal had first conducted a pilot study looking at the online research activities of children (Bilal, 1998), then enlarged on the pilot. As noted earlier, such pilot testing is strongly recommended when working with special populations. Three papers (Bilal, 2000, 2001, 2002) were published examining different aspects of the results, providing a very rich foundation for future studies.

Bilal (2000, 2001, 2002) drew from the theoretical literature in the field of education but also incorporated findings from previous studies of children's use of CD-ROM and online databases. An initial question arose about whether what was known about behavior with these resources was applicable to behavior in an Internet-based environment.

Bilal (2000, 2001, 2002) was interested in seventh-grade students and developed a sampling frame that consisted of all the seventh-grade students in a particular school. Because she limited her sampling frame to a single school, the results of the study should be generalized further than that school's students only with caution. Because Bilal provided descriptions of the school and its socioeconomic environment, other researchers can compare their own samples/populations with hers to evaluate their similarities and differences.

Permission from the parents was required by the school for Internet use, so this process had to be completed prior to selecting study participants. Thus an initial pool of 90 students took home permission slips. It is not clear that these permission slips included a request for the parents' consent to have their child participate in the study, but we can assume this was the case. When working with minors, it is standard practice to get informed consent for study participation from the child's parents. Next, permission was sought from the students themselves. This type of procedure is common when the children in the sample are judged to be old enough to be able to assent to their study participation. Twenty-five students agreed to participate. Three were used for an initial pilot study, leaving a total of 22 participants in the study reported.

The study procedures took place in the library's computer lab. Each student searched Yahooligans! to complete an assignment from their science teacher ("How long do alligators live in the wild, and how long in captivity?"). Bilal (2000, 2001, 2002) collected data about search behavior, search retrieval success, and use of navigation methods using a software program that recorded keystrokes. Follow-up interviews used three instruments: an Internet/Web quiz, an exit interview, and teachers' assessments of student characteristics. It's a good idea to build in methods to triangulate your data by confirming or enriching it with another method, as Bilal did in this study.

In summary, Bilal's (2000, 2001, 2002) work provides an example of how the information behaviors of children can be studied. As Bilal stated in the introduction, the information activities of children are infrequently studied. Because she was working with a special population, Bilal was careful to draw connections between what is known about this population and then to look for differences and similarities between the findings. She was sensitive to issues of place and the role those issues might play in the study's outcome. Finally, her approach to inquiry was strongly grounded in both education and in information science, rendering the study's findings meaningful to librarian-educators, teachers, and search engine designers.

CONCLUSION

Both Agada (1999) and Bilal (2000, 2001, 2002) used their close observations of two unique populations to craft their approaches to research, gaining entrance by enlisting the support and participation of local gatekeepers—in the Agada study, by consulting supervisors for the names of specific individuals, and in the Bilal study, by working through the school librarian and science teacher. They also mined the existing research literature for information specific to similar populations, using what they found to shape their inquiries and clearly stating what gaps they perceived in the understanding of these populations. These methods, along with a sensitivity to the need to protect potentially vulnerable special populations, contributed to the success of these two studies.

NOTE

1. Based on the scope of the Libraries Serving Special Populations Section of ALA, http://www.acrl.org/ala/mgrps/divs/ascla/asclaourassoc/asclasections/lssps/lssps.cfm.

WORKS CITED

Agada, J. (1999). Inner-city gatekeepers: An exploratory survey of their information use environment. *Journal of the American Society for Information Science, 50*(1), 74–85.

Bilal, D. (1998). Children's search processes in using World Wide Web search engines: An exploratory study. In *Proceedings of the 61st ASIS Annual Meeting (October 25–29, Pittsburgh, PA)* (Vol. 35, pp. 45–53). Medford, NJ: Published for the American Society for Information Science by Information Today.

Bilal, D. (2000). Children's use of the Yahooligans! Web search engine: I. Cognitive, physical, and affective behaviors on fact-based search tasks. *Journal of the American Society for Information Science, 51*(7), 646–665.

Bilal, D. (2001). Children's use of the Yahooligans! Web search engine: II. Cognitive and physical behaviors on research tasks. *Journal of the American Society for Information Science, 52*(2), 118–136.

Bilal, D. (2002). Children's use of the Yahooligans! Web search engine: III. Cognitive and physical behaviors on fully self-generated search tasks. *Journal of the American Society for Information Science, 53*(13), 1170–1183.

Chatman, E. A. (1996). The impoverished life-world of outsiders. *Journal of the American Society for Information Science, 47*(3), 193–206.

Lofland, J., & Lofland, L. H. (1995). *Analyzing Social Settings: A Guide to Qualitative Observation and Analysis* (3rd ed.). Belmont, CA: Wadsworth.

Sudman, S., & Kalton, G. (1986). New developments in the sampling of special populations. *Annual Review of Sociology, 12*, 401–429.

Taylor, R. S. (1991). Information use environments. *Progress in Communication Sciences, 10*, 217–255.

PART IV

METHODS FOR DATA COLLECTION

16

Historical Research

Chad Morgan and Barbara M. Wildemuth[1]

History is rarely a magical tool for achieving any of our fondest goals. In fact, quite often historical knowledge seems an impediment to what we desire.
— Paul K. Conkin and Roland N. Stromberg (1971)

INTRODUCTION

Many of us have a stereotype of scientists that see them in their white lab coats, working in a controlled environment where hypotheses are tested in isolation from the outside world. In contrast, the relevant metaphor for the historian is of the detective following a trail of evidence, trying to divine which clues are useful and pertinent in a chaotic and complicated world (Conkin & Stromberg, 1971). One clue leads to another, and then another, until the historian is able to tell his or her (always imperfect) story—a story recreating the past. Such a method yields necessarily flawed conclusions—a historian's laboratory is a past where contingencies are always cropping up and where isolating variables is impossible. But for all the complications implicit in working with a messy past, it is the imperfectness of their conditions for accumulating and evaluating evidence which allows historians to approach questions that other social sciences cannot penetrate.

One peculiar feature of historical research is its necessarily iterative nature. With many other methods of inquiry, data collection follows hypothesis formation and precedes interpretation of the evidence. It is a discrete step in the process. Not so with historical research, which is more like a journey down a winding path. Initial gathering of evidence points one in the direction of more evidence. And unlike the scientist, the historian formulates no single hypothesis to be tested all at once or over several preplanned phases. Instead, like the detective, he or she comes up with an ever evolving working theory of what happened, which is valid only until the next round of evidence leads to its modification. All of which is to say that in historical research, there are no discrete phases; hypothesis formation and the collection and interpretation of evidence (both inductively and deductively) are all integrated with one another. Indeed, given the iterative nature of historical research and the need to constantly revise one's working theory, it may reasonably be said that hypothesis formation and interpretation of evidence often amount to the same thing in history.[2]

Historical research is likewise unique in the range of phenomena that it can be used to investigate. If one considers everything up to the present moment fair game for historical inquiry, in fact, there may be said to be no real limits on what historians can research. They can investigate little, apparently insignificant events encompassing a few hours or days or chronicle a single life. Alternatively, they can choose to examine the course of entire nations, cultures, or civilizations. All of which makes pinning down their method the more difficult because presumably, one's method varies depending on the questions he or she is trying to answer.

For a variety of reasons, we could say that historical inquiry is not really research in the scientific sense at all. And if we consider history as a method (as opposed to a subject, i.e., "the study of the past"), there is no controlling for variables nor any attempt to build a strictly scientific case. There are researchers who consider themselves historians who would dispute this. But methodologically, they would have to be considered some species of social scientist; their first principles are not those of the historian. History's epistemological foundations are chaos and contingency. Historical researchers start from the assumption that human affairs are endlessly complex and that no factor or reasonably finite set of factors can be adduced to explain a given action or phenomenon. Consider, as an example, the old chestnut about how much the length of Cleopatra's nose changed the course of history. Had it been shorter, had the queen not been so alluring to Caesar and then Antony, who can say how history would have been different? That so small and seemingly insignificant a contingency could have had so profound an effect on the course of antiquity's greatest empire should be a humbling reminder to anyone tempted to construct an overly mechanistic, deterministic model for how and why human affairs unfold as they do. But neither is historians' emphasis on contingency only an epistemological concern. It is also an evidential one: to term the detritus of the past, anything so scientific as data would be an unsustainable pretension, and historians must always be drawing on imperfect and incomplete sources (at least relative to what once existed) to form their conclusions.

Given these two factors—the potential great importance of apparently trivial matters in shaping history and the fact that only a portion of historical evidence survives—the historical researcher could despair. What if, as seems likely, the small thing on which so much hinges is not to be found in the historical record? This, however, is the wrong perspective to take. As a condition of the nature of your historical research, you must accept that you will never recreate a past world "as it essentially was," in the words of nineteenth-century German historian Leopold von Ranke.[3] But if von Ranke would have been disappointed in the necessary incompleteness of historical knowledge, contemporary historians need not be (Conkin & Stromberg, 1971). Indeed, the knowledge can be liberating. Freed from the possibility that you can fully know the past, you are free to recreate that portion of the past, however small, which is knowable.

METHODS

Since the introduction of this chapter was largely dedicated to the problem of incompleteness—of evidence, of knowledge—it may surprise you that the chief practical difficulty the prospective historian will face is one of abundance. To wit, there are almost limitless topics that the historical researcher may choose to investigate. And within many, if not most, of those topics, there exists a similarly limitless universe of resources on which the historian-detective may draw. For recent eras at least, historical sources can only be considered scarce in comparison with all the sources that once existed and have since been destroyed or lost.

For the sake of clarity and usefulness, what follows is a step-by-step guide to conducting historical research.[4] It focuses on gathering sources, but also includes some advice on finding a subject and interpreting the evidence found.

Finding a Subject

Given an abundance of possible topics and research materials, the first thing you must do is clearly delineate your subject. The chief criteria for choosing a research topic must be your personal interest in and the wider relevance of the subject. Let us assume that you are interested in the history of libraries. The first test this subject must pass is whether there is a professional or popular audience for it and whether its wider relevance is sufficient to merit its study. Let us further assume that it is.

The next step for you to take is to pare the subject down to a manageable form. While it is true that someone may, due to hubris or pressure from a publisher, one day write a work titled *The History of Libraries*, no such work can be what it purports to be.[5] That is because any general history of the library implies a number of different histories. Would it include a history of the paper and printing technologies? Of different phases of cataloging? Of the evolution of librarianship as a craft and a profession? Would it incorporate all the libraries of the world? We could go on, but you get the point: there are many different histories that would bear on this central theme, and it is not practicable for one person to create all of them in a lifetime. It is therefore crucial for you to prune your subject to a manageable size from the outset. An appropriately circumscribed topic makes both the collection and interpretation of data easier. As an example, let us say that you want to investigate the origins of library education in North Carolina, which seems a suitable topic for a monograph-length work.

Gathering Sources

Now the task becomes one of accumulating source material. The first stage of this process is compiling and mastering the relevant secondary literature. As we shall see with primary sources, you must exhaust a number of avenues of inquiry before you can be said to have completed this project. The first stages may involve an informal, ad hoc search. One of the best ways to begin the process and isolate the most important works is to ask colleagues with similar interests for their recommendations. This will, it is hoped, lead you to several seminal and not so seminal articles, monographs, and comprehensive studies. While reading them, you will want to mine these works for other sources that are cited. Having chased down all relevant sources in the footnotes (and academic histories almost always have footnotes or endnotes), you will want to repeat the process with the new works. At some point, chasing down references may bring one to works that are too old or outmoded to be considered useful, but that is up to your discretion. In any event, this process of chasing down sources from within the literature will accomplish several things at once. All that reading will acquaint you with the principal issues surrounding your topic. Moreover, it will provide you with a good start on accumulating secondary sources. Finally, reading how often works are cited and whether with approval or disapproval will give you a good general impression of the relative value of the works.

To return to our example of a history of library education in North Carolina, you will probably learn early on in your efforts of Robert S. Martin's (1988) University of North Carolina (UNC) dissertation *Louis Round Wilson at the University of North Carolina, 1901–1932*, a landmark work (and one of the examples to be examined later in this chapter). Reading through the footnotes of that work, you will find reference to an obscure but germane master's paper by David Gunn (1987) titled "A History of Library Extension at the University of North Carolina at Chapel Hill, 1912–1958," which may well not have turned up in other searches. The references and footnotes in your secondary sources will often lead you to items that could not have been located by any other means.

Yet a strictly informal search is insufficient. For one thing, scholars in different fields often write about the same phenomena without realizing that parallel discussions are going on in other disciplines. Chasing down footnotes in one discipline may thus lend itself to a type of tunnel vision that prevents you from picking up on these parallel academic currents. This process, furthermore, only leads you back in time. And the further you chase, the more likely it is that you will find your sources too old to be very useful. Any effort to discover the latest scholarship relevant to a particular topic must therefore transcend the early informal effort. It may seem obvious to say so now—we can assure you that it is less so when you are actually doing this secondary reading—but it is important to keep in mind that just because you have read a lot of books and articles does not mean that your search is complete.

Having completed your informal search for secondary materials, then, you must enter a more formal, exhaustive phase, utilizing library catalogs and e-research tools. However advanced our tools for cataloging and retrieving information have been and may yet become, this step will always require some critical thought on the part of the researcher if only to imagine all the ways in which his or her topic may be labeled. Barzun (1992) describes the deployment of imagination in using a library catalog in this way:

One who wants information about the theory of the divine right of kings arrives at the term "Monarchy." One might conceivably have reached the same result by looking up "Right, divine," or even possibly "Divine Right," if the library owns a book by that title or is fully cross-indexed. What is certain is that there is little chance of success if one looks up "King" and no hope at all if one looks up "Theory." In other words, one must from the very beginning *play* with the subject, take it apart and view it from various sides in order to seize on its outward connections. (p. 19)

On the face of it, this may seem perfectly intuitive, and Barzun's (1992) reference to libraries being "fully cross-indexed" may seem quaint. But it does contain a home truth, namely, that no amount of cataloging sophistication will help the researcher who has not thoroughly thought through the subject of interest and all its connections. At UNC, a catalog keyword search on "North Carolina" and "library education" retrieves 54 items, not one of them Martin's aforementioned dissertation on Louis Round Wilson (although the Louis Round Wilson papers in the Southern Historical Collection are included in the search results). So having looked at the 54 hits and having determined which are useful, you will want to continue to play with your topic. This may involve casting a wider net or making a more precise search, depending on the results of your initial query.

Once you've identified some materials through the library catalog, you can use them to lead you to other materials. Specifically, be sure to check which subject headings have been assigned to those materials that you find useful. Then conduct a search using those subject headings. They are likely to lead you to other useful materials.

After scouring your library's catalog, there remain a few other means by which to ferret out secondary sources. I refer to online databases that are used mainly to search for journal articles. The most important for information and library science (ILS) topics will be Library and Information Science Abstracts (LISA) and Library Literature and Information Science. A LISA search on "North Carolina" and "library education" yields five articles, two of which would be relevant to our notional project on the history of library education in that state. Again, you will want to conduct several related searches to be sure that all materials are found. Before moving on, you may also want to check into other databases with some relevance to your subject. For a project such as our hypothetical one, it might be appropriate to search the America: History and Life database. In addition, for the example topic, you may want to investigate the Web sites of the current ILS programs in North Carolina to see if they include any information about their histories that might be useful to you.

After gathering all your secondary sources, you will want to take some time to read and assimilate that literature. This does not mean reading every word of every book and article necessarily, but it does mean reading enough that you are completely conversant with the key issues surrounding your topic. This step is crucial because it will inform your search for primary sources.

The identification of primary sources is both more difficult and, at least for historians, much more fun than the compilation of secondary literature. One reason it is more difficult is that primary sources are likely to be scattered across numerous archives and manuscript collections. Depending on the geographic scope of your topic, this could involve extensive travel, although for a state study like ours, most of the research should not take one across the borders of North Carolina. Furthermore, most archives of any size have a large backlog of unprocessed collections for which no adequate finding aid has been written. For the researcher, unfortunately, these sources are essentially impossible to find, and you must reconcile yourself to the fact that, however thorough your search may be, there are probably important materials out there that you simply cannot access.

Again, you will want to start by asking colleagues for recommendations and mining secondary works for useful collections. Turning to Robert Martin's dissertation on Louis Round Wilson once more, one finds in his selected bibliography a series of Wilson interviews stored in various repositories at UNC-Chapel Hill but which do not avail themselves to the researcher without very specific catalog queries. As a general rule, even if a document or collection has been cited scores of times in scholarly publications, you will still want to examine it for yourself to see if your interpretation squares with existing ones. Also, it is wholly conceivable that your subject and perspective will allow you to see old sources in a new light.

In recent years, ferreting out primary sources has been made somewhat easier by the introduction of online finding aids by most major archives and manuscript collections. Depending on their quality, finding aids will give you anything from an excruciatingly precise inventory to a vague-to-the-point-of-uselessness description of a given collection; levels of control vary markedly between institutions. Either way, you will want to look at the Web sites of relevant repositories to see what and what kind of online finding aids they make available. This seems the appropriate place to mention the subscription service ArchiveGrid (http://www.archivegrid.org), which aims to gather as many of the world's electronic collection descriptions together as possible. It already boasts "nearly a million collection descriptions" from thousands of repositories around the world, including many, if not most, of the preeminent American archives and manuscript collections. An ArchiveGrid search on "library history" and "North Carolina" turns up 9 collections, while a search on "Louis Round Wilson" turns up 24. Hopefully, ArchiveGrid will one day realize its potential and become something closer to "one-stop shopping" for the historical researcher. For the moment, though, it is also important to check out individual archive Web sites because many still exist outside the ArchiveGrid umbrella.

Similarly, it remains important to mine the expertise of archivists and librarians in special collections. They will often have worked in their respective institutions for years, if not decades, and have a knowledge of its holdings that far outstrips what can be gleaned from finding aids. Developing a relationship with the archivists or librarians in key collections can be extremely helpful to your research.

Unfortunately, and unavoidably, this description of evidence collection makes the process look more linear than it is in fact. The truth of the matter is that every meaningful piece of evidence will influence what comes after it. A new piece of evidence may make you see existing evidence in a different light and may cause you to go off in search of sources you could not have anticipated needing at the outset. To give only one example, if you find that a North Carolina librarian who you have been investigating was heavily involved in, say, advancing the cause of women's suffrage, you may need to look at that movement in the context of the state and examine the records of suffrage organizations in which he or she was active. Similarly, this fact could cause you to view other facts about your subject's life through a different lens.

Interpreting the Evidence

In historical research, the interpretation of the evidence collected from the sources reviewed involves a significant amount of creativity. However, it is not an act of creation, but of re-creation: you will "endeavor to imagine what the past was like" and "present the results of [your] imaginative reconstruction of that past in ways that do no violence either to the records or to the canons of scientific imagination" (Gottschalk, 1945, p. 8). Perhaps this process is best summed up by Conkin and Stromberg (1971), when they say, "A *history* is, at the very least, a story. . . . But obviously a history is a special kind of story, for it is both a purportedly true story and also always a story about the past" (p. 131).

There are a number of ways that telling a story that re-creates the past can incorporate fallacies of fact or logic. Barzun (1992) identified four common historical fallacies and the ways in which they may be avoided:

1. Generalization: This fallacy occurs when the researcher claims more for his argument than his or her evidence warrants. Usually, it is a case of careless language (e.g., using universals such as *all* or *every*), rather than sloppy reasoning (although the former could be considered a species of the latter). Just as overgeneralization is usually caused by careless language, it can be remedied by attention to language. Specifically, one can correct most overgeneralizations through use of qualifiers (e.g., *most, often, nearly*, etc.) or qualifying phrases (e.g., *in general* or *as a rule*).

2. Reduction: This fallacy consists in the attribution of complex, multifaceted phenomena to single causes or factors. An example might be, "The Vietnam War was caused by Communist expansionism." This statement is not false precisely—Communist expansionism did have a part in bringing about the Vietnam conflict—but it is reductionist to the extent that it implicitly shuts out other factors from consideration. As with overgeneralization, this fallacy can be avoided by the careful use of language.

3. Tautology: A tautology is the needless (and often hidden) repetition of an idea. An example (from one of Morgan's own student papers) is, "Southern pride required Confederate soldiers to fight until the end." Assuming that the reference is to the end of the war, it is redundant to say that they had to fight to the end.

4. Misplaced literalism: This is the trickiest of the four most common historical fallacies, and it comes down to this: people, historical and otherwise, often do not say what they mean. They are often facetious and, even more often, inconsistent. One must be wary to accord everything its appropriate level of importance or any person will appear a mass of contradictions.

In summary, when conducting historical research, you will want to use every means at your disposal to identify secondary and primary resources that can provide evidence concerning the subject of interest. Recommendations from colleagues, references, and footnotes in secondary sources and the library catalog and databases can all yield useful materials. As you interpret this evidence, you should also try to avoid some of the fallacies that can mar historical research: overgeneralization, reduction, tautologies, and misplaced literalism.

EXAMPLES

Two examples of historical research will be examined here. The first (Martin, 1988) is a historical study of the contributions of a leader in librarianship and library science education, Louis Round Wilson. It is organized chronologically and written as a PhD dissertation. The second (Buckland, 1992) makes an argument based on historical evidence and was published as a reasonably brief journal article. These two examples illustrate the wide range of forms that historical research can take.

Example 1: A History of One Man's Contributions to His Field

For his dissertation research, Robert S. Martin (1988) wrote a history of Louis Round Wilson's work at the University of North Carolina, 1901–1932. This dissertation represents a certain type of history—a monograph on a narrowly defined topic based on exhaustive primary research.

By most of the criteria described previously, Martin's (1988) dissertation succeeds as history. To begin, he made a judicious choice of subject. Not only did he limit himself to the life of one person, a wholly manageable subject, but he also chose a particular portion of that life that was exceedingly well documented. What was more, most of the primary sources that Martin would need were housed on the campus where he was completing his doctoral program. Finally, Louis Round Wilson was a person of sufficient historical importance that, although one published biography already existed (Tauber, 1967), his enormous accomplishments in North Carolina alone—including the founding of the library school at Chapel Hill, the establishment of the UNC Press, and a more than fivefold increase in the university library's holdings—merited further and closer study.

It may safely be said that Martin (1988) left no stone unturned in ferreting out primary sources. He sought out collections in archives and special collections in Atlanta, Georgia; Austin, Texas; Chapel Hill, North Carolina; Madison, Wisconsin; New York City; and Urbana, Illinois. He conducted three oral history interviews himself as well as drawing on others housed in the Southern Oral History Program in Chapel Hill. He consulted over 150 works published by Wilson during the latter's prodigious career. Finally, he appears to have mastered all relevant secondary literature and demonstrates a solid understanding not only of the specific events of Wilson's life but also of the wider historical context in which he operated. We say appears to have, because most histories, including this one, do not have explicit methods sections, and we really cannot know the ways in which Martin hunted down sources. But the reader can generally infer the thoroughness with which a given work was researched by perusing the footnotes and bibliography. In this case, Martin's expansiveness and level of sheer detail make it obvious what an enormous amount of legwork went into making his dissertation.

It is worth looking at one of Martin's (1988) footnotes as an example of historical documentation. In so doing, we acknowledge that history often does not document its sources in the same way as other disciplines. To wit:

"Report of the Librarian," *University Record*, no. 171 (December 1919): 95–96; Wilson to Snead and Co., August 8, 1918, November 9, 1918, and January 18, 1919, Librarian's Records, Box 3; "Memorandum of the North Carolina Collection, May 16, 1919," Mary L. Thornton Memorabilia, North Carolina Collection, UNC Library (VC027.7 N87un2; C. H. Hastings to Thornton, November 11, 1918, Thornton Memorabilia. (n. 103)

The first thing that strikes the reader is the multiple sources used by Martin, which one rarely sees in citations for other social sciences. The reason for this is that Martin, like many historians, chooses to footnote only at the end of paragraphs. This requires him to give all the sources he used for the entire paragraph. Historians do this so that footnotes will not break up the rhythm of their narrative. This circumstance often requires that a footnote carry a heavy documentation burden. The upshot, as in the preceding example, is a form of citation where readers sometimes have to puzzle out where the use of one source ends and the next begins. Thankfully, in recent years, it has become more common for historians to make explicit what quote or fact a given source backs up by, say, writing "first quote" in parentheses after a citation. If you want to leave no chance of confusion over which sources document which facts, it is probably better to footnote immediately after the relevant sentence.

In general, the writing of history tends to fall along a continuum. At one end of the continuum is thesis-driven, argumentative history. This kind of history is associated with the professionalization of the discipline in the late nineteenth and early twentieth centuries and emphasizes interpretation over description. At the other end of the continuum is descriptive, narrative history, which hearkens back to the dawn of Western civilization and today is often allied more closely with the journalistic tradition in the United States. Narrative history is usually organized by chronology—as opposed to what serves the argument—and its main preoccupation is with the telling of a (usually densely detailed) story. Of course, description and analysis can never be disentangled from one another; the act of deciding which details to include and which to discard in the telling of a story is eminently an act of interpretation. Martin's (1988) situation of Louis Round Wilson within the context of progressive era politics and mainline Protestantism demonstrates a deft analytic touch.

At bottom, though, Martin's (1988) history of Louis Round Wilson at the University of North Carolina seeks to construct a narrative. It seeks to document the deeds and accomplishments of a man of undeniable importance in the history of American academic librarianship; its argument is somewhat secondary to this other purpose. "This study examines in detail Wilson's career before Chicago," Martin writes in his prologue, by way of summarizing the book's purpose. "That career began in 1901 when he was appointed librarian at the University of North Carolina. During the next thirty years, he played a major role in the transition of that University from a small liberal arts school to a major research institution. Even beyond the campus, Wilson's activities in the professional associations demonstrated his capabilities as a leader and spokesman for education in general and libraries in particular" (Martin, 1988, p. 3). There is no doubt that Martin proves this argument many times over in the course of his nearly 800-page opus. On the other hand, we do not think anyone would take an opposing position, and it does not take a dissertation to prove this proposition. A critic might carp at Martin's failure to problematize his thesis, but that rather misses the point. For Martin, the primary objective is the account itself – the telling of an important story – and it is a task at which he succeeds brilliantly.

Example 2: Rethinking the Contribution of Bush's Memex

Buckland's (1992) work is the opposite of Martin's (1988) Wilson biography in almost every way. It is an article rather than a book-length study. At 10 pages long, it comes in at 782 fewer pages than Martin's work. Whereas Martin did extensive research in archives, for his research, Buckland consulted just over 80 articles and books (many of which might be considered primary sources). Finally, while Martin was content to document a life and make a very modest argument, Buckland speculated about "the background of information retrieval" during the first half of the twentieth century. Clearly Buckland's article falls at the other end of the continuum from Martin's dissertation.

Buckland's (1992) work is an instructive example of a *think piece* that makes an important and cogent argument without claiming too much for his evidence. Such think pieces often have the effect of moving debate forward and stimulating further research either in service of their argument or as a way of refuting it. Buckland seeks to reexamine the historical context of the publication of Vannevar Bush's (1945) seminal (or so the received wisdom has it) article "As We May Think," from the *Atlantic Monthly*. In that article, Bush imagined an information machine of the future, the "Memex." The Memex would be a "workstation containing the stored documents such that individual pages could be projected on to a screen at will." In addition, the machine would have the capacity of "adding new images to the store of microfilm," and "the ability not merely to locate a known record but to identify and select all and every record with any specified coding" (Buckland, 1992, p. 285). Some 50 years before the rise of widespread Internet use, Bush imagined a machine that allowed users to display all manner of media at will and not only to follow but also to establish links between works. Taken together, these links could form "associative trails," which to some observers prefigured technologies as far in the future as hypertext, wikis, social software networks, and even the semantic Web.

Given its apparent prescience, Bush's article has become something of a cultural touchstone since the Web's emergence as a daily fact of life in industrial and postindustrial societies. Ever since its publication, information scientists "constantly viewed and cited [it] in relation to *subsequent* developments in computing, information retrieval, and hypertext" (Buckland, 1992, p. 284). Buckland seemed to regard the omnipresence and significance attributed to Bush's article as oppressive or, at least, overstated. His aim in this article, therefore, was to try to introduce some context to Bush's article. When seen strictly as a bold and eerily accurate prediction of a new information age, "As We May Think" appears "strikingly original and visionary" (p. 284); if one just looks at what came later, Bush's forecasting ability may appear almost supernatural. But, Buckland contends, when one looks at what other information scientists were saying at the time, ideas that approximated the Memex were very much in the air.

Buckland (1992) focuses particularly on the vision of kinetics and photography scholar Emanuel Goldberg. Born in Russia in 1881, Goldberg had by the first decade of the twentieth century acceded to the German professorate, which at the time was in the process of inventing graduate education. His substantial scientific contributions "included a zinc plating process, the first handheld movie camera (the Kinamo), early involvement in television technology, and a well-received book *Der Aufbau des Photographischen Bildes* (The Construction of the Photographic Image)" (Buckland, 1992, pp. 288–289). For Buckland, though, Goldberg's greatest contribution may have been an obscure paper he delivered in 1932 that "describe[d] the design of a microfilm selector using a photoelectric cell. It [was], perhaps, the first paper on electronic document retrieval and describe[d] what seems to have been the first functioning document retrieval system using electronics" (p. 288). Buckland attributes the paper's continuing and undeserved obscurity to poor translations and Germany's fraught political environment at the time (pp. 288–290). Buckland furthermore argues that Goldberg's invention and its potential led European documentalists, including Paul Otlet, to make predictions about the future every bit as far-reaching and prescient as Bush's would appear to be a decade later. Finally, Buckland establishes that Goldberg's ideas were well known enough in the United States in the 1940s that Vannevar Bush would almost certainly have known about them and yet did not then or later credit his precursor. In other words, according to Buckland, Bush's article was less a watershed than many current-day information scientists make it out to be.

Obviously, Buckland is making an important argument here, and his historical detective work is a model for other scholars. In just over 10 pages, he makes a convincing case for a dramatic reconsideration of the legacy of a father of American information science. He was able to do so because (1) he chose a small enough (but simultaneously important enough) topic that was appropriate to an article-length treatment, (2) he thoroughly examined all the available evidence, and (3) he was able to situate his topic within the relevant historical context in such a way as to illuminate his argument. If one can do those three things in writing a historical article, she can be assured that the result will be successful.

CONCLUSION

Historical research is somewhat unique among the research methods covered in this book. Often it is more subject focused than question focused. It may result in a book with many footnotes or in a journal article. It may be organized chronologically or may be based on a particular thesis or argument. The review of sources and collection of evidence happen over a period of time, and each new piece of evidence leads to additional effort and additional evidence that pertains to the subject of the investigation. Such effort yields dividends by providing us with a better understanding of our profession's past and ideas for moving forward.

NOTES

1. We wish to thank Barry W. Seaver and Katherine M. Wisser for their feedback on an earlier draft of this chapter. While their feedback contributed to its quality, any misconceptions of fact or perspective are solely the responsibility of the authors.

2. In this chapter, collection of evidence will be emphasized over an *explicit* treatment of question formation and interpretation of evidence. While those processes are important to historical research, they are tightly integrated into and inform evidence collection. In focusing on evidence collection, therefore, we necessarily treat the others, to some extent.

3. Novick (1988) points out that the German phrase *Wie es eigentlich gewesen*, which has always been translated "as it really was" by von Ranke's detractors, is more properly rendered "as it essentially was." This interpretation would seem to make von Ranke's claim less unambiguously positivist than those wishing to set up von Ranke as a straw man might wish.

4. The guide is roughly based on the method put forward by Barzun (1992).

5. Even Michael H. Harris' work, *History of Libraries in the Western World* (1995), provides only an overview of libraries in one part of the world.

WORKS CITED

Barzun, J. (1992). *The Modern Researcher: The Classic Work on Research and Writing* (5th ed.). New York: Harcourt Brace Jovanovich.

Buckland, M. (1992). Emanuel Goldberg, electronic document retrieval, and Vannevar Bush's Memex. *Journal of the American Society for Information Science, 43*(4), 284–294.

Bush, V. (1945). As we may think. *Atlantic Monthly, 176*(1), 101–108.

Conkin, P. K., & Stromberg, R. N. (1971). *The Heritage and Challenge of History.* New York: Dodd, Mead.

Gottschalk, L. (1945). The historian and the historical document. In L. Gottschalk, C. Kluckhohn, & R. Angell (Eds.), *The Use of Personal Documents in History, Anthropology, and Sociology* (pp. 1–75). New York: Social Science Research Council.

Gunn, D. L. (1987). *A history of library extension at the University of North Carolina, 1912–1958.* Master's paper, School of Information and Library Science, University of North Carolina at Chapel Hill.

Martin, R. S. (1988). *Louis Round Wilson at the University of North Carolina, 1901–1932.* Unpublished doctoral dissertation, University of North Carolina at Chapel Hill.

Novick, P. (1988). *That Noble Dream: The "Objectivity Question" and the American Historical Profession.* New York: Cambridge University Press.

Tauber, M. F. (1967). *Louis Round Wilson: Librarian and Administrator.* New York: Columbia University Press.

ADDITIONAL RECOMMENDED READING

Appleby, J., Hunt, L., & Jacob, M. (1995). *Telling the Truth about History.* New York: W. W. Norton.

Berkhofer, R. F., Jr. (1997). *Beyond the Great Story: History as Text and Discourse.* Cambridge, MA: Belknap Press.

Carr, E. H. (1967). *What Is History?* New York: Vintage.

17

Existing Documents and Artifacts as Data

Barbara M. Wildemuth

Documents create a paper reality we call proof.
—Mason Cooley (1989)

The familiar material objects may not be all that is real, but they are admirable examples.
—Willard Van Orman Quine (1960)

INTRODUCTION

People often leave traces of their behavior in the documents they create or on the artifacts with which they interact. For example, a memo justifying the purchase of some computer equipment may provide the author's reasoning about the purposes for the purchase and plans for use of the equipment, and this representation of the author's reasoning may be as accurate and complete as an interview conducted after the equipment has been acquired. In another situation, the Post-it notes attached to various parts of someone's work space may allow a researcher to draw some conclusions about the work-arounds that that person has developed to complete particular work tasks most efficiently. Thus existing documents or traces of physical evidence may be a source of data about people's information behaviors.

The primary reason that documents or artifacts might be used as a source of data for a research study is that they exist. More important, the process of data collection will not influence their content in the same way that more intrusive methods (such as interviewing someone or directly observing her) have an effect on the information behaviors being studied. For this reason, these data are often referred to as nonreactive measures or as data collected through unobtrusive methods. A second reason for incorporating such data into your study is that, at least in some instances, this type of data could be a more accurate representation of the phenomenon of interest than data collected through self-report (as through an interview or questionnaire; Hodder, 2000). Because the person exhibiting the information behavior is not aware that the behavior will be the object of study in the future, he or she will be unguarded—that behavior will be truly "natural" (Neuman, 2006). It is this aspect of such data that leads Gray (2004) to describe it as "dead" data (p. 263) because it is preexisting and can no longer be altered by its creator (or by the researcher).

When considering the use of such data, there are two primary steps (Neuman, 2006). The first is to clearly conceptualize the phenomenon of interest. It might be the amount of user interest in a particular section of a Web site or the amount of use of a portion of a library's collection. It might be a historical time line of a series of events or the evolution of a wiki entry. In any case, you first need to be clear about the definition of the phenomenon in which you're interested. Second, you need to define the link between the phenomenon of interest and the documents or physical traces you will use to study it. If you are interested in the amount of use of a particular section of a library collection, you might physically examine the due dates stamped in the books in that section. Alternatively, you might examine the online circulation records for that portion of the collection. This second method would likely be considered superior because the first method misses data on all the books currently circulating. As part of your study design, you will need to provide a clear rationale for the link between the phenomenon of interest and the documents or artifacts observed. In addition, you will need to be able to rule out alternative causes (other than the phenomenon of interest) for the physical or documentary evidence you observe.

DOCUMENTS AS DATA

Every day, many documents are created. As defined by Scott (1990), a document is "an artefact which has as its central feature an inscribed text" (p. 5); to be considered a document (rather than just an artifact), the text must contain an intentional message, fulfilling a particular purpose of its creator. Such documents may later be of interest as the source for data for a research study. While they were not created to support the study, they are useful to it. These documents are of many different types and published in many different forms and media (both physical and virtual). They include, but are not limited to, the following:

- Public/official documents, for example, birth and death records, legislation, court records
- Financial documents of an organization, for example, SEC filings, annual financial statements
- Official statements and reports, for example, an organization's annual report, project reports, press releases, organizational charts
- Memos or other communications within organizations, for example, internal memos, e-mail, minutes of meetings
- Diaries (discussed in a separate chapter) and personal records created for individual use
- Images or video recordings, for example, photos, videos, maps, floor plans of office settings

As you can see from this list, some of these documents are relatively "official" within an organizational context, while others are very informal and semiprivate. As Denscombe (2003) notes, the more official records have two characteristics that make them particularly attractive to researchers: they're created and stored in a relatively systematic way, and they're likely to be available to a researcher. Documents created for a more private purpose are often episodic (Gray, 2004) and less likely to be accessible to a researcher.

Working with documents as a data source raises two important issues. The first is that the documents exist (Platt, 1981). While this is what makes them attractive as a data source, it also means that the researcher cannot control what they cover, how they were created, and/or whether they survive to be included in the study's data set. Thus the researcher must consider issues of sampling very carefully to understand whether the documents at hand are representative of the population of documents of interest for a particular study. Even if a set of documents is known to exist, the researcher may be restricted from using them through lack of access or concerns about their confidentiality (Denscombe, 2003; Patton, 2002). The second issue is that, to interpret the meaning of a document correctly, the researcher must know quite a bit about the social context in which it was created. In some cases, the document itself must be authenticated to ensure it is what it seems to be (Scott, 1990). In all cases, the researcher will need to consider whether the document is "telling the truth" in what it says. Documents are "socially contructed realities" (Miller, 1997, p. 77), and it is very possible that a particular document presents "a particular interpretation of what happened" (Denscombe, 2003, p. 214), related to the purpose for which it was created. As Hodder (2000) notes, "meaning does not reside in a text, but in the writing and reading of it" (p. 704). Keeping these issues in mind, you can plan for the way in which you will incorporate documentary evidence in your study.

ARTIFACTS AS DATA

As people interact with information, they often leave physical traces of their behavior behind (Bernard, 2000). Classic indicators of use are the wear on the flooring tiles around a particular museum exhibit or the number of smudges and annotations in a book. In information and library science, we are also likely to be interested in people's online information behaviors and can instrument our information systems to capture traces of such behaviors. Nicholson (2005) argues that use of such data is analogous to an archaeologist's examination of physical objects left behind by a particular culture and proposes *bibliomining* as an approach to studying people's use of a digital library. Because transaction logs are so frequently used as an indicator of online user behaviors, they are discussed in detail in a separate chapter (Chapter 18). Here we will focus on other types of artifacts and physical trace data.

Most physical trace data can be categorized as either erosion or accretion. Erosion is "degree of selective wear on some material" and accretion is "the deposit of materials" (Webb et al., 2000, p. 36). It should be noted that with the advent of digital information objects, both erosion and accretion from their use may be less visible than when all information objects were physical (Gray, 2004).

With either erosion or accretion, the evidence may be categorized as natural or controlled. Most often, it is natural, in the sense that it was created during the subject's normally occurring activities. However, the researcher can exert some influence on the data production or capture processes. For example, the researcher might place a small, slightly adhesive sticker between two pages of a magazine to be able to tell whether the reader opened those pages. More often in information and library science, the researcher is likely to instrument a computer or a Web site to be able to more accurately capture user interactions with it.

As with handling documents, treating artifacts as sources of data raises particular issues. The first of these is access—does the researcher have access to the physical traces that can be used as data? For example, if you were trying to study people's reading habits by examining the books they have on their own bookshelves, you would need to obtain permission to enter each study participant's home. Access becomes less of an issue when studying information behaviors performed in public spaces such as libraries, museums, or on a Web site. The second issue that is particular to working with artifacts is the validity of the measure being used. Any physical artifact "has to be interpreted in relation to a situated context of production, use, discard, and reuse" (Hodder, 2000, p. 706). As noted earlier, the researcher must explicitly link the physical evidence being observed to the phenomenon of interest. If we return to the example given previously, where the phenomenon of interest is the level of use of a particular portion of a library collection, we could use several different types of physical trace data. We already mentioned the use of due dates stamped in each book and online circulation records as indicators of each book's circulation. However, if we want to define "book use" as reading the book (rather than as checking it out of the library), we might want to use indicators such as the amount of wear on the pages or the amount of underlining and annotation on each page. For each study, you will need to carefully define your phenomenon of interest, then make sure that the physical indicators of that phenomenon (erosion or accretion) are valid measures of it.

ANALYZING DATA OBTAINED FROM DOCUMENTS AND ARTIFACTS

In speaking about using documents as a data source, Platt (1981) rightly comments that documentary research "can hardly be regarded as constituting a method, since to say that one will use documents is to say nothing about *how* one will use them" (p. 31). Documents and physical trace data are so varied in their forms and meanings that methods for analyzing the data gathered will need to be designed for each study. Most often, these methods will include some form of content analysis (see Chapters 29 and 30), but in some cases, other types of statistical or qualitative analysis methods are more appropriate. In essentially every study, data obtained from documents or artifacts will need to be analyzed in combination with data obtained using other methods. This approach is often called *triangulation*, as data from multiple sources are integrated to draw more valid conclusions. For example, memos describing the development of a new information system might be triangulated with interviews conducted with system developers to draw more valid conclusions about the process. In another study, data drawn from library circulation records about use of the science materials in the university library might be triangulated with a survey of science faculty and graduate students to draw more valid conclusions about the use of that portion of the library collection. Thus other data sources can be used to validate and cross-check the findings drawn from use of documents and artifacts (Patton, 2002). In this way, some of the weaknesses of data drawn from documents and artifacts can be minimized.

EXAMPLES

Three examples will be discussed here. The first (Maxwell, 2005) is a typical example of the use of publicly available documents to understand, in this case, the construction of the meaning of the term *homeland security*. The second (Buchwald, 2000) illustrates the way in which documents created within an organization can be used to study that organization, particularly if the researcher is a member of that organization. The third

(Dube, 2005) combines the use of documents and other artifacts as evidence of the way in which a university communicates to its students and faculty about health issues.

Example 1: Public Documents as Data

Relying on the texts in publicly available documents, Maxwell (2005) traced the development of the term *homeland security* (first used in a 2000 report of the U.S. Commission on National Security) and how its meaning changed over time and across different groups. Maxwell based his analysis on published and publicly available documents. His sample was a set of 286 documents that were related to this concept. The sample included reports, recommendations, journal articles, and press releases. It included 96 documents published by U.S. government agencies, identified on the Web sites of the Department of Homeland Security and the White House as well as through Lexis-Nexis searches on those agencies; 112 documents from the General Accounting Office (GAO) collection on homeland security, retrieved from the GAO Web site; 68 documents from academic and nonprofit organizations, "retrieved from the Social Sciences Abstracts database, the *Public Administration Review* and searches on organizational Web sites mentioned in Congressional hearings, news reports, Web searches, and government and organizational studies" (Maxwell, 2005, p. 159); and 10 local government reports, retrieved from local government association Web sites and Web searches. This procedure for identifying relevant documents is appropriate. It is unclear how documents were selected from those identified as potentially useful; presumably all the documents in the data set, at a minimum, included the phrase *homeland security* and provided some discussion of it.

Each text was assumed to take a particular perspective on homeland security. They were analyzed in multiple phases. First, relevant concepts and the terms used to represent them were identified by analyzing the texts with concordance software. This process resulted in the identification of 73 coding terms, such as the term *oversight*, which was coded as representing an instance of control in interorganizational behavior, or the term *constructive conflict*, which was coded as representing an instance of responsive change in change orientation. Using this coding scheme, the texts were then fully coded (using AtlasTi software). From this point, factor analysis based on the use of codes within individual documents was used to reduce the number of terms to be examined in further analysis. For example, the terms *mutual aid*, *coordination*, and *facilitation*, among others, were combined into one concept, *cooperative relationships*. Finally, an analysis of variance compared the codes associated with different agencies and/or authors and found that different agencies did have different understandings of the concept *homeland security*.

In summary, "this study has explored the homeland security symbol from two perspectives: First, as the structure and outcome of a debate in the political sphere that institutionalized the symbol in legislation and administrative mandates; and secondly, as an organizing theme through which stakeholders in the administrative knowledge creation process debated the requirements of cooperation, coordination, and action within inter-governmental networks" (Maxwell, 2005, p. 166). It used a computer-supported type of content analysis to understand the many concepts related to the term *homeland security* in a variety of types of documents created by both government agencies and academic researchers. Thus it is an example of the collection and analysis of publicly available documents.

Example 2: Use of Organizational Documents by a Member of the Organization

This second example[1] is also set within the context of the public sector and focuses on "the role of a public interest group, Canada's Coalition for Public Information, in the federal information policymaking process for the information highway" (Buchwald, 2000, p. 123), with particular emphasis on universal access policies. In this study, the use of data from documents was incorporated within a naturalistic research design that also incorporated participant observation and interviews. Participant observation occurred primarily at the monthly Coalition for Public Information (CPI) steering committee meetings, but also at other meetings and through observation of the messages on the CPI Listserv. Initial interviews were conducted with three members of the steering committee executive group, followed by 22 additional interviews with participants in the policy-making process.

The documents included in the data set were primarily those created by CPI and were collected as they were created. As a participant, Buchwald (2000) was able to collect many of these documents from their creators and so was able to include many documents that would not have been available to an outside researcher. The final set of documents in the data set included "submissions to government hearings, correspondence among members via the internet, internet correspondence among public interest groups, and correspondence with federal government ministers... [CPI] meeting minutes, flyers, position papers, responses to reports, interventions to the CRTC, and its seminal policy document *Future-Knowledge*" (p. 130). In this study, it is likely that the author was able to collect all or almost all the relevant documents. In addition, this set of data was not too big to include in its entirety. Thus issues related to sampling and representativeness were resolved because the entire population of relevant documents was included in the analysis.

An inductive qualitative approach to analyzing the content of these documents was taken, incorporating them into the full data set, which included field memos (documenting the observations) and interview transcripts. In addition, the author was explicit in triangulating her findings, across sources (observations, interviews, and documents) and across creators (CPI, government agencies, industry participants, etc.). In addition, Buchwald (2000) followed Hodder's (2000) recommendation that the conclusions drawn from a study must be internally coherent and must also correspond to the available theoretical frameworks (of which two—policy community theory and policy process theory—were used by Buchwald).

In summary, this example demonstrates how analysis of documents can be integrated into a study that also draws data from other sources such as observation and interviews. It is also an example of a very naturalistic research design, incorporating a thematic analysis of the document content.

Example 3: Artifacts as Evidence of Information Communication Behaviors

The purpose of Dube's (2005) study was to investigate "the framework, nature and scope of HIV/AIDS information communication strategies employed by higher education institutions in South Africa" (p. 315). Thirty-six institutions of higher education in South Africa were surveyed about the ways in which they communicated information about HIV/AIDS to their students; 33 responded. The respondents in each institution "were the HIV/AIDS service providers/intermediaries, institutional libraries and health centres" (p. 318), though it was not clear whether multiple people at each institution responded to similar questionnaires, or one person at each institution responded on behalf of that institution.

In addition to the survey data, Dube (2005) collected data through campus site visits, directly observing the "billboards, signs, posters, pamphlets, brochures, slogans, etc." (p. 319) that were visible on each campus. An observation guide was used to capture data about these artifacts, making the findings comparable across institutions. While I am depicting these objects as artifacts, they might more accurately be described as documents because, in Scott's (1990) words, their "central feature [is] an inscribed text" (p. 5). From another perspective, they (in particular, the billboards, signs, and posters) can be seen as a measure of accretion, with their visible presence on campus being treated as an indicator of the institution's communication behaviors.

Since two visits were made to each campus to observe the communication media in use, we can assume that the sample of artifacts observed was relatively complete and representative. It is not as clear how they were interpreted. Dube (2005) does not clearly differentiate the findings based on these observations and the findings based on the survey results. While the concept of triangulation is mentioned, it is not clear how the observation data were juxtaposed against the survey data to provide a more accurate picture of each campus's communication behaviors.

In summary, this study is a good example of the way that artifacts can be directly observed and incorporated into a study that also uses other data collection methods (i.e., a survey). The use of an observation guide to ensure the reliability of the data gathered across campuses is a strength of this study's methods. It would also have been useful to include a more explicit discussion of the ways in which the observation data and the survey data supported or conflicted with each other.

CONCLUSION

The use of evidence gathered directly from preexisting documents or artifacts can greatly strengthen a study. If an appropriate sample can be gathered, this nonreactive approach to data collection can allow the researcher to see some aspects of a situation that could not be detected through more intrusive data collection methods such as interviews or questionnaires. While it has some advantages, this data collection approach is rarely used alone; it is more often used to provide a different perspective on a particular phenomenon. In this way, findings from multiple data sources can be used to draw more valid conclusions about the phenomenon of interest.

NOTE

1. This work was the recipient of the 2000 Eugene Garfield Doctoral Dissertation Award from the Association for Library and Information Science Education.

WORKS CITED

Bernard, H. R. (2000). *Social Research Methods: Qualitative and Quantitative Approaches.* Thousand Oaks, CA: Sage.

Buchwald, C. C. (2000). A case study of Canada's Coalition for Public Information in the information highway policy-making process. *Library and Information Science Research*, 22(2), 123–144.

Cooley, M. (1989). *City Aphorisms: Sixth Selection*. New York: Pascal Press.

Denscombe, M. (2003). *The Good Research Guide for Small-Scale Social Research Projects* (2nd ed.). Maidenhead, England: Open University Press.

Dube, L. (2005). Insights into the diffusion of HIV/AIDS information in higher education institutions in South Africa. *International Information and Library Review*, 37(4), 315–327.

Gray, D. E. (2004). *Doing Research in the Real World*. London: Sage.

Hodder, I. (2000). The interpretation of documents and material culture. In N. K. Denzin & Y. S. Lincoln (eds.), *Handbook of Qualitative Research* (2nd ed., pp. 703–716). Thousand Oaks, CA: Sage.

Maxwell, T. A. (2005). Constructing consensus: Homeland security as a symbol of government politics and administration. *Government Information Quarterly*, 22(2), 152–169.

Miller, G. (1997). Contextualizing texts: Studying organizational texts. In G. Miller & R. Dingwall (eds.), *Context and Method in Qualitative Research* (pp. 77–91). Thousand Oaks, CA: Sage.

Neuman, W. L. (2006). *Social Research Methods: Qualitative and Quantitative Approaches* (6th ed.). Boston: Pearson.

Nicholson, S. (2005). Digital library archaeology: A conceptual framework for understanding library use through artifact-based evaluation. *Library Quarterly*, 75(4), 496–520.

Patton, M. Q. (2002). *Qualitative Research and Evaluation Methods* (3rd ed.). Thousand Oaks, CA: Sage.

Platt, J. (1981). Evidence and proof in documentary research: I. Some specific problems of documentary research. *The Sociological Review*, 29(1), 31–52.

Quine, W.V.O. (1960). *Word and Object*. Cambridge: Technology Press of the Massachusetts Institute of Technology.

Scott, J. (1990). *A Matter of Record*. Cambridge, MA: Polity Press.

Webb, E. J., Campbell, D. T., Schwartz, R. D., & Sechrest, L. (2000). *Unobtrusive Measures* (Rev. ed.). Thousand Oaks, CA: Sage.

18

Transaction Logs

Laura Sheble and Barbara M. Wildemuth

Computers "remember" things in the form of discrete entries: the input of quantities, graphics, words, etc. Each item is separable, perhaps designated by a unique address or file name, and all of it subject to total recall. Unless the machine malfunctions, it can regurgitate everything it has stored exactly as it was entered, whether a single number or a lengthy document. This is what we expect of the machine.

—Theodore Roszak (1986)

INTRODUCTION

Many computer applications record people's interactions with the application in a transaction log (i.e., a log of each transaction that occurred).[1] For example, Web server logs commonly record several data elements for each transaction, including the client (or proxy) IP address, the date and time of each page request, and which files were requested. In addition to Web server logs, data obtained from proprietary sources, such as search engine or electronic resource companies, or data obtained from logging programs integrated into library systems are commonly analyzed in the information and library science field. Log data are used by researchers to study user-system interaction behaviors, such as search and browse behaviors, as well as system-mediated interpersonal interactions, such as reference and support chat services.[2]

It is possible to obtain both server-side and client-side log files. Server-side logs are those that are part of the server's software and record the transactions in which the server was involved. Client-side logs are those that are captured on the user's machine (i.e., laptop, desktop, or other similar computer) and can record all the user's actions, no matter which servers are accessed. The software necessary to capture client-side logs must usually be written for a particular study and then loaded on each machine that participants will use during the study. Server-side studies are much more prevalent, partly due to the higher costs and more complicated logistics associated with collecting client-side log data.

Use of transaction log analysis research has undergone relatively rapid development since its first cited use in the mid-1960s (Jansen, 2006; Peters, 1993). Transaction log analysis is used to study many different types of systems, including online library catalogs (e.g., Blecic et al., 1999), digital libraries (e.g., Jones et al., 2004), specific Web sites (e.g., Marchionini, 2002; Wang et al., 2003), and Web search engines (see Markey, 2007). Transaction log analysis is used with both inductive research (at the exploratory or even more in-depth analysis levels) and deductive research (i.e., hypothesis-testing) approaches (Buttenfield & Reitsma, 2002). Several researchers (e.g., Borgman et al., 1996; Jansen, 2006; Jansen & Pooch, 2001; Marchionini, 2002; Peters, 1993) have outlined domains of inquiry appropriate to transaction log analysis methods. These domains include evaluation of system performance or interface functionality (Hiramatsu, 2002), Web site use and navigation patterns (e.g., Catledge & Pitkow, 1995), information seeking behavior (see Borgman et al., 1996), social networks (e.g., Ravid & Rafaeli, 2004), and electronic resource use patterns (e.g., Goddard, 2007a, 2007b; Nicholas et al., 2005). In commercial and service environments, transaction logs are sometimes used as a source of feedback data to gauge immediate or potential resource allocation and as evidence for decision support (e.g., Atlas et al., 1997).

ADVANTAGES AND LIMITATIONS

Transaction log analysis (TLA), as a research approach, has several advantages. First, as discussed previously, the captured data represent a record of events as they actually occurred, without the reframing and recall errors prevalent in many other data collection methods. Using transaction logs, the quality of your data will not be dependent on the study participant's memory of the interaction or on his or her ability to describe the interaction. Second, it draws on large volumes of data collected from a great number of users. It can be conducted at a large scale and thus may be more representative of larger populations than some more intensive methods. Third, it can be used both to build quantitative models and to assist in qualitative interpretations of qualitative models (Borgman et al., 1996). Finally, it is appropriate to both experimental and field study research designs. Transaction logs can be captured during experimental sessions; usually, client-side logs are captured so that more control can be exerted on which data elements are included in the data set. Transaction logs can also be captured "in the wild" (e.g., from the server supporting a particular Web site).

Server-side logs also have several other advantages. Relatively few resources are required to gather log data, provided appropriate logging programs are available. Because interpersonal interactions are minimized during the data collection process, server-side logs are relatively objective in their representations of user behaviors. Because recording of transaction data occurs in the background, data capture is unobtrusive.

Client-side transaction logs differ significantly from server-side logs in that use of client-side logs can be very resource-intensive. Researchers must recruit participants, install and test logging programs on the participants' machines, and (sometimes) collect data from a variety of machines and users (Kelly, 2006a, 2006b; Yun et al., 2006). Additionally, client-side logging programs are not as readily available to researchers. Some (e.g., Kelly, 2006a, 2006b) have used logging programs developed for the spyware[3] market, and others (e.g., Yun et al., 2006) have developed customized applications or browsers to log client-side events. At the same time, client-side logging provides the opportunity to collect data sets that include details of user actions across a variety of applications and Web sites, whereas server-side logs are restricted to server-based events. Laboratory-based transaction log analysis studies (e.g., Card et al., 2001) may fall anywhere along the continuum between client-side and server-side TLA methods with respect to advantages and limitations in sample size and are not discussed in detail here. It should be noted, however, that laboratory-based designs differ notably from other types of TLA in that they are generally highly controlled, task-based approaches, rather than naturalistic field studies, and may augment the transaction logs with other data such as think-aloud protocols or eye tracking.[4]

When using transaction log analysis, it is important to be aware of the limitations represented by the data set. First, it must be recognized that information about the context in which events recorded in a log file occurred is not collected. Log files do not collect information about the experiential context of the event such as user motives, intentions, and satisfaction with results. The only way to overcome this limitation is to combine the capture of transaction logs with other types of data collection methods. For example, study participants may be interviewed, may respond to questionnaires, or may be asked to think aloud during their interactions with the information system. Unfortunately, combining data collection methods means that you sacrifice the unobtrusiveness and large scale with which studies can be conducted if they rely solely on transaction logs (Jansen, 2006). At the same time, the addition of context and data not accessible through transaction logs often outweighs these limitations.

There are also technical limitations with respect to how data are collected in the case of both server-side and client-side transaction logs. A major concern with server-side log files is that they do not capture page requests that are fulfilled by means of file copies cached on local machines or proxy servers. It has been estimated that as many as 45 percent of page requests are fulfilled from cached content (Nicholas, 2000). The proportion of page requests fulfilled from cached content will vary depending on a number of Web site structure, size, and use factors. There is not a formula to predict how much and which content will be retrieved from cached copies (Fieber, 1999). Thus researchers should be cautious about the conclusions they draw from server-side log studies.

Another challenge to using server-side log files is that unless servers artificially maintain a connection with the client, require logins, or send cookies, it is difficult to distinguish individual system users (Marchionini, 2002). While it may be appropriate to some research questions to identify groups of users by characteristics of viewed content (e.g., Keegan et al., 2006), researchers must generally rely on identifying user sessions through a combination of the date and time stamp and IP addresses. Furthermore, identified IP addresses may relate to use by an individual, by more than one individual on a shared or public machine, or by a proxy server.

Another limitation of transaction log data is that it can be very cumbersome to process and analyze large volumes of data. Processing and manipulating large volumes of data is becoming less of a concern with the development of tools that can be used to work with transaction log data. Furthermore, abundant use of transaction logs in research and private industry provides precedents with respect to data handling and processing. Also, with continuing interest in transaction log analysis, it is likely that some of the technology-related challenges associated with this method will at least be mitigated. For example, Jansen (2006) has recently developed a tool, the Wrapper, that can be used in remote naturalistic studies.

The unobtrusiveness of transaction log capture raises some concerns about the ethical issues associated with collecting and using data without informing participants. Some researchers may believe that transaction logs captured from a large, often international audience (as in studies of Web server logs) ensure anonymity for the people being studied; however, the courts do not agree.[5] Client-side log studies entail extensive contact and interaction between researchers and participants, so informed consent can easily be obtained. Both researchers who use client-side logging methods and those who use server-side log files need to be careful with respect to how personal information, including query strings, is handled, so that their study participants' privacy can be maintained.

PROCESS OF TRANSACTION LOG ANALYSIS

Three key steps in the process of transaction log analysis are discussed here: (1) identification of appropriate data elements and sources, (2) data collection, and (3) data cleansing and preparation. In practice, the steps outlined here might overlap, depending on the research question and study logistics.

Identification of Appropriate Data Elements and Sources

As noted previously, most research is conducted using log data captured by existing logging programs. Data collected by a logging program should be reviewed with respect to the research questions. In some cases, it may be possible and appropriate to adjust the configuration of a logging program prior to data collection to collect the desired data. In studies that examine data over an extended period of time (e.g., Wang et al., 2003), previously collected log data may enforce constraints on data that are analyzed in subsequent studies. The length of time for which data collection will occur should also be determined. In TLA studies, this varies greatly, from multiple years, as in one study of an academic Web site (Wang et al., 2003), to one day, as in the Excite search engine studies of Jansen et al. (1998a, 1998b).

Additional steps might also be taken at this stage, such as the development of a coding scheme to categorize Web pages or Web page types according to content or expected use variables, or identification of IP addresses or ranges of IP addresses that are of interest. Supplementary data sources, such as Web site topology, might also be identified at this time. If not previously determined, identification of research methods to complement TLA methods should also be identified.

Data Collection

Data collection should be a relatively straightforward activity in the case of server-side transaction log studies. Nonetheless, researchers should monitor data logging and ensure that data are being captured as expected. In the case of client-side transaction log studies, data should be monitored and/or collected at regular intervals throughout the study. This is especially important because client-side studies require substantial resources per case studied. In many cases, this is also the appropriate time to collect data from other previously identified data sources and data from complementary methods.

Data Cleansing and Preparation

Data cleansing and preparation is a critical stage of transaction log studies. Two important activities are performed during the data cleansing process: (1) corrupt and extraneous data are discarded and (2) raw data files are processed to obtain secondary data sets based on desired units of analysis such as user sessions, query sessions, or term occurrences. The exact steps taken to process data will depend on the nature of the research question and the composition of the collected data set. Commonly, data are imported into a relational database, a spreadsheet application is used, text processing scripts are run on the data, or a combination of these methods is applied. Generally, it is a good idea to assign a unique ID to entries at the beginning of the data cleansing process. It may also be useful to produce and record summary statistics related to discarded data.

After corrupt data are discarded, it is necessary to achieve a uniform and useful definition of page accesses. When server-side logs record transactions, there are often numerous lines associated with the download and display of one page. Often, researchers discard files of specific types, such as log file entries initiated by spiders or search bots as well as entries associated with image files, server-side includes, and other embedded files that compose a page. Eliminating the former reduces entries to those that were likely to have been created by humans, and the latter reduces transaction counts to a single entry for each requested page. In studies where images are the primary focus, it might be better to retain image files of a given type and/or size and discard log entries associated with display of other elements. Rather than specific file types, files can be selected for inclusion or exclusion based on a list of specific file names (Cooley et al., 1999). Alternatively, some researchers choose to encode pages based on the content they contain or based on presuppositions related to the primary function(s) of each page. Page coding, along with user identification, session identification, query term–based data sets, and path completion, are discussed briefly later.

User and Session Identification

Identification of unique users, users of interest, or groups of users, such as those from a range of IP addresses of public access terminals or some other characteristic, is necessary for most data analyses. It is likely that you'll want to limit your data set to those actions taken by individual users (rather than robots) on single-user terminals. Jansen (2006) suggests that in Web query analysis, you can identify the relevant transactions based on the search engine–assigned user ID set by a cookie and a threshold to the number of transactions (e.g., less than 101). In studies that use Web log data that do not have user identification markers, such as cookies or login data, IP addresses can be used in conjunction with other data.

The goal of session identification is to divide a stream of transactions into individual sessions. Once you've identified a particular user's transactions, you can apply a threshold to define the maximum reasonable session length (see Jansen et al., 2007, for an investigation of methods for defining a session). If the time between transactions exceeds a predefined threshold, it can be assumed that the user started a new session. Many studies use 30 minutes as a threshold. Determining a temporal threshold for session identification should not be arbitrary because subsequent analysis will rely on how sessions are identified. Defining sessions too narrowly will result in single user sessions being divided into multiple sessions, and defining sessions too broadly will group single user sessions together. Though it is nearly inevitable that a single threshold cannot define sessions with complete accuracy, knowledge of site use, content, and experience from studies in related domains should all be used to inform threshold identification and derive a so-called reasonable level. As an example of a variation from the common 30-minute threshold, Keegan et al. (2006) defined a 60-minute threshold for their study, which examined search behaviors of users of a bilingual newspaper digital library based on language use characteristics. Other studies have set thresholds as low as five minutes. Together, user identification and session identification will allow you to divide your data into individual user sessions.

Classifying and Coding Information Behaviors

In each session, the study participant will have exhibited particular information behaviors, as captured in the logs. If the research question is relatively straightforward (e.g., which terms are used most often in Web queries?), you are ready to proceed to data analysis (e.g., Pu et al., 2002; Spink et al., 2000). However, for many research questions (e.g., how did the study participant formulate and reformulate a search strategy?), the individual actions captured in the log need to be classified, grouping similar types of behaviors. Seen from another perspective, each behavior is assigned a code from a small set of well-defined codes.

Various coding schemes have been devised for use in studying searching behaviors. Of particular note are the early schemes developed by Bates (1979) and Fidel (1985), based on the types of behaviors seen in professional searchers' interactions with literature databases. Shute and Smith (1993), taking a similar approach, devised a knowledge-based scheme that could be applied across different types of databases (see Wildemuth, 2004, for further discussion). Development of coding schemes is continuing, with Rieh and Xie (2006) recently taking a faceted approach. You will want to examine various possible coding schemes prior to data analysis and select a scheme that will serve your study's purposes. Be sure to pay attention to both the content of the coding scheme (so that it matches the aspects of the logged information behaviors in which you're interested) and its granularity (so that further analysis is at the appropriate level of generality).

Classifying and Coding Pages and Their Characteristics

The focus of your research question may be on the characteristics of the pages viewed. For some studies, you will be interested only in which pages among a set of pages (e.g., a Web site) were viewed and the frequency with which they were viewed. For other studies, you might be interested in the navigation path of the user (i.e., the sequence of pages viewed). For either of these purposes, you may want to classify or code pages so that you can draw conclusions about the *types* of pages viewed, rather than about individual pages.

Page coding can be performed at a number of levels based on page content, the relationship between the page and the overall system, and/or page functionality. Some common examples of page coding include classification of Web site pages according to site topology or according to page function. For example, Cooley et al. (1999) suggested that Web site pages could be classified based on whether a page is the head (i.e., home) page, a content page, a navigation page, a look-up page, or a personal page. Other commonly used page coding approaches include categorization of a page according to its position in a results set, based on the document or file type in a database or digital library, or based on its position and function with respect to a user process such as a search session (e.g., Mat-Hassan & Levene, 2005). Other methods of page coding could be based on the ratio of links to text, the proportion of image files, average reference length, relevant information contained in page metadata, and so on.

Path Completion

Path completion is used in Web log mining applications to add missing page references to a log so that important page accesses that are not recorded due to page caching are included in the refined log that will be analyzed. Path completion algorithms examine navigation patterns based on site topology and time- or session-delimited page access histories. If a given navigation sequence includes a highly unlikely sequence that has been determined to have been within the session of a given user, the algorithm adds an entry or entries for the most recently visited requested pages that trace the path of that user back to a point in the site directly linked to the page in question. Time stamps can also be added to the created log entry based on the average reference length for a page or page type (Cooley et al., 1999; Pitkow, 1997).

Analysis

Once the data have been cleaned and prepared, analysis can begin. Such analysis may range from simple frequency distributions of query terms to advanced methods for sequential analysis. See Part 5 for a discussion of some analysis possibilities.

EXAMPLES

We will examine two studies that relied on transaction logs as a source of data. The first (Jörgensen & Jörgensen, 2005) examines the image-searching behaviors of image professionals searching a stock photography Web site. Their results included frequency distributions of searches, search terms, types of terms and Boolean operators used, query modifications, and browsing of results. In the second example, Davis (2004) examined the ways in which chemists reached particular articles in a database produced by the American Chemical Society (ACS). The focus of the analysis was on the referral URLs, "a Web address that directs (or refers) a browser to another address" (p. 327), reporting the frequency with which different types of referrals occurred over a three-month period.

Example 1: Image Professionals Searching a Stock Photography Web Site

Jörgensen and Jörgensen (2005)[6] investigated the image-searching behaviors of image professionals (e.g., those engaged in advertising, marketing, graphic design, etc.) as they accessed a commercial stock photography site on the Web. The researchers were given access to one month's logs for their study. Because they wanted to code some of the search behaviors manually, they selected two samples from this full data set. Their final samples each included 5 percent of the search sessions conducted over a month (415 sessions in the first sample and 426 sessions in the second sample). Sessions were identified by a system-assigned session ID; it was also confirmed during the manual coding process. Each session might consist of one or more searches, with a search being defined as "a set of related queries all addressing the same subject or topic" (p. 1349). "As a general guideline if more than 2 minutes elapsed between the last session action and the next query, a new search was presumed to have started" (p. 1349). Sample 1 included 679 searches (made up of 1,439 queries) and sample 2 included 692 searches (made up of 1,371 queries). Even with the selection of small random samples from the logs, Jörgensen and Jörgensen (2005) were analyzing data on a much larger scale than most experimental studies of searching behaviors. In addition, they had the advantage of capturing naturalistic data, with the study participants conducting searches for real questions.

These transaction logs required minimal cleaning; unnecessary characters were removed, then the data were imported into a spreadsheet for coding and further analysis. The researchers noted when a new search was initiated, which searches were successful (i.e., they retrieved one or more images), the number of terms in each query, the type of query term, spelling errors in the query terms, and modifications to the query during the search. The types of query terms were primarily based on parts of speech and included adjectives, nouns, and verbs. In addition, some terms were classified as "concept terms" when they represented abstract concepts and as "visual constructs" when a specific image was described in the query. Proper nouns and dates were also coded. As the authors pointed out, this type of specificity required manual coding; none of the current automatic methods can reliably apply codes based on these types of semantic definitions. Thus the authors chose to work with a smaller sample so that a richer coding scheme could be used.

Though query modifications were coded and their frequencies tabulated, no sequential analysis of search tactics was conducted. The coding scheme used for query modifications would have supported such an analysis. It included the addition of a term to the query, the elimination of a term, and changing a term. In addition, the nature of the change was coded, when a term was added or changed, as a narrower, broader, or related term. This coding scheme is similar to the coding scheme used by both Wildemuth (2004) and Rieh and Xie (2006); it would have been useful if one of the earlier schemes had been employed so that these image search behaviors could be compared directly to studies of other types of searching behaviors.

While there are some ways in which this study might have been expanded, it was successful in providing some baseline data concerning image searching by image professionals. As the authors pointed out, their results helped to fill a gap in our understanding of people's searching behaviors.

Example 2: Information Seeking Behavior of Chemists—An Analysis of Referral URLs

Davis (2004) analyzed server-side transaction logs to better understand the tools and pathways used by Cornell University scientists to locate electronic journals hosted by the ACS. Davis was particularly interested in referral data, that is, the Web addresses recorded when a user's Web browser is directed to the ACS e-journal server via a link. Potential referral sources include any Web page with a link to the ACS e-journal server, the library catalog, bibliographic databases with links to full-text articles, external full-text articles with a link to another article, and Web-based e-mail messages containing embedded links. Referral addresses are not provided when a user connects by using a browser's bookmark, when the link is located on the same server, when the referral comes from a non-Web application, or when the link is directly typed or pasted into the URL address bar of a browser. Thus the data set cannot be considered complete for the purposes of understanding how chemists were referred to particular items in the ACS database. Transaction logs were obtained from the ACS and consisted of three months of data (December 2002 to February 2003) for all Cornell IP addresses connecting to the ACS servers. During this period, there were 15,876 log entries containing referral URLs from 1,630 unique IP addresses.

Referral data from nonjournal ACS sites (5,927 entries from 39 unique IP addresses) were discarded, leaving 9,949 referrals from 1,591 unique IP addresses. Users were approximated by IP address, and known Cornell Library Proxy Server IP addresses were treated as aggregate users. Each referral URL was categorized based on the type of referral: article link, bibliographic database, electronic journal list, e-mail, library catalog, Web page, Web search, or other. Additionally, each referral source was associated with an Internet domain name. Descriptive statistics were performed on referral data with respect to referral type based on the coding schema, by Internet domain name of the referral, and by IP address of the user(s).

In summary, Davis extended a minimal amount of data to reveal some interesting trends in how users of ACS e-journals locate the journals. At the same time, this study would have benefited from a more rigorous understanding of who the users were who were locating the journals. These data, if not extractable from logs, might have been collected via a questionnaire, though that method of data collection would likely not have been as accurate as the data provided in the logs. Alternatively, Davis might have obtained data that related IP addresses more precisely to departments likely to use ACS journals. Analysis of referrals from such a limited and targeted subset of IP addresses might have more accurately reflected e-journal use by a particular set of chemists but may have raised ethical issues related to privacy. In addition, it may have excluded some users in the target population such as graduate students and others who were not assigned university computers to use.

CONCLUSION

It is clear from these examples that transaction log analysis is a useful tool in understanding people's information behaviors. This method allows the researcher to capture and analyze large amounts of data and is a reasonably accurate representation of system users' behaviors. However, its primary weakness is that it cannot tell us anything about the users' cognitive or affective responses during the system interaction.

NOTES

1. For a more detailed discussion of this method, see Jansen (2006).

2. This chapter will focus on logs that capture the basic characteristics of a transaction. Because the analysis of chat logs and library reference service software use different approaches than other types of logs, they will not be discussed here. Ethical considerations (i.e., anonymity) are critical for handling analysis of such content-bearing logs; in all other aspects, content analysis methods are appropriate.

3. Spyware is "a client-side software component that monitors the use of client activity and sends the collected data to a remote machine" (Warkentin et al., 2005, p. 80).

4. Eye tracking is discussed in more detail in the chapter on direct observation (Chapter 20).

5. When the government subpoenaed Google, asking for two months of search records, a U.S. District Court ruled that Google did not have to provide them. The original subpoena is available at http://www.google.com/press/images/subpoena_20060317.pdf, and the court's ruling is at http://www.google.com/press/images/ruling_20060317.pdf. In spite of this ruling, AOL released the queries of over 650,000 users in August 2006 (McCullagh, 2006), later withdrawing that data with an apology.

6. Corinne Jörgensen, the first author of this article, was the recipient of the 2004 OCLC Library and Information Science Research Grant from the Association for Library and Information Science Education.

WORKS CITED

Atlas, M. C., Little, K. R. & Purcell, M. O. (1997). Flip charts at the OPAC: Using transaction log analysis to judge their effectiveness. *Reference and User Services Quarterly, 37*(1), 63–69.

Bates, M. J. (1979). Information search tactics. *Journal of the American Society for Information Science, 30*(4), 205–214.

Blecic, D. D., Dorsch, J. L., Koenig, M. H., & Bangalore, N. S. (1999). A longitudinal study of the effects of OPAC screen changes on searching behavior and searcher success. *College and Research Libraries, 60*(6), 515–530.

Borgman, C., Hirsh, S. G., & Hiller, J. (1996). Rethinking online monitoring methods for information retrieval systems: From search product to search process. *Journal of the American Society for Information Science, 47*(7), 568–583.

Buttenfield, B. P., & Reitsma, R. F. (2002). Loglinear and multidimensional scaling models of digital library navigation. *International Journal of Human-Computer Studies, 57*(2), 101–119.

Card, S. K., Pirolli, P., van der Wege, M., Morrison, J. B., Reeder, R. W., Schraedley, P. K., & Boshart, J. (2001). Information scent as a driver of Web behavior graphs: Results of a protocol analysis method for Web usability. In *Proceedings of the SIGCHI Conference on Human Factors in Computing Systems (Seattle, WA)* (pp. 490–497).

Catledge, L. D., & Pitkow, J. E. (1995). Characterizing browsing strategies in the World-Wide Web. In *Proceedings of the 1995 World Wide Web Conference (Darmstadt, Germany, 10–13 April, 1995)* (pp. 1065–1073).

Cooley, R., Mobasher, B., & Srivastava, J. (1999). Data preparation for mining World Wide Web browsing patterns. *Knowledge and Information Systems, 1*(1), 5–32.

Davis, P. M. (2004). Information seeking behavior of chemists: A transaction log analysis of referral URLs. *Journal of the American Society for Information Science and Technology, 55*(4), 326–332.

Fidel, R. (1985). Moves in online searching. *Online Review, 9*(1), 61–74.

Fieber, J. (1999, May 25). *Browser caching and Web log analysis.* Paper presented at the ASIS Midyear Conference, Pasadena, CA. Retrieved November 27, 2007, from http://ella.slis.indiana.edu/~jfieber/papers/bcwla/.

Goddard, L. (2007a). Getting to the source: A survey of quantitative data sources available to the everyday librarian. Part I: Web server log analysis. *Evidence Based Library and Information Practice, 2*(1), 48–67.

Goddard, L. (2007b). Getting to the source: A survey of quantitative data sources available to the everyday librarian. Part II: Data sources from specific library applications. *Evidence Based Library and Information Practice, 2*(1), 68–88.

Hiramatsu, K. (2002). Log analysis of map-based Web page search on Digital City Kyoto. In M. Tanabe, P. van den Besselaar, & T. Ishida (eds.), *Digital Cities II: Second Kyoto Workshop on Digital Cities, Kyoto, Japan, October 18–20, 2001. Revised Papers* (pp. 233–245). Lecture Notes in Computer Science 2362. Berlin: Springer.

Jansen, B. J. (2006). Search log analysis: What it is, what's been done, how to do it. *Library and Information Science Research, 28*(3), 407–432.

Jansen, B. J., & Pooch, U. (2001). A review of Web searching studies and a framework for future research. *Journal of the American Society for Information Science and Technology, 52*(3), 235–246.

Jansen, B. J., Spink, A., Bateman, J., & Saracevic, T. (1998a). Real life information retrieval: A study of user queries on the Web. *SIGIR Forum, 32*(1), 5–17.

Jansen, B. J., Spink, A., Blakey, C., & Koshman, S. (2007). Defining a session on Web search engines. *Journal of the American Society for Information Science and Technology, 58*(6), 862–871.

Jansen, B. J., Spink, A., & Saracevic, T. (1998b). Failure analysis in query construction: Data and analysis from a large sample of Web queries. In *Proceedings of the 3rd ACM Conference on Digital Libraries (Pittsburgh, PA, June 24–27, 1998)* (pp. 289–290).

Jones, S., Cunningham, S. J., McNab, R., & Boddie, A. (2004). Transaction log analysis of a digital library. *International Journal of Digital Librarianship, 3*(1), 152–169.

Jörgensen, C., & Jörgensen, P. (2005). Image querying by image professionals. *Journal of the American Society for Information Science and Technology, 56*(12), 1346–1359.

Keegan, T. T., Cunningham, S. J., & Apperley, M. (2006). Indigenous language usage in a bilingual interface: Transaction log analysis of the Niupepa Web site. In L. E. Dyson, M. Hendriks, & S. Grant (eds.), *Information Technology and Indigenous People* (pp. 175–188). Hershey, PA: IGI Global.

Kelly, D. (2006a). Measuring online information seeking context, part 1: Background and method. *Journal of the American Society for Information Science and Technology, 57*(13), 1729–1739.

Kelly, D. (2006b). Measuring online information seeking context, part 2: Findings and discussion. *Journal of the American Society for Information Science and Technology, 57*(14), 1862–1874.

Marchionini, G. (2002). Co-evolution of user and organizational interfaces: A longitudinal case study of WWW dissemination of national statistics. *Journal of the American Society for Information Science and Technology, 53*(14), 1192–1211.

Markey, K. (2007). Twenty-five years of end-user searching, part 1: Research findings. *Journal of the American Society of Information Science and Technology, 58*(8), 1071–1081.

Mat-Hassan, M., & Levene, M. (2005). Associating search and navigation behavior through log analysis. *Journal of the American Society of Information Science and Technology, 56*(9), 913–934.

McCullagh, D. (2006, August 7). AOL's disturbing glimpse into user's lives. *C/NET news.com.* Retrieved February 1, 2009, from http://news.cnet.com/AOLs-disturbing-glimpse-into-users-lives/2100–1030_3–6103098.html.

Nicholas, D. (2000). *Assessing Information Needs: Tools, Techniques and Concepts for the Internet Age* (2nd ed.). London: Europa Publications.

Nicholas, D., Huntington, P., & Watkinson, A. (2005). Scholarly journal usage: The results of deep log analysis. *Journal of Documentation, 61*(2), 248–280.

Peters, T. A. (1993). The history and development of transaction log analysis. *Library Hi Tech, 11*(2), 41–66.

Pitkow, J. (1997). In search of reliable usage data on the WWW. *Computer Networks and ISDN Systems, 29*(1997), 1343–1355.

Pu, H.-T., Chuang, S.-L., & Yang, C. (2002). Subject categorization of query terms for exploring Web users' search interests. *Journal of the American Society for Information Science and Technology, 53*(8), 617–630.

Ravid, G., & Rafaeli, S. (2004). Asynchronous discussion groups as small world and scale free networks. *First Monday, 9*(9). Retrieved November 27, 2007, from http://firstmonday.org/issues/issue9_9/ravid/index.html.

Rieh, S. Y., & Xie, H. (I.) (2006). Analysis of multiple query reformulations on the Web: The interactive information retrieval context. *Information Processing and Management, 42*(3), 751–768.

Roszak, T. (1986). *The Cult of Information.* New York: Pantheon.

Shute, S. J., & Smith, P. J. (1993). Knowledge-based search tactics. *Information Processing and Management, 29*(1), 29–45.

Spink, A., Wolfram, D., Jansen, B. J., & Saracevic, T. (2000). Searching the Web: The public and their queries. *Journal of the American Society for Information Science and Technology, 52*(3), 226–234.

Wang, P., Berry, M. W., & Yang, Y. (2003). Mining longitudinal Web queries: Trends and patterns. *Journal of the American Society for Information Science and Technology, 54*(8), 743–758.

Warkentin, M., Luo, X., & Templeton, G. F. (2005). A framework for spyware assessment. *Communications of the ACM, 48*(8), 79–84.

Wildemuth, B. M. (2004). The effects of domain knowledge on search tactic formulation. *Journal of the American Society for Information Science and Technology, 55*(3), 246–258.

Yun, G. W., Ford, J., Hawkins, R. P., Pingree, S., McTavish, F., Gustafson, D., & Berhe, H. (2006). On the validity of client-side vs. server-side Web log data analysis. *Internet Research, 16*(5), 537–552.

19

Think-aloud Protocols

Sanghee Oh and Barbara M. Wildemuth

A friend is a person with whom I may be sincere. Before him, I may think aloud.
—Ralph Waldo Emerson (1841/1889)

INTRODUCTION

Think-aloud protocols are a research method used to understand the subjects' cognitive processes based on their verbal reports of their thoughts during experiments (Ericsson & Simon, 1984/1993). The method of instruction in the protocol is simple: you request subjects to speak aloud, reporting what they are thinking while they are performing tasks during an experiment. The purpose of the protocol is to obtain information about what happens in the human mind when it processes information to solve problems or make decisions in diverse contexts (Payne, 1994; Russo et al., 1989; van den Haak et al., 2003). The terms *verbal reports* and *verbal protocols* may be used interchangeably with *think-aloud protocols*.

Think-aloud protocols have several advantages. First, they are relatively easy to collect. After receiving some simple instructions, the subjects do what they would normally do and speak aloud what they are thinking at the same time. Second, this method makes it possible to investigate the reactions, feelings, and problems that the subjects experience during task performance. It would be difficult to observe these characteristics using other methods (Larkin & Rainard, 1984; Nielsen, 1993; Robins, 2000; Tenopir et al., 1991). Third, the protocol data allow you to observe the sequential steps of the subject's cognitive processes over a given time period, rather than obtaining a general description at the end of a process (Crutcher, 1994; Ericsson & Simon, 1984/1993). As a result, this method leads to significant increases in the detail of the data collected (Ericsson & Simon, 1984/1993; Payne, 1994).

There are also several drawbacks to the protocol, raising concerns about its validity. First, task performance speed may be slower than usual because the subjects need some time to transfer their thoughts into words during the experiment. Thus there is a chance that the think-aloud protocols influence the thinking process related to the task itself, either to disrupt or improve the "normal" task performance (Nielsen, 1993). Second, conflicts between theory and practice have been reported (Boren & Ramey, 2000). Ericsson and Simon (1984/1993) established specific procedures for conducting think-aloud protocols, with the goal of minimizing the disruption of the subject's cognitive processes. However, these procedures are often compromised, with researchers using questions and prompts that negatively affect the validity of the think-aloud protocol. The strengths and weaknesses of think-aloud protocols will be discussed further in the next section, on the evolution of the method.

In information and library science (ILS), think-aloud protocols have been used to investigate the search tactics, processes, and strategies of people who are seeking information (Branch, 2001; Hsieh-Yee, 1993; Rieh, 2002; Robins, 2000; Tenopir et al., 1991) and the interactions of people with particular information systems, for example, library online catalogs (Sullivan & Seiden, 1985; Kiestra et al., 1994; van den Haak et al., 2004; Guha & Saraf, 2005), electronic databases (Nahl & Tenopir, 1996; Shaw, 1995), or information resources, either print or electronic (Branch, 2001; Shaw, 1996; Wang et al., 2000). Usability tests incorporating think-aloud protocols have been used to identify how users view a particular information system, how they understand its interface, and what misconceptions they hold about the system (Nielsen, 1993). There are also studies evaluating the work processes of librarians or information specialists in managing information resources (Pomerantz, 2004). These examples illustrate the ways in which think-aloud protocols can be useful in ILS studies.

EVOLUTION OF THE PROTOCOL METHOD

In the early part of the twentieth century, verbal protocols were widely used in psychological research, based on introspective methods. This traditional approach collected data about the subjects' information processing indirectly, through the observations of trained psychologists and the psychologists' verbal reports (Crutcher, 1994; Ericsson & Simon, 1984/1993; Payne, 1994). This method was criticized because (1) it depends too much on the skills of interpretation of the observers, rather than a more direct representation of the subjects' cognitive processes (Crutcher, 1994), and (2) it is hard to replicate the studies and obtain consistent results, even in the same settings, because the conclusions vary depending on who conducts the observation (van Someren et al., 1994).

Ericsson and Simon (1980) suggested a new strategy, obtaining the verbal data directly from the subjects without the intervention of the observers. This approach held great promise for the field. Their work responded to concerns about the use of verbal data in research being raised in mid-century. Verplanck (1962) was concerned with the disruption caused by the verbalization and task reinforcement; he believed that the verbal protocols would significantly affect performance and change people's behaviors. Nisbett and Wilson (1977) were concerned with people's ability to report their cognitive processes. They provided a comprehensive review of the case studies in which people had difficulty articulating the cognitive processes of justification, generating inferences, and changing one's views.

Ericsson and Simon (1984/1993) disagreed with these criticisms and pointed out that many of the problems were related to the ways the think-aloud protocols were collected. They emphasized that the effectiveness of the think-aloud methods can be enhanced by choosing appropriate tasks and by setting up proper experimental conditions. First, the verbal data should be captured from the immediate responses from the subjects while they are performing tasks or solving problems. Thus the subjects should be engaged only in simple verbal expressions of the steps being performed or their thought sequences, without interpreting what they are doing or why they are doing it. Second, it is important to collect the verbal data concurrently with the thinking process or immediately after the process is completed. Verbal protocols mostly depend on the information that resides in short-term memory. The more time that passes, the less accurate and complete the data will be.

Despite Ericsson and Simon's (1984/1993) defense of the method, it has been continually challenged in recent years, as it has only rarely been implemented as Ericsson and Simon suggested. On the basis of a review of a number of usability tests/studies, Boren and Ramey (2000) found that experimenters carried out the protocol, not with the instruction to subjects to report only what they were thinking but, rather, encouraging explanations and consulting with the subjects about their problems or concerns during the process of task completion. Thus Boren and Ramey suggested speech communication theory as an alternative theory of the protocol. With this theoretical foundation, verbal protocols are seen as one type of human communication, with the experimenters and the subjects situated in a much more natural environment of conversation. The debates surrounding the validity of this method and how, exactly, it should be implemented are likely to continue and to result in improvements in the use of think-aloud protocols. Yang (2003) has proposed a modification of the protocol in its later stages, as the researcher segments and analyzes the transcripts of the participants' verbalizations. Ericsson and Simon (1984/1993) urged researchers to analyze/code each segment or unit independently to avoid the bias that might arise from imposing a particular theoretical perspective on the data. Yang (2003) argues that "if a segment is large enough to make sense, then more often than not, it contains the potential for multiple categories. But, if it is small enough to reflect only a single category, then it is too small to make sense" (p. 105). Thus he urges researchers to analyze each segment within the context in which it was verbalized.

PRACTICAL TIPS FOR USING THE PROTOCOLS

Assuming that you want to use think-aloud protocols in the way originally specified by Ericsson and Simon (1980, 1984), there are a couple of ways to improve the outcomes of your data collection. First, you can prepare a couple of warm-up tasks in which subjects can practice thinking aloud, or you can show a video tutorial of someone thinking aloud while performing a sample task (Nielsen, 1993). Practicing the protocol with a very simple task that people usually do, such as how to replace staples in a stapler, could be useful in helping subjects to understand the process. Second, you should minimize the interaction between the experimenters and subjects during task performance. Begin with a very straightforward request for the subject to think aloud. For example, you might say, "Please solve the following problems, and while you do so, try to say everything that goes through your mind" (van Someren et al., 1994, p. 43). You shouldn't prompt the subject further unless he or she stops talking. Then, you might say something like, "Please keep talking." By restricting your interactions with the subject, you will minimize disruptions to the subject's cognitive processes.

If you find that Boren and Ramey's (2000) suggestion (i.e., to use speech communication theory to underlie your use of verbal protocols) is more appropriate for your study, then you will take a somewhat different approach to the process of data collection. Rather than trying to disappear (figuratively) from the subject's view, you will try to establish "a highly asymmetrical speaker/listener relationship, one which maximizes the speakership of the participant and minimizes the speakership" (p. 267) of the researcher. The subject is seen as the expert in performing the task and will be an active speaker; the researcher is seen as a learner and active listener. After your initial instructions to the subject, you will want to maintain an active listening stance by acknowledging what the subject is saying (e.g., with responses of "OK" or "yeah"). Boren and Ramey have additional advice about the types of "acknowledgement tokens" you use and how frequently they should be interspersed with the subject's comments.

Whichever theoretical stance you take, you will want to capture the full think-aloud protocol in a way that is synchronized with the subject's task performance. Audio or video recordings are often used to capture the data; taking notes is another option but is not complete enough for many research purposes. At some point, all or parts of these recordings will be transcribed; their synchronization with the task behaviors should be maintained during the transcription process.

METHOD VARIATIONS

Variations of think-aloud protocols have their own benefits and drawbacks. It is important to understand the characteristics of each method and select the one that is most appropriate for your research questions and the context of the study. A number of variations are possible, but three will be the focus of our discussion: concurrent versus retrospective protocols, individual versus collaborative protocols, and alternatives to face-to-face protocols.

Concurrent versus Retrospective Protocols

Depending on whether the subjects are asked to think aloud while performing tasks or after completing tasks, think-aloud protocols can be divided into two types of protocols: *concurrent protocols* and *retrospective protocols*. The concurrent protocols follow the general procedures of the protocol, asking the subjects to think aloud while working on tasks or solving problems. Retrospective protocols—also called *retrospective testing* (Nielsen, 1993), *aided subsequent verbal protocols* (Henderson et al., 1995), or *thoughts after* (Branch, 2000)—allow the subject to first complete tasks without saying anything. After the task performance is completed, subjects are asked to verbalize their thoughts, feelings, and/or opinions about the session. Retrospective protocols are most effective if the user's responses are stimulated by a recording (video or transaction log) of his or her behaviors during task performance.

There are strengths and weaknesses for each protocol, and generally, the strengths of one protocol are the weaknesses of the other. The concurrent protocol has the benefit that it collects the real-time responses of the subjects, but there is the possibility that the protocol itself influences task performance. The subjects could work better (or worse) as they speak about what they are thinking during the session. Thinking aloud may (or may not) help the subjects to think systematically about solving problems or completing tasks (Russo et al., 1989; Schooler et al., 1993).

On the other hand, the retrospective protocol allows the subjects to complete the tasks in a more natural way—without interruptions—as they would usually do if they were working alone. Thus it is possible to capture the so-called normal performance of the subjects. Moreover, subjects can provide their reflections on the tasks as well as their memories about the tasks and their thoughts while completing the tasks. The validity of the retrospective protocol, however, depends on what the subjects remember from their task performance sessions. It's possible that the subject will not recall exactly what he or she was originally thinking and so provide an incomplete or inaccurate report (Payne, 1994). Subjects are likely to blend their later thoughts on the process with those that occurred earlier, or even provide misleading responses about their performance. To help subjects recall their thoughts more accurately, video recordings, screen captures, or transaction logs can be used to stimulate recall (van den Haak et al., 2003). You can also use these stimulus materials to interview the subjects about their actions or thoughts, without disturbing the original performance (Nielsen, 1993).

Individual versus Collaborative Protocols

While think-aloud protocols were first designed to investigate the thought processes of an individual's mind, this method has also been adapted for use with pairs or small groups of subjects working together to complete a task or solve a problem. These are called *paired think-aloud protocols*, *collaborative think-aloud protocols*, or *constructive interactions*.

Nielsen (1993) argued that the collaborative approach can be more realistic in capturing cognitive behaviors than individual administration of a verbal protocol because people naturally verbalize their thoughts when they have a conversation with others. Rather than solely narrating what they are thinking, the participants are engaged in more talking as they communicate with their partners, asking and answering questions and discussing directions, issues, and problems associated with task completion. In terms of time and cost, however, the collaborative approach may not be as efficient as individual sessions because it requires recruitment of more than one person per session and the discussion and compromising process among participants may take more time.

The collaborative approach to think-aloud protocols has been used in several ILS studies. It has been found to be an effective method for involving children in evaluating system usability. Because children can be easily distracted and have difficulty focusing on free exploration tasks, a paired or constructive interaction with peers or instructors can help them concentrate on task completion (Als et al., 2005; Benford et al., 2000; Cassell & Ryokai, 2001). In addition, it has been used to investigate the interactions between end users and intermediaries in online information seeking (Robins, 2000; Saracevic & Su, 1989) as well as how people work collaboratively with other coworkers when they seek, search, and use information in workplaces (Fidel et al., 2000).

Alternatives to Face-to-Face Protocols

Verbal protocols are usually collected with the researcher and the subject in the same physical space (i.e., face-to-face). However, as communication technology has evolved, there have been various trials of think-aloud protocols collected via telephone, online chat services, or other computer-mediated technology. Edlin (2005) compared the effectiveness of two different types of think-aloud protocols collected for a remote usability study. One version was collected via phone; the researcher was on the phone with the subject as the subject interacted with the system being tested. The other version used an instant message session for communication between the researcher and the subject. She found that the think-aloud protocols collected via phone were much richer and more detailed than those collected via instant messaging. Another example of verbal protocols collected via phone (Pomerantz, 2004) is discussed later in this chapter.

Protocols Used in Combination with Other Methods

In many ILS studies, multiple methods are used to collect a diverse data set. Think-aloud protocols have been used with other methods in various ways, depending on the context and research designs of the studies. Think-aloud protocols are often used in combination with transaction logs to investigate and/or evaluate users' interactions with systems (Griffiths et al., 2002; Hancock, 1987; Hancock-Beaulieu, 1990). Using these two methods in combination enables the researcher to collect a comprehensive set of data, including both the verbal statements of what the subjects were thinking about and the log data about what the subjects actually did while interacting with the system and how the system responded. Interviews also are often used with think-aloud protocols for collecting background information about the subjects or other data about their experiences related to the experiment (Hirsh, 1999). Interviews are also used to debrief subjects after a think-aloud protocol, allowing the researcher to probe interesting issues that came up during task performance. There are also many studies that combine more than one method with verbal protocols. For example, Rieh (2002) combined three methods of data collection—think-aloud protocols, search transaction logs, and postsearch interviews—to investigate people's perceptions of the authority of Web resources. There have also been recent trials of biometric methods (e.g., eye tracking) used in combination with think-aloud protocols (Cooke & Cuddihy, 2005).

EXAMPLES

As noted previously, two examples of the use of think-aloud protocols will be discussed here. The first (Branch, 2001) examines the cognition of junior high students as they searched an electronic encyclopedia. Both concurrent and retrospective think-aloud protocols were collected and analyzed. The second example (Pomerantz, 2004) collected think-aloud protocols from reference librarians as they conducted triage on digital reference questions. Because the librarians were scattered geographically, the protocols were collected by phone. Thus each of these studies employs a variation of the basic think-aloud protocol.

Example 1: Junior High Students' Use of an Electronic Encyclopedia

Branch (2001) collected verbal protocols during junior high students' use of an electronic encyclopedia. The 12 Canadian students, nominated by their teachers to develop a diverse sample of study participants, included boys and girls, aged 11 to 15, with varying degrees of academic success and various ethnic backgrounds. Each student participated in three search sessions. In the first session, the student completed searches on four researcher-generated questions; in the second session, the student completed searches on four teacher-generated questions; and in the final session, the student completed searches on four of his or her own questions. During the search sessions, the student was asked to think aloud while conducting the searches; these verbal protocols were audio recorded. In addition, the computer screen was videotaped during the session, and the searches were then replayed and retrospective verbal protocols collected. The final transcripts that formed the data set included the 144 original think-aloud protocols (one for each search by each student), the retrospective protocols, and notes about the searcher's actions during the verbalizations.

Branch's (2001) study had two distinct research purposes. The first was to understand the process through which the students conducted their searches of the encyclopedia. To accomplish this goal, the transcripts were segmented; there were 2,221 segments generated during the 144 verbal protocols. Then, each segment was coded as cognition associated with defining, planning, monitoring, or evaluating—a coding scheme based on Biemiller and Meichenbaum's (1992) earlier work. The frequency with which each of these types of cognitions occurred was analyzed across individual study participants and across the three search sessions (representing the three different sources of search questions). While this type of quantitative analysis was appropriate in the context of this study, it was unusual. In most cases, verbal protocols are analyzed qualitatively, to identify particular incidents of interest in the interaction (e.g., particularly important usability problems) or themes within the participants' comments.

Branch's (2001) second research purpose was to understand the differences in the students' abilities to produce verbal protocols. During the data collection process, she noticed that some of the verbal protocols were "incomplete" (p. 113). In other words, they were either very brief (i.e., very few statements were made) or they were almost completely procedural (i.e., the participant's only statements were merely descriptions of the actions they took). She attributes these differences to the students' differing levels of self-direction as learners (in line with Biemiller and Meichenbaum's, 1992, earlier findings), with those in the third/consultation phase being most able to generate complete verbal protocols.

In many ways, Branch's (2001) use of verbal protocols was typical of how they have been used in other ILS studies. A small number of study participants were engaged in a particular information behavior that was mediated by a computer/information system. Concurrent verbal protocols were collected during the interactions. These were then tran-scribed, annotated with notes about the interaction behaviors, and analyzed. However, there were several points on which Branch diverged from the norm. First, she augmented the concurrent verbal protocols with retrospective protocols, supported by the viewing of a videotape of the interactions. This method imposed a slightly greater burden on the study participants because each data collection session was longer, but it undoubtedly improved the completeness of the data collected. Second, she used a preexisting coding scheme for analyzing the data. There is nothing wrong with this approach, but it is more common for a researcher to induce a coding scheme from verbal protocol data. Finally, she analyzed the data quantitatively, while most verbal protocol data will be analyzed qualitatively.[1] In spite of these differences from typical implementations of think-aloud protocols, this study can serve as a model for future research using this method.

Example 2: Digital Reference Triage

Pomerantz (2004) used think-aloud protocols to investigate factors that influence decision-making processes during digital reference triage. Triage is the process of routing and assigning questions received by a digital reference service as well as filtering out repeated questions or out-of-scope questions (Pomerantz et al., 2003). This task must be performed, either manually or automatically, to ensure that each question is addressed by a qualified answerer.

Prior to this think-aloud study, Pomerantz et al. (2003) conducted a Delphi study, also focused on identifying the factors that influence decision making during triage. Pomerantz (2004) argued that the Delphi study was limited in its ability to elicit all the possible factors that influence triage decisions and that people could identify more factors if they were asked about the decisions during their performance of triage tasks. Thus he conducted this follow-up study, in which he collected concurrent think-aloud protocols.

Pomerantz recruited 28 triagers from various digital reference services in libraries and AskA services. He arranged a time to meet with each participant, based on the participant's regular schedule for performing triage on incoming reference questions. At each session, the participant triaged all the reference questions waiting for processing; a total of 185 questions were included in the data set. When possible, Pomerantz (2004) was physically present with the triager during the think-aloud protocol; when that was not possible (i.e., when travel to the site was not possible), the think-aloud protocol was collected via phone. Eight protocols were collected face-to-face and 20 were collected via phone. In both situations, the participant was "instructed to think aloud while performing triage, with specific attention to factors that affect their triage decisions" (Pomerantz, 2004, p. 245). Thus Pomerantz implemented think-aloud protocols with a slight compromise of Ericsson and Simon's (1993) suggested procedures—he asked for more detailed explanations of the factors that influenced the triage decision making, rather than just asking the participants to think aloud. Each protocol was recorded on audiotape. After completing the think-aloud protocol, a short interview about the demographic characteristics of each participant was carried out. The verbal protocols and interview were later transcribed. In addition, the original reference questions that inspired the think-aloud protocols were collected and synchronized with the transcriptions.

The data were imported into ATLAS.ti (http://www.atlasti.com/) for analysis. The data were coded in terms of the factors that influenced the triage decisions. Some of the codes were generated in the earlier Delphi study (Pomerantz et al., 2003), while others were induced from the current data set. The 2003 study identified 15 factors (general influences, influences on the routing or assignment of a question to an answerer, and influences on routing questions to another service); the current study identified 38 factors (including attributes of the question, the answer, the patron, the patron's current information need, the triaging service, and the receiving service, if forwarded, or the answerer). It appears that Pomerantz's argument, that concurrent think-aloud protocols would elicit more factors than the earlier Delphi study, was supported by the results.

Triagers are library reference experts who know their work relatively well, but they are not likely to have experience thinking aloud while they are doing their work. Van Someren et al. (1994) pointed out that in most cases, experts have difficulty verbalizing the routine processes of their work since they are usually doing it "very fast" and because their expert knowledge has been internalized to the point that it is implicit. Thus Pomerantz's role in the think-aloud protocols was to encourage the triagers not to miss any aspect of the process, as each step was important in this study.

In this study, an additional complication was that the verbal protocol was often conducted by phone. In the phone-based protocols, Pomerantz (2004) had only the verbal channel to use to encourage the subjects to talk, without being able to see the subjects' facial expressions (e.g., of puzzlement) or their physical actions. As more and more computer-mediated communication technologies become commonplace, it may be possible to supplement the phone with video of the research subject or the viewing of his or her screen in real time. Particularly in think-aloud protocols that are more interactive, as suggested by Boren and Ramey (2000), these new technologies will be useful in creating a communicative environment for data collection.

CONCLUSION

In this chapter, the theory and practice of think-aloud protocols used in various settings of studies were reviewed. Compared to other data collection methods, the process of collecting think-aloud protocols is simple, but you will be able to collect valid data only when your study is designed well. Choose appropriate think-aloud protocol methods, taking into account the subject population and the situation in which the study will be conducted. Try to minimize the cognitive load on the participants, allowing them to perform the task in a naturalistic way. Either minimize your interactions with the subjects (as recommended by Ericsson and Simon, 1984/1993) or treat your interactions with the subjects as a particular, asymmetrical form of speech communication (as recommended by Boren and Ramey, 2000). It is hoped that the examples presented in this chapter will enable you to use think-aloud protocols to achieve your research objectives.

NOTE

1. See Chapters 29 and 30 for further consideration of these last two points.

WORKS CITED

Als, B. S., Jensen, J. J., & Skov, M. B. (2005). Comparison of think-aloud and constructive interaction in usability testing with children. In *Proceedings of the 2005 Conference on Interaction Design and Children* (pp. 9–16).

Benford, S., Bederson, B. B., Akesson, K.-P., Bayon, V., Druin, A., Hansson, P., et al. (2000). Designing storytelling technologies to encourage collaboration between young children. In *Proceedings of the Conference on Human Factors in Computing Systems (CHI' 2000)* (pp. 556–563).

Biemiller, A., & Meichenbaum, D. (1992). The nature and nurture of the self-directed learner. *Educational Leadership, 50,* 75–80.

Boren, M. T., & Ramey, J. (2000). Thinking aloud: Reconciling theory and practice. *IEEE Transactions on Professional Communication, 43*(3), 261–278.

Branch, J. L. (2000). Investigating the information seeking processes of adolescents: The value of using think alouds and think afters. *Library and Information Science Research, 22*(4), 371–392.

Branch, J. L. (2001). Junior high students and think alouds: Generating information seeking process data using concurrent verbal protocols. *Library and Information Science Research, 23,* 107–122.

Cassell, J., & Ryokai, K. (2001). Making space for voice: Technologies for supporting children's fantasy and storytelling. *Personal and Ubiquitous Computing, 5*(3), 169–190.

Cooke, L., & Cuddihy, E. (2005). Using eye tracking to test the validity and accuracy of think-aloud protocol. In *Proceedings of the IEEE International Professional Communication Conference, July 200, Limerick, Ireland* (pp. 653–658).

Crutcher, R. (1994). Telling what we know: The use of verbal report methodologies in psychological research. *Psychological Science, 5*(5), 241–244.

Edlin, A. L. (2005). *The effectiveness of instant messaging versus telephone communication for synchronous remote usability evaluations.* Master's paper, University of North Carolina at Chapel Hill. Retrieved June 19, 2008, from http://ils.unc.edu/MSpapers/3045.pdf.

Emerson, R. W. (1889). Friendship. In *Essays* (1st series). Philadelphia: David McKay. (Original work published 1841)

Ericsson, K. A., & Simon, H. A. (1980). Verbal reports as data. *Psychological Review, 87,* 215–251.

Ericsson, K. A., & Simon, H. A. (1984). *Protocol Analysis: Verbal Reports as Data.* Cambridge, MA: Bradford Books / MIT Press.

Ericsson, K. A., & Simon, H. A. (1993). *Protocol Analysis: Verbal Reports as Data* (Rev. ed.). Cambridge, MA: Bradford Books / MIT Press. (Original work published 1984)

Fidel, R., Bruce, H., Pejtersen, A. M., Dumais, S., Grudin, J., & Poltrock, S. (2000). Collaborative information retrieval (CIR). *The New Review of Information Behaviour Research, 1,* 235–247.

Griffiths, J. R., Hartley, R. J., & Wilson, J. P. (2002). An improved method of studying user system interaction by combining transaction log analysis and protocol analysis. *Information Research, 7*(4), Article 139. Retrieved December 10, 2007, from http://informationr.net/ir/7-4/paper139.html.

Guha, T. K., & Saraf, V. (2005). OPAC usability: Assessment through verbal protocol. *The Electronic Library, 23*(4), 463–473.

Hancock, M. (1987). Subject searching behaviour at the library catalogue and at the shelves: Implications for online interactive catalogues. *Journal of Documentation, 43*(4), 303–321.

Hancock-Beaulieu, M. M. (1990). Evaluating the impact of an online library catalogue on subject searching behaviour at the catalogue and at the shelves. *Journal of Documentation, 46,* 318–338.

Henderson, R. D., Smith, M. C., Podd, J., & Varela-Alvarez, X. (1995). A comparison of the four prominent user-based methods for evaluating the usability of computer software. *Ergonomics, 38,* 2030–2044.

Hirsh, S. (1999). Children's relevance criteria and information seeking on electronic resources. *Journal of the American Society for Information Science, 50,* 1265–1283.

Hsieh-Yee, I. (1993). Effects of search experience and subject knowledge on the search tactics of novice and experienced searchers. *Journal of the American Society for Information Science, 44*(3), 161–174.

Kiestra, M. D., Stokmans, M. J., & Kamphuis, J. (1994). End-users searching the online catalogue: The influence of domain and system knowledge on search patterns. *The Electronic Library, 12,* 335–343.

Larkin, J. H., & Rainard, B. (1984). A research methodology for studying how people think. *Journal of Research in Science Teaching, 21*(3), 235–254.

Nahl, D., & Tenopir, C. (1996). Affective and cognitive searching behavior of novice end-users of a full-text database. *Journal of the American Society for Information Science, 47*(4), 276–286.

Nielsen, J. (1993). *Usability Engineering.* Boston: AP Professional.

Nisbett, R. E., & Wilson, T. D. (1977). Telling more than we can know: Verbal reports on mental processes. *Psychological Review, 84,* 231–259.

Payne, J. W. (1994). Thinking aloud: Insights into information processing. *Psychological Science, 5*(5), 241–248.

Pomerantz, J. (2004). Factors influencing digital reference triage: A think-aloud study. *Library Quarterly*, *74*(3), 235–264.

Pomerantz, J., Nicholson, S., & Lankes, R. D. (2003). Digital reference triage: An investigation using the Delphi method into the factors influencing question routing and assignment. *Library Quarterly*, *73*(2), 103–120.

Rieh, S. Y. (2002) Judgment of information quality and cognitive authority in the Web. *Journal of the American Society for Information Science and Technology*, *53*(2), 145–161.

Robins, D. (2000). Shifts of focus on various aspects of user information problems during interactive information retrieval. *Journal of the American Society for Information Science*, *51*(10), 913–928.

Russo, J. E., Johnson, J., & Stephens, D. L. (1989). The validity of verbal protocols. *Memory and Cognition*, *17*, 759–769.

Saracevic, T., & Su, L. (1989). Modeling and measuring user-intermediary-computer interaction in online searching: Design of a study. *Proceedings of the 52nd Annual Meeting of the American Society for Information Science*, *26*, 75–80.

Schooler, J. W., Ohlsson, S., & Brooks, K. (1993). Thoughts beyond words: When language overshadows insight. *Journal of Experimental Psychology*, *122*, 166–183.

Shaw, D. (1995). Bibliographic database searching by graduate students in language and literature: Search strategies, system interfaces, and relevance judgment. *Library and Information Science Research*, *17*(4), 327–345.

Shaw, D. (1996). Undergraduate use of CD-ROM databases: Observation of human-computer interaction and relevance judgments. *Libraries and Information Science Research*, *18*(3), 261–274.

Sullivan, P., & Seiden, P. (1985). Educating online catalog users: The protocol assessment of needs. *Library Hi Tech*, *10*, 11–19.

Tenopir, C., Nahl-Jakobovits, D., & Howard, D. L. (1991). Strategies and assessments online: Novices' experience. *Library and Information Science Research*, *13*, 237–266.

van den Haak, M. J., de Jong, M. D. T., & Schellens, P. J. (2003). Retrospective versus concurrent think-aloud protocols: Testing the usability of an online library catalogue. *Behaviour and Information Technology*, *22*(5), 339–351.

van den Haak, M. J., de Jong, M. D. T., & Schellens, P. J. (2004). Employing think-aloud protocols and constructive interaction to test the usability of online library catalogues: A methodological comparison. *Interacting with Computers*, *16*, 1153–1170.

van Someren, M. W., Barnard, Y., & Sandberg, J. (1994). *The Think Aloud Method—A Practical Approach to Modeling Cognitive Processes*. London: Academic Press.

Verplanck, W. S. (1962). Unaware of where's awareness: Some verbal operants-notates, moments and notants. In C. W. Eriksen (ed.), *Behavior and Awareness—A Symposium of Research and Interpretation* (pp. 130–158). Durham, NC: Duke University Press.

Wang, P., Hawk, W. B., & Tenopir, C. (2000). Users' interaction with World Wide Web resources: An exploratory study using a holistic approach. *Information Processing and Management*, *36*(2), 229–251.

Yang, S. C. (2003). Reconceptualizing think-aloud methodology: Refining the encoding and categorizing techniques via contextualized perspectives. *Computers in Human Behavior*, *19*(1), 95–115.

20

Direct Observation

Barbara M. Wildemuth

The office of the scholar is to cheer, to raise, and to guide men by showing them facts amidst appearances. He plies the slow, unhonored, and unpaid task of observation. . . . He is the world's eye.

—Ralph Waldo Emerson (1837/1849)

INTRODUCTION

As Tenopir (2003) has suggested, essentially every method for collecting data about people can be categorized as either observing them or asking them questions. In this chapter, we'll focus on a set of methods for directly observing people. For many research questions, observation has significant advantages over interviews or questionnaires (or other forms of asking people questions). First, direct observation allows you to gather accurate information about events (McCall, 1984). As O'Leary (2005) points out, "there are times when you need to 'see it for yourself'" (p. 119) to be able to understand what happened. Even a participant's report of an event may not give you the full picture. And in many cases, people who "live" in a particular setting may not be able to see some of the things that occur there; some things are just taken for granted and are not noticed by those most familiar with and knowledgeable about them (Patton, 2002). Second, direct observation enables you to gather more precise data about the timing, duration, and/or frequency of particular behaviors as well as their sequence. The observer can take note of these characteristics of the behaviors of interest, even while the participants in an interaction may not be fully aware of them.

Given these strengths, it is clear that the primary purpose of observation is to find out what people do; that is, this method of data collection is focused on the behaviors of participants in a particular setting. This also means that observation is only an appropriate method of data collection when there really is something to watch—the actions or behaviors to be observed must be overt (Denscombe, 2003). As Wilson and

Streatfield (1980) found during Project INISS, watching someone write a report may not be very informative, but watching him or her sort through and respond to the mail can tell the researcher a lot about the information and communication flows of the person being observed.

There are a couple of different ways to distinguish direct observation methods. First, *participant observation* (discussed in Chapter 21), in which the observer also has a role as a participant in the setting being observed, can be distinguished from *nonparticipant observation*, in which the observer is there *only* to observe. Different observation methods also vary on the amount of structure imposed on the observation (O'Leary, 2005). In this chapter, we're specifically concerned with formal observation, defined by Wilkinson (1995) as "the planned and systematic application of a system of procedures for conducting the observations or gathering the data.... It usually involves an unintrusive observer who makes field notes and/or times, counts or rates behaviours or events" (p. 216). While we'll focus on observation in this chapter, it should be noted that observation methods are often combined with interviews or other methods for investigating the reasons behind the study participants' behaviors.

OBSERVATION PROCEDURES

The first step in conducting an observation is to select and gain access to the setting in which the behaviors of interest are likely to occur. The setting might be a library, a study participant's office, or even a grocery store, depending on the goals of the study and the research question(s) being asked. Once a setting is selected, you will need to gain access to it. Even if it's a relatively public space, it may be a challenge to gain permission to observe people in that space. For instance, if you were studying the ways in which people select fiction in libraries and in bookstores, you would need the permission of both the library's management and the bookstore's management to conduct your study. Once that permission is obtained, you would need to obtain the consent of the individuals you would be observing. You would need to establish at least a minimum level of rapport with the study participants. You should plan carefully how you will introduce yourself and your study to the study participants and make sure that your actions are consistent with the role that you are taking in relation to your participants (Patton, 2002).

Your next decision concerns the sample of data you will collect. You cannot observe everything that happens in a particular setting, 24 hours a day, seven days a week, for any period of time. So you will need to develop a plan for collecting a sample of data that is appropriate for the goals of your study. Such sampling plans are usually based on either time or events (Mason & Bramble, 1997; McCall, 1984). Time sampling involves collecting observations over particular time intervals. For example, you might be interested in the ways that people use library services, so you observe people's use of the library for two-hour intervals, purposively selected from the library's open hours to include those that have the highest levels of traffic. Whichever behaviors or events occur during those periods are intended to be representative of library use patterns. The second approach is event sampling, based on the occurrence of particular behaviors or events. Using this approach, you will predefine which behaviors or events are of interest; these definitions must be clear enough so that you can be certain when the behavior or event is starting and stopping. Then you will gather observation data only when those behaviors or events occur. For example, you might be interested in people's use of library computers for searching the library catalog. You would not collect data about their use of the computers if they were doing e-mail, searching the Web, or completing other tasks; your observations would be focused only on the behaviors of interest.

In addition to these high-level questions about your sample, you will need to decide which people in the setting will be observed and which of their behaviors will be observed—how each unit of behavior is defined and what you want to know about it, for example, its frequency, its duration, or its quality (McCall, 1984). In addition, you need to decide how much detail you will capture about the context of the behaviors such as the physical appearance or arrangement of the setting (Gray, 2004; Neuman, 2006). It is wise to make some decisions in advance about what you want to watch for so that you are not biased in your observations (Wilkinson, 1995). It is very easy to filter unconsciously what you see, based on your own expectations. Use your observation schedule or coding/categorizing definitions to minimize the potential for bias in your observation data.

During the observation periods, you will be recording data about what you observe. There are several ways in which you can record the data. The most obvious approach is to watch what is happening and to use an observation schedule or checklist to record the needed data. As Mason (2002) notes, "simply 'hanging around' in an unfocused way can be notoriously time-consuming, unproductive, exhausting and sometimes embarrassing or risky" (p. 90). The purpose of using an observation schedule is to improve the reliability of the data collected (Denscombe, 2003), minimizing as much as possible the variability between observers over time. An existing observation schedule may serve your purposes, or you may need to develop one specific to your study. The quality of the observation schedule you use can have a significant impact on the quality of the data you collect, so it is worthwhile to plan and pilot test it carefully and to make sure that all observers are well trained in its use (Curry, 2005; Wilson & Streatfield, 1980). Even so, you will need to be flexible enough so that the observation schedule can be adapted as unexpected behaviors or events are observed (Wilson & Streatfield, 1980). In addition, you may need to augment the observation schedule with field notes, maps or drawings, photos of the setting or participants, and so on.

Video and audio recordings are sometimes used to capture observation data. However, this approach is not common because there are some significant disadvantages. They can be even more obtrusive than an observer taking notes. Often people are wary of their behavior being recorded, particularly if they can be recognized in the recording. While video recording might be useful for capturing intermittent behaviors without being present all the time, such an approach raises serious ethical issues related to the informed consent of the study participants. So, overall, these techniques for data capture are more often used to augment interviewing and similar data collection methods (e.g., think-aloud protocols) than they are used for studies relying predominantly on observation.

For some studies, eye tracking is an appropriate method for capturing behavioral data. Two types of data can be captured with eye tracking equipment: the movement of the eyes from place to place and pupil dilation, the latter being interpreted as indicating increased cognitive load (Granholm et al., 1996) and/or affective response (Partala & Surakka, 2003). Rayner (1998) concluded that eye tracking is "very valuable in studying reading and other information processing tasks" (p. 404) and so may be particularly useful in information and library science (ILS) studies focused on the behaviors of reading, particularly on-screen, and interacting with information retrieval systems. If you decide to incorporate eye tracking into your study methods, be sure to take account of the possibility that you may suffer from sample attrition due to difficulties in calibrating the eye tracking equipment. While this is less of a problem with the current generation of eye trackers than it was in the past, researchers (e.g., Joachims et al., 2007; Lorigo et al., 2006) have reported losing from 15 to 35 percent of their willing participants because the equipment could not be calibrated.

Several other methods for capturing observational data are discussed in other chapters in this book. These include transaction log analysis (in which the study participant's online behaviors are captured by the system with which the participant is interacting; Chapter 18), think-aloud protocols (a particular style of verbal protocol, usually accompanied by video capture of the study participant's behaviors; Chapter 19), participant observation (in which the researcher takes on a participant role as well as the observer role; Chapter 21), and diaries (in which the study participant records his or her own behaviors for later analysis by the researcher; Chapter 22).

Once the observational data have been captured, there is usually a pre-analysis phase prior to the actual analysis of the data. In most cases, you will need to categorize or code the data, transforming the raw data into a sequence of events or abstracting in some other way the data points that are useful in accomplishing your research goals. Either an interpretive, qualitative approach may be taken during the analysis phase, or a quantitative approach may be taken. If the analysis is qualitative, it is expected to result in a rich description of the behaviors observed and the context in which they occurred. As Patton (2002) notes, "the quality of observational reports is judged by the extent to which that observation permits the reader to enter into and understand the situation described" (p. 262). If the analysis is quantitative or very structured, you will need to make sure that each category of behavior is clearly defined and that the categorizing of individual behaviors or events can be conducted reliably.

The final step is "leaving the field." During studies employing observation for data collection, it is easy for the researcher to develop strong relationships with those being observed, particularly if the observations were done in person and over an extended period of time. While it is necessary, it is not always easy to disengage, both physically and emotionally (Gray, 2004). You will need to plan ahead to accomplish this step gracefully.

ISSUES IN DIRECT OBSERVATION

There are several issues that will arise as you plan for a study involving direct observation. They include the fact that many information behaviors are intermittent and so are hard to catch; that the context of the information behavior of interest may be relevant to the study but may be difficult to observe; that being watched is often bothersome to people; and that additional ethical issues may arise during the observation. Each of these is discussed in the following paragraphs.

The challenge in trying to observe many information behaviors is that they are intermittent; they occur infrequently and at unpredictable times. Thus it is difficult for the observer to be at the right place at the right time to observe the behavior of interest. You can, of course, schedule observation times when the information behaviors are most likely to occur. For example, if you wanted to observe the responses of reference librarians to the questions they receive, you might observe at the times of day/week when the reference desk traffic is the heaviest. Or if you wanted to observe someone conducting Web searches for planning his or her vacation, you could schedule an observation session in advance and ask the person to begin only when you are present. For other studies, you may be able to simulate the situation of interest to see how people behave in the simulation (Wilkinson, 1995). For example, in controlled studies of online searching, Borlund (2003) recommends that you ask people to complete simulated task situations, that is, realistic tasks set in a realistic context. As you plan your study, consider how you will be able to be present when the information behaviors of interest are occurring.

During an observation, your attention will be focused on particular information behaviors. In addition, the context within which those behaviors occur may be of great interest. For some types of behaviors, you can directly observe that context. For example, Fisher's study (Pettigrew, 2000) of the information sharing between community health nurses and their elderly clients was observed within its natural context, and she took some time before and after each observation to understand further the background of each nurse and the physical context in which the information exchange occurred. But for other studies, there may be things happening outside your view that are pertinent to the information behaviors of interest. For example, an observation of behaviors at the reference desk cannot "see" what motivated the question presented by the library user. Mason (2002) suggests that you continually ask yourself, What are you missing? and Patton (2002) encourages researchers to make notes about what doesn't occur when you would expect it to occur. Both these strategies will help you to discover aspects of the context that may be important to your study.

One of the most obvious issues that arises with observational studies is the obtrusiveness of being watched. The biggest danger is that observed people change their behavior because of the presence of the observer, that is, the *Hawthorne effect* (see Kumar, 2005, p. 120, for a brief discussion of this phenomenon). While there is some evidence that this effect fades as the observer is present for a longer period of time (McCall, 1984; Wilson & Streatfield, 1980), you will want to "retain the naturalness of the setting" as much as possible (Denscombe, 2003, p. 199) or become "wallpaper" (Cooper et al., 2004). To achieve this goal, pay attention to where you are positioned, avoid unnecessary interaction with those being observed, develop a basic level of trust with your study participants before you begin observing them, and spend sufficient time at the site so that those observed become accustomed to your presence. Even if you've taken these precautions, there is no way to avoid completely the fact that you are present as an outsider. You should be prepared for "observing, participating, interrogating, listening, communicating, as well as a range of other forms of being, doing and thinking" (Mason, 2002, p. 87) that will help you achieve your study goals.

Even if you have permission to observe in a particular location and have received permission from those being observed, additional ethical issues may arise. For example, other people may be in the same location who are not the focus of your observation but will be in your view or will be captured with your data-recording equipment. These might include patients when you're studying health care workers (Cooper et al., 2004) or students when you're studying teachers. Be sure to consider the issues of informed consent for study participation before you begin your observation and protect the privacy and confidentiality of both your study participants and those others who inhabit the same spaces.

EXAMPLES

You'll need to resolve these issues for your own study; here we'll examine the way that three different researchers/teams resolved them. The first example (Shoham &

Shemer-Shalman, 2003) supplemented observations with interviews and questionnaires to map the ways in which students move about school libraries. The second example (Curry, 2005) conducted intentionally unobtrusive observation of service at library reference desks; it is particularly interesting for the methods used in overcoming ethical issues related to unobtrusive observation. The third (Lorigo et al., 2006) used eye tracking to observe user behaviors during Web searching.

Example 1: Mapping Student Seating Choices and Movement in the Library

A recent study by Shoham and Shemer-Shalman (2003) investigated some specific behaviors of junior high and high school students in Israel. Specifically, they examined the connection between the physical attributes of the library and the students' seating choices as well as the students' "territorial behaviors." The observations were conducted in the libraries of four different comprehensive high schools and were augmented with student questionnaires and interviews with librarians and students.

Four visits were made to each school. The first occurred during a break period, when the students were not present. This allowed the researchers to become very familiar with the physical space to be observed. A map of the library space in each school was drawn, to be used during the later observation periods. The three-day-long observation periods in each library captured "the movements of the students entering the library, the seating location they chose and their way of sitting, and the students' various activities in the library" (Shoham & Shemer-Shalman, 2003, p. 5). Interviews were later conducted with all the librarians and with a small random sample of students who were present in the library (five in each school). After all the observations had been completed, questionnaires were distributed to the students in all the schools who had spent time in the library, asking about their choice of seating location and about their attitudes toward the library's physical facilities. Of the 1,222 students who were observed in the library, 394 also completed questionnaires. The analysis consisted of coding the seating or standing locations selected by students as they entered the library (e.g., in the corners versus a central location), with special attention to the locations used in the reading area (e.g., near friends versus near the part of the library collection being used). The development of the coding scheme was inductive, though it was partially based on the initial diagrams made on the first visit to each site. Students' body language and the arrangement of their belongings were also noted and were interpreted as indicators of territorial behavior.

The goals of this study required that the observer focus on particular actions and ignore others. For example, the use of study materials to mark off a particular study territory was of interest and noted. Other behaviors, such as the content of the books being used, was not included in the observation notes. For some observation studies, the researcher will be working with a research question that clearly defines which behaviors or aspects of the site will be of interest and which will not; for other studies, the researcher will need to induce these definitions through repeated visits to the observation site or repeated observations of the behavior of interest.

Issues related to the obtrusiveness of the observation were not discussed in this article. It would be useful to know whether the students were aware that they were being observed (it is assumed that the librarians were aware of the observers and their study's purpose). In particular, it seems likely that the observer's position in the library would have influenced students' behaviors in relation to choosing that location for sitting. Because this study was not conducted in the United States, procedures for protecting the students' rights in relation to participation in the study were not enforced. If the study had been conducted in the United States, it would have been considered of minimal risk to the participants, but prior parental and student notification of the study would have likely been required. It is not clear how this notification might have affected student behavior, and so the researchers might have argued for a waiver of prior consent to be followed by a debriefing for the students at the end of the study.

The pairing of the observation methods with the student questionnaires allowed the researchers to overcome one serious weakness of observation: it doesn't tell you anything about the motivations behind the behaviors observed. In this study, the researchers were able to ask students about the meanings behind their actions. For example, the questionnaire asked about why the student selected a particular location to sit. This study, then, is a typical example of using two methods—one watching the study participants and one asking them questions—to get a more complete picture of a phenomenon.

Example 2: Unobtrusive Observation at the Reference Desk

The purpose of Curry's (2005) study was to investigate the quality of reference services provided by Vancouver area libraries to gay, lesbian, bisexual, or transgender (GLBT) or questioning young people. Specifically, she wanted to see whether reference librarians were following the Reference and User Services Association (RUSA) guide-lines for reference service when responding to questions from GLBT or questioning youth.

Curry (2005) wanted to conduct unobtrusive observations (i.e., observations of the reference librarians without their knowing that they were being observed) to capture their normal behaviors. She believed that this approach was very important for the goals of her study, to avoid a Hawthorne effect. In addition, deception was involved because a student was hired to play the part of a lesbian youth and would be asking preplanned questions, rather than her own questions. Principles of research ethics normally require that researchers not deceive their study participants and that study participants be asked for their consent prior to their participation. Thus Curry had to convince her local ethics review board that the value of the study outcomes would offset the potential for harm to the librarians who would be observed. In the end, she was successful in including three methods that normally are not allowed/followed: (1) the research assistant was allowed to deceive the librarians by pretending to be a lesbian youth asking an authentic question; (2) prior informed consent was not obtained; and (3) the participating librarians were later debriefed as a group with only the aggregate data. Curry argued that this third component would reduce the potential for harm to the participating librarians because none of them or their libraries would be singled out in the results or through an individual debriefing process. These negotiations with the ethics review board took approximately eight months, so researchers wishing to use this approach should be aware that they will need to allow for extra time in the planning stages of their research.

The research assistant who interacted with the reference librarians was a 19-year-old college student who looked several years younger; it was expected that the librarians would believe she was about 16. (The ethics review board would not approve someone younger than 18 playing this role in the study.) She approached a librarian at the reference desk that served young adults in each library being studied. In 10 of the 11 library systems studied, this service was provided at the adult reference desk. She asked the same question at each of 20 libraries: "I am planning to start a club at my high school. A gay-straight alliance. What books do you have that could help me out?" (Curry, 2005, p. 69). A question about gay-straight alliances was used because this type of activity had received media coverage over the previous few years and because resources existed to support a response. Immediately after each interaction, the research assistant used an observation schedule to record what happened and what resources were recommended. In addition, the schedule included questions based on the RUSA guidelines. The observation data were analyzed in terms of these guidelines, and Curry concluded that "in some areas, the librarians scored quite well; in only three of twenty interactions did [the research assistant] detect definite censure of her gay- and lesbian-related questions. But in most other areas, there was room for improvement" (p. 73).

This example highlights several of the decisions a researcher must make when using observational methods. The context of the observation was natural, and the information behavior of interest was one that could be evoked by the research assistant. The data were captured through an observation schedule filled out immediately after each interaction. While more detail could have been provided about the observation schedule, its underlying rationale was made clear. The study violated several of the commonly enforced ethical principles intended to protect study participants, but the researcher was careful to overcome these difficulties by providing alternative approaches to study participant protection. Overall, this study is a good model for how to conduct an unobtrusive observation.

Example 3: Eye Tracking during Web Retrieval

Lorigo and colleagues (2006) used technology to assist with direct observation of their study participants' interactions with search results returned by a Web search. Each of 23 graduate students conducted Web searches on 10 close-ended tasks (5 navigational and 5 informational). Each search task was read aloud to the study participant so that no eye movement was needed to read the task. Transaction logs were captured, and an Applied Sciences Laboratory (ASL) 504 eye tracker, with the ASL GazeTracker software, was used to capture fixations, saccades, pupil dilation, and scan paths as the participants reviewed the results of each search. These data were used to analyze the sequence and patterns with which people evaluate Web search results lists.

Eye tracking is a useful technique for this type of study because the researcher cannot directly observe eye movements and the study participant cannot accurately report them. Yet eye movements provide a very fine-grained view of how people interact with information content. Thus, while the equipment and software require a significant investment in the research effort, this investment is necessary for some types of research studies.

With the use of an eye tracker, one of the first steps of the research protocol is to calibrate the equipment so that it will accurately record the eye movements of the current participant. While new equipment has improved in its ability to be calibrated for a wider range of study participants, there are still some people for whom the eye tracker cannot be calibrated. In this study, the original sample of 36 graduate students was reduced to 23 due to "inability of some subjects to be calibrated and additional equipment and setup errors" (Lorigo et al., 2006, p. 1125). Thus, if you are planning to capture eye movements, plan to overrecruit so that you can meet your goals for an adequate sample size.

Four types of data were captured with the eye tracking equipment and software. The first were the fixations of each person's eye, "defined as a spatially stable gaze lasting for approximately 200–300 ms, during which visual attention is directed to a specific area of the visual display" (Lorigo et al., 2006, p. 1126). Researchers usually interpret a fixation as an indicator of attention to that point on the display. For example, if you fixate on the previous two sentences, it is assumed that you are paying special attention to them. Second, the researchers captured saccades, the rapid movements between fixations. It is assumed that little cognitive processing of the Web page content is occurring during a saccade. Third, the researchers used the sequences of fixations to draw a scan path, that is, a diagram of the participant's eye movements from place to place in sequence. Fourth, the researchers captured measures of pupil dilation. It is assumed that pupil dilation is an indicator of arousal during the task and so is interpreted as an indicator of more cognitive effort being expended on examining the content on which the participant is fixated. In combination, these eye movement metrics helped Lorigo and colleagues (2006) understand the ways in which people review Web search results.

Eye tracking has been used in a few studies in ILS since the field became interested in people's use of online systems. The first studies gathering these data required that the study participant sit very still, usually using a chin rest to hold the eyes in one place to enable tracking their movement. A later generation of equipment used a head tracker in combination with an eye tracker. The head tracker was mounted on a head band and enabled the eye tracking equipment to follow the participant's eyes over a larger area. The most recent generation of equipment has become even more robust to head movement and no longer requires simultaneous head tracking. In addition, its software creates scan paths automatically from the data collected. This technology will continue to develop and is an important tool for ILS research.

CONCLUSION

These three examples have demonstrated that observation methods can be used for a wide range of research questions. An observer present at the site being observed is still quite frequently used, but automatic methods for capturing some types of behaviors are also becoming more common. As long as we are interested in people's information behaviors, direct observation will be a useful research method.

WORKS CITED

Borlund, P. (2003). The IIR evaluation model: A framework for evaluation of interactive information retrieval systems. *Information Research, 8*(3), Article 152. Retrieved November 2, 2007, from http://informationr.net/ir/8-3/paper152.html.

Cooper, J., Lewis, R., & Urquhart, C. (2004). Using participant or non-participant observation to explain information behaviour. *Information Research, 9*(4), Article 184. Retrieved November 5, 2007, from http://informationr.net/ir/9-4/paper184.html.

Curry, A. (2005). If I ask, will they answer? Evaluating public library reference service to gay and lesbian youth. *Reference and User Services Quarterly, 45*(1), 65–75.

Denscombe, M. (2003). Observation. In *The Good Research Guide for Small-scale Social Research Projects* (pp. 192–212). Philadelphia: Open University Press.

Emerson, R. W. (1849, August 31). *The American scholar* [Speech presented to the Phi Beta Kappa Society, Harvard University]. *Nature*, Addresses and Lectures. (Original work presented 1837.)

Granholm, E., Asarnow, R. F., Sarkin, A. J., & Dykes, K. L. (1996). Pupillary responses index cognitive resource limitations. *Psychophysiology*, *33*, 457–461.

Gray, D. E. (2004). *Doing Research in the Real World*. London: Sage.

Joachims, T., Granka, L., Pan, B., Hembrooke, H., Radlinski, F., & Gay, G. (2007). Evaluating the accuracy of implicit feedback from clicks and query reformulations in Web search. *ACM Transactions on Information Systems*, *25*(2), Article 7.

Kumar, R. (2005). *Research Methodology: A Step-by-Step Guide for Beginners* (2nd ed.). London: Sage.

Lorigo, L., Pan, B., Hembrooke, H., Joachims, T., Granka, L., & Gay, G. (2006). The influence of task and gender on search and evaluation behavior using Google. *Information Processing and Management*, *42*(4), 1123–1131.

Mason, E. J., & Bramble, W. J. (1997). *Research in Education and the Behavioral Sciences: Concepts and Methods*. Madison, WI: Brown and Benchmark.

Mason, J. (2002). *Qualitative Researching* (2nd ed.). London: Sage.

McCall, G. J. (1984). Systematic field observation. *Annual Review of Sociology*, *10*, 263–282.

Neuman, W. L. (2006). *Social Research Methods: Qualitative and Quantitative Approaches* (6th ed.). Boston: Pearson.

O'Leary, Z. (2005). *Researching Real-world Problems: A Guide to Methods of Inquiry*. London: Sage.

Partala, T., & Surakka, V. (2003). Pupil size variation as an indication of affective processing. *International Journal of Human-Computer Studies*, *59*, 185–198.

Patton, M. Q. (2002). *Qualitative Research and Evaluation Methods*. Thousand Oaks, CA: Sage.

Pettigrew, K. E. (2000). Lay information provision in community settings: How community health nurses disseminate human services information to the elderly. *Library Quarterly*, *70*(1), 47–85.

Rayner, I. (1998). Eye movements in reading and information processing. *Psychological Bulletin*, *124*, 372–422.

Shoham, S., & Shemer-Shalman, Z. (2003). Territorial behavior in the school library. *School Libraries Worldwide*, *9*(2), 1–23.

Tenopir, C. (2003). Information metrics and user studies. *Aslib Proceedings*, *55*(1/2), 13–17.

Wilkinson, J. (1995). Direct observation. In G. M. Breakwell, S. Hammond, & C. Fife-Schaw (Eds.), *Research Methods in Psychology* (pp. 213–230). London: Sage.

Wilson, T. D., & Streatfield, D. R. (1980). *"You can observe a lot . . ."* A study of information use in local authority social services departments conducted by Project INISS (Occasional Publication No. 12). Sheffield, England: University of Sheffield, Postgraduate School of Librarianship and Information Science. Retrieved October 4, 2007, from http://informationr.net/tdw/publ/INISS/.

21

Participant Observation

Barbara M. Wildemuth

In the fields of observation chance favors only those minds which are prepared.
—Louis Pasteur (1854/1954)

DEFINITION

Directly observing information behaviors in the context in which they "naturally" occur is a potentially useful method to learn about how people experience information needs, seek information, or use the information found. A data collection method developed primarily in anthropology and qualitative sociology, *participant observation* has been defined in several ways:

- "Participant observation is a method in which a researcher takes part in the daily activities, rituals, interactions, and events of a group of people as one of the means of learning the explicit and tacit aspects of their life routines and their culture" (DeWalt & DeWalt, 2002, p. 1)
- "Participant observation aims to generate practical and theoretical truths about human life grounded in the realities of daily existence" (Jorgensen, 1989, p. 14)
- Participant observation involves "being in the presence of others on an ongoing basis and having some nominal status for them as someone who is part of their daily lives" (Schwartz & Jacob, 1979, p. 46)
- Participant observation involves "prolonged, personal contact with events in a natural setting" (Chatman, 1984, p. 426)

These definitions point out that in participant observation, (1) the researcher is a participant in the setting, (2) such participation leads to a better understanding of the people and social processes that occur within that setting, and (3) this understanding can lead to better theories about social processes in that setting and similar settings.

In spite of the potential usefulness of this data collection method to address research questions in information and library science (ILS), "comparatively few information needs [and other ILS] studies have made use of observation techniques, and of these, most have used non-participant observation techniques" (Cooper et al., 2004, para. 2). It is hoped that this chapter will help those wishing to conduct studies using participant observation because a variety of questions can be addressed with the data resulting from such observations (DeWalt & DeWalt, 2002). The method is used most often for descriptive studies, both those that are exploring a new area of research interest and those that are intended to generate empirically grounded theories. In addition, participant observation can be useful in studies that are intended to help interpret or explain the results of prior empirical work. For example, a survey of academic library reference practices may find that reference librarians report a decrease in the number of requests for assistance in online database searching; participant observation may be used to follow up such a study to understand the social processes leading to such a change in activity level.

The choice of participant observation as a data collection method is often motivated by the researcher's epistemological stance. While the participant observer may espouse one of a number of theoretical orientations (Patton, 2002), it is most likely that he or she is working within an interpretive or phenomenological research paradigm. In such a paradigm, it is assumed that reality is socially constructed, though not completely subjective. The participant observer usually assumes that "some sort of consensus of common knowledge about meaning exists in groups and is sustained over time by social processes" (Schwartz & Jacob, 1979, p. 37) and, importantly, the meanings that are pertinent to a particular setting can be understood if the observer can take on the role of a participant in that setting.

THE RESEARCHER'S ROLE

The researcher's role is "the characteristic posture researchers assume in their re-lationship with respondents" (Chatman, 1984, p. 429). In participant observation, the researcher simultaneously takes on two roles: that of participant and that of observer. For a particular study, the researcher should consider carefully how these two roles will be balanced. Schwartz and Jacob (1979) depicted this balancing act as one of finding one's position on a continuum between involvement and detachment. Patton (2002) pro-posed that researchers exhibit empathic neutrality. By taking this stance, the researcher experiences empathy with the other participants, gaining both an affective connection with them as well as a cognitive understanding of the setting. The researcher also main-tains neutrality; that is he or she "does not set out to prove a particular perspective or manipulate the data to arrive at predisposed truths" (Patton, 2002, p. 51).

Spradley's (1980) classic discussion of participant observation points out the many ways that participant observers differ from the other participants in the setting. First, they have a dual role: to both participate and observe. Second, the participant observer is explicitly aware of what is happening in the setting, while the other participants routinely employ "selective inattention" (p. 55). Third, the participant observer tends to define the setting more broadly, in an attempt to understand how the culture's context influences the culture itself. Fourth, the participant observer is an outsider as well as an insider. Fifth, the participant observer records notes on what is observed and reflects on what is observed. These activities are not generally undertaken by the other participants in the setting.

Most discussions of participant observation consider the researcher's dual role in terms of the level of participation undertaken. At one end of the spectrum is the situation in which the researcher is only a participant in the sense that he or she is actually present in the setting. This level of participation has been called *passive participation* by Spradley (1980), *participant-as-observer* by Gold (1958), and *limited* observation by Ely (1991). At the other end of the continuum, the participant observer is fully involved as a participant in the setting. Spradley (1980) describes this level of involvement as *complete* participation, where the observer is a true member of the culture being studied. For example, a librarian employed in a library may also study the culture of that library. Other authors refer to similar levels of involvement as *full membership* (Adler & Adler, 1987) or *active participant* (Ely, 1991). While most texts on ethnography list and describe discrete levels of participation, the level of participation can be situated at any point on a continuum between the two extremes. Each researcher must determine which participation level is most appropriate for a given study.

There are several considerations that should be taken into account when determining the appropriate level of participation. First, the fit between the characteristics of the researcher and the characteristics of others in the setting must be considered. The personality or the interpersonal communication skills of the researcher may or may not allow him or her to participate in a particular setting. The demographic characteristics of the researcher (such as race or sex) may allow the researcher to participate only as an "outsider" in some settings, limiting the type of participatory roles that can be assumed. Second, the range of roles available to the researcher will affect his or her level of participation. For example, if the researcher wants to study the corporate culture of a start-up technology firm, the roles available for active participation are limited, and the researcher will need some technical expertise or administrative skills to assume a "real" participant's role. The ability of the researcher to enter and, later, to leave the setting should also be considered as a participatory role is selected.

THE PROCESS OF PARTICIPANT OBSERVATION

Participant observation happens over a period of time and in a number of phases, including entering the field, establishing rapport, performing the selected role, making and recording observations, and withdrawing from the field. These phases usually overlap, and the relationship between the researcher and other participants in the setting will evolve during each phase.

Entering the field has a variety of difficulties that must be negotiated successfully for the study to progress. First, you must select the setting. In some cases, access to a setting will affect the questions to be asked; in others, the questions to be asked will motivate the choice of a setting. Before gaining access to the selected setting, you will need to obtain permission to enter the setting. In many settings, a member (or multiple members) of the culture play the role of gatekeeper. For instance, if a library is selected as the setting, the library director will need to grant permission for the study to take place. Once permission to conduct the study has been granted, you will need to explain the research to the other participants in the setting. These initial contacts and explanations are important for establishing the role that you will play in the culture. When you finally begin to enter the setting as a participant observer, it is possible that you will first be approached by that culture's "professional stranger-handlers" (Agar, 1996), who officially or unofficially serve as communicators with outsiders. While people in this role may be useful informants, they may also serve as a second set of gatekeepers, intending to keep outsiders on the outside. Thus, to move forward with the study, you must enter the field with great care.

The next task of the participant observer is to establish rapport with members of the culture being studied. As Chatman (1984) notes, "rapport is the sense of closeness field researchers need to establish with their informants in order to be able to talk with, and observe them in somewhat unguarded situations" (p. 432). Rapport is based on mutual respect, which can be expressed in a number of ways such as being interested in other members of the culture, conversing with members of the culture (including self-revelation), and working to fit in with the routines of the culture. The expression of reciprocity is also a strategy for developing and maintaining rapport. You can informally help people out and, through regular interaction, can develop empathy for the other participants in the culture. Developing rapport will allow you to observe the culture more closely, and developing empathy is a natural outcome of attempts to see a culture from its members' perspectives.

As a participant observer, you will take on some role within the culture being observed. The higher the level of participation, the more important role performance becomes as a method for learning about the culture (Jorgensen, 1989). You will learn the language of the culture being studied (i.e., you'll learn to talk the talk), and you'll learn how to behave properly in the culture (i.e., you'll learn to walk the walk). During the learning process, it is very likely that you will make mistakes in your role performance, only some of which can be gracefully repaired. Such mistakes are inevitable, and their repair has the potential to increase your understanding of the culture. One role that provides an opportunity to learn appropriate role performance is the apprentice role (Coy, 1989; Ely, 1991). Often used in anthropological studies, this role is also recommended as part of the contextual inquiry approach to systems analysis and design (Beyer & Holtzblatt, 1998).

While participating in the culture, you are also observing the culture and recording those observations. A variety of things may be observed and recorded: the physical arrangement of places and objects, sequences of events and where they occur, who participates in which activities, who communicates with whom, and the conversations that occur within the setting. Remembering what is observed is aided by a variety of types of field notes, which are a "form of *representation*, that is, a way of reducing just-observed events, persons and places to written accounts" (Emerson et al., 2001, p. 353). Such notes include jot notes or scratch notes taken in the field, logs of daily activities and questions, expanded field notes that describe what was observed in more detail, methodological notes, analytical notes that try to interpret what was observed, and diaries and journals, in which you will reflect on your personal reactions to what you observed.

You will continue participating in the culture and observing the culture until theoretical saturation has been reached (i.e., when you are learning nothing new and of importance to the goals of the study). Data collection and some analysis occur while you are still in the field, but at some point, you must leave the setting. Withdrawing from the field may be easy or difficult, depending mostly on the role taken in the culture. In most cases, you will want to depart from the field gradually, leaving the opportunity for follow-up, if necessary.

PITFALLS TO WATCH FOR

As with any other method of data collection, participant observation has certain inherent characteristics that can cause a researcher to stumble. Three of these pitfalls will be mentioned here: (1) the effects of the observer on the setting being observed, (2) the possibility that members of the culture will lead you to incorrect conclusions, and (3) the barriers that characteristics of the setting and method can place in the way of collecting data systematically.

The most obvious concern for those considering participant observation as a data collection method is the effect that you might have on the culture being observed. Clearly one cannot enter a culture without affecting it, whether you are a researcher or playing some other role. There are two ways in which the researcher can guard against invalid conclusions biased by participation in the culture. First, you should make every effort to fit in to the culture, rather than disrupting it. This can be aided by choosing an appropriate role to play and working hard to learn to perform that role correctly. Second, you must reflect on the effect of your participation in the culture, just as the participation of other cultural members is the subject of your reflections. The diaries or journals that you keep should include notes about your own conversations, actions, and reactions as well as the conversations, actions, and reactions of other members of the culture. These notes, then, become part of the data to be analyzed during the study.

A second pitfall is that some members of the culture may, intentionally or unintentionally, lead you to incorrect conclusions about the culture. In the worst case, an informant may lie to you (Becker, 1958). In other cases, a "professional stranger-handler" may urge you to focus in one direction and avoid a direction that the culture would prefer to protect from outsiders. This pitfall can be overcome by a lengthier and more active participation in the culture. Importantly, participant observation has an advantage over interviews alone in avoiding this pitfall, because what is observed can be compared to what informants tell you, allowing you to "call into question the relationship between words and deeds" (Schwartz & Jacob, 1979, p. 46). When interviews and observations conflict, each should be carefully considered within its own context.

A third pitfall is that the setting or events in the setting may interfere with collecting data systematically (Becker, 1958). Unlike many other data collection methods, a participant observer does not ask every member of the culture the same set of carefully designed questions. Participant observation is opportunistic—the participant observer is at a certain place at any given moment and events unfold within that situation (DeWalt & DeWalt, 2002). To overcome this pitfall, you should use your current understanding of the culture to place yourself at the right places at the right times, increasing the likelihood that objects, events, and people of interest to the study can be observed frequently.

EXAMPLES

Two examples of participant observation will be considered here. In the first, Westbrook (1995) studies women's studies faculty members' use of periodicals by participating in their work lives (serving as their librarian) and by directly observing their information seeking behaviors. In the second, McKechnie (1996) took on the role of a "student" in a library, while observing young girls during their visits to the public library. Each of these studies was conducted as dissertation research, hinting at the labor-intensive nature of participant observation.

Example 1: Women's Studies Faculty's Use of Periodicals

Westbrook (1995) used participant observation, among other methods, for her dissertation research on the information seeking experiences of faculty in women's studies. She describes the study as exploratory and naturalistic, using a grounded theory approach (Glaser & Strauss, 1967; Strauss & Corbin, 1990). The full study combined multiple data collection methods: content analysis of a pertinent Listserv, in-depth interviews with faculty at two universities, and follow-up observation of the faculty at one of the universities. The dissertation was revised and published in book form in 1999 (not uncommon for large-scale interpretive studies) and in an article in 1998. This discussion will focus on the observation methods used.

The process of selecting the two settings (i.e., universities) to be studied is not described in either the dissertation or the book. However, the ways in which the two sites differ on theoretically important dimensions are described in some detail in the book (Westbrook, 1999). The two universities were similar in size and in the library support available, but they differed in terms of research funding, number of patents received, and general character. The women's studies departments at the two universities were markedly different in age, size, and status.

Interviews and follow-up observations both were conducted at just one of the sites: a midwestern university. Westbrook (1995) obtained assistance in entering the field there by receiving a list of faculty meeting the study's inclusion criteria from the Women's Studies Program office. The chair of the program provided a cover letter for Westbrook's invitation to participate in the study, mailed to each of 27 eligible faculty members. Westbrook followed up to arrange the interview and get the scholar's consent to participate in the study; nine faculty members agreed to participate.

Data at the midwestern university were collected through an initial interview, in which the scholar discussed one project in detail, and observation of information seeking work. Altogether, Westbrook (1995) met 30 times with the nine participants, audiotaping and taking notes during these meetings. In addition to transcribing the audiotapes, three types of field notes were kept: an activity log, describing her research activity; a methodology log, with notes about the methods used; and a reflexive log, with notes about the researcher's reactions to what she was learning. In addition, analytical notes were recorded in memos as the data collection was ongoing.

Combining these data with interview data collected at another university and the analysis of an international Listserv strengthens this study. It allowed Westbrook (1995) to triangulate the findings from the multiple data sources, testing the validity of each against the others. Even with the two data collection methods used at the midwestern university, Westbrook had the capability of testing the information seeking approaches reported by the faculty participants against what she observed as they conducted information seeking work. Under these conditions, it is much less likely that the results would describe information seeking as the scholars believe it "should" be done, rather than as they actually do it.

Westbrook (1995) was able to adopt a very natural role in relation to those faculty observed: she was a librarian in the university and served these faculty occasionally. In this case, instead of adopting a new participant role to undertake the study, Westbrook needed to adapt her current role in relationship to these faculty members. The interviews and observations were to be conducted in the work setting of the study participants (i.e., their offices), not in the work setting that they shared (i.e., the library). Thus, while this study can be correctly described as including participant observation, Westbrook's participation in the culture of the participating scholars was limited.

While her already existing relationship with these faculty made it easy to adopt a participant observer role, it also created a potential obstacle for successful completion of her study. First, she had to establish her role as a researcher, in addition to being a librarian. Second, she needed to communicate to her study participants that she was interested in exploring the full range of information seeking approaches they used, not just those supported by the library. Westbrook (1995) verified that she was successful in defining her role and the scope of the study to the participants because a number of them described and allowed her to observe such information seeking activities as use of their personal collections or contacts with other people.

A challenge faced by most ILS researchers who would like to use participant observation as a data collection method is the timing of information behaviors. While people, in some sense, interact with information frequently throughout the day, the types of information behaviors that are of research interest occur much less frequently. Also, they often occur spontaneously—something happens that motivates an unplanned information seeking episode. The anthropological style of participant observation, where the researcher observes a culture while "living" in it, requires a significant amount of time to be used to observe a relatively small number of episodes of information behavior. In addition, many information behaviors are exhibited by solitary individuals, rather than social groups. There is no "natural" way for a researcher to observe these behaviors because they normally occur when the subject of the study is alone. Westbrook (1995) faced this methodological challenge by scheduling an observation session chosen by the faculty member "on the basis of 'having something for [her] to observe' " (p. 85). The scheduling of these sessions in advance probably limited the types of information seeking that were observed to only those that could be anticipated by the faculty member. The alternative—shadowing the faculty member for particular days, in the hope that some information seeking would occur on those days—would have been less efficient for Westbrook, with only small gains in the validity of the results.

Another challenge associated with participant observation is the protection of the study participants from any risk associated with their participation in the research. Generally, some type of anonymity or confidentiality guarantees must be made by the researcher to encourage informants to reveal their lives fully. Typically, pseudonyms are used for individual study participants, and the identity of their organization is masked. In her dissertation, Westbrook (1995) followed these practices. In her later article (Westbrook, 1998), the identities of the participating universities were revealed, but the comments from the participants were reported only in the aggregate; that is, no individual quotes from the interviews were included. In her book (Westbrook, 1999), the universities are identified by name and the real names of the study participants are used, even with individual quotes. As a researcher, you will need to make a decision in advance of the study about whether and how participants are to be protected. In many studies, the information revealed by the participants, either through their actions or through their words, is not sensitive and they are not at risk in any way if their identities are revealed. However, great caution should be exercised. For example, if one of Westbrook's scholars had been extremely critical of the university administration and its support of women scholars on campus, would Westbrook have had the power to ensure that the participant would not be treated differently within her department? Because it is rarely within the researcher's power to provide such protection for subjects, it is recommended that pseudonyms be used for all individual participants. Organizations may be identified under two conditions: that permission has been given by a responsible person in the organization and that identification of the institution will not lead to identification of individual participants.

As noted earlier, Westbrook's (1995) study was reported in three versions. While duplicate publication of results is discouraged in general, it is often the case for studies involving participant observation that multiple publications are necessary. The original work was conducted in completing Westbrook's dissertation, in 1995. As a published dissertation, the results were made available, but it is expected that they will be reported in other venues in addition to the dissertation to receive wider dissemination. The article in *The Serials Librarian* appeared next, in 1998. This article can be seen as a niche publication: well focused to inform a particular audience. It focused on those findings of interest to readers of that journal and could only report them in aggregated form, due to typical limitations on the length of journal articles. The next year, in 1999, the book appeared. It is a completely rewritten version of the study, intended for the professional reader, rather than Westbrook's dissertation committee. The language is oriented toward the discourse of the profession, and the book is reorganized to emphasize the findings (placing the methods description in appendices). Because the data resulting from participant observation is rich and qualitative, such a book-length report of the findings is quite appropriate.

In many ways, Westbrook's (1995) study can be considered typical of the way in which participant observation can be fruitfully applied to the study of information behaviors, particularly in academic settings. Access is not usually difficult to arrange because the focus of the study is usually not sensitive. There are a number of viable participant roles that can be assumed by the researcher, including an information provider role or an apprentice role. The researcher must overcome the challenge of the sparse occurrence of the behaviors of interest in people's lives. However, this difficulty is outweighed by the advantage of being able to observe people's information behaviors directly, rather than just hearing reports of them. The researcher needs to take precautions to protect study participants because they will be revealing many aspects of their lives. Finally, the results will probably need to be reported in multiple venues, one of which may be of book length.

Example 2: Preschool Girls' Use of the Public Library

McKechnie (1996), in her dissertation research,[1] applied participant observation to the study of public library use by preschool girls. In addition, she was interested in a couple of questions related to the context of their use: the role of adults (parents, librarians) in the girls' use of the library and the ways in which library use encouraged learning. In addition to publishing the results in her dissertation, McKechnie has published a methodological article (McKechnie, 2000) describing this work.

While describing the study as "exploratory" (McKechnie, 1996, p. 2), she did use two theoretical frameworks to focus her attention. The first was Dervin's *Sense-Making Theory* (Dervin & Frenette, 2001); McKechnie expected that the adults in the setting might serve the girls in addressing their information-related gaps. The second was Vygotsky's (1978) concept of the *zone of proximal development*, in which the library could be seen as a learning environment in which the adults provide scaffolding for the learners. These theories helped McKechnie to focus her attention without overly limiting her investigation of the girls' behaviors.

The selection of a setting in which to conduct the study was done in two phases. In the first, McKechnie (1996) chose a public library system in an urban setting. The library system met certain inclusion criteria such as accepting the American Library Association role of "Preschooler's Door to Learning" (McClure et al., 1987). Permission to conduct the study was obtained from the library system director. In the next phase, four individual libraries were selected for participation. Libraries that did not have a full-time children's librarian or whose communities did not include a large number of English-speaking children were excluded from consideration. From the remaining libraries, four were selected, and permission to conduct the study was obtained from their directors. In addition, the researcher met with the library staff to introduce them to the purpose and procedures of the study.

The 30 four-year-old girls who participated in the study were recruited through a variety of means, with almost half of them recruited through flyers posted in the participating libraries. The participants had to meet a number of inclusion criteria: having language skills strong enough to provide data, having used the library at least once per month for the six months prior to the study, and having family and demographic characteristics that were typical of the Canadian population. The eligibility of the child was determined through a phone interview with each mother. McKechnie (1996) focused on girls' behaviors, excluding boys, partly because she wished to compare her results with those of an earlier study that included only girls (Tizard & Hughes, 1984) and so replicated many of that study's design decisions.

Prior to the observation session, McKechnie (1996) met with the study participants (child and mother) at their home or at the library. During this session, McKechnie worked to establish some rapport with the child and her mother, "gave the child an opportunity to observer [her] in a non threatening environment" (p. 53), allowed the child to handle and become familiar with the recording equipment to be used during the study, obtained consent from the mother and assent from the child, and scheduled a library visit. The initial meeting with the mother and child provided an opportunity for her to move from the status of complete stranger to someone recognizable, even in a different place (i.e., the library). Working with children introduces a very obvious status/power differential between the researcher and the study participant. It was McKechnie's hope that the initial meeting might alleviate the aspects of that status differential, which could interfere with naturalistic observation.

McKechnie's (1996) work is an excellent example of a researcher identifying and developing a participant role that is natural for the setting of the study. During the library visits (i.e., the observation periods), McKechnie took on the formal role of "student" (McKechnie, 1996, p. 50). This role allowed her to take notes during the observation period, because that is what students often do in a library, and with the added purpose of gracefully warding off social interactions with the child during the library visit, which were undesirable because they would not be typical of a library visit by that child. She augmented this effort to be unobtrusive by asking "the families to do what they would normally do during their visit" (McKechnie, 1996, p. 61) and trying to observe the child while remaining out of the child's line of sight.

A variety of types of data were collected in this study, as is typical of studies incorporating participant observation. Prior to any observation sessions, McKechnie (1996) visited and mapped out each of the four library sites. During the library visits, the child was asked to wear a special shirt; a pocket for an audiotape recorder was sewn on the back, with the microphone attached to the front. Most of the children accepted this intervention well, though some objected. There were also a few early cases of the girls accidentally turning off the recorder while somersaulting through the library; this problem was resolved with cardboard padding around the recorder. Using this method of recording the children's natural speech during the visit resulted in detailed transcripts. McKechnie also observed the children while they were in the library, thus gaining access to their nonverbal behaviors—an important aspect of their library use. Her observations were recorded in descriptive notes, methods notes (with particular attention to possible observer effects), and a diary/journal of her feelings and impressions. After the library visit, mothers were asked to keep diaries of incidents related to the library visit or use of library materials. The mothers were then interviewed about their diary entries about one week after the visit. The diaries were an attempt to vicariously observe the child's activities. As McKechnie (2000) notes, "the technique of observation by the researcher in the child's home was rejected as impractical because of the difficulty of finding subjects who would have agreed to a stranger observing their family life for several days or more" (p. 67). Thus the full set of data included maps of the sites, recordings of the children's talk while in the library, notes from the observations of the children's behavior while in the library, and diary-interviews with the mothers.

Working with children presents special challenges related to protecting them from any risks associated with study participation. McKechnie's (1996) handling of these issues has already been described previously. In addition, they were partially alleviated because a parent was present at all times during the data collection. An additional confidentiality issue associated with participant observation was raised in this study. The children were wearing tape recorders to record their speech during the visit; however, if they interacted with a librarian or other person in the setting, new study participants were added without gaining their prior consent. McKechnie appropriately handled this issue with the methods she used to gain access to the site. She got permission from each library director and also informed the library staff of the details of the procedures. In addition, library staff members are not identified in the reports of the findings, protecting their anonymity. A final step that McKechnie took was to post signs about the study in the children's area whenever an observation session was occurring; these signs alerted other library users of the study.

McKechnie's (1996) careful attention to the methodological issues associated with participant observation led to the successful completion of her study. In addition, both her publications discuss these methodological challenges, how they were addressed, and whether the methods used were successful or not. For example, she spends a dozen pages in her dissertation (and three pages in the article) discussing various types of observer effects, her attempts to overcome them, and evidence from her data that they were or were not overcome. Through such frank self-evaluation, her readers can assess the validity of her findings, and researchers can learn about methods that they can use to overcome the obstacles associated with participant observation.

CONCLUSION

As can be seen from these two examples, participant observation is a rigorous form of in-depth qualitative research, requiring significant advance planning and significant time in the field. If done well, it looks like the researcher is just part of the setting (i.e., is just "hanging out" among the others within the setting). But that superficial view of the researcher's activities does not take into account the many layers of data collection and interpretation that occur to successfully complete the study. Thus participant observation can yield a very rich description of a particular setting and the information behaviors that occur within it.

NOTE

1. For this work, McKechnie was the winner of the 1997 Eugene Garfield Doctoral Dissertation Competition administered by the Association for Library and Information Science Education.

WORKS CITED

Adler, P. A., & Adler, P. (1987). *Membership Roles in Field Research*. Newbury Park: Sage.

Agar, M. H. (1996). *The Professional Stranger: An Informal Introduction to Ethnography* (2nd ed.). San Diego, CA: Academic Press.

Becker, H. S. (1958). Problems of inference and proof in participant observation. *American Sociological Review, 23*(6), 652–660.

Beyer, H., & Holtzblatt, K. (1998). The master/apprentice model. In *Contextual Design: Defining Customer-centered Systems* (pp. 42–46). San Francisco: Morgan Kaufmann.

Chatman, E. A. (1984). Field research: Methodological themes. *Library and Information Science Research, 6*, 425–438.

Cooper, J., Lewis, R., & Urquhart, C. (2004). Using participant and non-participant observation to explain information behaviour. *Information Research, 9*(4), Article 184. Retrieved June 29, 2008, from http://informationr.net/ir/9-4/paper184.html.

Coy, M. (1989). Introduction. In *Apprenticeship: From Theory to Method and Back Again* (pp. xi–xv). Albany: State University of New York Press.

Dervin, B., & Frenette, M. (2001). Sense-making methodology: Communicating communicatively with campaign audiences. In R. Rice & C. K. Atkin (Eds.), *Public Communications Campaigns* (pp. 69–87). Thousand Oaks, CA: Sage.

DeWalt, K. M., & DeWalt, B. R. (2002). *Participant Observation: A Guide for Fieldworkers*. Walnut Creek, CA: AltaMira Press.

Ely, M. (1991). *Doing Qualitative Research: Circles within Circles*. London: Falmer Press.

Emerson, R. M., Fretz, R. I., & Shaw, L. L. (2001). Participant observation and fieldnotes. In P. Atkinson, A. Coffey, S. Delamont, J. Lofland, & L. Lofland (Eds.), *Handbook of Ethnography* (pp. 352–368). London: Sage.

Glaser, B. G., & Strauss, A. L. (1967). *The Discovery of Grounded Theory: Strategies for Qualitative Research*. Chicago: Aldine.

Gold, R. L. (1958). Roles in sociological field observations. *Social Forces, 36*(3), 217–223.

Jorgensen, D. L. (1989). *Participant Observation: A Methodology for Human Studies*. Newbury Park, CA: Sage.

McClure, C. R., Owen, A., Zweizig, D. L., Lynch, M. J., & Van House, N. A. (1987). *Planning and Role Setting for Public Libraries: A Manual of Options and Procedures*. Chicago: American Library Association.

McKechnie, L. (E. F.). (1996). *Opening the "preschoolers' door to learning": An ethnographic study of the use of public libraries by preschool girls*. Unpublished doctoral dissertation, University of Western Ontario.

McKechnie, L. (E. F.). (2000). Ethnographic observation of preschool children. *Library and Information Science Research, 22*(1), 61–76.

Pasteur, L. (1954). Inaugural lecture as professor and dean of the faculty of science, University of Lille, Douai, France, December 7, 1854. In H. Peterson (Ed.), *A Treasury of the World's Great Speeches* (p. 473). New York: Simon and Schuster. (Original work presented 1854.)

Patton, M. Q. (2002). *Qualitative Research and Evaluation Methods* (3rd ed.). Thousand Oaks, CA: Sage.

Schwartz, H., & Jacob, J. (1979). *Qualitative Sociology: A Method to the Madness.* New York: Free Press.

Spradley, J. P. (1980). *Participant Observation.* New York: Holt, Rinehart and Winston.

Strauss, A. L., & Corbin, J. (1990). *Basics of Qualitative Research: Grounded Theory, Procedures, and Techniques.* Newbury Park, CA: Sage.

Tizard, B., & Hughes, M. (1984). *Young Children in Learning.* Cambridge, MA: Harvard University Press.

Vygotsky, L. (1978). *Mind in Society: The Development of Higher Psychological Processes.* Cambridge, MA: Harvard University Press.

Westbrook, L. (1995). *The information seeking experiences of women's studies faculty.* Unpublished doctoral dissertation, University of Michigan.

Westbrook, L. (1998). Using periodicals in women's studies: The faculty experience. *The Serials Librarian, 35*(1/2), 9–27.

Westbrook, L. (1999). *Interdisciplinary Information Seeking in Women's Studies.* Jefferson, NC: McFarland.

ADDITIONAL RECOMMENDED READING

Angrosino, M. V., & de Pérez, K.A.M. (2000). Rethinking observation: From method to context. In N. K. Denzin & Y. S. Lincoln (Eds.), *Handbook of Qualitative Research* (2nd ed., pp. 673–702). Thousand Oaks, CA: Sage.

Grover, R., & Glazier, J. D. (1985). Implications for application of qualitative methods to library and information science research. *Library and Information Science Research, 7*(3), 247–260.

Grover, R., & Glazier, J. D. (1992). Structured participant observation. In J. D. Glazier & R. R. Powell (Eds.), *Qualitative Research in Information Management* (pp. 105–121). Englewood, CO: Libraries Unlimited.

Jacob, E. (1987). Qualitative research traditions: A review. *Review of Educational Research, 57*(1), 1–50.

Lincoln, Y. S., & Guba, E. G. (1985). *Naturalistic Inquiry.* Beverly Hills, CA: Sage.

Lofland, J., & Lofland, L. H. (1995). *Analyzing Social Settings: A Guide to Qualitative Observation and Analysis* (3rd ed.). Belmont, CA: Wadsworth.

Newhouse, R. C. (1989). Librarian-researchers: Perspectives on a methodology. *Library Quarterly, 59*(1), 22–26.

22

Research Diaries

Laura Sheble and Barbara M. Wildemuth

One day we share this opinion and the next day we take a different view. Then we write
many things into that [diary] and they are valid some day and some other time they are not
and the conclusion drawn from it can even be totally wrong.
—Interviewee from a diary contributor at a paper mill (quoted in Auramaki et al., 1996)

A DIVERSE METHOD

Diaries capture life as it is lived by an individual over time. The diary author's thoughts
and the internal and external events he or she experiences are fixed in a medium to
"provide a record of an ever-changing present" (Elliott, 1997, ¶2.4). Other forms of
writing about the self, such as autobiography and letters, are closely related to the diary,
but diaries are distinct in that time structures their creation, layering text and objects into
a chronological composite of snapshots and reflections a few minutes, a day, or a week
at a time. Construed broadly, a diary might be a collage of text and nontext or consist
solely of nontextual materials (Allport, 1942; Plummer, 2001).

Research diaries (i.e., diaries solicited specifically for research) comprise a varied set
of data collection instruments and techniques that range from descriptive event logs to
narrative personal accounts. The research diary can conceptually and physically resemble
other data collection methods such as the questionnaire, the interview, or observation.
What makes diary methods distinct from other methods is that diary protocols require
participants to make self-reports repeatedly over time (Bolger et al., 2003). Thus diaries
range from highly structured logs to unstructured narratives.

HISTORY

The tradition of diaries spans a murky history with an unascertained origin. Extant
autobiographical diaries[1] date from the first century CE in China. Though diary keeping
among adults has been cited as an activity with a diminishing number of practitioners

(Bloom, 1976), an ever increasing variety of autobiographical everyday life texts and material/digital objects is being created. Plummer (2001) argues that photography has supplanted traditional text diaries to become the de facto medium of choice to chronicle personal life. Online diaries, including blogs (weblogs), have evolved from simple text documents in the mid-1990s[2] to composite works in many media, and they continue to gain in popularity (Serfaty, 2004).

Social scientists began using research diaries to collect data in the early twentieth century (Black & Crann, 2002; Szalai, 1972; Wheeler & Reis, 1991), but their use in social science research is still infrequent (Plummer, 2001; Toms & Duff, 2002). In information and library science (ILS) research, the diary method has been used mainly in studies of information seeking (such as the Byström & Järvelin, 1995, study discussed later) and human-computer interaction (e.g., from Rieman, 1993, to Ryan & Valverde, 2005).

TYPES OF RESEARCH DIARIES

Several classifications of diary types have been developed. The time an experience is written about with respect to when it occurred and the practice of collecting repeat entries are key concepts in the definition of a diary. Why a diary was written, that is, whether it was solicited for research, is of primary importance. *Solicited* diaries are often considered independently of *unsolicited* diaries with respect to research methods because study design and content vary greatly based on whether a diary was solicited. When a diary is solicited for research, an audience—that of the researcher, and potentially, the audience of the researcher's work—is imposed on the diarist. Structured diaries overtly recognize the presence of the researcher. Participants often directly acknowledge that they are aware of the "presence" of the researcher through what they write or when asked in subsequent interviews (Elliott, 1997; Toms & Duff, 2002).

Within the realm of solicited diaries, classifications focus on one or more key aspects of the diary such as (1) the degree of structure and (2) how a diarist knows when to record, or the basis for recording schedules. On the basis of structure, diaries are classified as *unstructured*, *semistructured*, or *structured* and may also be described as a *log*. Unstructured diaries are open ended, and the diarist is given little or no guidance regarding the content that should be included, or its shape or form. Structured diaries, on the other hand, are very specific regarding these aspects. Most diaries are semistructured, falling somewhere in the middle of the continuum. Logs are diaries with a list or tablelike format and may be more or less structured.

The second characteristic used for classification, how a diarist knows when to record, or the basis for recording schedules, speaks to the same point from two different perspectives. Wheeler and Reis (1991) based their classification on the former characteristic, which considers the diary experience from the point of view of the diary writer or participant. According to their schema, diaries can be classified as (1) interval-contingent, (2) signal-contingent, or (3) event-contingent based on the triggers—the passing of time, an external prompt, or an experienced event—that instigate self-reporting by the participant. In interval-contingent diaries, entries are made at regular intervals, for example, daily or weekly. In signal-contingent diaries, entries are made based on the receipt of some external signal. For example, a study of librarians' professional work may require that the librarians wear a timer; when the timer goes off, at random intervals during the day, the librarian is to make a diary entry about the work in which he or she is currently engaged. In event-contingent designs, responses are prompted by internal or external events that meet a preestablished definition such as the occurrence of an information seeking episode.

STRENGTHS AND WEAKNESSES

Research diaries are especially effective when used to study phenomena that would not otherwise be accessible to researchers because they are internal, situationally inaccessible, infrequent and/or rare, or because the physical presence of the researcher would significantly impact the phenomenon of interest (Bolger et al., 2003; Elliott, 1997; Wheeler & Reis, 1991). Diary methods are more likely to capture ordinary events and observations that might be neglected by other methods because participants view them as insignificant, take them for granted, or forget them (Elliott, 1997; Wheeler & Reis, 1991). Diary methods also have potential for research related to temporal dynamics and time-based phenomena (Bolger et al., 2003).

One of the great strengths of diary methods is that information about events is captured at or close to the time of occurrence (Wheeler & Reis, 1991). Thus diaries have fewer recall and reframing errors compared to other methods that capture events a significant period after their occurrence. Because the researcher need not be present during data collection, diary studies have the potential to constitute a relatively unobtrusive form of data collection—provided participant burden is minimized. Otherwise, they have the potential to be very intrusive in terms of participant time requirements (Berg, 2004; Bolger et al., 2003; Symon, 2004).

One of the most obvious aspects of a diary, one that could be construed as a potential benefit or limitation, is that potential research participants are familiar with the concept (Breakwell & Wood, 1995). On one hand, this may be a benefit to research because participants are likely to be familiar with the basic form of a diary and with the concept of recording narratives repeatedly over time. At the same time, preconceived notions of what constitutes a diary could inhibit recording of responses according to the research protocol if the protocol differs substantially from the participants' preexisting notion of a diary. Diarists themselves are also likely to vary in their tendencies as autobiographical writers. The degree of intimacy and reflection exhibited varies on an individual basis: some diarists tend simply to report events, while others offer detailed accounts of their reflections. The degree to which a diarist focuses on topics of primary interest to the researcher is also likely to vary.

Diary studies impose a significant burden on participants and researchers alike. It is generally time consuming to pretest diary methods, train respondents, keep diaries, and analyze the data. Many potential participants assume that diary studies will be time consuming, which can inhibit participant recruitment, retention, and the quality of data collected. Getting study participants to make the requested entries can be a challenge (Breakwell & Wood, 1995). Underreporting, content selection bias, behavior modification, and partial recording errors occur in diaries. Recall and reframing errors increase as time between an experience and its recording increase (Corti, 1993; Rieman, 1996). Other potential weaknesses of diary studies are derived from the tools and instruments that are used to collect data. For example, questions in a structured or semistructured diary instrument can affect how the participant conceptualizes responses or perceives events, or, in extreme cases, may alter long-term views held by the participant. The act of keeping a diary may have some therapeutic effect itself, but the degree to which this could affect the data collected is not well understood (Bolger et al., 2003).

RESEARCH DESIGN OPTIONS

Generally, to minimize the limitations and maximize the strengths of a diary study, it is helpful to (1) establish periodic and continually available lines of communication with participants, (2) carefully select motivated participants and seek ways to maximize motivation, (3) collect portions of diary data as they are completed or at intervals throughout the study, and/or (4) pretest the diary protocol. Beyond these general heuristics for designing diary studies, you will need to consider several other aspects of your study design, including (1) the degree of structure imposed on the diary, (2) the trigger that prompts a participant to make a diary entry, (3) the length of time a diary is kept, (4) the length of time between recordings and when events are recorded with respect to their occurrence, and (5) the technologies used. Each of these considerations is discussed here, followed by a brief overview of how diaries are often integrated with interviews.

The Amount of Structure to be Imposed on the Diary Entries

The data collected through a diary will be shaped by the oral and written instructions provided to the participants by the researcher. The degree of structure imposed through these instructions guides participants in selecting or omitting material. The benefits and limitations of imposing structure will vary according to the aims of the research study. Structure may be introduced through the format and design of the diary instrument, through written and/or oral instructions, or through the context in which the diary is written. There are several reasons to employ structured diary approaches. Structure guides respondents to include information that is of interest to the researcher and also reduces the burden on participants because participants need to make fewer decisions about what to include in the diary and may need to record only abbreviated amounts of information in response to short answer and closed-ended questions. Even in diary instruments that are semistructured, it is common to include some structured elements such as rating scales. Depending on the goals of the research, however, a less structured, open-ended diary may be of more value (Elliott, 1997). A less structured diary can encourage the priorities of the participant to rise to the top, presenting events as they are perceived by the diarist, and the diarist can participate more independently of the researcher's initial perspectives, assumptions, and frames of reference.

Record-Making Triggers, or how A Respondent Knows When to Respond

As evidenced by the classifications of diary studies provided by Wheeler and Reis (1991) and Bolger et al. (2003), the trigger that prompts the diary keeper to record is an important attribute of the diary. Fixed-schedule, time-based diary studies that require the participant to report at fixed intervals are often used to study phenomena that are thought to occur regularly with respect to the interval chosen. For many fixed-schedule interval studies, an interval of one day or one workday is adopted. This approach is the least disruptive form of diary because participants can anticipate when they are expected to record their response and, at least to a degree, can potentially accommodate diary writing into their daily schedule (Bolger et al., 2003).

Variable-schedule, time-based diary studies (i.e., signal-contingent studies) are sometimes used to reduce the number of times a respondent is asked to respond. The researcher and participant should agree on acceptable time blocks that both accommodate the research goals and minimize potentially intrusive interruptions for the participant.

In event-contingent diary studies, participants are prompted to make diary entries based on the occurrence of a phenomenon designated by the researcher. Communication events, consultation of an information resource, or completion of a task are all examples of events that might be used to trigger diary recordings. When event-based triggers are used to prompt diary recordings, participants must clearly understand the criteria of the defined phenomenon in for the study to meet the research goals. Event-contingent designs are often well suited to studies of isolated and/or rare phenomena (Bolger et al., 2003).

How long should the Diary be Kept?

To determine the length of time a diary should be kept, it is necessary to have a clear idea of the type of information to be collected. If a phenomenon has a cycle or is closely related to a cyclic event, it is ideal for a diary to capture at least one full cycle. For example, in an educational setting, weeks, terms, and academic and calendar years are cyclic periods that might affect what is being studied. In such a case, it is best to identify the most important cycles and base the data collection period(s) on these cycles. Generally, if the phenomenon of interest is related to a specific project or similar series of events, diaries will be kept for the length of the project. The norm for work diaries tends to be a period of one or, more frequently, two weeks. The value of these strategies should be evaluated in terms of the overall context of the study.

Studies that seek to document rare phenomena or phenomena thought to occur according to longer cycles, or qualitative studies that seek to elicit reflective diary entries, may extend for a period of weeks, months, or longer. When designing diary studies that extend over long periods of time, it is necessary to be realistic about the level of participant commitment and motivation required and to tailor other aspects of the study accordingly. The importance of establishing and maintaining communication with the participants during the study is even greater when studies stretch out for long periods of time. If possible, it is also a good idea to collect diary submissions at regular intervals throughout the study.

Frequencies and Intervals

The length of time between when an event occurs and when a diarist writes about the event is very important. Usually, it is preferable to make the diary entry immediately after the event, provided it does not interfere with the phenomenon that is being investigated or become overly intrusive. Diary entries that are recorded close to the event will minimize the likelihood of recall errors, which may lead to "retrospective 'aggregate' responses that reflect faulty reconstruction of the phenomena of interest" (Bolger et al., 2003, p. 585). On the other hand, when longer periods of time pass between an experience and the recording of that experience, diary study participants tend to be more reflective and selective in what is recorded. Therefore studies that seek to elicit reflections generally instruct participants to record their entries over longer intervals such as a week or even less frequently. Another alternative is for the researcher to ask a diary keeper to record a particular event and reflect on that event at a later time.

Technologies for Capturing Diary Entries

Technological developments have been and should be expected to continue to expand capacities for both performing diary-based studies and analyzing the results. Audio, visual, biometric, and mobile recording and communication technologies can greatly expand the range of information that can be relatively easily collected in so-called natural contexts. While predigital analogs of these recording technologies have been in existence for some time, portability, ease of use, automation of time and (in some cases) location data recording, compatibility with computer applications, and other features make the digital versions more compatible with research diary studies (Bolger et al., 2003; Carter & Mankoff, 2005).

The development and proliferation of Web-based diaries is a trend that has been hard to miss. While the discussion here excludes methods related to unsolicited documents and those that more closely resemble focus groups, solicited diaries also have a place online. Online diaries or logs have a number of advantages, including the automation of data collection; capture of electronic text, images, and other objects; the ability to track changes; and simultaneous access. Online diaries have also facilitated the construction of group or organizational diaries such as the one quoted at the beginning of this chapter. Whether using the Web or paper as a technology platform for a research diary, you should keep in mind the preferences and abilities of your study participants. Some groups of participants may be more comfortable with electronic diary recording technologies than they are with paper, while others may be more comfortable with paper diaries (as found by Toms & Duff, 2002).

Another major use of technology in diary studies is as a means to prompt or remind participants to record a diary entry. Signaling is useful both as a memory aid in fixed study designs (e.g., Tapia, 2004) and as a means to sample the experiences of participants according to a variable schedule (random or simply unknown to the participant) within prespecified time blocks. It is especially important that researchers using potentially intrusive signaling techniques prearrange acceptable time periods for sampling during the early stages of working with the participants.

The Diary-Interview Method

Diary methods are often used in conjunction with other research methods (e.g., questionnaires, observation, or interviews) to provide a rich description of the phenomenon under study or as a means of triangulation. Questionnaires, observation, interviews, and critical incident methods have all been used alongside diary methods. One of the most widely followed diary study research designs is the diary-interview method described by Zimmerman and Wieder (1977), pairing diary reports with an interview. The technique, however, is much stronger than the sum of its parts because the interview is grounded in and expands on information captured in the diary. Used conservatively, the interview provides the opportunity to clarify and draw out selected diary entries. More liberally, the interview may employ diary entries as a point of departure to explore in-depth topics presented in the diary. For example, a researcher could ask questions directed at learning what alternative actions a subject considered before deciding on the particular action recorded in the diary and why these alternative choices were rejected.

EXAMPLES

Two examples of the use of research diaries in work settings are discussed in the following sections. The first study (Hernon et al., 2004) examined the activities conducted by academic library directors. The second study (Byström & Järvelin, 1995) examined the information seeking behaviors of city administrative staff while completing their work-related tasks. In both cases, semistructured diaries were kept for a period of two weeks; however, the study similarities end there. The different ways in which the studies used research diaries will be discussed here.

Example 1: How Do Academic Library Directors Spend Work Time?

Hernon et al. (2004) employed the diary-interview method to explore how academic library directors spend their work time. They were interested in learning about (1) the activities in which directors engage, (2) which activities are most common, (3) whether the range of activities encompasses both management and leadership, and (4) how the reported activities compare with the attributes and activities previously reported as important. Twelve college or university library directors were recruited to participate in this study; 11 of them completed the diary for the two-week study period. Diaries were seen as a means to provide the authors the opportunity to compare the daily activities of academic library directors with previous, more general descriptions of their work.

The diary method was well suited to this study for two reasons. First, it would have been impossible to take the time to shadow each director for the two-week period (including one weekend) of the data collection. In addition, direct observation would have been intrusive. Second, the geographical locations of the participants made it financially impossible to visit each site. These two problems were overcome by asking the directors to complete diaries.

The form of the diaries was pretested with three library directors. In its final form, it collected data on two types of work activities: routine and nonroutine. The directors were asked to complete one diary entry for each activity. The diaries were semistructured, with both open and closed questions designed to document the work time activities of library directors based on the questions, Who? What? When? Where? and How? Additionally, participants were asked to make connections between activities when they occurred. For nonroutine activities (illustrated by the form in the article's appendix), directors were also asked to rate how typical the given activity was for a "typical" workweek. The diary entries were made on printed forms. Checkboxes included in the forms minimized the time required to complete a diary entry and elicited specific information the researchers wanted to capture. Additionally, the respondent was given the opportunity to expand on his or her response.

Respondents were directed to record activities on diary forms as they had time throughout the day; thus this is a loosely defined interval-contingent schedule for recording entries. While this approach might not work well with respondents who are likely to forget, it was beneficial here because it decreased the burden on participants by allowing them leeway with respect to when entries were recorded and because it emphasized that the reports should be made throughout the day, at least relatively close to the time an activity occurred. By basing the forms on activities, rather than time intervals, the researchers focused participants on each performed activity and its context and characteristics. The authors note that the participants were instructed not to report "routine, personal activities (e.g., coffee breaks or meals)...unless those activities related to work" (Hernon et al., 2004, p. 540). Stressing the inclusion of all work activities, including those that occurred away from the workplace and outside of normal hours, on the other hand, helped construct a picture of how academic library directors distribute work activities across time.

The participants were not explicitly instructed on how to handle overlapping or simultaneous activities (e.g., the secondary activity of browsing through a journal while performing the primary activity of speaking on the phone). These activities are important here because they directly relate to one of the secondary research questions, concerning multitasking. While participants could have reported such activities, it might not have occurred to them that they should make such entries. Thus such activities could only be identified systematically during the follow-up interviews.

Interviews[3] were used to flesh out and probe details omitted from the written diary, including attitudes, beliefs, knowledge, and consequences of actions. The authors write that the interviews were used to "expand on activities that either the directors or the authors had selected." In this sense, the diary authors and the researchers became "collaborators in the construction of the account" (Elliott, 1997, ¶4.18) because each had a stake in the research experience. Particularly with a sample of library directors, this type of collaboration strengthens the study findings.

In summary, Hernon and colleagues (2004) successfully adapted the diary-interview method to fit their specific research goals and the needs of their study participants. They used semistructured diaries and allowed the participants some flexibility in the schedule for recording entries to decrease the burden on the participants. The diary was kept for two weeks. Then interviews were conducted to fill in the details of the library directors' work lives.

Example 2: Does Task Complexity Affect Information Seeking and Use?

Byström and Järvelin (1995) used semistructured diaries paired with questionnaires to study how task complexity affects information seeking and use. Unlike many of the published diary studies in ILS literature, this study was not characterized as an exploratory or preliminary study. On the contrary, the use of diaries was seen as an opportunity to advance theoretical development in information seeking research. The diary method provided rich, detailed accounts of information seeking associated with particular tasks, from the worker's viewpoint.

Questionnaires and diaries were used sequentially for data collection. Questionnaires were administered first and provided background information on individual workers (education, experience), information-related aspects of their job functions, and the organization. Diaries were then used to gather in situ information related to the cognitive characteristics of the information seeking experience as it related to specific work tasks.

The diary entry form, included in the article, consists primarily of open-ended questions asking for a description of the task and the situational factors associated with it. However, a critical section, where the participant lists the information resources associated with a task, is structured into a table, with columns for the source or channel, why it was chosen, the participant's success in using that source, and whether the information found was applicable to the task. Entries in the diary were event based in that each entry was focused on a particular task, no matter when it occurred. The participant was to add to the diary entry as different information sources were used to complete the task. The goal was to collect entries on the information sources used during completion of a variety of tasks. On the basis of the number of participants involved, it would have been reasonable to think that two weeks would be sufficient to collect a variety of tasks over this period.

Instruction in the use of the diaries and diary terms was critical to the success of this study. Review of the diary entry form suggests that without careful instruction, the participants could have easily misinterpreted diary items or gone on at great length in response to some of the open-ended questions. One portion of the instruction included definition of terms and concepts (e.g., *source*, *channel*, and *task*) as well as the purpose and scope of the study. Though it might not always be beneficial to give such in-depth instruction to participants regarding diary data collection, it was necessary in this case.

Participants were asked to select the tasks that would be described in the diary entries, with the goal of representing "the variety of their tasks as well as possible" (Byström and Järvelin, 1995, p. 198). Over the two-week period, the 14 participants described 94 tasks. However, during the analysis phase, Byström and Järvelin reduced the number of tasks considered for analysis to 25. A task was eliminated from analysis if information seeking was only incidental or if the task was not well described (18 occurrences), if a very similar task had already been described by that participant (30 occurrences), or if a very similar task had already been described by another participant (21 occurrences). While these screening procedures reduced the sample size dramatically, they did result in a final sample of 25 unique tasks.

A more interesting aspect of this study was the authors' use of diary data to analyze a dynamic process, converting it to quantitative data prior to analysis. They began with a theoretical framework that defined particular variables and levels of those variables. A thorough content analysis of the diaries' content allowed them to analyze and represent the dynamic temporal nature of information use, thus drawing on the diary's strength in capturing temporally ordered data (Breakwell & Wood, 1995). In addition, the relationships between task complexity and the information resources used could be clarified.

In summary, diaries were well suited to this study for several reasons. First, the diaries were completed throughout the information seeking process, as it was happening, and were therefore apt to accurately and dynamically portray elements of the process. The diary method, as used here, avoided recall errors as much as was possible. Second, because the work of interest was cognitive work, it could not be directly observed, even if the researchers could have been present. Thus it was necessary for the participants to supply information about their cognitive activities themselves. Third, the researchers sought to collect relatively complete and detailed information about a variety of specific tasks that could span one or more work sessions. During a two-week period, 14 workers generated diary entries for 94 tasks. It would not be possible to collect this much information from as many study participants through either observation or interviews. The data collected through diaries were then used to further develop the authors' theoretical model of information seeking.

CONCLUSION

Diary study methods comprise a diverse set of techniques and approaches that can be used for exploratory, in-depth, and theory-building research. Through diary methods, researchers—or their diary surrogates—are able to gain entry to places they might not otherwise be able to go such as personal homes, the minds of individuals, and geographically dispersed locations. Though there are limitations to diary studies, particularly regarding the significant amount of time and commitment they can require from participants and researchers, careful design can mitigate these limitations.

NOTES

1. *The Diary Junction* (http://www.pikle.demon.co.uk/diaryjunction.html), compiled by P. K. Lyons, is a useful online resource that includes brief descriptions of significant diaries and diarists.

2. Several early Internet diaries, from 1995 on, are available from the Online Diary History Project (http://www.diaryhistoryproject.com/).

3. It is not clear whether the interviews were conducted face-to-face or by phone.

WORKS CITED

Allport, G. W. (1942). *The Use of Personal Documents in Psychological Science*. New York: Social Science Research Council.

Auramaki, E., Robinson, M., Aaltonen, A., Kovalainen, M., Liinamaa, A., & Tuuna-Vaiska, T. (1996). Paperwork at 78kph. In *Proceedings of the 1996 ACM Conference on Computer Supported Cooperative Work (Boston, MA)* (pp. 370–379).

Berg, B. L. (2004). *Qualitative Research Methods*. Boston: Allyn and Bacon.

Black, A., & Crann, M. (2002). In the public eye: A mass observation of the public library. *Journal of Librarianship and Information Science, 34*(3), 145–157.

Bloom, L. Z. (1976). The diary as popular history. *Journal of Popular Culture, 9*(4), 794–807.

Bolger, N., Davis, A., & Rafaeli, E. (2003). Diary methods: Capturing life as it is lived. *Annual Review of Psychology, 54*, 579–616.

Breakwell, G. M., & Wood, P. (1995). Diary techniques. In G. M. Breakwell, S. Hammond, & C. Fife-Schaw (Eds.), *Research Methods in Psychology* (pp. 293–301). London: Sage.

Byström, K., & Järvelin, K. (1995). Task complexity affects information seeking and use. *Information Processing and Management, 31*(2), 191–213.

Carter, S., & Mankoff, J. (2005). When participants do the capturing: The role of media in diary studies. In *Proceedings of the SIGCHI Conference on Human Factors in Computing Systems (Portland, OR)* (pp. 899–908).

Corti, L. (1993). Using diaries in social research. *Social Research Update, 2*. Retrieved October 10, 2007, from http://sru.soc.surrey.ac.uk/SRU2.html.

Elliott, H. (1997). The use of diaries in sociological research on health experience. *Sociological Research Online, 2*(2). Retrieved October 10, 2007, from http://www.socresonline.org.uk/2/2/7.html.

Hernon, P., Powell, R. R., & Young, A. P. (2004). Academic library directors: What do they do? *College and Research Libraries, 65*(6), 538–563.

Plummer, K. (2001). *Documents of Life 2: An Invitation to a Critical Humanism*. Thousand Oaks, CA: Sage.

Rieman, J. (1993). The diary study: A workplace-oriented research tool to guide laboratory efforts. In *Proceedings of InterCHI'93* (pp. 321–326).

Rieman, J. (1996). A field study of exploratory learning strategies. *ACM Transactions on Computer-Human Interaction, 3*(3), 189–218.

Ryan, G., & Valverde, M. (2005). Waiting for service on the internet: Defining the phenomenon and identifying the situations. *Internet Research: Electronic Networking Applications and Policy, 15*(2), 220–240.

Serfaty, V. (2004). Online diaries: Towards a structural approach. *Journal of American Studies, 38*(3), 457–471.

Symon, G. (2004). Qualitative research diaries. In C. Cassell & G. Symon (Eds.), *Essential Guide to Qualitative Methods in Organizational Research* (pp. 98–113). Thousand Oaks, CA: Sage.

Szalai, A. (Ed.). (1972). *The Use of Time: Daily Activities of Urban and Suburban Populations in Twelve Countries* (in collaboration with P. E. Converse, P. Feldheim, E. K. Scheuch, & P. J. Stone). The Hague: Mouton.

Tapia, A. (2004). The power of myth in the IT workplace: Creating a 24-hour workday during the dot-com bubble. *Information Technology and People, 17*(3), 303–326.

Toms, E. G., & Duff, W. (2002). "I spent $1^{1}/_{2}$ hours sifting through one large box . . . ": Diaries as information behavior of the archives user: Lessons learned. *Journal of the American Society for Information Science and Technology, 53*(14), 1232–1238.

Wheeler, L., & Reis, H. T. (1991). Self-recording of everyday life events: Origins, types, and uses. *Journal of Personality, 59*, 339–354.

Zimmerman, D. H., & Wieder, D. L. (1977). The diary: Diary-interview method. *Urban Life, 5*(4), 479–499.

23

Unstructured Interviews

Yan Zhang and Barbara M. Wildemuth

There is no such thing as a worthless conversation, provided you know what to listen for. And questions are the breath of life for a conversation.

—James Nathan Miller (1965)

Ideal conversation must be an exchange of thought, and not, as many of those who worry most about their shortcomings believe, an eloquent exhibition of wit or oratory.

—Emily Post (1922)

INTRODUCTION

Interviews are a widely used tool to access people's experiences and their inner perceptions, attitudes, and feelings of reality. On the basis of the degree of structuring, interviews can be divided into three categories: structured interviews, semistructured interviews, and unstructured interviews (Fontana & Frey, 2005). A *structured interview* is an interview that has a set of predefined questions, and the questions would be asked in the same order for all respondents. This standardization is intended to minimize the effects of the instrument and the interviewer on the research results. Structured interviews are similar to surveys (see Chapter 26), except that they are administered orally, rather than in writing. *Semistructured interviews* (see Chapter 24) are more flexible. An interview guide, usually including both closed-ended and open-ended questions, is prepared, but in the course of the interview, the interviewer has a certain amount of room to adjust the sequence of the questions to be asked and to add questions based on the context of the participant's responses. This chapter will focus on unstructured interviews as a qualitative research method for data collection.

The *unstructured interview* technique was developed in the disciplines of anthropology and sociology as a method to elicit people's social realities. In the literature, the term is used interchangeably with the terms *informal conversational interview*, *in-depth interview*, *nonstandardized interview*, and *ethnographic interview*. The definitions of an unstructured interview are various. Minichiello et al. (1990) defined them as interviews in which neither the question nor the answer categories are predetermined; instead, they rely on social interaction between the researcher and the informant. Punch (1998) described unstructured interviews as a way to understand the complex behavior of people without imposing any a priori categorization, which might limit the field of inquiry. Patton (2002) described unstructured interviews as a natural extension of participant observation because they so often occur as part of ongoing participant observation fieldwork. He argued that they rely entirely on the spontaneous generation of questions in the natural flow of an interaction.

While the definitions are not the same, there is more agreement about the basic characteristics of unstructured interviews. The researcher comes to the interview with no predefined theoretical framework and thus no hypotheses and questions about the social realities under investigation; rather, the researcher has conversations with interviewees and generates questions in response to the interviewees' narration. As a consequence, each unstructured interview might generate data with different structures and patterns. The intention of an unstructured interview is to expose the researcher to unanticipated themes and to help him or her to develop a better understanding of the interviewees' social reality from the interviewees' perspectives. While unstructured interviews can be used as the primary data collection method (as in the two example studies discussed later in this chapter), it is also very common to incorporate unstructured interviews into a study primarily based on participant observation (see Chapter 21).

Just because unstructured interviews don't use predefined questions doesn't mean that they are random and nondirective. Unstructured interviews cannot be started without detailed knowledge and preparation, if you hope to achieve deep insight into people's lives (Patton, 2002). The researcher will keep in mind the study's purpose and the general scope of the issues that he would like to discuss in the interview (Fife, 2005). The researcher's control over the conversation is intended to be minimal, but nevertheless, the researcher will try to encourage the interviewees to relate experiences and perspectives that are relevant to the problems of interest to the researcher (Burgess, 1984).

The decision to use unstructured interviews as a data collection method is governed by both the researcher's epistemology[1] and the study's objectives. Researchers making use of unstructured interviews often hold a constructivist point of view of social reality and correspondingly design studies within an interpretive research paradigm. They believe that to make sense of a study participant's world, researchers must approach it through the participant's own perspective and in the participant's own terms (Denzin, 1989; Robertson & Boyle, 1984). No hypothesis should be made beforehand, and the purpose of inquiry is theory development, rather than theory testing.

In an ideal unstructured interview, the interviewer follows the interviewees' narration and generates questions spontaneously based on their reflections on that narration. It is accepted, however, that the structure of the interview can be loosely guided by a list of questions, called an aide-mémoire or agenda (Briggs, 2000; McCann & Clark, 2005; Minichiello et al., 1990). An aide-mémoire is a broad guide to topic issues that might be covered in the interview, rather than the actual questions to be asked. It is open ended and flexible (Burgess, 1984). Unlike interview guides used in structured interviewing, an aide-mémoire doesn't determine the order of the conversation and is subject to revision based on the responses of the interviewees. Using an aide-mémoire in an unstructured interview encourages a certain degree of consistency across different interview sessions. Thus a balance can be achieved between flexibility and consistency.

Unstructured interviews can be very useful in studies of people's information seeking and use. They are especially useful for studies attempting to find patterns, generate models, and inform information system design and implementation. For example, Alvarez and Urla (2002) used unstructured interviews to elicit information requirements during the implementation of an enterprise resource planning system. Due to their conversational and nonintrusive characteristics, unstructured interviews can be used in settings where it is inappropriate or impossible to use other, more structured methods to examine people's information activities. For example, Schultze (2000) used unstructured interviews, along with other ethnographic methods, in her eight-month field study in a large company investigating their production of informational objects.

Although unstructured interviews can generate detailed data and enable in-depth understanding of a phenomenon, they are still underused in information and library science, compared to surveys and semistructured interviews. Fortunately, as observed by Ellis and Haugan (1997), a shift has been occurring in the study of information use toward a more holistic view. The effects of this shift are reflected in a change in data collection approaches "from a macro-approach, studying large groups via questionnaires or structured interviews, to a micro-approach, studying small groups via observation or unstructured interviews" (Ellis & Haugan, 1997, pp. 384–385). If Ellis and Haugan are correct, we will see an increasing use of unstructured interviews in information behavior research.

THE ROLE OF THE INTERVIEWER

The interviewer has a unique position in an unstructured interview. He or she is an integral part of the research instrument in that there are no predefined frameworks and questions that can be used to structure the inquiry. To a great extent, the success of the interview depends on the interviewer's ability to generate questions in response to the context and to move the conversation in a direction of interest to the researcher. Thus an unstructured interview is more open to interviewer effects than its structured and semistructured counterparts. To become a skillful interviewer takes knowledge and experience (Minichiello et al., 1990).

The role that an interviewer adopts is critical to the success of an unstructured interview. The choice of roles is constrained by many characteristics of the interviewer such as gender, age, social status, race, and ethnicity. Even so, it is generally preferable that the interviewer present himself or herself as a learner, a friend, and a member of the interviewee's group who has sympathetic interest in the interviewee's life and is willing to understand it (Burgess, 1984). Adopting this kind of role makes building rapport between the interviewer and interviewees possible; it further makes in-depth understanding of the interviewees' lives possible.

The merit of an unstructured interview lies in its conversational nature, which allows the interviewer to be highly responsive to individual differences and situational changes (Patton, 2002). This characteristic of unstructured interviews requires interviewers to have a rich set of skills. First, the interviewer should be able to listen carefully during the conversation. The interviewer often starts the interview with a very broad and open question, such as, "How do you feel about the . . . ?" The interviewee then can take over and lead the conversation. In such conversations, the interviewer usually listens and reflects more than he or she talks. Second, to adjust the interview direction in response to the individual interview context, the interviewer has to be able to "generate rapid insights [and] formulate questions quickly and smoothly" (Patton, 2002, p. 343).

Most important, interviewers should be good at questioning, probing, and adjusting the flow of conversations at an appropriate level. This skill is reflected in three aspects of the interviewer's questioning tactics. First, interviewers should be adept at using the appropriate type of question, based on the specific interview context. The kinds of questions posed are crucial to the unstructured interview (Burgess, 1984). Spradley (1979) identified three main types of questions: (1) *descriptive questions*, which allow interviewees to provide descriptions about their activities; (2) *structural questions*, which attempt to find out how interviewees organize their knowledge; and (3) *contrast questions*, which allow interviewees to discuss the meanings of situations and make comparisons across different situations. Each type of question is used at different points in the interview to encourage interviewees to talk or to probe for more details. Second, interviewers should be able to monitor and control the directiveness of their questions, comments, and even gestures and actions (Burgess, 1984). It is important for interviewers not to ask directive questions when initiating the interview because directive questions may bias the data by leading interviewees to respond in a way that they thought was expected or desired by the researcher. Patton (2002) cautioned that interviewers should "guard against asking questions that impose interpretations on the situation" (p. 343). Denzin (1989) also pointed out that a "sympathetic identification" (p. 109) with interviewees' points of view is necessary, but the interviewer should avoid giving advice and/or passing judgment on respondents. Whyte (1960) provided a six-level scale to evaluate the degree of directiveness in any question or statement made by the interviewer by examining it in the context of what immediately preceded it during the interview. Controlling and adjusting the directiveness of questions and statements is a big challenge for interviewers, especially for those with little interviewing experience. Third, interviewers should be able to maintain control of the pace and direction of the conversation. While the interviewer allows the interviewee to raise new topics or move the conversation in directions that the interviewee believes are important, it is the interviewer's responsibility to engage the interviewee in the conversation and keep the conversation focused on the researcher's concerns. As Minichiello et al. (1990) note, an unstructured interview is "always a controlled conversation, which is geared to the interviewer's research interests" (p. 93). A productive conversation is possible when a balance of control is achieved.

CONDUCTING AN UNSTRUCTURED INTERVIEW

There are no official and agreed on guidelines for how to conduct an unstructured interview. But in practice, many researchers comply with the following steps (Fontana & Frey, 2005; Punch, 1998) when planning and conducting unstructured interviews:

1. Getting in: accessing the setting. Various difficulties in gaining access to research settings have been documented, especially when the researcher is an outsider in the environment. Negotiation techniques and tactics are required in this situation. The researcher also has to take into consideration the possible political, legal, and bureaucratic barriers that may arise during the process of gaining access to the setting (Lofland et al., 2006).
2. Understanding the language and culture of the interviewees. A primary focus of an unstructured interview is to understand the meaning of human experiences from the interviewees' perspectives. Thus unstructured interviews are governed by the cultural conventions of the research setting. This requires that the researcher can understand the interviewees' language

and, further, its meanings in the specific cultural context of the research setting (Fife, 2005; Minichiello et al., 1990).

3. Deciding on how to present oneself. An unstructured interview is a two-way conversation. The quality of the conversation is influenced, to a great extent, by how the interviewer represents himself or herself. The interviewer's self-representation will depend on the context he or she is in, but in all cases, the interviewer is a "learner" in the conversation, trying to make sense of the interviewee's experiences from his or her point of view.

4. Locating an informant. Not every person in the research setting will make a good informant. The informant (i.e., the interviewee) will be an insider who is willing to talk with you, of course. But even more important, the informant must be knowledgeable enough to serve as a guide and interpreter of the setting's unfamiliar language and culture (Fontana & Frey, 2005).

5. Gaining trust and establishing rapport. Gaining trust and establishing rapport is essential to the success of unstructured interviews. Only when a trustful and harmonious relationship is established will the interviewee share his or her experience with the interviewer, especially if the topic of the conversation is sensitive. When endeavoring to cultivate rapport, the interviewer might need to be careful: it's easy to become so involved with your informants' lives that you can no longer achieve your research purposes (Fontana & Frey, 2005).

6. Capturing the data. Note taking is a traditional method for capturing interview data. But in an unstructured interview, note taking is likely to disrupt the natural flow of the conversation. Thus, when possible, it is preferable to audio record the interviews by tape or digital recorder. In situations where only note taking is possible, you will need to take brief notes during the interview, writing up more detailed notes immediately after each interview (Fontana & Frey, 2005; Lofland et al., 2006). As you develop your interviewing skills, you also will want to practice a variety of memory techniques to be able to capture as much detail as possible from each interview.

THE CHALLENGES OF UNSTRUCTURED INTERVIEWS

While the flexibility of unstructured interviews offers a number of advantages, there are three main challenges that researchers face when using unstructured interviews as a data collection method. The first challenge is that this method requires a significant amount of time to collect the needed information (Patton, 2002), especially when the researcher first enters the field and knows little about the setting. It takes time to gain trust, develop rapport, and gain access to interviewees. Because each interview is highly individualized, the length of each unstructured interview session also might be longer than structured or semistructured interview sessions (Arksey & Knight, 1999).

The second challenge for researchers is to exert the right amount and type of control over the direction and pace of the conversation. It is difficult to control the degree of directiveness of the questions and statements proposed during the conversation. This issue was discussed in the previous section. Also, when a new topic emerges in the discussion, it is difficult for the researcher to know whether to follow it and risk losing continuity, or to stay on the major theme and risk missing additional useful information (Patton, 2002). Furthermore, when the interviewee moves the conversation/interview in a direction that is not useful, the interviewer will need to decide when and how to interrupt the conversation gracefully, to return it to a topic of interest for the purposes of the research (Whyte, 1960). Researchers agree that to develop your skills in sensitively controlling unstructured interviews, both training and experience are important.

The third challenge is analyzing the data gathered by unstructured interviews. The questions asked in each unstructured interview were dependent on the context of the interview and so can vary dramatically across multiple interviews. Different questions will generate different responses so that a great deal of effort has to be made to analyze the data systematically, to find the patterns within them (Patton, 2002).

EXAMPLES

Two studies that relied primarily on unstructured interviews will be discussed here. In the first, Cobbledick (1996) investigated the information seeking behaviors of artists by interviewing four of them about their information needs and the sources they used to address those needs. In the second example, Attfield and Dowell (1997) investigated the work-related information behaviors of newspaper journalists in London. In each case, the interviews were based on a list of the study's main research questions, rather than on a more detailed interview guide.

Example 1: Artists' Information Seeking Behavior

While artists constitute a significant proportion of the nation's educated professional class, their information needs have been largely ignored by information professionals (Bates, 2001). This situation leads to the first purpose of this study: to investigate the context of artists' information seeking and their sources of information so as to draw some tentative conclusions about artists' information seeking behaviors. The information sources used by artists are extremely diverse, so a structured and standardized questionnaire with little flexibility would not be an effective tool for data collection. This leads to the second purpose of the study: to establish a basic framework for developing standardized questionnaires. Given the complexity of the research phenomenon and the exploratory nature of the research, Cobbledick (1996) chose to conduct unstructured interviews, which she called *in-depth interviews*, with a limited number of subjects, hoping that the unconstrained and in-depth discussions allowed by unstructured interviews could expose her to "the emergence of the unexpected" (p. 347).

Since the study was exploratory, the sample that Cobbledick (1996) chose was quite small but represented some of the diversity in the population of interest. Two male artists and two female artists participated in the study. They were a sculptor, a painter, a fiber artist, and a metalsmith, thus representing different media. Furthermore, they represented two main traditions: fine art and crafts. They were all faculty in the same university in the Midwest, so they shared many goals, tasks, facilities, and information sources on campus. In addition, they all had access to the public libraries, the museums, and the other academic libraries in the surrounding area.

Cobbledick's (1996) two research objectives shaped her planning for the interviews. Drawing on several years of personal observation, she proposed a systematic structure to guide the line of questioning in the interviews. The structure included eight research issues that she wanted to cover: (1) the processes that place the finished work of art in a community, (2) technical information needs, (3) visual information needs, (4) inspirational information needs, (5) libraries, (6) books, (7) technology, and (8) keeping up with contemporary developments in the visual arts. In an unstructured interview, this type of structure, also called an aide-mémoire or agenda, serves as a reminder for researchers to make sure that all the issues in which they are interested are covered.

The amount of structure incorporated in the interviews in this study is very close to that of semistructured interviews in terms of the level of control imposed by the researcher. Nevertheless, these interviews would be regarded as unstructured interviews in the sense that the wording of the questions and the order of the questions to be asked were not predetermined. Similar to other unstructured interviews, the researcher had to ask questions based on the individual context of the conversation.

Unstructured interviews based on an aide-mémoire, as outlined previously, would produce more consistent and structured data across different interviewees than interviews conducted without any preexisting structure. Imposing structure on the interviews can make data analysis easier (though you are likely to sacrifice some diversity in the interviewees' responses). Burgess (1984) advocated this approach when he argued that "interviewers need to ensure that similar topics are covered in interviews where the data are to be used to make comparisons" (p. 111). In this study, the data collected in the course of these interviews were organized into the eight categories outlined in the aide-mémoire. On the basis of the data analysis, tentative conclusions about artists' information seeking behaviors were made, and a questionnaire was developed. The questionnaire was organized into eight topical sections, some of which corresponded to the issues outlined in the aide-mémoire, while others were induced directly from the interview data.

Ensuring confidentiality to protect interviewees from the possible risks of participating in a study is a concern for all studies involving human subjects, including studies incorporating unstructured interviews. In this study, only four subjects were interviewed, and their sexes were identified, together with their major disciplines. They were also identified as the art faculty of a large midwestern university with a strong art program. While it's possible that someone could identify the participants from these demographic characteristics, it's unlikely. Cobbledick (1996) masked the identity of the university, which makes the identification of the individual participants difficult and, to a certain degree, ensures their anonymity.

Cobbledick (1996) did not provide details on many aspects of how she implemented unstructured interviews in this study. She did not report, in this article, where the interviews took place, how long the interviews lasted, or what method was used to record the interviews. She also did not mention how she probed issues of particular interest during the interview process, how she controlled the direction and pace of the interviews, or how she handled the emergent issues or discussions that were not expected in advance. This lack of detailed description of her interviewing procedures might be due to the fact that the focus of the article was on reporting the findings, rather than elaborating on methodological concerns. However, we hope that other researchers will provide detailed information about how they implemented their research methods. Only through this practice can studies be repeated in the future by other researchers, as they continue the work or verify the findings.

Example 2: Information Seeking and Use by Journalists

Our second example (Attfield & Dowell, 1997) explored information seeking and use behaviors by journalists at a London-based national newspaper, *The Times*, by using unstructured interviews. It was part of a project aiming to specify system requirements and design implications for an integrated information retrieval and authoring system based on an understanding of journalistic information behaviors. The sample consisted of 25 journalists: 19 home news writers, 4 feature writers, 1 obituary writer, and 1 systems editor. Follow-up e-mails were used to collect additional data, when necessary. To ensure confidentiality, the interviewees' identities were not revealed.

The purpose of this study was to provide a rich account of the information behaviors of journalists working at *The Times*—not only the journalists' observable behaviors, but also the cognition behind their behaviors. In particular, Attfield and Dowell (2003) were interested in journalists' information activities, such as their location, management, relocation, and use of information, in terms of the constraints imposed by their working context as well as the motivations behind the activities. Furthermore, they intended to probe why, when, and how each information activity would be undertaken within the working context of the journalist. They did not have a preconceived theoretical framework for this study; they did not propose categories of information activities beforehand; and they did not have predefined hypotheses to test. It was the researchers' intention to gain an understanding of the reality of the information activities of journalists and to build a model representing the information seeking and use behaviors involved in the journalistic research and writing process. The intensive and detailed data required by the research goals led to the selection of unstructured interviews as a data collection method.

Interviews were conducted at the journalists' workplace, and each lasted 20 to 40 minutes. Attfield and Dowell (1997) did not use a predefined question list, but did focus each interview on the research purpose: to understand journalists' work-related information seeking and use. A typical interview started with the researcher asking the journalist to describe his or her work assignment process—a very general request. Because it is logically the beginning of journalists' information seeking and because it focused on a very familiar part of the journalists' work routine, this request not only helped reveal contextual information about the journalists' information activities, but also presented the researcher to the interviewees as a learner wanting to understand their work processes. Thus this broad question served as a good starting point to engage the journalists in the conversation. As the interview progressed, the researcher could steer the discussion toward more specific issues related to the journalists' information seeking and use activities. By using this questioning strategy, the interview became a focused conversation. Unfortunately, more details about what kinds of questions the researchers used to pursue the issues in which they were particularly interested and how they controlled the direction of conversations were not reported in the paper.

The authors captured the interviews by audio recording them[2] and then transcribed them for analysis. Unstructured interviews often generate data with different patterns and structures from one session to another, which makes the data analysis very intensive and time consuming. The data were analyzed using a grounded theory approach, which is a data-driven emergent approach for building models from qualitative data (Corbin & Strauss, 2008; Strauss, 1987). Open coding (i.e., using codes induced from the data) was used to identify concepts about information-related activities that were of particular interest to the researchers. Then axial coding was used to identify relationships between the concepts, with the intention of contextualizing the identified phenomena.

When using unstructured interviews, one of the researcher's goals is to understand the language and cultural of the interviewees from the interviewees' perspectives. In the work processes of a journalist, some words have meanings different from their commonly understood (i.e., standard English) meanings. In this paper, Attfield and Dowell (1997) used those terms in the way that journalists use them, providing notes at the end of the paper to explain their meanings. In this way, Attfield and Dowell helped us to follow their own process of learning about the language and culture of these journalists.

In summary, this study identified the information activities of newspaper journalists. Attfield and Dowell (1997) generated a rich description of the journalists' motivations for these behaviors within the context of the requirements of journalistic work, which included the information products they created, the situation within which each was produced, and the resources that provided the means for production. This description was further developed into a model of the newspaper article research and writing process.

CONCLUSION

Unstructured interviews are most useful when you want to gain an in-depth understanding of a particular phenomenon within a particular cultural context. In addition, they are most appropriate when you are working within an interpretive research paradigm, in which you would assume that reality is socially constructed by the participants in the setting of interest. On the basis of this underlying assumption, you will want to understand the phenomenon of interest from the individual perspectives of those who are involved with it. If these are your research goals, then it is useful to allow the interview/conversation to be mutually shaped by you and the interviewee. Imposing too much structure on the interview will inhibit the interviewee's responses, and you are likely to come away with only an incomplete understanding of the phenomenon of interest.

Unstructured interviews are not useful when you already have a basic understanding of a phenomenon and want to pursue particular aspects of it. If your research goals are well defined, then you can use other methods (e.g., semistructured interviews or surveys) to collect the needed data more efficiently.

NOTES

1. Interpretive research and its epistemological stance is also discussed in Chapter 21.
2. Attfield and Dowell (2003) did not explicitly describe their methods of data capture. Because they did say that they transcribed the interviews, we are assuming that they were originally audio recorded.

WORKS CITED

Alvarez, R., & Urla, J. (2002). Tell me a good story: Using narrative analysis to examine information requirements interviews during an ERP implementation. *The DATA BASE for Advances in Information Systems, 33*(1), 38–52.

Arksey, H., & Knight, P. (1999). *Interviewing for Social Scientists: An Introductory Resource with Examples.* Thousand Oaks, CA: Sage.

Attfield, S., & Dowell, J. (1997). Information seeking and use by newspaper journalists. *Journal of Documentation, 59*(2), 187–204.

Bates, M. J. (2001). *Information needs and seeking of scholars and artists in relation to multimedia materials* (Extracted from a report submitted to the Getty Research Institute, Los Angeles, CA, in 1999). Retrieved June 30, 2008, from http://www.gseis.ucla.edu/faculty/bates/scholars.html.

Briggs, C. (2000). Interview. *Journal of Linguistic Anthropology, 9*(1–2), 137–140.

Burgess, R. G. (1984). *In the Field: An Introduction to Field Research.* London: Unwin Hyman.

Cobbledick, S. (1996). The information seeking behavior of artists: Exploratory interviews. *The Library Quarterly, 66*(4), 343–372.

Corbin, J., & Strauss, A. (2008). *Basics of Qualitative Research: Techniques and Procedures for Developing Grounded Theory* (3rd ed.). Los Angeles: Sage.

Denzin, N. K. (1989). The sociological interview. In *The Research Act: A Theoretical Introduction to Sociological Methods* (pp. 102–120). Englewood Cliffs, NJ: Prentice Hall.

Ellis, D., & Haugan, M. (1997). Modelling the information seeking patterns of engineers and research scientists in an industrial environment. *Journal of Documentation, 53*(4), 384–403.

Fife, W. (2005). *Doing Fieldwork: Ethnographic Methods for Research in Developing Countries and Beyond.* New York: Palgrave Macmillan.

Fontana, A., & Frey, J. H. (2005). The interview: From neutral stance to political involvement. In N. K. Denzin & Y. S. Lincoln (eds.), *The Sage Handbook of Qualitative Research* (3rd ed., pp. 695–728). Thousand Oaks, CA: Sage.

Lofland, J., Snow, D., Anderson, L., & Lofland, L. H. (2006). *Analyzing Social Settings: A Guide to Qualitative Observation and Analysis.* Belmont, CA: Wadsworth.

McCann, T., & Clark, E. (2005). Using unstructured interviews with participants who have schizophrenia. *Nurse Researcher, 13*(1), 7–18.

Miller, J. N. (1965, September). The art of intelligent listening. *Reader's Digest,* p. 127

Minichiello, V., Aroni, R., Timewell, E., & Alexander, L. (1990). *In-depth Interviewing: Researching People.* Hong Kong: Longman Cheshire.

Patton, M. Q. (2002). *Qualitative Research and Evaluation Methods.* Thousand Oaks, CA: Sage.

Post, E. (1922). *Etiquette.* New York: Funk and Wagnalls.

Punch, K. F. (1998). *Introduction to Social Research: Quantitative and Qualitative Approaches.* Thousand Oaks, CA: Sage.

Robertson, M.H.B., & Boyle, J. S. (1984). Ethnography: Contributions to nursing research. *Journal of Advanced Nursing, 9,* 43–49.

Schultze, U. (2000). A confessional account of an ethnography about knowledge work. *MIS Quarterly, 24*(1), 3–41.

Spradley, J. P. (1979). *The Ethnographic Interview.* New York: Holt, Rinehart and Winston.

Strauss, A. (1987). *Qualitative Analysis for Social Scientists.* New York: Cambridge University Press.

Whyte, W. F. (1960). Interviewing in field research. In R. N. Adams & J. J. Preiss (Eds.), *Human Organization Research* (pp. 352–374). Homewood, IL: Dorsey Press.

24

Semistructured Interviews

Lili Luo and Barbara M. Wildemuth

Interviewing is rather like a marriage: everybody knows what it is, an awful lot of people do it, and yet behind each closed door there is a world of secrets.

—Ann Oakley (1981)

INTRODUCTION AND DEFINITION

As used by professionals in various settings, interviews have been employed as part of hiring and personnel review processes to determine patients' or clients' needs for health or social services, or in support of library reference services. By contrast, this chapter is concerned with interviewing as a data collection method within the context of research studies. Basically, an interview is a particular type of purposeful conversation (Skopec, 1986). Unlike casual conversations, interviews are more organized and well planned. Both parties are aware of the purpose of the interview and attempt to accomplish the goal through oral communication consisting of questions and answers. A more complete definition of *interview* is proposed by Millar et al. (1992): "A face-to-face dyadic interaction in which one individual plays the role of interviewer and the other takes on the role of interviewee, and both of these roles carry clear expectations concerning behavioral and attitudinal approach. The interview is requested by one of the participants for a specific purpose and both participants are willing contributors" (p. 2). This definition contains the essence of the interview by pointing out its three central facets: the dyadic nature of interview, the different roles played by the two parties involved, and the interview's clear purpose.

Because we will consider interviews only as a data collection method in this chapter, it is necessary to also present a definition from this perspective. The *research interview* is defined as "a two-person conversation initiated by the interviewer for the specific purpose of obtaining research-relevant information and focused by him on content specified by research objectives" (Cannell & Kahn, 1968, p. 530).

Generally, an interview is a face-to-face encounter. However, in a broader sense, an interview can be conducted through other channels such as telephone or e-mail. Telephone interviews are a popular way of administering surveys. E-mail interviews are particularly useful for reaching a population who could not be easily reached at a predetermined time or place. With the increasing availability of Web-based instant messaging applications, this might become another means of conducting interviews with people who are frequent users of these tools.

A major typology of interviews distinguishes among structured, semistructured, and unstructured interviews. This distinction is based on the extent of formality/structure imposed on the interaction and (often) on the depth of response sought in the interview (Robson, 2002). The structured interview employs a list of preestablished questions in a fixed order and using standardized wording, usually with only a limited number of response alternatives available. These interviews are essentially the same as personally administered surveys, so you are referred to the chapter on survey research for a detailed discussion of Robson's data collection method (Chapter 26). Unstructured interviews provide greater flexibility and breadth throughout the interviewing process, allowing the conversation to develop within the general focus of the investigation. The questions and follow-up probes must be generated and adapted to the given situation to uncover in-depth, open-ended responses (Berg, 2001). See the earlier chapter on unstructured interviews (Chapter 23) for a detailed discussion of this method.

Structured and unstructured interviews are two extremes of a continuum. Located somewhere in between are semistructured interviews. This type of interview "has predetermined questions, but the order can be modified based upon the interviewer's perception of what seems most appropriate. Question wording can be changed and explanations given; particular questions which seem inappropriate with a particular interviewee can be omitted, or additional ones included" (Robson, 2002, p. 270). Semistructured interviews give the interviewer considerable freedom to adjust the questions as the interview goes on and to probe far beyond a particular respondent's answers to the predetermined questions. Researchers often choose to use semistructured interviews because they are aware that individuals understand the world in varying ways. They want to elicit information on their research topics from each subject's perspective. The interviewer will begin with a list of topics and associated questions as a loosely structured interview guide. The interviewer can go on to use probes to have subjects clarify or elaborate particular topics (Berg, 2001). In a word, semistructured interviews involve less rigidity and more leeway than structured interviews but are more organized and systematic than unstructured interviews in developing the conversation.

There are several steps required to incorporate semistructured interviews into your study. They include developing the interview guide, conducting the interview, and capturing and analyzing the data. Each of these steps will be discussed here.

DEVELOPING THE INTERVIEW GUIDE

Once you determine the nature and objectives of your study, you will need to construct an interview guide. An interview guide is not like the questionnaire that makes up a structured interview or survey. It is a list of questions, but it does not require the interviewer to follow the wording of the questions strictly or to always ask them in the same order. It is up to the interviewer to decide how closely to follow the guide and how much depth to seek in a subject's responses (Kvale, 1996).

The process of developing an interview guide usually begins with an outline of major topics related to the study's objectives. For each topic, you will list the questions that need to be asked. Next, you will decide on the preferred order of the major topics and the order of the questions associated with each topic. Even though you will use the guide as a basis for the interviews, you can vary the sequencing and wording of the questions, based on the responses of the subjects.

As you develop the specific questions in the interview guide, take into account the characteristics of the population from which your subjects were selected to create questions that are appropriate for them. Berg (2001) proposed four types or styles of question that should be included in an interview guide: essential questions, extra questions, throw-away questions, and probing questions. *Essential questions* are questions that address the central focus of the research. They may be clustered together or spread through the interview. In either case, they all have the same function: eliciting the key information related to the research question. *Extra questions* are the questions that can be considered equivalent to certain essential questions but use different wording. They may be used as alternative expressions of the essential questions if a study participant did not understand the original wording. They also may be used to check on the reliability of responses and gauge the possible impact caused by the change of wording. *Throw-away questions* are those used to develop rapport at the beginning of the interview, to adjust the pace, or to switch question focus throughout the interview. They are not crucial in collecting important information for the study, but they are indispensable in building up a bond between the interviewer and the subject and so can have a significant impact on the overall success of the interview. *Probing questions*, or *probes*, are employed to ask subjects to elaborate on their answers to a given question, for example, Can you tell me more about that? Would you please explain that more fully? and so on. For the same question, different first responses might trigger different probes, but their purpose is the same: to elicit more information from the subjects on a specific question.

Besides the four types of questions that should be incorporated in the interview, Berg (2001) also suggested that researchers avoid using three kinds of problematic questions: affectively worded questions, double-barreled questions, and complex questions. *Affectively worded questions* arouse inappropriate emotional responses from the subjects. Although the question was not intended to be offensive, inappropriate wording can easily hinder the interview process. *Double-barreled questions* incorporate two issues in a single question. Such questions can confuse the subjects and also make it difficult to analyze the responses. *Complex questions* also create difficulties. Brief, concise and to-the-point questions are more efficient than complex ones in obtaining clear responses from the subjects.

It is highly recommended that the interview guide be pretested. Berg (2001) suggested two steps to be included in the pretest. First, the interview guide should be examined by people who are experts in relation to the research topic. Their goal will be to identify technical problems with the interview guide such as wording. Second, it should be tested with people who are potential subjects to assess the applicability of questions and procedures in a real study setting. On the basis of the pretest results, the interview guide can be revised and improved.

Two Specific Interviewing Techniques

Two specific interviewing techniques are particularly useful for collecting data about information behaviors: time-line interviews and the critical incident technique. Each is briefly described here.

Time-line interviewing—more specifically, the *micromoment time-line interviewing technique*—is frequently associated with Dervin's *sense-making theory* (Dervin, 1999; Savolainen, 1993). Sense making is "behavior, both internal (i.e., cognitive) and external (i.e., procedural), which allows the individual to construct and design his/her movement through time-space" (Dervin, 1983, ¶3). Dervin and her colleagues developed this interviewing technique to directly capture the time dimension of people's sense-making behaviors. As the basis for the interview, study participants are asked to describe a particular situation of interest to the research study's purpose. A time line of events is established based on the participant's description of the situation. Then a series of questions is asked about each event in the time line, e.g., "What questions arose at this step? What thoughts? What feelings?" (Dervin & Frenette, 2001, p. 77). For each question that is identified, the interviewer asks the participant to elaborate further, concerning how this question arose, what barriers were faced in resolving it, and how it was resolved. This basic form for the interview can be varied, as described by Dervin and Frenette (2001) and Schamber (2000). Using this technique, the interviewer can gain an in-depth understanding of the sequential events in a cycle of sense making and the multiple facets of each event.

The critical incident technique was developed by Flanagan (1954). His definition of an *incident* is quite broad, including "any observable human activity that is sufficiently complete in itself to permit inferences and predictions to be made about the person performing the act" (p. 327). Selecting the critical incidents on which to focus is an important decision for your study. Flanagan recommends selecting extreme incidents, such as the most successful occurrence and the least successful occurrence, because these incidents are most easily recalled in detail and are most efficient in characterizing the general behavior of interest. In studies of information behaviors, this technique is especially useful for collecting data about events or behaviors that happen infrequently and so cannot be observed directly. For example, you may want to study the ways in which engineers use information during new product development (as in Kraaijenbrink, 2007). Kraaijenbrink asked each engineer to describe one example of successful information usage and one example of unsuccessful information usage during new product development. By focusing on a specific example, the engineer could recall it in more detail and provide concrete examples of the information used for particular purposes. Thus the descriptions of the engineers' information usage behaviors were more accurate and more detailed than data collected by other means. Once the detailed description has been collected, you can ask for additional explanations of the participant's behavior or his or her reflections on it. Asking for participants to describe one successful and one unsuccessful incident, as Kraaijenbrink did, is the most common framework for a critical incident interview; however, you can also focus on other types of critical incidents such as the most recent occurrence of the behavior of interest (see Johnson, 2004, for an example of this approach). Using this technique, then, can be particularly useful for gathering data about information behaviors, particularly if they occur only occasionally. By focusing on a particular critical incident, the study participants are aided in remembering it more clearly than if they had been asked about their information behaviors in general.

CONDUCTING THE INTERVIEW

Before an interview is carried out, careful preparation is required. Preparing for an interview includes selecting an appropriate location, setting up the interview time, confirming arrangements, rescheduling in case of any emergent absence, sending out a reminder to the subject of the scheduled interview a couple of days in advance, and so on. Recording tools, either an audio recorder or a note taker, should also be arranged before the interview (Robson, 2002).

Once these plans are in place, you're ready to conduct the interviews. Robson (2002) proposed a sequence of steps that the interviewer needs to go through in conducting an interview. Suppose you are interviewing a library user concerning his or her evaluation of an online catalog system. The following procedures exemplify the general process for such an interview:

1. Introduction. At the beginning of the interview, the interviewer would introduce himself or herself and explain the purpose of the study. This introductory portion of the interview includes describing the ways in which the interviewer will assure the anonymity of the user, asking permission to record the interview, and answering the user's questions about the nature of the study.
2. Warmup. This stage is a rapport-building step for both the interviewer and the user to get settled down for the interview. For example, the interviewer can say something like, "This is a nice place, isn't it?," if the interview is conducted in a nicely built library.
3. Main body of the interview. In this stage, the interviewer starts asking questions according to the interview guide, exploring the user's subjective evaluation of the online catalog system.
4. Cool-off. When the interviewer gets to the end of the interview, he or she can direct the conversation to be more casual, to ease out of the interview. Remarks like, "It's been good to talk to you," or "Your input is of great help to our study of this online catalog system," can be made.
5. Closure. This is the end of the interview, which can be closed by, "Thank you very much for your time and good-bye."

When conducting the interview, the interviewer should also be aware of his or her tone of voice. Since the interviewer communicates with the subject face-to-face, the way he or she asks questions or reacts to the subject's responses can affect the subject's responses and introduce bias in the data collected. Therefore the interviewer should remain neutral throughout the interview (Leedy & Ormrod, 2001).

DATA CAPTURE AND PREANALYSIS

Because the information exchanged through verbal communication during an interview can be slippery, it is best to record the interview. Permission from the subject is needed when the interview is to be recorded. With the rapid growth of use of computer and digital information, a digital voice recorder is frequently used in recording interviews because the recording can easily be converted to computer-readable formats, which would facilitate transcription and analysis.

Following the interview, transcribing is usually the next step, which results in a literal transcript of what has been said. The transcript will constitute the basis for further analysis. You will need to decide whether to transcribe the full text of the interview, or transcribe parts and take notes on the rest. Because full transcription is so labor-intensive, partial transcription is recommended. As you proceed with analysis, you can always go back and transcribe additional portions of the subject's words, if needed.

EXAMPLES

Two examples of the use of semistructured interviews will be discussed. The first researcher (Hara et al., 2003) interviewed scientists about their collaborations, which had been explored earlier using a sociometric survey. The second researcher (Rieh, 2004) interviewed people about their home use of the Internet, with a particular focus on Web-based searching. The interviews were based on research diaries recording the Web searches of the participants. These two studies are typical of well-designed semistructured interview studies, each based on a clearly articulated interview guide formulated from prior work with the study participants.

Example I: Collaboration in Scientific Research

Hara et al. (2003) did a study of scientific collaboration in a newly established research center. They used semistructured interviews to elicit information on scientists' perceptions regarding collaboration and factors that affect collaboration. Analysis of the full data set (including the interview data) resulted in the development of a framework that incorporates different types of collaborations and the factors that influence collaborative relationships.

The study was conducted in the context of a multidisciplinary, geographically dispersed research center distributed among four universities. Participants in the study included faculty, postdoctoral fellows, and students who were members of four research groups, ranging from 14 to 34 members each. Prior to interviewing the participants, a sociometric survey was conducted to collect basic information about the participants' collaborative experiences in the research center, such as with whom they interacted, what they interacted about, how they interacted, and how long they had been interacting. This preliminary data provided a solid foundation for Hara and colleagues (2003) to develop their interview guide.

According to the results of the sociometric surveys, three of the four research groups had abundant collaborations, while in the fourth group, collaborations were sparse. The authors were intrigued by the contrast between these two situations. Why did collaborative relationships develop in three teams, but not the fourth? This question made them decide to start from the negative case in conducting the semistructured interviews. What they found out from the interviews with this group was verified by later interviewing the other three groups.

Hara and colleagues (2003) provided a strong rationale for using semistructured interviews as a principal data collection technique. They argued that the free-flowing structure of a semistructured interview makes the interview feel like an informal conversation. They opened the interviews with a broad question and encouraged the participants to tell their stories regarding collaboration, from which the researchers were able to gain valuable qualitative insight. Their strategy was to begin with questions concerning an example of a collaboration, then move to questions about a particular collaboration in the research group and/or the center. This plan was reflected in their interview guide, which was basically a list of questions grouped under three top-level topics: (1) "Perceptions Regarding Collaboration in General," where four questions asked for examples of successful and unsuccessful collaborations and what made them so; (2) "Collaboration in the Research Group and Center," where the questions started getting specific to elicit experiences and perceptions of collaboration in this specific research environment; and (3) "Organizational Context of Collaboration," under which a few questions were asked about participants' ideas of how collaboration was perceived by other people in the organization, and potential barriers to collaboration in the center. Guided by this step-by-step sequence of primary topics, interviewers were aware of the principal research concerns, and the list of questions for each topic reminded them of different aspects of that topic that they needed to explore in the interview.

Any gaps in the interview guide were filled in with follow-up questions. Probes, as exemplified in their interview guide, were frequently used to gain further information from the participants. For example, one typical question-and-probe combination was, "Have you had any problems with collaborating with others in your research group/the center? If so, could you tell me about them?" The first part of the question was looking for a closed-ended answer. If the answer was yes, the second part of the question, or probe, would naturally encourage the participant to elaborate on what the problems were and why he or she had those problems. Thus the interview guide employed in this study not only had the topic question hierarchy to inform the interviewers of key aspects of the research question, but it also used probes to obtain more information from the participants.

Each interview lasted from 45 to 75 minutes. Most interviews were conducted in the participants' offices. Selecting the offices as the location for the interviews was reasonable because the participants were researchers, so sitting in the office and talking about something related to their research work would allow them to feel comfortable. The authors had approval from all but one participant to tape-record the interview. In case of recorder failure, they also took notes during the interview. For the one who did not wish to have the interview recorded, extensive notes were taken and shared with the participant after the interview to make sure the data accurately reflected the participant's words.

In reporting the interview results in this article, the authors used pseudonyms to protect the privacy of the participants. This approach prevented the participants from most risks associated with the study. However, in this study, the participants were from the same research center and knew each other. When reporting the results, the researchers also needed to be cautious in protecting the participants from the potential harm that might be caused by people they knew such as their coworkers or bosses. The risks of exposing participants' identities by revealing what they said had to be taken under consideration as quotes or notes were selected for inclusion in the research report.

This study illustrates the way that semistructured interviews can be successfully applied. The authors' careful preparation laid the groundwork for conducting the interviews. The interview guide is a good example of a method for collecting data on people's perceptions and experiences regarding a particular topic. The clear writing and organization of the methods section makes it well worth reading.

Example 2: Information Seeking in the Home Environment

Rieh (2004)[1] conducted a study of people's information seeking and Web search behaviors in the home environment. She used semistructured interviews to collect data on people's Web search activities and analyzed them on four levels: the home environment, the subjects' information seeking goals, the information retrieval interaction, and the specific query. Her findings suggested that the home provided a social context—beyond the physical setting alone—where people seek information in ways different from those of the workplace.

In this study, a convenience sample of 12 residents of northern California was recruited. All the subjects had computers and high-speed Internet connections at home. Before the interview, Rieh (2004) asked each subject to keep a diary of his or her Web information seeking activities over a three- to five-day period. In this diary, subjects were instructed to make notes of the date and time of activities, what kind of information they were looking for, the duration time, the starting point of the search, and whether the search was successful or not. These activity logs formed a preliminary data set, on which the interviews were based. While this study resembled the Hara et al. (2003) study, in terms of collecting a set of data before conducting the interviews, this study used the diary data in a different way than Hara and her colleagues used the results of their sociometric survey. In this study, the diary data were used more directly—as a stimulus for the interviews. Rieh scanned the diaries, and both she and the subjects could refer to the diary entries during the course of the interview.

The interviews took place in the subjects' homes because the home environment of information seeking was the focus of the study. A two-person team was present for each interview: the researcher and a transcriber. On arrival, they were taken to the room where the computer was placed and the Internet was accessed. Before the researcher started asking questions, she explained the purpose of the study and the data collection process to the subject and asked him or her to sign a consent form, as suggested by Robson (2002). A brief introduction of the study purpose prior to the interview gave the subjects a clear idea of the interview context and purpose.

Because the subject was going to be asked to conduct searches during the interview and Rieh (2004) wanted to capture as much information as possible about the subjects' search behaviors, the transcriber used a camcorder to record the computer screen and the interviews. In addition, the transcriber took notes during the interview. In this way, the researcher could focus on conducting the interview, without worrying about capturing data at the same time.

The interview guide was organized based on the four research questions raised in this study. For example, the first research question focused on environmental factors that affect searching from home; the accompanying 11 interview questions asked about the amount of time spent searching from home, motivations for getting broadband access to the Internet, other family members who searched from home, the kinds of searches conducted, and the positive and negative aspects of searching from home. The other three research questions were investigated with two to five interview questions each. The structure of this kind of interview guide facilitated answering the research questions in a very direct way.

In some ways, the semistructured interview employed in this study resembled a time-line interview. The Web search activities of each subject were recorded in sequential order in the research diary, which was used as a time line of events to establish a situation-oriented frame of reference (Schamber, 2000). For each Web search activity entered in the diary, the subject was asked to recall that event and answer a set of questions (though not the same set of questions that Dervin & Frenette, 2001, recommend). Finally, this study was naturalistic, collecting data in a real-world setting. It "did not apply pre-existing concepts of home information environments nor operationalize context and situation" (Rieh, 2004, p. 751). Using a time-line interview instrument encouraged the subjects to focus on real-life situations, which was helpful in avoiding bias and obtaining reliable and valid results (Schamber, 2000).

In summary, Rieh (2004) successfully gleaned data on people's home-based information seeking behavior by conducting semistructured interviews. She used diaries of subjects' Web search behaviors as a basis for the interviews and also had them conduct online searches during the interviews. Her careful planning and preparation for the interviews provide an excellent example for studies of search behaviors.

CONCLUSION

Semistructured interviews are one of the most useful data collection methods for studying a wide range of information behaviors. It is frequently the case that structured interviews or surveys are too structured—they limit the kinds of open-ended response that are sought in many studies. At the other extreme, the researcher often wants to impose some structure on the data collection process, rather than leaving it as open ended, as is allowed (and expected) using ethnographic interviewing techniques. To receive the full benefit of this research method, however, you need to plan your interview guide carefully and fully pretest it before conducting your interviews. In addition to the value of pretesting the guide for the purpose of improving it, the pretesting process will provide you with a means for improving your interviewing skills.

NOTE

1. This paper was the winner of the 2005 John Wiley Best *JASIST* Paper Award, administered by the American Society for Information Science and Technology.

WORKS CITED

Berg, B. L. (2001). *Qualitative Research Methods for the Social Sciences.* Boston: Allyn and Bacon.

Cannell, C. F., & Kahn, R. L. (1968). Interviewing. In G. Lindzey & E. Aronson (Eds.), *The Handbook of Social Psychology* (Vol. 2, pp. 526–595). Reading, MA: Addison-Wesley.

Dervin, B. (1983, May). *An overview of sense-making research: Concepts, methods and results to date.* Paper presented at the annual meeting of the International Communication Association, Dallas.

Dervin, B. (1999). On studying information seeking methodologically: The implications of connecting metatheory to method. *Information Processing and Management, 35*(6), 727–750.

Dervin, B., & Frenette, M. (2001). Sense-making methodology: Communicating communicatively with campaign audiences. In R. E. Rice & C. K. Atkin (Eds.), *Public Communication Campaigns* (3rd ed., pp. 69–87). Thousand Oaks, CA: Sage.

Flanagan, J. C. (1954). The critical incident technique. *Psychological Bulletin, 51*(4), 327–358.

Hara, N., Solomon, P., Kim, S., & Sonnenwald, D. H. (2003). An emerging view of scientific collaboration: Scientists' perspectives on collaboration and factors that impact collaboration. *Journal of the American Society for Information Science and Technology, 54*(10), 952–965.

Johnson, C. A. (2004). Choosing people: The role of social capital in information seeking behaviour. *Information Research, 10*(1), Article 201. Retrieved June 23, 2008, from http://informationr.net/ir/10-1/paper201.html.

Kraaijenbrink, J. (2007). Engineers and the Web: An analysis of real life gaps in information usage. *Information Processing and Management, 43,* 1368–1382.

Kvale, S. (1996). *Interviews: An Introduction to Qualitative Research Interviewing.* Thousand Oaks, CA: Sage.

Leedy, P. D., & Ormrod, J. E. (2001). *Practical Research: Planning and Design* (7th ed.). Upper Saddle River, NJ: Merrill Prentice Hall.

Millar, R., Crute, V., & Hargie, O. (1992). *Professional Interviewing.* London: Routledge.

Oakley, A. (1981). Interviewing women: A contradiction in terms. In H. Roberts (Ed.), *Doing Feminist Research* (pp. 30–61). London: Routledge and Kegan Paul.

Rieh, S. Y. (2004). On the Web at home: Information seeking and Web searching in the home environment. *Journal of the American Society for Information Science and Technology, 55*(8), 743–753.

Robson, C. (2002). *Real World Research: A Resource for Scientists and Practitioner-Researchers* (2nd ed.). Malden, MA: Blackwell.

Savolainen, R. (1993). The sense-making theory: Reviewing the interests of a user-centered approach to information seeking and use. *Information Processing and Management, 29*(1), 13–28.

Schamber, L. (2000). Time-line interviews and inductive content analysis: Their effectiveness for exploring cognitive behaviors. *Journal of the American Society for Information Science, 51*(8), 734–744.

Skopec, E. (1986). *Situational Interviewing.* New York: Harper and Row.

ADDITIONAL RECOMMENDED READING

Powell, R. R. (1997). *Basic Research Methods for Librarians* (3rd ed.). Greenwich, CT: Ablex.

Silverman, D. (2000). Analyzing talk and text. In N. K. Denzin & Y. S. Lincoln (Eds.), *Handbook of Qualitative Research* (2nd ed., pp. 821–834). Thousand Oaks, CA: Sage.

Warren, C.A.B. (2001). Qualitative interviewing. In J. F. Gubrium & J. A. Holstein (Eds.), *Handbook of Interview Research: Context and Method* (pp. 83–102). Thousand Oaks, CA: Sage.

25

Focus Groups

Barbara M. Wildemuth and Mary Wilkins Jordan

Things come in kinds; people come in groups.

—Chinese proverb

INTRODUCTION

Focus group methods originated in marketing studies but are rapidly being adopted in the social sciences, including information and library science (ILS). As defined by Powell and Single (1996), "a focus group is a group of individuals selected and assembled by researchers to discuss and comment on, from personal experience, the topic that is the subject of the research" (p. 499). On the surface, focus groups appear to be group interviews, but that is not all there is to it. Agar and MacDonald (1995) describe them as somewhere between a meeting and a conversation. Because the focus group members are encouraged to talk with each other as well as the researcher, the data produced by a focus group are more than just the answers to an interviewer's questions (Krueger & Casey, 2009). They are a set of intertwined voices, and you will need to pay particular attention to the voices opposing the group consensus as well as the voices that truly synthesize the group's ideas (Kitzinger & Barbour, 1993).

One of the core strengths of focus groups is that participants can compare their views with those of other participants in the group, rather than simply reporting their views to an interviewer. In this process, group members will make their differences of opinion explicit and will also voice their agreement with others' views. Thus, rather than having to infer similarities and differences in the participants' views from their individual statements, you will be able to directly observe them in your data. Because the group members challenge each others' views, the discussion in a focus group has often been found to reveal a more nuanced perspective on a topic than could have been discovered through individual interviews.

A related strength of focus groups is that their social nature mimics the setting in which people often form their opinions and attitudes (Millward, 1995). In some cases, at least, group members' views will be shifting as they hear and consider the views of other group members. For example, as a group of public library users discusses the length of the loan period, they may learn from each other about the effects of the loan period on peers in different life situations. This could clarify or, possibly, change their views on what the library's loan period should be. As Millward (1995) notes, "people will become more aware of their own perspective when confronted with active disagreement and be prompted to analyze their views more intensely" (p. 277).

A third strength of focus groups is the efficiency with which they can be used to generate new ideas (Gaiser, 1997). For example, a small number of focus groups may generate as many different ideas about a topic as a dozen or more individual interviews. The corresponding weakness is that each of these ideas may not be as fully developed as it might be if it were explored through individual interviews or participant observation. As noted previously, people's behaviors in a focus group will be similar to their behaviors in a meeting or conversation, both of which consist of rapid turn taking and short individual contributions.

While focus groups have been and will continue to be used as the sole data collection approach for some studies, they are a much stronger research tool if used in combination with other methods such as in-depth individual interviews, direct observation, or surveys. Agar and MacDonald (1995) illustrated this point when they used a focus group in combination with a series of ethnographic interviews. As can be seen from their report, they were able to interpret the focus group data with much more confidence when it was juxtaposed with data collected through other methods (Reed & Payton, 1997). Thus it is recommended that you consider augmenting your focus group data with data collected through other methods, or that you augment data collected through other methods with focus group data.

ISSUES TO CONSIDER IN CONDUCTING FOCUS GROUP RESEARCH

There are a number of issues that arise when conducting focus group research. The most critical of these issues will be discussed in terms of the stage of the research: planning the topic and developing a moderator's guide, selecting a moderator, identifying and recruiting participants, conducting the group sessions, and analyzing your results.

Putting the Focus in Your Focus Group

As with any type of research, you need to carefully consider what question you are asking with your study and what kinds of answers will be useful to you. In other words, you need to set the objectives for the study (Greenbaum, 1998). As Langer (2001) notes, "getting it right in the beginning means that the study will have value and credibility at the end" (p. 46).

There are a variety of purposes for which focus groups have been or could be used in studies of ILS (Glitz, 1997, 1998). Just a few examples of the purposes for which focus groups have been or could be used in libraries or other information organizations include the following:

• Evaluating the effectiveness of library services, for example, reference services
• Determining how satisfied people are with a new information service

- Evaluating the usability of a Web site
- Evaluating the strengths and weaknesses of library systems, for example, the online catalog
- Assessing students' needs for academic library services
- Identifying staff training needs
- Gathering ideas for the design or marketing of a new service or system
- Understanding the effects of Internet-based book reviews on whether people will purchase a book
- Developing plans for a new library building or evaluating the library's space needs from the users' perspective
- Providing input about long-term needs to a strategic planning process
- Understanding how people seek information and/or use libraries
- Determining members' attitudes toward a professional association and its services

For focus group research, decisions about your research questions are most often embodied in a moderator's guide or topic guide—the outline that the moderator will use to structure each focus group session (Knodel, 1993; Morgan, 1997). Developing a moderator's guide is an important step because it is very possible for an entire group to get off track and provide you with no usable or useful results. The guide will include a plan for introducing the moderator to the group and the group members to each other, some warm-up discussion topics related to the research questions (possibly including a discussion-starter question), discussion topics more specifically related to the research questions, and a closing or summary discussion. In general, the flow is from more general discussion of the topic of interest, to more specific discussion. For example, in an evaluation of a university's library services, the discussion might begin with discussions of the participants' earliest experiences with libraries, later eliciting participants' reactions to the particular library sponsoring the study, and concluding with questions about specific library services (if they have not already come up in the discussion). The guide should include the topics to be covered, a plan for the general sequence or flow of the discussion and how much time should be devoted to each topic area, and the materials needed during the session (Langer, 2001). Development of the moderator's guide should be done in consultation with your moderator.

In some cases, the research goals focus on a particular product, system, service, situation, or event. If useful, a concrete stimulus can be used to provide a springboard for the discussion. For example, if you were evaluating a new Web site design, it could be demonstrated or screen shots could be made available. Clearly this approach will be most effective if the focus of the research is on a concrete object.

Selecting a Moderator

The moderator of the focus group plays an important role in its success (or lack of it). Greenbaum (1998) argues that your choice of moderator is one of the three most important decisions you will make in developing and executing your research (along with the creation of the moderator guide and recruitment of the participants). The moderator is the one who keeps the discussion on track and away from becoming an unfocused conversation. He or she must achieve the right balance between controlling the flow of the discussion and allowing the participants free rein. He or she encourages the quiet members to speak up and controls the impact of the more dominant members. "If a respondent answers a question and it doesn't make sense, it's the moderator's job to understand why" (Langer, 2001, p. 108). In summary, a good moderator can bring order to the swirl of comments a focus group makes, helping you to get the best results. Using an inexperienced moderator, even one with the best of intentions, could result in missed opportunities during the research.

While some libraries have used professional moderators for focus group research, some have also used their own staff and been satisfied with the outcome (Glitz, 1997). This is not a simple yes-or-no decision. One possibility is to hire a market researcher to conduct the research. With this approach, the moderator will be responsible for managing the entire research process, including the preparation of the moderator's guide, development of the plan for recruitment, moderating the focus group sessions, analyzing the results, and writing up the final report (Greenbaum, 1998). It is important that the moderator you hire be well versed in the topic of the research as well as experienced in managing focus groups. Brown University took this approach and found it to be very effective (Shoaf, 2003, discussed later). A second possibility is to take on some of these activities in-house, hiring a moderator only for managing the sessions. In this situation, you will be responsible for developing the moderator's guide (in collaboration with the moderator), recruiting the participants and arranging for the logistics of the session (e.g., location, recording of the session), and analyzing and writing up the results. It is still important that your moderator be experienced in focus group research and knowledgeable about the topic of the research. The third possibility is to manage the focus group research yourself. This approach has been used in many focus group studies conducted in libraries and other information settings (e.g., the Large & Beheshti, 2001, study discussed later). However, it carries some risks beyond the obvious weakness from lack of experience. Most important, using a moderator known to the participants as a member of your organization or your research project could inhibit people's responses if they have negative comments to make. Nevertheless, using a member of your staff who is experienced with focus group research may be the most appropriate approach to take.

Identifying and Recruiting Appropriate Participants

The first step in this process is to define the characteristics of the people you would like to have participate in your focus groups (these are called *control characteristics* by Knodel, 1993). As Goebert and Rosenthal (2002) note, the "primary consideration is who will provide the most insightful information" related to the topic (p. 11), or, as Krueger and Casey (2009) put it, you want to recruit the most "information-rich" participants. Like other qualitative/intensive research approaches, you will want to purposefully se-lect a sample to participate in your focus groups. Morgan (1997) advises that you should "think in terms of minimizing sample bias rather than achieving generalizability" (p. 35). By this, he means that you should strive for a sample that includes an array of people representing different views, making sure that one particular perspective is not overrep-resented (Greenbaum, 1998). For example, if you were developing a Web site that would serve as a portal on nutrition and diet information, you would want to include people who had no weight problems as well as those who have recently lost significant amounts of weight, those who weigh too little, and those whose weight increases and decreases over time.

Because data collection occurs in a group setting, how your participants are distributed over the groups is also important. Some focus groups consist of a mixture of people from different backgrounds and having different characteristics. Such diversity within a group may be a good thing, to generate different ideas. However, most often, a segmentation approach (adapted from marketing) is used so that each group represents a relatively distinct (and homogeneous) segment of the intended audience for the product or service that is the focus of the research (Morgan, 1996, 1997). For example, a study of library services offered by a university library might segment by status (i.e., faculty in one group and students in another) or, as in the study by Widdows et al. (1991), by academic discipline (with science library users in one group and humanities library users in another). In general, you will want to limit the number of attributes used in segmentation (called *break characteristics* by Knodel, 1993) so that the number of groups does not exceed your ability to conduct the study.

Many authors recommend that members of a focus group should be strangers to each other, to avoid the political effects (e.g., not wanting to disagree with someone who has more power or status) and social effects (e.g., not wanting to disagree publicly with a friend) of existing relationships. However, the decision whether to recruit strangers or to work with people who are already acquainted will depend on the goals of your study. In most cases, there are no advantages to having intact groups serve as focus groups. However, in some cases (e.g., a study of the views of members of a particular department), your research goals will necessitate groups made up of acquaintances, colleagues, and so on. In these cases, the moderator will need to be especially sensitive to issues of confidentiality because he or she cannot guarantee that comments made in the group will not be communicated outside the group.

Sample size, for focus group research, has two dimensions: the size of each group and the number of groups. Most groups include 8 to 12 members, but some studies may need to use smaller groups (called minigroups by Langer, 2001). If participants have a lot of involvement with the topic, then you can use a smaller group; each person will have plenty to contribute. If participants have less involvement with the topic, you may need a larger group to keep the discussion going. Also, a larger group may yield a more diverse set of ideas about the topic (Morgan, 1996). The number of groups you use will depend on the goals of your study and also on the resources available to you: more groups require more resources. "In general, the goal is to do only as many groups as are required to provide a trustworthy answer to the research question" (Morgan, 1997, p. 44). Most projects include 4 to 6 groups (Morgan, 1996), though Millward (1995) suggests you won't see significant redundancy[1] in your data until about 10 groups have been completed. Such data redundancy is the most important indication that you have collected data from enough groups.

Many of the focus group studies reported in the literature note that recruiting participants is the most difficult aspect of this method, and several authors recommend that you overrecruit by 20 to 25 percent for each group (Millward, 1995; Powell & Single, 1996). It is entirely appropriate to offer incentives (such as refreshments, gift certificates, and/or cash) for participation (Krueger & Casey, 2009); such incentives are typical for focus group research. In addition, it may be appropriate to offer assistance with transportation costs or child care. If you use some type of gatekeeper (i.e., someone who has better access to the intended participants than you do) to assist with your recruiting, then be sure that he or she is fully informed about the study and accurately represents it to potential participants. As you recruit participants, you may also need to screen them to make sure that they have the characteristics required for inclusion in a particular group (the specified break characteristics) or in the study generally (the specified control characteristics).

During the Focus Group Session

Prior to the group session, you will need to select a site. It should be easily accessible for the participants. It should be quiet and comfortable, and private enough so that the session is free from interruptions. Because sessions typically last one to two hours, refreshments are typically provided; sharing them before the session allows participants to become comfortable with each other informally.

The moderator is responsible for the content of the session. The primary issue is the level of moderator control (Morgan, 1996). If the moderator takes a more structured approach, he or she will be asking the questions specified in the moderator's guide, keeping the discussion on topic, encouraging those who might otherwise say little and limiting those who would dominate the discussion. A less structured approach is also possible. In it, the moderator allows the group to move to topics not included in the moderator's guide or to skip topics they do not consider important. Participants may talk as much or as little as they please, and the group dynamics control the flow of the discussion. Each of these approaches can be effective, if it is well matched to the purposes of the research.

You will need to decide how to record the group's discussion. There are three methods that are most often used. The first is to audiotape the discussion. While it is a challenge to sort out the different speakers based on only their voices, this approach is the one that is most often used because it is a good midpoint between the other two possibilities: having a scribe present during the session or videotaping the session. In some sites specifically developed for focus group research, videotaping may be feasible. However, the obtrusiveness of the equipment, the need to get special permission from the participants, and/or the need for a specially designed room make this approach less attractive than simple audiotaping. A scribe is more feasible and is often used in conjunction with audiotaping. Used in combination with audiotaping, the scribe can pay special attention to which speaker raises which idea. Another way to use a scribe is for the scribe to record all the main points on flip charts for the group, to assist in its discussion (a role that may also be played by the moderator). If you simultaneously take notes and audiotape, you can later augment your notes with details from the recording (Bertrand et al., 1992). This approach achieves the dual goals of developing a rich data set and completing the process efficiently.

Understanding Your Results

The process of analyzing your data and understanding your results is, unfortunately, "the least agreed upon and the least developed part of focus group methodology" (Powell & Single, 1996, p. 502). Nevertheless, some advice can be gathered from experienced focus group researchers. In general, you will be working with qualitative data—transcriptions of or detailed notes on the group discussions (Krueger & Casey, 2009). Thus the same basic methods can be applied to these data as qualitative data gathered using other data collection methods. In general, you will code the data based on the themes that emerge from the participants' comments. However, there are a few particular points to keep in mind with focus group data, all related to the fact that the data are the result of group discussion, rather than interviews or documents from individuals. First, it is not always easy to follow the dialogue in the group. Consult with your moderator as you are doing your analysis if you are not sure how some comments fit into the flow of the discussion. Pay particular attention to agreement and disagreement within the group; these views often shift in the course of a discussion. Second, you will need to balance the views of all the participants, not just a few talkative ones (Greenbaum, 1998). Make sure that the themes that you identify represent the views of the group, rather than the strongly held opinions of just one or two participants (Kidd & Parshall, 2000). Third, some themes are embodied in a single comment, while others are embodied in a dialogue between multiple participants (Morgan, 1997; Reed & Payton, 1997). You can't be too rigid about the basic unit of analysis (e.g., defining the unit of analysis as a single comment made by a single participant), or you will lose ideas that were generated across multiple participants. As Kidd and Parshall (2000) note, "analyzing group discourse as though it was merely a concatenation of individual statements may only yield a laundry list of contradictory statements . . . or lead to erroneous conclusions" (p. 295). Fourth, you will want to compare the themes that emerge within each group with those themes that emerged from other groups. This aspect of focus group research adds a layer to the analysis phase. Fifth, you will need to distinguish between what participants believe is important and what they believe is interesting (Morgan, 1997). Just because they spend a lot of time discussing a particular topic does not mean that they think it is a critical point. Finally, if the group members knew each other prior to the research session, pay special attention to who contributed each idea. The existing relationships among participants will influence what gets contributed by whom (Reed & Payton, 1997).

Once you've analyzed the data from the group sessions, you will produce a report, written or oral (Krueger & Casey, 2009). Often this is a brief summary, meant to spur administrative action. However, this brief summary will not document the richness of your data. You should also provide a back-up report, providing evidence of each theme and thoroughly discussing the implications of each theme in terms of the original research question.

CONDUCTING FOCUS GROUPS ONLINE

Conducting your focus groups online may be particularly appropriate for studies of online social phenomena (Gaiser, 1997) or evaluations of Web sites or other online systems (Schneider et al., 2002), but they might also be used for other research purposes, particularly if the population of interest is geographically dispersed. A variety of tools are available to support focus group research conducted online. They include synchronous communication tools, such as conferencing software, chat (IRC), or a multiuser domain (MUD), or asynchronous tools, such as Listservs, electronic bulletin boards, and so on. Each software platform has slightly different characteristics, so you'll need to select the one that most closely meets your research needs. If you're planning to conduct focus groups online, you will still need to consider all the issues raised earlier. In addition, you may want to consider the ways in which the online communication medium will differ from what you would expect in a face-to-face focus group.

Several studies have compared online and face-to-face focus groups (see Chase & Alvarez, 2000, for a review) and have found differences in the ways that people interact. The most obvious is that online groups work best for people who are comfortable expressing themselves through written text, and face-to-face groups work best for people who are more comfortable expressing themselves orally. A second difference is that in an online discussion group, people cannot interrupt each other. Each person's complete comment is posted whenever it is entered into the discussion (Schneider et al., 2002).

Some tools are better than others at keeping the discussion threads organized, but it will be clear from the transcript that the online conversation is different than the conversation that would have occurred in a face-to-face session. In directly comparing face-to-face and online focus groups, Schneider et al. (2002) found that those in the online groups made more comments (though not more comments per minute), made shorter comments (and so may need to be asked to elaborate on their ideas), and made more brief statements of agreement (equivalent to a head nod in a face-to-face group). Participation was more evenly distributed in the online groups, providing a more balanced view of the group's opinions. There was no difference between the two types of groups in the number of off-topic comments made. A later study by Underhill and Olmsted (2003) confirmed the difference in number of comments but found that it did not translate into a difference in number of unique ideas generated. From these studies, we can conclude that online focus groups are likely to be very effective for some types of studies but that the medium of communication will need to be taken into account when the data are analyzed.

EXAMPLES

Two studies based on focus groups will be discussed here. The first (Shoaf, 2003) evaluated the performance of an academic library (at Brown University) and used a professional market researcher as the moderator. The goal of the second (Large & Beheshti, 2001; Large et al., 2002) was to understand children's perspectives on the design of Web search engines. Both were successful in achieving their goals, and each illustrates different decisions made about the design of the study by the researchers.

Example 1: Understanding Academic Library Performance

The User Needs Team in the Brown University Library decided to use focus groups to investigate their customer service processes (Shoaf, 2003). Their goal was to gather more specific input from library users, to evaluate their library services, and to support decision making about changes in those services. They had conducted previous user surveys but wanted the richer qualitative data that could be acquired through focus groups to help them interpret the survey results.

After reviewing focus group procedures, the group decided they did not have anyone on the library staff who would be capable of moderating the focus groups. They argued that "a professional librarian cannot simply follow the book on focus group surveys and expect good results" (Shoaf, 2003, p. 126). Therefore they decided to bring in outside expertise. They first looked within the university, but there was no one available. They then looked into the market research companies in their area and ended up hiring a Brown graduate who was interested in the library. The consultant was responsible for drafting the moderator's guide, conducting the focus group sessions, analyzing the data, and reporting the results to the library staff; the library staff handled some of the administrative aspects of the research such as booking the meeting room, providing refreshments, and recruiting the participants. Shoaf emphasizes that the decision to hire a consultant as a moderator was not entered into lightly—it cost several thousand dollars. In addition, the library staff spent time orienting the consultant to the library and its current services and facilities. In spite of the need for this up-front investment, they felt strongly that they needed professional assistance to achieve their research goals. As Shoaf pointed out in the literature review, hiring an outside consultant as a moderator is not often done by libraries conducting focus group research. As you plan your own research, you will need to weigh the resource investment required to hire a professional moderator against the improvement in data quality that may be achieved.

One important thing the consultant did was to draft a moderator's guide. "This printed report covered the topics to be discussed in the focus group meetings and outlined talking points for the participants" (Shoaf, 2003, p. 127). Both the library and the consultant brought ideas to this document, and it provided them with a way to plan the structure of the sessions and to articulate the points that should be discussed in the sessions. Although focus group sessions are going to be relatively free flowing, a good moderator will try to "focus" the participants on providing answers to the questions you believe are most important.

The library staff was responsible for recruiting participants; it was an uphill battle. Eventually, they were able to conduct five focus group sessions, with a minimum of five participants in each group. The recruiting plan segmented the target population on two break characteristics: status (faculty versus graduate student) and discipline (sciences versus humanities). They were basically successful in maintaining the use of status to differentiate the groups: two groups were made up of faculty and three were made up of graduate students. They were less successful in maintaining the use of discipline to differentiate the groups, and "eventually efforts were directed toward securing attendance of a sufficient number of participants," regardless of discipline (Shoaf, 2003, p. 127). While these challenges are not unusual, it did mean that each group was more heterogeneous than originally planned.

The library staff used two different recruiting methods: one for faculty and one for graduate students. All the participants came from the same initial pool: those who had responded to a prior library user survey and indicated that they would be willing to participate in a follow-up study. The faculty members were then invited, by phone, to participate in a focus group. Those who agreed received a follow-up e-mail and a reminder phone call the day before the session. The graduate students received the initial invitation via e-mail and received a follow-up e-mail and a phone call to confirm attendance and the reminder phone call the day before the session. Even with these relatively strenuous efforts at recruiting and the added offer of a $25 gift certificate as an incentive, prospective participants sometimes did not attend the scheduled sessions.

The procedure for the meetings themselves occurred as planned, with one exception. After the first couple of sessions, they discovered that people were not willing to attend the planned early evening sessions, so they switched the schedule to hold the sessions in the afternoon. While this did not alleviate all the difficulty of recruiting, it did make the study possible to complete.

The moderator tape-recorded the sessions, with permission from the participants. About two months after the five sessions were completed, the consultant submitted a final report. As part of that report, the consultant discussed the process of the focus group sessions and commented on the validity of the findings. This was a very important part of the final report, particularly because the results were much more negative than the earlier surveys had been. Because of the staff's reaction to the results, the consultant was asked to meet with them to put the criticisms of the library into the context of the focus group discussion and help the library translate the findings into plans of action for the future. This extra effort resulted in the study having more impact on the library's planning process than would have been the case if there were questions about the validity of the findings or if the consultant had not been able to explain the basis for the study's conclusions.

The Brown University Library learned several lessons from this experience, all of which would be valuable for anyone trying to conduct his or her own focus group research. The first is that you get what you pay for. Brown was very pleased with its consultant and felt that the money expended was well worth it. However, Shoaf (2003) also noted that it is very important that the consultant be very familiar with the topic of the research as well as focus group methods. If you are not able to find a moderator in your organization with the appropriate experience and knowledge, you should consider looking outside. If budgets are a problem for you, consider negotiating with a moderator to decrease the fees—you may have something you can trade instead of money (labor, good publicity, offering your location for further research, and so on). The importance of planning ahead was another lesson learned, but it was balanced by the accompanying need to be flexible. As Brown University Library learned, you need to be prepared to change your plans if it appears that something is not working. And in the end, the Brown University Library learned that satisfaction is a job well done. Sometimes just the process of trying to find out more about your research issue is helpful. Getting negative feedback gives you a place to start to work on improving your organization's effectiveness. Getting positive comments lets you know you are on the right track with your ideas and can give you encouragement for the future.

Example 2: Children's Views of Web Portal Design

Large et al. (2002) Large and Beheshti (2001) used focus groups made up of children to understand how Web portals might be designed to better serve children. They had four small groups of friends, age 10 to 13, search on assigned questions using four Web portals: Ask Jeeves for Kids, KidsClick, Lycos Zone, and Yahooligans! The children took turns controlling the computer, while the whole group commented on the strengths and weaknesses of each portal and how its design might be improved. During their interactions with the portals, a moderator guided their discussion.

The researchers created a strong focus for the group's discussion by having the children interact with each of the portals during the session. They were asked to find information on a particular topic with each of the portals; the order of the topics and portals was rotated across the four group sessions. This use of Web portals as the focal point of the group's discussion should be distinguished from a demo of a Web site provided by the moderator, as is often the case. Here, the children were conducting realistic searches on operational Web portals and thus had a more direct, concrete experience of the design features of those portals. As they worked through the search problems, they were quite uninhibited in pointing out where and why they experienced problems or how the portal designers might improve their designs. As the authors note, "the experience therefore was interactive as well as discursive" (Large & Beheshti, 2001, p. 83). This use of a stimulus to focus the discussion increases the likelihood that the participants in a focus group will interact with each other, yielding valuable data.

As noted previously, the selection of a moderator for the focus groups is a critical decision. In this study, the moderator was not experienced in managing focus groups. To prepare, he read the literature on focus group methods and "met with an experienced, professional moderator" (Large et al., 2002, p. 85). In addition, the moderator conducted several mock sessions with the research team. This is an idea not often seen in the literature, but the idea of rehearsals is a good one. Particularly, as in this case, when the moderator is inexperienced, it would be a good idea to run through your planned procedures to ensure they actually work the way you think they will. In most research, the idea of a pilot study is important. When using focus groups, you may indeed set up one group as a pilot study. However, given the difficulty many researchers have had in recruiting enough subjects to take part in their focus groups, it's most likely that you will need to run your pilot study with participants who are not in your target audience, saving all the potential participants for your "real" data collection efforts. While trying to bring an inexperienced moderator up to speed through training and rehearsal may not be ideal, it's a reasonable way to conduct focus groups in situations where a professional moderator is not available or the use of a professional moderator is not feasible.

The idea of using children in focus groups is not common in ILS research, though it is not unique to this study (see, e.g., Waters, 1996). The general social science research literature on using focus groups with children recommends that the session length be limited to about an hour, that each group be homogeneous in terms of the children's age and sex, that the participants be strangers to each other (as with adults), and that the focus groups be held in a location that is *not* in an institution controlled by adults. The current study followed most of this advice but deviated from it in some cases. Those points related to the sample will be discussed first, followed by those points related to how the focus group sessions were conducted.

All the children participating in this research had certain characteristics in common. They were between the ages of 10 and 13, and they had Internet access at home and were familiar with Web portals, but none of them had used any of the four portals being evaluated in this study. The groups were formed so that each included children of only one sex: two groups of boys and two groups of girls. The evidence suggesting that, with children of this age, single-sex groups would be more effective was corroborated with this study. The authors concluded that the boys' groups were more aggressive and expressed doubt that they would have learned as much from the girls in mixed-sex groups. In addition, the design ideas generated by the boys' groups were different than those generated by the girls' groups, suggesting that "a gender effect requires further investigation" (Large et al., 2002, p. 92).

The method of selecting/recruiting children was unusual because the child participants could not be recruited directly. The first contact was made with the parent of a potential child participant (in all cases, the mother). If the mother was willing to host a focus group in her home, she was asked to see if her child was willing to participate and to invite five friends to participate also. Once cooperation from a parent and child was attained, then formal consent was obtained from all participants and their parents. Thus each group consisted of a small group of friends, rather than the group of strangers most often recommended in the literature. The difficulty that may arise in groups of friends is that the children would be particularly susceptible to the so-called group-think problem through peer pressure. While the authors initially developed this recruitment strategy to simplify the process, they now argue that recruiting preexisting groups of friends "was the best decision in terms of getting an immediate group coherence and in encouraging all children to speak out" (Large & Beheshti, 2001, p. 85). In the four individual groups, there was some unanimity of opinion, but there were also many diverse opinions expressed as well. The authors believed that the fact that these children all knew each other and were friends actually helped the free-flowing expression of ideas and increased the number of diverse ideas generated. Other researchers using focus groups with children should give this decision careful consideration because arguments can be made for either approach. Alternative approaches to recruitment might rely on contact in a local school or the local public library. If there are other organizations in your area that work with children, you might approach them about recruiting children through them. Obviously, when dealing with recruitment of children, especially children who are strangers to you, you need to be particularly careful to clearly explain the purposes and procedures to their parents.

Each focus group session was conducted in the home of one of the child participants, with one exception: one group was held in the workplace of a child's parent. In each case, there was a room where the group could have access to a computer and would be uninterrupted for the session. Because these children were accustomed to visiting each others' homes, it is likely that this choice of location made them more at ease than if they had traveled to a neutral but unfamiliar site.

Locating the study in one child's house also brings up the issue of parental involvement and consent. In this study, there was no parental involvement in the actual focus group itself. However, with children, you need to consider how they are getting to and from your study—likely with a parent transporting them. Thus you need to consider where the parents will be during the study so they do not interfere with the interaction. It is not clear how these issues were handled in this study.

The sessions themselves were audio recorded; in addition, an assistant was taking notes. The authors stated that the children were not disturbed by the microphone, and this is generally true with the audio recording of focus groups. You should be sure to obtain explicit permission to record the sessions.

The groups in this study met for an hour. If you are working with children, you will need to consider how long their attention can reasonably be focused on your topic. These were older children, but it is an important topic to consider regardless of the ages of your participants. You need to let the groups go on long enough that you can get them settled into your topic and can get all the information you need, but you cannot keep people so long that they start to get restless and frustrated. The researchers broke up the time by allowing each child to take a turn on the computer and rotating the portals, so that all four portals were examined in every group. Children not in control of the computer were encouraged to contribute verbally to the work being done on the computer and to offer comments as they went through the process.

At the conclusion of the research session, the researchers provided pizza to all participants, along with free movie passes. Both refreshments and some type of incentive are expected in focus group research. Even relatively small tokens of appreciation, such as were given in this study, can help to encourage participation. If your budget is tight, consider talking with local businesses to see if they would donate incentives (such as gift certificates or coupons) for your research project. If you can show them the value of the research, they may be surprisingly helpful to you.

In general, this study did a good job of planning and conducting focus group sessions with children aged 10 to 13. Recruiting groups of friends to interact with Web portals in one of their homes served to put the children at ease, and the authors found these sessions to be much more fruitful than earlier individual interviews they had conducted with children of similar ages (Large & Beheshti, 2000). While these decisions about the sample and recruiting methods need to be reconsidered in future studies conducted for other purposes, they were implemented successfully here.

CONCLUSION

Focus groups can be a good choice for data collection if you believe that value will be obtained in the participants' interactions with each other, rather than through individuals responding to questions from you, the researcher. As several of the authors cited in this chapter have argued, people form their opinions in a social setting, so it is appropriate to gather data about those opinions in a social/group setting. While focus groups are not an ideal data collection method for every situation, they can provide you with a wealth of information, both as a follow-up to another research method (e.g., individual interviews or direct observation) and as a stand-alone method.

NOTE

1. In most forms of qualitative data collection, you are attempting to identify a wide range of ideas or perspectives. Redundancy is achieved when your new/additional participants are repeating ideas already expressed by other participants, without adding any new ideas to the data set.

WORKS CITED

Agar, M., & MacDonald, J. (1995). Focus groups and ethnography. *Human Organization, 54,* 78–86.

Bertrand, J. T., Brown, J. E., & Ward, V. M. (1992). Techniques for analyzing focus group data. *Evaluation Review, 16*(2), 198–209.

Chase, L., & Alvarez, J. (2000). Internet research: The role of the focus group. *Library and Information Science Research, 22*(4), 357–369.

Gaiser, T. J. (1997). Conducting on-line focus groups: A methodological discussion. *Social Science Computer Review, 15*(2), 135–144.

Glitz, B. (1997). The focus group technique in library research: An introduction. *Bulletin of the Medical Library Association, 85*(4), 385–390.

Glitz, B. (1998). *Focus Groups for Libraries and Librarians.* New York: Forbes.

Goebert, B., & Rosenthal, G. (2002). *Beyond Listening: Learning the Secret Language of Focus Groups.* New York: John Wiley.

Greenbaum, T. L. (1998). *The Handbook for Focus Group Research* (2nd ed.). Thousand Oaks, CA: Sage.

Kidd, P. S., & Parshall, M. B. (2000). Getting the focus and the group: Enhancing analytical rigor in focus group research. *Qualitative Health Research, 10*(3), 293–308.

Kitzinger, J., & Barbour, R. S. (1993). Introduction: The challenge and promise of focus groups. In R. S. Barbour & J. Kitzinger (Eds.), *Developing Focus Group Research: Politics, Theory and Practice* (pp. 1–20). Thousand Oaks, CA: Sage.

Knodel, J. (1993). The design and analysis of focus group studies: A practical approach. In D. L. Morgan (Ed.), *Successful Focus Groups: Advancing the State of the Art* (pp. 35–50). Newbury Park, CA: Sage.

Krueger, R. A., & Casey, M. A. (2009). *Focus Groups: A Practical Guide for Applied Research* (4th ed.). Thousand Oaks, CA: Sage.

Langer, J. (2001). *The Mirrored Window: Focus Groups from a Moderator's Point of View.* New York: Roper Starch Worldwide.

Large, A., & Beheshti, J. (2000). The Web as a classroom resource: Reactions from the users. *Journal of the American Society for Information Science, 51*(12), 1069–1080.

Large, A., & Beheshti, J. (2001). Focus groups with children: Do they work? *Canadian Journal of Information and Library Science*, *26*(2/3), 77–89.

Large, A., Beheshti, J., & Rahman, T. (2002). Design criteria for children's Web portals: The users speak out. *Journal of the American Society for Information Science and Technology*, *53*(2), 79–94.

Millward, L. J. (1995). Focus groups. In G. M. Breakwell, S. Hammond, & C. Fife-Schaw (Eds.), *Research Methods in Psychology* (pp. 274–292). London: Sage.

Morgan, D. (1996). Focus groups. *Annual Review of Sociology*, *22*, 129–152.

Morgan, D. L. (1997). *Focus Groups as Qualitative Research* (2nd ed.). Thousand Oaks, CA: Sage.

Powell, R. A., & Single, H. M. (1996). Methodology matters—V: Focus groups. *International Journal for Quality in Health Care*, *8*(5), 499–504.

Reed, J., & Payton, V. R. (1997). Focus groups: Issues of analysis and interpretation. *Journal of Advanced Nursing*, *26*, 765–771.

Schneider, S. J., Kerwin, J., Frechtling, J., & Vivari, B. A. (2002). Characteristics of the discussion in online and face-to-face focus groups. *Social Science Computer Review*, *20*(1), 31–42.

Shoaf, E. C. (2003). Using a professional moderator in library focus group research. *College and Research Libraries*, *53*(2), 124–132.

Underhill, C., & Olmsted, M. G. (2003). An experimental comparison of computer-mediated and face-to-face focus groups. *Social Science Computer Review*, *21*(4), 506–512.

Waters, M.R.T. (1996). From the mouths of the young: What children and young people think about the public library. *Public Library Quarterly*, *15*(4), 3–16.

Widdows, R., Hensler, T. A., & Wyncott, M. H. (1991). The focus group interview: A method for assessing users' evaluation of library service. *College and Research Libraries*, *52*(4), 352–359.

26

Survey Research

Carolyn Hank, Mary Wilkins Jordan, and Barbara M. Wildemuth

> The job is to ask questions—it always was—and to ask them as inexorably as I can. And to face the absence of precise answers with a certain humility.
>
> —Arthur Miller (1964)

INTRODUCTION AND DEFINITION

Surveys have become a common part of everyday American life. On any given day, you can expect to be asked to respond to a survey in your grocery store, when you check your e-mail, and via a phone call during dinner. Though survey research is a popular, commonplace method, it does not mean surveys are simple to design and administer. Effective survey research involves extensive planning. You will need to carefully consider your research objectives as you plan for participant recruitment, design and administration of the survey, and data analysis.

Survey research is a useful method, enabling researchers to statistically "estimate the distribution of characteristics in a population," based on a sample that is only a fraction of that population (Dillman, 2007, p. 9).[1] Survey research designs are appropriate to investigate many different information and library science research scenarios, from program quality to worker satisfaction to information behaviors. Survey research supports the collection of a variety of data, including the beliefs, opinions, attributes, and behaviors of the respondents (Babbie, 1990; Dillman, 2007).

Surveys can take many different forms. The methods introduced in this chapter are intended for those studies attempting direct assessments, posed in a straightforward manner, for which singular, nonscalar responses for measurement purposes are appropriate.[2] In general, such surveys use one survey question to collect responses on each variable of interest. Questionnaires intending to gather data on attitudes, individual/subjective perceptions, and other psychological constructs will benefit from a scalar measurement instrument.

CONDUCTING SURVEY RESEARCH

The design of effective survey research involves "many decisions which need to fit together and support one another in a way that encourages most people to respond and minimizes inaccurate or inadequate answers" (Dillman, 2007, p. 13). Survey research design is dependent on careful planning that necessitates attention to a series of critical components to ensure effective data collection and implementation. Here we will focus on survey design; pretesting and pilot testing, with revision as necessary; survey administration; and data analysis.

Designing the Survey Instrument

A survey, simply, is a set of items, formulated as statements or questions, used to generate a response to each stated item. Designing the survey instrument is a critical task in planning survey research because it will influence the number of responses you receive and the validity of those responses (Czaja & Blair, 2005; Dillman, 2007). A good survey is appropriately brief and simple to complete, both in terms of wording and organization, so as not to demand too much effort on the part of respondents. Survey design is an iterative process, involving thoughtful drafting and organization of questions and response categories, then subsequent evaluation and revision, as necessary, until it's ready for distribution.

Before you even begin drafting your survey, examine the literature in your area of interest. Consult other studies that may have posed similar questions. Refer to Web sources like the American Library Association (ALA; http://www.ala.org) or the Pew Research Center (http://www.pewinternet.org), where the results of professionally conducted surveys are collected. Consider using or revising the surveys used in those studies. If appropriate, you may want to contact the authors of previous studies to get more information on their study procedures.

Many texts are available that offer guidance for constructing the survey instrument. For example, Peterson (2000) provides a seven-step framework for survey construction, and Dillman (2007) offers 19 principles to consider when composing questions. A few suggestions are summarized here:

- Ask only what can be answered, and ask only what is necessary to satisfy the objectives of the research investigation.
- Questions should be asked in complete sentences, diminishing the risk of misinterpretation.
- Use neutral language, avoiding words that could be misconstrued as subordinating, biased, or offensive.
- Give consideration to the specificity of your questions. Questions should not be so specific as to impede the ability to arrive at an appropriate response or so vague that they lead to confusion or frustration.
- Avoid double-barreled questions. For example, the question "Should the library invest in new electronic databases that allow patrons to access the databases remotely?" actually asks two questions: first, should the library buy new databases, and second, if so, should these databases be licensed so that they permit remote access by patrons? Make sure that each query posed is only asking one question of respondents.
- Participation in most survey research is voluntary, and as such, respondents should be in control of the extent of their participation. Do not burden respondents by requiring that each question

be answered before respondents are allowed to continue with the survey (Dillman, 2007; Sue & Ritter, 2007).

Surveys comprise two types of questions: open-ended and closed-ended. Closed-ended questions are more commonly applied in surveys because they require less time and effort from the respondent and it is easier to analyze the results (Czaja & Blair, 2005). They present respondents with a limited number of predetermined response categories. You'll need to pay attention to developing both the question and the list of possible responses. Don't provide more responses than necessary, but make sure to provide all the responses that might be selected. When necessary (e.g., when you're not confident that you've identified all the possible responses), the list of responses may include an "other" category, accompanied by space for an explanation.

Open-ended questions do not present respondents with any response categories; rather, respondents compose and submit their own responses. An example open-ended question might be, What would you do if the library no longer provided remote access to the library's electronic database collection? There is no way the researcher could reasonably construct response categories to this question because it would be impossible for the researcher to know all the possible responses. Open-ended questions are appropriate for many different research purposes, particularly for exploratory studies. Instruction should be clear in what is being asked of the respondents, offering parameters to help respondents devise answers that are appropriate in length, content, and detail.

In addition to developing the individual questions to be included in your survey, you need to organize them appropriately. Peterson (2000) recommends arranging the survey into three sections: an introduction, a substantive questions section, and a classification questions section. The introduction section is the respondents' first interaction with the survey. It should engage respondents in the survey, encouraging continued participation and building rapport. The first questions should also be relatively easy to answer (Dillman, 2007; Peterson, 2000). Questions essential to the research initiative are presented next, in the substantive questions section. This section is considered the heart of the survey. Within this section, related questions should be grouped together. If you have any questions that ask respondents to divulge sensitive information, place those at the end of this section. Classification questions, the final section, gather basic information such as demographic information. These questions should be positioned at the end of the survey because, for the most part, the information collected is not essential to the research investigation and, second, answering usually requires little exertion on the part of respondents (Peterson, 2000).

In addition to organizing the questions themselves, consider the physical appearance of your survey. For paper-based surveys, the layout should be attractive, using an appropriate amount of space between questions and sections, and selecting font sizes and styling that are easy for respondents to read. For Web-based and e-mail surveys, different computers and different e-mail applications and browsers may alter the intended display. Surveys to be distributed by these means should be designed with these renderability concerns in mind. Other design considerations for Web-based surveys include the use of a progress bar so respondents will be made aware of their progress as they move through the survey.

Pretesting and Pilot Testing

Evaluation of the survey instrument prior to administering it to the study sample can ensure that the survey is both reliable and valid. There are a couple of approaches to evaluating your survey instrument before you administer it to the sample of interest. Here we'll classify these approaches into two groups: pretesting and pilot testing. By *pretesting*, we mean the review of the survey instrument by experts or by members of the target audience. By *pilot testing*, we mean a realistic administration of the survey to a sample from the target audience (not the sample for the real administration).

Pretesting provides the opportunity to uncover any problems, such as misleading questions or incomplete response categories or grammatical errors and misspellings. A pretest involves administering the survey to a small group of evaluators; the evaluators may be experts in the topic of the research or members of the target audience. In its simplest form, the pretest will ask the evaluators for suggestions for improving the survey. Alternatively, particularly if you're using members of the target audience, you might have the evaluators "think aloud" as they respond to the survey; that is, they verbalize their thoughts about the questions as they are answering. Using these methods, you can ensure that the survey items are being interpreted as you had intended.

A pilot test, if appropriate, would follow the pretesting. In the pilot test, you would replicate the administration of the full-scale survey research design, but to a small sample from your target audience. Depending on the research enterprise, pilot testing may not be possible or pragmatic because it demands more time, effort, and resources than a pretest. Particularly if your target audience is somewhat small, you may not want to pilot test because it decreases the number of people eligible for the survey research itself (Czaja & Blair, 2005).

Administering the Survey

There are a variety of ways to administer a survey. They include the following:

- Mailing the survey to the respondents and asking them to respond by mail
- E-mailing the survey to the respondents and asking them to respond by e-mail
- E-mailing a request to fill out the survey and asking respondents to go to a Web site to respond
- Arranging to administer the survey via a synchronous online chat session
- Posting the survey on a Web site and inviting visitors to the site to respond to the survey
- Phoning the potential respondents and asking them to respond on the phone
- Automatically phoning the respondents and asking them to respond by Interactive Voice Response or Touch-tone Data Entry
- Other variations on these approaches

While there is "no one best method" for data collection, there are benefits and disadvantages associated with each different technique (Czaja & Blair, 2005, p. 33). When choosing the method for data collection, it is important to consider a number of factors, including available resources, time frame, staffing, and cost, among others. To consider the advantages and disadvantages of different approaches, we'll distinguish self-administered surveys from other administered surveys (Peterson, 2000), and we'll take into account the technology used to deliver the survey and collect the responses.

It is very likely that the content of your survey, in terms of the types and number of questions included, will influence your decisions about administration. E-mail surveys may be ideal for very brief, simple surveys, while Web-based or printed surveys may be more appropriate for longer or more complex surveys (Dillman, 2007). In addition, Web-based surveys can generally provide more control over user responses (e.g., enforcing the requirement that only one item on a response list be selected). By contrast, administration via phone or face-to-face may be more appropriate when you have a large proportion of open-ended questions. Personal interactions between the interviewer and the respondents may contribute to more thorough responses, and the interviewers may be able to capture nonverbal cues such as pauses, facial movements, and body gestures. Such personal interactions also may motivate sample members to participate.

Self-administered questionnaires, on paper or on the Web, allow respondents flexibility in deciding when, where, and at what pace to complete the survey. This form of questionnaire also allows it to be distributed over a wide geographic area (Czaja & Blair, 2005). While conducting face-to-face interviews limits the geographical reach of the study, phone interviews allow the researcher to cast a wider net. However, the lack of available resources, such as funds to support long-distance calling or use of automated dial systems, may limit the study's geographical scope.

Web-based surveys have become increasingly popular because of their lower costs when compared to other approaches to survey administration (Czaja & Blair, 2005; Dillman, 2007). While some costs will be incurred, including Internet service, survey software subscription, and others, these are usually less than costs associated with other techniques, including the cost of paper, postage, and data entry for mailed surveys, and travel or phone service, staffing, and transcription services for interview surveys. An additional cost advantage is that the responses to Web-based surveys can be automatically captured, avoiding the cost of data entry.

The elapsed time for completing the study also gives the advantage to Web-based or e-mail surveys. Czaja and Blair (2005) estimate that data collection times for Internet-administered surveys are brief, approximately 1 to 3 weeks, while the time frame for telephone surveys is 2 to 4 weeks, and mailed surveys take approximately 10 weeks. Face-to-face interview surveys typically require the most time to complete—4 to 12 weeks—and are the most expensive data collection activity.

On the other hand, Web-based and e-mail surveys require that your respondents have easy access to this technology and are comfortable using it. For example, a Web-based survey may be an effective method for a sample of college students, but a paper-based mail survey may be more appropriate for a sample comprising senior citizens. Phone surveys also require that the respondents have access to a phone; while phones are common, survey administration may be hampered by call blocking or by lack of access to cell phone numbers.

Taking all these considerations into account, you will need to choose the survey method that is right for your study. On the basis of your particular research question, the answer may be obvious. Or, based on the amount and types of resources available for the study, you may be compelled to select one option or another. You may also want to consider combining methods: you could mail out printed surveys, then follow up with e-mail copies to slow responders, and finally phone people who have not returned the survey. You may want to consider which format will give you the most flexibility for yourself, or which one your staff can help you administer, or which one you think the respondents will enjoy the most. Consider which method you believe will bring in the highest number of valid responses. The important thing is to select a method that will bring you success in answering your research question.

Methods for Increasing Your Response Rate

Most likely, you will have administered your survey to a sample from the population in which you're interested. (See Chapter 13 for a full discussion of sampling.) Because surveys are relatively inexpensive to administer (either by mail, e-mail, or the Web), it's likely that you distributed the survey to a large number of potential respondents (Dane, 1990). To understand the validity of any generalizations you make from the survey, you will need to calculate your response rate, defined as "the number of eligible sample members who complete a questionnaire divided by the total number of eligible sample members" (Czaja & Blair, 2005, p. 37). Several ways to increase your response rate will be discussed here.

One way to increase the response rate is to contact potential respondents multiple times. Dillman (2007) suggests a five-contact framework, including a short, prenotice contact; initial distribution of the survey; a thank-you/reminder about 1 week after initial distribution; a second reminder a couple of weeks later; and a fifth follow-up contact using a different means for contact (e.g., phoning those who have not responded to an e-mail survey). All contacts, regardless of type, should be personalized, when possible, and written in such a way as to build participant interest in the research enterprise.

Another strategy for increasing your response rate is to collaborate with relevant organizations or individuals to sponsor the study, and to make the relationship known to potential respondents. Sponsorship is an effective strategy because "it is shown that people are more likely to comply with a request if it comes from an authoritative source; that is, one whom the larger culture defines as legitimate to make such requests and expect compliance" (Dillman, 2007, p. 15). Caution should be taken in seeking sponsorship from persons that may be perceived as superiors because it may give the impression that participation is required, rather than optional, and resulting responses may negatively affect the integrity of the data collected.

A final approach to increasing your response rate is to provide an incentive for participation. You can provide a small, but concrete, incentive for each respondent. Even a nominal reward—a pencil, a bookmark—can help encourage people to respond to your survey.

Analyzing the Responses

An important characteristic of survey research is that the data may be analyzed for both descriptive and comparative purposes (Czaja & Blair, 2005). Careful consideration of strategies for conducting your analysis should begin in the earliest stages of designing your survey. Closed-ended questions afford more convenience and ease for analysis by presenting results that can be easily converted to numerals and calculated using statistical software applications. Even with closed-ended questions, you will want to carefully plan your response options to optimize the ways in which you can analyze the results. Analysis of responses to open-ended questions requires an additional step—analyzing and categorizing the responses—before additional quantitative analysis can be completed. In addition, the form of your data collection methods will affect the ease of the preanalysis steps. Face-to-face and phone interviews as well as printed surveys require that response data be manually entered into whatever computer application will be used for analyzing data. Web-based surveys, on the other hand, compile the data at the point of data collection, removing a time-consuming step.

Your survey was administered to be able to answer your research question. Be prepared: sometimes the answer is not what you expected. Sometimes, despite your fondest hopes and wishes, the people you survey will hate your new system, kill your chances for expansion of a program, or tear the heart out of your research project. While you are taking a moment to bounce back from the shock of learning that not everyone agrees with you, try to remember that at least you figured it out now—before you had too much invested in your project. This can be the true power of surveys. Having this kind of information will help you make an informed choice about your next steps.

EXAMPLES

Three examples of survey research will be discussed. The first (Marshall, 1992) used a mail survey to evaluate the relevance of particular hospital library services as well as the impact of library services on physicians' clinical work. The population of interest was staff in 15 hospitals in one region of New York State. The second example (D'Elia et al., 2002) reports on a telephone survey of several thousand citizens, designed to investigate the consumer market for public library services and Internet services. The third example (Hirsh & Dinkelacker, 2004) is a Web-based survey distributed to researchers within a single large, high-tech company.

Example 1: Impact of Hospital Libraries on Physician Decision Making

In this article, Marshall (1992)[3] reports on a survey research study evaluating the relevance of hospital library services and the impact of librarian-provided information on physicians' clinical decision making. The study was conducted in response to changes to legislation that no longer required hospitals to maintain a library for Medicare and Medicaid eligibility, with the intent of demonstrating the need for hospital libraries and to provide evidence of the positive impact of library services on patient care.

The study was initiated by the Hospital Library Services Program advisory board, a program within the Rochester (New York) Regional Library Council (RRLC). A planning meeting for the study, described as a "grass-roots effort," was held in March 1990 and involved a group of participants representing Rochester-area hospital librarians, the RRLC staff, and Marshall—at the time, a University of Toronto researcher serving as research director for the study. The planning group decided to base the research design on a similar study that took place in Chicago in the mid-1980s, so the research director for the Chicago study was retained by the Rochester group to refine and revise the Chicago methodology, including the survey instrument, for the Rochester study. To increase their survey response rates, the Rochester group contacted participants prior to the study to solicit participation; enlisted the cooperation of local medical associations to serve as sponsors; and used unique identifiers to distinguish between respondents and nonrespondents to aid in sending reminders and identifying the reasons for nonresponse. The planning group also hired a research assistant, based in Rochester, to perform sampling, recruitment, and data collection activities.

The population of interest was the practicing physicians and residents at the 15 hospitals (7 urban and 8 rural) in a five-county area. The urban hospitals had on-site hospital libraries, and the rural hospitals were served by a circuit librarian program. The sampling frame totaled 2,750 members, after the removal of duplicates. The planning group decided to calculate how many members from each hospital would be selected for the sample based on type of hospital and number of active physicians. This was done to diversify the sample as well as to avoid taxing certain hospital libraries with information requests if a disproportionate number of physicians and residents at particular locations were selected for the sample. Also, because the planning group was particularly interested in the use of hospital library services by residents and by physicians in rural libraries, these members represented a larger proportion (30%) of the sample. The final sample size was 448, comprising 207 urban physicians, 85 rural physicians, and 156 residents. On the basis of the guidelines in standard texts on survey research design, this sample size would provide reliable results at a plus or minus 4 percent sampling error, based on a 95 percent confidence interval.

A list of each hospital's active physicians and residents was used to randomly select participants. The research assistant contacted each selected sample member by phone to invite him or her to participate. If a physician or resident declined to participate or could not be reached after four attempts, the research assistant substituted another member of the population from the sampling frame. Furthermore, if a physician or resident declined participation, the reason was noted, when made available. Reasons reported included lack of time, lack of interest, or lack of library use. Overall, 1,600 telephone calls were made, with an average of three calls required to confirm willingness to participate.

The survey instrument from the Chicago study was revised to meet the Rochester study objectives. The goal in drafting the survey was to keep it as brief as possible. The survey directed participants to request library information on a recent clinical case and assess the impact it had on that patient's care. Participants were instructed not to identify themselves as study participants when making information requests to librarians. That was a necessary step to ensure the credibility of the data. If librarians were aware that information requests were made as part of the study, then it may have influenced how those requests were handled. While the survey itself may have been brief, this activity called for a considerable amount of effort on the part of physicians and residents.

The paper-based survey, to be administered through the mail, went through iterative drafting procedures. Each draft was reviewed by members of the planning group and was pretested by a group of physicians at rural hospitals. Further pretesting was performed at the University of Toronto, under Marshall's direction. The substantive questions section sought to collect data on the impact of library-supplied information on clinical decision making, and three new impact questions were created in response. For example, one question asked whether library-provided information changed particular aspects of patient care. Respondents replied yes, no, or not applicable to each category in the response set—(1) handled situation differently, (2) diagnosis, (3) choice of tests, (4) choice of drugs, (5) choice of other treatment, (6) length of stay (reduce), (7) posthospital care or treatment, and (8) changed advice given to patient.

Data collection took place between September 1990 and March 1991. To improve response rates, senior medical staff members at each hospital were recruited to serve as study facilitators, supporting data collection activities at their respective locations. After the initial contact by telephone, participants were mailed the survey packet. The mailing of the packets was staggered so that hospital librarians would not receive a noticeable increase in information requests. Contents of the packets included a letter of support for the study from the local medical society, an information sheet on the study, one page of instructions, the two-page survey, a listing of study facilitators, and a stamped return envelope. Nonrespondents were mailed a second packet approximately one month after the initial mailing. Those not responding to the follow-up mailing were contacted by telephone by the Rochester-based research assistant. Additionally, study facilitators were requested to contact nonrespondents at their respective hospitals.

From the 448 mailed surveys, 227 surveys were received. The importance of follow-up activities in the survey research design is evidenced by the fact that 37 percent were received after the follow-up activities were implemented. The total number of complete, useable surveys was 208, resulting in a response rate of 46 percent. The 19 discarded surveys were returned blank or incomplete, some with notations by participants that they did not have enough time to respond. Overall, findings showed that physicians and residents perceive information received from hospital librarians as having a significant impact on their decision making regarding patient care.

Overall, the survey research design employed in this study was successful. Many factors contributed to this success. First, the study benefited from the support and cooperation of several stakeholder groups, including hospital librarians, senior medical staff, and local medical societies. Second, this study was modeled on a similar study, rather than starting from scratch. This decision resulted in a well-vetted instrument and a multiple-contact framework for facilitating data collection. Third, the study team had available resources to staff the research activity, including the hire of a consultant and two research assistants. Additionally, these resources were supplemented by a grant from the Medical Library Association to support the numerous follow-up activities.

While the 46 percent response rate was slightly lower than the Chicago study, it was a satisfactory rate of response considering the survey population and the effort required to complete the survey. The survey did not call for simply checking a series of boxes on a paper-based survey and mailing the results. Completing the survey involved identification of a clinical case, contacting the library and requesting information, and reviewing and evaluating the information received as a result of the request. Ease of access to information may have also played a role in nonresponse. Residents were the least represented group among the sample, with only 33 percent responding. One possible explanation for this low response may be that residents had free access to the MEDLINE database. Given the occupational demands of physicians and residents and the extensive steps that had been implemented to induce participation, it seems likely that a higher response rate would have been impossible to achieve.

Example 2: Public Library Services in the Internet Era

D'Elia et al.'s (2002) article[4] reports on a random digit dialing (RDD) telephone survey of 3,097 English- and Spanish-speaking adults, undertaken by the authors in 2000. The objective of the survey was to collect descriptive information on the consumer market for public library services and Internet services. The research was conducted in response to the need to negotiate the role of libraries with the emergence of the Internet because "to date, there has been little data on which to base an understanding of the Internet," and "which may result in potential shifts in consumer demands for the types of information and services provided by libraries" (D'Elia et al., 2002, p. 803). To frame their investigation, D'Elia and his colleagues devised a two-dimensional market segment model for use as a conceptual grounding. The first dimension was library use (library users, nonusers); the second dimension was related to Internet access (Internet access and use, Internet access and nonuse, and no Internet access).

The researchers outsourced survey administration activities to Goldhaber Research Associates. The sample consisted of 3,097 adults, representing residents of 48 contiguous states in the United States. The sampling error for a sample this size was plus or minus 1.8 percent based on a 95 percent confidence level.[5] The RDD survey limited contact to residential telephone numbers and, due to cost considerations, English- and Spanish-speaking participants. While other languages were not supported, support for the two most commonly spoken languages in the United States enabled the inclusion of more participants than would have been possible if the survey was only made available in English. Electing to base your sample on residential telephone listings also excludes those members of the population who do not have home telephone service, reported by the authors to be about 6 percent, based on 1998 figures from the Department of Commerce.

Overall, the survey was designed to collect information on respondents' access to information resources, why they elect to use one type of service—library service or Internet service—as opposed to the other, and their evaluation of the services selected. The survey was constructed following an extensive review of other information resources, including literature reviews of similar studies and consultation with the study's advisory committee, a national group of public and special library directors. Two other steps merit specific mention. First, survey design was informed by a series of focus groups. The researchers conducted four focus group sessions with representatives from four of the six segments of their consumer market model, resulting in a "particularly rich pool of information that assisted [us] in creating the questionnaire" (D'Elia et al., 2002, p. 805). Second, the researchers consulted previously deployed surveys for collecting information. For example, demographic questions on racial heritage were asked based on categories used in the 1990 National Census. Questions to meet objective 2, "to describe why people use the library and to determine if use of the Internet affects the reasons why people use the library," and objective 8, "to describe the information requirements of people who do not use the library and who do not have access to Internet," were taken from the service response categories developed by the Public Library Association (D'Elia et al., 2002, p. 805). Cumulatively, these procedures allowed the researchers to draw comparisons between the data collected in their study and those collected by similar studies using comparable questions and response categories.

In addition to carefully planning the survey design, three pilot studies were conducted to test, assess, and revise the instrument. Filtering questions were used at the outset of the survey to collect demographic information and determine where respondents fit in relation to the consumer market model. On the basis of these responses, each respondent was assigned to one of the model's six segments. This design was made more efficient by use of a computer-assisted telephone interview (CATI) system, automating respondents' assignment to one of the six segment groupings. Next, the substantive questions section consisted of eight sets of questions[6] for collecting more detailed information on selection and evaluation of information resources.

Those respondents identifying themselves as library users accounted for 66 percent of the complete sample, with 34 percent identifying themselves as nonlibrary users. Forty percent of all respondents used both the public library and the Internet for information seeking activities. Thus it can be concluded that use of the public library and the Internet are complementary. However, findings also showed emerging differences in consumer preferences for Internet services and public library services such as ease of access. The researchers encouraged subsequent monitoring of these consumer preferences and concluded by promoting replication of the study for continued assessment of these trends.

Taken as a whole, the planning and design of this research study was extensive and allowed the research team to effectively meet the research objectives. D'Elia and colleagues (2002) acknowledge several limitations of their research design, including exclusion of the population segment without telephone service and exclusion of minors. These limitations, however, when placed in the context of the complete study design, do not take away from the overall research activity. Several aspects of the study design strengthened the outcomes. Design of the survey instrument benefited from the use of focus groups prior to design and the implementation of three pilot studies for testing the instrument. Outsourcing the survey administration activities allowed a more sophisticated approach, including use of the CATI system for filtering the respondents, than would have been possible in most academic settings. It should be kept in mind, however, that the procedures that strengthened the study required substantial resources. This particular study was made possible by an initial grant of $154,324 from the Institute of Museum and Library Services.

Example 3: Looking at Information Seeking Behavior at Hewlett Packard Labs

Hirsh and Dinkelacker (2004) used a survey to examine the ways that information was collected and disseminated at the Hewlett Packard (HP) labs. HP and Compaq had recently merged (in 2001), each with a history of research and a need for productive research to continue, creating a unique and dynamic environment in which to study potentially shifting research information needs.

The authors distributed their Web-based survey to roughly 180 lab researchers in different disciplines within the company. For this project, the authors decided to survey researchers in six labs, three former HP labs and three former Compaq labs, to balance the perspectives of the two companies. The surveys were distributed at the three main research centers: 77 percent in Palo Alto, California; 10 percent in Cambridge, Massachusetts; and 7 percent in Bristol, England. More people who had originally worked for HP were in the sample than those who had originally worked for Compaq as there had been more premerger HP lab workers overall.

"Company policy prohibits disclosing the specific number of employees in the Labs, or their distribution geographically" (Hirsh & Dinkelacker, 2004, p. 810). This is a small point in the article but illustrates a situation to be cognizant of when designing any type of research—confidentiality may be a very important issue in regard to questions, to participants, and/or to specific results. As you are in the planning stages, be aware of how it can affect your research and your ability to disseminate your findings.

The survey included both closed-ended and open-ended questions. It asked about the researchers' information seeking and their "production of information assets" (Hirsh & Dinkelacker, 2004, p. 810) as well as their understanding of the organizational factors that affected those activities and their suggestions for improvement. Among the closed-ended questions, the survey included some questions that asked for only a single response choice and others that allowed participants to select multiple response choices (e.g., more than one type of use for each information resource). It is easier to control the way people respond with a Web survey, in comparison with a printed survey; for example, you can use radio buttons to let them choose only one response or check boxes to allow more than one response. Be sure to think through this situation in advance so you will allow multiple choices only when it's appropriate. This is one more way in which the design of your survey will affect the analysis of your results.

While the exact questions were not provided as part of the article, the authors grouped the results to examine three primary research questions:

- What types of information resources were used by R&D researchers?
- What factors influenced their selection of information resources?
- What approaches were used in the production of new information assets? (Hirsh & Dinkelacker, 2004, p. 810)

After going through the quantitative results for these questions, the authors discussed the results from the open-ended questions. When you are designing your survey, you may need to use both types of questions, but consider in advance how this will affect your analysis of the results. If you need answers that are clear-cut, you may choose to avoid open-ended questions. If, however, your research purpose is more exploratory and you are seeking responses in uncharted territory, open-ended questions can help you bring out that information.

In summary, this study is a good example of the use of a Web survey to collect data from a geographically dispersed, but well-defined, target audience. A combination of closed-ended and open-ended questions was used to find out more about the information seeking and information capital production of corporate researchers, and the results were used to improve library services for this group.

CONCLUSION

Survey research is a very common method in information and library science, partly because it seems to be very straightforward—you ask people some questions, and you get answers. But it isn't really that simple. You need to design your survey instrument carefully, including both the individual items and how they are organized into the survey as a whole. You need to carefully select a sample (Chapters 13 and 14) and use a variety of methods to ensure that your sample responds to the survey. You need to administer the survey in a form that is accessible to and comfortable for your sample members. If you take these steps in planning and executing your survey, you will succeed in addressing your research questions.

NOTES

1. Sample survey research differs from a census in that a census is conducted with an entire population, while a sample survey is conducted with only a segment of the survey population (Fowler, 2002).

2. Some questionnaires may employ measurement scales, asking a series of questions to assess a singular variable or construct, such as attitude, through use of scaled and precoded responses.

For example, "Likert-type scales are designed to show a differentiation among respondents who have a variety of opinions about an attitude object" (Busha & Harter, 1980, p. 74). For a discussion of techniques for developing and using such measurement scales to assess complex constructs, see the next two chapters.

3. This article received the 1993 Ida and George Eliot Prize from the Medical Library Association.

4. This article was the winner of the 2001 Bohdan S. Wynar Research Paper Competition, sponsored by the Association for Library and Information Science Education, and the 2003 Jesse H. Shera Award for Excellence in Published Research, sponsored by the American Library Association.

5. The confidence level is our own calculation, based on the sample size and relative standard error.

6. The actual number of items in the survey was not stated in the article.

WORKS CITED

Babbie, E. (1990). *Survey Research Methods* (2nd ed.). Belmont, CA: Wadsworth.

Busha, C. H., & Harter, S. P. (1980). *Research Methods in Librarianship: Techniques and Interpretation.* Orlando, FL: Academic Press.

Czaja, R., & Blair, J. (2005). *Designing Surveys: A Guide to Decisions and Procedures.* Thousand Oaks, CA: Pine Forge Press.

Dane, F. C. (1990). *Research Methods.* Pacific Grove, CA: Brooks / Cole.

D'Elia, G., Jorgensen, C., & Woelfel, J. (2002). The impact of the Internet on public library use: An analysis of the current consumer market for library and Internet service. *Journal of the American Society for Information Science and Technology, 53*(10), 802–820.

Dillman, D. A. (2007). *Mail and Internet Surveys: The Tailored Design Method* (2nd ed.). Hoboken, NJ: John Wiley.

Fowler, F. J. (2002). *Survey Research Methods* (3rd ed.). Thousand Oaks, CA: Sage.

Hirsh, S., & Dinkelacker, J. (2004). Seeking information in order to produce information: An empirical study at Hewlett Packard Labs. *Journal of the American Society for Information Science and Technology, 55*(9), 807–817.

Marshall, J. G. (1992). The impact of the hospital library on clinical decision making: The Rochester study. *Bulletin of the Medical Library Association, 80*(2), 169–178.

Miller, A. (1964, January 20). On *After the Fall*, quoted in *National Observer.*

Peterson, R. A. (2000). *Constructing Effective Questionnaires.* Thousand Oaks, CA: Sage.

Sue, V. M., & Ritter, L. A. (2007). *Conducting Online Surveys.* Thousand Oaks, CA: Sage.

ADDITIONAL RECOMMENDED READING

Alreck, P. L., & Settle, R. B. (2004). *The Survey Research Handbook* (3rd ed.). New York: McGraw-Hill / Irwin.

Barnett, V. (1991). *Sample Survey Principles and Methods.* New York: Oxford University Press.

Braverman, M. T., & Slater, J. K. (Eds.). (1996). *Advances in Survey Research.* San Francisco: Jossey-Bass.

Fink, A., & Kosecoff, J. (1998). *How to Conduct Surveys: A Step-by-Step Guide* (2nd ed.). Thousand Oaks, CA: Sage.

Nardi, P. M. (2003). *Doing Survey Research: A Guide to Quantitative Methods.* Boston: Allyn and Bacon.

Patten, M. L. (2001). *Questionnaire Research: A Practical Guide* (2nd ed.). Los Angeles: Pyrcak.

Punch, K. F. (2003). *Survey Research: The Basics*. London: Sage.

Rea, L. M., & Parker, R. A. (1997). *Designing and Conducting Survey Research: A Comprehensive Guide* (2nd ed.). San Francisco: Jossey-Bass.

Sapsford, R. (1999). *Survey Research*. London: Sage.

27

Measuring Cognitive and Affective Variables

Barbara M. Wildemuth

Numbers are the product of counting. Quantities are the product of measurement. This means that numbers can conceivably be accurate because there is a discontinuity between each integer and the next. Between two and three there is a jump. In the case of quantity, there is no such jump; and because jump is missing in the world of quantity, it is impossible for any quantity to be exact. You can have exactly three tomatoes. You can never have exactly three gallons of water. Always quantity is approximate.

—Gregory Bateson (1979/2002)

INTRODUCTION AND DEFINITION

Many studies in information and library science (ILS) involve cognitive or affective variables that cannot be directly observed. For example, a study might investigate the relationship between a person's cognitive style (not directly observable) and his or her use of a library catalog, or a person's affective responses (i.e., feelings) at various stages of the process of seeking information. In such situations, psychological assessment approaches can be used to measure cognitive or affective variables such as a person's attitudes, interests, beliefs, or feelings (Joint Committee on Standards for Educational and Psychological Testing [JCSEPT], 1999).

Trying to measure these invisible aspects of a person's thinking or feelings is more complex than asking straightforward questions about a person's age or amount of library use because the attribute being measured is hypothetical (Rust & Golombok, 1999). The object of measurement is called a *construct*: "something that scientists put together from their own imaginations, something that does not exist as an isolated, observable dimension of behavior" (Nunnally, 1978, p. 96). The construct, or variable, must first be defined, and then, in a separate step, it must be operationalized; that is, observable indicators of its presence and level must be identified (Pedhazur & Schmelkin, 1991). For many cognitive and affective variables, this operationalization process entails the development of an inventory. Once such an inventory is developed and administered, numbers can be systematically assigned to the construct of interest to represent each person's level of that construct (McDonald, 1999; Reckase, 2000). While Yuan and Meadow (1999) have argued that "the information retrieval field has not matured enough to have established standards of measurement" (p. 140), the goal of this chapter is to encourage ILS professionals and researchers to incorporate reliable and valid measures in their studies of cognitive and affective variables.

The development of a new inventory is a process that involves significant effort, and the methods for such development are discussed in the next chapter. An alternative strategy is to identify an appropriate inventory used in past studies of the same variable. If appropriate, the existing inventory can be applied in the planned study; otherwise, it can be adapted as necessary. This approach is described subsequently, with particular emphasis on assuring that the selected inventory is reliable and valid.

IDENTIFYING AN APPROPRIATE INVENTORY

There are a couple of important advantages to identifying an appropriate existing inventory for your study, instead of trying to develop an inventory yourself. The primary advantage is that to develop a reliable and valid inventory takes significant time and effort. In most cases, it is not feasible to develop an inventory and apply it in a study within a reasonable amount of time. Second, using an existing inventory will allow you to evaluate its strengths and weaknesses based on its application in past studies. You can see whether it has been used with a sample that is similar to yours or for studying similar questions. The reports of past studies using the inventory will describe its use and any problems that were experienced. In particular, it is likely that past reports of the inventory's use will provide empirical data concerning its reliability and validity.

Given these advantages, your efforts will be focused on identifying the particular inventory that is most appropriate for your study. In preparation for your study, you have been reading other studies focused on similar research questions. Check these studies first to see how they measured each variable of interest. It's very likely that you will want to select an inventory that has been used in one of them. If you need to search further for an appropriate inventory, begin with databases of the literature in ILS, but also consider databases of the literature in psychology, education, and other disciplines related to your research question. In addition, there are a few sources that focus specifically on indexing measures of this type, including the *Mental Measurements Yearbook* (available in print and online) and the Educational Testing Service Test Collection's Test Link database (http://www.ets.org/testcoll). The available inventories will vary in their form, their length, their approach to operationalizing the construct in which you're interested, and, most important, their reliability and validity. You will want to identify several possibilities and then compare them in terms of their usefulness for your study.

ASSESSING THE RELIABILITY AND VALIDITY
OF AN INVENTORY

Assessing the reliability of each inventory is the starting point for considering its quality. In general, the reliability of an inventory is the consistency with which it measures the construct in which you're interested (Janda, 1998; JCSEPT, 1999). Prior studies evaluating an inventory's reliability will most likely report Cronbach's (1951) alpha, a statistic that is based on the intercorrelations among the items and can range from 0 to 1. As you consider adopting an inventory for your study, keep in mind that Cronbach's alpha should be at least 0.70 for it to be considered sufficiently reliable for use in research studies (Nunnally, 1978).

Once you have determined that the inventory you are considering is sufficiently reliable for your purposes, you are ready to consider its validity. As with your assessment of its reliability, you will want to gather and examine the evidence of its validity that is available from past studies using the inventory. Given the variety of types of validity that may have been investigated (see the next chapter for a more detailed discussion), you will want to pay attention to several types of indicators of validity. There may be reports of the face validity of the inventory. If so, consider the number and qualifications of the experts who were asked to evaluate items. There may be results from a factor analysis. If so, examine the factor loadings and make your own judgments of the convergent validity of the inventory. There may be reports of correlations between your inventory and other measures. If so, examine the theoretical basis for the researchers' assessment of whether these correlations support the validity of the measure or not. It's likely that much of this evidence will be somewhat complex and require some statistical expertise for its interpretation. You should consult with a statistician or psychometrician if you have difficulty with understanding this evidence; it's important to the strength of your study results to make sure that you are using a valid inventory.

EXAMPLES

The two example studies discussed here illustrate the appropriate use of an existing inventory in a study of information behaviors. The first example (Ford et al., 2005a) used a commercial instrument, the Cognitive Styles Analysis inventory, to investigate whether cognitive style has an effect on a person's Web search strategies. The second example (Ryker et al., 1997) used a research instrument, originally developed and later refined by a number of researchers, to measure user satisfaction with a particular information system.

Example 1: A Measure of Cognitive Style

Ford, Miller, and Moss recently completed a study (published as a series of articles) examining the relationships between various individual differences and the Web search strategies those individuals employed. The first article (Ford et al., 2003) focused on the participants' approaches to studying; the second (Ford et al., 2005a), to be the focus of our discussion here, examined the study participants' cognitive styles, demographic attributes, and perceptions of and preferred approaches to Web-based information seeking. The third article (Ford et al., 2005b) integrates and summarizes the analyses initially reported in the first two articles.

Here we will examine the way in which these researchers used the Cognitive Styles Analysis (CSA) inventory to measure cognitive style. The CSA was developed by Riding (Riding & Cheema, 1991) and consists of three subscales (i.e., three short inventories). The first two are intended to distinguish those with a holistic style from those with an analytic style. In the first subscale, respondents are asked to judge the similarity (the same or different) of two geometric figures. In the second subscale, respondents try to "determine whether a simple shape is contained within a more complex geometrical figure" (Ford et al., 2005a, p. 746). The third subscale is intended to distinguish verbalizers from imagers. Respondents are asked to decide whether particular statements are true or false; half of the statements represent conceptual relationships and half represent visual relationships. For each of the three subscales, the respondents' response times are used to generate a score. A fast response time on the first subscale indicates a holistic style; on the second, an analytic style; and on the third subscale, fast times on the conceptual statements indicate a verbalizer and fast times on the visual statements indicate an imager. The complete inventory is administered via a computer and is available for a fee from Learning and Training Technology (http://www.learningandtrainingtechnology .com).

Ford and his colleagues have used these measures in a number of studies conducted since the mid-1990s. In his first article citing the CSA, Ford (1995) discussed its advantages and disadvantages in relation to an alternative measure of field dependence/ independence (a construct that he and Riding both now argue is equivalent to holistic/analytic cognitive styles). In that article, he also empirically examined the CSA's relationship with a measure of Pask's holist/serialist styles. His arguments for selecting the CSA include its improved validity over standard measures of field dependence/ independence and the increased precision afforded by the fact that it is computer administered. While no reliability data are reported in the 1995 study or in the 2005 study being examined, Ford and his colleagues have taken great pains to examine the CSA's predictive and construct validity.

In summary, this example illustrates how a commercially available measure may be incorporated into a study of information behaviors. The validity of the CSA was the primary consideration in its selection, and further investigations of its validity were conducted by the authors across several studies over the past decade. The track record of the CSA in these and other ILS studies makes it an appropriate candidate for use in future studies.

Example 2: A Measure of User Satisfaction

In designing their study, Ryker et al. (1997) assumed that user expectations of an information system affect a user's satisfaction with that system. They focused their investigation on the influences on a user's expectations to see which of those influences had the most impact on user satisfaction. They considered external influences (TV commercials, technical journals, training at a college or technical school, friends outside of work, and vendor personnel), internal influences (coworkers and information systems staff), and past experience with hardware and software. The 252 participants from a variety of organizations ranked the top three items "that most influenced their expectations" (Ryker et al., 1997, pp. 533–534); the top-ranked item was used to divide the respondents into three groups (external, internal, and experience) for comparison.

User satisfaction was the dependent variable in this study and is the focus of our discussion here. It was measured using the 13-item (short) version of the user satisfaction measure developed by Ives et al. (1983), based on a longer inventory developed by Bailey and Pearson (1983). This measure consists of Likert scales[1] related to three underlying constructs: the information product, provider staff and services, and knowledge and involvement. In addition, a further check of the measure's validity was taken with a single-item overall assessment of the respondents' satisfaction with their information systems. The 13-item measure and the additional validity-check item are included in the appendix of the Ryker et al. (1997) paper.

Let's examine the evolution of this user satisfaction inventory, beginning at the beginning. This measurement instrument began as a 39-item measure (with each item composed of four semantic differential rating scales), developed by Bailey and Pearson (1983). Ives et al. (1983) further developed the scale and investigated its reliability and validity. They began by confirming the reliabilities of each of the original scales, using Cronbach's alpha to assess internal consistency. They found that all of the scales had good reliability, with Cronbach's alpha values ranging from 0.75 to 0.98.[2] They noted, however, that the format of the scales (all the items in each inventory listed together, and all laid out so that positive scores were on the same side) may have artificially inflated their reliability.

Ives et al. (1983) investigated the predictive validity of Bailey and Pearson's (1983) original measure in two ways. First, each of the 39 items was correlated against an independent measure of satisfaction; all the correlations were statistically significant ($p < 0.001$) and ranged from 0.22 to 0.54. Second, an overall score from the 39 items was correlated with the independent satisfaction measure ($r = 0.55$, $p < 0.001$). In addition, a factor analysis was conducted to investigate the measure's construct validity. It identified five factors composed of 22 of the 39 items.

Ives et al. (1983) also developed a short form of the measure—the form later used in the Ryker et al. (1997) study—by selecting "representative" items from the original measure. To verify the validity of the short form, they correlated its score with the remaining items ($r = 0.90$, $p < 0.001$). The short form was also correlated with the independent satisfaction measure ($r = 0.55$, $p = 0.001$). This extensive development process, conducted by two teams of researchers, forms a strong foundation for this inventory, allowing it to be used in future studies such as the one conducted by Ryker and colleagues.

The form of the inventory used by Ryker et al. (1997) was adapted from the short form published by Ives et al. (1983). A comparison of the two versions of a particular item will illustrate the transformation (see Figure 27.1). As noted previously, the original measure used four semantic differential items for each scale; in the adapted version, the scale was converted to a single Likert scale item. While this transformation has face validity, the reliability and validity of the new scale format should be reconfirmed within the context of the Ryker et al. study. A pilot study of the full battery of measures was conducted, with 10 participants with different organizational roles completing the measures and being interviewed about any aspects of the instrument that were unclear. Minor changes in the measurement instrument were made as a result of the pretest but are not described in the article. A "single-item 5-point overall measure of user satisfaction" (Ryker et al., 1997, p. 534) was also administered to the full study sample, but the correlation between this item and the full satisfaction measure is not reported. The value of Cronbach's alpha in the 1997 study was also not reported. In particular, the reporting of the correlation between the single-item satisfaction measure and the 13-item measure (or its subscales) and the reporting of Cronbach's alpha for each of the subscales would have helped readers to evaluate the quality of the measure actually used in the study.

As noted earlier, the satisfaction measure consisted of three subscales: information products, provider staff and services, and knowledge and involvement (three of the five factors originally identified by Ives et al., 1983). In analyzing the study data to test the study hypotheses, the results from each of the three subscales are reported separately. Such an analysis is very appropriate. An assumption underlying psychological

Scales as originally published in Bailey and Pearson (1983) and Ives et al. (1983):

Processing of requests for changes to existing systems

fast :___:___:___:___:___:___:___: slow

timely :___:___:___:___:___:___:___: untimely

simple :___:___:___:___:___:___:___: complex

flexible :___:___:___:___:___:___:___: rigid

Item as used by Ryker et al. (1997):

The people who provide me computer products and services process my requests

for changes to existing systems quickly.

Strongly Agree   Agree   Neutral   Disagree   Strongly Disagree

Figure 27.1. Sample scale/item.

assessment methods is that each measurement instrument is unidimensional (i.e., it is measuring only one construct); in this case, each of the three subscales is assumed to represent a single dimension of user satisfaction. If this assumption is accepted, then it is less appropriate to also analyze the data for the combination of the three subscales/ factors. Ryker et al. (1997) did conduct this additional analysis, but its validity must be questioned.

In spite of violating the assumption that a measure is unidimensional, and in spite of the unvalidated adaptation of the items, Ryker et al.'s (1997) use of this measure of satisfaction is a positive example and can appropriately be emulated by other researchers in ILS. Future researchers should follow their lead in applying a well-constructed and frequently used measure to the study of the relationship between influences on those users and their satisfaction with their information systems. Measures of many constructs of interest to ILS researchers have been developed within our field and in related disciplines. The use of these existing measures will, in the long run, contribute to the development of the field by clarifying the definitions of particular constructs and by allowing the comparison of results across studies.

CONCLUSION

For the research findings in ILS to form a strong foundation for improving practice, any measurements that are taken must be reliable and valid. This is particularly important when we want to measure constructs that are not directly observable such as a library user's satisfaction or a Web user's cognitive style. The most efficient way to ensure that our measures are reliable and valid is to use existing measures that have been implemented and evaluated in past studies. The two examples discussed here illustrate that this approach is feasible in ILS research and can lead to a stronger knowledge base in ILS.

NOTES

1. A Likert scale begins with a statement, and asks the respondent to report their level of agreement or disagreement with the statement. Most Likert scales, as is the case here, have five levels of responses, from strongly agree to strongly disagree.

2. Recall that Nunnally (1978) argued that inventories with Cronbach's alpha values greater than 0.70 are reliable enough for use in research studies.

WORKS CITED

Bailey, J. E., & Pearson, S. W. (1983). Development of a tool for measuring and analyzing computer user satisfaction. *Management Science, 29*(5), 530–545.

Bateson, G. (2002). Every schoolboy knows. In *Mind and Nature: A Necessary Unity*. Cresskill, NJ: Hampton Press. (Original work published 1979.)

Cronbach, L. J. (1951). Coefficient alpha and the internal structure of tests. *Psychometrika, 16*(3), 297–334.

Ford, N. (1995). Levels and types of mediation in instructional-systems—An individual-differences approach. *International Journal of Human-Computer Studies, 43*(2), 241–259.

Ford, N., Miller, D., & Moss, N. (2003). Web search strategies and approaches to studying. *Journal of the American Society for Information Science and Technology, 54*(6), 473–489.

Ford, N., Miller, D., & Moss, N. (2005a). Web search strategies and human individual differences: Cognitive and demographic factors, internet attitudes, and approaches. *Journal of the American Society for Information Science and Technology, 56*(7), 741–756.

Ford, N., Miller, D., & Moss, N. (2005b). Web search strategies and human individual differences: A combined analysis. *Journal of the American Society for Information Science and Technology, 56*(7), 757–764.

Ives, B., Olson, M. H., & Baroudi, J. J. (1983). The measurement of user information satisfaction. *Communications of the ACM, 26*(10), 785–793.

Janda, L. H. (1998). *Psychological Testing: Theory and Applications*. Boston: Allyn and Bacon.

Joint Committee on Standards for Educational and Psychological Testing. (1999). *Standards for educational and psychological testing*. Washington, DC: American Educational Research Association, American Psychological Association, and National Council on Measurement in Education.

McDonald, R. P. (1999). *Test Theory: A Unified Treatment*. Mahwah, NJ: Erlbaum.

The Mental Measurements Yearbook. Highland Park, NJ: Gryphon Press.

Nunnally, J. C. (1978). *Psychometric Theory*. New York: McGraw-Hill.

Pedhazur, E. J., & Schmelkin, L. P. (1991). *Measurement, Design, and Analysis: An Integrated Approach*. Hillsdale, NJ: Erlbaum.

Reckase, M. D. (2000). Scaling techniques. In G. Goldstein & M. Hersen (Eds.), *Handbook of Psychological Assessment* (3rd ed., pp. 43–61). Amsterdam: Pergamon.

Riding, R. N., & Cheema, I. (1991). Cognitive styles—An overview and integration. *Educational Psychology, 11*, 193–215.

Rust, J., & Golombok, S. (1999). *Modern Psychometrics: The Science of Psychological Assessment* (2nd ed.). London: Routledge.

Ryker, R., Nath, R., & Henson, J. (1997). Determinants of computer user expectations and their relationships with user satisfaction: An empirical study. *Information Processing and Management, 33*(4), 529–537.

Yuan, W., & Meadow, C. T. (1999). A study of the use of variables in information retrieval user studies. *Journal of the American Society for Information Science, 50*(2), 140–150.

28

Developing New Measures

Songphan Choemprayong and Barbara M. Wildemuth

Since we are assured that the all-wise Creator has observed the most exact proportions of number, weight and measure in the make of all things, the most likely way therefore to get any insight into the nature of those parts of the Creation which come within our observation must in all reason be to number, weigh and measure.

—Stephen Hales (1727)

INTRODUCTION

Cognitive and affective constructs, such as satisfaction or cognitive style, are particularly difficult to measure because they cannot be directly observed. The most effective way to incorporate these types of variables into a study is to use (possibly with minor adaptation) a measurement instrument that has been carefully developed and whose reliability and validity have been adequately evaluated. This approach was discussed in the previous chapter. But what if you cannot find an appropriate measure for a variable that you want to include in your study? Then you may need to start developing a new instrument that could provide a valid measure of the variable or construct in which you're interested.

There have been only a handful of measures developed in the field of information and library science (ILS). For example, recent efforts have resulted in measures of library anxiety (Bostick, 1992), information literacy self-efficacy (Kurbanoglu et al., 2006), and online privacy concern and protection on the Internet (Buchanan et al., 2007). We can also expand our perspective by looking at examples from related disciplines, particularly business (e.g., measures of perceived usefulness and perceived usability developed by Davis, 1989) and informatics in a variety of application areas. Nevertheless, you may be faced with a situation in which you will need to develop a measure; this chapter is intended to guide you through the basics of that process as well as to discuss issues related to the construction and validation of the measure.

APPROACHES TO MEASUREMENT

The main objective of measurement, especially measurement of cognitive and affective attributes, is to quantify the amount or level of a particular construct associated with each study participant. In psychological measurement, Nunnally (1978) defines a construct as "something that scientists put together from their own imaginations, something that does not exist as an isolated, observable dimension of behavior" (p. 96). A variety of cognitive and affective constructs are of interest in ILS. They include satisfaction with or attitudes toward information systems and services, the relevance of search results for a particular use, the degree of frustration experienced during an information interaction, an individual's interests and motivations for information seeking, information literacy/competency, and prior knowledge in a particular domain, among other constructs.

Such cognitive and affective variables cannot be directly observed. Thus they need to be measured by establishing definitions by which numbers can be assigned particular meanings. The first step in this process is to define the construct of interest. This definition can then be operationalized; in other words, a rule will be established for assigning particular numbers to particular levels of the presence of the construct. For example, for a measure of satisfaction with a library's services, 1 could be defined as "completely dissatisfied" and 5 could be defined as "completely satisfied." The most common method for specifying these rules or definitions is to develop a scale or inventory.

A scale, as defined by Boyce et al. (1994), is the logical structure of the assignment rule that represents the relationship between the numbers and the presence of the construct of interest. To turn the construct into meaningful numeric values, it may involve specific actions such as selecting a response, ranking a number of possibilities, or assigning a score. The most common forms of such scales include Likert scales and similar rating scales, and semantic differential scales.

Likert Scales and Similar Rating Scales

One of the most commonly used formats for measuring psychological constructs is a Likert scale. It is based on Likert's (1932; Albaum, 1997) work on measurement of levels of agreement. Each item begins with a statement; the respondent is asked to rate his or her agreement with the statement on a 5-point scale, ranging from "strongly agree" to "strongly disagree." While Likert's original work included only a 5-point scale, researchers have used differing numbers of response options on similar scales. For example, when the researcher does not want to allow a neutral response, the most common approach is to use a 4-point response scale. This format is very flexible and has been used widely in ILS and many other disciplines. A measurement instrument using this format would include several individual items/statements, each rated separately. The scores would then be aggregated (i.e., summed or averaged) to obtain each respondent's measure on the construct of interest. The Bostick (1992) Library Anxiety Scale, presented as an example later in this chapter, uses Likert scales.

Some researchers have developed rating scales that resemble Likert scales in their format but are not focused on agreement or disagreement with a statement. For example, one could ask a respondent to rate his or her levels of proficiency with particular computer tools using a 5-point rating scale. While the format would resemble a Likert scale, the "stem" of the item would not be a statement and the "anchors" for each of the ratings would more likely range from "not proficient" to "highly proficient," rather than from "strongly agree" to "strongly disagree." Such rating scales are usually described as being Likert-like scales, and the results generated from them can usually be analyzed in the same way that results from a Likert scale can be analyzed.

Another decision you will need to make about your rating scale is whether to anchor (i.e., label) each point on the scale or only the end points. For example, if you decided to label each point on a 5-point Likert scale, you might use anchors like "strongly disagree," "disagree," "neutral," "agree," and "strongly agree." At first glance, it might seem like labeling each point on the scale will help people interpret it. However, it does risk the possibility that people will interpret it as if it were an ordinal scale, rather than an interval scale.[1] An important disadvantage of labeling each point, then, is that your options for data analysis may be restricted to those that are appropriate for ordinal data.

For Likert scales and similar rating scales, one of the sources of bias that may appear in the responses is a phenomenon called *response style* (also called *response mode* or *response set*). For example, some respondents may move down the column of items, marking the same rating each time, or some respondents may be more prone to use the extreme points on the rating scale, while others use only the middle points. All types of response styles are problematic because they lead to results that are measuring an individual characteristic other than the construct of interest. A common technique for avoiding the lack of variability caused by respondents always marking the same rating is to "reverse" the wording of some of the items. For example, a Likert scale statement/stem could be worded, "I found this system difficult to use," rather than "I found this system easy to use." Placement of one or two of these reversed items near the beginning of the inventory will minimize the possibility of this type of response style. Similarly, one of the reasons to use a 4-point range for Likert scales (rather than the typical 5-point range) is to force people out of the middle. These and other techniques can be applied to semantic differential scales and other types of rating scales as well as Likert scales.

Semantic Differential Scales

A semantic differential scale is another approach to measuring the connotative meaning of particular things (i.e., objects, events, people, etc.) to the people responding to the scale. This response format consists of a word or phrase as stimulus and several pairs of adjectives that are opposites from each other (e.g., *good* versus *bad*). Each adjective pair is presented on a continuum, marked off in some number of degrees (usually 7 or 11). The respondents are expected to express their attitudes toward the stimulus by placing a mark at a point on each continuum.

This type of scale is based on Osgood et al.'s (1957) work. They proposed three dimensions of the judgments to be made: evaluation (good–bad), potency (strong–weak), and activity (active–passive). They suggested that this technique is suitable for use in measuring multidimensional constructs because different dimensions can be represented by the different adjective pairs.

Semantic differential scales have been adapted widely in the area of user acceptance of technology and usability of information systems. For instance, Spacey et al. (2004) used semantic differential scales to measure the attitudes of public library staff toward using the Internet at work. Their measure included the stimulus "Internet use at work" and five adjective pairs, as shown in Figure 28.1. In other situations, a different stimulus

Internet use at work

negative	_____ : _____ : _____ : _____ : _____	positive
unpleasant	_____ : _____ : _____ : _____ : _____	pleasant
unenjoyable	_____ : _____ : _____ : _____ : _____	enjoyable
unnecessary	_____ : _____ : _____ : _____ : _____	necessary
optional	_____ : _____ : _____ : _____ : _____	required

Figure 28.1. Example of semantic differential scales (Spacey et al., 2004).

and difference adjective pairs could be used, but the reliability and validity of any set of scales should be evaluated prior to using the scales in a study.

OTHER APPROACHES TO MEASURING COGNITIVE AND AFFECTIVE CONSTRUCTS

A variety of other approaches might be (and have been) used to measure cognitive and affective constructs that are important to ILS. For example, measures of self-efficacy might ask a person whether he or she believes that he or she can accomplish a particular task (yes or no) and also to rate his or her confidence in that ability (e.g., Downey & McMurtrey, 2007). People have been asked to rank Web sites in terms of their usefulness for a particular topic (Toms & Taves, 2004), and people have been asked to "grade" (as in an academic setting) the quality of Web sites based on specified criteria (Chao, 2002). Whichever approach or scale format you choose to use, you are encouraged to follow the process of scale development outlined subsequently and to thoroughly evaluate your measurement instrument's reliability and validity before using it in a study.

THE PROCESS OF DEVELOPING A MEASUREMENT INSTRUMENT

There are four basic steps in the development of measurement scales or inventories: (1) defining the construct, (2) developing the items, (3) creating an inventory from the set of items, and (4) pilot testing the inventory, including evaluating its reliability and validity. Depending on the outcomes of the pilot testing, the previous steps may be repeated. Each of these steps is briefly described in the following sections.

Defining the Construct

When you're trying to develop a measure of a particular construct (i.e., a cognitive or affective characteristic of interest), you should focus your attention on clearly defining what it is that you want to measure and the goals of that measurement (Sethi & King, 1991). A variety of types of constructs can be measured, including achievement, attitudes, and emotions (Dillman, 1978). Once you've decide what you want to measure, put it in writing. Develop a brief definition of your construct, including its scope (i.e., what it is and what it is not) and any subcomponents that are to be included (Joint Committee on

Standards for Educational and Psychological Testing [JCSEPT], 1999). It is likely that definitions of your construct already exist in prior research studies or more theoretical literature. Be sure to draw on these as much as possible as you develop your definition. (This investigative work may also lead you to a measurement instrument that already suits your purposes, saving you the work of developing a new one.)

Once you have written a clear definition of the construct, the next step is to operationalize it. You've already decided *what* you want to measure; this step focuses on *how* to measure it. For most of the constructs of interest in ILS, you'll need to consider different types of questions or rating scales to which your study participants can respond. In general, you should ask yourself what kinds of responses would be clear indicators of the respondent's level or amount of the construct of interest.

Developing the Item Pool

A typical measurement instrument uses multiple similar items, in combination, to obtain a reliable measure of the construct of interest (Reckase, 2000). Thus the development of an initial item pool involves identifying or generating a much larger number of items that can then be evaluated for their validity and usefulness. You will want to collect all the existing items that appear to fit your construct's definition to represent all dimensions of the construct. Typically, the individual items are derived from previous studies and existing related scales found in the literature, and you may also want to confer with experts in the field. If necessary, you may also develop items on your own. During the creation of additional items, you should consider items that have slightly different shades of meaning (Churchill, 1979), which may represent the missing dimensions of the construct. You should next review all the items in your initial item pool for "content quality, clarity and lack of ambiguity" (JCSEPT, 1999, p. 39).

Given the variety of sources from which your initial item pool was collected, you'll next want to consider the consistency of response format across the items. While it is possible, it is awkward to combine multiple types of scales within the same instrument. Therefore you will want to consider which format will work the best for your instrument. While Likert scales, or similar rating scales, or a semantic differential scale are most frequently used, you can consider other options.

Creating an Inventory from the Set of Items

Once you have assembled the entire pool of items, you will want to structure them as an inventory. The first consideration is their order. If you are measuring several related subcomponents of a construct, you will most likely want to intermingle the items from the different scales so that they seem less repetitious to your respondents.

Next, you need to decide how you will administer the inventory: on paper or on a computer. For some samples (e.g., those who are not comfortable with computers) or some study designs (e.g., a study where administration of the inventory on the computer would interrupt the flow of other interactions with the computer), you may want to administer the inventory on paper. Otherwise, computer administration has many advantages. In particular, if administered on a computer, the inventory responses can be automatically recorded as the respondent enters them. In addition, you have the capability of administering the inventory remotely. (See Chapter 26 for additional discussion of these considerations.)

The final decisions related to administration of the inventory are concerned with the instructions to the respondents. There should be instructions with each section of the inventory; they should be brief and clear.

Prior to pilot testing your draft inventory, you should do an informal pretesting of it. Identify a small number of people who are similar to the intended sample for the inventory but who will not be included in the actual sample involved in the pilot test or later use of the inventory. Ask each evaluator to individually complete the inventory, with you present. During this process, ask him or her to think aloud (see Chapter 19, on think-aloud protocols). This type of evaluation will help you to identify items that are not clear, items that are being interpreted in ways that are different from what you intended, and instructions that are vague or ambiguous. Use this feedback to improve the inventory before pilot testing it.

Pilot Testing the Inventory

The main purposes of a pilot test are to identify weaknesses in the inventory items and to improve the reliability and validity of the inventory. This is an iterative evaluation process. In other words, there will be several pilot tests conducted, and after each test, the results will be used to further improve the inventory. In most cases, these improvements will include dropping or modifying any items that are not contributing to the quality of the inventory. The iterative process can stop when the inventory is of sufficient quality for its intended purposes.

During the pilot testing, you need to administer the inventory in conditions that are as similar to the real data collection conditions as possible. You are simulating a real study in which the inventory would be used, so develop your research procedures using the same process as if you were designing a real study. In particular, your sampling plan and your data collection procedures should be similar to those that will be used in your future studies using this inventory. After the data are collected, the data analysis will be focused on analyzing the characteristics of each item and on evaluating the inventory's reliability and validity.

Item Analysis

Two characteristics of the individual items may be of particular interest and can be evaluated with the data gathered during a pilot test. First, you will want to understand the discriminability of each item. Can this particular item distinguish those with high amounts of the characteristic of interest (e.g., library anxiety) from those with low amounts of that characteristic? The inventory as a whole will be more efficient if it is made up of items that can make such discriminations accurately. To evaluate the discrim-inability of each item, you will examine the scores achieved on that item in relation to the scores achieved on the inventory as a whole. Those items with scores that most closely resemble the whole-inventory scores will be most valuable to retain in the final version of the inventory.

You might also be concerned with the difficulty of an item if the inventory is meant to measure achievement or performance. For example, you may be interested in studying the effectiveness of a bibliographic instruction module. To evaluate its effectiveness, you may be developing a test of the knowledge or skills covered by the module. In such a case, you will want to have an inventory that is sufficiently challenging so that not all the study participants can score at the very top. But, for efficiency's sake, you also want an inventory that allows those who learned the module's material to get a high performance score. Usually, item difficulty is calculated as the proportion of study participants who answer an item correctly. For a particular inventory, you will want to include items at different levels of difficulty.

Reliability

The reliability of a measurement is its consistency (Janda, 1998; JCSEPT, 1999). As Sethi and King (1991) note, scores on an inventory "must not vary unreasonably because of irrelevant factors (such as the way question are asked)" (p. 456). In the physical world, an unreliable measure is the equivalent of a rubber ruler; if you want to measure the height of a book, you want to use a ruler that will give you a reliable measurement each and every time and a measurement that is comparable from one book to another. Therefore the purpose of reliability analysis is to eliminate any items that are inconsistent, in relation to the other items of the inventory or in relation to administrations of the inventory at different points in time.

Most often, inventories are evaluated in terms of their internal consistency. In most cases, inventories measuring cognitive or affective constructs will be made up of three or more items/questions. The inventory's internal consistency, then, addresses the issue of whether all the items are measuring the same construct. Internal consistency is usually evaluated with Cronbach's (1951) alpha, a statistic calculated from the correlations among the inventory items. It can range from 0 to 1. The minimum acceptable level of reliability depends on the purpose of the research project for which the inventory is being used (Moore & Benbasat, 1991; Nunnally, 1978). Although Janda (1998) argued that Cronbach's alpha should be at least 0.80, Nunnally (1978) argued that, especially in the early stages of research, reliabilities of 0.70 would suffice, and that increasing reliability much beyond 0.80 is often wasteful of time and funds. It should be noted that inventories with fewer items are usually less reliable; statistical methods for estimating the reliability of a shorter version of an inventory are available. Alternative approaches to evaluating internal consistency include alternate-form reliability (correlating different forms of the inventory with each other) and split-half reliability (dividing the items into two groups and correlating one half with the other half).

A second type of reliability to consider is the inventory's stability over time, called test-retest reliability. The assumption is that if a measure of a stable construct is administered at two points in time, the two measurements should be the same. For instance, if I measure the height of a book today and one year from now, I would expect the ruler to show that the book is the same number of inches high each time. This type of reliability is not emphasized in ILS because many of the constructs in which we're interested are not expected to be stable over time; in such cases, it is not appropriate to evaluate test-retest reliability. If it is appropriate to evaluate test-retest reliability, the correlation between the two scores collected at different points in time is examined.

Validity

Validity is "the extent to which the test score measures the attribute it was designed to measure" (McDonald, 1999, p. 63). There are a number of approaches to evaluating the validity of an inventory, all of which relate to the extent to which the inventory measures the construct it is intended to measure. For example, if I were to measure your satisfaction with the library by asking you a number of questions about your home life, you would likely question the validity of my inventory.

In this way, we can consider the first approach to assessing the validity of an inventory: *content validity*. Using this approach, a judgment is made about the adequacy of the content of the individual items in representing the construct of interest. Typically, an assessment of content validity is implemented by having a knowledgeable person examine the items themselves (i.e., their face validity). As the Joint Committee on Standards for Educational and Psychological Testing (1999) notes, the assessment of content validity should be construed broadly, to consider "the themes, wording, and format of the items, tasks, or questions on a test, as well as the guidelines for procedures regarding administration and scoring" (p. 11).

A second type of validity is called *criterion-related validity*. It is appropriately evaluated when scores on a particular measure are expected to be strongly related to an established criterion, for example, scores on some other measure. One form of this type of validity is predictive validity, in which scores on one measure should be able to predict the scores on another measure. For example, you might expect that if you introduced a new information system to a group of users, their scores on an attitude inventory would be highly correlated with the amount of their later use of the system. A second type of criterion-related validity is concurrent validity, in which scores on one inventory are highly correlated with the scores of another inventory measuring the same or a similar construct. For example, if two library satisfaction inventories are measuring the same construct, their scores should be highly correlated.

A third, more theoretically oriented type of validity is *construct validity*, which refers to the degree to which the individual completing the inventory actually possesses the attribute or construct being measured by the inventory. Most often, this type of validity is evaluated through factor analysis. Factor analysis (Kim & Mueller, 1978) is a statistical technique that examines a set of items and evaluates the validity of treating the combined set of items as a single measure of the same construct (Pedhazur & Schmelkin, 1991). Exploratory factor analysis is used to identify the underlying dimensions of a data set, when an inventory is first under development; confirmatory analysis is used to test hypotheses regarding the number of dimensions and the relationships among them. These approaches are focused on the convergent validity of an inventory, that is, the use of multiple items to measure the same construct.

Evaluating discriminant validity, another form of construct validity, focuses on differentiating two distinct constructs. It and convergent validity can be simultaneously assessed through examination of the correlations in a multitrait-multimethod matrix (Campbell & Fiske, 1959; Churchill, 1979; Pedhazur & Schmelkin, 1991). The items in your inventory are expected to be highly correlated with each other (demonstrating convergent validity) and have only low correlations with other constructs measured at the same time (demonstrating discriminant validity).

Alternatively, construct validity can be assessed by placing the construct of interest within a known theoretical framework and determining whether the scores obtained from the inventory fit within that theoretical framework. In other words, an analysis is undertaken to investigate whether relationships between the construct and other constructs in the framework are related in the ways that the theory specifies.

CHALLENGES TO BE ANTICIPATED

The most significant challenge in developing a new measure is in the operationalization of the construct to be measured. If no existing inventories were found to be acceptable, it's likely that the construct is not well understood. Therefore it will be difficult to develop a clear and unambiguous definition of it, and even more difficult to operationalize that definition. Even so, it's important to take the first steps in this process, acknowledging the possibility that later work may supersede your efforts. Through this iterative process, carried on by multiple researchers, our understanding of the construct will gradually improve.

A related challenge is the role of wording in the development of the inventory items. Even small changes in wording can affect the reliability or validity of the inventory. For instance, when anchoring the points on a rating scale, the definitions given at each point (e.g., "very good," "quite good," "somewhat good") may not be clearly distinguishable to your respondents (Pedhazur & Schmelkin, 1991). Ambiguity, unfamiliar terms, and jargon may also cause confusion with the item stems or questions. For example, while it's important to include some negatively worded items to avoid a response style of rating every item the same, negatively worded items can be difficult to write so that they are clear.

Another challenge is related to the length of the inventory. In general, a longer instrument is a more reliable instrument. However, a longer instrument also imposes a greater burden on its respondents and, in the extreme, will result in a lower response rate. In such a case, you're working with a very reliable inventory, but you've jeopardized the value of your study results because of the negative effects on the representativeness of your sample of respondents. As you develop a new inventory, you will need to balance the need for increased reliability with the need for minimizing the burden on respondents.

Finally, you should keep in mind that undertaking the development of a new inventory is a significant commitment of resources such as time and funds. The process could take from months to years to complete. Therefore you should be certain that there is no existing inventory that will serve your purposes before you begin developing a new inventory.

EXAMPLES

While there are not as many examples of inventory development in the ILS literature as one might hope, several examples were identified. The two examples discussed here include the Library Anxiety Scale, developed during Bostick's (1992) dissertation work, and the Online Privacy Concern and Protection Scale, developed by Buchanan et al. (2007). The development process for each inventory will be summarized, as will the data on its reliability and validity.

Example 1: The Library Anxiety Scale

Library anxiety is an important construct in ILS because those experiencing this affective response to libraries are unlikely to use them and thus are unlikely to benefit from the services they offer. The Library Anxiety Scale (LAS) was developed by Bostick (1992, 1993; Onwuegbuzie et al., 2004) during her doctoral work at Wayne State University. The scale has been used in a number of studies (e.g., Jerabek et al., 2001; Onwuegbuzie & Jiao, 2004; Van Scoyoc, 2003) and was further developed by several researchers and practitioners (e.g., Van Kampen, 2004).

Bostick's (1992) work was motivated by Mellon's (1986) development of a grounded theory of the library anxiety experienced by college students. Mellon likened library anxiety to similar experiences (e.g., test anxiety and math anxiety), thus arguing that this construct should be theoretically situated within the broader context of studies of anxiety, generally. While Bostick's (1992) literature review discussed various types of anxiety further, she did not provide a succinct definition of the construct of library anxiety.

On the basis of Mellon's (1986) theoretical work, Bostick (1992) began developing items for the LAS. Because Mellon's work did not provide sufficient detail to support the development of an inventory, Bostick specified the key components of library anxiety through an extensive review of the related literature; discussions with an unspecified number of students, faculty, and librarians; and her own professional experience. An initial list of 268 statements was grouped into five sections: "staff, resources, technology, reference, and policies and procedures" (Bostick, 1993, p. 2). It was sent to 11 experts (reference librarians, library administrators, and library school faculty) to review. This was an initial check on the instrument's face validity, intended to improve the inventory prior to pilot testing. On the basis of the experts' feedback, a sixth section, "psychological factors," was added to the list; after all the changes were made, the list consisted of 294 statements. In the inventory, the respondent's level of agreement with each statement was to be rated using a 5-point Likert scale.

Once the inventory had been drafted, it was ready for pilot testing. Students ($n = 281$) from four colleges and universities in Michigan and Ohio responded to the 294 statements in the pilot instrument—an instrument that was 13 pages long and took 45 minutes to complete. An exploratory factor analysis was conducted to assess its construct validity. Unfortunately, the computer memory required to complete the analysis was not available in the early 1990s, even on the mainframe computers at Wayne State, the University of Michigan, or the University of Toledo. To complete the analysis, the items were divided up into their original six components, and each component was analyzed separately to determine whether it was unidimensional. Any items that had factor loadings greater than 0.30 were retained for the next version of the inventory. While this compromised approach to the assessment of the pilot instrument's validity was necessary, it was certainly not desirable and would not need to be employed with today's computing capacity. In addition, the sample size was not really sufficient to reach stable results. Nunnally (1978) recommends that you have "at least 10 times as many subjects as variables" (or items; p. 421), though some statisticians believe that you could complete a factor analysis if you had as few as four times as many respondents as there are items on the instrument. In the case of this first pilot study, the sample size would have needed to be at least 1,200 students to reach a stable solution.

An evaluation of the pilot instrument's reliability was also conducted using only the 88 items that were to be retained for the next iteration of development. Bostick (1992) reports that Cronbach's alpha was 0.80 for these 88 items. While this level of internal consistency is more than adequate, it is not really appropriate to expect that a multidimensional scale (i.e., one with the six dimensions, or components, hypothesized for the LAS) will be internally consistent. It would have been better to postpone an evaluation of the instrument's reliability until its factor structure had been confirmed.

Using the 88 items retained from the first study, a second pilot study was performed, with 415 students completing the instrument. This sample size was sufficient to achieve stable results from the two factor analyses that were conducted. The first analysis was forced to identify six factors (based on the original six components used to develop the items); in the second analysis, a four-factor solution was sought. The results from both analyses were used to reduce the number of items in the inventory to 43.

A third pilot test was conducted to further investigate the reliability and validity of the 43-item LAS. In addition to calculating Cronbach's alpha to assess internal consistency, Bostick (1992) evaluated the test-retest reliability of the inventory. Sixty-nine students in three classes in three institutions completed the inventory twice, three weeks apart. The reliability of each of five components was evaluated by examining the correlation coefficients between the two administrations of the LAS. The correlations ranged from 0.19 to 0.75; all were statistically significant. The test-retest reliability of the full scale was 0.70 and was judged to be sufficient.

The construct validity of the LAS was again investigated through factor analysis. As in the first pilot study, the sample size was insufficient to consider these results to be stable because only 69 students responded to the 43 items (a minimum sample size of 172 students might have been sufficient). Nevertheless, Bostick (1992) concludes that there are five factors (or dimensions) represented in this inventory: barriers with staff (e.g., "The reference librarians are unhelpful"), affective barriers (e.g., "I'm embarrassed that I don't know how to use the library"), comfort with the library (e.g., "I feel safe in the library"), knowledge of the library (e.g., "I want to learn to do my own research"), and mechanical barriers (e.g., "The copy machines are usually out of order"). This 43-item inventory and scoring instructions for it are available in the appendices of Onwuegbuzie et al. (2004).

Since its development, this instrument's quality has been further evaluated in a number of studies, illustrated with just a few examples here. Its concurrent validity was evaluated in terms of its relationship with computer anxiety (Jerabek et al., 2001). Its predictive validity was evaluated in terms of its ability to predict students' performance in writing a research proposal (Onwuegbuzie, 1997). Its construct validity was further investigated in terms of the way the construct fits in the *anxiety-expectation mediation model* of library anxiety (Onwuegbuzie & Jiao, 2004).

In summary, Bostick (1992) followed very appropriate procedures in the development of the LAS. She began with some theoretical grounding for defining the construct of interest, augmenting that work with a review of the literature and other sources of input. Before pilot testing the inventory, she asked experts to evaluate the items for their face validity. She then conducted a series of pilot tests, each time refining and shortening the inventory. There were two important ways in which her work might have been improved. First, her evaluations of the reliability of the inventory at each stage should have focused on the internal consistency of each of the five subscales, rather than the overall inventory. Second, her evaluations of the construct validity of the inventory, using factor analysis, should have used larger samples of respondents to obtain stable findings about the factor structure of the inventory. In spite of these weaknesses in the development process, this instrument's usefulness is demonstrated by its continuing use in studies of library anxiety.

Example 2: The Online Privacy Concern and Protection Scale

People's concern about their privacy while using the Internet is one of domains that have been investigated by many poll organizations and scholars over the past decade. However, none of the inventories used in these studies has been thoroughly examined in terms of its reliability and validity. Buchanan and colleagues (2007) recently took on this challenge by developing and evaluating an inventory measuring people's concerns and behaviors regarding privacy on the Internet.

The first step in this process was to define the construct(s) to be measured. The authors drew on previous definitions of related constructs: informational privacy, accessibility privacy, expressive privacy, and Westin's (1967) definition of privacy concerns: "the desire to keep personal information out of the hands of others" (Buchanan et al., 2007, p. 158). On the basis of these construct definitions and items from previously developed measures of them, an initial item pool of 82 items was developed. These items were intended to represent a variety of aspects of online privacy, including attitudes toward informational privacy, accessibility, physical privacy, expressive privacy, and the benefits of surrendering one's privacy as well as behaviors intended to safeguard one's privacy. Forty-eight of the items were concerned with online privacy attitudes, and the remaining 34 items were related to online privacy behaviors. Responses to the items were collected via 5-point rating scales. The attitudinal items were rated from "not at all" to "very much"; the behavioral items were rated from "never" to "always." The initial item pool was not evaluated by experts outside the research team; instead, an initial pilot test was conducted.

Students at Open University ($n = 515$) were recruited to participate in the pilot test by e-mail invitation. The inventory was administered via the Web. Note that Web-based administration has its own advantages and disadvantages. The target population of this instrument is Internet users in general, so Web-based administration would seem appropriate. Nevertheless, some of the intended audience may be concerned about the privacy issues associated with Web-based questionnaires (Gunn, 2002) and so may choose not to participate in the study. This could lead to instrument bias, in which those most concerned about the privacy issue would be missing from the study sample. The authors tried to address this problem by assuring respondents that "all the information they provided would be confidential" (Buchanan et al., 2007, p. 160), so it's likely that this type of bias, if it is present at all, is minimal.

A preliminary analysis of the results investigated the range of response to each item to ensure that the full 5-point rating scale was used for each item. If the full scale was not used for a particular item, it would be an indication that the item was not as useful as other items. In this case, only one item did not have scores ranging from 1 to 5 (and its scores ranged from 2 to 5), so no items were excluded from the inventory on this basis.

To test the validity of the inventory, principal component analyses (a type of factor analysis) were conducted separately for the behavioral and attitudinal items. It is noteworthy that this study did meet the minimum criterion for sample size; for the behavioral items, there were 15 times as many study participants as items, and for the attitudinal items, there were almost 11 times as many participants as items. This sample size will result in a stable result from the factor analysis.

Three factors were initially identified from the behavioral items. Selecting those items that had a factor loading of at least 0.3 and had at least twice as large a loading as on the other factors, six items remained in each of the first two factors, and four items remained in the third factor. Next, the reliability (i.e., internal consistency) of each factor was separately evaluated. Cronbach's alpha for each of the first two factors, general caution and technical protection, was acceptable (i.e., higher than 0.70), while Cronbach's alpha for the third factor was only 0.44, indicating that this factor was unreliable. On the basis of this result, and because this third factor explained little of the variation in the overall ratings, this factor was dropped.

The principal component analysis results for the attitudinal items indicated that they may represent as many as 11 different factors. When statistical techniques were used to identify a small number (two to five factors), the researchers had difficulty in interpreting them. This example clearly illustrates one of the challenges of using factor analysis methods: while the statistical techniques may find a parsimonious solution for reducing the dimensionality of an instrument, that solution may not make sense in terms of the construct definition being used. Buchanan et al.'s (2007) resolution of this problem was very appropriate. They elected to use only the first and primary factor identified. It accounted for 27 percent of the variance in the ratings, while the other factors accounted for very little additional variance. In addition, the 16 items included in the factor were very consistent with each other (Cronbach's alpha = 0.93). This subscale was labeled "Privacy Concern."

This initial pilot study provided some valuable results concerning the reliability and validity of the new inventory. In addition, the authors conducted two more pilot studies to further investigate the instrument's validity. The second study investigated whether the inventory could discriminate between technically oriented students and those without particular technical background. The researchers recruited participants by using the course bulletin boards of two technology-related classes and one social science class. Sixty-nine students completed the instrument online, and t tests were used to compare the ratings of the two sample groups. The results indicated that the technical group's ratings were significantly different from the nontechnical group's ratings on the General Caution scale and the Technical Protection scale. There was no difference in ratings on the Privacy Concern scale; the authors argued that this lack of difference was to be expected because past studies have found that people with technical expertise are only moderately concerned about their privacy because they have already implemented many privacy protection measures.

To test the convergent validity of the three subscales, intercorrelation analyses were conducted. The results from all the analyses indicated that the Privacy Concern scale (attitudes) was significantly correlated with the General Caution scale (behaviors) but not significantly correlated with the other behavioral scale, Technical Protection. Thus the second pilot study provided additional support for the instrument's validity.

The third pilot study assessed the instrument's criterion-related validity by correlating it with two preexisting similar measures: the Westin Privacy segmentation questionnaire (Kumaraguru & Cranor, 2005), with 3 items each rated on 4-point scale, and the Internet Users Information Privacy Concerns scale (IUIPC; Malhotra et al., 2004), with 10 items each rated on 7-point scale. All items from the three measures were pooled into one questionnaire, and 1,122 Open University students responded to it. Pearson's correlations among the measures were reported; they ranged from 0.051 to 0.305, and all but one were statistically significant. While the authors argued that these correlations support the validity of their instrument, they do not comment on the weakness of the correlations; it might have been expected that they would be in the 0.40 to 0.50 range, given the similarity in the underlying constructs.

This instrument was developed only recently, but the authors have already provided evidence of its reliability and validity. It is hoped that other researchers will investigate it further and also apply it in their studies of online privacy concerns.

CONCLUSION

It is important for the development of ILS as a field to base our studies on reliable and valid measures of constructs of interest. However, when you are beginning a study, an appropriate instrument may not be available. In such a case, it will be worth the time and effort required to develop a new instrument and to make it available to other researchers.

While such research efforts are oriented toward methodological issues, rather than other types of research questions, they are of great importance to research and evaluation in ILS.

NOTE

1. There are four levels of measurement: categorical, ordinal, interval, and ratio. Categorical data are grouped into categories, but the categories are not ordered. Ordinal data are in ordered categories, e.g., ratings of the frequency of your computer use as daily, weekly, or monthly. Interval data are ordered and at equal intervals. Because Likert scales are most often represented as the numerals 1 through 5, we can assume that people interpret them as being distributed at equal intervals (i.e., 1 is the same distance from 2 as 2 is from 3). Ratio data, in addition, have a zero point, so that we can argue that 4 is twice as much as 2. A person's age is a variable that could be considered to be measured on a ratio scale.

WORKS CITED

Albaum, G. (1997). The Likert scale revisited: An alternate version. *Journal of the Market Research Society, 39*(2), 331–348.

Bostick, S. L. (1992). *The development and validation of the Library Anxiety Scale.* Unpublished doctoral dissertation, Wayne State University.

Bostick, S. L. (1993). The development and validation of the library anxiety scale. In M. E. Murfin & J. E. Whitlatch (Eds.), *Research in Reference Effectiveness* (pp. 1–7). Chicago: Reference and Adult Service Division, American Library Association.

Boyce, B., Meadow, C. T., & Kraft, D. H. (1994). *Measurement in Information Science.* San Diego, CA: Academic Press.

Buchanan, T., Paine, C., Joinson, A. N., & Reips, U. (2007). Development of measures of online privacy concern and protection for use on the Internet. *Journal of the American Society for Information Science and Technology, 58*(2), 157–165.

Campbell, D. T., & Fiske, D. W. (1959). Convergent and discriminant validation by the multitrait–multimethod matrix. *Psychological Bulletin, 56,* 81–105.

Chao, H. (2002). Assessing the quality of academic libraries on the Web: The development and testing of criteria. *Library and Information Science Research, 24*(2), 169–194.

Churchill, G. A., Jr. (1979). A paradigm for developing better measures of marketing constructs. *Journal of Marketing Research, 16*(1), 64–73.

Cronbach, L. J. (1951). Coefficient alpha and the internal structure of tests. *Psychometrika, 16*(3), 297–334.

Davis, F. D. (1989). Perceived usefulness, perceived ease of use, and user acceptance of information technology. *MIS Quarterly, 13*(3), 319–340.

Dillman, D. A. (1978). *Mail and Telephone Surveys: The Total Design Method.* New York: John Wiley.

Downey, J. P., & McMurtrey, M. (2007). Introducing task-based general computer self-efficacy: An empirical comparison of three general self-efficacy instruments. *Interacting with Computers, 19*(3), 382–396.

Gunn, H. (2002). Web-based surveys: Changing the survey process. *First Monday, 7*(12). Retrieved July 11, 2007, from http://firstmonday.org/issues/issue7_12/gunn/index.html.

Hales, S. (1727). Introduction. In *Vegetable Staticks, or, An account of some statical experiments on the sap in vegetables: being an essay towards a natural history of vegetation: also, a specimen of an attempt to analyse the air by a great variety of chymio-statical experiments which were read at several meetings before the Royal Society.* London: Printed for W. and J. Innys . . . and T. Woodward.

Janda, L. H. (1998). *Psychological Testing: Theory and Applications.* Boston: Allyn and Bacon.

Jerabek, J. A., Meyer, L. S., & Kordinak, S. T. (2001). "Library anxiety" and "computer anxiety": Measures, validity, and research implications. *Library and Information Science Research, 23,* 277–289.

Joint Committee on Standards for Educational and Psychological Testing. (1999). *Standards for educational and psychological testing.* Washington, DC: American Educational Research Association, American Psychological Association, and National Council on Measurement in Education.

Kim, J., & Mueller, C. W. (1978). *Introduction to Factor Analysis: What It Is and How to Do It.* Beverly Hills, CA: Sage.

Kumaraguru, P., & Cranor, L. F. (2005). *Privacy Indexes: A Survey of Westin's Studies* (CMU-ISRI-5-138). Pittsburgh, Pa: Institute for Software Research International, School of Computer Science, Carnegie Mellon University. Retrieved July 11, 2007, from http://reports-archive .adm.cs.cmu.edu/anon/isri2005/CMU-ISRI-05-138.pdf.

Kurbanoglu, S. S., Akkoyunlu, B., & Umay, A. (2006). Developing the information literacy self-efficacy scale. *Journal of Documentation, 62*(6), 730–743.

Likert, R. (1932). A technique for the measurement of attitudes. *Archives of Psychology, 140,* 44–53.

Malhotra, N. K., Kim, S. S., & Agarwal, J. (2004). Internet users' information privacy concerns (IUIPC): The construct, the scale and a causal model. *Information Systems Research, 15,* 336–355.

McDonald, R. P. (1999). *Test Theory: A Unified Treatment.* Mahwah, NJ: Erlbaum.

Mellon, C. A. (1986, March). Library anxiety: A grounded theory and its development. *College and Research Libraries, 47,* 160–165.

Moore, G. C., & Benbasat, I. (1991). Development of an instrument to measure the perceptions of adopting an information technology innovation. *Information Systems Research, 2*(3), 192–222.

Nunnally, J. C. (1978). *Psychometric Theory* (2nd ed.). New York: McGraw-Hill.

Onwuegbuzie, A. J. (1997). Writing a research proposal: The role of library anxiety, statistics anxiety, and composition anxiety. *Library and Information Science Research, 19,* 5–33.

Onwuegbuzie, A. J., &. Jiao, Q. G. (2004). Information search performance and research achievement: An empirical test of the anxiety expectation mediation model of library anxiety. *Journal of the American Society for Information Science and Technology, 55*(1), 41–54.

Onwuegbuzie, A. J., Jiao, Q. G., & Bostick, S. L. (2004). *Library Anxiety: Theory, Research, and Applications.* Lanham, MD: Scarecrow Press.

Osgood, C. E., Suci, G. J., & Tannenbaum, P. H. (1957). *The Measurement of Meaning.* Urbana: University of Illinois Press.

Pedhazur, E. J., & Schmelkin, L. P. (1991). *Measurement, Design, and Analysis: An Integrated Approach.* Hillsdale, NJ: Erlbaum.

Reckase, M. D. (2000). Scaling techniques. In G. Goldstein & M. Hersen (Eds.), *Handbook of Psychological Assessment* (3rd ed., pp. 43–61). Amsterdam: Pergamon.

Sethi, V., & King, W. R. (1991). Construct measurement in information systems research: An illustration in strategic systems. *Decision Sciences, 22*(3), 455–472.

Spacey, R., Goulding, A., & Murray, I. (2004). Exploring the attitudes of public library staff to the Internet using the TAM. *Journal of Documentation, 60*(5), 550–564.

Toms, E. G., & Taves, A. R. (2004). Measuring user perceptions of Web site reputation. *Information Processing and Management, 40,* 291–317.

Van Kampen, D. J. (2004). Development and validation of the multidimensional library anxiety scale. *College and Research Libraries, 65*(1), 28–34.

Van Scoyoc, A. M. (2003). Reducing library anxiety in first-year students: The impact of computer-assisted instruction and bibliographic instruction. *Reference and User Services Quarterly, 42*(4), 329–41.

Westin, A. (1967). *Privacy and Freedom.* New York: Atheneum.

PART V

METHODS FOR
DATA ANALYSIS

29

Content Analysis

Kristina M. Spurgin and Barbara M. Wildemuth

A word is not a crystal, transparent and unchanged, it is the skin of a living thought and may vary greatly in color and content according to the circumstances and the time in which it is used.

—Oliver Wendell Holmes (*Towne v. Eisner*, 1918)

WHAT IS CONTENT ANALYSIS?

Content analysis is a research method with a long history of use in journalism/mass communication. It is also used in information and library science (ILS). The primary foci of our field are recorded information and people's relationships with it. We must understand the features and laws of the recorded-information universe to facilitate access to the right information at the right time (Bates, 1999). Since content analysis focuses on the features of recorded information, it has been adopted as a useful ILS research technique (White & Marsh, 2006).

Content analysis is "the systematic, objective, quantitative analysis of message characteristics" (Neuendorf, 2002, p. 1). The meaning of the term *message* in content analysis is broad. The word is used in a similar way in Shannon and Weaver's (1963) theory of information. This theory conceptualizes information as a message that travels from source to destination. Any information captured and recorded in a fixed manner on paper, digitally, or in an analog audio or video format can be considered a message; thus it can be examined using content analysis. Content analysis was originally developed to analyze texts such as journal articles, newspapers, books, responses to questionnaires, and transcribed interviews. In journalism/mass communication, the procedures of content analysis have also been used to analyze graphical, aural, and video messages such as advertisements, television, and film. While the Web's multimedia form presents special challenges, its content can also be analyzed.

Regardless of the content, its analysis should be systematic and follow the scientific method. A hypothesis or question—based on theory, previous research, or observation—is formed about a body of messages. Then the content analysis is carried out, usually on a sample of messages selected from a larger population. The analysis procedures should be unbiased, valid, reliable, and replicable. On the basis of the results of the content analysis, the original hypothesis is tested or the research question addressed. The study's conclusions are assumed to be generalizable to a larger population of content.

The quantitative form of content analysis discussed in this chapter (hereafter referred to just as content analysis) differs in many ways from thematic, qualitative content analysis (discussed in the next chapter). Content analysis is interested only in content characteristics related to the hypothesis or research question. A set of codes to capture those characteristics is developed and finalized before analysis begins. The qualitative approach allows themes to emerge from the data throughout the process of analysis: the coding framework is continually shaped by emerging information. Content analysis is a deductive approach, while qualitative/thematic analysis is an inductive approach. Content analysis can deal with large, randomly selected samples. The results are numerical, statistically manipulable, and often generalizable. In contrast, qualitative/thematic content analysis requires relatively small, purposively selected samples. Its results are textual descriptions, typologies, and descriptive models.

USES OF CONTENT ANALYSIS

Content analysis can describe a message pool. An example of this use of the method is Järvelin and Vakkari's (1993) longitudinal examination of the topical distribution of and methods used in international ILS research. Content analysis can also identify relationships between message characteristics. In a longitudinal analysis of job advertisements appearing in *American Libraries*, Zhou (1996) examined the relationships among library size, type of position, and degree of demand for computer-related skills. Descriptive and relational research questions are the types of questions most often investigated with content analysis in ILS. Allen and Reser (1990) conducted a content analysis of ILS content analyses and described the use of the method in our field in more detail.

Applied in combination with other methods, content analysis can be used to infer or predict outcomes or effects of messages. To do so, characteristics of message content are linked to measures of human response or other measures taken from outside the message content. This application of content analysis is rare in ILS; one example is Bucy et al.'s (1999) exploratory examination of the relationship between the complexity of a Web site and the amount of Web traffic it attracts. Among the study's findings was a relationship between the amount of asynchronous interactive elements on a Web page and the number of page views it received. This study is examined in more depth later in this chapter.

MANIFEST AND LATENT CONTENT

Messages can be analyzed for different types of content: manifest and latent. Manifest content exists unambiguously in the message. It is easily observable and countable. For example, the occurrence of a given word in a text is manifest content. Whether a photograph on a Web site is color or black and white is manifest content. Carlyle and Timmons's (2002) examination of what machine readable cataloging (MARC) fields appear in the default record view of online library catalogs considered only manifest content: either a field appeared, or it did not.

Latent content is conceptual and cannot be directly observed in the messages under analysis. It is difficult—if not impossible—to count. An example of latent content is the level of research anxiety present in user narratives about their experiences at the library.[1] Perhaps it seems that you could easily tell whether a narrative expresses research anxiety. Is your interpretation of the text the same as someone else's? How do you quantify the expression of anxiety? Should you distinguish high levels of research anxiety from low levels? How? As you can see, it is problematic to examine latent content directly using content analysis.

In Berelson's (1954) strict definition, content analysis can be concerned only with manifest content. But most content analysis methodologists agree that content analysis may be used to examine latent content characteristics that can be measured using manifest indicators (Neuendorf, 2002; Shapiro & Markoff, 1997). Manifest indicators are manifest content characteristics that are assumed to indicate the presence of latent content. The latent content of interest informs which manifest content is coded and analyzed. Results of the manifest content analysis are interpreted to make claims about the latent content. To continue our example, psychological research has identified words people use when feeling anxious or recounting experiences of anxiety. You might count the manifest presence of these words in your library experience narratives to learn something about library users' research anxiety.

The challenge of this approach is that the validity of your results might be questionable. Are you certain the manifest indicators you are measuring are related to the latent content in the way you think they are? Should you include additional indicators? How strong is the psychological research from which you drew your anxiety-signifying words? Are the findings of that research applicable to the context of your analysis? Attention to these issues is important in the design of a content analysis study using manifest indicators to examine latent content.

IDENTIFYING THE UNITS FOR ANALYSIS

There are two basic types of units of content to define after you have chosen a research question: sampling units and recording units (Riffe et al., 2005). The first relates to what you will sample from the overall population of the text or other media of interest. To compare librarians' and computer scientists' mental models of the World Wide Web, you might analyze articles from each profession's popular literature. Each article would be a unit within your sampling frame.

Recording units are the elements of content that are coded. There are several types of recording units: physical (e.g., code each paragraph), conceptual (e.g., code each assertion), or temporal (e.g., code each minute of video). In our example, the recording unit might be any sentence that refers to or describes the Web. In this case, the coder would classify the content of the sentence. An alternative recording unit might be the article (the sampling and recording units can be the same). Here the coder would classify the article.

Some recording units are straightforward. Others are not. A third possible recording unit for our example study could be each description of the Web—a conceptual unit. Each description must be identified so that it can be coded. It is important to demonstrate that your recording unit can be identified reliably. You might have two or more coders independently mark all the descriptions in a subset of the papers. Ideally, the marked passages would be identical across all coders. Usually they are not. If there is little agreement, you will need to clarify the definition of your recording unit. A strong content analysis study will report on the intercoder agreement on recording unit identification, when appropriate.

SAMPLING

The population of some message types is small enough that a census content analysis is possible. In a census study, all members of the population are included, so sampling is not necessary. In the majority of cases, however, a sample of the population must be drawn. Content analysis calls for you to obtain a representative sample so that the results of your work will be generalizable to the population. Typically, you can use the same types of sampling methods you would use to draw a sample of study participants from a population of interest (see Chapter 13, on sampling for extensive studies).

There are some special considerations when sampling messages for content analysis. In particular, be aware of patterns that occur in publications and changes in those patterns. For example, choosing equal numbers of articles per year from a journal that increased its publication frequency will result in a sample that overrepresents the earlier years of publication.

In their content analysis of ILS content analyses, Allen and Reser's (1990) sample consisted of all results for a search on "content analysis" in three ILS-focused bibliographic databases. This is a common approach to building a sampling frame, but it can be problematic. No bibliographic database covers the whole of any particular literature. The bias of any database is transferred to your sampling frame. Meho and Spurgin (2005) detailed issues of bibliographic database bias in ILS. Deacon (2007) examined issues of validity and reliability in using keyword searching and database content to construct a sampling frame. Consult these sources if you are planning to use database searches to develop your sampling frame.

Sampling Web content can be highly problematic. On the Web, it is often impossible to identify all members of the population. The populations of particular types of Web documents or Web pages on a specific topic are unknowable. There is no registry, for example, of all blogs written by librarians. In such cases, you cannot be assured of a truly representative sample, so compromises will need to be made. McMillan (2000) and Weare and Lin (2000) offer some suggestions for sampling from particular segments or populations of documents on the Web as well as discussions of some practical logistical issues to consider when analyzing Web content.

CODING SCHEME DEVELOPMENT

Coding is the process of reducing the entire content of the messages in your sample into quantitatively analyzable data describing only the variables in which you are interested. The coding scheme is the instruction book and data collection instrument for use in conducting a content analysis. The first step in developing a coding scheme is to identify the critical variables you wish to examine, a step that you began as you defined the units for analysis. Ideally, your choice of variables is grounded in prior research and theory. If coding schemes related to your research questions already exist, strongly consider using them in the interest of comparability of results.

Sometimes there is no existing theory or research on your message population; you may not know what the important variables are. The only way to discover them is to explore the content. This emergent process of variable identification is described by Neuendorf (2002). This process is similar to the induction used to identify themes in qualitative content analysis, but the variables are identified and indicators defined using only a subset of the sample. The coding scheme is then determined and the entire sample is coded and analyzed. Overall, the study remains deductive and quantitative.

After you identify the variables in your study, you must choose or define indicators for those variables. Indicators are what you will code for and count. They are often the manifest content indicating the presence of latent variables. Indicators are measures and as such require attention to reliability, validity, accuracy, and precision. Indicators in content analysis commonly take two forms: definitions of content characteristics or features that will be counted (e.g., word frequency, number of hyperlinks on a Web page) and sets of categories or levels used to record codes representing the content of a message. A coding scheme must be clear; multiple coders should be able to apply it consistently. Revision and editing of the scheme during coder training is typically expected and necessary for the improvement of the scheme. Coder training is the process of explaining the coding scheme to coders and attempting to move all coders to the same mental frame of reference regarding the scheme and its application. The scheme must be finalized before the coding of your sample begins.

There are two other points to keep in mind about developing coding schemes. First, the categories must be exhaustive. If necessary, this requirement can be satisfied by adding a category such as "other," "not present," or "cannot determine." The categories must also be mutually exclusive. No recording unit should belong in more than one category of a particular variable.

MULTIPLE CODERS AND INTERCODER AGREEMENT

Any time humans observe phenomena or interpret meaning, there is bias. Content analysis strives for objectivity and replicability. Thus employing more than one coder is essential to demonstrate that your results are not skewed by a single coder's subjective judgments and bias. Given the same content, coding scheme, and training, any coder's work should result in the same data. High measures of intercoder agreement indicate the reliability of the results of the coding process (Lombard et al., 2002).

In ILS research, coding by more than one person is rare and reporting of intercoder agreement measures is poor. It is hoped that recent studies have improved in this regard, but Allen and Reser (1990) found that only 7 percent ($n = 2$) of ILS content analyses conducted between 1984 and 1989 involved coding by a person other than the researcher. Neither of those studies reported intercoder agreement. Ironically, the Allen and Reser article itself is coauthored but does not state that both authors coded the articles under analysis; rather, it implies that one author developed the category scheme, while the other coded the material using that scheme. The article does not report intercoder agreement, though it contains a recommendation to do so. In their review of content analysis and its use in ILS research, White and Marsh (2006) relegate discussion of this topic to a footnote. Our discipline's lack of methodological rigor in this area is truly unfortunate, for "failure to report reliability virtually invalidates whatever usefulness a content study may have" (Riffe et al., 2005, p. 155).

Perhaps few ILS content analyses report intercoder agreement measures because a great deal of confusion surrounds the issue. Several measures of intercoder agreement exist, but methodologists disagree about which measure is the best to use.[2] The discussion of this topic in the literature is too voluminous and mathematically dense to cover in any detail here. However, a core list of guidelines has emerged. First, select an appropriate measure of agreement. Do not use percentage agreement because it does not account for chance agreement between coders. In studies with two coders, a large sample, and only nominal data, Scott's pi is acceptable. In all other cases, methodologists recommend Krippendorff's alpha. Second, you must choose a minimum acceptable level of reliability for the measure you have chosen. The appropriate level depends on the context of your research. If you must be able to rely on your data (i.e., if the results directly affect people), set the level high. Exploratory research allows for a lower level of agreement. Understand the meaning of the number that will result from your intercoder agreement calculation and set the required level accordingly. Third, assess reliability informally during coder training, formally in a pilot test, and formally as a part of the actual coding task. The procedures for selecting subsamples for reliability assessment, deciding the appropriate number of messages to be coded by multiple coders, and conducting these reliability tests are clearly outlined by Riffe et al. (2005). Finally, you should clearly report your method for measuring agreement and the results from that measure when you write up your research. You should be able to justify your choices and decisions. Lombard et al. (2002, 2005) and Krippendorff (2004b) discuss these recommendations in a detailed yet readable manner and include references to further discussions of the topic. Remember that despite what you see in most ILS content analyses, these steps are not optional. In a good content analysis, you must have at least two coders analyze at least a portion of the data, and you must measure and report intercoder agreement.

ANALYSIS OF CODED DATA

Once the messages have been coded, you will have a set of numerical data to analyze. One of the most common practices in content analysis is to report frequencies for each category. While this is informative and descriptive, it is not all that you can do. A wide range of statistical tests can be performed on the data resulting from coding. Of course, the analysis method chosen should match the questions in which you are interested. Likewise, your data must meet the assumptions of the statistical methods you use. Remember that there is no need to use inferential statistics in a census study because you cannot infer beyond the bounds of your data—the entire population of messages of interest. Later chapters in Part 5 address useful data analysis techniques. Neuendorf (2002, pp. 170–171) provides a useful table for the selection of appropriate statistical tests for use in content analysis.

COMPUTER-SUPPORTED CONTENT ANALYSIS

Advances in lexical processing promise that computers will be increasingly useful for supporting content analysis (Shapiro, 1997). Computers can quickly and inexpensively code manifest content in enormous message samples. That said, computer coding may not be appropriate for every content analysis; some types of analysis may be better suited to computer-supported analysis than others. Results of human- and computer-coded analyses of the same data set have had significantly different findings.

Since the computer objectively interprets the coding rules it is given, there is no question of intercoder reliability. There are questions about the internal consistency of the rule sets and the possibility that other researchers could reliably devise rules that would get the same results with the same data. Currently there is scant research on assessing the quality and development of coding rules (Conway, 2006). Part of the challenge of conducting a computer-supported content analysis is technical. You should choose the right software tool for the job. You should also have a good understanding of how the software works so that you can recognize any problems or anomalies in your results. Reviews of available text analysis tools are regularly published in *Social Science Computer Review*. These quickly go out of date, so check your library for the most recent issues.

SUMMARY

Our discussion so far has presented an overview of content analysis, the types of questions it can answer, and the procedures for conducting a study. You may have decided that content analysis is appropriate for your research project, and you are ready to begin designing your study. If so, pause and get ready to do a bit more reading. In the interest of clarity, this chapter has presented a rather simplified, general form of content analysis. Various methodologists have set forth different and conflicting guidelines for the proper procedures and applications of the method. Shapiro and Markoff (1997) compare definitions of content analysis in well-known methodological works on the topic. They discuss differences in opinion about such basic issues as what types of content can be analyzed and what the products of a content analysis can be. Riffe et al. (2005), Krippendorff (2004a), and Neuendorf (2002) are relatively recent and easy-to-read hands-on guidebooks on how to apply the method.

EXAMPLES

Two examples of content analysis are discussed here. The first is a straightforward example of coding manifest content from brief texts written by study participants. In it, Kracker and Pollio (2003) analyzed college students' descriptions of their library experiences. The second (Bucy et al., 1999) illustrates a more complex analysis of the content and features of Web pages.

Example 1: Users' Experiences with Libraries

Kracker and Pollio (2003) provide an example of the use of content analysis in a mixed-method study aimed at understanding how people experience libraries. The other method used in the study is a phenomenological thematic analysis (a method discussed in the next chapter), so the article provides a good contrasting example of the two approaches.

One hundred eighteen freshmen psychology students at a major university were recruited for the study. Each student listed three specific memorable library experiences. The experiences could have occurred at any library at any time in their life. A longer narrative about one of the incidents was requested from each student. The thematic analysis of these narratives is not discussed here.

Content analysis was used to reduce the short library experience descriptions to data on two variables: students' school level at the time of the incident and the type of library in which the incident occurred. Students were asked to "name and locate" the library in their responses, but the variable of interest was library type. Coders inferred the type of library from the information given—it was not manifest content. Over 10 percent of the 354 incidents analyzed ($n = 48$) were coded "unclear as to type." This may be an area where the study design could have been improved by providing more structure in the data collection instrument.

Two researchers coded the data. The first coded all the data. The second performed coding on the 48 unclear cases and a randomly selected 10.1 percent of the clear cases. Holsti's (1969) method for calculating intercoder agreement was used to evaluate the reliability of the coding of the unclear cases (70.8%) and the clear cases (94.4%). It is commendable that more than one researcher participated in coding and that agreement was calculated. Holsti's method, like simple percentage agreement, does not take into account chance agreement and is therefore not as informative as other intercoder agreement statistics. Given the large sample size of 354 incidents, two coders, and data at the nominal level, Scott's pi would have been a better choice.

The frequency and percentage of the incidents at each school level and in each library type are presented clearly in tables. The content analysis data were used to find differences (by grade level and by library type) between themes identified in the other portion of the study. Even this simple example of content analysis moved past pure description, helping us to understand what factors may affect users' experiences with libraries.

Example 2: Web Page Complexity and Site Traffic

As mentioned previously, Bucy et al. (1999) went beyond content analysis by analyzing data on human behavior—measures of site traffic—in relation to content characteristics of Web pages. Though the study does not attempt to predict site traffic from Web page characteristics, the underlying assumption is that the presence of certain Web page characteristics influences human behavior.

Bucy et al. (1999) give a thorough explanation of the sampling methods they used. As discussed, sampling is a particularly thorny issue on the Web. The researchers used a proprietary service to get a list of the top 5,000 sites by amount of Web traffic. Five hundred sites were selected from this list for coding. The selection process was a systematic random sample of every tenth URL on the list of 5,000 URLs. This method is appropriate if one assumes that there is no pattern in the list that would result in a biased sample. The study did not address any potential bias introduced by including only sites monitored by the proprietary service. Given the goals of the proprietary service, it is unlikely that any meaningful bias was introduced from this source. The study intended to generalize to the Web overall; however, it is more appropriate to generalize to other top-ranked Web sites. The entire Web is made up of innumerable sites, most of which receive very little traffic, and many of which will share few of the Web page characteristics under study.

This study is an example of using content analysis of manifest indicators associated with latent variables. Researchers hypothesized that the level of complexity on a Web page is related to its site traffic. But how does one measure complexity? Is your definition of Web page complexity the same as mine? Bucy et al. (1999) identified and counted the presence on Web pages of several manifest content variables that they conceptualized as indicators of complexity. These included structural aspects of the page, graphical elements, dynamic elements (moving or blinking text), asynchronous interactive elements (links or survey forms), real-time interactive elements (chat functionality), and background color. The paper describes the coding scheme and shows all the categories in the tables of results. There is sufficient discussion of the development of the coding scheme, including justifications for including particular categories. However, we can still question the comprehensiveness and validity of this conceptualization of Web page complexity.

Multiple undergraduate student coders were used. While the total number of coders is not explicitly stated, we can assume it was approximately 35 because each coder was responsible for 15 sites. Percentage agreement was used to measure agreement on binary nominal variables; Krippendorff's alpha was used for interval and ratio-level data. Intercoder agreement is reported for each variable. In addition, agreement averaged over all variables and agreement for individual variables are reported. Individual variables that fall below acceptable levels of agreement can be hidden by reporting only a sufficient overall agreement; this study instead details the five variables that fell below 70 percent agreement and considers why this might have occurred. Capturing snapshots of the homepages or downloading all of them at one point in time would eliminate some of the variability that may have occurred because live Web pages were coded over a period of time during this study. This study addresses intercoder agreement better than most ILS content analyses, but there is still room for improvement. Percentage agreement and Krippendorff's alpha are two different measures. The authors do not explain how their values were averaged across all variables. As previously mentioned, percentage agreement does not consider chance agreement and is therefore less informative than other statistics. Finally, percentage agreement can only be calculated between two coders, not the multiple coders used here. For all these reasons, it would have been better to use Krippendorff's alpha to calculate agreement on all the variables.

The tables in the article clearly present the frequencies (and percentages) resulting from the analysis for categories overall, for the top 20 percent (by traffic) of sites in the sample, and by domain qualifier (.com, .net, etc.). While more details of the analysis of the relationships between site traffic and the interactivity variables would be useful, this article can serve as a model for conducting content analysis of Web content.

CONCLUSION

Content analysis is a systematic approach to learning about particular aspects of a body of text or other messages (e.g., pictures or video). As you design a study involving content analysis, you will first choose sampling units and ensure that your sample is an unbiased representation of all the texts of interest. Next, you will define recording units to be analyzed. In some cases, these units can be defined objectively, but when coder judgment is required, the reliability of those judgments should be evaluated. Finally, you will develop a coding scheme that can be applied to the recording units in the study sample. The reliability of the application of your coding scheme must be evaluated. With careful attention to definition of the sample and the coding scheme, content analysis can be an effective way to understand the meaning embodied in a wide variety of texts.

NOTES

1. This example is inspired by Kracker and Wang's (2002) content analysis. That study is not discussed here because it analyzes projective content—a subset of latent content proposed by Potter and Levine-Donnerstein (1999). Discussion of the analysis of projective content is beyond the scope of this chapter as it is not in line with the recommendations of most content analysis methodologists.

2. The most well known of these include Krippendorff's (2004a) alpha, Scott's (1955) pi, and Cohen's (1960) kappa. Numerous modifications of each have been proposed (Banerjee, 1999; Cohen, 1968; Popping, 1988).

WORKS CITED

Allen, B., & Reser, D. (1990). Content analysis in library and information science research. *Library and Information Science Research*, *12*, 251–262.

Banerjee, M. (1999). Beyond kappa: A review of interrater agreement measures. *Canadian Journal of Statistics*, *27*, 3–23.

Bates, M. J. (1999). The invisible substrate of information science. *Journal of the American Society for Information Science*, *50*(12), 1043–1050.

Berelson, B. (1954). Content analysis. In G. Lindzey (Ed.), *Handbook of Social Psychology* (Vol. 1, pp. 488–522). Reading, MA: Addison-Wesley.

Bucy, E. P., Lang, A., Potter, R., & Grabe, M. E. (1999). Formal features of cyberspace: Relationships between Web page complexity and site traffic. *Journal of the American Society for Information Science*, *50*(13), 1246–1256.

Carlyle, A., & Timmons, T. E. (2002). Default record displays in Web-based catalogs. *Library Quarterly*, *72*(2), 179–204.

Cohen, J. (1960). A coefficient of agreement for nominal scales. *Educational and Psychological Measurement*, *20*(1), 37–46.

Cohen, J. (1968). Weighted kappa: Nominal scale agreement with provision for scaled disagreement of partial credit. *Psychological Bulletin*, *70*(4), 213–220.

Conway, M. (2006). The subjective precision of computers: A methodological comparison with human coding in content analysis. *Journalism and Mass Communication Quarterly*, *83*(1), 186–200.

Deacon, D. (2007). Yesterday's papers and today's technology: Digital newspaper archives and "push button" content analysis. *European Journal of Communication*, *22*(1), 5–25.

Holsti, O. R. (1969). *Content Analysis for the Social Sciences and Humanities*. Reading, MA: Addison-Wesley.

Järvelin, K., & Vakkari, P. (1993). The evolution of library and information science 1965–1985: A content analysis of journal articles. *Information Processing and Management*, *29*(1), 129–144.

Kracker, J., & Pollio, H. R. (2003). The experience of libraries across time: Thematic analysis of undergraduate recollections of library experiences. *Journal of the American Society for Information Science and Technology*, *54*(12), 1104–1116.

Kracker, J., & Wang, P. (2002). Research anxiety and students' perceptions of research: An experiment. Part II. Content analysis of their writings on two experiences. *Journal of the American Society for Information Science and Technology*, *53*(4), 295–307.

Krippendorff, K. (2004a). *Content Analysis: An Introduction to Its Methodology*. Thousand Oaks, CA: Sage.

Krippendorff, K. (2004b). Reliability in content analysis: Some common misconceptions and recommendations. *Human Communication Research, 30*(3), 411–433.

Lombard, M., Snyder-Duch, J., & Bracken, C. C. (2002). Content analysis in mass communication: Assessment and reporting of intercoder reliability. *Human Communication Research, 28*(4), 587–604.

Lombard, M., Snyder-Duch, J., & Bracken, C. C. (2005). *Practical resources for assessing and reporting intercoder reliability in content analysis research projects.* Retrieved November 30, 2007, from http://astro.temple.edu/~lombard/reliability/

McMillan, S. J. (2000). The microscope and the moving target: The challenge of applying content analysis to the World Wide Web. *Journalism and Mass Communication Quarterly, 77*(1), 80–98.

Meho, L. I., & Spurgin, K. M. (2005). Ranking the research productivity of library and information science faculty and schools: An evaluation of data sources and research methods. *Journal of the American Society for Information Science and Technology, 56*(12), 1314–1331.

Neuendorf, K. A. (2002). *The Content Analysis Guidebook.* Thousand Oaks, CA: Sage.

Popping, R. (1988). On agreement indices for nominal data. In W. E. Saris & I. N. Gallhofer (Eds.), *Sociometric Research: Vol. 1. Data Collection and Scaling* (pp. 90–115). London: Macmillan.

Potter, W. J., & Levine-Donnerstein, D. (1999). Rethinking validity and reliability in content analysis. *Journal of Applied Communication Research, 27*, 258–284.

Riffe, D., Lacy, S., & Fico, F. G. (2005). *Analyzing Media Messages: Using Quantitative Content Analysis in Research.* Mahwah, NJ: Erlbaum.

Scott, W. A. (1955). Reliability of content analysis: The case of nominal scale coding. *Public Opinion Quarterly, 19*, 321–325.

Shannon, C. E., & Weaver, W. (1963). *The Mathematical Theory of Communication.* Urbana: University of Illinois Press.

Shapiro, G. (1997). The future of coders: Human judgments in a world of sophisticated software. In C. W. Roberts (Ed.), *Text Analysis for the Social Sciences: Methods for Drawing Statistical Inferences from Texts and Transcripts* (pp. 225–238). Mahwah, NJ: Erlbaum.

Shapiro, G., & Markoff, J. (1997). A matter of definition. In C. W. Roberts (Ed.), *Text Analysis for the Social Sciences: Methods for Drawing Statistical Inferences from Texts and Transcripts* (pp. 9–34). Mahwah, NJ: Erlbaum.

Towne v. Eisner, 245 U.S. 425 (1918).

Weare, C., & Lin, W. Y. (2000). Content analysis of the World Wide Web: Opportunities and challenges. *Social Science Computer Review, 18*(3), 272–292.

White, M. D., & Marsh, E. E. (2006). Content analysis: A flexible methodology. *Library Trends, 55*(1), 22–45.

Zhou, Y. (1996). Analysis of trends in demand for computer-related skills for academic librarians from 1974 to 1994. *College and Research Libraries, 57*, 259–272.

30

Qualitative Analysis of Content

Yan Zhang and Barbara M. Wildemuth

If there were only one truth, you couldn't paint a hundred canvases on the same theme.
—Pablo Picasso (1966; as quoted in Parmelin, 1969)

INTRODUCTION

As one of today's most extensively employed analytical tools, content analysis has been used fruitfully in a wide variety of research applications in information and library science (ILS; Allen & Reser, 1990). Similar to other fields, content analysis has been primarily used in ILS as a quantitative research method until recent decades. Many current studies use qualitative content analysis, which addresses some of the weaknesses of the quantitative approach.

Qualitative content analysis has been defined as

- "a research method for the subjective interpretation of the content of text data through the systematic classification process of coding and identifying themes or patterns" (Hsieh & Shannon, 2005, p. 1278)
- "an approach of empirical, methodological controlled analysis of texts within their context of communication, following content analytic rules and step-by-step models, without rash quantification" (Mayring, 2000, p. 2)
- "any qualitative data reduction and sense-making effort that takes a volume of qualitative material and attempts to identify core consistencies and meanings" (Patton, 2002, p. 453)

These three definitions illustrate that qualitative content analysis emphasizes an integrated view of speech/texts and their specific contexts. Qualitative content analysis goes beyond merely counting words or extracting objective content from texts to examine meanings, themes, and patterns that may be manifest or latent in a particular text. It allows researchers to understand social reality in a subjective but scientific manner.

Comparing qualitative content analysis with its rather familiar quantitative counterpart can enhance our understanding of the method. First, the research areas from which they developed are different. Quantitative content analysis (discussed in the previous chapter) is used widely in mass communication as a way to count manifest textual elements, an aspect of this method that is often criticized for missing syntactical and semantic information embedded in the text (Weber, 1990). By contrast, qualitative content analysis was developed primarily in anthropology, qualitative sociology, and psychology to explore the meanings of underlying physical messages. Second, quantitative content analysis is deductive, intended to test hypotheses or address questions generated from theories or previous empirical research. By contrast, qualitative content analysis is mainly inductive, grounding the examination of topics and themes, as well as the inferences drawn from them, in the data. In some cases, qualitative content analysis attempts to generate theory. Third, the data sampling techniques required by the two approaches are different. Quantitative content analysis requires that the data be selected using random sampling or other probabilistic approaches so as to ensure the validity of statistical inference. By contrast, samples for qualitative content analysis usually consist of purposively selected texts, which can inform the research questions being investigated. Last, but not least, the products of the two approaches are different. The quantitative approach produces numbers that can be manipulated with various statistical methods. By contrast, the qualitative approach usually produces descriptions or typologies, along with expressions from subjects reflecting how they view the social world. By this means, the perspectives of the producers of the text can be better understood by the investigator as well as the readers of the study's results (Berg, 2001). Qualitative content analysis pays attention to unique themes that illustrate the range of the meanings of the phenomenon, rather than the statistical significance of the occurrence of particular texts or concepts.

In real research work, the two approaches are not mutually exclusive and can be used in combination. As suggested by Smith (1975), "qualitative analysis deals with the forms and antecedent-consequent patterns of form, while quantitative analysis deals with duration and frequency of form" (p. 218). Weber (1990) also pointed out that the best content-analytic studies use both qualitative and quantitative operations.

INDUCTIVE VERSUS DEDUCTIVE

Qualitative content analysis involves a process designed to condense raw data into categories or themes based on valid inference and interpretation. This process uses inductive reasoning, by which themes and categories emerge from the data through the researcher's careful examination and constant comparison. But qualitative content analysis does not need to exclude deductive reasoning (Patton, 2002). Generating concepts or variables from theory or previous studies is also very useful for qualitative research, especially at the inception of data analysis (Berg, 2001).

Hsieh and Shannon (2005) discussed three approaches to qualitative content analysis, based on the degree of involvement of inductive reasoning. The first is *conventional qualitative content analysis*, in which coding categories are derived directly and inductively from the raw data. This is the approach used for grounded theory development. The second approach is *directed content analysis*, in which initial coding starts with a theory or relevant research findings. Then, during data analysis, the researchers immerse themselves in the data and allow themes to emerge from the data. The purpose of this approach usually is to validate or extend a conceptual framework or theory. The third approach is *summative content analysis*, which starts with the counting of words or manifest content, then extends the analysis to include latent meanings and themes. This approach seems quantitative in the early stages, but its goal is to explore the usage of the words/indicators in an inductive manner.

THE PROCESS OF QUALITATIVE CONTENT ANALYSIS

The process of qualitative content analysis often begins during the early stages of data collection. This early involvement in the analysis phase will help you move back and forth between concept development and data collection, and may help direct your subsequent data collection toward sources that are more useful for addressing the research questions (Miles & Huberman, 1994). To support valid and reliable inferences, qualitative content analysis involves a set of systematic and transparent procedures for processing data. Some of the steps overlap with the traditional quantitative content analysis procedures (Tesch, 1990), while others are unique to this method. Depending on the goals of your study, your content analysis may be more flexible or more standardized, but generally, it can be divided into the following steps, beginning with preparing the data and proceeding through writing up the findings in a report.

Step 1: Prepare the Data

Qualitative content analysis can be used to analyze various types of data, but generally, the data need to be transformed into written text before analysis can start. If the data come from existing texts, the choice of the content must be justified by what you want to know (Patton, 2002). In ILS studies, qualitative content analysis is most often used to analyze interview transcripts to reveal or model people's information-related behaviors and thoughts. When transcribing interviews, the following questions arise: (1) should all the questions of the interviewer or only the main questions from the interview guide be transcribed, (2) should the verbalizations be transcribed literally or only in a summary, and (3) should observations during the interview (e.g., sounds, pauses, and other audible behaviors) be transcribed or not (Schilling, 2006)? Your answers to these questions should be based on your research questions. While a complete transcript may be the most useful, the additional value it provides may not justify the additional time required to create it.

Step 2: Define the Unit of Analysis

The unit of analysis refers to the basic unit of text to be classified during content analysis. Messages have to be unitized before they can be coded, and differences in the unit definition can affect coding decisions as well as the comparability of outcomes with other similar studies (De Wever et al., 2006). Therefore defining the coding unit is one of your most fundamental and important decisions (Weber, 1990).

Qualitative content analysis usually uses individual themes as the unit for analysis, rather than the physical linguistic units (e.g., word, sentence, or paragraph) most often used in quantitative content analysis. An instance of a theme might be expressed in a single word, a phrase, a sentence, a paragraph, or an entire document. When using theme as the coding unit, you are primarily looking for the expressions of an idea (Minichiello et al., 1990). Thus you might assign a code to a text chunk of any size, as long as that chunk represents a single theme or issue of relevance to your research question(s).

Step 3: Develop Categories and a Coding Scheme

Categories and a coding scheme can be derived from three sources: the data, previous related studies, and theories. Coding schemes can be developed both inductively and deductively. In studies where no theories are available, you must generate categories inductively from the data. Inductive content analysis is particularly appropriate for studies that intend to develop theory, rather than those that intend to describe a particular phenomenon or verify an existing theory. When developing categories inductively from raw data, you are encouraged to use the constant comparative method (Glaser & Strauss, 1967) because it is not only able to stimulate original insights, but is also able to make differences between categories apparent. The essence of the constant comparative method is (1) the systematic comparison of each text assigned to a category with each of those already assigned to that category, to fully understand the theoretical properties of the category, and (2) integrating categories and their properties through the development of interpretive memos.

For some studies, you will have a preliminary model or theory on which to base your inquiry. You can generate an initial list of coding categories from the model or theory, and you may modify the model or theory within the course of the analysis as new categories emerge inductively (Miles & Huberman, 1994). The adoption of coding schemes developed in previous studies has the advantage of supporting the accumulation and comparison of research findings across multiple studies.

In quantitative content analysis, categories need to be mutually exclusive because confounded variables would violate the assumptions of some statistical procedures (Weber, 1990). However, in reality, assigning a particular text to a single category can be very difficult. Qualitative content analysis allows you to assign a unit of text to more than one category simultaneously (Tesch, 1990). Even so, the categories in your coding scheme should be defined in a way that makes them as internally homogeneous as possible and as externally heterogeneous as possible (Lincoln & Guba, 1985).

To ensure the consistency of coding, especially when multiple coders are involved, you should develop a coding manual, which usually consists of category names, definitions or rules for assigning codes, and examples (Weber, 1990). Some coding manuals have an additional field for taking notes as coding proceeds. Using the constant comparative method, your coding manual will evolve throughout the process of data analysis and will be augmented with interpretive memos.

Step 4: Test Your Coding Scheme on a Sample of Text

If you are using a fairly standardized process in your analysis, you'll want to develop and validate your coding scheme early in the process. The best test of the clarity and consistency of your category definitions is to code a sample of your data. After the sample is coded, the coding consistency needs to be checked, in most cases through an assessment of intercoder agreement. If the level of consistency is low, the coding rules must be revised. Doubts and problems concerning the definitions of categories, coding rules, or categorization of specific cases need to be discussed and resolved within your research team (Schilling, 2006). Coding sample text, checking coding consistency, and revising coding rules is an iterative process and should continue until sufficient coding consistency is achieved (Weber, 1990).

Step 5: Code All the Text

When sufficient consistency has been achieved, the coding rules can be applied to the entire corpus of text. During the coding process, you will need to check the coding repeatedly, to prevent "drifting into an idiosyncratic sense of what the codes mean" (Schilling, 2006, p. 33). Because coding will proceed while new data continue to be collected, it's possible (even quite likely) that new themes and concepts will emerge and will need to be added to the coding manual.

Step 6: Assess Your Coding Consistency

After coding the entire data set, you need to recheck the consistency of your coding. It is not safe to assume that if a sample was coded in a consistent and reliable manner, the coding of the whole corpus of text is also consistent. Human coders are subject to fatigue and are likely to make more mistakes as the coding proceeds. New codes may have been added since the original consistency check. Also, the coders' understanding of the categories and coding rules may change subtly over time, which may lead to greater inconsistency (Miles & Huberman, 1994; Weber, 1990). For all these reasons, you need to recheck your coding consistency.

Step 7: Draw Conclusions from the Coded Data

This step involves making sense of the themes or categories identified and their properties. At this stage, you will make inferences and present your reconstructions of meanings derived from the data. Your activities may involve exploring the properties and dimensions of categories, identifying relationships between categories, uncovering patterns, and testing categories against the full range of data (Bradley, 1993). This is a critical step in the analysis process, and its success will rely almost wholly on your reasoning abilities.

Step 8: Report Your Methods and Findings

For the study to be replicable, you need to monitor and report your analytical procedures and processes as completely and truthfully as possible (Patton, 2002). In the case of qualitative content analysis, you need to report your decisions and practices concerning the coding process as well as the methods you used to establish the trustworthiness of your study (discussed later).

Qualitative content analysis does not produce counts and statistical significance; instead, it uncovers patterns, themes, and categories important to a social reality. Presenting research findings from qualitative content analysis is challenging. Although it is a common practice to use typical quotations to justify conclusions (Schilling, 2006), you also may want to incorporate other options for data display, including matrices, graphs, charts, and conceptual networks (Miles & Huberman, 1994). The form and extent of reporting will finally depend on the specific research goals (Patton, 2002).

When presenting qualitative content analysis results, you should strive for a balance between description and interpretation. Description gives your readers background and context and thus needs to be rich and thick (Denzin, 1989). Qualitative research is fundamentally interpretive, and interpretation represents your personal and theoretical understanding of the phenomenon under study. An interesting and readable report "provides sufficient description to allow the reader to understand the basis for an interpretation, and sufficient interpretation to allow the reader to understand the description" (Patton, 2002, pp. 503–504).

Computer Support for Qualitative Content Analysis

Qualitative content analysis is usually supported by computer programs such as NVivo (http://www.qsrinternational. com/products_nvivo.aspx) or ATLAS.ti (http://www.atlasti. com/). The programs vary in their complexity and sophistication, but their common purpose is to assist researchers in organizing, managing, and coding qualitative data in a more efficient manner. The basic functions supported by such programs include text editing, note and memo taking, coding, text retrieval, and node/category manipulation. More and more qualitative data analysis software incorporates a visual presentation module that allows researchers to see the relationships between categories more vividly. Some programs even record a coding history to allow researchers to keep track of the evolution of their interpretations. Any time you will be working with more than a few interviews or are working with a team of researchers, you should use this type of software to support your efforts.

TRUSTWORTHINESS

Validity, reliability, and objectivity are criteria used to evaluate the quality of research in the conventional positivist research paradigm. As an interpretive method, qualitative content analysis differs from the positivist tradition in its fundamental assumptions, research purposes, and inference processes, thus making the conventional criteria unsuitable for judging its research results (Bradley, 1993). Recognizing this gap, Lincoln and Guba (1985) proposed four criteria for evaluating interpretive research work: credibility, transferability, dependability, and confirmability.

Credibility refers to the "adequate representation of the constructions of the social world under study" (Bradley, 1993, p. 436). Lincoln and Guba (1985) recommended a set of activities that would help improve the credibility of your research results: prolonged engagement in the field, persistent observation, triangulation, negative case analysis, checking interpretations against raw data, peer debriefing, and member checking. To improve the credibility of qualitative content analysis, researchers not only need to design data collection strategies that are able to adequately solicit the representations, but also to design transparent processes for coding and drawing conclusions from the raw data. Coders' knowledge and experience have significant impact on the credibility of research results. It is necessary to provide coders precise coding definitions and clear coding procedures. It is also helpful to prepare coders through a comprehensive training program (Weber, 1990).

Transferability refers to the extent to which the researcher's working hypothesis can be applied to another context. It is not the researcher's task to provide an index of transferability; rather, he or she is responsible for providing data sets and descriptions that are rich enough so that other researchers are able to make judgments about the findings' transferability to different settings or contexts.

Dependability refers to "the coherence of the internal process and the way the researcher accounts for changing conditions in the phenomena" (Bradley, 1993, p. 437). *Confirmability* refers to "the extent to which the characteristics of the data, as posited by the researcher, can be confirmed by others who read or review the research results" (Bradley, 1993, p. 437). The major technique for establishing dependability and confirmability is through audits of the research processes and findings. Dependability is determined by checking the consistency of the study processes, and confirmability is determined by checking the internal coherence of the research product, namely, the data, the findings, the interpretations, and the recommendations. The materials that could be used in these audits include raw data, field notes, theoretical notes and memos, coding manuals, process notes, and so on. The audit process has five stages: preentry, determinations of auditability, formal agreement, determination of trustworthiness (dependability and confirmability), and closure. A detailed list of activities and tasks at each stage can be found in Lincoln and Guba (1985, appendix B).

EXAMPLES

Two examples of qualitative content analysis will be discussed here. The first example study (Schamber, 2000) was intended to identify and define the criteria that weather professionals use to evaluate particular information resources. Interview data were analyzed inductively. In the second example, Foster (2004) investigated the information behaviors of interdisciplinary researchers. On the basis of semistructured interview data, he developed a model of these researchers' information seeking and use. These two studies are typical of ILS research that incorporates qualitative content analysis.

Example 1: Criteria for Making Relevance Judgments

Schamber (2000) conducted an exploratory inquiry into the criteria that occupational users of weather information employ to make relevance judgments on weather information sources and presentation formats. To get firsthand accounts from users, she used the time-line interview method to collect data from 30 subjects: 10 each in construction, electric power utilities, and aviation. These participants were highly motivated and had very specific needs for weather information. In accordance with a naturalistic approach, the interview responses were to be interpreted in a way that did not compromise the original meaning expressed by the study participant. Inductive content analysis was chosen for its power to make such faithful inferences.

The interviews were audiotaped and transcribed. The transcripts served as the primary sources of data for content analysis. Because the purpose of the study was to identify and describe criteria used by people to make relevance judgments, Schamber (2000) defined a coding unit as "a word or group of words that could be coded under one criterion category" (p. 739). Responses to each interview were unitized before they were coded.

As Schamber (2000) pointed out, content analysis functions both as a secondary observational tool for identifying variables in text and as an analytical tool for categorization. Content analysis was incorporated in this study at the pretest stage of developing the interview guide as a basis for the coding scheme as well as assessing the effectiveness of particular interview items. The formal process of developing the coding scheme began shortly after the first few interviews. The whole process was an iteration of coding a sample of data, testing intercoder agreement, and revising the coding scheme. Whenever the percentage of agreement did not reach an acceptable level, the coding scheme was revised (Schamber, 1991). The author reported that, "based on data from the first few respondents, the scheme was significantly revised eight times and tested by 14 coders until inter-coder agreement reached acceptable levels" (Schamber, 2000, p. 738). The 14 coders were not involved in the coding at the same time; rather, they were spread across three rounds of revision.

The analysis process was inductive and took a grounded theory approach. The author did not derive variables/categories from existing theories or previous related studies, and she had no intention of verifying existing theories; rather, she immersed herself in the interview transcripts and let the categories emerge on their own. Some categories in the coding scheme were straightforward and could be easily identified based on manifest content, while others were harder to identify because they were partially based on the latent content of the texts. The categories were expected to be mutually exclusive (distinct from each other) and exhaustive. The iterative coding process resulted in a coding scheme with eight main categories.

Credibility evaluates the validity of a researcher's reconstruction of a social reality. In this study, Schamber (2000) carefully designed and controlled the data collection and data analysis procedures to ensure the credibility of the research results. First, the time-line interview technique solicited respondents' own accounts of the relevance judgments they made on weather information in their real working environments, instead of in artificial experimental settings. Second, nonintrusive inductive content analysis was used to identify the themes emerging from the interview transcripts. The criteria were defined in respondents' own language, as it appeared in the interviews. Furthermore, a peer debriefing process was involved in the coding development process, which ensures the credibility of the research by reducing the bias of a single researcher. As reported by Schamber (1991), "a group of up to seven people, mostly graduate students including the researcher, met weekly for most of a semester and discussed possible criterion categories based on transcripts from four respondents" (pp. 84–85). The credibility of the research findings also was verified by the fact that most criteria were mentioned by more than one respondent and in more than one scenario. Theory saturation was achieved as mentions of criteria became increasingly redundant.

Schamber did not claim transferability of the research results explicitly, but the transferability of the study was made possible by detailed documentation of the data processing in a codebook. The first part of the codebook explained procedures for handling all types of data (including quantitative). In the second part, the coding scheme was listed; it included identification numbers, category names, detailed category definitions, coding rules, and examples. This detailed documentation of the data handling and the coding scheme makes it easier for future researchers to judge the transferability of the criteria to other user populations or other situational contexts. The transferability of the identified criteria also was supported by the fact that the criteria identified in this study were also widely documented in previous research works.

The dependability of the research findings in this study was established by the transparent coding process and intercoder verification. The inherent ambiguity of word meanings, category definitions, and coding procedures threaten the coherence and consistency of coding practices, hence negatively affecting the credibility of the findings. To make sure that the distinctions between categories were clear to the coders, the codebook defined them. To ensure coding consistency, every coder used the same version of the scheme to code the raw interview data. Both the training and the experience of the coder are necessary for reliable coding (Neuendorf, 2002). In this study, the coders were graduate students who had been involved in the revision of the coding scheme and thus were experienced at using the scheme (Schamber, 1991). The final coding scheme was tested for intercoder reliability with a first-time coder based on simple percentage agreement: the number of agreements between two independent coders divided by the number of possible agreements. As noted in the previous chapter, more sophisticated methods for assessing intercoder agreement are available. If you're using a standardized coding scheme, refer to that discussion.

As suggested by Lincoln and Guba (1985), confirmability is primarily established through a comfirmability audit, which Schamber (2000) did not conduct. However, the significant overlap of the criteria identified in this study with those identified in other studies indicates that the research findings have been confirmed by other researchers. Meanwhile, the detailed documentation of data handling also provides means for comfirmability checking.

When reporting the trustworthiness of the research results, instead of using the terms *credibility, transferability, dependability*, and *confirmability*, Schamber (2000) used terms generally associated with positivist studies: *internal validity, external validity, reliability*, and *generalizability*. It is worth pointing out that there is no universal agreement on the terminology used when assessing the quality of a qualitative inquiry. However, we recommend that the four criteria proposed by Lincoln and Guba (1985) be used to evaluate the trustworthiness of research work conducted within an interpretive paradigm.

Descriptive statistics, such as frequency of criteria occurrence, were reported in the study. However, the purpose of the study was to describe the range of the criteria employed to decide the degree of relevance of weather information in particular occupations. Thus the main finding was a list of criteria, along with their definitions, keywords, and examples. Quotations excerpted from interview transcripts were used to further describe the identified criteria as well as to illustrate the situational contexts in which the criteria were applied.

Example 2: Information Seeking in an Interdisciplinary Context

Foster (2004) examined the information seeking behaviors of scholars working in interdisciplinary contexts. His goal was threefold: (1) to identify the activities, strategies, contexts, and behaviors of interdisciplinary information seekers; (2) to understand the relationships between behaviors and context; and (3) to represent the information seeking behavior of interdisciplinary researchers in an empirically grounded model. This study is a naturalistic inquiry, using semistructured interviews to collect direct accounts of information seeking experiences from 45 interdisciplinary researchers. The respondents were selected through purposive sampling, along with snowball sampling. To "enhance contextual richness and minimize fragmentation" (Foster, 2004, p. 230), all participants were interviewed in their normal working places.

In light of the exploratory nature of the study, the grounded theory approach guided the data analysis. Foster (2004) did not have any specific expectations for the data before the analysis started; rather, he expected that concepts and themes related to interdisciplinary information seeking would emerge from the texts through inductive content analysis and the constant comparative method.

Coding took place in multiple stages, over time. The initial coding process was an open coding process. The author closely read and annotated each interview transcript. During this process, the texts were unitized, and concepts were highlighted and labeled. On the basis of this initial analysis, Foster (2004) identified three stages of information seeking in interdisciplinary contexts—initial, middle, and final—along with activities involved in each stage. Subsequent coding took place in the manner of constantly comparing the current transcript with previous ones to allow the emergence of categories and their properties. As the coding proceeded, additional themes and activities emerged—themes and activities not covered by the initially identified three-stage model. Further analysis of emergent concepts and themes and their relationships to each other resulted in a two-dimensional model of information seeking behaviors in the interdisciplinary context. One dimension delineates three nonlinear core processes of information seeking activities: opening, orientation, and consolidation. The other dimension consists of three levels of contextual interaction: cognitive approach, internal context, and external context.

The ATLAS.ti software was used to support the coding process. It allows the researcher to code the data, retrieve text based on keywords, rename or merge existing codes without perturbing the rest of the codes, and generate visualizations of emergent codes and their relationships to one another. ATLAS.ti also maintains automatic logs of coding changes, which makes it possible to keep track of the evolution of the analysis.

As reported by Foster (2004), coding consistency in this study was addressed by including three iterations of coding conducted over a period of one year. However, the author did not report on the three rounds of coding in detail. For example, he did not say how many coders were involved in the coding, how the coders were trained, how the coding rules were defined, and what strategies were used to ensure transparent coding. If all three rounds of coding were done by Foster alone, there was no assessment of coding consistency. While this is a common practice in qualitative research, it weakens the author's argument for the dependability of the study.

The issue of trustworthiness of the study was discussed in terms of the criteria suggested by Lincoln and Guba (1985): credibility, dependability, transferability, and confirmability. Credibility was established mainly through member checking and peer debriefing. Member checking was used in four ways at various stages of data collection and data analysis: (1) at the pilot stage, the interviewer discussed the interview questions with participants at the end of each interview; (2) during formal interviews, the interviewer fed ideas back to participants to refine, rephrase, and interpret; (3) in an informal postinterview session, each participant was given the chance to discuss the findings; and (4) an additional session was conducted with a sample of five participants willing to provide feedback on the transcripts of their own interview as well as evaluate the research findings. Peer debriefing was used in the study to "confirm interpretations and coding decisions including the development of categories" (Foster, 2004, p. 231). No further details about who conducted the debriefing or how it was conducted were reported in the paper.

The transferability of the present study was ensured by "rich description and reporting of the research process" (Foster, 2004, p. 230). Future researchers can make transferability judgments based on the detailed description provided by Foster. The issues of dependability and confirmability were addressed through the author's "research notes, which recorded decisions, queries, working out, and the development results" (Foster, 2004, p. 230). By referring to these materials, Foster could audit his own inferences and interpretations, and other interested researchers could review the research findings.

The content analysis findings were reported by describing each component in the model of information seeking behaviors in interdisciplinary contexts that emerged from this study. Diagrams and tables were used to facilitate the description. A few quotations from participants were provided to reinforce the author's abstraction of three processes of interdisciplinary information seeking: opening, orientation, and consolidation. Finally, Foster (2004) discussed the implications of the new model for the exploration of information behaviors in general.

CONCLUSION

Qualitative content analysis is a valuable alternative to more traditional quantitative content analysis, when the researcher is working in an interpretive paradigm. The goal is to identify important themes or categories within a body of content and to provide a rich description of the social reality created by those themes/categories as they are lived out in a particular setting. Through careful data preparation, coding, and interpretation, the results of qualitative content analysis can support the development of new theories and models as well as validating existing theories and providing thick descriptions of particular settings or phenomena.

WORKS CITED

Allen, B., & Reser, D. (1990). Content analysis in library and information science research. *Library and Information Science Research, 12*(3), 251–260.

Berg, B. L. (2001). *Qualitative Research Methods for the Social Sciences*. Boston: Allyn and Bacon.

Bradley, J. (1993). Methodological issues and practices in qualitative research. *Library Quarterly, 63*(4), 431–449.

Denzin, N. K. (1989). *Interpretive Interactionism*. Newbury Park, CA: Sage.

De Wever, B., Schellens, T., Valcke, M., & Van Keer, H. (2006). Content analysis schemes to analyze transcripts of online asynchronous discussion groups: A review. *Computer and Education, 46,* 6–28.

Foster, A. (2004). A nonlinear model of information seeking behavior. *Journal of the American Society for Information Science and Technology, 55*(3), 228–237.

Glaser, B. G., & Strauss, A. L. (1967). *The Discovery of Grounded Theory: Strategies for Qualitative Research*. New York: Aldine.

Hsieh, H.-F., & Shannon, S. E. (2005). Three approaches to qualitative content analysis. *Qualitative Health Research, 15*(9), 1277–1288.

Lincoln, Y. S., & Guba, E. G. (1985). *Naturalistic Inquiry*. Beverly Hills, CA: Sage.

Mayring, P. (2000). Qualitative content analysis. *Forum: Qualitative Social Research, 1*(2). Retrieved July 28, 2008, from http://217.160.35.246/fqs-texte/2-00/2-00mayring-e.pdf.

Miles, M., & Huberman, A. M. (1994). *Qualitative Data Analysis*. Thousand Oaks, CA: Sage.

Minichiello, V., Aroni, R., Timewell, E., & Alexander, L. (1990). *In-depth Interviewing: Researching People*. Hong Kong: Longman Cheshire.

Neuendorf, K. A. (2002). *The Content Analysis Guidebook*. Thousand Oaks, CA: Sage.

Patton, M. Q. (2002). *Qualitative Research and Evaluation Methods*. Thousand Oaks, CA: Sage.

Parmelin, H. (1969). Truth. In *Picasso Says* London: Allen and Unwin.

Schamber, L. (1991). *Users' criteria for evaluation in multimedia information seeking and use situations*. Unpublished doctoral dissertation, Syracuse University.

Schamber, L. (2000). Time-line interviews and inductive content analysis: Their effectiveness for exploring cognitive behaviors. *Journal of the American Society for Information Science, 51*(8), 734–744.

Schilling, J. (2006). On the pragmatics of qualitative assessment: Designing the process for content analysis. *European Journal of Psychological Assessment, 22*(1), 28–37.

Smith, H. W. (1975). *Strategies of Social Research: The Methodological Imagination.* Englewood Cliffs, NJ: Prentice Hall.

Tesch, R. (1990). *Qualitative Research: Analysis Types and Software Tools.* Bristol, PA: Falmer Press.

Weber, R. P. (1990). *Basic Content Analysis.* Newbury Park, CA: Sage.

31

Discourse Analysis

Barbara M. Wildemuth and Carol L. Perryman

Men's thoughts are much according to their inclination, their discourse and speeches according to their learning and infused opinions.

—Francis Bacon (1626)

The true mirror of our discourse is the course of our lives.

—Michel de Montaigne (1595)

INTRODUCTION

Since information and library science (ILS) work is so centrally focused on information, it is logical that we, as researchers, would concern ourselves with its communication. Much ILS research focuses on direct and nonnuanced content, perhaps looking at literacy levels and issues related to particular resources, but there are other dimensions to explore that can greatly enrich our understanding and practice. We understand implicitly that words carry far more than their literal meaning. Discourse analysis is a tool that can be used to uncover those other meanings—meanings that we negotiate in our everyday and professional interactions but that are rarely made explicit within those interactions.

Discourse analysis, on the surface, is just what its name implies—the analysis of discourse. But we need to look behind this superficial definition to maximize the potential of this research method for ILS research. First, we need to understand what kinds of communication, or discourse, might be analyzed. Broadly defined, discourse includes "all kinds of spoken interaction, formal and informal, and written texts of all kinds" (Potter & Wetherell, 1987, p. 7). ILS studies using discourse analysis have tended to focus on either particular types of conversations (e.g., the reference interview) or more formal texts (e.g., the professional literature). Such units of information comprise social texts (i.e., the expressions of our society) and function to support interpersonal relationships, institutions, and ideologies within that society.

Emphasizing the variety embodied in these texts, discourse is sometimes depicted as embodying interpretative repertoires, which are "recurrently used systems of terms used for characterizing and evaluating actions, events and other phenomena" (Potter & Wetherell, 1987, p. 149). These repertoires obviously include what is said in a particular text, but may also include the silences and hesitations related to particular topics or concepts (Talja, 1999). As Johnstone (2008) notes, "what is not said or cannot be said is the background without which what is said could not be heard" (p. 70). It is common that groups who share a common space or purpose also share interpretative repertoires. Each individual selects from the available interpretative repertoires as part of the communication process. Identifying the interpretative repertoires in use is the initial task of discourse analysis (Talja, 1999).

An important assumption underlying discourse analysis is that speech acts are constructive. People use speech/text to *construct* versions of their social world; they are shaped by the speech acts in which they engage, and they use those speech acts to shape their world (Coyle, 2000; Johnstone, 2008). One implication of this assumption is that discourse is not of interest for its representation of an objective reality but, instead, for the ways in which it functions to create a social reality (Coyle, 2000). "Discourse or social texts are approached in *their own right* and not as a secondary route to things 'beyond' the text like attitudes, events or cognitive processes" (Potter & Wetherell, 1987, p. 160). Thus most studies using discourse analysis view social phenomena as the products of discourse, and the research questions tend to focus on how and why discourse is used to construct the social world of the relevant actors (Hammersley, 2003).

A corollary of the assumption that speech is used to construct a social reality is that different individuals might use different interpretative repertoires and thus construct different social realities. In addition, one individual might use multiple interpretative repertoires and thus hold multiple perspectives on his or her social world. Discourse analysis is particularly attuned to making these interpretative conflicts and ambiguities visible (Talja, 1999). While many methods for social science data analysis focus on identifying the agreed on themes within a body of text, discourse analysis goes beyond this goal and also focuses on differences within a single text or across texts. Potter and Wetherell (1987) highlight these dual goals of discourse analysis, describing them as the search for variability, as well as the search for consistency, in people's worldviews.

Because speech is an action and is constructive of social realities, discourse analysis may also be used to conduct a more critical (rather than merely descriptive) investigation of the objects of a study. Many authors (e.g., Parker, 1992) have used discourse analysis to examine the ways in which powerful groups can use speech acts to maintain their power, or the ways in which less powerful groups can try to gain power through speech. Similarly, speech acts can be used to support institutional goals or to promote (or overthrow) particular ideologies. Discourse analysis can be used to investigate any of these types of dynamic phenomena.

Discourse analysis, as a method,[1] can be compared to a variety of other methods, including content analysis (both quantitative and qualitative), conversation analysis, and hermeneutics. It differs from *content analysis* in some of its underlying assumptions and in the status given to the text itself. Discourse analysis assumes that the role of speech is to construct the speakers' (and, potentially, listeners') social world. Content analysis does not necessarily make this assumption. In addition, discourse analysis regards speech as an act in itself and is focused on analyzing the functions and outcomes of speech acts. In most cases, content analysis regards text as a description of an external reality and focuses on discerning that reality through its description in selected texts. For example, you might use content analysis to examine chat reference transcripts to see whether the patron was explicit about need or whether the librarian cited sources in giving information. If you were to apply discourse analysis to the same texts, it is likely that you would be investigating the ways that interpretative repertoires differ between librarians and their patrons, and how those differences affect and are affected by the power differences between the two groups. Content analysis methods, both quantitative and qualitative, are discussed in separate chapters in Part 5.

Conversation analysis is generally limited to the analysis of conversations (i.e., transcripts of them). Conversation analysis may focus on linguistic phenomena, such as turn-taking, and structures of speech often ritualized within their context (e.g., consider the conventions followed in answering the phone). Alternatively, it may focus on trying to understand what people say to be understood by others (Budd, 2006). Clearly there is an emphasis on dialogic speech and the interactions between the speakers (Budd & Raber, 1996). Both discourse analysis and conversation analysis require a very fine grained reading of the texts under consideration, though conversation analysis is much more likely to include the specification of pauses and nonverbal utterances in the conversation transcript and to directly interpret these portions of the data.

In *hermeneutics*, the goal is "to identify the horizons that surround and define a particular phenomenon . . . and to describe the interpretive community or communities for which it is meaningful" (Smith, 1996, p. 29). The researcher begins with particular preunderstandings of the concept of interest, informed by his or her prior everyday experiences with the concept. On the basis of this preunderstanding, the researcher examines the texts of interest, with particular focus on the relationships between the different texts. The reflexive character of this method of analysis gives rise to the concept of the hermeneutical circle, in which the whole body of text influences your interpretation of each part of the text, and each part of the text influences your understanding of the whole. A hermeneutical approach has rarely been used in ILS research; Smith's (1999) dissertation is an example that combines content analysis and hermeneutics. Hermeneutics resembles discourse analysis in that both are subjective and both look at culture's influence on texts; a signal difference is that, in using discourse analysis, the intent is not to view how participants understand their environment, but instead, how it is expressed through their discourse.

DISCOURSE ANALYSIS METHODS AND TOOLS

Being a relatively new method to ILS research, there are not many examples of discourse analysis in the literature. The introductory section to Potter and Wetherell's (1987) classic, *Discourse and Social Psychology*, mentions the new researcher's bewilderment at encountering discourse analysis and the dawning recognition that the steps used in conducting this type of research actually consist of incrementally building a series of intuitions. As they put it, "there is no analytic method, at least as the term is understood elsewhere in social psychology. Rather, there is a broad theoretical framework, which focuses attention on the constructive and functional dimensions of discourse, coupled with the reader's skill in identifying significant patterns of consistency and variation" (Potter & Wetherell, 1987, p. 169). Thus, instead of using scales or counting occurrences of terms, the toolbox for discourse analysis includes the works of theorists within ILS and outside of it; careful, close reading of the discourse/texts being analyzed; and an exhaustive, repetitive framing and reframing of the data until conclusions can be drawn that are well supported.

In spite of their ambivalence about specifying procedures for discourse analysis, Potter and Wetherell (1987) do suggest a number of steps that will be taken during discourse analysis. These steps are not set in stone and, in fact, are sometimes overlapping, merging, or even completely absent.

The first step is to construct your research question. No matter what the topic, your question will address how discourse is constructed, what is gained by it, and what the relationship of the discourse structure might be to its function. Examples of ILS research questions that can be addressed by discourse analysis include the ways in which people talk about female librarians or the ways in which they talk about the roles of libraries—two examples discussed in depth later in this chapter.

The second step is to select a sample of discourse to study. Sampling, in this context, is similar to sampling for the purposes of other types of intensive studies (see Chapter 14). Keep in mind that you are making decisions about what to exclude as well as what to include in your sample. You may conduct a set of interviews (with a sample of interviewees) to generate texts; you may be selecting a sample from preexisting texts. Because the process of discourse analysis is quite labor-intensive, it is likely that you'll want to limit the size of your sample. A small sample is often sufficient because a large number of linguistic patterns are likely to emerge from just a few people or sources. "What is important is to gather sufficient text to discern the variety of discursive forms that are commonly used when speaking or writing about the research topic" (Coyle, 2000, p. 256). Radford and Radford (1997), discussed later, examined a small sample of texts from a large and diverse array of text resources. As Potter and Wetherell (1987) note, "the value or generalisability of results depends on the reader assessing the importance and interest of the effect described and deciding whether it has vital consequences for the area of social life in which it emerges and possibly for other diverse areas" (p. 161).

The next step is to collect the records and documents you will analyze. You may be working with preexisting texts. These may be public documents, such as published articles, but they may also include personal documents. Be sure to attend to any ethical issues that arise when seeking access to letters, diaries, or other private documents. Alternatively, you may have conducted interviews for the purposes of your study and will analyze the transcripts. If so, be sure to keep your interview questions as open ended as possible and to encourage the interviewee to address the issues of concern from multiple angles. In addition, your own questions in the interview are also part of the discourse and should be examined. If you are using interview data or data recorded from meetings or other events, you will need to transcribe the recordings before you can proceed further. The only issue to consider here is how much detail to incorporate into the transcript. Potter and Wetherell (1987) estimated that you will spend about 10 hours transcribing each hour of interview,[2] if you only include the words that were said. If you include such things as pauses and their length, overlaps between speakers, and intonation, the transcription effort can easily double. As with your initial decisions about the sample of texts to analyze, your decisions about the level of detail in your transcription should be guided by the needs of your research question.

Once you've got all the texts in printed form, you're ready to code the data. The process of coding consists of identifying themes within categories that emerge and take shape as you examine the texts. These categories and themes may occur within one text, within multiple texts from the same source, or across a variety of texts. In developing the category scheme, you should aim for broad inclusion, as opposed to stringent narrowness. Segments of text can be categorized into more than one code to more fully characterize the discourse. While coding is not a mandatory step, it is a tool that can provide easy entry into the analysis of what may seem impenetrable text.

In many ways, all the steps to this point can be considered preanalysis. So once they have been completed, you're ready to analyze your data. The success of your analysis is very much predicated on your close reading and rereading of the texts. To do this, what's needed is not the kind of reading for gist we've learned to do in school, but rather an extremely microfocused and repetitive examination. You are not looking for an overall sense of the text, but for nuance, contradictions, or areas of vagueness or ambivalence. First, search for patterns in the text, then look for similarities across different areas of an individual text and/or different texts. Next, look for variations and contradictions. In these initial readings, your goal is to identify the interpretative repertoires in use in the body of discourse being analyzed. It's common to have to consider and reconsider patterns—consider this an important part of learning about the discourse in depth. Try to identify assumptions that underlie a particular way of talking about a phenomenon. Ask yourself how differences are accounted for, and then try to identify and annotate textual proof of this behavior (Coyle, 2000). Formulate one or more hypotheses about the form and functions of the text based on your analysis. Search back through the text yet again to find evidence for and against your hypotheses, making careful note of where they do not fit as well as where they do fit. Look carefully for ways that contradictory evidence can be explained. During this process, it's also important to ask yourself about your *own* presuppositions and how they are affecting your interpretation of the text. Once you've completed the analysis, you will be in a position to draw conclusions related to your research question(s).

A final step is to validate your findings. In other types of social science research, there are standard methods for evaluating the reliability and validity of your findings. In discourse analysis, you will want to focus your attention on the coherence of your conclusions and on their fruitfulness (Coyle, 2000; Potter & Wetherell, 1987). *Coherence* means that the outcomes of your analysis should add clarity and focus to the text of the discourse you have examined. Exceptions should always be noted and are valuable in producing a fuller accounting of this sample of discourse. Note any instances of in-text (community-created) recognition of variability and inconsistencies. These work to lend support to your own recognition of the same. Also look for instances of what Potter and Wetherell (1987) have called "the sequential constructions of issues arising because of the use of interpretative repertoires" (p. 171). The example they give is that a car engine converts chemical energy to propulsion but then requires that the heat created in the process must be dealt with by having a fan. The fan would not need to exist without the engine having fulfilled its function. The *fruitfulness* of your findings is the extent to which they provide insight that might be useful in the analysis of new kinds of discourse. In an applied field like information and library science, your study may also be fruitful if it has clear implications for the improvement of the practice of the information professions.

As in every other part of research, clarity is key in presenting the results in such a way that not only your findings, but also your analytical procedures, can be understood by your intended audience. In addition, examples from your data should be presented so that your readers can comprehend the discourse of interest and judge the validity of your conclusions for themselves. Weaknesses in discourse analysis can arise from the subjectivity with which every step in the process is imbued. Less than careful reading, lack of rigor in categorization, and the nonrepresentative selection of texts can all destroy the validity of your study.

EXAMPLES

Two examples of discourse analysis will be discussed here. In the first example, Radford and Radford (1997) examined the stereotype of the female librarian, as expressed in popular literature and media, and analyzed it in terms of the ways this discourse defines the relationships between librarians and social systems of power and rationality. The second example is Frohmann's (1997) analysis of the writings of Melvil Dewey, with emphasis on librarians' and libraries' roles in recommending books for readers. In addition to these two examples, you may want to examine Frohmann's (1994) classic analysis of the discourse in ILS theory. Neither of the examples discussed here is based on interviews as the source of the textual data to be analyzed; for more detail on this form of discourse analysis, please refer to Talja's (1999) discussion.

Example 1: Discourse on Female Librarians

Radford and Radford (1997) began by outlining the stereotype of a female librarian. They use images from TV commercials and other popular media as well as critiques of the stereotype published in the professional literature. In general, the stereotype portrays female librarians as middle-aged spinsters with an unfashionable appearance, whose only responsibilities are to keep the people in the library quiet and to check out books. Others have examined the stereotype directly, and in more detail, but that was not Radford and Radford's goal. Instead, they applied both Foucault's ideas and feminist theory to the analysis of the function of this stereotype as it shapes a particular social reality. They saw these two philosophical streams as converging in their ability to provide an appropriate analytical lens for the two research questions to be addressed in this study:

(a) How is the portrayal of women librarians related to the role of discourse in producing and sustaining hegemonic power? and (b) How is the stereotype related to the manner in which universals such as truth, freedom, and human nature are made and privileged by masculine elites? (p. 252)

While Radford and Radford (1997) didn't explicitly describe their methods as discourse analysis, their research goals were clearly in line with this approach. They identified several interpretative repertoires in the stereotype of the female librarian and used Foucaultian/feminist theories to elaborate the ways in which those repertoires create a particular social reality.

They moved, first, to the connection between the hyperorderliness embodied in the librarian stereotype to its opposite: madness, or "the breakdown of systematicity and the unconstrained production of discourse" (Radford & Radford, 1997, p. 255). Society requires that the library (with its stereotypical librarian) exist to protect it from chaos. The ideal of orderliness also results in an ideal of the completeness of the collection: every book in its place. This ideal is in tension with the professional ideal of providing access, in the sense that the most orderly library is the library in which every book is on the shelf. Thus the librarian is expected to order and to protect the texts in the library.

Because the use of the library disrupts the order in it, the user of the library is in an oppositional relationship to the stereotypical librarian. This relationship also embodies a power differential: the librarian knows the mystery of the order within the library, while the user does not. This provides the librarian with power over the user. As Radford and Radford (1997) described this power relationship, the librarian is a god, "the guardian of rationality and knowledge, whose domain of order the user dares to violate, and who has the power to render discipline and punishment" (p. 259).

But wait! We know that librarians are not seen as gods by their users. So what's happening? This was the point in the argument where Radford and Radford (1997) called on feminist theory and Foucault's ideas. It was argued that Foucault sees the library as an institution that manages society's "fundamental fear of *discourse* and the dangers that *uncontrolled discourse* may give rise to" (p. 260). Librarians, as gatekeepers of a collection of discourse/texts, serve both to reflect and neutralize the potential dangers associated with those texts. The very orderliness of the library calms society's fears of the disorderliness that might ensue if the texts were uncontrolled. Yet the stereotypical librarian also serves as a warning about the power of those texts.

The article concluded with unanswered questions, which are even more appropriate as the object of discourse analysis than the original questions were:

Who is speaking through the stereotype of the female librarian, and to what ends? What interests does the stereotype serve (certainly not those of women)? (Radford & Radford, 1997, p. 263)

There are a number of things Radford and Radford (1997) did not do in this study, which are worth a brief mention. First, they did not explicitly perform coding, although they did visibly categorize discourse about the stereotype. Second, although they did not include a methods section, as we might understand it, they constantly revisited and reexamined their evidence for consistency within the literature of ILS and other theories. As you practice close reading of this work, you will be rewarded by its depth of analysis and impressed by the careful sequencing of logic employed.

Example 2: Dewey's Discourse on the Role and Functioning of Libraries

Frohmann (1997) analyzed a tension in the writings of Melvil Dewey, using discourse analysis as his analytical tool. He found that "Dewey's rhetoric was in fact an unstable mixture of the old and the new" ideas about the library's role (p. 352). We will briefly summarize his findings here to demonstrate how this method of analysis can be used to identify and understand multiple/conflicting interpretative repertoires used in the writings of a single person.

Frohmann (1997) focused on Dewey's writings that addressed the idea of the means for getting the "best books" to each reader. In addition, he augmented Dewey's writings with some of the writings of Dewey's contemporaries to make the tension in Dewey's ideas clearer.

One of the ideas that Dewey espoused was in agreement with most of the library leaders of the time: a goal of the library is to provide readers with the best books available. This view is based on "the library's traditional social mission in the service of high culture" (Frohmann, 1997, p. 350). Most of Dewey's contemporaries[3] argued that librarians had a responsibility to work with their patrons, leading them from their current state toward a state in which they would appreciate the reading of books considered highly valuable to society. The librarian was to teach the patron about what to read and how to read it. The library took on an educational role, with the best books taking the place of lecturers.

The concept of "best books" is a node in the discursive network of the view just described. However, it's also a node in a different discursive network: that of Dewey's push for a more businesslike and standardized approach to librarianship. When taking this rhetorical stance, Dewey argued that the best books are those that the reader selects for himself or herself. Library collection development decisions should be made by those with common sense and experience, rather than those with literary training. This view supports Dewey's articulation of the need for a standardized library catalog, with a standardized description of each book. In this way, by knowing the classification number of interest, the user can select books without guidance from a librarian. Even Dewey's description of readers as wanting "information" is an indicator that he is using a interpretative repertoire oriented toward the systematic management of information resources as capital assets.

Some previous biographies of Dewey (such as that by Miksa, as cited in Frohmann, 1997) have reconciled these two contrasting views by proposing a means-end relationship: the systematic description and organization of a library's holdings are the means to the goal of providing readers with the best books. However, rather than working to make these conflicting views internally consistent, discourse analysis brings into focus the differences between them.

CONCLUSION

As you can see from the preceding discussion, discourse analysis is simultaneously complex and powerful. The examples provided here provide strong proof that discourse analysis has a place in our toolbox. It offers ILS researchers the potential to explore paths of inquiry that can provide us with a far greater understanding of some of the phenomena that affect us all. However, as with other qualitative methods for inquiry, engaging in its practice will require rigor, clarity, and even self-inquiry.

NOTES

1. Some authors argue that discourse analysis is a research paradigm, rather than just a particular social science data analysis method. While we recognize the merits of this argument, we side with Hammersley (2003), when he argues that discourse analysis will be more widely useful if it is not inextricably linked to some of the epistemological and ontological requirements associated with its use as a research paradigm.

2. This estimate is likely too high, given that use of digital recordings and word processors has made this process more efficient than it was in 1987.

3. Frohmann incorporates the writings of William Fletcher, Frederic B. Perkins, and Justin Winsor in his analysis.

WORKS CITED

Bacon, F. (1626). Of custom and education. In *Essays of Francis Bacon, or Counsels, Civil and Moral*.

Budd, J. M. (2006). Discourse analysis and the study of communication in LIS. *Library Trends*, 55(1), 65–82.

Budd, J. M., & Raber, D. (1996). Discourse analysis: Method and application in the study of information. *Information Processing and Management, 32*, 217–226.

Coyle, A. (2000). Discourse analysis. In G. M. Breakwell, S. Hammond, & C. Fife-Schaw (Eds.), *Research Methods in Psychology* (2nd ed., pp. 251–268). London: Sage.

de Montaigne, M. (1595). Of the education of children. In *The Essays (Les Essais), Book I* (chap. 26). Paris: Abel Langelier.

Frohmann, B. (1994). Discourse analysis as a research method in library and information science. *Library and Information Science Research, 1*(2), 119–138.

Frohmann, B. (1997). "Best books" and excited readers: Discursive tensions in the writings of Melvil Dewey. *Libraries and Culture, 32*(3), 349–371.

Hammersley, M. (2003). Conversation analysis and discourse analysis: Methods or paradigms? *Discourse and Society, 14*(6), 751–781.

Johnstone, B. (2008). *Discourse Analysis*. Malden, MA: Blackwell.

Parker, I. (1992). *Discourse Dynamics: Critical Analysis for Social and Individual Psychology*. London: Routledge.

Potter, J., & Wetherell, M. (1987). *Discourse and Social Psychology: Beyond Attitudes and Behaviour*. London: Sage.

Radford, M. L., & Radford, G. P. (1997). Power, knowledge, and fear: Feminism, Foucault, and the stereotype of the female librarian. *Library Quarterly, 67*(3), 250–266.

Smith, M. M. (1996). *Information ethics: An hermeneutical analysis of an emerging area in applied ethics*. Unpublished doctoral dissertation, University of North Carolina at Chapel Hill.

Talja, S. (1999). Analyzing qualitative interview data: The discourse analytic method. *Library and Information Science Research, 21*(4), 459–477.

32

Analytic Induction

Kristina M. Spurgin and Barbara M. Wildemuth

> The problem of induction is not a problem of demonstration but a problem of defining the difference between valid and invalid predictions.
>
> —Nelson Goodman (1955)

INTRODUCTION

Induction is one of the main forms of scientific logic. It is best understood in contrast with the other main form of scientific logic: deduction. *Deductive reasoning* is the logical process of arriving at specific facts that must be true, given a set of broader tenets that are assumed to be true. For example, suppose you accept the fact that college students use the library. You also know that Rosemary is a college student. Given this information, you may deduce that Rosemary uses the library. *Induction*, on the other hand, is the logical process of arriving at a general conclusion by examining a set of specific facts. Suppose we observe that Stella, Daphne, and Sandy are all college students. We also know that they all use the library. We may then induce that college students use the library.

Analytic induction is a specific form of inductive reasoning used to analyze qualitative data. It is a formalized method for developing and refining a theory or hypothesis, directly from the data. It also can be used for clearly specifying the definitions of variables or phenomena. The hypotheses and definitions resulting from analytic induction must apply to all cases in your sample (Katz, 2001). Depending on your goals, analytic induction may be a fruitful method for analyzing your data. The technique is suitable for analyzing data such as those gathered in multiple case studies, ethnographic observations, participant observation, or semistructured or unstructured interviews. The method can lead to answers to *how* questions, as in, How do people do this particular thing? (Becker, 1998). The researcher doing analytic induction attempts to explain the essential features of a phenomenon. These features will occur when the phenomenon occurs and will not occur when the phenomenon does not occur (Manning, 1982).

Denzin (1989) stressed the strength of analytic induction for developing theory. There are several approaches for theory development from qualitative data. Analytic induction is different than other methods because it allows for the generation, testing, and disproving of theories. These may be preexisting theories about a phenomenon or theories generated by the researcher during the analytic induction process. Analytic induction also provides a framework for testing whether existing theories can be combined or incorporated in new ways.

THE PROCESS OF ANALYTIC INDUCTION

In his dissertation work on the social psychology of embezzlement, Cressey (1950, 1953) outlined the process of analytic induction. This section will roughly follow Cressey's outline and provide an example based on a hypothetical library science research project.

First, formulate a rough definition of the phenomenon you would like to explain. For example, you may want to explain how undergraduate students use the print journal collection in the university library. Here, you must define what you mean by "use of the print journal collection." Your initial definition might be as follows: "a student uses the print journal collection when he or she removes bound volumes from the shelf for reading or copying."

Next, develop a hypothetical explanation of the phenomenon. In our example, you might begin by hypothesizing that students use the print journal collection to complete their course assignments. When facing your real-life research problem, you may construct the initial definition and hypotheses before beginning to examine cases. In this situation, a careful review of the literature, your experience, and your informal observations will guide you. Alternatively, you may define your phenomenon and begin to build your initial hypothesis from the first case you examine. The latter situation is more aligned with the idea of letting the data speak for itself. By generating the hypothesis from the data itself, you avoid imposing artificial and external theory or structure on the phenomenon at hand. This is a more purely inductive approach.

However you derive your initial definition and hypothesis, you will continue by choosing cases and studying them to see if the information that emerges is consistent with your hypothesis. Analytic induction requires the inclusion of likely negative cases. Considering negative cases forces you to refine your definitions and hypotheses. The more they are refined, the more likely they are to accurately describe the phenomenon of interest. If you do not make an effort to include negative cases, your work is simply a collection of data to support your view of the phenomenon without testing that view. When you write up your project, it is important to explicitly address how you included negative cases in your analysis. You should also explain how you accounted for them. Accounting for negative cases is the focus of the rest of the analytic induction process.

In our example, you may believe that students who are heavy users of the print journal collection are using it to complete their course assignments. In light of this hypothesis, you might conduct an interview with just such a student. From that interview, you learn that the student works for a professor who sends him to make copies of journal articles using her copy card. This is an example of a negative case. It does not fit with your hypothesis regarding student use of the print journal collection.

The discovery of a negative case requires one of two actions. You may either redefine the phenomenon to exclude the negative case or reformulate the hypothesis. In our example, you may decide that this student's use of the print collection is not representative of the use you are interested in explaining. In this case, you would redefine the phenomenon. Your new definition of print journal collection use might be as follows: "a student uses the print journal collection when, on his or her own time, he or she removes bound volumes from the shelf for reading or copying. If copies are made, they are paid for with the student's funds." The new definition of the phenomenon becomes more precise and specific. Your explanation at this point remains that students use the print journal collection *in this particular way* to support the completion of course assignments.

Examination of cases that appear to fall within the bounds of your described phenomenon will reveal negative cases. You will also want to examine some known negative cases that are obviously not examples of the phenomenon in question. They are of use to you because finding support for your hypothesis in these cases will indicate that your hypothesis is not enough to explain your phenomenon. If you examine cases outside your phenomenon and do not find that your hypothesis applies to them, you can begin to make the argument that your hypothesis explains the phenomenon you are studying.

In our example, we may want to look at cases from students who do not use the print journal collection, but who do use the electronic journal collection. Examination of such cases may reveal that these students are using the electronic journal collection to complete course assignments. You have discovered that students use both the print and electronic journal collections to complete course assignments. Therefore the hypothesis that "students use the print journal collections to complete course assignments" does not adequately explain why students use the print collection as opposed to the electronic collection. The hypothesis should be modified. Reanalysis of examined cases in light of this may reveal a difference between the uses of these collections. You would modify your hypothesis based on this difference so that it explains the distinction between these different types of use. For example, your new hypothesis might be that students use the print collection to complete assignments when they are required by their professors to use articles from specific journals not available electronically.

The process of examining cases and reformulating definitions and hypotheses continues until you have developed an explanation of the phenomenon in your sample. If you are sampling iteratively during the study, knowing when to stop looking for more cases may be difficult. You may find, after examining a small number of cases, that your hypothesis is supported, but you must make efforts to the fullest extent possible to identify and take into account negative cases. If you have predefined a sample for the study, you must examine and account for all of those cases.

We have given you a contrived and simplistic example of analytic induction for the purpose of giving you a basic understanding of what is involved in this method. If you are interested in using this method, it is important that you read about how it has been used in the classic studies that are commonly cited as examples of its use: Cressey's (1953) work on embezzling, Lindesmith's (1947) work on opiate addiction, Becker's (1963) work on marijuana use, and Manning's (1971) work on abortion.

A BIT OF HISTORY

Since analytic induction is an unfamiliar method in information and library science (ILS), a brief history is necessary. Analytic induction has primarily been a sociological method. Within that field, it has had an interesting development as far as accepted appropriate applications of the method are concerned. Induction in general has been used to make sense of data and observation since ancient times, but sociologist Florian Znaniecki is most often cited for formalizing and naming analytic induction.

In the early twentieth century, Znaniecki (1934a, 1934b) made sweeping claims for the powers of analytic induction. He proposed analytic induction as a method of deriving certain proof and cause from qualitative data. He claimed that analytic induction was superior to enumerative (statistical) approaches, which deal in probability, because analytic induction results in theories, hypotheses, or definitions that apply, with certainty, to all cases. Most of the criticisms of analytic induction rightly stem from these extreme claims.

Several criticisms have been leveled against analytic induction. Robinson (1951) identified a gaping hole in Znaniecki's original description of the method. In this description, only cases that were examples of the phenomenon would be examined. As discussed previously, this design provides no evidence of an adequate explanation of the phenomenon of interest. The classic analytic induction studies did not follow Znaniecki on this point. They examined nonexamples of the phenomena at hand to arrive at explanations that were specific to their questions.

Znaniecki claimed that analytic induction could prove the cause of a phenomenon with certainty. This is overreaching as the method can only truly identify sequential patterns or co-occurring conditions (Robinson, 1951). This does not mean that analytic induction is not a useful tool for exploring possible causation. Remember that statistical techniques, such as correlation, can only tell us about patterns or relationships, but they are virtually unanimously regarded as useful and acceptable (Lindesmith, 1952).

If analytic induction does not determine causation, as Znaniecki claimed, what does it do? An undisputed strength of the method is in developing clear and specific definitions of phenomena and in identifying different types of phenomena (Turner, 1953). The method has been criticized for resulting only in definitions (Goldenberg, 1993; Robinson, 1952), with the implication that such results are simplistic or frivolous. Others feel that there is value in rigorously defining or describing a phenomenon, even if you can predict or prove nothing with your findings.

Bear in mind that analytic induction is a qualitative analysis method that emerged before such methods began to be more accepted and commonly used in the late 1970s and early 1980s. Qualitative and quantitative methodologies have different assumptions and requirements. To judge one on the basis of the other is of little use. The problem with analytic induction is that Znaniecki (1934a, 1934b) wrote that it was the "true method" of science, and that, done correctly, it should replace the traditional enumerative induction methods used in sociology at the time. This statement is sure to annoy quantitatively oriented researchers, and by the criteria of empirical experimental design and statistical analysis, analytic induction hardly looks scientific. It does not use representative sampling (Robinson, 1951), and its findings cannot be generalized in the typical manner (Goldenberg, 1993). Williams (2000) made a case for a limited and appropriate type of generalization from qualitative inquiry, called *moderatum generalization*, and discussed the generalizability of analytic induction in a more even-handed manner.

Robinson (1951) suggested that since analytic induction could not replace enumerative methods, it should be combined with them. Years later, Miller (1982) described how this could be done. Lindesmith (1952) claimed that analytic induction was not supposed to replace or be combined with enumerative induction because the two approaches work for different types of questions and have different places in the research process. He suggested that analytic induction be used as a preliminary to an enumerative approach to the same phenomenon. Thus analytic induction's definitions and hypotheses can be used to design strong experiments for empirical hypothesis testing (Turner, 1953).

Most researchers who have used analytic induction have not perpetuated Znaniecki's claims for the power of the method. Instead, its use has been more moderate. Also, modifications have been introduced to the method by various researchers to address particular criticisms or concerns in their own work. Today, analytic induction seems to enjoy general acceptance as an exploratory method or when used within the interpretive paradigm. Denzin (1989) recommended it as a way to achieve a triangulation of methods. Be aware, however, that there are still some methodological purists who will discount any research that is not in line with their views. They seem to be relatively rare in ILS, however.

CHALLENGES IN USING ANALYTIC INDUCTION

The issue of when to stop examining more cases in a rigorous application of analytic induction is a difficult one. Even armed with much knowledge of the phenomenon, it is impossible for a researcher to know where all negative cases might be lurking. It is impossible to examine all cases that are examples of a phenomenon, so the idea of examining all existing cases that are *not* examples of a phenomenon is even more ridiculous. In modified form, analytic induction may used be to find explanations for all cases in a given sample. A carefully chosen sample bounds the number of cases that you will examine.

Denzin (1989) noted that analytic induction has difficulty accounting for continuous variables. Our preceding example was concerned with use and nonuse of the library's print journal collection. Either students use the collection, or they do not. This is a binary distinction that works well in analytic induction. In real life, however, few things are so clear-cut. Consider the issue that arises if we want to study some aspect of how frequent users of the collection work with library resources. There is no clear and natural distinction between frequent and nonfrequent users. It is difficult to take into account a continuous variable like frequency of library use without introducing quantitative measures. Such measures violate the purely qualitative nature of rigorous analytic induction. Your research design and data-gathering techniques should account for this.

Perhaps analytic induction's greatest strength as a method is that the researcher analyzes all cases in great depth. Achieving results inclusive of all cases requires many iterations of intensive analysis. This aspect also proves to be one of the challenges with applying analytic induction: the method requires a considerable investment of time and effort. Only relatively small numbers of cases can realistically be considered. Rettig et al. (1996) cautioned that "researchers who intend to use analytic induction should be prepared for its time intensiveness and the resulting mental exhaustion that may occur" (p. 217). When designing your project, be sure not to overestimate how many cases you will be able to consider.

Writing the results of your analytic induction may be challenging. First, the nature of analytic induction results in research reports is very different from the results you're used to reading. Manning (1982) explained that "the 'public' readjustment of definitions, concepts, and hypotheses is in a sense an intrinsic feature of the approach" (p. 233).

The traditional method of describing the analytic induction process involves showing how your initial and subsequent ideas were wrong and were adjusted in the course of the study. Understandably, some feel uncomfortable with this transparency in writing a research report. Second, describing any qualitative, inductive analysis process in such a way that your thought processes can be followed by a reader is a difficult task. This is especially true when there are length restrictions on your write-up, as is the case with most journal articles. Third, you should not expect the hypotheses and definitions that result from analytic induction to be short, simple statements. Because of the qualifications and specifications that arise in the process of analytic induction, your findings may require paragraphs to state clearly.

Finally, analytic induction has been used relatively infrequently, especially in ILS. Because of this, you should be prepared to write a stronger rationale for using the method than you would with more well-known methods. If you use analytic induction, you will need to be able to explain what it is and why you used it. If you use a modified analytic induction approach, you should state how your approach is different from traditional analytic induction and what the implications of your modifications are. Your background reading on the method will be of value here. Informed by the classic examples and the methodological dialogue from the literature, you should be able to explain your choice of method and how you applied it.

EXAMPLES

Analytic induction does not seem to be currently or historically used in ILS. However, we believe that analytic induction may be a potentially useful technique for the analysis of qualitative data in our field. For this reason, we would like to include it here. To do this, we will discuss two examples that use analytic induction in other social science disciplines.

Example 1: The Role of Dynamic Capabilities in E-Business Transformation

This paper (Daniel & Wilson, 2003) is from the domain of management of information systems, a domain that is closely related to ILS. The overall research question of the study was, How do organizations make successful e-business transformations? In this case, the organizations were brick-and-mortar businesses that developed and implemented e-business plans to complement their extant traditional businesses. In this multiple case study, researchers conducted semistructured interviews with 13 managers from five businesses. Analytic induction was used to analyze the transcripts of those interviews. The researchers were looking for a set of core qualities or practices present in traditional businesses that allowed them to successfully add e-business to their structure. As discussed previously, analytic induction is good for developing explanations of what is necessary for a phenomenon to occur a certain way.

The researchers found theories from related domains that could be logically combined in a particular way to describe the process of e-business transformation. The study then tested whether this hybrid theory fit the new hybrid business situation. Exploration of whether or not a theory is a good description of the actual phenomenon is a good use of analytic induction. If theory does not fit, the negative cases allow the researcher to modify the theory. This is an example of analytic induction's theory generation and testing capabilities.

The businesses included in this study were carefully chosen to maximize the chances for discovery of negative cases. Management and business theory outlines various dimensions or qualities that influence an organization's ability to adapt to change. The five businesses in the sample were purposefully chosen to represent different positions on the various dimensions known to be salient in e-business. This fulfills analytic induction's requirement of diversifying the cases examined to attempt to find negative cases.

The authors explain their choice of method and summarize the overall steps of the method. To do this, they adapt Cressey's summary of the steps of analytic induction to the context of their study. The study identified eight distinct capabilities and five practices in the cases. Not all capabilities and practices identified were present in all cases, but the conclusion of the paper draws together inferences that applied to all cases, which is required by analytic induction.

This article is clear and informative about why analytic induction was used as a method, how cases were chosen, and the findings that emerged from the data. It is relatively murky, however, about the precise logical steps used to arrive at those findings. Earlier studies employing analytic induction tend to be clear about the theory and definition modification process at each step of the analysis. For instance, Cressey's (1950, 1953) work on embezzlement begins by explaining the initial hypothesis and why it was made. From there, the reader can follow his line of thought through the analysis. Later studies follow a more ethnographic, narrative reporting convention (Katz, 2001). As mentioned previously, it is a challenge to write a transparent account of the analytic induction process in the space allotted in a typical journal article.

Daniel and Wilson (2003) clearly state the limitations of this study. One of the weaknesses of analytic induction is that only limited numbers of cases may be analyzed. Each additional case may provide a valuable chance to refine the findings of the analysis. Since the researchers must, at some point, cease collecting data and performing analysis, there is always a chance that an important case has been missed. Positioning such a study as exploratory and in need of further research to refine and extend the findings is wise.

This study is somewhat distant from core work in ILS; however, it is easy to see how such methods could apply to case studies of transformations in libraries. For example, you might ask what practices or capabilities lead to successful ILS system migrations? Or to successful implementation of chat reference services? There are also other broad *how* questions in ILS that could be informed by analytic induction. How do people make relevance judgments? How is knowledge created and shared within organizations? While analytic induction is unlikely to provide us with acceptable final answers for any of these questions, it may be a useful exploratory method for developing definitions of phenomena that we can build on and test further.

Example 2: Using Pattern Matching and Modified Analytic Induction in Examining Justice Principles in Child Support Guidelines

This paper (Rettig et al., 1996) is even further away from the core subject matter of ILS but is included here for two reasons. First, it is an example of a not-so-rigorous form of analytic induction, as discussed previously. The authors identify it as "modified analytic induction." Second, the paper reports the use of analytic induction for the refinement of definitions for use in a research project. This early methodological stage of research is not commonly written about and published in journals, so this paper offers a peek into the process of using analytic induction at a preliminary stage in research. This is a stage at which this method may be of use to ILS researchers.

This example is a methodological piece of a larger study investigating the perceived injustices of child support guidelines and the child support system. This paper is mainly concerned with problems of theoretical definitions for use in the research study. It draws on the theory of both procedural justice and distributive justice. Each of these bodies of theory includes a typology of justice principles, and the two typologies overlap. For the purposes of their larger research project, the researchers needed to code informant perceptions of injustice into the proper types of injustice for analysis. To facilitate this, the definitions and boundaries of the different justice types and principles required clear delineation. Analytic induction was used as one method for clarifying these definitions.

This application of analytic induction differs from classical, rigorous analytic induction in two main ways. First, the sample for this study consisted of quotations describing perceptions of injustice. These quotes were extracted from transcriptions of taped public hearings on how child support guidelines affected parents and children. All of the quotations in the sample were analyzed, but since the overall study was not an emergent design—the researchers developed their research question after learning about the existence of this data—there was no option to find more negative cases to test against the definitions. As mentioned earlier, classic analytic induction depends on theoretical sampling, in which decisions about which cases to include in the sample continue to be made throughout the analysis.

Second, Rettig et al. (1996) did not use the entire process of analytic induction. It does not result in a hypothesis inclusive of all cases explaining when injustice is perceived. The researchers state that they are not looking for causes and do not intend their definitions to be universal. They used the method of analytic induction only to pare the definitions of different types of injustice to their necessary components and to identify the quotations that do not fit into the theoretical definitions. This demonstrates that, depending on your research goals, you may not need to use the entire process of rigorous classical analytic induction to achieve results. Decisions on how to use or modify the method should be informed and well reasoned. An explanation of any modifications or omissions of steps should be included in the write-up of your project.

Finally, this is another example of the use of analytic induction to test theory. In our previous example, analytic induction was used to bridge two bodies of theory, generate new theory to connect them, and test whether that theory applied in selected cases. Again, we have two bodies of theory—procedural justice theory and distributive justice theory—that have not been combined in this way before. In this case, analytic induction was used as a way to begin to reconcile the two complementary but overlapping bodies of theory in such a way that theory-based definitions can be used in further research.

Rettig et al. (1996) intended to use analytic induction to a fuller extent but reported stopping the analysis sooner than expected due to the time and labor intensity of the method, illustrating one of the problems with the method. This difficulty could be due to the large number of quotations in the sample as well as the number of definitions to be examined and refined. In doing analytic induction, you will delve deeply into rich qualitative data, so you must be realistic about how many cases you will be able to examine within the time you have for conducting your research.

CONCLUSION

As noted previously, analytic induction is an analysis method that has not been used in ILS studies yet. However, it holds promise for application to research questions in our field. We are often working with qualitative data. We often are trying to develop definitions or examine hypotheses from these qualitative data. Its rigorous examination of both positive and negative cases of a phenomenon make analytic induction a valuable, though labor-intensive, tool for ILS research.

WORKS CITED

Becker, H. S. (1963). *Outsiders: Studies in the Sociology of Deviance*. New York: Free Press.

Becker, H. S. (1998). *Tricks of the Trade*. Chicago: University of Chicago Press.

Cressey, D. R. (1950). *Criminal violation of financial trust*. Unpublished doctoral dissertation, Indiana University.

Cressey, D. R. (1953). *Other People's Money*. Glencoe, IL: Free Press.

Daniel, E. M., & Wilson, H. N. (2003). The role of dynamic capabilities in e-business transformation. *European Journal of Information Systems*, *12*, 282–296.

Denzin, N. K. (1989). *The Research Act: A Theoretical Introduction to Sociological Methods*. Englewood Cliffs, NJ: Prentice Hall.

Goldenberg, S. (1993). Analytic induction revisited. *Canadian Journal of Sociology*, *18*(2), 161–176.

Goodman, N. (1955). *Fact, Fiction, and Forecast*. Cambridge, MA: Harvard University Press.

Katz, J. (2001). Analytic induction. In N. J. Smelser & P. B. Baltes (Eds.), *International Encyclopedia of the Social and Behavioral Sciences* (pp. 480–484). New York: Elsevier.

Lindesmith, A. (1947). *Opiate Addiction*. Bloomington, IN: Principia Press.

Lindesmith, A. (1952). Two comments on W. S. Robinson's "The logical structure of analytic induction." *American Sociological Review*, *17*, 492–493.

Manning, P. K. (1971). Fixing what you feared: Notes on the campus abortion search. In J. Henslin (Ed.), *The Sociology of Sex* (pp. 137–166). New York: Appleton-Century-Crofts.

Manning, P. K. (1982). Analytic induction. In R. B. Smith & P. K. Manning (Eds.), *A Handbook of Social Science Methods* (Vol. 2, pp. 273–302). Cambridge, MA: Ballinger.

Miller, S. I. (1982). Quality and quantity: Another view of analytic induction as a research technique. *Quality and Quantity*, *16*, 281–295.

Rettig, K. D., Tam, V. C.-W., & Magistad, B. M. (1996). Using pattern matching and modified analytic induction in examining justice principles in child support guidelines. *Marriage and Family Review*, *24*(1–2), 193–222.

Robinson, W. S. (1951). The logical structure of analytic induction. *American Sociological Review*, *16*, 812–818.

Robinson, W. S. (1952). Rejoinder to the logical structure of analytic induction. *American Sociological Review*, *17*, 492–494.

Turner, R. H. (1953). The quest for universals in sociological research. *American Sociological Review*, *18*, 604–611.

Williams, M. (2000). Interpretivism and generalization. *Sociology*, *34*, 209–224.

Znaniecki, F. (1934a). Analytic induction. In F. Znaniecki (Ed.), *On Humanistic Sociology* (pp. 125–132). Chicago: University of Chicago Press.

Znaniecki, F. (1934b). *The Method of Sociology*. New York: Farrar and Rinehart.

33

Descriptive Statistics

Barbara M. Wildemuth

Like dreams, statistics are a form of wish fulfillment.

—Jean Baudrillard (1990)

DESCRIBING A PHENOMENON WITH STATISTICS

When you first develop your research question and plan the way you will carry out your study, you should also plan your data analysis, "proceed[ing] logically from purpose to measurement to analysis to conclusions" (Spirer et al., 1998, p. 13). One of the first steps in your data analysis is to summarize your results; this is the role of descriptive statistics. In this chapter, we will focus on describing the results related to a single variable; for example, you may want to know how much Internet experience the college students in your sample have.

There are a number of statistics you can use for summarizing data. The simplest is a frequency distribution. Since handling this type of data is the basis for creating and evaluating contingency tables, frequency distributions are discussed with cross-tabulation and chi-square analysis in the next chapter. Here we will focus on two types of statistics. The first type focuses on how the values of a particular variable cluster together; these statistics are called *measures of central tendency*. The second type focuses on how the values of a particular variable spread apart and are called *measures of dispersion* (Weaver, 1989). Each of these two types of statistics will be discussed, after a review of what we mean by variables and their levels of measurement.

VARIABLES AND THEIR LEVELS OF MEASUREMENT

A *variable* is a property of an object, person, or event that can take on different values (Howell, 2004); that is, its value can vary. Variables can be defined and operationalized at different levels of measurement. A variable's level of measurement is a mathematical characteristic (Healey, 2007) and tells us which types of analysis can be performed on that variable. There are four possible levels of measurement: nominal, ordinal, interval, and ratio.

Nominal variables (also called categorical variables) are those whose possible values are categories, with no true numerical value that can be assigned to them. Each category is named, but even if its name is a number, you can't perform any arithmetic operations on it. Some common examples of nominal variables include sex (in which the possible values are male and female), country of origin (in which the possible values are country names), or Internet browser being used to access a Web site (in which the possible values are browser names). The set of possible values for a particular nominal variable must be both exhaustive and mutually exclusive. In other words, every observation must fit into one, and only one, category.

Ordinal variables are those for which the "values can be rank ordered" (Bernard, 2000, p. 43). Some common examples of ordinal variables include your study participants' levels of education (e.g., grade school, high school, college, etc.) or their rankings of their favorite online bookstores (e.g., Amazon ranked as 1, Barnes & Noble as 2, etc.). In each of these cases, you can see that the different observations can be put in order—the hallmark of an ordinal variable. You should also be sure to notice that the distance between the variable's possible values is not necessarily uniform. For example, one person may like Amazon much better than Barnes & Noble, while another person may see them as almost exactly the same, with only a slight preference for Amazon.

Interval variables are also ordered but have the advantage of a uniform distance between the possible values. The most common example of an interval-level variable is a rating scale. To understand the idea of equal intervals, imagine a 5-point rating scale to measure your attitudes toward an online class you just completed. By saying that this is an interval scale, I am arguing that 1 is as far from 2 as 2 is from 3, and so forth through the whole scale. With such variables, we can perform some basic arithmetic operations (addition and subtraction), thus supporting a variety of data analysis methods.

Ratio-level variables, in addition to being ordered and having values at equal intervals, "have a true zero point" (Bernard, 2000, p. 43). With these variables, ratios can be calculated (Howell, 2004). For example, age is a ratio-level variable; thus saying that I am twice as old as you is a sensible statement. Such statements cannot be made about interval-level variables. Ratio-level variables support the widest possible range of data analysis methods.

MEASURES OF CENTRAL TENDENCY

It is ideal if you can calculate or identify one number that summarizes your entire data set. Thus measures of central tendency are "concerned with identifying a typical value that best summarizes the distribution of values in a variable" (David & Sutton, 2004, p. 272). There are three measures of central tendency from which you can choose: the mean, the median, and the mode. Your choice of which one of these to use will be primarily based on the level of measurement of the variable you're trying to summarize. If you have only nominal data, you can only use the mode. If you have ordinal data, the median is most commonly used, though the mode is also a possibility. If you have interval or ratio data, you can use any of the three, but the mean is the most commonly used. Each of these three measures is described here, followed by a further discussion about their relative strengths and weaknesses.

Mean

The mean is likely to be familiar to you. It is "the sum of the individual scores in a distribution, divided by the number of scores" (Bernard, 2000, p. 512). In other words, it is the average score or value for the variable that you're trying to summarize. The primary advantage (and disadvantage) of the mean is that it takes every observation into account. This characteristic is an advantage because it allows the mean to represent all the observations collected. It is a disadvantage if a few of the observations were very extreme. For example, if you are collecting data on a group of 30 college students, and 2 of them are nontraditional students and over 50 years old, your calculation of the mean age of the group will be skewed. Such extreme scores are called outliers, and you will need to decide whether it makes more sense to include them in your data analysis or exclude them.

Median

The median is "the middle value when all the valid values for a variable are placed in ascending order" (David & Sutton, 2004, p. 272). In other words, if you put all the observations in order, half of the values would be above the median and half below the median (Bernard, 2000; Howell, 2004). The median may also be called the fiftieth percentile, because 50 percent of the values are below it. If you are working with ordinal data, then the median is your best choice. It may also be appropriate for interval or ratio data, particularly if there are outliers in your data set.

Mode

The mode is the value that occurs most frequently among your observations. Ideally, there is only one mode in your data set, and it is near the center of the distribution of scores. However, there may be two modes if two different values occur with the same frequency. This is called a bimodal distribution. It's also possible that there is no mode, if each value occurs only once. The mode is the weakest measure of central tendency but is the only appropriate one if you are working with nominal data. It is usually reported as the proportion of the sample with that value of the variable.

Choosing which Measure of Central Tendency to use

Except in very rare cases, the three measures will differ in value (see Gross & Saxton, 2002, table 1, for a display of all three from the same data set); thus you will need to select which one best summarizes your data set. Examine all of them that are available to you (i.e., that are appropriate for the level of measurement of the variable you're summarizing). If you are working with nominal data, your only choice is the mode. If you are working with ordinal data, you may use the mode or the median. If you are working with interval or ratio data, you may use any of the three (Healey, 2007).

Next, consider the characteristics of each and what it can tell you about your data set. The mean is the most stable estimate of the population central tendency. Means calculated from different samples will vary less than medians from those samples or modes from those samples. The mean is also the easiest to incorporate into further data analysis because it can be incorporated directly into algebraic formulae (Howell, 2004).

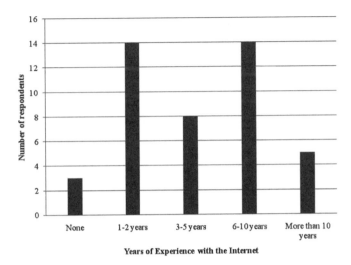

Figure 33.1. Example of a bimodal distribution.

However, as noted earlier, the mean can be skewed if there are some outliers in your sample. A few outliers with low values will negatively skew the distribution; a few outliers with high values will positively skew the distribution. In either case, you will need to compare the median and the mean to see if the mean remains a good measure of central tendency. If the distribution is highly skewed, the median may be a better choice.

The biggest advantage to the mode is that it is an actual score from an observation in your sample. Also, like the median, it is not affected by outliers. In addition, if the distribution is bimodal, like that shown in Figure 33.1, then the two modes are a better summarization of the data set than either the mean or the median. In this example, using the median (the only other alternative for this ordinal data) would not be as accurate a summarization of the data set as reporting that 14 people had used the Internet for 1 to 2 years and 14 for 6 to 10 years, making up 64 percent of the entire sample.

MEASURES OF DISPERSION

While an accurate measure of central tendency is the best single-number summarization of your data set, most people interested in your research will also want to know how far the scores spread out around that central point (Rubin, 2007). For this purpose, you will want to report a measure of dispersion for each variable. If you've already selected the measure of central tendency that is most appropriate, your decision about which measure of dispersion to report will follow from that earlier decision. If you chose to use the mode or the median, you'll want to use the range or interquartile range as a measure of dispersion. If you chose to use the mean, you'll want to report the standard deviation, which is calculated from the distribution's variance. In addition to describing these measures of dispersion, this section will also touch on confidence intervals, a way to represent the confidence you have in the accuracy with which you can predict the population statistics from your sample statistics.[1]

Range and Interquartile Range

The range is "the distance from the lowest to the highest score" (Howell, 2004, p. 76), calculated by subtracting the lowest value from the highest value in your data set. It is particularly useful as a measure of dispersion for ordinal data. However, if your data set includes some outliers, you may want to report the interquartile range instead. The interquartile range is "the range of the middle 50% of the observations" (Howell, 2004, p. 76). It is the difference between the value at the twenty-fifth percentile and the value at the seventy-fifth percentile. (You may recall the concept of a percentile from your college admissions tests; if you were at the ninetieth percentile, it meant that 90 percent of the students taking the test scored lower than you did.)

Variance and Standard Deviation

If you are using the mean as a measure of central tendency, then you will want to report the standard deviation as a measure of dispersion. The standard deviation is the square root of the variance of the distribution. The variance is the "average squared deviation from the mean" (Bernard, 2000, p. 526); to calculate it, you subtract the mean from each individual score, square that result, and average all those individual squared results. Unfortunately, this method of calculation leaves us with "squared" units that are difficult to understand. For example, if you were reporting on the years of work experience among systems analysts in large corporations, and your sample of study participants had worked an average of 8.5 years, the variance would be "squared" years. By reporting the square root of the variance—the standard deviation—you are back in your original metric, years. If there were a lot of variation among your respondents, the standard deviation could be something like 7.8 years; if there were very little variation, it might be something like 1.3 years. This "unsquaring" step (Rubin, 2007) makes the standard deviation relatively straightforward to interpret as a measure of dispersion.

Confidence Intervals

At times, you want to be able to say that, based on your sample mean, you predict that the mean of the population of interest is within a certain range. In addition, you'd like to be able to report the level of confidence you have in the accuracy of your prediction. Confidence intervals will help you do this. A confidence interval is "an estimated range of values with a given high probability of covering the true population value" (Hays, 1988, p. 206). The confidence interval calculated based on any particular sample can be thought of as the range of "good" estimates of the population parameter of interest.

The standard error is used to calculate the confidence interval (Phillips, 1999). If you drew multiple samples from a particular population and calculated the mean for each sample, you could then analyze this set of means. The standard deviation of this set of means is the standard error. Using the standard error as a measure of dispersion for the sample means, you could make a statement such as, "I can predict, with 95 percent confidence, that the mean of the population is between 5.8 and 7.3." This statement is based on the mean from your study sample and the confidence intervals around it. You can narrow the confidence interval by increasing your sample size (Hays, 1988).

Table 33.1. Frequency of communication between distance learners

	Mean	Median
Month 1	14	8
Month 2	20	13
Month 3	21	10
All three months	50	24

SUMMARY

When you begin to analyze the data from your study, you will need to summarize it with a few simple statistics. You should include at least one measure of central tendency (the mean, the median, or the mode) and one measure of dispersion (standard deviation or range). These two statistics will help you to interpret your findings so that you can draw valid conclusions from the data. In addition, you may want to use graphs to represent your findings. A variety of basic charts and graphs are reviewed in the next chapter, on frequency distributions, so that discussion will not be repeated here.

EXAMPLES

Three example studies are discussed here, focusing on one variable from each study. We will emphasize the way in which the descriptive statistics are reported for these selected variables. The first example, from a study of communication patterns among distance education students (Haythornthwaite, 1998), reports both the mean and median frequency with which pairs of students communicated during the course of a semester. In the second example (Weise & McMullen, 2001), a variety of statistics about the compensation of systems librarians in medical libraries are reported. They include both measures of central tendency and measures of dispersion. The third example (Carter & Janes, 2000) reports on the time required to respond to reference questions posed to the Internet Public Library and uses both descriptive statistics and a chart to report their findings. It is recommended that you examine the tables and figures in each example, as you review this discussion of their use of descriptive statistics.

Example 1: Communication Patterns among Distance Education Students

Haythornthwaite (1998)[2] examined the social networks that developed among 14 distance education students enrolled at the University of Illinois at Urbana-Champaign. For analysis, the data were organized into 182 pairs among these students. The students were asked how often, within the past month, they had worked with another class member on class work, received or given information or advice about class work, socialized with another class member, and exchanged emotional support with another class member. For our purposes here, we will closely examine a portion of the data reported in Haythornthwaite's (1998) first table because it is typical of the data reported throughout the paper.

Table 33.1 includes both the mean frequency of communication and the median frequency of communication for each month and for the three-month period. Note that all the median values are lower than the mean values. This tendency would indicate that the distribution of communication frequency is skewed positively; in other words, some members of the class communicated much more frequently than the majority of the class members. No measure of dispersion is reported. Thus we can only guess at the shape of the distribution on this variable (i.e., communication frequency).

In this article, the results were complex and multifaceted. Thus the author provided less detail about each variable than might ordinarily be recommended. Means and medians were routinely reported, but no measures of dispersion were provided, nor were any graphs provided to help us visualize the distribution of the data on each variable. In a simpler study, with fewer variables, it would be expected that more descriptive statistics would be provided.

Example 2: Compensation for Systems Librarians in Medical Libraries

Weise and McMullen (2001)[3] studied the compensation of medical library professionals performing information technology (IT)-related roles. Fourteen "model" jobs were defined (e.g., reference librarian and systems librarian), and a survey related to these jobs was distributed to 550 medical library directors. Of those, 179 surveys were returned and analyzed. A compensation data table was created for each of the model jobs; the table for the systems librarian job is reported as table 1 in the Weise and McMullen (2001) article. An excerpt from it is included here, as Table 33.2, and will be discussed.

This is a very complex table, loaded with information. Though it's broken down by type of library (hospitals versus academic medical centers) and size of library (small, medium, and large, based on staff size), we'll focus our attention on the first row of the table, which reports data for "all participants." First, it indicates that 42 organizations responded, with 50.8 incumbents in systems librarian positions. The next several columns provide descriptive statistics for the base salary for systems librarians. The twenty-fifth, fiftieth, and seventy-fifth percentiles are reported as well as the mean. As expected, the fiftieth percentile (i.e., the median) did not match the mean exactly: the median was $38,000, and the mean was $39,934. These two figures would indicate a slight positive skew in this distribution; you can tell that it's only a slight skew because the mean is fairly well centered in the interquartile range (bounded by the twenty-fifth percentile salary of $32,000 and the seventy-fifth percentile salary of $45,000).

The survey respondents were asked about the proportion of time spent doing IT work; the median value for systems librarians is reported as 95 percent. The next two columns examine the relationship between base salary and amount of time spent doing IT work. The mean base salary was calculated, separately, for those with a light concentration on IT work (less than 25% of time spent on IT work) and those with a heavy concentration on IT work (greater than 25%). The cutoff point of 25 percent was selected because it was the median for all respondents for all 14 model jobs. For the systems librarians, the "light" column is empty, presumably because there were no cases to average. The "heavy" column shows an average base salary of $41,078, slightly higher than the systems librarians overall. It is not clear why this figure differed from the mean for all systems librarians. The final column of the table reports the percentage of systems librarians who have some responsibility for managing people. This figure was 24 percent.

The complete table in the Weise and McMullen (2001) article provides rich data concerning base salaries for a particular job in a medical library setting. It includes two measures of central tendency (mean and median) for the base salary as well as a measure

Table 33.2. Excerpts from "Systems librarian" (Weise & McMullen, 2001, table 1). Reprinted with permission from *The Journal of the Medical Library Association*.

	No. of organizations	No. of incumbents	Base salary				Median time in IT work	Average base salary by time in IT work		% of jobs managing people
			P25	P50	P75	Average		Light	Heavy	
All participants	42	50.8	$32,000	$38,000	$45,000	$39,934	95%		$41,078	24%
Hospitals										
All hospitals										
1–2 medical library staff (FTEs)										
3–5 medical library staff (FTEs)										
6+ medical library staff (FTEs)										
Academic medical centers										
All academic medical centers										
...										

of dispersion (interquartile range). In addition to the base salary data, it provides data on several variables expected to affect base salary such as the amount of time spent performing IT work and whether the librarian has responsibility for managing others. This well-designed table can serve as an example of how to provide a large amount of data compactly.

Example 3: Time Spent Answering Digital Reference Questions

Carter and Janes (2000) analyzed the logs of over 3,000 questions posed to the Internet Public Library in early 1999. They investigated the questions asked, the ways those questions were handled, and whether/how they were answered or rejected. We will focus our discussion on their analysis of the time required to answer those questions; these results are reported in table 11 and figure 1 of their paper.

Patrons of the Internet Public Library are promised that they will receive a response to their questions within one week, so the time required to respond to questions was an important operational question to examine. On average, it took 2.96 days to answer a question (the mean reported with figure 1). The figure also indicates that the standard deviation of this variable was 2.70, indicating a fairly wide range of variability. This variability is further illustrated in the figure, which charts the number of questions answered within each daylong time interval.

The accompanying table reports the mean and standard deviation (duplicating the information reported with the figure). It also provides the twenty-fifth and seventy-fifth percentiles and the median. The median of 2.05 days can be compared with the mean of 2.96 days, and we can conclude that the distribution is positively skewed (a conclusion supported by the chart in figure 1). In addition, a statistic indicating the amount of skew is reported in the table.

In summary, this paper reports two measures of central tendency (mean and median) for this variable as well as measures of dispersion (standard deviation and interquartile range). From these statistics, we get a very clear picture of how much time it took to respond to this sample of digital reference questions.

CONCLUSION

Descriptive statistics are the most essential view of your study findings and so are critical components of any report of your research. For each variable of interest, you should report both a measure of central tendency (the mean, the median, or the mode) and a measure of dispersion (standard deviation, range, or interquartile range). While it is likely that you will go on to do further statistical analyses, these basic measures are your starting point for understanding your findings and for communicating them to your audience.

NOTES

1. For more details on samples and populations, see Chapter 13, on sampling for extensive studies.

2. A closely related paper was the winner of the 1999 Bohdan S. Wynar Research Paper Competition administered by the Association for Library and Information Science Education.

3. This paper was the recipient of the 2003 Ida and George Eliot Prize administered by the Medical Library Association.

WORKS CITED

Baudrillard, J. (1990). *Cool Memories*. New York: Verso.

Bernard, H. R. (2000). *Social Research Methods: Qualitative and Quantitative Approaches*. Thousand Oaks, CA: Sage.

Carter, D. S., & Janes, J. (2000). Unobtrusive data analysis of digital reference questions and service at the Internet Public Library: An exploratory study. *Library Trends*, *49*(2), 251–265.

David, M., & Sutton, C. D. (2004). *Social Research: The Basics*. London: Sage.

Gross, M., & Saxton, M. L. (2002). Integrating the imposed query into the evaluation of reference service: A dichotomous analysis of user ratings. *Library and Information Science Research*, *24*(3), 251–263.

Hays, W. L. (1988). *Statistics* (4th ed.). Fort Worth, TX: Holt, Rinehart and Winston.

Haythornthwaite, C. (1998). A social network study of the growth of community among distance learners. *Information Research*, *4*(1), Article 49. Retrieved November 19, 2007, from http://informationr.net/ir/4-1/paper49.html.

Healey, J. F. (2007). *The Essentials of Statistics: A Tool for Social Research*. Belmont, CA: Thomson Wadsworth.

Howell, D. C. (2004). *Fundamental Statistics for the Behavioral Sciences* (5th ed.). Belmont, CA: Brooks / Cole.

Phillips, J. L. (1999). *How to Think about Statistics* (6th ed.). New York: W. H. Freeman.

Rubin, A. (2007). *Statistics for Evidence-based Practice and Evaluation*. Belmont, CA: Brooks / Cole.

Spirer, H. F., Spirer, L., & Jaffe, A. J. (1998). *Misused Statistics* (2nd ed.). New York: M. Dekker.

Weaver, D. H. (1989). Basic statistical tools. In G. H. Stempel III & B. H. Westley (Eds.), *Research Methods in Mass Communication* (pp. 49–89). Englewood Cliffs, NJ: Prentice Hall.

Weise, F. O., & McMullen, T. D. (2001). Study to assess the compensation and skills of medical library professionals relative to information technology professionals. *Bulletin of the Medical Library Association*, *89*(3), 249–262.

34

Frequencies, Cross-tabulation, and the Chi-square Statistic

Barbara M. Wildemuth

Science is feasible when the variables are few and can be enumerated; when their combinations are distinct and clear.

—Paul Valéry (1932/1970)

What is to be sought in designs for the display of information is the clear portrayal of complexity. Not the complication of the simple; rather the task of the design is to give visual access to the subtle and the difficult—that is, the revelation of the complex.

—Edward R. Tufte (1983)

FREQUENCY DISTRIBUTIONS

When analyzing nominal (i.e., categorical) data,[1] you most often will begin by counting "how many cases there are in a particular category of a particular variable" (Rubin, 2007, p. 32). These counts can then be organized and displayed in a table, referred to as a *frequency distribution* (Hafner, 1998).

You may also want to display the relative frequency of each category of the variable. These would be shown as the percentage of cases in each category. Percentages allow for easier comparison of two data sets, particularly if the sample sizes are not the same. You should calculate the relative frequencies of the categories only when your sample size is reasonably large; otherwise, they can be misleading (Rubin, 2007). For example, if you have a sample size of five, it can be misleading to say that 20 percent of the cases are in a particular category; that would be only a single case.

In situations where you have many categories for a particular variable, you may need to group them to help you interpret your findings. This will simplify your table of the frequency distribution, making it easier for both you and your audience to understand. However, be very careful in grouping categories together. Both Hays (1988) and Janes (2001) pointed out the dangers associated with grouping the categories during the data analysis phase (i.e., after the data have been collected and the original category definitions established). In particular, this type of post hoc grouping may disrupt the random selection that was incorporated into the original sampling plan. If you do decide that it's necessary to group the categories, make sure you have a strong rationale for each grouping and that each grouped category has a clear definition.

TWO-WAY FREQUENCY DISTRIBUTIONS: CROSS-TABULATION TABLES

Simple frequency distributions display the frequencies of the categories of a single variable. This idea can be extended to a two-way table (also called a cross-tabulation table, a contingency table, or a bivariate table), with the categories of one variable shown as rows and the categories of a second variable shown as columns. In this way, the relationship between the two variables can be described. In each cell of the table, you would report the number of cases that belong in that cell (i.e., the number of cases that fit in that particular category of each of the two variables). You may also want to report the relative frequency (i.e., percentage) in each cell.

Designing informative tables takes careful thought. Wainer (1997) suggested three guidelines for the design of useful tables. First, you should consider the order of the rows and columns. You will want to "order the rows and columns in a way that makes sense" (p. 96). Second, you will want to round the numbers off to a point where they can be easily interpreted. With simple frequency counts, you will display only integers. With the percentages, report only one decimal place (e.g., 33.3% for one-third of the cases). Finally, you should provide a meaningful summary of each row and column. Usually, this will consist of a total for each row (shown in the rightmost column) and a total for each column (shown in the bottom row), plus a grand total of all the cases/observations. These totals are usually called marginal totals because they appear at the margins of the table.

THE CHI-SQUARE STATISTIC

A frequency distribution table describes the data you have collected, but just viewing the table doesn't tell you whether a relationship exists between two variables (or, in the case of a one-way table, whether the cases are distributed as expected). For this purpose, you can use the chi-square statistic,[2] which tests whether the frequency distribution is likely to occur by chance. If it is unlikely to occur by chance, then you can conclude that there is an underlying relationship between the variables that is the basis for the frequency distribution you observed.

The *chi-square statistic* "measures the difference between what was observed and what would be expected in the general population" (Byrne, 2007, p. 41). Chi-square is calculated for each cell of the table, then summed to get the overall chi-square statistic. Your frequency distribution is the frequencies observed, so to calculate chi-square, you need to estimate the frequencies you would have expected if there were no relationship between the variables. These calculations are based on the marginal totals in the two-way table. For a particular cell, the row total and the column total, in combination, will tell you what proportion of the grand total you would expect to fall in that cell. You simply multiply the row total by the column total and divide by the total sample size (the grand total). In a one-way table, you would simply divide the grand total by the number of cells to test the hypothesis that the cases are evenly distributed over the variable's categories.

The next step is to subtract the cell's expected value from the observed value, square the difference, and then divide the squared difference by the expected value. This calculation will yield the value of chi-square for each cell. You then sum all these chi-square values to get the overall chi-square for the table.

Once you have the chi-square statistic, it can be used to test the null hypothesis that there is no relationship between the two variables or the hypothesis that the cases are distributed evenly over the variable categories in a one-way table. Any statistical analysis software will calculate the chi-square statistic, the degrees of freedom (df) associated with your table (a necessary component of the significance testing process), and the p value (i.e., the probability that you would be incorrect if you rejected the null hypothesis). Through these methods, you are really testing "the null hypothesis that the variables are independent in the population" (Healey, 2007, p. 236).

Unfortunately, while "chi-square tests are among the easiest for the novice in statistics to carry out, and they lend themselves to a wide variety of social and behavioral data . . . there is probably no other statistical method that has been so widely misapplied" (Hays, 1988, p. 780). I would urge caution in three particular areas. First, use of the chi-square statistic for hypothesis testing may not be valid if many of your table cells have expected values that are low (i.e., less than 5). If you are working with a two-row-by-two-column table, then you can use Fisher's exact test as a substitute for the chi-square test (Rubin, 2007). It provides an accurate estimate of the probability of observing the particular distribution you obtained. If you are working with a different size table, you may want to consider grouping categories to increase the expected frequencies in the table cells. However, keep in mind the warnings about grouping categories given previously. The second problem associated with the chi-square test of significance is that with a large enough sample size, you can detect relationships that are not really meaningful (Healey, 2007). The value of the chi-square statistic increases in proportion to sample size. So, even though the chi-square statistic increases to the point where you find a statistically significant result, you may not be able to interpret that relationship. As Denham (2002) notes, "with cross-tabulation and chi-square analysis, practically anything can prove 'significant' with enough observations" (p. 163). A final area in which you should exercise caution in using chi-square tests is in the interpretation of your findings. Using chi-square as a test of statistical significance is the first step, but it only tells you that a relationship is very likely to exist; it does not tell you anything about the nature of that relationship. Further examination of the individual cell values is needed to interpret the relationship. Examination of cell percentages in relation to column percentages is a useful tool for such interpretation (Healey, 2007).

VISUALIZATIONS OF YOUR DATA SET

Tables of the frequency of occurrence of particular categories provide you with a detailed summary of your data set, and the chi-square statistic can tell you the likelihood of a relationship between two variables. In addition, graphical representations may help both you and your audience more thoroughly understand that relationship. Graphical displays of data should show the data clearly, make large data sets coherent, present many numbers in a small space, and avoid distorting what the data have to say (Tufte, 1983). While graphs and charts are useful for visualization, they should, in most cases, be accompanied by the original statistics (the frequency distributions) that they're illustrating (Janes, 1999).

As Tufte (1983) notes, "at their best, graphics are instruments for reasoning about quantitative information" (p. 7). The most important reason to use graphs and charts is to help you understand your own data. Once you understand the data and can draw valid conclusions from it, you can use graphs and charts to communicate those conclusions to your readers (Howell, 2004). While it is easy to "lie" with charts and graphs (just as it is easy to "lie" with statistics), you should do your best to avoid distorting what the data have to say (Tufte, 1983; Wainer, 1997).

We'll first review some basic types of charts and graphs here. Pie charts and bar charts are most useful for displaying nominal or ordinal data. Histograms, line graphs, and box plots are more useful for interval or ratio data. The section will conclude with some suggestions for avoiding charts and graphs that misrepresent your data.

Pie Charts

The use of pie charts is most appropriate when you're trying to understand how a particular variable is distributed. As Janes (1999) notes, they're "useful for showing proportions, especially when there are not very many categories" (p. 403).

There are two situations in which you should avoid pie charts. The first is when you want to visualize the distribution of responses to a question where each respondent may have selected more than one of the response choices. For example, you may have conducted a survey that included a question such as, "Mark all those databases that you have used within the last week," followed by a list of 10 or more databases. From this question, you hope to find out which databases are used most frequently. However, because each person may have marked multiple databases, a pie chart is inappropriate; you should, instead, use a bar chart for displaying this data set. The second situation is when there are many possible values of a variable. Most authors (e.g., David & Sutton, 2004; Janes, 1999) recommend that pie charts be used to display no more than six categories. With more categories of data, the chart becomes so cluttered that it no longer communicates your findings clearly.

Bar Charts

Bar charts are very flexible in terms of being able to represent a variety of different types of distributions. They are particularly useful for making comparisons across categories or for seeing trends across categories or time periods. In a bar chart, each bar represents a category of the variable, and its length or height represents the number of instances in that category. In general, the categories are represented on the horizontal axis (i.e., the x axis) and the frequencies or percentages are represented on the vertical axis (i.e., the y axis). In designing a bar chart, be sure to put the categories along the x axis in a logical order (Hafner, 1998).

Histograms

A histogram is similar to a bar chart in appearance, but it is slightly different in meaning. The appearance differs in that the bars in the chart touch each other. This difference in appearance is meant to convey the idea that the variable on the x axis is a continuous variable,[3] with each bar representing an interval within the possible values

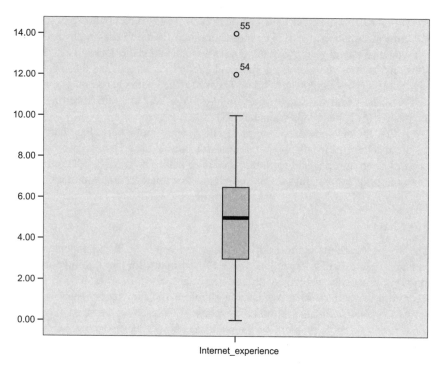

Figure 34.1. Box plot displaying level of Internet experience among 55 study participants.

of that variable. As with a bar chart, the length or height of the bar represents the number of observations within that interval.

Line Graphs

Line graphs can be used in place of either bar charts or histograms and are especially useful when there are more than five categories or intervals to be represented on the *x* axis. They are formed by placing a point on the *y* axis to represent the frequency or percentage observed at each point on the *x* axis, then connecting those points. Line graphs are an especially "effective way to show the general tendency of a variable to rise or fall" (Hafner, 1998, p. 107).

Box Plots

Box plots (also called box-and-whisker plots) can be used to visualize the central tendency and dispersion of a data set.[4] Because this type of visualization is less frequently used in information and library science, an example is shown in Figure 34.1. The variable depicted is Internet experience (in years). The questionnaire responses from 55 student participants are included in the graph. The dark bar in the middle of the box marks the median of the distribution (five years), and the edges of the box mark the interquartile range. The ends of the "whiskers" illustrate the range of the distribution, excluding the two outliers; participants 54 and 55 had much more Internet experience than the other study participants and are shown with individual dots.

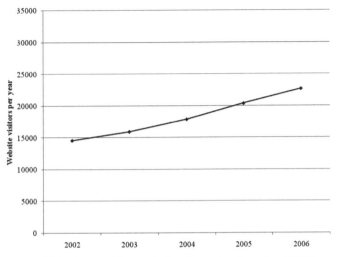

Figure 34.2. Graph with a vertical scale ranging from 0 to 35,000.

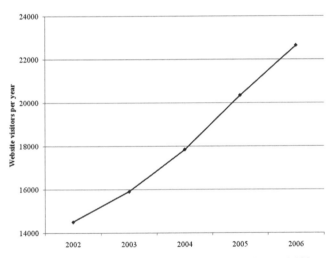

Figure 34.3. Graph with a vertical scale ranging from 14,000 to 24,000.

"Lying" with Graphs

Even though each of these charts is relatively straightforward, they are being misused whenever they do not aid the viewer in understanding the data set accurately. This problem can occur for a variety of reasons, almost all of them unintentional. One possible misuse is to develop a graph that is so complex that it hides the truth it is trying to reveal. Another possibility is that the developer of the graph has manipulated the vertical scale in a way that over- or understates the differences between categories. For example, compare the two graphs shown in Figures 34.2 and 34.3. They are based on exactly the same data; the only difference is in the scale used on the *y* axis. Yet the first graph seems to show that the increase in number of Web site visitors over time is only modest, and the second graph seems to show that the trend is sharply upward. You can only decide on the appropriate scale for the vertical axis of such a graph *after* you have concluded your analysis and are confident in the validity of your conclusions. A final misuse of graphs is to include two vertical axes on the same graph because it is almost impossible to make them unbiased. For example, Wainer (1997) uses simple transformations of a graph that demonstrates (in one version) that college entrance exam scores *are* related to spending in education and (in another version) that they *are not* related to spending in education. Just as the misuse of the vertical scale in any graph can lead the viewer to draw incorrect conclusions, this same problem is compounded when there are two vertical axes on the same graph.

EXAMPLES

Two of the examples we'll examine here are studies related to health information seeking behaviors. The third is a study of ways that Internet users can protect their privacy, and the fourth is a study of astronomers' reading patterns. Each of these examples illustrates an aspect of analyzing and reporting frequency distributions.

The first example (Harris et al., 2006) reports relative frequencies and uses a chi-square test to analyze them further. It does an excellent job of reporting the results of the chi-square tests in the text of the paper. The second example (Morey, 2007) reports frequencies and relative frequencies in a bivariate table and uses chi-square to examine the relationship between the two variables. It uses these findings to draw conclusions about the fit of the data to theories about the strength of weak ties in a social network. The third example (Wang et al., 2003) illustrates the ways in which frequency distributions can be displayed graphically. The fourth (Tenopir et al., 2005) uses a variety of tables and graphs (including bar charts and pie charts) to present the study results.

Example 1: Health Information Seeking in Canada

Harris et al. (2006) conducted semistructured phone interviews with 187 adults in a rural county in Ontario, Canada. Almost three-quarters (74%) of the respondents had "looked for medical or health information within the past year" (¶9). Those respondents were then asked about the sources of health information they used (with particular emphasis on Internet access and use, including the impact of government e-health initiatives) and how they use health information.

Throughout the paper, the relative frequency of each response is reported as a percentage of the respondents who used a particular source or used health information for a particular purpose. These data are reported in one-way tables. It would have been useful if the frequencies had also been reported.

Further statistical analyses included a chi-square test of the differences between men and women on their use of doctors and the Internet as information sources. The results of these analyses are presented clearly and concisely in the text: "Overall, there was no difference in the proportion of women and men who sought health information from a doctor ($\chi^2 = .124$, df $= 1$, p $= .725$) and no difference in the proportion of women and men who consulted a doctor (and no other source) for health information ($\chi^2 = .416$, df $= 1$, p $= .838$). However, the women who participated in the study were more likely than male respondents to have used the Internet to search for health information

Table 34.1. Excerpts from "Closeness of relationship for source of health information last six months" (Morey, 2007, table 6). Reprinted with permission of the author.

Source	Closeness of relationship							
	Very close		Somewhat close		Not close		Total	
	n	$\%$	n	$\%$	n	$\%$	n	$\%$
Health service professional								
Family living with								
...								
Librarian								
Coworker								
Total								

($\chi^2 = 4.28$, df $= 1$, p $= .039$)" (Harris et al., 2006, ¶11). This explanation of their findings can serve as a model for reporting the results of a chi-square test.

Example 2: Health Information Seeking in an African American Community

Morey (2007), in her study of health information seeking in an African American community, used social network theory to frame her research questions. In particular, she was interested in "the association between the source of health information as related to demographics and tie strength between individuals" (abstract). Like Harris and colleagues (2006), Morey (2007) collected her data via phone interviews. The interview questions were adapted from a Pew Internet and American Life Project questionnaire (Fox & Rainie, 2000) and another study of tie strength (Princeton Research Associates, 2006).

Morey's (2007) examination of the relationship between the use of particular interpersonal sources of health information and the closeness of the respondent's relationship with that source is displayed in table 6 of her paper. The column headings and some of the row headings are excerpted here (in Table 34.1), to illustrate the design of this table of results.

This table is an excellent example of a bivariate display. Here the two variables are information source (shown in the rows; excerpted here) and closeness of relationship. The frequencies (n) and relative frequencies ($\%$) are shown for each level of closeness to each source. Both rows and columns are totaled at the table's margins. The labels on the table clearly indicate the meanings of the values in each cell.

Morey (2007) went on to use a chi-square test of the relationship depicted in the table. She found that there was a statistically significant relationship between the closeness of the tie (e.g., health professionals were considered "somewhat close," and family living with the respondent were considered "very close") and the sources used for seeking health information. Morey concluded that these findings supported the strength of weak ties theory because people relied heavily on health professionals for health information. In summary, this study provides an excellent example of a two-way contingency table and its analysis.

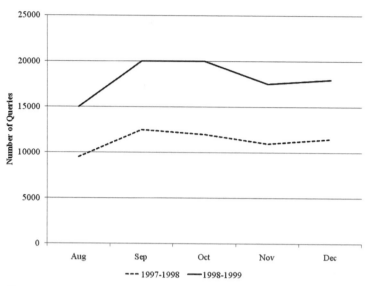

Figure 34.4. Excerpts from "Monthly query plots of two academic years" (Wang et al., 2003, figure 2). Reprinted with permission of John Wiley & Sons, Inc.

Example 3: Analysis of Web Queries

Wang et al. (2003) presented their results both with tables and with graphs. Wang and her colleagues analyzed over 500,000 queries submitted to an academic Web site between 1997 and 2001. Their goals were to understand users' query behaviors, to identify problems experienced by these users, and to develop appropriate methods for analyzing this type of data. We'll focus our attention on figure 2, a line graph, and figures 3A, 3B, and 3C, including both line graphs and bar charts, from their paper. Each of the figures displays the same variable (number of queries) on the vertical axis and displays some measure of time (days or months) on the horizontal axis.

Figure 2 from their paper is a line graph showing the number of queries, by month, over a two-year period, and a portion of that figure is recreated here as Figure 34.4. An unusual aspect of this graph is that instead of the years being plotted, one after the other, on the horizontal axis, each year is plotted over the same 12-month range on the horizontal axis (only five months are shown in our excerpt). In other words, the horizontal axis in the full graph includes 12 months, and each year's data is plotted on that 12-month axis. For the purposes of this research, the decision to overlap the two years' data was appropriate, so that the monthly variations in number of queries could be more easily compared across the two years. While a 24-month horizontal axis would have made the long-term trend more visible, it would have made comparisons of the same month from the two years (e.g., January 1998 versus January 1999) more difficult.

Figure 3 in the original paper consists of three sections: A, a bar chart comparing the number of queries each day during a week in March with those during a week in October; B, a similar bar chart comparing the number of queries submitted each day during the winter holiday period in each of two years; and C, two line graphs (comparable to figure 2) comparing the career-related queries submitted each month and the football-related queries submitted each month.[5] It is not at all clear why bar charts were chosen for some of the figures and line graphs for others. The bar charts were used when the horizontal axis represented days, and line graphs were used when the horizontal axis represented months. Though on a different scale, the horizontal axis is always representing a period of time. Since time is a continuous variable, line graphs would have been the best choice for all the figures.

Each of the individual graphs in Wang et al. (2003) has a different vertical scale. The full data set, shown in figure 2, is displayed on a vertical axis, which ranges from 0 to 30,000 queries, at intervals of 5,000. The subset of data with the lowest frequencies, the data on football queries, is displayed in figure 3C; its vertical axis ranges from 0 to 300 queries, at intervals of 50. In general, the decisions made about the vertical axes in these figures were appropriate. All of them are scaled so that the maximum frequency to be displayed is very near the top of the chart and the minimum point on each axis is 0. All of the charts are comparing two sets of data, and so both are displayed side by side (with two sets of bars on the bar charts and with two lines on the line graphs). In figure 3C, there is an additional comparison being made. Each line graph in figure 3C shows two years of queries on a particular topic, so each graph contains two lines. In addition, we want to compare the career-related queries in the first graph to the football-related queries in the second graph. For this comparison, it might have been useful to use the same scaling on the two graphs' vertical axes; in the paper, one scale ranges from 0 to 900 and one from 0 to 300. My assumption is that the authors wanted to show the differences in cyclic behavior between the two queries (with the career-related query peaking early in each semester and the football-related query peaking in early fall). However, the peak of the football-related query is much lower than that of the career-related query—a fact hidden by the difference in vertical axis scales.

In spite of this one potential flaw, this paper does a very nice job of displaying significant amounts of frequency data through a series of graphs. The graphs communicate the study's findings much more clearly than a table could, allowing the reader to see trends and differences in various subsets of the data.

Example 4: Reading Patterns of Astronomers

Tenopir et al. (2005)[6] surveyed members of the American Astronomical Society (AAS) about the ways in which they use journals and the features of those journals they prefer. Two surveys were administered via the Web. The first, concerned with the astronomers' reading behaviors, was sent to a random sample of 2,200 AAS members; 517 (23.5%) responded. The second, concerned with particular electronic journals and databases available to AAS members, was sent to a second, independently drawn random sample of 2,200 AAS members; 491 (22.3%) responded. The results from these two surveys are reported in a variety of tables and graphs. The discussion here will focus on a few of those that illustrate particular techniques not seen in the other examples in this chapter.

Let's begin by looking at table 5 from the original paper; the column and row headings are excerpted in Table 34.2. Two variables are represented in this table: the type of source for the materials read by astronomers, and the format of the source. For example, a print journal received by the astronomer as a personal subscription would be counted in the first ("Personal subscriptions") row of the "Print" column. With this table, the authors were able to understand the interaction between the type of source and the format in which it was received. They concluded that "astronomers still rely on print personal

Table 34.2. Excerpts from "Astronomer reading by the source and format of the article read" (Tenopir et al., 2005, table 5). Reprinted with permission of John Wiley & Sons, Inc.

	Source format					
	Electronic		Print		Total	
	n	%	n	%	n	%
Personal subscriptions						
Library collection						
Separate copy and other						
Total						

subscriptions, but almost entirely on electronic format for the other sources" (Tenopir et al., 2005, p. 795).

There are two other points that may be made about this table. First, as recommended, the row and column totals are shown, as well as the overall total number of cases ($n = 228$) included in the table. In addition, the authors add a table note, indicating that these data came from the survey of AAS members and that 508 of the astronomers responded to this question on the survey. Knowing the number of respondents and the number of cases they reported is useful in more fully understanding the implications of the data shown in the table. A second point is that no chi-square test was reported to indicate the likelihood that the conclusion was correct. While the raw data do seem to support the authors' conclusion, it would have been useful if they had also reported the results of a chi-square test of the statistical significance of the relationship between these two variables.

Next, I would draw your attention to figure 5 in the Tenopir et al. (2005) paper. It is a simple bar chart that indicates the amount of time spent reading, per year, by engineers, medical faculty, astronomers, physicists, and chemists. The data on astronomers were from the current study and were augmented by data from an earlier study of other scientists (Tenopir & King, 2002). Thus this is an example of how data from multiple studies can be compared through an appropriate visualization. Another thing to notice about this figure is that the actual value associated with each bar is shown on the bar. This technique allows you to overcome the problem that graphs are usually not detailed enough so that the reader can recover the actual data on which they are based.

Finally, let's examine figure 6 and table 7 from the Tenopir et al. (2005) paper. This is an example of including both the base data and a graphic that illustrates them; both the graphs and the table illustrate the same set of data. The topic of both is the age of the articles read by astronomers and other scientists. In the table, the three sources of data (AAS members in the current study, scientists in a study conducted in 1960, and scientists in a study conducted in the period 2000–2003) are represented in the columns. In the figure, these three data sources are shown in three pie charts. The rows of the table (and the segments of each pie chart) represent the age of the articles: 1 year, 2 years, 3 years, 4–5 years, 6–10 years, 11–15 years, or 15+ years. The pie chart is an effective visualization because it makes it very clear that across all three data sources, scientists are focusing their reading on articles less than one year old. While the pie charts have more segments than is usually recommended (i.e., seven segments, rather than the five to six usually recommended), they are quite readable and serve the purposes of this study quite well.

Overall, this example provides numerous tables and figures, illustrating the ways that frequency data can be represented clearly. In each case, the authors have drawn some conclusions based on their data, and they effectively use the tables and graphs to help the reader understand the data and evaluate those conclusions.

CONCLUSION

No matter what the purpose of a particular study, it's worthwhile to report descriptive statistics on its findings, including frequency distributions on key categorical variables. Most often, these frequency distributions should be reported in tables that include the frequency and relative frequency in each cell. In addition, row and column totals should be displayed. The chi-square statistic can be used to test the statistical significance of a possible relationship between the variables shown in a two-way table. In some cases, especially when it's important to make some comparisons or to understand trends in the data, a graphical display of the frequencies will be useful. With these tools, the researcher can more clearly understand the study results and communicate those results to his or her audience.

NOTES

1. See the previous chapter for a review of levels of measurement.
2. Chi-square is written as χ^2 when using the Greek letter.
3. A variable may be continuous or discrete. "As mathematicians view things, a discrete variable is one that can take on a countable number of different values, whereas a continuous variable is one that can take on an infinite number of different values" (Howell, 2004, p. 130). An example of a discrete variable is the frequency with which someone visits the public library (i.e., daily, weekly, monthly, etc.). An example of a continuous variable is the amount of time needed to complete a search (which can be measured in hundredths of seconds or in even smaller increments).
4. See the previous chapter on descriptive statistics.
5. It is highly recommended that you examine the original graphs as you read through this discussion of them.
6. The first author was the recipient of the 2002 Research in Information Science Award, and the second author was a recipient of the 1987 Award of Merit, both administered by the American Society for Information Science and Technology.

WORKS CITED

Byrne, G. (2007). A statistical primer: Understanding descriptive and inferential statistics. *Evidence Based Library and Information Practice, 2*(1), 32–47.

David, M., & Sutton, C. D. (2004). *Social Research: The Basics*. London: Sage.

Denham, B. E. (2002). Advanced categorical statistics: Issues and applications in communication research. *Journal of Communication, 52*(1), 162–176.

Fox, S., & Rainie, L. (2000). *The Online Health Care Revolution: How the Web Helps Americans Take Better Care of Themselves*. Washington, DC: Pew Internet and American Life Project. Retrieved November 21, 2007, from http://www.pewinternet.org/report_display.asp?r = 26.

Hafner, A. W. (1998). *Descriptive Statistical Techniques for Librarians* (2nd ed.). Chicago: American Library Association.

Harris, R. M., Wathen, C. N., & Fear, J. M. (2006). Searching for health information in rural Canada: Where do residents look for health information and what do they do when they find it? *Information Research, 12*(1), Article 274. Retrieved November 20, 2007, from http://informationr.net/ir/12-1/paper274.html.

Hays, W. L. (1988). *Statistics* (4th ed.). Fort Worth, TX: Holt, Rinehart and Winston.

Healey, J. F. (2007). *The Essentials of Statistics: A Tool for Social Research.* Belmont, CA: Thomson Wadsworth.

Howell, D. C. (2004). *Fundamental Statistics for the Behavioral Sciences* (5th ed.). Belmont, CA: Brooks / Cole.

Janes, J. (1999). Descriptive statistics: Where they sit and how they fall. *Library Hi Tech, 17*(4), 402–408.

Janes, J. (2001). Categorical relationships: Chi-square. *Library Hi Tech, 19*(3), 296–298.

Morey, O. T. (2007). Health information ties: Preliminary findings on the health information seeking behaviour of an African-American community. *Information Research, 12*(2), Article 297. Retrieved November 20, 2007, from http://informationr.net/ir/12-2/paper297.html.

Princeton Research Associates. (2006). *The Strength of Internet Ties.* Washington, DC: Pew Internet and American Life Project. Retrieved November 21, 2007, from http://www.pewinternet.org/PPF/r/172/report_display.asp.

Rubin, A. (2007). *Statistics for Evidence-Based Practice and Evaluation.* Belmont, CA: Brooks / Cole.

Tenopir, C., & King, D. W. (2002). Reading behavior and electronic journals. *Learned Publishing, 15*(4), 259–266.

Tenopir, C., King, D. W., Boyce, P., Grayson, M., & Paulson, K.-L. (2005). Relying on electronic journals: Reading patterns of astronomers. *Journal of the American Society for Information Science and Technology, 56*(8), 786–802.

Tufte, E. R. (1983). *The Visual Display of Quantitative Information.* Cheshire, CT: Graphics Press.

Valéry, P. (1970). Analects, Volume 14. In J. Mathews (Ed.), *Collected Works.* Princeton, NJ: Princeton University Press. (Original work published 1932.)

Wainer, H. (1997). *Visual Revelations: Graphical Tales of Fate and Deception from Napoleon Bonaparte to Ross Perot.* New York: Copernicus, Springer.

Wang, P., Berry, M. W., & Yang, Y. (2003). Mining longitudinal Web queries: Trends and patterns. *Journal of the American Society for Information Science and Technology, 54*(8), 743–758.

35

Analyzing Sequences of Events

Barbara M. Wildemuth

The events in our lives happen in a sequence in time, but in their significance to ourselves they find their own order . . . the continuous thread of revelation.

—Eudora Welty (1984)

INTRODUCTION

Information behaviors happen over time, in a sequence of individual steps or events. While their sequential nature is an inherent aspect of information behaviors, it is also a challenge to study, just because time is a "ubiquitous constituent and context of *all* human action" (Savolainen, 2006, p. 122; emphasis added). The temporal aspects of information behaviors tend to be taken for granted. Nevertheless, a recent increase in researchers' interest in the context of social behaviors in general, and information behaviors specifically, has included an interest in the "temporal context" of those behaviors (Abbott, 1995, p. 94; Savolainen, 2006). Abbott (1990) argued that questions about event sequences are of "three kinds: questions about the pattern of the sequences, questions about independent variables that affect those patterns, and questions about the dependent variables affected by the patterns" (p. 377). The first of these kinds of questions is the most central and will be the focus of the analysis methods discussed in this chapter. Only if patterns can be found in the event sequences can the other two types of questions be addressed.

Any sequence of events can be analyzed using sequential analysis methods. While the methods have been derived from biological analyses of DNA and RNA strings as well as string manipulation techniques in computer science they have been applied to research areas as diverse as birdsong and folk dancing. In information and library science (ILS), they have most often been applied in the analysis of searching and browsing behaviors, but they also have been applied in studies of other information seeking behaviors (e.g., Yoon, 2007) and organizational processes (Wildemuth, 1992).

Sanderson and Fisher (1994) provided an overview of the process of working with sequential data.[1] The first step in the process is to capture a record of the raw sequences of the behavior of interest. For many information behaviors, these may be video recordings or transaction logs; they also may be the results from time-line or similar interviewing techniques. The next step is to transform this raw data into a form that can be analyzed. Most often, this entails the classification of the events into a small number of types, maintaining the sequence in which they occurred. In other words, the raw sequences of events are transformed into coded sequences. The final step is to conduct analyses of the sequences so that statements can be made in response to the original research question(s). This chapter will focus on these last two steps: coding and analysis.

CODING THE DATA

No matter which approach to analyzing the data you undertake, you will need to abstract the raw data into a coded form.[2] The first step in this process is selection (Hilbert & Redmiles, 2000). This step involves selecting those events that are of interest and excluding those that are not of interest. Your decision about which events to include will depend on your research question. For example, if you were interested only in the way in which people use terms as they formulate and reformulate their search strategies, you might decide to exclude all the printing- and viewing-related actions in the event stream. However, if you were interested in the feedback provided by the references viewed, you would want to include all the viewing-related actions. While it seems like it would be wiser just to include *all* the study participants' actions, that choice may make the actions of interest less visible and cloud the later analysis. So keep your research question in mind, and think through the implications of including or excluding each type of action.

The next step is chunking. Sanderson and Fisher (1994) defined *chunks* as "aggregates of adjacent data elements that the analyst views as cohering" (p. 266). For instance, using the same example provided in the previous paragraph, you might decide to include all the viewing-related actions. You could decide to code the viewing of a single document surrogate as a chunk, or you could decide to code the viewing of a list/page of document surrogates as a chunk. Many of your decisions at this step will relate to a stream of similar events and whether you want to differentiate them.

The final step is to assign codes to the events. Sanderson and Fisher (1994) defined *codes* as "syntactically structured labels that are usually linked to data elements or chunks" (p. 266). For example, you might code all the viewing actions as "V" and the entry of search terms as "S." As with other types of data coding, your coding scheme should cover all the possible events/actions in the sequence, and each category/code should be mutually exclusive. In addition, you are encouraged to use only a small number of codes. My own experience with coding search moves leads me to recommend that you work with a coding scheme that consists of 6 to 12 different categories of events. (For a further discussion of the granularity of a coding scheme for search moves, see Wildemuth, 2004, p. 256.)

APPROACHES TO SEQUENTIAL EVENT ANALYSIS

Sequential event analysis methods fall into two types: those based on state transitions and those based on optimal matching algorithms. The first type is based on the transitions from one event to another (i.e., the transition from one state to the next) and has been frequently used in ILS studies of information behaviors, particularly search behaviors.

Table 35.1. Example
first-order transition matrix

	S	H	P
S		2	
H	1	1	2
P		1	

The second type of approach, based on optimal matching, has not been widely used in ILS studies but holds potential for investigation of sequences of information behaviors. In addition to the two primary analysis approaches, I will point to some ways to visualize the event sequences being analyzed.

Rather than using one of these two primary approaches to sequential analysis, some ILS studies have taken a qualitative approach to analysis. These are usually intensive studies with a small number of study participants (see, e.g., Barry, 1997; Rose, 2006). Because the qualitative analysis methods used are unique to each study, they will not be discussed here.

Markov Models: Examining Sequences Step by Step

Analyzing event sequences via Markov models and state transition matrices focuses on the movement from one event to the next. These analyses assume that there are dependencies among the events in a sequence (Abbott, 1995); in other words, event occurrence is a stochastic process "governed by probabilistic laws" (Pao & McCreery, 1986, p. 7). A Markov model is a very simple type of stochastic process, in which the conditional probability of the occurrence of a certain event depends only on the event immediately preceding it (Pao & McCreery, 1986). These types of models were originally developed in 1907 by Andrei Andreevich Markov, a Russian mathematician (Pao & McCreery, 1986). They have been in use for ILS studies of online searching behaviors since the mid-1970s (e.g., Penniman, 1975; Tolle & Hah, 1985).

To illustrate how you can use Markov models to analyze sequential data, let's use a simple example. Assume that a person interacting with an information-rich Web site can enter a search (S), can traverse a hyperlink (H), or can print the current page/document (P). One person's sequence of events, then, might be to enter a search, traverse a hyperlink, print the page, return via a hyperlink, traverse another hyperlink, enter a new search, traverse a hyperlink, and print a page. This sequence consists of the following events: SHPHHSHP.

The simplest form of a Markov model is called a zero-order model. It is simply the frequency with which each state occurred. In our example, H occurred four times, and S and P each occurred twice. While we often want to know about the frequency of occurrence of particular events, a zero-order Markov model does not really tell us anything about the *sequence* in which the events occurred. Therefore we will develop a first-order Markov model, also called a state transition matrix. The seven transitions in our example are laid out in the transition matrix shown in Table 35.1. The three rows represent the origins of the transitions; the three columns represent the destinations of the transitions.

Because we generally want to use the data on state transitions to predict how those transitions will occur in the future (Pao & McCreery, 1986), we often want to report a

Table 35.2. Example first-order probability transition matrix

	S	H	P
S		100%	
H	25%	25%	50%
P		100%	

Table 35.3. Example second-order transition matrix

	S	H	P
SH			2
HP		1	
HH	1		
HS		1	
PH		1	

probability transition matrix (Gottman & Roy, 1990). In such a matrix, the value in each cell is converted to a percentage of all the transitions in the row (i.e., each row sums to 100%) and can be interpreted as "the probability of going from the corresponding row state to the column state" (Qiu, 1993, p. 413). Using this approach to interpret our sample data would lead us to the conclusion that the probability of someone traversing a hyperlink immediately after traversing a hyperlink is one in four (i.e., 25%), while the probability of someone printing the page after traversing a hyperlink is two in four (i.e., 50%), as shown in Table 35.2. When a large sample of transition data is analyzed, it may be appropriate to generalize these probabilities to predict the behavior of the population from which our sample was drawn.

First-order Markov models are the types of models most frequently found in the ILS literature. Higher-order models can also be created and evaluated. A second-order Markov model takes into account the previous two states in trying to predict the next state, and so forth. For example, the second-order transition matrix for our sample data would look like Table 35.3; a more complete analysis, showing second-, third-, and fourth-order Markov chains, is described by Chapman (1981). Which model fits the data set the best can be tested; for example, Qiu (1993) found that a second-order Markov model was the best fit to a data set consisting of people's interactions with a hypertext system.

Several methods can be used to further analyze the Markov models that can be created by sequential data; they include loglinear and logit analysis, time series analysis, lag sequential analysis, and Pathfinder analysis (Abbott, 1990; Cooke et al., 1996). In general, the purpose of these methods is to test the statistical significance of a particular Markov model in predicting future states within the sequence of interest. For example, if you are studying search moves, you can use one of these methods to determine how confident you should be that your observations can be generalized from the sample from which they were obtained to a larger population of searchers. Buttenfield and Reitsma (2002) took just such an approach. They created a three-dimensional state transition matrix in which each transition (from one page of a Web site to another) was recorded within a particular time interval (the third dimension of the matrix). They then

Table 35.4. Example replacement cost matrix

		Cost of replacement
S	H	0.5
S	P	1.0
H	P	1.0

used loglinear modeling to detect patterns in the transitions and used multidimensional scaling to visualize those patterns. Using these methods, they could detect (and test the statistical significance of) differences in the search behaviors of different groups of users. These more advanced techniques have only rarely been used in ILS studies but do hold potential as an addition to the field's research tool kit.

Optimal Matching Approaches: Comparing Whole Sequences

While state transition matrices and Markov models are relatively easy to understand and do focus on the sequence of the events in a particular process, they suffer from the fact that the researcher needs to break apart the sequences to analyze them. By looking at the process one step at a time, a researcher loses the "information contained in the actual paths" of the users (Buttenfield & Reitsma, 2002, p. 105). An alternative approach attempts to directly compare the similarity (or dissimilarity) of two complete sequences (Abbott, 1990).

This approach was called the *optimal matching approach* by Abbott (1990). First, you would create a "replacement cost matrix" (Abbott & Tsay, 2000, p. 6). In other words, you would assign a level of dissimilarity to each pair of elements in the sequence. For example, in our sequence used as an example earlier (SHPHHSHP), you might decide that S and H are more similar to each other than either is to P. So, you might set up a replacement cost matrix, as shown in Table 35.4.

This table would then be used to compare the original sequence with another sequence; for our example, we'll assume that another person interacting with the Web site took the following actions: SHSHPHHP. You would then calculate the amount of dissimilarity between the pair of sequences by determining the minimum cost of the insertions, deletions (collectively called *indels*), and substitutions needed to convert one sequence to the other (Forrest & Abbott, 1990). The basic approach for this step is to break down the differences between the two sequences into a set of individual simple differences (Kruskal, 1983), illustrated in Figure 35.1. Often there are multiple ways to convert one sequence to another; the method with the lowest cost is the preferred method. Several different algorithms have been proposed for carrying out this calculation for large data sets (Djikstra & Taris, 1995; Elzinga, 2003; Forrest & Abbott, 1990). The outcome of this algorithmic process is a distance matrix, showing the distance between each pair of sequences in your data set. This distance matrix can then be further analyzed using multidimensional scaling or cluster analysis. This type of approach is widely used in the biological sciences and has been incorporated into sociological research (Abbott & Tsay, 2000), but no examples of its use in information and library science were found.

While optimal matching approaches, as just described, have not yet been employed in studies of information behaviors, one difficulty in their use that might be anticipated is the variety in people's information behaviors. We know, from studies of user performance

```
SHPHHSHP
SHSHPHHP
                        Substitute S/P
SHSHHSHP
SHSHPHHP
                        Substitute P/H
SHSHPSHP
SHSHPHHP
                        Substitute H/S
SHSHPHHP
SHSHPHHP
                        Total distance/cost: 2.5
```

Figure 35.1. Calculating the distance/cost between two sequences.

with information systems, that it is not uncommon to see individual differences on the order of 10 to 1 (Borgman, 1989). It is likely that the individual actions that people take during this type of performance also vary significantly from one person to another. For this reason, it may be appropriate to select sequences from the data set that represent the information behaviors that occur most frequently, prior to proceeding with the analysis. Siochi and Ehrich's (1991) algorithm for identifying maximal repeating patterns (MRPs) among sequences of behavior is well suited for this purpose. They defined an MRP as "a repeating pattern that is as long as possible, or is an independently occurring substring of a longer pattern" (Siochi & Ehrich, 1991, p. 316). Thus the algorithm systematically identifies those sequences of events that occur repeatedly within the data set. From those, the researcher can select those that should be included in the analysis. For example, it is probably not worthwhile to include a sequence of 15 events that occurs only twice in a data set. Likewise, if you include all the sequences of only two events, you have reverted to an analysis based on first-order Markov chains. By looking at the distribution of MRPs in terms of the lengths of each MRP and the number of occurrences of each MRP, you can make a decision about which MRPs should be investigated further. MRP analysis has been conducted in a few studies of online searching behaviors, one of which (Goodrum et al., 2003) is discussed later in this chapter.

Visualizing Sequences of Events

Many studies of sequential events present their results by depicting one or more of the sequences of interest (e.g., the most frequently occurring sequence). The simplest form for such a visualization is a box-and-arrow diagram of some type. For example, Ju and Burnett (2007) used concept maps of the error sequences they discovered in people's interactions with a geographic information system, and time-line maps were used by Barry (1997) to illustrate scholars' research activities. An example of such a graphic, based on the SHPHHSHP search sequence discussed previously, is shown in Figure 35.2.

In addition to creating such diagrams manually, there are some computer-based tools that can assist you. The Pathfinder algorithm (Schvaneveldt, 1990) and the MacSHAPA software (Sanderson, http://ritter.ist.psu.edu/dismal/macshapa.html) are designed to create flow diagrams (i.e., box-and-arrow diagrams) directly from your coded data set,

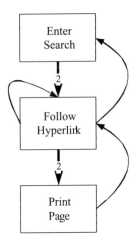

Figure 35.2. Example visualization of a first-order Markov model.

taking a step-by-step approach to analyzing the sequential data. The LifeLines interface, developed at the University of Maryland's Human-Computer Interaction Lab (Plaisant et al., 1998), is also intended to help you visualize streams of events across cases, though it does not directly correspond to any of the data analysis techniques discussed here. Finally, there are also statistical methods that might be used to help you visualize your sequential data set. For example, if you had created some type of distance matrix (either a probability transition matrix or the outcome of an optimal matching algorithm), you could use multidimensional scaling to create a two-dimensional map that could help you visualize and understand your findings.

SUMMARY

There are advantages and disadvantages to each of the analysis approaches that have been discussed here. Some of the statistical analyses may be beyond your level of statistics expertise. Nevertheless, I encourage you to work toward systematizing your analysis of sequential data to achieve the purpose of understanding the temporal aspects of the information behaviors under study. I conducted a side-by-side comparison of first-order Markov models and maximal repeating patterns analyses, applied to the same data set (Wildemuth, 2004). Before making a decision about which approach to use in your study, you may want to examine that analysis of sequences of search moves.

EXAMPLES

Three studies will be examined here to illustrate different approaches to the analysis of sequential events and some of the challenges you'll face when you try to undertake such an analysis. The first example (Koch et al., 2006) investigated people's navigation behaviors as they used Renardus, a European gateway/portal providing access to high-quality information resources. This study used first-order Markov chains to understand people's behaviors, illustrating their results with flow graphs. The second example (Chen & Cooper, 2002) investigated people's use of the University of California's MELVYL library catalog system. The study used both first-order and higher-order Markov chains to analyze the data, and the authors also compared the patterns they discovered across different user groups. The third example (Goodrum et al., 2003) investigated the ways that college students searched for images on the Web. The study included the analysis of both first-order Markov chains and maximal repeating patterns. In the discussion of each of these studies, I will focus on the coding of the raw data and on the methods used to analyze the coded sequences of events.

Example 1: Browsing in a Web Portal

Koch et al. (2006) investigated the ways that people navigated within Renardus, "a distributed Web-based service which provides integrated searching and browsing access to quality controlled Web resources from major individual subject gateway services across Europe" (p. 165). They captured the transaction logs from the system's use from summer 2002 through late fall 2003. After deleting the actions of robots, the data set consisted of 464,757 actions/events to be analyzed.

Each action was classified into one of 11 types of actions. Those that occurred most frequently were defined as the following:

- General Browse: browsing of the system hierarchy, based on the Dewey Decimal Classification (DDC) scheme
- Graphical Browse: browsing through a graphical fish-eye view of the DDC hierarchy
- Search Browse: entry into the browsing hierarchy through a search
- Advanced Search: use of the advanced search page to conduct a search
- Home Page: visits to the site home page
- Other: visits to other project documentation pages

Using these codes, the raw transaction logs were converted to a coded sequence of actions. The authors also incorporated two different approaches to chunking the sequences prior to further analysis. For most of the analyses, consecutive identical actions were collapsed, as if they had occurred only once. For example, if a Graphical Browse action was followed immediately by a Graphical Browse action, it would have been coded as only a single action. For a more detailed analysis of browsing behavior, the authors also developed a data set that included "immediate repetitions of the same activity" (Koch et al., 2006, p. 173). As you code your data, you will always face this decision: should you combine consecutive actions of the same type, or treat them as separate actions in the event sequence? You should base your decision on the purposes of your study and the nature of the events/actions being analyzed.

The analyses included calculation of both simple frequencies and state transitions. The results, however, were not presented in tables or state transition matrices. Instead, the authors used a box-and-arrow diagram to present both these sets of results (see figure 1 in the original paper). In the diagram, each type of action was shown as a circle, and the size of each circle indicated the frequency with which that type of action was taken. Each circle also was annotated with the percentage of actions associated with the relevant action. The state transition analysis results were presented as arrows connecting the circles in the diagram. The thickness of the arrow line represented the overall frequency of that transition; in addition, the percentage was written near the line. It should be noted that these percentages are not equivalent to the probabilities generated by a first-order Markov chain analysis. You will recall that in a transition matrix generated during a Markov chain analysis, each percentage is a row percentage; it represents the probability of moving to a particular next state, given a particular current state. Koch et al. (2006) instead used overall percentages—the proportion of *all* the transitions, rather than just those originating in the node that was the source of the arrow. Either of these two approaches to representing the transitions is appropriate, but to interpret the results correctly, you need to be sure which approach is being used.

In summary, this study did not incorporate some of the advanced methods we have discussed in this chapter. However, it does provide an interesting illustration of many of the issues and questions you might face when conducting sequential analysis. In particular, this study highlights the decision about whether to combine or separate consecutive actions of the same type and also provides an alternative way to visually represent the state transitions discovered.

Example 2: Searching an Online Library Catalog

Chen and Cooper (2002) investigated the way that people searched the MELVYL online library catalog. They captured the transaction logs of catalog use between mid-February and mid-March 1998. The data to be analyzed consisted of 126,925 search sessions. There were, on average, 4.6 searches in each session, and 22.6 Web pages were requested in each session (Chen & Cooper, 2001).

Each action was automatically coded. The state space of the system was first defined, based on the types of Web pages that might be displayed. Twelve possible states were included in this analysis and were represented by alphabetical codes:

- G: index access or search attempt activity
- H: search with retrievals
- I: search without retrievals
- J: modify search
- K: screen display or multiple-record display
- L: record display or single-record display
- M: change display format
- N: record processing
- O: error
- P: help
- Q: profile
- R: miscellaneous action

There are 26 possible actions in the entire state space. The authors selected these 12 actions, rather than including all 26, because of the high computational costs associated with more states. The 12 selected states were in the middle range of the system structure's hierarchy. They were decompositions of the higher-level states, such as search and display, and two of them (modify search and record processing) could be more fully decomposed (e.g., record processing could be further decomposed into printing, mailing, downloading, and saving records). Thus this study focused on a medium level of granularity in the codes used as the basis for the analysis.

In addition to limiting the number of codes to be used, Chen and Cooper (2002) decided to eliminate multiple consecutive occurrences of the same state; that is, "multiple occurrences of a state in succession in a session were replaced with a single occurrence of the state" (p. 539). They chose to combine consecutive states because they believed that the full sequence of events would be too fine grained to be useful.

On the basis of a prior study (Chen & Cooper, 2001), the sessions were grouped into six clusters, each cluster representing a different usage pattern. On the basis of the coded sequences, Chen and Cooper then went on to analyze each cluster of sessions in terms of Markov chains of up to four orders (i.e., chains of events that take into account up to four prior events in trying to predict the next event). They did not investigate any higher-order chains due to the high computational cost. They tested the fit of the sequential dependencies at each order and found that for five of the clusters, the third-order Markov chain was the best fit; for the remaining cluster, the fourth-order Markov chain was the best fit.

Chen and Cooper (2002) were also interested in the time spent in each state—not just the sequence in which the states occurred. For this purpose, they used semi-Markov chains, rather than the more frequently used discrete-time Markov chains. In a discrete-time Markov chain, each event is seen within its sequential context. Semi-Markov chains also take into account the amount of time between state changes. Thus, for each usage pattern, Chen and Cooper were able to report the proportion of transitions into each state (i.e., the zero-order Markov chain results), the proportion of time in the state, and the mean duration of the stay in each state (see table 4 in the original article). Given the interest in the amount of time needed to conduct a search, you're encouraged to consider the use of this approach in your studies.

Finally, Chen and Cooper (2002) reported the top 20 sequences in each of the six usage patterns, using the results from the Markov model analysis of the proper order (i.e., third-order for five of the usage patterns and fourth-order for the remaining usage pattern). Examination of the frequently used sequences in each usage pattern cluster helps to further illuminate each usage pattern. For instance, many of the sequences in cluster 7 (characterized as "relatively unsophisticated" searches, p. 544) included the I state, search without retrievals. It is particularly noticeable that many of the search modifications (state J) are followed by state I. This pattern is in contrast to the sequences identified in cluster 6 (characterized as "knowledgeable and sophisticated usage," p. 543), none of which contained an I state. From this discussion, you can see that a careful quantitative analysis of event sequences can provide a firm foundation for a rich, qualitative discussion of the behaviors observed.

In summary, the Chen and Cooper (2002) study is an excellent illustration of some very mathematically sophisticated analyses of event sequences that represent library catalog searches. Applying Markov chain analysis and cluster analysis to this data set provided us with a clear view of users' interactions with the catalog.

Example 3: Searching for Images on the Web

The third example (Goodrum et al., 2003) illustrates the analysis of a sequential data stream to identify MRPs. In the preceding discussion, I suggested using MRP analysis as a selection step before implementing optimal matching algorithms. In this example, MRP analysis was used to augment state transition analysis.

Eighteen graduate students were asked "to conduct [Web] searches for five images to illustrate a lecture on one of six topics" (Goodrum et al., 2003, p. 282). As a result,

71 searches were conducted, composed of 1,046 state transitions. Each state was coded with one of 18 codes. A few examples are defined here:

- Original Collection (CO): used for opening moves in a particular collection
- Original Search Engine (SO): used for opening moves in a general search engine
- Original Query Text (QOT): used when an opening query is submitted without an image designation
- Original Query Image (QOI): used when an opening query consists of image features such as color, texture, and shape
- Web Site Surrogates (WS): used for lists of Web sites retrieved in response to a query
- Image Surrogates (IS): used for groups of images retrieved in response to a query
- Image (I): used when moving from an image/Web site surrogate to an individual image

You have probably noticed that 18 is more than the 12 codes used by Cooper and Chen (2002) and earlier recommended as a maximum number. The further analyses conducted in this study do not seem to have been harmed by this large number of codes. However, it is likely that fewer MRPs were identified because the data set was spread out over more, different codes.

The authors first reported the results of a first-order Markov model (see table 3 in the original paper). A number of these single-step transitions were associated with browsing among the results retrieved. For instance, the most frequently occurring transition was between a Web site surrogate and the actual Web site, and the second was from one page of image surrogates to another page of image surrogates.

While these findings are useful, they don't tell us much about the search strategies being used (i.e., about the longer sequences of search actions that these students took). To address this question, MRP analysis is useful. The overview of the MRP results (table 5 in the original article) shows us the number of MRPs identified and the number of times they occurred. It groups MRPs by length so that we can see that there were 13 MRPs of length 7 (i.e., made up of seven actions), and altogether, those 13 MRPs occurred 36 times within the full data set. In general, this type of display is useful for determining which MRPs should be analyzed further. There are very few long MRPs (length > 8), so those could be excluded because they occur so infrequently. In addition, the 44 MRPs of length 2 could be eliminated because they are equivalent to a first-order Markov analysis and do not add anything to the analysis already conducted. Goodrum et al. (2003) did *not* eliminate any MRPs from their further analysis.

Of greater interest is which MRPs occurred most frequently (shown in table 6 of the original paper). The most frequently occurring MRP represented "rapid browsing of image thumbnails" (Goodrum et al., 2003, p. 289); it was made up of a string of five consecutive IS (image surrogate viewing) actions and occurred 27 times. Here we can see that Goodrum et al. did *not* eliminate consecutive occurrences of the same action/event from their analysis, as was done in our other two examples. The next most frequently occurring MRP represented starting a search with a text query, then viewing Web site surrogates and individual Web sites. It consisted of the following sequence: START (beginning of search)—SO (entering a search into a general search engine)—QOT (entering a text query)—WS (viewing a Web site surrogate)—W (going to the individual Web site). It occurred 18 times. From these two examples, you can see what you can gain from an MRP analysis. Rather than specifying the length of sequential dependencies in advance (as in a particular order of Markov chain), you can identify the sequences of *any* length that occur most frequently in a particular data set. Either as the end point of your analysis (as in this study) or as an intermediate point (as when MRP analysis is used prior to optimal matching or to select sequences for Markov chain analysis), MRP analysis can be quite useful.

CONCLUSION

The sequences of events that occur as people enact information behaviors are of interest to many researchers in ILS. It's not enough to know which behaviors/actions occur most frequently—we also need to know the sequence of those actions and which sequences occur most frequently. The methods discussed in this chapter can be used to analyze sequential data. You can use a step-by-step approach through simple first-order Markov models and transition matrices, look for frequently occurring longer sequences using maximal repeating patterns analysis, or focus directly on the similarity between sequences through optimal matching algorithms. Most of the past ILS research on sequences of events has focused on search moves and search strategies, using Markov models to analyze the data. This data analysis method can and should be applied to additional types of information behaviors, and additional methods/approaches can and should be applied to the analysis of search moves and other sequential data.

NOTES

1. A more detailed, but introductory, overview of sequential analysis techniques is provided by van Hooff (1982).

2. For additional discussion of coding data gathered via computer transaction logs, see Chapter 18, on transaction log analysis.

WORKS CITED

Abbott, A. (1990). A primer on sequence methods. *Organization Science, 1*(4), 375–392.

Abbott, A. (1995). Sequence analysis: New methods for old ideas. *Annual Review of Sociology, 21*, 93–113.

Abbott, A., & Tsay, A. (2000). Sequence analysis and optimal matching methods in sociology—review and prospect. *Sociological Methods and Research, 29*(1), 3–33.

Barry, C. A. (1997). The research activity timeline: A qualitative tool for information research. *Library and Information Science Research, 19*(2), 153–179.

Borgman, C. L. (1989). All users of information retrieval systems are not created equal: An exploration into individual differences. *Information Processing and Management, 25*(3), 237–251.

Buttenfield, B. P., & Reitsma, R. F. (2002). Loglinear and multidimensional scaling models of digital library navigation. *International Journal of Human-Computer Studies, 57*(2), 101–119.

Chapman, J. L. (1981). A state transition analysis of online information seeking behavior. *Journal of the American Society for Information Science, 32*(5), 325–333.

Chen, H.-U., & Cooper, M. D. (2001). Using clustering techniques to detect usage patterns in a Web-based information system. *Journal of the American Society for Information Science and Technology, 52*(11), 888–904.

Chen, H.-U., & Cooper, M. D. (2002). Stochastic modeling of usage patterns in a web-based information system. *Journal of the American Society for Information Science and Technology*, *53*(7), 536–548.

Cooke, N. J., Neville, K. J., & Rowe, A. L. (1996). Procedural network representations of sequential data. *Human-Computer Interaction*, *11*(1), 29–68.

Dijkstra, W., & Taris, T. (1995). Measuring the agreement between sequences. *Sociological Methods and Research*, *24*(2), 214–231.

Elzinga, C. H. (2003). Sequence similarity: A nonaligning technique. *Sociological Methods and Research*, *32*(1), 3–29.

Forrest, J., & Abbott, A. (1990). The optimal matching method for studying anthropological sequence data: An introduction and reliability analysis. *Journal of Quantitative Anthropology*, *2*(2), 151–170.

Goodrum, A. A., Bejune, M. M., & Siochi, A. C. (2003). A state transition analysis of image search patterns on the Web. In E. M. Bakker et al. (Eds.), *Image and Video Retrieval: Proceedings of the International Conference on Image and Video Retrieval (CIVR)* (pp. 281–290). Lecture Notes on Computer Science, 2728. Berlin: Springer.

Gottman, J. M., & Roy, A. K. (1990). *Sequential Analysis: A Guide for Behavioral Researchers*. Cambridge: Cambridge University Press.

Hilbert, D. M., & Redmiles, D. F. (2000). Extracting usability information from user interface events. *ACM Computing Surveys*, *32*(4), 384–421.

Ju, B., & Burnett, K. (2007). Comparison of human performance by knowledge domain: Types, frequency, and sequencing of errors made while interacting with an information system. *Library and Information Science Research*, *29*(4), 471–494.

Koch, T., Golub, K., & Ardö, A. (2006). Users' browsing behaviour in a DDC-based Web service: A log analysis. *Cataloging and Classification Quarterly*, *42*(3/4), 163–186.

Kruskal, J. B. (1983). An overview of sequence comparison. In D. Sankoff & J. B. Kruskal (Eds.), *Time Warps, String Edits, and Macromolecules: The Theory and Practice of Sequence Comparison* (pp. 1–44). Reading, MA: Addison-Wesley.

Pao, M. L., & McCreery, L. (1986). Bibliometric application of *Markov* chains. *Information Processing and Management*, *22*(1), 7–17.

Penniman, W. D. (1975). *Rhythms of dialogue in human-computer conversation*. Unpublished doctoral dissertation, Ohio State University.

Plaisant, C., Shneiderman, B., & Mushlin, R. (1998). An information architecture to support the visualization of personal histories. *Information Processing and Management*, *34*(5), 581–597.

Qiu, L. (1993). Markov models of search state patterns in a hypertext information retrieval system. *Journal of the American Society for Information Science*, *44*(7), 413–427.

Rose, M. (2006). The information activity of rail passenger information staff: A foundation for information system requirements. *Information Research*, *12*(1), Article 275. Retrieved February 3, 2009, from http://informationr.net/ir/12-1/paper275.html.

Sanderson, P. M., & Fisher, C. (1994). Exploratory sequential data analysis: Foundations. *Human-Computer Interaction*, *9*(3/4), 251–317.

Savolainen, R. (2006). Time as a context of information seeking. *Library and Information Science Research*, *28*(1), 110–127.

Schvaneveldt, R. W. (1990). *Pathfinder Associative Networks: Studies in Knowledge Organization*. Norwood, NJ: Ablex.

Siochi, A. C., & Ehrich, R. W. (1991). Computer analysis of user interfaces based on repetition in transcripts of user sessions. *ACM Transaction on Information Systems*, *9*(4), 309–335.

Tolle, J. E., & Hah, S. (1985). Online search patterns: NLM CATLINE database. *Journal of the American Society for Information Science, 36*(2), 82–93.

van Hooff, J. A. R. A. M. (1982). Categories and sequences of behavior: Methods of description and analysis. In K. R. Scherer & P. Ekman (Eds.), *Handbook of Methods in Nonverbal Behavior Research* (pp. 362–439). Cambridge: Cambridge University Press.

Welty, E. (1984). *One Writer's Beginnings.* Cambridge, MA: Harvard University Press.

Wildemuth, B. M. (1992). An empirically grounded model of the adoption of intellectual technologies. *Journal of the American Society for Information Science, 43*, 210–224.

Wildemuth, B. M. (2004). The effects of domain knowledge on search tactic formulation. *Journal of the American Society for Information Science and Technology, 55*(3), 246–258.

Yoon, K. (2007). A study of interpersonal information seeking: The role of topic and comment in the articulation of certainty and uncertainty of information need. *Information Research, 12*(2), Article 304. Retrieved February 3, 2009, from http://informationr.net/ir/12-2/paper304.html.

36

Correlation

Barbara M. Wildemuth

The cause is hidden; the effect is visible to all.

—Ovid, *Metamorphoses*

Even the most remarkable encounters are related in casual, everyday ways in fairy tales.

—Bruno Bettelheim (1975)

OVERVIEW

Correlation is a statistical analysis method that helps you to examine the relationship between two variables. Specifically, it is the proportion of the variability in one variable that is explained by the variability in the other variable. If two variables are perfectly correlated, then all the variability in one variable is explained by the variability in the other; if two variables are not at all correlated, then none of the variability in one variable is explained by the variability in another. Calculation of the correlation statistic assumes that the two variables being studied are linearly related and that the data are ordinal, interval, or ratio data.[1]

Correlation can be graphically represented by a scatter diagram. Each variable is represented by an axis of a two-dimensional plot. Each instance in the data set is represented by a dot at the intersection of the two values representing the two variables under study. For example, an examination of the correlation between the time spent by a searcher in preparing for a search (e.g., in checking a thesaurus and developing a search strategy) and the time spent in conducting the search might be represented as in Figure 36.1, which illustrates a correlation of −0.85.

The *direction* of the relationship is indicated by the sign of the correlation statistic. If the statistic is positive, it indicates that as one variable increases, the other variable also increases. If the statistic is negative, it indicates that as one variable increases, the other variable decreases. In the example shown in Figure 36.1, the correlation statistic is negative, indicating that as the amount of time spent in preparing for a search increases, the amount of time spent conducting the search decreases, and vice versa.

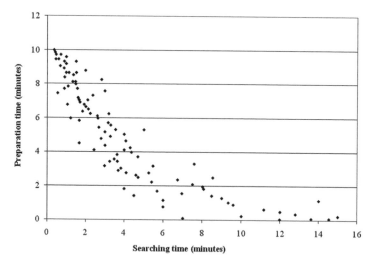

Figure 36.1. Correlation between preparation time and searching time.

The *strength* of the relationship is indicated by the absolute value of the correlation statistic. It can range from 0 to 1. The larger the absolute value, the stronger the relationship between the two variables. In other words, as the absolute value of the correlation statistic increases, more of the variability in one variable is associated with the variability in the other variable. In the example shown in Figure 36.1, the relationship between time spent preparing for the search and time spent conducting the search is quite strong.

Before interpreting a correlation statistic, you should check to see whether it is statistically significant. Statistical analysis software usually provides the p value associated with a correlation statistic. The p value represents the likelihood that you will be wrong if you say that there is a relationship between the two variables. The statistical significance of the correlation statistic is related to the sample size and the strength of the correlation. For more details on interpreting the p value, see Chapter 37, on comparing means.

SELECTING THE APPROPRIATE CORRELATION STATISTIC

There are several different correlation statistics, each having different properties. Your choice of a particular correlation statistic should be based on the level of data available. If both variables are interval or ratio data, then the Pearson product-moment correlation, or Pearson's r, is used; if one or both of the variables are ordinal data, then Spearman's rho or Kendall's tau should be used.

Pearson's r can be calculated with interval or ratio data but also assumes that the data are more nearly continuous than discrete. The data used in Figure 36.1 illustrate the case in which this assumption is correct; both measures of time are continuous. The example shown in Figure 36.2 illustrates the case in which one of the variables is clearly continuous (time spent searching) and the other is not (scores on a 5-point rating scale). While Pearson's r can be used in situations like that shown in Figure 36.2, Spearman's rho or Kendall's tau would be more appropriate.

Both Spearman's rho and Kendall's tau can be used to calculate the relationship between two ordinal variables. As recommended by Weaver (1989), Spearman's rho is more appropriate if the data are distributed across a large number of ranks (eight or

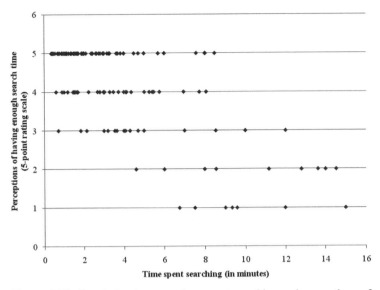

Figure 36.2. Correlation between time spent searching and perceptions of having enough time.

more), while Kendall's tau is more appropriate if it is known that the intervals between the ranks are unequal and that there are a few cases with very high or very low ranks. The calculation of Spearman's rho is equivalent to the calculation of Pearson's r, treating the ranks as scores (Lane, 2003). Kendall's tau is calculated by comparing the ordering of the individual observations on each of the two variables (Nie et al., 1975).

SOME CAUTIONS FOR INTERPRETING THE CORRELATION COEFFICIENT

The most common mistake in interpreting correlation coefficients is to presume that any relationship found indicates that one of the variables causes the other. While one variable causing another may result in a correlation being found, the finding of a statistically significant correlation does not support the conclusion that one of the variables caused the other. If such a conclusion can be drawn, it must rely on additional evidence such as that provided by a strong theoretical framework or logical necessity.

Using the data shown in Figure 36.2 as an example, we found that there is a strong negative correlation (Spearman's rho $= -0.55$) between time spent searching and the searcher's perception of having enough time to complete the search. Which of these two variables might be causing the other? The correlation statistic itself does not favor one as the cause and the other as the effect. If there were an existing theoretical framework that posited that those who search more efficiently (i.e., in less time) are more likely to feel that they have enough time to complete their searches, then that theoretical framework could be used in combination with the empirical finding to argue for causality. Similarly, if there was some logical necessity, such as one of the variables preceding the other in its occurrence (not true in this example), then an argument of causality might be made. However, you should keep in mind that the correlation statistic, in and of itself, does not support conclusions concerning cause and effect.

A second consideration in interpreting correlation coefficients is the range of values represented in the data. If the range of data collected is small, that is, it does not cover the range of possible values, it is likely that the correlation may be underestimated. For example, in the example shown in Figure 36.2, the actual scores on perceptions of having enough time ranged from the theoretical minimum of 1 to the theoretical maximum of 5. In another study, such ratings might have ranged only from 3 to 5, truncating the range of values for that variable. As you try to interpret the meaning of a correlation coefficient, be sure to look at the range of values on each of the two variables being examined.

Finally, you should remember that your interpretation of a correlation coefficient is dependent on the quality of the measures of the two variables. If one or both of the measures is unreliable, the false variability in that measure may result in an underestimate or overestimate of a correlation coefficient. If the measures are reliable but not valid, the correlation statistic itself is easily interpretable, but its implications for the research question may be hidden.

EXAMPLES

Two studies using correlation in their data analysis will be discussed here. The first (Duy & Vaughan, 2003) investigates a question inspired by a common problem in libraries: how to know whether to trust usage data supplied by database vendors. To address this question, they examined the relationship between locally collected and vendor-collected data on use of the same databases. The second example (Pennanen & Vakkari, 2003) focuses on a more theoretical question: whether students' conceptual structure of a particular domain, their search processes when seeking information in that domain, and the outcomes of their searches are related. In this study, the authors are particularly interested in whether there are causal links between these constructs.

Example 1: The Relationship between Locally-Collected and Vendor-Collected Usage Data

Libraries that have licensed electronic resources from their vendors are interested in understanding whether and how much those resources are being used. Vendors typically (though not always) provide usage data; however, the way in which these data are compiled differs from vendor to vendor and is usually not rigorously defined, and may differ from the library's conceptualization of use. In an attempt to determine whether vendor-provided usage data are reliable and valid, Duy and Vaughan (2003) examined the relationship between usage data gathered locally, at North Carolina State University, and those provided by vendors. The data were collected monthly, from March 2001 through February 2002, and included data on 28 products (e.g., Philosopher's Index from SilverPlatter and ScienceDirect from Elsevier Science) from 15 vendors/ providers.

Correlation was used to investigate the relationship between the data provided by each vendor (across all of that vendor's products) and the data collected locally. A combination of Pearson's r and Spearman's rho was used for the analysis, based on whether the data were normally distributed: Pearson's r was used for data that were normally distributed and Spearman's rho was used for data that were not normally distributed. The correlations ranged from $r = 0.06$ (for the data from Project Muse) to $r = 0.98$ (for the data from ProQuest). Of the 15 correlation statistics calculated, 10 were statistically significant ($p < 0.05$), from which the authors concluded that the locally collected data showed similar usage patterns to the vendor-provided data.

The authors appropriately go further in investigating the relationship between the two data sources by creating a new metric: the ratio between the locally collected data and the vendor-provided data. They then examined these ratios, finding that "six out of the 15 vendors had ratios between 0.75–1.25, indicating that the two sets of values were fairly close" (Duy & Vaughan, 2003, p. 19). Such an examination is appropriate because it is possible that the two data sources could be very highly correlated and, simultaneously, quite different in their raw values. For example, there was a very strong correlation (Pearson's $r = 0.95$) between the locally collected data and the data provided by ISI, but the mean ratio between the data points was 0.606, indicating that the ISI data on use were consistently higher than the locally collected usage data for ISI products.

In summary, this example illustrates an appropriate use of correlation as a tool of analysis. The authors took into account the distribution of their data when selecting which correlation statistic to use—one of the considerations for selecting a correlation statistic. They also realized the limitations of correlation in understanding the phenomenon under study and so augmented correlation with other methods of analysis.

Example 2: Relationships between Students' Conceptual Structure, Search Process, and Outcomes While Preparing a Research Proposal

Pennanen and Vakkari's (2003) research question was much more complex than the question investigated in the first example. They were interested in the relationships between students' conceptual structure, search process, and outcomes while preparing a research proposal. Specifically, they hoped to identify aspects of students' conceptual structure, knowledge level, search goals, query facets and terms, and search tactics that were related to the utility of their search results, at two points during the research process. Twenty-two undergraduate students in psychology participated in the study. Their progress through proposal writing was measured using Kuhlthau's (1993) questionnaire, scoring each student as in stage 1 (initiation) through stage 6 (presentation). Conceptual structure was measured by analyzing the students' topic descriptions, identifying the main concepts and subconcepts included in them. Students reported their own knowledge level. The measure of search goals was based on students' ratings of their desire to find five different types of information—two general types (e.g., theories or models) and three specific types (e.g., information about methods); a composite measure was calculated to indicate "expected contribution of the information in a continuum from general to specific" (Pennanen & Vakkari, 2003, p. 762). Measures of search behaviors included the number of query facets, the number of query terms, and the frequency of the two most frequently used search tactics. A utility rating for each document viewed was also collected.

Pearson's r was used to examine the relationships between these variables at two points in time: at the beginning session and at the end session of a two-semester seminar on preparing a research proposal. The variables used for these analyses were all interval data. In a few cases, it could be argued that the variable more nearly approximated ordinal data, and so it might have been wiser to use Spearman's rho or Kendall's tau as the correlation statistic. These variables included (1) progress in proposal writing (a 6-point rating scale), (2) knowledge level (a 4-point rating scale), and (3) the rating of utility (a 4-point rating scale). While progress in proposal writing was measured with a multiple-item questionnaire, the scores were then reduced to place each student in one of only six stages. It is not clear that these stages are at equal intervals, so a conservative approach would be to consider this variable to be ordinal data. The ratings of knowledge level and document utility would be considered interval data; however, the low number of possible values makes these scales discrete, rather than continuous, making Spearman's rho or Kendall's tau a better choice of correlation coefficient.

Pennanen and Vakkari (2003) found a number of statistically significant relationships at each of the two sessions. Just a few of these relationships will be examined more closely here. First, let's look at a relationship that would be expected in this data set, based on a logical link between the two variables. The relationship between number of query facets and number of query terms is such a relationship because there is a logical link between a query facet and its representation in specific terms. A strong positive relationship, as would be expected, was found at both sessions (Pearson's $r = 0.78$ at the first session and $r = 0.75$ at the second session).

More interesting are relationships that are not necessarily expected to exist. It is in these relationships that new research questions can be seen. One example of this type of relationship occurred at the first session, between the students' conceptual structure and their search outcomes. Specifically, there was a correlation between the proportion of concepts articulated in a student's query and the number of useful references (judged as totally, partially, or potentially useful) retrieved (Pearson's $r = 0.43$). To help the reader fully appreciate this relationship, the authors point out that coverage of concepts was *not* related to the total number of concepts or the proportion of subconcepts represented in the conceptual structure of the student's research question. Coverage of the concepts was also not related to the overall number of terms used in the queries. By ruling out these other possible linkages, the relationship between concept coverage and search outcomes can be interpreted directly: "students' ability to express their knowledge structure in query terms affects search success directly without the mediation of the number of facets and terms or the search tactics used" (Pennanen & Vakkari, 2003, p. 764). You may have noticed that this interpretation does imply a cause-and-effect relationship between concept coverage and search outcomes. While the correlation alone does not support this inference, it is appropriate to use the correlation in combination with the sequencing of the two variables to draw this conclusion. In other words, the possibility that search outcomes cause the students' coverage of concepts can be ruled out because the sequence of events does not allow it: search outcomes occur only after the concepts have been specified. The lack of correlation among other variables in the sequence of events also helps to rule out causal explanations other than the direct relationship between concept coverage and search outcome. While it is still possible that there is an alternative causal explanation, the authors' discussion of these specific results provides a good example of using correlation to understand cause and effect, without reaching beyond the limitations of the statistic.

The authors were careful in limiting the inferences they drew from the correlation just discussed, but they may have stretched their data a little too far in the causal models shown in figures 1 and 2. These figures depict the statistically significant correlations found at each session and suggest causal links that may be inferred from the correlations. As with the correlation discussed previously, the inferences are supported by the sequencing of events, from student conceptual structure and stage of research, to search process variables, to search outcome variables. This sequencing of events makes the linkages represented in the two figures plausible. However, the reader should be cautioned to understand these figures more as hypotheses than as findings.

A final lesson that can be learned from this example is the importance of the measures underlying the variables that are being examined via correlation. For the correlations to be valid, the measure of each variable must also be reliable and valid. Let's examine Pennanen and Vakkari's (2003) measure of search goals as a positive example of developing a measure for a construct that is difficult to measure. They define a search goal as the "specific search results a user hopes to obtain" (p. 762), drawing on Xie (2000). The students provided ratings of their desire for their literature searching to yield particular types of information: general information (i.e., general background knowledge and theories, models, and definitions) and specific information (i.e., information about methods, empirical research results, and particular specific information). The difference between general and specific information was then used as "an indicator of the expected contribution of the information in a continuum from general to specific" (Pennanen & Vakkari, 2003, p. 762). The complexity of this measure is both its strength and its weakness. By aggregating multiple ratings from the students, the measure is likely to be more reliable—that is its strength. By manipulating the ratings in fairly complex ways, the measure is more difficult to understand—that is its weakness. When correlated with other measures, understanding the correlation relies on understanding each variable involved in it. This variable was correlated positively with the stage of the research process (Pearson's $r = 0.40$) and negatively with the number of useful references retrieved (Pearson's $r = -0.54$) in the second session. Interpreting these relationships becomes more difficult because the measurement of search goal is complex. Thus it is important for information and library science researchers to continue to develop new measures for constructs that are relevant for our research questions; however, you should keep in mind that each measure should also be defined clearly for others interested in similar research questions.

In summary, this study provides a good example of the extensive use of correlation to investigate a number of relationships between three classes of variables: students' conceptual structure, their search behaviors, and their search outcomes. The authors did a very good job of overcoming some of the difficulties encountered in studying such a complex research question, and the choice of correlation as the primary method of statistical analysis helped make the results accessible for a broad audience. There are a few ways in which the application of correlation analysis might be improved further, but none of us would go wrong in emulating this example.

CONCLUSION

Many research questions are oriented to discovering whether there is a relationship between two variables and, if there is, how strong that relationship is. Even more to the point, the question is likely to be focused on whether one variable, in some sense, causes the other. While the statistical methods of correlation cannot directly address this latter question, they can provide evidence of a relationship between two variables. From there, you will need to use other types of evidence, combined with your correlation results, to argue that one of the variables is the cause of the other.

NOTE

1. If you are working with nominal/categorical data, then you will need to use chi-square to investigate the possibility of a relationship among your variables; see the previous chapter.

WORKS CITED

Bettelheim, B. (1989). Fairy tale versus myth: Optimism versus pessimism. In *The Uses of Enchantment* (pp. 35–40). New York: Vintage.

Duy, J., & Vaughan, L. (2003). Usage data for electronic resources: A comparison between locally collected and vendor-provided statistics. *Journal of Academic Librarianship, 29*(1), 16–22.

Kuhlthau, C. (1993). *Seeking Meaning: A Process Approach to Library and Information Services.* Norwood, NJ: Ablex.

Lane, D. M. (2003). *HyperStat Online Textbook.* Retrieved July 7, 2008, from http://davidmlane .com/hyperstat/.

Nie, N. H., Hull, C. H., Jenkins, J. G., Steinbrenner, K., & Bent, D. H. (1975). *SPSS: Statistical Package for the Social Sciences* (2nd ed.). New York: McGraw-Hill.

Pennanen, M., & Vakkari, P. (2003). Students' conceptual structure, search process, and outcome while preparing a research proposal: A longitudinal case study. *Journal of the American Society for Information Science and Technology, 54*(8), 759–770.

Weaver, D. H. (1989). Basic statistical tools. In G. H. Stempel III & B. H. Westley (Eds.), *Research Methods in Mass Communication* (2nd ed., pp. 49–89). Englewood Cliffs, NJ: Prentice Hall.

Xie, H. (2000). Shifts of interactive intentions and information seeking strategies in interactive information retrieval. *Journal of the American Society for Information Science, 51,* 841–857.

37

Comparing Means: *t* Tests and Analysis of Variance

Abe J. Crystal and Barbara M. Wildemuth

> Statistical analysis is a tool, not a ritualistic religion. It is for use, not for reverence, and it should be approached in the spirit that it was made for [researchers] rather than vice versa.
>
> —Jacob Cohen (1965)

OVERVIEW

Often in your research, you will want to compare different groups of people in terms of the mean (average) values of particular variables. For example, suppose you are testing a new online catalog interface and want to determine whether users prefer it to the existing interface. After giving a questionnaire to people who have used one or the other interface, you want to compare the responses of the two groups. Two statistical techniques—the *t* test and analysis of variance (ANOVA)—help you make these types of comparisons.

Why do we need statistical techniques to do this? Can't we just look at the questionnaires and see which group had higher scores? Unfortunately, it's not that simple. You need to be able to distinguish *actual* effects from *chance* effects (what statisticians call *sampling error*). This problem is especially acute when studying people because individual people are inherently so different from each other—they think differently, feel differently, and act differently, even in similar situations. These basic differences introduce large random variations (or so-called noise).

There are two steps to dealing with the problem of random variation. First, you must define an appropriate sample (see Chapter 13, on sampling for extensive studies). The sample must be large enough to allow you to detect the differences that interest you (in other words, your sample must have sufficient power, discussed later). Second, you must use and carefully interpret the appropriate statistics. This chapter will explain how to calculate and interpret statistics for comparing means.

COMPARING TWO GROUPS: THE t TEST

The t test (also called *Student's t*) gives the probability that the difference between two means can be attributed to chance. The test relies on three basic ideas. First, large differences are more meaningful than small differences. The bigger the difference between the two groups, the larger the value of t. Second, small variances are more reliable than large variances. The smaller the variance of responses within the groups, the larger the value of t. Finally, large samples are more reliable than small samples. The larger the size of the samples being compared, the larger the value of t.

The actual t statistic is calculated by dividing the difference between the means by the standard error. The standard error is found by dividing the standard deviation of your sample by the square root of n, the size of the sample.

The t value itself is not particularly interesting—what you really want is the p value, which is the *probability* that the difference between the two means is caused by chance. The larger (in absolute terms) the t value, the smaller the p value. Statistical software will calculate a p value for you.

Technically, you should not be using a t test unless your data meet two important assumptions: equal variances and normal distributions. The first assumption means that if you're comparing group A and group B, the two groups should have responses that are dispersed around the mean in a generally similar way. The second assumption means that the data for each group are expected to come from a normally distributed population. The good news is that violating these assumptions isn't a fatal flaw in your analysis. The t test is known to be robust to minor violations of these assumptions. As long as you don't have extremely unequal or skewed distributions, the t statistic will generally be valid.

To illustrate how a t test works, let's return to the example of evaluating a new online catalog interface. Suppose you have 20 participants—10 using the old interface and 10 using the new one. After using the interface, each person answers 10 questions (such as "I felt comfortable using this system") on a 1 to 5 rating scale. You add up the scores for each person and enter them into your statistical software.[1] The results show that group A (the old interface) had a mean score of 35.6; group B (the new interface) had a mean score of 40.5; the standard error was 1.6. It looks like the new interface received higher scores, but maybe this result was due to chance variations in these groups. Your software reports a t value of -3.046 and a p value of 0.007. This means that there is only a 7 in 1000 chance that the difference between group A and group B is due to sampling error alone—so it's almost certainly a real, measurable difference.

INTERPRETING THE RESULTS OF A t TEST

Statistically Significant Results

If you read many social science research articles, you've undoubtedly encountered statements like this: "The difference was statistically significant, $p < 0.05$." Often, such a statement appears in the context of null hypothesis testing. The null hypothesis is that no difference exists between the two groups being compared. If the t test yields a p value below some established level (typically 0.05 or 0.01), it is said that the null hypothesis was rejected, and the alternative hypothesis (that there is some real difference) supported. (Note that in contrast to the older technique of looking up "critical values" in tables, statistical software now reports exact *p* values. You can examine these directly and should report them in a write-up of your research.)

The basic idea of statistical significance is extremely important. If you have a finding with a *p* value of, say, 0.20, that means there is a 20 percent chance that the difference you observed is due to random variability. This should cause you to carefully consider how useful the finding is. Even if you have a result with a very low *p* value, you are not finished with your interpretation of that finding. You need to go on to consider the effect size and practical significance of your finding, rather than just its statistical significance (Cohen, 1994; Wilkinson, 1999).

One reason to emphasize the next step of interpretation is that it's surprisingly easy to obtain statistically significant results of no practical significance whatsoever. Think back to the three ideas behind the *t* test: size of the difference, amount of variance, and size of the sample. You can often achieve statistical significance by simply increasing the size of the sample. This amounts to establishing a tiny effect, but with great certainty—knowing something for sure about very little. (See the Toms and Taves, 2004, example later in this chapter for a more detailed discussion of this problem.)

You should consider both the magnitude of the results you obtain and the implications of the results for the problems with which you're concerned. If your major concern is to evaluate the quality of the new online catalog interface, you should think about whether the questionnaire findings really convince you that the new interface is superior. Furthermore, you should consider whether the results are really good, in a broader sense, or merely a small improvement on a poor baseline.

Many statistical experts have also recommended various effect size statistics as a supplement to significance testing. Effect size statistics attempt to measure the magnitude of a treatment effect or other manipulation. For example, Cohen's *d* is a widely used measure of effect size. It is calculated by dividing the difference between the means by the pooled standard deviation across the two samples. A *d* of 0.8 or greater is considered large, while 0.2 or less is considered small. This is a useful heuristic, and effect sizes (including more complex measures based on correlation or shared variance) are the foundation of meta-analysis. But computing effect sizes is no substitute for consideration of practical significance. A well-controlled study can have low standard deviations and, therefore, a high effect size, but still represent an effect that has little importance to actual behavior or operations.

Nonsignificant Results

Another common problem is how to interpret nonsignificant findings (by convention, $p > 0.05$). In one sense, the interpretation is straightforward: no effect was found. But does this mean there's *really* no effect, or just that you couldn't measure it effectively in your study? Let's return to the example of comparing two online library catalog interfaces. Suppose that you ran the study with only two participants in each condition. As before, the mean score for group A was 35, and the mean for group B was 40. The *t* test reports a *p* value of 0.29. Apparently, there's no difference between the two interfaces. Clearly, though, your sample is too small to say for sure. If you test more participants and see a similar pattern of results, a statistically reliable difference will become apparent.

Statisticians would say the study design with only four total participants lacked *power*. Power refers, technically, to the ability to reject the null hypothesis at a given significance level. Intuitively, it is the ability to detect a difference where one really exists. Lack of power is a major problem in many social scientific research designs. Because of this, methodologists recommend estimating power before conducting a study. Good estimates of power depend on having access to approximate characteristics of the effect that interests you, for a particular population. Unfortunately, this is often difficult, particularly in fields such as information and library science, where methods and measures are diverse. If you are conducting formal, controlled research—and particularly if you are seeking external grant funding—you should attempt to estimate the power of your design.[2]

COMPARING MULTIPLE GROUPS: ANOVA

ANOVA extends the *t* test to situations where you have more than two groups to compare. ANOVA takes its name from the mathematical approach that underlies it—comparing the amount of variance within and between groups. But just like the *t* test, ANOVA is used to compare *means*.[3] How does analyzing variance help us compare means? ANOVA treats the variance between groups as the "signal" and the variance within each group as "noise." If there is a lot of signal, but not much noise, we can be confident that there are meaningful differences among the means. If, instead, the signal is low and the noise is high, then no difference is likely.

Just as the *t* test relies on *t* values, ANOVA uses an *F* test, which relies on *F* values. Given a set of data points associated with different groups, statistical software will calculate an *F* value and its associated *p* value. In terms of hypothesis testing, we can say that if the *p* value is lower than an established level (such as 0.05 or 0.01), then there is a difference between the means. Technically, we reject the null hypothesis that there is *no* difference between the means.

A hypothetical example will illustrate how ANOVA works. Suppose you add a third condition to your online catalog study. Participants in the third condition interact with a librarian, instead of the computer interface. You can't compare all three conditions using a *t* test, so you run ANOVA using your statistical software. The mean response of the new group C is 42.2. The results from your ANOVA indicate that the *F* value is 4.64, and the associated *p* value is 0.011. These results provide strong evidence that the groups differ.

In addition to testing differences between three or more means, ANOVA enables analysis of complex experimental designs (see Chapter 12, on experimental studies), including factorial and repeated-measures designs. *Factorial* designs involve studying different levels of the experimental factors in combination. For example, suppose you were interested in how training affects different-aged students' use of an online encyclopedia. You could design a study with four conditions: training or no training, third graders or fifth graders. This 2×2 factorial design would enable you to test both the independent (or main) effects of training (all those with training compared to all those with no training) and grade (all third graders compared to all fifth graders, regardless of whether training was received), and their combined (or interaction) effect: no training/third-grade students, no training/fifth-grade students, training/third-grade students, training/fifth-grade students. *Repeated-measures* (also known as *within-subjects*) designs assign each participant to multiple conditions, rather than just one. For example, you could have designed the online catalog study to have each participant use *both* interfaces, rather than just one. A variation of ANOVA can be used with such designs.

INTERPRETING THE RESULTS FROM ANOVA

Calculating the overall F statistic using ANOVA only provides a general finding: whether or not the means of the groups differ. Because ANOVA is used when you have multiple groups, you are bound to wonder whether (and how) specific subsets of the groups differ, for example, group A versus group B, or group B versus group C. A quick look at the means (either in a table or graph) will help you understand the pattern of results. To establish statistical significance, you will need to conduct specific *pairwise* tests, such as directly comparing group A and group B.

These pairwise tests are exactly like the t tests discussed previously. In fact, you can use t tests to make pairwise comparisons after the overall F test. But there's a big potential problem: the more comparisons you make, the greater the possibility of a chance finding (i.e., a Type I error—falsely concluding that there is an effect where none exists). Suppose your research design enables you to make 14 comparisons. If you adopt a 0.05 significance level, there's roughly a 50–50 chance that you will find a significant result, just by chance.

Numerous statistical techniques have been developed to cope with this problem of multiple comparisons. Fisher's least significant difference (LSD) test, if used in conjunction with the omnibus F statistic, helps reduce the incidence of chance findings. Bonferroni's inequality test is also used in this context. Tukey's honestly significant difference (HSD) test can be used to test all possible pairs, regardless of the F statistic. Scheffe's test is appropriate for data mining—looking for significant findings amid a large collection of possible comparisons.

Understanding the nuances of these techniques is important for some formal research, particularly when publishing in a journal that expects clear delineation of significant and nonsignificant results. In such a case, it is important to understand the appropriate use of liberal (e.g., the t test) versus conservative (e.g., Scheffé's test) measures. Liberal tests err on the side of significance; conservative tests err on the side of nonsignificance.[4] For most studies, though, it's more important to focus on the magnitude of the effects and their practical significance. In addition, you should strive to reduce the possibility of chance findings by minimizing the number of variables you manipulate and measure (Cohen, 1990).

In our example study, comparing different means of access to an online library catalog, you might use your statistical software to compare the means of the three groups using Tukey's HSD. The results show that group A (the original interface) is rated significantly lower than groups B (the new interface) and C (interacting with a librarian). However, groups B and C are not significantly different from each other. From these findings, you would conclude that people are just as satisfied using the new interface as they are when working with a librarian.

EXAMPLES

Comparing means is a routine part of most social science research. ANOVA and t tests are useful tools for making these comparisons. Here we'll look at two example of their use. The first example (Toms & Taves, 2004) compares the quality of the Web sites retrieved by different search engines. Because there are four search engines to be compared, ANOVA is used for the analysis. The second example (Wildemuth et al., 2003) also compares four means—in this case, they represent four different speeds

Table 37.1. Comparison of mean ratings of Web site reputation

Variable	Links	Semantics	$F(1, 4597)$	p value
Trustworthiness	3.60	3.50	30.563	<0.001
Authoritativeness	3.50	3.25	52.835	<0.001
Aboutness	3.75	3.55	40.007	<0.001

for playing a fast-forward video surrogate. In each case, the authors want to know not only whether there is a difference among the means, but where the break point is between high and low. ANOVA, combined with a post hoc analysis, is useful for this purpose.

Example 1: Evaluating a System Design to Identify Reputable Web Sites

Imagine you arrive at an unfamiliar Web site, say, http://www.trust-us.com. Perhaps you received a link to the site in an e-mail or found it while searching the Web. Do you trust the site? Do you see it as credible? Authoritative? People face this problem of assessing a Web site's credibility, or reputation, every day and would likely appreciate a search engine that retrieved only reputable sites. Toms and Taves's (2004) study was designed to assess whether a new search engine, TOPIC, could retrieve sites that were more reputable, on average, than the sites retrieved by other search engines. TOPIC was designed to automatically find so-called reputable sites on the Web by analyzing which sites have the most in-links (similar to Google's PageRank algorithm). To evaluate its effectiveness, Toms and Taves conducted a study designed to address the research question, Do link-based search engines (such as TOPIC and Google) output more reputable Web sites than other search engines?

A challenge in designing a study of this sort is choosing the actual sites to evaluate. Toms and Taves (2004) chose 12 general-interest topics (such as "movie reviews" and "gardening") and searched for information on those topics using four search engines: TOPIC, Google, Altavista, and Lycos. They took the top five sites returned by each search engine for each topic. They grouped the 12 topics into four sets, with 3 topics in each set, so each set contained 60 distinct Web sites (20 Web sites/topic × 3 topics).

They recruited 80 study participants, who were divided into four groups of 20 people each. Each group worked with one set of topics (i.e., 60 Web sites). Each participant was asked to briefly (for no more than two minutes) browse the 60 Web sites. Then, the participant filled out a questionnaire about the site, rating it as "trustworthy," "authoritative," and "about the topic," on a scale from 1 to 5 and indicating whether they would return to the site in the future and whether they would recommend it to a friend. In total, the study participants made 4800 distinct assessments (80 participants × 60 Web sites), which were then analyzed.

For the analysis, Toms and Taves (2004) grouped the four search engines into two categories: links (Google and TOPIC, which analyze hyperlink structure) and semantics (Altavista and Lycos, which rely on statistical analysis of text). They wanted to *compare the mean evaluations* of Web sites returned by the two different types of search engines. They used ANOVA to make this comparison and found that the links engines were superior (see Table 37.1;[5] note that identical findings would have resulted from the use of a *t* test instead of ANOVA).

The *p* value for each comparison indicates that all the differences were statistically significant—*p* values less than 0.001 indicate that there is essentially no probability (less than one in one thousand) that the results were due to chance. Next, we can examine the actual mean values. They tell us that on average, sites returned by the search engines using link analysis were rated as more trustworthy, more authoritative, and more about a given topic than links returned by the search engines using semantic analysis.

Given that the results are statistically significant, the next question to ask is, How meaningful is the difference? The low *p* values would suggest a strong finding. But with this large a sample, a low *p* value is almost routine. We can be confident that the effect they are reporting is real, but that doesn't mean it's particularly strong. We need to look at the actual differences between the two types of search engines. Sites from the links engine were rated, on average, 3.6 on the trustworthiness measure, while sites from the semantics engine were rated 3.5, a difference of only 0.1 points on a 5-point scale. This supposedly highly significant finding, then, represents a very small difference. Whenever you are evaluating or conducting social science research, carefully consider all the findings in terms of effect size, not just statistical significance.

In addition to comparing the search engine types, Toms and Taves (2004) also compared the four individual search engines. First, they performed both an overall ANOVA and found statistically significant ($p < 0.001$) differences in assessment ratings among the four search engines. This result, however, doesn't tell us which site was most effective. For example, suppose you were interested in whether Google or TOPIC output more authoritative sites. A post hoc comparison of the mean ratings of the sites retrieved by these two engines would tell us whether there is a statistically significant difference between them. Toms and Taves compared the means on the authoritativeness, trustworthiness, and aboutness ratings using the Bonferroni post hoc technique. The Bonferroni technique is quite conservative—this gives us confidence in their findings but also means that some significant results may have been overlooked. The post hoc comparisons indicated that Google was the overall "winner"—its ratings were higher on all measures. Toms and Taves did not provide numerical means for these ratings, so it is not clear whether this statistically significant finding was of a magnitude that would be meaningful to Web searchers.

What lessons can we learn from Toms and Taves's (2004) research? First, ANOVA is a valuable analytical tool that can quickly make sense of large data sets. Second, looking for statistical significance with large samples is a risky game. Weak findings can be made to look strong by trumpeting *p* values and downplaying actual magnitudes. It is worth noting that no effect sizes were reported in this article—they might be very small. Perhaps the simplest advice is this: use statistical tests to assess the reliability of your results, but not their importance (Abelson, 1995). Take a careful look at a tabular or graphical display of the key descriptive data. Then ask yourself, is this a meaningful finding?

Example 2: Designing a Fast-forward Video Surrogate

When you search for a book using a library catalog, or a Web page using a search engine, you typically get many results. The system represents each result with a *surrogate*—something that stands in for the actual item. So a book is represented by its title, author, year of publication, and so on. A Web page is often represented by its title and a brief extract of its text. But what sort of surrogate would be most useful in representing a video?

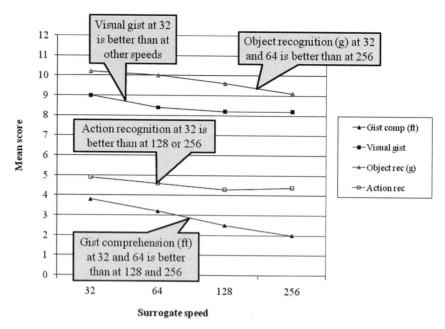

Figure 37.1. Effects of surrogate speed on performance (from Wildemuth et al., 2003).

For the Open Video project, a digital library of videos, this problem was not just theoretical. The project team had built a collection of hundreds of videos and wanted people to be able to search the collection effectively. They developed "fast-forwards," a video surrogate that mimics the fast-forward function on a VCR. In the study discussed here (Wildemuth et al., 2003),[6] the team compared different fast-forward surrogates. In one sense, faster is better because the user can see the whole video in less time. But if the surrogate is *too* fast, it becomes gibberish. Negotiating this trade-off required empirical evidence.

Surrogates were created at four different speeds: 32×, 64×, 128×, and 256× (i.e., 32 times as fast a normal playing speed, etc.). Forty-five study participants were asked to view one video's surrogate at each speed (i.e., this was a within-subjects experimental design). The order in which the videos and different fast-forward speeds were presented was counterbalanced to avoid order effects. Thus each fast-forward speed received 45 unique evaluations, which were evenly distributed among four different videos. After viewing each surrogate, participants completed six tasks such as "textual object recognition" (select objects seen in the surrogate from a list of nouns) and "full-text gist comprehension" (write a brief summary of the video, based on the surrogate). In essence, these measures tested participants' ability both to recognize and recall information in the video surrogate.

The researchers used ANOVA to analyze the effects of surrogate speed on user performance. They found that surrogate speed had a significant effect on four of the measures: linguistic gist comprehension, visual gist comprehension, action recognition, and object recognition. They then conducted post hoc analysis using Duncan's multiple range test to determine whether the differences between the four speeds were statistically significant. Figure 37.1 (reproduced from the original article) illustrates the trade-off between surrogate speed and user performance. The differences identified in Figure 37.1 are all statistically significant according to Duncan's test (specific p values were not reported).

Many statistical experts recommend against using Duncan's test. Its primary weakness is that, as you compare more and more means, it has a higher and higher chance of reporting a significant result by chance alone—not necessarily a problem here because only four means were being compared for each variable. Even so, more recently developed procedures, such as Tukey's HSD and Scheffé's test, avoid this problem and so are safe to use with any number of comparisons. Naturally, they are also more conservative, meaning they may fail to detect some meaningful effects.

What are the practical implications of these findings? Users performed well on most of the tasks. For example, they were able to recognize more than 70 percent of the objects in the video. In general, performance at $128\times$ and $256\times$ was poorer than at $64\times$ and $32\times$. Given these data, Wildemuth and colleagues (2003) argued that fast-forwards are effective surrogates and suggested using the $64\times$ speed as a default, while allowing users to choose a faster or slower speed if they prefer. This argument provides a clear and useful example of how research can inform practice.

CONCLUSION

Many research questions in information and library science involve making comparisons: comparing the effectiveness of different systems or services, comparing the performance of one group with the performance of another group, and so on. When tackling one of these research questions, you've usually calculated a mean for each group or entity that you want to compare. The problem is that because you probably are using a sample from your population of interest, you need to take into account the variability across different samples and within each sample. The t test and ANOVA are designed to address this problem. They can tell you the likelihood that the difference you observed will hold true across the entire population of interest.

If you find that you have observed a statistically significant difference, then you will need to examine the size of the difference more directly. Keep in mind that you can have a statistically significant difference that is so small that it is not meaningful for any practical purpose. Thus you can think of the t test and ANOVA as the first of two important steps in the interpretation of your results.

NOTES

1. See Gerhan (2001) for a clear discussion of how to enter and analyze data using SPSS, or see http://www.graphpad.com/quickcalcs/ttest1.cfm for a simple t test calculator.

2. For a discussion of power and the factors that need to be considered in determining if your study design has sufficient power, see Chapter 13, on sampling for extensive studies.

3. Mathematically, ANOVA is considered a general linear model technique, like linear regression. Some software refers to ANOVA as general linear model, or GLM, analysis.

4. When you get to this point in designing your analysis, you may want to consult with a statistician.

5. Note that the numerical means have been approximated because the article provides only a figure.

6. This paper received the 2003 Best Conference Paper Award at the Joint Conference on Digital Libraries.

WORKS CITED

Abelson, R. P. (1995). *Statistics as Principled Argument*. Hillsdale, NJ: Erlbaum.

Cohen, J. (1965). Some statistical issues in psychological research. In B. B. Wolman (Ed.), *Handbook of Clinical Psychology* (pp. 95–121). New York: McGraw-Hill.

Cohen, J. (1990). Things I have learned (so far). *American Psychologist, 45*, 1304–1312.

Cohen, J. (1994). The earth is round ($p < .05$). *American Psychologist, 49*, 997–1003.

Gerhan, D. (2001). Statistical significance: How it signifies in statistics reference. *Reference and User Services Quarterly, 40*(4), 361–374.

Toms, E. G., & Taves, A. R. (2004). Measuring user perceptions of Web site reputation. *Information Processing and Management, 40*, 291–317.

Wildemuth, B. M., Marchionini, G., Yang, M., Geisler, G., Wilkens, T., Hughes, A., & Gruss, R. (2003). How fast is too fast? Evaluating fast forward surrogates for digital video. In *Proceedings of the ACM/IEEE 2003 Joint Conference on Digital Libraries (JCDL 2003)* (pp. 221–230).

Wilkinson, L. (1999). Statistical methods in psychology journals: Guidelines and explanations. *American Psychologist, 54*, 594–604.

ADDITIONAL RECOMMENDED READING

David, M., & Sutton, C. D. (2004). Inferential statistics and hypothesis testing. In *Social Research: The Basics* (pp. 309–319). London: Sage.

Lane, D. (2004). *HyperStat*. Retrieved November 3, 2004, from http://davidmlane.com/hyperstat/.

Mason, E. J., & Bramble, W. J. (1997). Making inferences from data. In *Research in Education and the Behavioral Sciences: Concepts and Methods* (pp. 185–259). Madison, WI: Brown and Benchmark.

Trochim, W. (2004). *The Research Methods Knowledge Base*. Retrieved November, 3, 2004, from http://davidmlane.com/hyperstat/.

Vaughan, L. (2001). *Statistical Methods for the Information Professional*. Medford, NJ: Information Today.

PART VI

CONCLUSION

38

Putting It All Together

Barbara M. Wildemuth

The main satisfaction we're getting . . . is the intellectual excitement. For me, that's plenty. Isn't that really the driving force of science?

—David R. Nelson (as quoted in Browne, 1985)

By the worldly standards of public life, all scholars in their work are of course oddly virtuous. They do not make wild claims, they do not cheat, they do not try to persuade at any cost, they appeal neither to prejudice nor to authority, they are often frank about their ignorance, their disputes are fairly decorous, they do not confuse what is being argued with race, politics, sex or age, they listen patiently to the young and to the old who both know everything. These are the general virtues of scholarship, and they are peculiarly the virtues of science.

—Jacob Bronowski (1953/1990)

STARTING OVER FROM THE BEGINNING

Unless you're one of those people who begins reading mysteries by going directly to the last page, you've arrived at this chapter *after* having read several of the other chapters in this book. The chapters in Part 2 outline some of the ways in which you might have arrived at your research question. You may be motivated by an issue that arose in your professional life, by your desire to be able to more accurately describe a particular entity or process, by your interest in the relationships among two or more phenomena, or by an important theoretical question. Part 3 considers research designs and sampling and offers a number of alternatives, including both quantitative and qualitative approaches. Part 4 describes a number of different approaches to data collection. For most studies, you'll use multiple methods of data collection to avoid the bias that can result from using only one method. Finally, Part 5 contains a number of chapters on data analysis techniques, covering a broad spectrum of the methods that are most frequently used in information and library science (ILS).

Parts 2 to 5 were necessarily divided into short chapters, thus splintering the methods that would normally be used together. Unfortunately, this means that none of the chapters explicitly addressed the challenges of how to integrate multiple methods into a single study. We will try to deal with those challenges in this chapter, primarily by examining some examples in which a single study integrates a set of data collection and analysis techniques into a well-designed whole.

SOME EXAMPLES OF HOW A STUDY CAN BE PUT TOGETHER

This set of three examples was selected to represent a diverse set of approaches to designing a robust study. The first (Abels et al., 2002, 2004) was conducted in several phases, with the goal of developing a taxonomy of the contributions that hospital libraries can make to the success of their parent organizations. This example integrates several small studies to create and validate the taxonomy. The second example (Blake & Pratt, 2006 a, 2006b) uses naturalistic methods to learn how teams of biomedical scientists go about conducting systematic reviews. Two groups were studied, using observation, interviews, and examination of existing documents. The third example (Christel & Frisch, 2008) is a pair of experiments comparing the effectiveness of two different versions of a digital archive of oral history interviews. Each of these examples illustrates how a researcher can use multiple methods to design an effective study.

Example 1: Developing a Taxonomy of Library Contributions to Health Care Institutions' Performance

Abels et al. (2002)[1] pointed out that "many hospitals and academic health sciences centers have questioned their investment in library and information services" (p. 276). Because these doubts may put library and information services at risk, the researchers were highly motivated to find out what value library and information services provide to their sponsoring institutions and how their most important organizational contributions might be communicated. Thus the research questions investigated in the studies discussed here (Abels et al., 2002, 2004) are strongly oriented to the practice of librarianship and will address an important issue in the management of hospital libraries.

The study was conducted in five phases: a literature review, intended to develop an initial taxonomy of the contributions of library and information services units to their parent organizations; the drafting and pilot testing of the taxonomy; interviews designed to validate the taxonomy and further explore the ways in which the contributions of library and information services can be communicated to organizational leaders; a focus group with the same purpose as the interviews; and a survey of a larger sample of library directors and hospital administrators, also intended to validate the taxonomy. The overall goal of the study was to develop and validate a taxonomy of contributions so that it could be used by individual libraries to develop their own evaluation/communication programs. After briefly describing the first two phases of the study, the discussion here will focus on its last three (empirical) phases.

On the basis of the literature review and some pilot-test interviews with just a few administrators, a draft taxonomy was developed. It was based on the *balanced scorecard* approach (Kaplan & Norton, 1992) to evaluating organizational performance and included four perspectives: financial, internal business, customer, and learning and innovation. As part of the development process, the draft taxonomy was validated through "two pretest interviews with [library and information services] directors and institutional administrators in a community hospital and an academic health sciences center" (Abels et al., 2002, p. 278). It's not clear which or how many administrators in each setting were included in the interviews.

In the third phase of the study, semistructured interviews were conducted with 12 library and information services directors and institutional administrators in three hospitals and three academic health sciences centers. In addition to validating the taxonomy, these interviews asked the administrators about best practices in communicating the contributions of library and information services in these types of settings. The selection of participants for this phase was based on three inclusion criteria. First, each participant was from an institution in the mid-Atlantic states so that face-to-face interviews would be feasible. Second, institutional reputation was considered so that only the top-ranked institutions on two lists of top hospitals were included in the sample. Third, only those institutions providing significant support to the library and information services unit were included; level of support was calculated as "the library's total budget normalized by the number of beds in the affiliated hospital" (Abels et al., 2002, p. 278). Because of space limitations, the full interview guide was not included in either the 2002 or the 2004 article. The content of the interviews was analyzed qualitatively. The researchers found that the taxonomy was generally valid but that library directors and institutional administrators did differ in the emphasis they placed on particular aspects of the taxonomy. Before modifying the taxonomy, the next phase of the research was conducted.

In the fourth phase of the research, a focus group was conducted with five hospital administrators attending the 2001 meeting of the Maryland Hospital Association. While all of the participants in the phase 3 interviews supervised library directors, that was not necessarily true of the administrators in the focus group. Thus the sample providing input for the taxonomy was expanded in a theoretically interesting way. It is not clear how this sample was selected, so we can presume it was a convenience sample. The structure of the focus group was not provided, but we can assume that it followed the structure of the interviews fairly closely because it served the same general purpose.

On the basis of the input from the interviews and the focus group, the taxonomy was modified. The generic approach of the balanced scorecard approach was tuned to be more specific to the needs of health care institutions. The resulting taxonomy included five categories of possible library and information service contributions, depicted as organizational mission concepts: (1) clinical care, (2) manage operations, (3) education, (4) research and innovation, and (5) service. While these still resemble the original four categories of the balanced scorecard, it is clear that the interviews and the focus group enabled Abels and colleagues (2002, 2004) to make the taxonomy much more relevant to the health care settings in which they were interested.

The fifth phase of the study was described by Abels et al. (2004). Two Web-based questionnaires were administered, one to library directors and one to institutional administrators. The sample of library directors was randomly selected from Hospital Libraries section members of the Medical Library Association ($n = 60$ nonuniversity hospital libraries) and library directors at institutional members of the Association of American Medical Colleges ($n = 60$ university hospitals); thus 120 library directors were invited to participate. Institutions represented in the samples of previous phases were excluded. The library directors in the selected institutions provided the names and addresses of hospital administrators, plus deans of the selected medical colleges were invited to participate. Administrators who did not want to participate were excluded, so the final sample of administrators included 25 nonuniversity hospital administrators, 25 academic hospital administrators, and 51 deans of medical education programs. Almost 60 percent of the library directors responded to the questionnaire; 34 percent of the institutional administrators responded.

Both questionnaires focused on 15 organizational goals, rather than the 42 possible library and information service contributions included in the full taxonomy. This decision was made to reduce the burden on the respondents. The full questionnaires were not included in the article, but the content was described. Each questionnaire consisted of three sections. The first asked the respondents to rate the extent to which library and information services could contribute to each of the 15 organizational goals. The second section consisted of open-ended questions and asked about ways to communicate the contributions of library and information services to organizational success. In addition, the respondents were asked to describe three to five indicators of library and information service contributions that they would find most meaningful. The third section consisted of demographic questions.

On the basis of the responses to the questionnaire, the authors were able to compare the views of the different subgroups in the sample. For instance, they could compare the number of library directors who believed that libraries contribute to promoting clinical learning with the number of hospital administrators who held the same belief. Not surprisingly, more library directors than hospital administrators agreed that libraries contributed to the 15 organizational goals; even so, at least 35 percent of the hospital administrators agreed that libraries contributed to each of the goals. In addition, an open-ended question asking for additional ways that libraries contribute to organizational goals did not elicit any new items for the taxonomy. The larger sample size contacted via the questionnaires increased the validity of these findings.

The authors concluded that the taxonomy is complete and that to use it, each institution will need to select those organizational goals and library contributions that are most pertinent for the particular setting. In this way, the taxonomy can serve as the basis for an assessment of a particular library's contributions to its parent institution. The authors concluded with suggestions for a process through which the contributions of library and information services can be assessed and communicated.

Example 2: Studying Teams of Scientists as They Synthesize Information

Blake and Pratt (2006 a, 2006b)[2] investigated the behaviors of biomedical scientists as they work in teams to develop systematic reviews. Medical experts use an established process to conduct such reviews, with the goal of integrating and interpreting the findings from many clinical studies investigating the same research question. Blake and Pratt's goal was to increase our understanding of the process by which a team of researchers collaboratively conducts such reviews. Since such reviews typically integrate the findings from hundreds or thousands of studies and can often take over two years to complete, Blake and Pratt's long-term goal was to develop an information system that would support and streamline the systematic review process. Thus we can see that the original research question is descriptive in nature (i.e., it is an attempt to accurately describe the current systematic review process) and was motivated by an issue that arose in practice (i.e., the time-consuming nature of the current process). In addition, Blake and Pratt situated their work within the context of current theories of cognition and information seeking.

The design of this study might best be described as a qualitative field study, and it also might be viewed as two case studies. Because they were interested in describing a naturally occurring process, Blake and Pratt (2006 a, 2006b) designed their study to be able to investigate that process. They selected two groups in which to conduct the study. It is not clear exactly how they selected which groups to include. The two groups differed from each other in theoretically interesting ways such as the topics on which the reviews were conducted and the health/medical domain of the group, the size of the group, and the motivations for conducting the systematic review(s). However, it seems most likely that the groups were selected because they were available, rather than because they fulfilled particular selection criteria.

Each group was either at the beginning or in the midst of conducting a systematic review. The first group, the medical group, was made up of eight people with various types of expertise, collaboratively developing a review on complementary and alternative approaches to medicine. The second group, the public health group, consisted of 11 people with differing types of expertise, including graduate and undergraduate students. This group was engaged in some stage of conducting two systematic reviews (one on the relationship between smoking and impotence and one on utility estimates and AIDS) and development of a database on lifesaving and cost-effectiveness data.

Blake and Pratt (2006 a, 2006b) gathered data from each group over an extended period. Three distinct data collection methods were used. The first was direct observation. The meetings of the medical group were directly observed and recorded. Interactions with the public health group were more intensive and might be considered participant observation; Blake worked at their offices for two days a week for several months. Blake and Pratt found that direct observation provided them with a better understanding of the systematic review process than would have been possible through interviews or surveys alone. The second method of data collection was interviews; a variety of types of interviews were conducted with a variety of people. The domain expert in the medical group and the director of the public health group responded to semistructured interviews; a separate semistructured interview was held with the public health director and the group's statistician together; the programmer-statistician in the public health group responded to phone and e-mail interviews as well as to a short face-to-face interview; and open-ended discussions were held with the public health group's undergraduate interns. Finally, Blake and Pratt analyzed existing documents. They collected and analyzed meeting minutes, team e-mail messages, lists of citations identified for the review, published literature recommended by the study participants, worksheets used during the knowledge extraction process, spreadsheets used to analyze the group's data, and final manuscripts of the systematic reviews. These various sources of data were integrated (i.e., triangulated) to develop the study's findings and recommendations.

The methods used to analyze this body of textual data (observation notes, interview transcripts, and existing documents) are not described. On the basis of the purpose and design of the study, we can assume that Blake and Pratt (2006 a, 2006b) used qualitative content analysis as their primary analysis method. The outcomes of the study were twofold: (1) a model of the process of collaborative information synthesis and (2) several recommendations for the design of a system that could support this process. These types of outcomes have brought us full circle, back to the original goals of the study. The model of the process provided an accurate description of the process, and the recommendations addressed the practical issues that originally motivated the study.

Example 3: Comparing Still versus Video Representations of Oral Histories

Christel and Frisch (2008)[3] conducted two experiments to investigate the differences between still-image and video representations of oral history interviews. Their studies were based on the HistoryMakers, an archive of "video oral history interviews highlighting the accomplishments of individual African Americans and African-American-led groups and movements" (p. 242). They compared the effectiveness of two versions of the system used to provide access to the interviews: one in which the full digital video of each interview could be played (the video system), and another in which a still image selected from the video was displayed, while only the audio portion of the interview was played (the still system). Results from two experiments were reported in this paper.

For the first experiment, 24 participants were recruited via an online study participant recruitment system, available to people in the Pittsburgh area. This convenience sample included both men and women, with a mean age of 23. They were not familiar with using African American oral history interviews, and while they were experienced Web searchers, they were not familiar with digital video retrieval systems. The subjects were paid $10 for their participation, plus cash prizes were given to the three who were most successful in completing the assigned tasks.

The experimental design was a within-subjects design, meaning that each participant interacted with both systems. The order in which they experienced the two systems was counterbalanced; half the subjects used the video system first, while the other half used the still system first. The way in which subjects were assigned to each of these two orders was not specified, but we can assume that the first subject was randomly assigned and that system order was alternated for the remaining subjects.

In the first experiment, each subject was instructed to find the one story that best answered or discussed each of 12 topics, using the first system to which they were assigned. For illustration, one of the topics asked for an interview showing and discussing a photo of a musician quartet in Singapore, and another asked for an interview that recalls scents of childhood holidays, including turkey, sweet potato pies, and the ocean. The "treasure hunt" was timed; each subject was allowed just 20 minutes to find the stories on all 12 topics. They then filled out a questionnaire of their perceptions about six different aspects of the system (e.g., its accuracy and whether it was historically meaningful). They then repeated the search process (with another 12 topics) using the other system and filled out the questionnaire on their perceptions of that system. They then completed a final questionnaire, directly comparing the two systems: which was easier to learn, which was easier to use, and which they liked the best. These ratings of the subjects' perceptions were augmented with performance data recorded in transaction logs. For example, later analysis compared the two systems in terms of the amount of time spent viewing/playing the interviews and the number of searches entered in each session.

A variety of descriptive statistics were reported, some in tables and some in the text of the paper. The mean scores on the six perception questions were reported in a table; the number of subjects expressing a preference for one system or the other as well as performance measures calculated from the transaction logs were reported in the text of the paper. The data analysis methods were not described in detail, but we can assume that Christel and Frisch (2008) used analysis of variance (ANOVA) to compare the two systems on the perceptual and performance measures. In this first experiment, there were no statistically significant differences between the two systems in either the subjects' performance (e.g., number of "correct" interviews retrieved) or their perceptions. The difference in subjects' perceptions of the systems' accuracy approached statistical significance ($p < 0.10$), with the video system perceived as more accurate.

Because the "treasure hunt" tasks were unlike the assignments that history professors would normally use to introduce their students to such a digital library, a second experiment was conducted. The design of this experiment was identical to the first, except that the task involved identifying oral history interviews that would be useful in preparing a report on the assigned topic. Only one topic was assigned for each system; one topic was to "identify characteristics that resulted in the leadership effectiveness of the interviewee," and the other was to "discuss the civil, social or political organizations that the interviewee. . . founded" (Christel & Frisch, 2008, p. 247). Fourteen subjects participated in this experiment. They had demographic characteristics similar to the participants in the first experiment. The subjects were paid $10 for their participation, but there was no additional cash incentive for performance.

Because the correctness of the interviews retrieved could not be scored, only the participants' perceptions and their other online behaviors were reported and compared. Analysis of variance was used to evaluate the statistical significance of any differences between means. The subjects perceived the video system to be more accurate than the still system. In addition, the preferences expressed in the final questionnaire were overwhelmingly in favor of the video system. In both experiments, Christel and Frisch (2008) used responses to open-ended questionnaire items to augment and discuss the results from the closed-ended items.

In their discussion, Christel and Frisch (2008) also made comparisons across the two experiments. Since the experimental procedures were so similar in the two studies, such comparisons are quite appropriate. In some ways, you could see the combination of the two experiments as a within-subjects design embedded within a between-subjects design. The two systems were compared within subjects, and the effects of the type of task ("treasure hunt" versus a more exploratory task) were compared between subjects. Thus Christel and Frisch's (2008) discussion of the effects of task on the search behaviors of their study participants was a valuable addition to this paper.

FINDING, OR WINDING, YOUR WAY THROUGH THIS BOOK

The three preceding examples illustrate the variety of types of research studies that are conducted in information and library science. The first was a multiphase study that used different data collection and data analysis methods in each phase to investigate the ways that library contributions to organizational success could be assessed and communicated to hospital administrators. If Abels et al. (2002, 2004) had used this book to assist them in developing this study, they would have consulted a number of chapters. The chapters on developing a research question and on questions originating in ILS practice would have gotten them started. They next would have used the chapters on naturalistic research and sampling for extensive studies to make some preliminary decisions about study design. To support the planning of their data collection methods, they would have consulted chapters on semistructured interviews, focus groups, and survey research. The chapters on content analysis and calculation of frequencies and chi-square would have been useful in working out their data analysis plans.

The second example was a strongly naturalistic study of the ways in which a team of researchers synthesizes findings from a large number of studies during the systematic review process. If Blake and Pratt (2006 a, 2006b) had used this book to help plan their study, they would probably have begun with the chapters on developing a research question and on questions related to the description of phenomena and settings. They would have found the chapters on case studies and naturalistic research, as well as the chapter on sampling for intensive studies, useful in designing their study. To support their planning for data collection, they might have consulted the chapters on the use of existing documents and artifacts as data, direct observation, unstructured interviews, and semistructured interviews. Their planning for data analysis would have been supported by the chapters on qualitative analysis of content and, possibly, analyzing sequences of events.

The third example included two experiments, designed to compare the effectiveness of two different versions of a digital archive. If Christel and Frisch (2008) had used this book in their planning, they would have begun with the chapters on developing a research question and testing hypotheses. The chapter on experimental studies would have been useful in designing their study, as would have been the chapter on sampling for extensive studies. They would have consulted the chapters on transaction logs and on measuring cognitive and affective variables to support the planning of their data collection. The chapters on descriptive statistics and on comparing means would have been useful in planning their data analysis.

Each time you use this book, you'll be taking a somewhat different path through it. In most cases, until you are a very experienced researcher, you will want to read or review the first chapter, on developing a research question. You will also want to examine one or more of the other chapters in Part 2, as you develop the question for a specific study. Once you have a sense of your research question, you'll need to make some decisions about your overall study design. For this purpose, you'll want to read one or more of Chapters 7 to 12, followed by reading one of the chapters on sampling. It's likely that you'll be using multiple methods of data collection (as in all the examples discussed previously), so you'll want to read over several of the chapters in Part 4, on data collection methods. Once you know what type of data you will collect, you're ready to plan your data analysis, supported by one or more of Chapters 29 to 37.

As you read each relevant chapter, you will see that each provides just a brief introduction to the method that is its focus. To further support your efforts, we've tried to reference works that will provide more depth to your understanding of the use of that method. In addition, the heart of each chapter is the examples discussed. Get the full text of those studies that are of particular interest to you, and study them in detail. All of the studies discussed in this book are excellent examples of the way a particular method should be used; you won't go wrong in mimicking the approach used in any of the selected examples.

PROVIDING EVIDENCE TO PROMOTE PROGRESS IN INFORMATION AND LIBRARY SCIENCE

As noted in the introduction to this book, its goal is to promote your participation in creating a body of evidence that can be used to improve practice in information and library science. Improvements in our professional practice should be based on a strong foundation of evidence about the effectiveness of different approaches. Unfortunately, we currently do not have a large enough body of evidence to address all the practical and theoretical questions that arise. Only if all of us work together to create this body of evidence can we put the ILS professions on a strong footing to move forward to the future.

NOTES

1. This paper was the winner of the 2004 Ida and George Eliot Prize from the Medical Library Association.

2. This pair of papers received the 2007 John Wiley Best *JASIST* Paper Award from the American Society for Information Science and Technology.

3. This paper was a finalist for the Best Paper Award at the 2008 Joint Conference on Digital Libraries.

WORKS CITED

Abels, E. G., Cogdill, K. W., & Zach, L. (2002). The contributions of library and information services to hospitals and academic health sciences centers: A preliminary taxonomy. *Journal of the Medical Library Association, 90*(3), 276–284.

Abels, E. G., Cogdill, K. W., & Zach, L. (2004). Identifying and communicating the contributions of library and information services in hospitals and academic health sciences centers. *Journal of the Medical Library Association, 91*(1), 46–55.

Blake, C., & Pratt, W. (2006 a). Collaborative information synthesis I: A model of information behaviors of scientists in medicine and public health. *Journal of the American Society for Information Science and Technology, 57*(13), 1740–1749.

Blake, C., & Pratt, W. (2006b). Collaborative information synthesis II: Recommendations for information systems to support synthesis activities. *Journal of the American Society for Information Science and Technology, 57*(14), 1888–1895.

Bronowski, J. (1990). The sense of human dignity (part 3) [Lecture]. In *Science and Human Values* (pp. 49–76). New York: Harper Perennial. (Original work presented 1953.)

Browne, M. W. (1985, July 30). Puzzling crystals plunge scientists into uncertainty. *New York Times*, sect. C, p. 1.

Christel, M. G., & Frisch, M. H. (2008). Evaluating the contributions of video representation for a life oral history collection. In *Proceedings of the 8th ACM/IEEE-CS Joint Conference on Digital Libraries (JCDL)* (pp. 241–250).

Kaplan, R. S., & Norton, D. P. (1992). The balanced scorecard: Measures that drive performance. *Harvard Business Review, 71*(1), 71–79.

Index of Authors of Examples Discussed

Subject Index

About the Contributors

LEO L. CAO is a doctoral student in the School of Information and Library Science at the University of North Carolina at Chapel Hill, and is a Gates Millennium Scholar. He holds a M.S.I. from the University of Michigan. His research interests focus on the use of gaming applications in education.

SONGPHAN CHOEMPRAYONG is a doctoral student in the School of Information and Library Science at the University of North Carolina at Chapel Hill. He holds a M.L.I.S. from the University of Pittsburgh and was previously an information scientist at the Thailand Creative & Design Center in Bangkok. His research interests include information-seeking behavior in social crises and critical incidents, information policy related to digital divides, information and library science education, and the library workforce.

ABE J. CRYSTAL is the Chief Research and Strategy Officer at MoreBetterLabs, Inc., in North Carolina. He holds a Ph.D. from the University of North Carolina at Chapel Hill; his dissertation is titled, "Design research for personal information management systems to support undergraduate students." He is also president emeritus and continues to be active in the Triangle (NC) chapter of the Usability Professionals Association.

CAROLYN HANK is a doctoral student in the School of Information and Library Science at the University of North Carolina at Chapel Hill. She holds a M.L.I.S. from Kent State University and was previously a research assistant at OCLC's Office of Research. Carolyn is a graduate research assistant for the DigCCurr project (Preserving Access to Our Digital Future: Building an International Digital Curation Curriculum, http://www.ils.unc.edu/digccurr/). Her research interests focus on digital preservation and appraisal of blogs.

LILI LUO is an Assistant Professor in the School of Library and Information Science at San José State University. She holds a Ph.D. in information and library science from the University of North Carolina at Chapel Hill; her dissertation is titled, "Towards sustaining professional development: Identification of essential competencies and effective training techniques for chat reference services." Her primary research interests focus on information access and services in the digital age. She is interested in exploring more about how the advent of new technologies has affected the library world and library users. She teaches courses (via Second Life) in reference services and research methods.

CHAD MORGAN is a doctoral student and teaching fellow in the School of Information and Library Science at the University of North Carolina at Chapel Hill. He holds a Ph.D. in history from the University of North Carolina at Chapel Hill, and teaches a course on the history of the book. His research interests focus on the effects of library and information science programs on career trajectories.

SANGHEE OH is a doctoral student and teaching fellow in the School of Information and Library Science at the University of North Carolina at Chapel Hill. She holds a M.L.I.S. from the University of California, Los Angeles. Sanghee is a graduate research assistant for the Digital Libraries Curriculum Development project (http://curric.dlib.vt.edu/), which is developing a curriculum framework and modules for teaching graduate courses in digital libraries. Her dissertation research will focus on the motivations of question answerers in social question-answering Web sites. She teaches a course in retrieving and analyzing information.

CAROL L. PERRYMAN is a doctoral student in the School of Information and Library Science at the University of North Carolina at Chapel Hill. She holds a M.S.L.I.S. from the University of Illinois at Urbana-Champaign. She is interested in evidence-based library and information practice, and her dissertation research will focus on the information-seeking behaviors used by librarians in the course of making management decisions.

LAURA SHEBLE is a doctoral student in the School of Information and Library Science at the University of North Carolina at Chapel Hill. She holds a M.L.I.S. from Wayne State University. Laura is a graduate research assistant for the VidArch project (http://www.ils.unc.edu/vidarch/), which is investigating ways to preserve a video work's context and highlight its essence, thus making it more understandable and accessible to future generations.

KRISTINA M. SPURGIN is a doctoral student and teaching fellow in the School of Information and Library Science at the University of North Carolina at Chapel Hill. She holds a M.L.S. from the State University of New York at Albany. She is currently the grants manager for Folkstreams.net (http://www.folkstreams.net/) at ibiblio (http://www.ibiblio.org/index.html). Her research is focused on personal information management, and she teaches a course on the organization of information.

MARY WILKINS JORDAN is a doctoral student and teaching fellow in the School of Information and Library Science at the University of North Carolina at Chapel Hill. Mary holds a J.D. from Case Western Reserve University and a M.L.I.S from the University of Wisconsin-Milwaukee. She is interested in the management of public libraries and teaches a course on the management of information professionals. She plans to pursue her dissertation research through an examination of the competencies needed by public library directors.

YAN ZHANG is a doctoral candidate and teaching fellow in the School of Information and Library Science at the University of North Carolina at Chapel Hill. She holds a M.S.I.S. from the University of Tennessee, Knoxville. Her dissertation research is focused on the ways in which people construct mental models of information-rich Web spaces, and she has published some of her studies in the *Journal of the American Society for Information Science and Technology* and *Information Processing and Management*. She teaches a course on retrieving and analyzing information.

About the Author

BARBARA M. WILDEMUTH is a professor in the School of Information and Library Science at the University of North Carolina at Chapel Hill. She received her Ph.D. from Drexel University and holds master's degrees from Rutgers University and the University of Illinois at Urbana-Champaign. Her research interests are focused on people's information behavior, particularly the ways that people seek and use information through computerized retrieval systems. She has conducted studies of the information behaviors of medical students and physicians, health services consumers, law students, and a variety of other groups. Her teaching responsibilities include courses in research methods, systems analysis, information ethics, and other related areas.